July 2, 1951

With deep regards
and best wishes
to
Bro. H. E. Wight—
Sincerely your brother
Milton R. Hunter

May this book give you as much
inspiration as I have received from
my Mission. To the best Dad in the
world with all my love.
Marg.
July 29, 1951.

ANCIENT AMERICA
AND
THE BOOK OF MORMON

Ancient America

and

THE BOOK of MORMON

by

Milton R. Hunter

Thomas Stuart Ferguson

KOLOB BOOK COMPANY
P. O. Box 1575
OAKLAND, CALIFORNIA
1950

First Edition

PRINTED IN U.S.A.
KOLOB BOOK COMPANY
P. O. Box 1575
OAKLAND, CALIFORNIA

FOREWORD

The unique confirmation of the truth of Joseph Smith's claims here presented makes this book (*Ancient America and the Book of Mormon*) of especial value to all Latter-day Saints.

The Spaniards who came to this continent and conquered the land with the sword brought with them priests who, in their zeal to establish Christianity among the native inhabitants, used their authority to destroy practically all written native records of the earlier peoples in the land. This defenseless action stands as an example of the wrong manner of carrying forward the work of the Lord.

The only records on ancient American history after this destruction were the carved or painted inscriptions on stone or wood. These could not be read, for the keys to the language were lost. It is really surprising that the vandals did not destroy every symbol that might some day be deciphered. A very few records, mostly in symbolic representation not yet fully understood, were overlooked. These have been and are being studied and may reveal the key of interpretation to the remaining symbols on stone and wood which then will give an understanding of life in ancient America.

Fortunately, at the time of this destruction or soon thereafter there lived men who remembered the contents of the destroyed records. One of these was Ixtlilxochitl who from memory and available materials wrote as best he could a history of ancient America. This history has been preserved and known for many years but generally overlooked. The authors have had this book translated into modern English and it is the first time that it has appeared in the English language.

By the use of paralleled quotations from the *Works of Ixtlilxochitl* and *The Book of Mormon,* striking similarities appear, which confirm to a remarkable degree the story of *The Book of Mormon.* These are printed in this volume, and make this volume an important and valuable document in the study of *The Book of Mormon.*

It is difficult to understand why we, a *Book of Mormon* people, have allowed this ancient book (the *Works of Ixtlil-xochitl*), a real opportunity for us, to slumber so long. But now we have it, and no doubt its testimony will be used by gospel students for years to come.

Not only are the comparisons of the two books given here, but the authors have skillfully added much historical and doctrinal information, to clarify the comparisons and to help the reader in his search for truth. This makes the volume doubly precious.

This additional information was drawn from such sixteenth-century native documents as the *Popul Vuh* and *Totonicapan*— Quiché-Maya Guatemalan writing — and the works of famous Catholic missionaries, also of the sixteenth century, such as Father Bernardino Sahagun and Father Juan de Torquemada. The late Sylvanus Morley and other outstanding authorities in the field of Mayan and Mexican archæology have also been quoted.

This volume is valuable to all lovers of *The Book of Mormon,* and to all who are seeking to establish in their hearts the truth of the gospel of the Lord Jesus Christ, as revealed by the Prophet Joseph Smith. We should be grateful to the authors who have gone to such pains to bring this information to our attention. May the book find a wide distribution. It will grace the library of every Gospel student.

JOHN A. WIDTSOE

Salt Lake City, Utah
October 20, 1950

ACKNOWLEDGEMENTS

During the writing and publication of this book, *Ancient America and The Book of Mormon,* the writers have received help from many different persons. Some of them assisted in translating sixteenth century Mexican, Spanish, and Guatemalan writings. Others assisted in translating material from French sources. Some contributed to the production of this book by helping in typing, editing, and proofreading the manuscripts, and art and illustration work. Also, very beneficial assistance and advice were liberally given by certain other friends. For all of these contributions the writers are very grateful.

Also, we wish to express deep appreciation to Dr. John A. Widtsoe of the Quorum of the Twelve Apostles for his careful reading of the entire manuscript and for offering many helpful suggestions. We are very grateful for the foreword of the book which he so generously prepared and for all of the advice and counsel that he gave throughout the entire production of this volume.

The writers are also grateful to Elder Ezra Taft Benson of the Twelve and to President Levi Edgar Young and President Antoine R. Ivins of the First Council of the Seventy for the generous use of their time in their reading the entire manuscript through, offering many helpful suggestions to the writers, and giving statements of endorsement of the book.

Also, acknowledgement is made of the vital help received from President J. Willard Marriott and Allie Mariott of Washington, D.C. in the production of this book. For many years they have also expressed much interest in the subject treated in this volume and in the archaeology of *Book of Mormon* lands.

The following persons have also assisted greatly in one or more of the above mentioned matters for which the writers are indeed appreciative: President Bruce R. McConkie; Dr. Arnulfo Rodriquez; Dr. Wells Jakeman; Dr. Hugh Nibley; Ester I. Ferguson; Ferne G. Hunter; M. Reed Hunter; Lois Aposhian; Dr. J. Poulson Hunter; Melvin Israelsen; Ralph Harding; Elrich B. Davis; Clyde Braegger; Jack Fitzpatrick; Louis Tremelling;

Mary Watkinson; Margaret Allen; Heber James Brown; Elmo R. Smith; Winona Farr; Margaret Meik; Donna Perry; Dean M. McDonald; Edward C. Hall; Howard Gerber; Ray Collier; and Marvin Wallin.

The writers also acknowledge the kind cooperation and consideration extended by the publishers listed below for generously allowing the use of copyrighted materials in this book: American Museum of Natural History; Alfred M. Knopf, Inc.; National Geographic Magazine; University of Oklahoma Press; Doubleday and Company, Inc.; Readers' Digest; The MacMillan Company; Harvard College; Stanford University Press; McGraw—Hill Book Company. Inc., New York; Peabody Museum, Harvard, University; and Chester Stock, Los Angeles County Museum.

MILTON R. HUNTER

THOMAS STUART FERGUSON

Salt Lake City, Utah
October 25, 1950

CONTENTS

ILLUSTRATIONS

EXPLANATION REGARDING FOOTNOTES
AND ABBREVIATIONS

ibid.	From the Latin *ibidem*, meaning "the same reference as last cited."
op. cit.	From the Latin *opere citato*, meaning "the work cited more than one note previously."
e. g.	From the Latin *exempli gratia*, meaning "for pages following."
ff.	From the German *folgende*, meaning "and the example."
f.	Meaning "and the page following."
pp.	Meaning "pages."
p.	Meaning "page."
2a.	Meaning the first portion of verse two.
5b.	Meaning the latter portion of verse five.
3:10; 4:6, 10, 16-20.	Meaning "chapter three, verse ten; chapter four, verses six, ten, sixteen to twenty."

JOSEPH SMITH, DECEMBER 23, 1805 - JUNE 27, 1844

Chapter 1

INTRODUCTION

PURPOSE AND NATURE OF THIS BOOK

When Christopher Columbus discovered America in 1492, a vast expanse of land was opened to the Europeans which was nearly as large as the then known world. As time passed, it was referred to as the "New World" or the western hemisphere. Since Columbus thought he had discovered the East Indies, the bronze-colored people found here were named Indians.

At the time of the discovery of America and on down to the present day, thousands and thousands of people have been intrigued by the natives of this land, and the following questions have been asked innumerable times: Who are the American Indians? What is their origin? What ancient races of people were their ancestors? Are the Indians indigenous to America or did their ancestors migrate from the other side of the world? Do all the Indians have a common ancestry or did people from various countries migrate to America in ancient times? If the past ages of the western hemisphere could speak, what is the story they would tell?

Hundreds of people have attempted to answer these questions and many other similar ones. The early missionaries who brought medieval European Christianity to the natives of America, beginning shortly after 1492 A. D., especially the Spanish Padres, gathered many traditions from the Indians. These traditions, generally speaking, assigned to the natives an Israelitic origin. Even intelligent and educated Indians, such as *Ixtlilxochitl* (pronounced Eesh-tleel-sho-cheetl), an Aztec prince of Mexico, and the Guatemalan author of the *Popol Vuh*, wrote books in which they gave the principal outline of the history and religious teachings of their ancestors. Such authors claimed to have had at their disposal the traditions and historical records of their people which had come down to them from their fathers, having been transmitted from father to son for many generations.

1

In addition to all these writings, during the past one hundred years archæologists have been probing in the earth in Peru, Central America, Yucatan, Guatemala, and Mexico, the portions of the western hemisphere where extensive evidence remains which bears testimony of high civilizations once having lived in those regions. The discoveries made by these scientists are continuing to throw much light on the story of ancient America.

But of all the books, articles, and statements that have come from the press since 1492 endeavoring to throw light on the history of this land, the greatest and most authentic is *The Book of Mormon*. Why should this be the case? The answer is important and it is as follows: because this book was written by holy prophets of God who received inspiration and revelations from the Eternal Father and His Only Begotten Son at the time the events occurred, and the writings cover a period from the time of the building of the Tower of Babel down to 421 A. D. Herein lies the most authoritative, true, and detailed history of ancient America and it bears the stamp of divine approval.

However, strange as it may seem, one hundred twenty years have passed since *The Book of Mormon* came from the press, and it has been almost completely ignored by those who should be interested in its claims because they profess to be seekers after truth. Reference is hereby being made to the archæologists and anthropologists, students of American antiquities.

Why should this condition have occurred? The answer is simple. A modern prophet named Joseph Smith claimed to have received "gold plates" or records from the hands of a holy angel who had been sent to the Prophet from the presence of God. From these ancient records, Joseph translated *The Book of Mormon*. A vast majority of the men and women who have turned their backs on that book without even giving it a hearing claim to be Christians; therefore, they readily accept the ministration of angels in ancient times to the Hebrew prophets. But they think, however, that it is unreasonable to believe that the same God who sent angels to visit those ancient prophets would be interested enough in the vast multitudes which constitute the human family in the world today to send angels to prophets in our day for the good of the inhabitants of the earth.

The purpose of this book is to correlate all of the principal sources which tell the story of ancient America. In many instances, the documents used, such as the *Works of Ixtlilxochitl,* have never heretofore appeared in Engilsh. The writers have had those documents translated into that language in order that they might be utilized in contributing to this story. A point of interest and of great importance is that practically all of the documents which can be classified as primary sources confirm each other and also sustain the account as revealed to the earth by an angel and published in *The Book of Mormon,* as will be shown in this book. Even the American anthropologists and archæologists, in the discoveries that they make from time to time, are continuing to pile up evidence which helps to sustain the divine authenticity of *The Book of Mormon.*

It is hoped by the writers of this book that a study of the same will result in many people making a re-evaluation of the ancient Nephite and Jaredite records which were translated and published by an American prophet, Joseph Smith.

This book is essentially a comparison of *The Book of Mormon* with an ancient Mexican history, known as the *Works of Ixtlilxochitl.* Both accounts deal, among other things, with the origins and histories of the people who developed the highest early cultures of the New World. Also, they both tell the story of the early formative eras of these high cultures. Both *The Book of Mormon* and the *Works of Ixtlilxochitl* devote much space to the history of the ancient American colonizers, known in *The Book of Mormon* as "the people of Bountiful" and in the Mexican history as "the people of *Tulan (Bountiful)."* *The Book of Mormon* account, also known as the Nephite record, ends in 421 A.D., whereas *Ixtlilxochitl* continues the history on down through the Spanish Conquest of Mexico.

The Book of Mormon was the first to come from the press, being published eighteen years before the *Works of Ixtlilxochitl.* The major portion of the Nephite record was compiled during the latter part of the fourth century A. D. by an ancient historian and prophet named Mormon.[1] The work was completed during

---

[1] *The Book of Mormon* (1920 edition), p. 460, (Mormon 1:1-5); pp. 132-133, (Words of Mormon 1:1-11); pp. 472-473, (Mormon 8:1-6); pp. 510, 520, 522, (Moroni 1:1, 4; 10:1-8, 34).

THE

BOOK OF MORMON :

AN ACCOUNT WRITTEN BY THE HAND OF MORMON, UPON PLATES TAKEN FROM THE PLATES OF NEPHI.

Wherefore it is an abridgment of the Record of the People of Nephi ; and also of the Lamanites ; written to the Lamanites, which are a remnant of the House of Israel ; and also to Jew and Gentile ; written by way of commandment, and also by the spirit of Prophesy and of Revelation. Written, and sealed up, and hid up unto the LORD, that they might not be destroyed ; to come forth by the gift and power of GOD, unto the interpretation thereof ; sealed by the hand of Moroni, and hid up unto the LORD, to come forth in due time by the way of Gentile ; the interpretation thereof by the gift of GOD ; an abridgment taken from the Book of Ether.

Also, which is a Record of the People of Jared, which were scattered at the time the LORD confounded the language of the people when they were building a tower to get to Heaven : which is to shew unto the remnant of the House of Israel how great things the LORD hath done for their fathers ; and that they may know the covenants of the LORD, that they are not cast off forever ; and also to the convincing of the Jew and Gentile that JESUS is the CHRIST, the ETERNAL GOD, manifesting Himself unto all nations. And now if there be fault, it be the mistake of men ; wherefore condemn not the things of GOD, that ye may be found spotless at the judgment seat of CHRIST.

BY JOSEPH SMITH, JUNIOR,
AUTHOR AND PROPRIETOR.

PALMYRA :

PRINTED BY E. B. GRANDIN, FOR THE AUTHOR.

1830.

Fig. 2: TITLE PAGE OF THE FIRST EDITION OF THE BOOK OF MORMON

It is to be noted that the following appears on the title page: "By Joseph Smith, Junior, Author and Proprietor." In all subsequent editions the statement reads: "Translated by Joseph Smith, Jun." The reason for the statement as it appears in the first edition was to meet the requirements of the copyright law in New York at that time.

ANTIQUITIES OF MEXICO:

COMPRISING

FAC-SIMILES

OF

ANCIENT MEXICAN PAINTINGS AND HIEROGLYPHICS,

PRESERVED

IN THE ROYAL LIBRARIES OF PARIS, BERLIN, AND DRESDEN ;

IN THE IMPERIAL LIBRARY OF VIENNA ;

IN THE VATICAN LIBRARY ;

IN THE BORGIAN MUSEUM AT ROME ;

IN THE LIBRARY OF THE INSTITUTE AT BOLOGNA ;

AND IN THE BODLEIAN LIBRARY AT OXFORD.

TOGETHER WITH

THE MONUMENTS OF NEW SPAIN,

BY M. DUPAIX:

WITH THEIR RESPECTIVE

SCALES OF MEASUREMENT AND ACCOMPANYING DESCRIPTIONS.

———

THE WHOLE ILLUSTRATED BY MANY VALUABLE

Inedited Manuscripts,

BY LORD KINGSBOROUGH.

THE DRAWINGS, ON STONE, BY A. AGLIO.

———

IN NINE VOLUMES.

VOL. IX.

———

LONDON:

PRINTED BY RICHARD AND JOHN E. TAYLOR, RED LION COURT, FLEET STREET.

PUBLISHED BY HENRY G. BOHN, YORK STREET, COVENT GARDEN

M.DCCC.XLVIII.

Fig. 3. TITLE PAGE OF VOL. IX OF LORD KINGSBOROUGH'S "MEXICAN ANTIQUITIES"

It was in this volume that the Works of Ixtlilxochitl were first published. The volume appeared in the year M.DCCC.XLVIII—1848, 18 years after the first edition of The Book of Mormon.

the early part of the fifth century A. D. by his son, Moroni. They compiled *The Book of Mormon* by making an abridgment of records which had been written by historians who had lived con-temporanously with the events as they occurred. In many sec-tions they included the unabridged original writings of their predecessor eyewitness historians. The Nephite account covers approximately one thousand years' time from 600 B. C. to 421 A. D.

Moroni, the latter of the two ancient historians, also abridged the history of a great people known as Jaredites. Their civilization flourished in America from the time of the building of the Tower of Babel until after the arrival of the Nephites. More than fourteen hundred years passed before the abridgment was trans-lated and published in English as a part of *The Book of Mormon*.

The first *Book of Mormon* was copyrighted in 1829 by the modern American prophet, Joseph Smith Jr. Several months later, March 26, 1830, it came from the press in a little town named Palmyra, located in the then frontier region of western New York.[2]

Joseph Smith did not lay claim to writing *The Book of Mormon*. He claimed that his material was derived from ancient authentic hieroglyphic writings. In fact, he did not lay claim to the authorship of a single word of *The Book of Mormon*, but rather stated that he merely served in the capacity of translator.

The ancient Mexican history, the *Works of Ixtlilxochitl,* was written in Mexico at about the close of the sixteenth century. *Ixtlilxochitl,* the author, derived his material from ancient authen-tic hieroglyphic writings which he had received from his ancestors. More than two hundred years passed before this ancient Mexican history was first published; and to the knowledge of the writers of this book, up to the present time it has not heretofore been published in English.

NO HELP FROM DOCUMENTARY SOURCES IN 1830

The *Works of Ixtlilxochitl* came from the press for the first time in 1848 in England. They were printed in the Spanish language. They appeared in volume nine of Lord Kingsborough's famous *Antiquities of Mexico*.[3] Volumes one to seven of Kings-

---

[2]*The Wayne Sentinel*, Palmyra newspaper, March 19, 1830, announced the date of the first sales. Cited in Francis W. Kirkham, *A New Witness for Christ in America* (1942 ed.), pp. 226-227.

borough's works were published in 1830-1831, but volumes eight and nine did not come from the press until seventeen years later.

As late as 1839 Lord Kingsborough's first seven volumes were still unavailable in the United States. On April 25, 1839, the great historian, William H. Prescott, while at work on his famous *Conquest of Mexico,* wrote, "I am daily expecting from Europe . . . the magnificent works of Lord Kingsborough. *There is not a copy, I believe, in the United States.*"[4] Of course it should be remembered that nine more years elapsed (1848) before Kingsborough's first edition of the *Works of Ixtlilxochitl* came from the press. The Prophet Joseph Smith had been dead for three years when Kingsborough's nine volumes had all been published; therefore, it can never be successfully maintained that he obtained material for *The Book of Mormon* from the *Works of Ixtlilxochitl.* Further, of the two accounts, only *The Book of Mormon* purports to be taken from eyewitness records contemporaneously with events related. As a general rule, it gives a more detailed account than does the *Works of Ixtlilxochitl.* It is also considered the more reliable of the two. Lord Kingsborough's complete set of nine volumes cost $1,350 (30 pounds sterling per volume),[5] a price beyond the means of most people, then and now.

The *Works of Ixtlilxochitl* still constitute the only documentary source, exclusive of *The Book of Mormon,* detailed enough and complete enough to have been of substantial assistance to anyone who might have attempted to write the history

[3]In the *Dictionary of National Biography,* published in London, 1892, vol. 31, pp. 130-131, the following appears:

Edward King, Viscount Kingsborough (1795-1837), born 16 Nov. 1795, was eldest son of George, third earl of Kingston, by Lady Helena Moore, only daughter of Stephen, first earl of Montcastle (Burke, *Peerage,* 1891, p. 789). After his father succeeded to the earldom in 1799 he was known by the courtesy title of Viscount Kingsborough. He matriculated at Oxford from Exeter College on 25 June 1814, and in Michaelmas term 1818 gained a second class in classics, but did not graduate (Foster, *Alumni Ox.* 1715-1886, ii, 794). In 1818 and again in 1820 he was elected M.P. for Cork county, but resigned his seat in 1826 in favour of his younger brother, Robert [Lists of Members of Parliament, pt. ii].

The sight of a Mexican manuscript in the Bodleian Library determined King to devote his life to the study of the antiquities of that country. He promoted and edited, with copious notes, a magnificent work entitled *Antiquities of Mexico,* comprising facsimilies of Ancient Mexico paintings and hieroglyphics preserved in . . . various libraries, together with the monuments of New Spain by M. Duplaix, with . . . accompanying descriptions. The whole illustrated by many valuable manuscripts by Augustine Aglio. 9 vols. imperial fol., London, 1830-1848, including 60 pages of a projected tenth volume. Four copies were printed on vellum, with the plates coloured. It is said that the work was undertaken by the encouragement and with the advice of Sir Thomas Phillips, in whose collection many of the manuscripts and drawings used in it were preserved (Macray, *Annals of the Bodleian Library,* 2nd edition p. 322).

The drift of King's speculations is to establish the colonization of Mexico by the Israelites. The book cost King upwards of 32,000 pounds and his life. Oppressed by debt, he was arrested at the suit of a paper manufacturer, and lodged in the sheriff's prison, Dublin, where he died of typhus fever on 27th Feb. 1837, and was buried at Mitchelstown. He was unmarried.

Gent. Mag. Newser, vii, 537-8; *Ann. Reg.* 1837; Webb's *Compendium of Irish Biog.,* p. 275; (Allibones *Dict.*)
[4]Victor Wolfgang Von Hagen, *Maya Explorer,* 1947, p. 77, citing letter from William H. Prescott to Manuel Najera, in Mexico, dated April 25, 1839.
[5]*Ibid.,* p. 78.

of the earliest cultured colonizers of the ancient New World. Joseph Smith received no help from that source nor from any other documents published by Lord Kingsborough. They were not available to him. Nor did Joseph Smith have access to the *Popol Vuh* or the *Titulo de los Señores de Totonicapan* or the other important native accounts of Guatemala. They were not available until after the death of the Prophet. In fact, no reliable documentary sources were available in New York in 1830.

The only other time the *Obras Historicas de Ixtlilxochitl* have appeared in print was in 1891-92 in which years they were published in a two-volume edition in Mexico as an homage from Mexico to Columbus on the fourth centenary of the discovery of America.[6] This edition was also in the Spanish language.

No Help from Archæology in 1830

Lord Kingsborough, when publishing his *Mexican Antiquities,* had no help from archæology. Nor did Joseph Smith, when presenting to the world *The Book of Mormon* in 1830, have archæological data to assist him.

In 1841 and 1843, approximately eleven and thirteen years respectively after the publication of *The Book of Mormon,* John Lloyd Stephens published his two great books on travel in Middle America.[7] His works were practically the first ones to come from the press dealing with the marvelous ancient ruins extant on this hemisphere; therefore, his works hold a memorable place in the study of the people who inhabited America during the past ages. Concerning Stephens, an eminent American archæologist recently wrote:

> Stephens' writings were chiefly responsible for bringing the great cities of the Maya civilization to the attention of the outside world. Before the publication of his two books, the very existence of these cities was unknown outside of Yucatan and northern Central America. But, after their appearance, knowledge of the Maya, who developed our greatest native American civilization, became general on both sides of the Atlantic. With Stephens also begins the period of modern exploration of this region.[8]

Oddly enough, the very science of archæology was born about the year 1840.[9] And yet, already in 1950—after but 110 years, *The Book of Mormon* and the *Works of Ixtlilxochitl* have been confirmed to a surprising degree by archæology.

---

[6] Alfredo Chavero, editor, *Obras Historicas de Ixtlilxochitl,* 2 vois., Mexico, 1891-1892.
[7] John Lloyd Stephens, *Incidents of Travel in Central America, Chiapas, and Yucatan,* 1841; *Incidents of Travel in Yucatan,* 1843.
[8] Sylvanus G. Morley, *The Ancient Maya,* 1944, p. viii.
[9] Glyn E. Daniel, *A Hundred Years of Archaeology* (1950 ed.), ch. 3 "The Birth of Archaeology, 1840-1870."

Subsequent to the initial publication of *The Book of Mormon* (1830) and the *Works of Ixtlilxochitl* (1848) great institutions of learning have been engaged, through countless technicians, in the task of ascertaining facts concerning the origins, cultures, languages, and histories of the higher civilizations of both the ancient Near East (from whence came the highest cultures of ancient America—according to both *Ixtlilxochitl* and *The Book of Mormon*) and ancient America. They have brought to light a vast amount of knowledge concerning the ancient inhabitants of the western hemisphere. Further, since 1830 a vast wealth of historical-documentary material has become available to the students interested in the higher civilizations of the ancient peoples of this land. None of this material was accessible to Joseph Smith on the frontier of western New York in 1830. Lord Kingsborough published all that was available to himself.

The fact that sources available to the wealthy, educated, and traveled John Lloyd Stephens in 1841-1843 were likewise meager is indicated in his books.

No Help from Historical Sources

Regarding the dearth of documentary material available to Stephens and his contemporary, Joseph Smith, the former's biographer recently wrote:

It was a simple bibliographic fact in 1839 that there was no literature available to the American reader on the ancient American civilizations other than those [Kingsborough's *Antiquities of Mexico,* Volumes 1-6], recently published, which Stephens had read. . . . The reports on the Maya, voluminous detailed investigations made by priests and soldiers, still lay unpublished in the Spanish archives, or if printed, had been issued in editions of such rarity that they were inaccessible to scholars in America. Actually, before one could attempt literary research on these pre-Columbian civilizations, or the history of the Conquest, one would have to create an entire manuscript library.[10]

Joseph Smith read the books of Stephens with great interest.[11] In connection with editorials in the *Times and Seasons,* published

[10]Von Hagen, *op. cit.,* 1947, p. 78.
[11]Joseph Smith mentioned Stephens' book, *Incidents of Travel in Central America, Chiapas, and Yucatan,* 1841, in editorials in *Times and Seasons,* published in Nauvoo, Ill., September 15, 1842, and October 1, 1842. J. M. Sjodahl, *Introduction to the Study of The Book of Mormon,* 1927, pp. 93-95.

in Nauvoo, Illinois, September 15, 1842, and October 1, 1842, "Extracts" from Stephens' *Incidents of Travel in Central America* were published by the Mormon prophet. To quote the words of one of the editorial comments:

> Mr. Stephens' great development of antiquities are made bare to the eyes of all the people by reading the history of the Nephites in *The Book of Mormon.* They lived about the narrow neck of land, which now embraces Central America, with the cities that can be found. Read [in *The Book of Mormon* about] the destruction of cities at the crucifixion of Christ. . . .[12]

In the next issue of the *Times and Seasons,* published two weeks later (October 1, 1842), another editorial appeared on Stephens' book, followed by some more extracts quoted from the same source. Part of this editorial will appear later on in Chapter 13.

JOHN LLOYD STEPHENS AND JOSEPH SMITH COMPARED

John Lloyd Stephens was born November 28, 1805; Joseph Smith was born December 23, 1805. Stephens spent his early youth in New York City; Joseph Smith spent his early youth in the wilderness country of Vermont and western New York. Stephens lived in luxury; Joseph Smith lived in poverty. Stephens attended the best schools in the land for fourteen years, including Columbia College where he studied under Professor Charles Anthon;[13] Joseph Smith attended the little country schools in Vermont and in Palmyra, New York. In the year 1828 some of the hieroglyphs which Joseph had translated were shown to Professor Anthon.[14] Stephens traveled in the Near East, Europe, Africa and Central America before producing his two books on the ancient civilizations of Middle America; Joseph Smith traveled from Palmyra, New York, to Colesville

---

[12]*Times and Seasons,* vol. 3, no. 22, September 15, 1842, p. 915.
  Joseph Smith, "Truth Will Prevail," *Times and Seasons,* vol. 3 (Nauvoo, Ill., September 15, 1842), p. 915.

[13] Von Hagen, *op. cit.,* pp. 13-14, 66.

[14] Martin Harris took a transcript of some of the hieroglyphs to Prof. Charles Anthon at Columbia College (now Columbia University, in New York City) in February, 1828. Prof. Anthon later wrote two letters, one dated February, 17, 1834, and a second dated April 3, 1841, acknowledging this visit. These are quoted in Kirkham, *op. cit.,* pp. 364-371. Anthon did not know the Egyptian language, much less the modified syllabic Egyptian in which *The Book of Mormon* was written. He therefore was not competent to identify the transcript. He taught the classics and published 50 textbooks. Von Hagen, *op. cit.,* pp. 13-14.

and Harmony, Pennsylvania, before sending *The Book of Mormon* to the printer. Stephens produced books on ancient America in 1841-1843; *The Book of Mormon* was ready for the critics in 1830 (when Joseph Smith was twenty-four years old).[15] Stephens' books are today read by relatively few persons; *The Book of Mormon* is read and carefully perused by a million Mormons, one of the most literate and self-reliant people in the world.[16]

THE BOOK OF MORMON AND WORKS OF IXTLILXOCHITL FAR AHEAD OF THE TIMES

When first published, both *The Book of Mormon* and the *Works of Ixtlilxochitl* were apparently far ahead of the times. They credited some of the ancients of certain parts of the New World with such things as sedentary agriculture, metallurgy, hieroglyphic writing, mathematics, an astronomical calendar, and city-states under theocratic governments. In 1830, to credit any of the pre-European peoples of America with such a civilization was unheard of in New York and England. This is clearly stated by the biographer of Stephens, who is emphasizing the advanced nature of the writings of Stephens:

The acceptance of an "Indian civilization" demanded, to an American living in 1839, an entire reorientation, for to him an Indian was one of those barbaric, tepee-dwellers against whom wars were constantly waged. A rude, subhuman people who hunted with the stealth of animals, they were artisans of buffalo robes, arrowheads, and spears, and little else. Nor did one ever think of calling the other indigenous inhabitants of the continent "civilized." In the universally accepted opinion, they were like their North American counterparts—savages. No one dreamed that throughout the tablelands of Mexico, in the tangled scrub-jungles of Yucatan, there stood, covered by jungle verdure, ruins of temples, acropolises, and stone causeways of a civilization as great in extent as Egypt's. . . . "Aztec," "Maya," "Toltec," and "Inca" were in no dictionary, and in few histories.

These civilizations were not only dead, for dead implied having once lived, but, even to the world immersed in searching out the antique, absolutely unknown.

---

[15] Victor Wolfgang von Hagen, *Maya Explorer;* John Henry Evans, *Joseph Smith an American Prophet.*
[16] Supt. J. D. B. Denlow, *Compendium of the Census of 1850,* p. 152; John Clifton Moffitt, *The History of Public Education in Utah* (1946); M. Lynn Bennion, *Mormonism and Education* (1939); Raymond M. Hughes, William H. Lancelot, *Education—America's Magic* (Iowa State College Press, 1946), pp. 6, 9-11, 48, 49, 51, 57, 63, 67, 70, 73, 77, 78; Dr. Edward L. Thorndike, "Origin of Superior Men," *The Scientific Monthly* (May, 1943); Dr. John A. Widtsoe, Richard L. Evans, "The Educational Level of the Latter-day Saints," *The Improvement Era* (July, 1947); preceding authorities taken from this last mentioned source.

This blanket of oblivion that covered these civilizations had, in part, been woven on the loom of the well-known William Robertson, the eighteenth century Scottish historian: "Neither the Mexicans nor Peruvians [were] entitled to rank with those nations which merit the name of civilized.[17]

Greater detail regarding the very early colonizers responsible for the highest cultures of ancient America is found in *The Book of Mormon* and in the *Works of Ixtlilxochitl* than in any other known sources. Each is entirely independent of the other and yet they are in substantial accord on the basic aspects, as well as on most of the unique secondary aspects that characterized those higher cultures. Also, *The Book of Mormon* and the *Works of Ixtlilxochitl* agree precisely on certain dates assigned to important early historical events. Further, there are striking parallels between the two accounts on historical place names and geography. Each tends to clarify some of the obscure geographical points in the other. Each is corroborated by numerous reliable sixteenth-century documentary sources as well as by recent archæolgocial findings.

NEITHER HAS BEEN FAIRLY APPRAISED

Notwithstanding the foregoing facts, both *The Book of Mormon* and the *Works of Ixtlilxochitl* have been almost completely ignored by the technicians and archæological fact-finders interested in the great cultures of ancient America.

When *The Book of Mormon* is mentioned by the archæologist, it is generally for the purpose of berating the record. And invariably such writers reveal their ignorance of the book. To date most archæologists have complacently swept aside *The Book of Mormon,* satisfied to pass final judgment and sentence without examining what a lawyer would call "the best evidence," the book itself. They have been content to rely only on the moth-eaten discredited hearsay lore of former generations in preparing their sweeping condemnations of *The Book of Mormon.* Such unfair and untrue denunciations are still being published. In the recent biography of John Lloyd Stephens it is said, ". . . The theory was advanced that the Indians were descendants of the lost Tribes of Israel. This fancy was to endure for four hundred

[17] Von Hagen, *op. cit.*, p. 75.

years and into our own century, for the doctrines of the Mormon church are based on it."[18]

In one of the quarterly journals of the professional archæologists, *American Anthropologist*, a statement recently appeared which is also representative. It indicates that *The Book of Mormon* "attributes New World civilization to the Ten Lost Tribes of Israel."[19] This, of course, is far from the truth. It is most unscientific and yet it comes from a scientist. The same flagrant misstatement appears in a recent book by another archæologist. To quote:

> Some time in the 1820's Lord Kingsborough, son of an Irish peer of great wealth, got it into his head that the Lost Tribes of Israel were the ancestors of the Maya and the Aztecs—*the same idea that animated Joseph Smith* and *The Book of Mormon;* and in 1830—the very year that Smith's American supplement to the Bible appeared—Kingsborough began the publication of the nine monumental and handsomely illustrated volumes, *Antiquities of Mexico,* which cost him £25,000 and ultimately—like Smith —his life. Quite as eccentric theories followed.[20]

The author of the foregoing statement is quite correct in saying that both Lord Kingsborough and Joseph Smith gave their lives for their books, but he is in error when he states that *The Book of Mormon* deals with the Lost Tribes of Israel. One need read only the first few pages in the Nephite record to recognize this fact.

Ixtlilxochitl has fared little better than *The Book of Mormon*. He virtually has been ignored by the archæologists. It was a surprise indeed when in 1944 one of the leading archæologists, Vaillant, wrote of him: "This sixteenth-century writer is underestimated."[21]

It is hoped that the present volume will lead to a fresh and conscientious re-examination of both *The Book of Mormon* and the *Works of Ixtlilxochitl*.

WHAT IXTLILXOCHITL AND THE BOOK OF MORMON DO NOT PURPORT TO COVER

Neither *Ixtlilxochitl* nor *The Book of Mormon* purports to cover New World history before 3100 B. C. What may have happened prior to that date is not the concern of this book. *The*

---

[18] *Ibid.*, p. 76.
[19] Julian H. Stewart, in *American Anthropologist* (January-March, 1949), p. 113.
[20] Kenneth MacGowan, *Early Man in the New World* (1950), p. 13.
[21] George C. Vaillant, *Aztecs of Mexico* (1944), note 2, p. 285.

Book of Mormon deals with events from about the time of the erection of the Tower of Babel to 421 A. D. *Ixtlilxochitl* covers a somewhat greater time span. He also began his account with the history of the emigrants who migrated from the "Great Tower" to America, but he continues his account down to the Spanish Conquest shortly after 1500 A. D.

Neither *Ixtlilxochitl* nor *The Book of Mormon* purports to cover events over the entire New-World hemisphere. For example, neither reports on happenings in Alaska to the far north nor in Tierra del Fuego to the far south. *Ixtlilxochitl's* account is confined to events in central and southern Mexico and in Guatemala—and *The Book of Mormon* story is centered in the middle portion of the hemisphere.

Neither *Ixtlilxochitl* nor *The Book of Mormon* claims to deal with all people who entered the New World in ancient times. Neither purports to explain and account for all of the ancestry of all of the peoples found in the New World when the Europeans came here in the sixteenth century. Neither purports to explain the ancestry of all those people who are referred to collectively as the "American Indians." It is clear that some of the ancestry of some of those people entered the New World from northeastern Asia by way of Bering Straits. They left a trail of primitive artifacts behind them. Others may have come by island-hopping from the south Pacific. We are not concerned with such cases for they are outside the scope of both *Ixtlilxochitl* and *The Book of Mormon*. Reputable anthropologists maintain that there was a heavy influx of orientals and other types after 400 A. D. *The Book of Mormon* closes with the year 421 A. D.

English Translations Used Herein

The English translation of *Ixtlilxochitl's* writings was made from the 1891 Spanish edition. It includes only those parts dealing with pre-conquest history. The translator was Arnulfo Rodriguez who, in 1939, when the translation was made, was an instructor in Spanish at the University of California. He was well qualified for the task, having spent many years in Mexico, the land of his birth, and having had training in old Spanish. Further, while he was engaged in making the translation he had not the slightest knowledge of the nature or content of *The Book of Mormon*. His work was completely unbiased and impartial. His translation has not been altered.

The English translation of *The Book of Mormon* used herein is that of Joseph Smith. Only the most minor changes have been made in punctuation and spelling since the Mormon Prophet completed his original translation. The quotations are drawn from the 1920 edition, the one in widest and most current circulation.

FERNANDO DE ALVA DE IXTLILXOCHITL

A brief sketch of the life of *Ixtlilxochitl,* as well as one of the life of Joseph Smith, will be worth while at this point.

Ixtlilxochitl ". . . was born about 1568: he was a student at the College of Santa Cruz in Tlateloco [Mexico]; . . . he was an interpreter in the court of justice of the Indians; and he died in 1648 at the age of eighty."[22] His first work was written about 1600 and the second about 1608.[23] He spent his entire life in Mexico. Hubert Howe Bancroft comments: "Fernando de Alva Ixtlilxochitl was a grandson of the last king of Texcuco, from whom he inherited all that were saved of the records in the public archives. His works are more extensive than those of any other native writer. . . ." Bancroft further indicates that Ixtlilxochitl ". . . wrote honestly, compiling from authentic documents in his possession."[24] In 1941 George C. Vaillant, distinguished archæologist and authority on early cultures of Mexico, said of him, "He was a descendant of the old Texcocan lineage and had access to many of the ancient records."[25]

JOSEPH SMITH

Joseph Smith was born on a farm at Sharon in Windsor County, Vermont, December 23, 1805. He died at Carthage, Illinois, on June 27, 1844. His life-story has been summarized as follows:

Here is a man who was born in the stark hills of Vermont; who was reared in the backwoods of New York; who never looked inside a college or high school; who lived in six States, no one of which would own him during his lifetime; who spent months in the vile prisons of the period; who, even when he had his freedom, was hounded like a fugitive; who was covered once with a coat of tar and feathers, and left for dead; who, with his followers, was driven by irate neighbors from New York to Ohio, from

---

[22] Alfredo Chavero, preface to *Obras Historicas de Don Fernando de Alva Ixtlilxochitl* (1891 edition), vol. 1, p. 6.
[23] *Ibid.,* pp. 6-7.
[24] Hubert Howe Bancroft, *The Native Races of the Pacific States of North America* (1876), vol. 5, p. 147.
[25] Vaillant, *op. cit.,* p. 285.

Ohio to Missouri, and from Missouri to Illinois; and who, at the unripe age of thirty-eight, was shot to death by a mob with painted faces.

Yet this man became mayor of the biggest town in Illinois and the state's most prominent citizen, the commander of the largest body of trained soldiers in the nation outside the Federal army, the founder of cities and of a university, and aspired to become President of the United States.

He wrote [sic] a book which has baffled the literary critics for a hundred years and which is today more widely read than any other volume save the Bible. On the threshold of an organizing age he established the most nearly perfect social mechanism in the modern world, and developed a religious philosophy that challenges anything of the kind in history, for completeness and cohesion. And he set up the machinery for an economic system that would take the brood of fears out of the heart of man—the fear of want through sickness, old age, unemployment, and poverty.

In thirty nations are men and women who look upon him as a greater leader than Moses and a greater prophet than Isaiah; his disciples now number close to a million [over a million], and already a granite shaft pierces the sky over the place where he was born, and another over the place where he is credited with having received the [records which he translated, *The Book of Mormon*.][26]

SUMMARY STATEMENT

Since Joseph Smith received no help from archæology or documentary sources—no such help having been available—it follows that he either fabricated *The Book of Mormon* or he took it from original tablets made available to him by the Lord, as he claimed. There could have been no middle scholastic ground in 1830. The writings of *Ixtlilxochitl*, which might have been of real aid to a scholar, which Joseph Smith was not, were not published until included in Lord Kingsborough's works, volume IX, in 1848. If the writings of either Joseph Smith or *Ixtlilxochitl*, or both, are fabrications, such should be readily apparent in the light of present-day knowledge derived from undisputed archæological and documentary sources brought to light since 1830-1848.

The Book of Mormon and the writings of *Ixtlilxochitl*, however, support, clarify and augment one another, and—in turn— are corroborated to an amazing degree by the earliest and best documentary sources available, as well as by recent archæological discoveries. It is time that both *Ixtlilxochitl* and *The Book of Mormon* were fairly appraised.

---

[26] John Henry Evans, *Joseph Smith an American Prophet* (1944), preface statement.

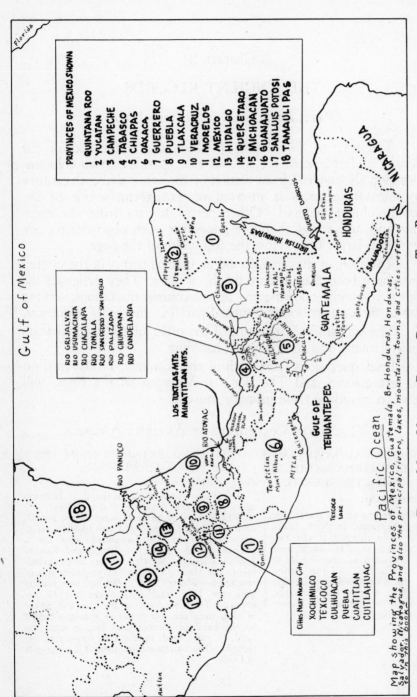

PROVINCES OF MEXICO SHOWN

1 QUINTANA ROO
2 YUCATAN
3 CAMPECHE
4 TABASCO
5 CHIAPAS
6 OAXACA
7 GUERRERO
8 PUEBLA
9 TLAXCALA
10 VERACRUZ
11 MORELOS
12 MEXICO
13 HIDALGO
14 QUERETARO
15 MICHOACAN
16 GUANAJUATO
17 SAN LUIS POTOSI
18 TAMAULIPAS

RIO GRIJALVA
RIO USUMACINTA
RIO CHACALAPA
RIO TONALA
RIO SAN PEDRO Y SAN PABLO
RIO PALIZADA
RIO CHUMPAN
RIO CANDELARIA

CITIES NEAR MEXICO CITY
XOCHIMILCO
TEXCOCO
CULHUACAN
PUEBLA
CUATITLAN
CUITLAHUAC

Gulf of Mexico

Pacific Ocean

Map showing the Provinces of Mexico, Guatemala, Br. Honduras, Honduras,
Salvador, Nicaragua, and also the principal rivers, lakes, mountains, towns and cities referred
to in this book.

Fig. 4: MAP—VARIOUS PLACES DISCUSSED IN THIS BOOK

Chapter 2

THE ANCIENT RECORDS

Pattern Followed in This Book

The text of *The Book of Mormon* and the text of the *Works of Ixtlilxochitl* are set out side by side in two columns. Occasionally material from certain of the other sixteenth-century documentary sources is inserted on *Ixtlilxochitl's* side of the double-column material. Other pertinent data from documentary and archæological sources, together with observations, are set out in larger type across the full width of the page.

The Roman numerals found at various points in the quoted texts have been placed there by the writers. They designate the topics discussed following the double-column quotations, serving also to direct attention to unusual parallels and cross references.

The writers have rearranged the order of the original texts for systematic and chronological handling.

Brief quotations from each of the accounts, *Ixtlilxochitl* on the left column, and *The Book of Mormon* on the right, will serve to introduce these primary sources.

I. Cultured Colonizers of Ancient America

HISTORICAL WORKS OF DON FERNANDO DE ALVA IXTLILXOCHITL:

Summary Account

Concerning all the things that have happened in New Spain, and many things that the *Tultecas*[1] understood and knew, from the Creation of the World to its destruction, and the coming of the third Chichimeca settlers to the coming of the Spaniards, taken from the original history of this New Spain.

HISTORICAL EXTRACTS FROM THE BOOK OF MORMON:

Book of Mormon Preface

An account written by the hand of Mormon upon plates taken from the Plates of Nephi.

Wherefore, it is an abridgment of the records of the people of Nephi, and also of the Lamanites—Written to the Lamanites, who are a remnant of the house of Israel; and also to Jew and Gentile—Written by way of commandment, and also by the spirit of prophecy and of revelation—Written and sealed up, and hid up unto the Lord, that they might not be destroyed—To come forth by the gift and power of God unto the interpretation thereof—Sealed by the hand of Moroni, and hid up unto the Lord, to come forth in due time by way of the Gentile—The interpretation thereof by the gift of God.

18

An abridgment taken from the Book of
Ether also, which is a record of the people of
Jared, who were scattered at the time the Lord
confounded the language of the people, when
they were building a tower to get to heaven—
Which is to show unto the remnant of the House
of Israel what great things the Lord hath done
for their fathers; and that they may know the
covenants of the Lord, that they are not cast off
forever—And also to the convincing of the Jew
and Gentile that JESUS is the CHRIST, the
ETERNAL GOD, manifesting himself unto all
nations—And now, if there are faults they are
the mistakes of men; wherefore, condemn not
the things of God, that ye may be found spotless
at the judgment-seat of Christ.

Ixtlilxochitl sometimes uses the name *"Tultecas"* in referring generally to all the highly cultured colonizers of ancient
Middle America. As we study the *Works of Ixtlilxochitl,* we
find that he gives an account of three separate groups of people
who came from across the ocean to colonize America. The first
of these, he claims, migrated to the New World from *"the very
high tower"* at the time of the confusion of tongues. He calls
this group by several different names. First he calls them *"Tultecas"* and he distinguishes them from the later Tultecas by calling
them *"the Ancient Ones."* He also refers to them as *"the
Giants."*

Later in his book he speaks of another group of advanced
people who came to Middle America by sea. These he also calls
Tultecas. These people are referred to in ancient Guatemalan
histories as the early *Nahuas* or *Nahuales.*

Ixtlilxochitl speaks of a third group of people who came
across the ocean to settle America. These he calls *Ulmecs.* The
spelling that is usually given for the name is *Olmecs.*

The Book of Mormon, like the *Works of Ixtlilxochitl,* also
gives an account of three groups of people who settled in ancient
America. The first settlers that *The Book of Mormon* speaks
of are called the "Jaredites." They, like *Ixtlilxochitl's* first settlers,
came from the "great tower" (Babel) at the time of the confusion of tongues. Their civilization flourished in America for more
than 2,000 years. These people seem to be the earliest Tultecas
(the Ancient Ones, the Giants) of Ixtlilxochitl's history.

The Book of Mormon, like *Ixtlilxochitl,* tells of the second
group of cultured people who settled ancient America. They
left the Near East about 600 B. C., arriving in the New World

several years later after enduring great hardships. They were led by a prophet named Lehi and his son Nephi. The people took upon themselves the name *"Nephites."* Their principal homeland was Bountiful-*Zarahemla* (bountiful plant land). This people seem to be the second "Tultecas," the "artisans," of *Ixtlilxochitl's* history. A number of sixteenth-century writers spoke of a group of early settlers of America whom they called the *"early Nahuas or Nahuales."* Note the close resemblance of the names "Nahuas" or "Nahuales" with that of "Nephites." It seems that those names may have been derived from *The Book of Mormon* name of the people of ancient Bountiful. These people flourished in a certain part of the New World, distin-guished by an advanced imported culture, for approximately 1,000 years and then their government and civilization collapsed in a destructive war in 385 A. D. The last event recorded in *The Book of Mormon* occurred in 421 A. D.

The Book of Mormon, like *Ixtlilxochitl*, tells of a third group of artisans who migrated to ancient America. This group likewise came from the Near East about 586 B. C. or fourteen years after the Nephites had come from the same locale. The most prominent member of this group was Mulek, a son (prob-ably in his infancy for he is not mentioned in the Old Testament story) of King Zedekiah of Jerusalem. Since Mulek was of the royal family, these people called themselves "Mulekites." About 200 B. C. the *Mulekites* and the *Nephites* merged together as one people in the central region of the hemisphere and from that time forward the combined people were known as Nephites. In some of the sixteenth-century accounts, there are references to a merger of two groups of people in ancient America. It seems possible that these writers are referring to the same merger that is described in the Nephites' records. The *Mulekites* of *The Book of Mormon* may be identical with the people that *Ixtlilxochitl* calls "Ulmecs." Observe the similarity in the names "Mulek" and "Ulmec."

A comparison and study of the texts of *Ixtlilxochitl* and *The Book of Mormon* will now be made.

Chapter 3

KNOWLEDGE OF CREATION AND FLOOD

Introductory Statement

According to Ixtlilxochitl, the earliest Tultecas, elsewhere referred to by him as "the Ancient Ones" or Giants, had a knowledge of the creation of the world and the great flood. *The Book of Mormon* credits the early emigrants from Babel with the same knowledge.

II. Creation of the World

IXTLILXOCHITL:

Creation[1a]

Concerning the creation of the World and the origin of the Indians, only God is the one who knows all things. But what has been able to be known easily, according to the Tultecas, is what follows:

The Tultecas understood and knew of the creation of the World[II] and how *Tloque Nahuaque* created it, and the other things that are in it, such as planets, mountains, animals, etc., and in the same manner they knew how God created a man and a woman from whom men descended and multiplied, and concerning this they add many fables that in order to avoid prolixity are not set here; and it is not to be wondered at, for the other nations of the world have done the same thing.

EXTRACTS—BOOK OF MORMON:[1]

Creation

1. And now I, Moroni, proceed to give an account of those ancient inhabitants who were destroyed by the hand of the Lord upon the face of this north country.

2. And I take mine account from the twenty and four plates which were found by the people of Limhi, which is called the Book of Ether.

3. And as I suppose that the first part of this record, which speaks concerning the creation of the world,[III] and also of Adam, and an account from that time even to the great tower, and whatsoever things transpired among the children of men until that time, is had among the Jews—

4. Therefore I do not write those things which transpired from the days of Adam until that time; but they are had upon the plates; and whoso findeth them, the same will have power that he may get the full account.

Ether 1:1-4.[2]

The quotation from *The Book of Mormon* clearly shows that the Jaredites—the earliest New-World colonists from Bible lands, having come from the Tower of Babel—had a knowledge of the creation of the world and of the early history of mankind.

[1a] The italicized words or phrases which appear immediately below "IXTLILXOCHITL" and "EXTRACTS—BOOK OF MORMON" were placed there by the writers for the purpose of pointing out to the readers the principal points to observe in the discussions that follow. They will serve as an outline.

[1] Generally speaking *The Book of Mormon* contains many more details than does *Ixtlilxochitl*; therefore, extracts have been selected. *Ixtlilxochitl's* full account is given on each topic throughout the book.

[2] See also *The Book of Mormon*, p. 190 (Mosiah 28:17); p. 131 (Omni 1:20-22).

21

The knowledge that the Jaredites knew those things was carried forward for 1,000 years throughout the entire course of Nephite history. And even after their destruction it continued to persist in the traditions of the Indians for 1,200 years more, even to the time of *Ixtlilxochitl*. That fact is made clear in the foregoing material presented from his writings, for he declares that the ancient Tultecas knew about God as the Creator of the world and also that He created man and woman who multiplied and filled the earth with their posterity.

Many other quotations could be taken from *The Book of Mormon* regarding the doctrine of the fall of man and God's relationship with the human family since the early periods of civilization. *Ixtlilxochitl's* statement is in accord with such statements in *The Book of Mormon*.

III. Deluge (Flood) and Ark of Noah

IXTLILXOCHITL:

Flood and Ark

And they say that the world was created in the year of the *ce Tecpatl,* and this epoch up to the *deluge*[III] they called *Atona-tiuh,* which means, *age of the sun of water,* because the world was destroyed by the deluge; and it is found in the Tulteca histories that this age and first world, as they called it, lasted 1716 years;[3] that men were destroyed by very great storms and lightnings from heaven, and the whole world without a thing remaining, and the highest mountains *Caxtolmoletltli,*[4] which are fifteen cubits, were covered with water; and they add likewise other fables, and how men began to multiply from a few that escaped this destruction within a *Toptlipetlacalli,* which almost means *closed ark.*[III]

EXTRACTS—BOOK OF MORMON:

Flood and Ark

7. And it came to pass that when they [the Jaredites] were buried in the deep there was no water that could hurt them, their vessels being tight like unto a dish, and also they were tight like unto the *ark of Noah;*[III] therefore when they were encompassed about by many waters they did cry unto the Lord, and he did bring them forth again upon the top of the waters.

Ether 6:7.

The Book of Mormon account agrees in detail with the *Works of Ixtlilxochitl* in the report of a universal flood or deluge and also in the reference made to the fact that a few of the people were saved from destruction in a "closed ark" or the "ark of

---

[3] According to *Ixtlilxochitl's* chronology, the creation took place about 5229 B. C. If the deluge took place 1716 years after the creation, the date of the deluge would be 3513 B. C., according to his reckoning. *The Book of Mormon* gives no date for the deluge or the building of the Tower of Babel.

[4] Should be spelled "Caxtolmolictli."

Noah." Furthermore, it is a significant fact that both of these accounts corroborate the story of Noah and the flood as contained in the Hebrew scriptures.

SUMMARY STATEMENT

Since the two accounts correspond very closely concerning the Creation and the Flood, some will suggest that *Ixtlilxochitl* obtained his information for this part of his account from the Spaniards who brought the book of Genesis with them to the New World. However, it will be seen throughout the book that there are innumerable parallels, equally as close, on the matters entirely unknown to the Spanish conquerors.

Ixtlilxochitl and *The Book of Mormon* each use the conjunction "and" with about the same frequency and regularity as did the ancient Semites of the Near East, it is observed.

Chapter 4

MIGRATION FROM THE GREAT TOWER

INTRODUCTORY STATEMENT

Both *Ixtlilxochitl* and *The Book of Mormon* declare that the earliest cultured settlers departed from the Old World at the time of the building of a tower. *Ixtlilxochitl* refers to this structure as "The Very High Tower," whereas *The Book of Mormon* refers to the structure as "The Great Tower." The term Babel, it is understood, is a comparatively recent appellation—so no anachronistic error is committed in either of our sources. Other details of the two accounts are in close agreement. Both refer to the confusion of tongues. *Ixtlilxochitl* dates the exodus from Babel at 3097 B. C.

The eminent Bernardino de Sahagun (1499-1590) in his *History of the Things of New Spain* discusses the coming of these settlers to ancient America and even fixes the place of landing at the mouth of the Panuco River, a point not far from the present city of Tampico, Mexico. Following *Ixtlilxochitl's* statement concerning these matters, we have inserted in the left-hand column Sahagun's observations.

BABEL, CONFUSION OF TONGUES AND MIGRATION TO AMERICA

IXTLILXOCHITL:	EXTRACTS—BOOK OF MORMON:
Zacualli, high tower, confusion of tongues, migration, fertile land	*Great tower, confusion of tongues, migration,, choice land*
And [the Tulteca history tells] how afterwards men, multiplying made a very tall and strong Zacualli,[IV] which means *the very high tower*,[V & IX] in order to shelter themselves in it when the second world should be destroyed.	33. . . . Jared came forth with his brother and their families, with some others and their families, from *the great tower*,[V & IX] at the time *the Lord confounded the language of the people*,[VI] and swore in his wrath that they should be *scattered upon all the face of the earth;* and according to the word of the Lord *the people were scattered.*[VI]
When things were at their best, *their languages were changed*[VI] and, not understanding each other, *they went to different parts of the world;*[VI] and the Tultecas, who were as many	34. And the brother of Jared being a large and mighty man, and a man highly favored of the Lord, Jared, his brother, said unto him: Cry unto the Lord, that he will not confound us that we may not understand our words.

24

as seven companions and their wives, *who understood their language among themselves,*[VII] came to these parts, having first crossed large lands and seas, *living in caves*[VIII] and undergoing great hardships, until they came to this land, which *they found good and fertile for their habitation.*[X]

* * *

It is the common and general opinion of all the natives of all this Chichimeca land, which is now called new Spain, besides appearing in the demonstration of their pictures, that their ancestors came from *Occidental parts,* and all of them are now called Tultecas, Aculhuas, Mexicanos; and other nations that are in this land say that they are of the lineage of the Chichimecas, and are proud of it; and the reason is, according as it appears in their histories, that the first king they had was called *Chichimecatl,* who was the one who brought them to this New World where they settled, who, as can be inferred, came from the great Tartary, *and they were of those of the division of Babylon,* as it is declared more at length in the history that is written.

And they say that they traveled for 104 years through different parts of the world until they arrived at *Huehue Tlapallan* their country, which happened in *ce Tecpatl,* for it had been 520 years[IX] since the Deluge had taken place, which are five ages.

35. And it came to pass that the brother of Jared did cry unto the Lord, and *the Lord had compassion upon Jared; therefore he did not confound the language of Jared; and Jared and his brother were not confounded.*[VI]

36. Then Jared said unto his brother; Cry again unto the Lord, and it may be that he will turn away his anger from them who are our friends, that he confound not their language.

37. And it came to pass that the brother of Jared did cry unto the Lord, and *the Lord had compassion upon their friends and their families also, that they were not confounded.*[VII]
Ether 1:33-37.

16. And the friends of Jared and his brother were in number about twenty and two souls; and they also begat sons and daughters before they came to the promised land; and therefore they began to be many. . . .

20. And accordingly the people were gathered together. Now the number of the sons and the daughters of the brother of Jared were twenty and two souls; and the number of sons and daughters of Jared were twelve, he having four sons.
Ether 6:14-16, 20.

40. And it came to pass that the Lord did hear the brother of Jared, and had compassion upon him, and said unto him:

41. Go to and gather thy flocks, both male and female, of every kind; and also of the seed of the earth of every kind; and thy families; and also Jared thy brother and his family; and also thy friends and their families, and the friends of Jared and their families.

42. And when thou hast done this thou shalt go at the head of them down into the valley which is northward. And there will I meet thee, and *I will go before thee into a land which is choice above all the lands of the earth.*[X]

43. And there will I bless thee and thy seed, and raise up unto me of thy seed, and of the seed of thy brother, and they who shall go with thee, a great nation. And there shall be none greater than the nation which I will raise up unto me of thy seed, upon all the face of the earth. And thus I will do unto thee because this long time ye have cried unto me.
Ether 1:40-43.

1. And it came to pass that Jared and his brother, and their families, and also the friends of Jared and his brother and their families, went down into the valley which was northward, (and the name of the valley was Nimrod, being called after the mighty hunter) with their flocks which they had gathered together, male and female, of every kind.

2. And they did also lay snares and catch fowls of the air; and they did also prepare a vessel, in which they did carry with them the fish of the waters.

3. And they did also carry with them deseret, which, by interpretation, is a honey bee; and thus they did carry with them swarms of bees, and all manner of that which was upon the face of the land, seeds of every kind.

4. And it came to pass that when they had come down into the valley of Nimrod the Lord came down and talked with the brother of Jared; and he was in a cloud, and the brother of Jared saw him not.

5. And it came to pass that the Lord commanded them that they should go forth into the wilderness, yea, into that quarter where there never had man been. And it came to pass that the Lord did go before them, and did talk with them as he stood in a cloud, and gave directions whither they should travel.

6. And it came to pass that they did travel in the wilderness, and did build barges,[VIII] in which they did cross many waters, being directed continually by the hand of the Lord.

7. And the Lord would not suffer that they should stop beyond the sea in the wilderness, but he would *that they should come forth even unto the land of promise, which was choice above all other lands, which the Lord God had preserved for a righteous people.*[X] . . .   Ether 2:1-7.

IV.[1a] ZACUALLI

It is noteworthy that *Ixtlilxochitl* defines the Mexican word, *Zacualli,* which he uses in naming *"the very high tower."* The *Book of Mormon* refers to the Tower of Babel in similar language, calling it *"the great tower."* In another place *Ixtlilxochitl* says of the earliest Tultecas, ". . . they were those of the division of Babylon, as it is declared more at length in the history that is written; and this their king, as he traveled on with them through the greater part of the world, arrived in this land, and the land seeming to them to be good, fertile, and abundant for human sustenance, as has been said, they settled the greater part of it [Mexico], especially that toward the north. . . ."

The Book of Mormon and the *Works of Ixtlilxochitl* explain, therefore, why the temple towers of Middle America are identical in style and purpose with those of the ancient Near East. The prototype was the Great Tower itself. The term *Babel* is from *babilu,* meaning "gate of God."[1]

[1a] The reader is reminded that the Roman numerals refer to material presented in the double columns.
[1] Hugo Gressman, *The Tower of Babel* (1928), pp. 5-8.

V. Earliest Toltecas, "The Ancient Ones"—(Jaredites) —Came From Tower of Babel

Certain other ancient native accounts from southern Mex' ico indicate that the earliest artisans of Middle America came from Babel in the Chaldean country. One of the most important was a hieroglyphic manuscript referred to by the Spaniards who knew of it as the *Probanza de Votan*, meaning "*Proof [of the genealogy] of Votan*." As late as the eighteenth century, it was in the hands of Nuñez de la Vega, a Catholic priest who had been Bishop in Chiapas in southern Mexico before publishing in Rome in 1702 his *Constituciones Diocesanas del Obispado de Chiappa*. In the latter work he refers to one of the earliest tradi' tional colonizers, Votan, as follows:

Votan is the third gentile placed on the calendar [of the *Tzendal Mayas*] and in the historical manuscript [*Probanza de Votan*] written in the Indian language are mentioned stops and towns where he was . . . and he is said to have seen the great wall, which is the Tower of Babel, which by the command of Noah, his grandfather, was made from the earth to the sky, and who was the first man God sent to divide and distribute this land of the Indies, and there where he saw the great wall, was given to each nation its different language.[2]

The hieroglyphic manuscript of Votan has been lost. Per' haps it was a victim of the ignorance that was responsible for many such tragic literary losses during the Spanish Inquisition. At any rate it disappeared, as did the most complete work com' piled directly from it, the historical writings of Don Ramon de Ordoñez y Aguiar. Ordoñez was a resident priest in the town Ciudad Real in Chiapas, one of the southernmost states of Mexico. Don Ramon wrote a two-volume work, the first on the history and the second on the religion of the ancients of the Chiapas region. About the year 1803, he sent his manuscript to Spain to be printed. He never saw it again and died not knowing what had become of it. It is posssible that it was sup' pressed.[3] However, the first portion which deals with the religion of the ancient Americans has survived in Mexico, apparently from a duplicate of the original which went to Spain. Thus, the title of his two-volume work has been preserved and from it we see that, working from the *Probanza de Votan*, Don Ramon tells

---

[2] Translated from Nuñez de la Vega, *Constituciones Diocesanas del Obispado de Chiappa*, written in 1692, published in Rome in 1702, Preamble, Paragraph 34 Sec. 30, p. 9.

[3] E. Charles Brasseur de Bourbourg, *Lettres Pour Servir d'Introduction a L'Histoire Primitive des Nacions*.

of the earliest emigrants coming across the ocean from Babylon
after the building of the Tower of Babel. The title of his works,
translated from the Spanish, reads:

"HISTORY OF THE CREATION OF THE
HEAVENS AND THE EARTH
according to the system of the American Gentility

THEOLOGY OF THE SERPENTS
represented in ingenious hieroglyphs, symbols,
emblems and metaphors,
Universal Deluge, Dispersion of Mankind

---

*True origin of the Indians: their departure from Chaldea: their
immigration to these southern parts: their crossing the ocean, and
the defeat which followed, until their arrival in Mexico*
Beginning of their empire, foundation and destruction of their
ancient and first court, discovered recently, and known by the
name city of Palenque[4]

Superstitious worship with which the ancient Palencans worshiped
the true God, pictured in those symbols and emblems, which
placed in the altars of their temples, lately degenerated into abominable idols

Books, all of the most venerable antiquity; some taken from the
forgotten past: others recently discovered: and their symbols,
emblems and metaphors interpreted according to the genuine
meaning of American phraseology."[5]

An effort has recently been made to locate the manuscript
of Ordoñez y Aguiar. Correspondence with the Vatican in
Rome, with the Archivo General de Indias in Seville, Spain,
and with the Manuscripts Section, National Library, Mexico,.
has resulted negatively.

Ordoñez y Aguiar apparently feared that the information
he was setting forth from the *Probanza de Votan* might be sup-
pressed. In his introduction to the portion of his writings which
survived he attempted to prepare the way and justify publication of his material. He stated that there was a basis for sup-
pressing the information in 1700 A. D. in the day of Nuñez

---

[4] Palenque is an existing community in the state of Chiapas, Mexico. A great ruined city of the ancient
Mayas is located near the village. The native accounts clearly indicated that somewhere in the
general vicinity of Palenque was located the great capital center of the second Toltecas settlers,
Tullan or *Tula*, "Bountiful" or "Bountiful plant-land." However, it is not likely that the Palenque
ruins visible today are to be identified with either Jaredites or Nephites for the standing monuments
date from the seventh century A. D. Ordoñez y Aguiar was in error in locating the first colonizers
from the Near East in the Palenque area.
[5] Translated from the only known edition, one published in Mexico about 1907.

de la Vega, when the natives were being "converted" from their ancient religion. But, he says, writing in about 1800, ". . . the Indians are no longer capable of understanding the errors of their paganism . . . and it would not be fair or just to deprive the scholars any longer of the rare and wonderful antiquities of which both sacred and profane American history abound, there being no reason whatever for withholding them."[6] Unfortunately, the *Probanza de Votan* is still not available, nor are the historical writings of the priest who understood that hieroglyphic document and who wrote a volume concerning the data therein.

VI. Confounding of Tongues and Scattering the People

The parallels between the two records—*The Book of Mormon* and *Ixtlilxochitl*—on the confusion of tongues at the Tower of Babel and scattering the people throughout the world are astounding. The fact that both of the records claim that the early colonizers of ancient Middle America came from Babel immediately following the time that the "Lord confounded the language of the people" is very significant. Such statements coming from two sources recorded twelve hundred years apart, both being in perfect agreement with each other, are evidence that both Mormon and *Ixtlilxochitl* drew their materials from earlier records which stem ultimately from the same source.

VII. Language of Ancient Americans Not Confounded

The readers are invited to compare the two records in their statements regarding the fact that God permitted the members of the entire party that first colonized ancient America from the Near East to retain their original tongue; therefore, they all spoke the same language. The language that they used has been referred to by some writers as the Adamic language.

It could never be maintained successfully that *Ixtlilxochitl* learned from the Spaniards that the language of the group of people who migrated to America from the Towel of Babel was not confounded. There is only one conceivable way that he could have learned such a fact and that way was through the traditions and histories of his forefathers. Ether, the last Jaredite

---

[6] Don Ramon Ordoñez y Aguiar, *Historia de la Creacion del Cielo y de la Tierra* . . . (Mexico), p. 15, translated from the Spanish.

prophet, recorded the foregoing fact in the Book of Ether; and the knowledge of it came down from age to age through the Nephites and their successors, the Lamanites, to the Mexican historian, *Ixtlilxochitl*. This is one more proof that he had at his disposal, as he claimed to have, reliable documents when he wrote his history.

BARGES, OCEAN VOYAGE, AND PROMISED LAND

EXTRACTS—BERNARDINO DE SAHAGUN, HISTORIA DE LAS COSAS DE NUEVA ESPAÑA:

Seven caves or ships, landing place, choice land

[*Sahagun, born in Spain in 1499, lived in Mexico from 1529 to 1590. He wrote this important and scholarly work in the latter part of the 16th century. It is one of the most reliable and comprehensive reports concerning the ancients of Middle America. His history was lost and unknown for 300 years after it was written. Finally it was discovered in a convent in Spain. The first publication appeared in Mexico in 1829. Lord Kingsborough published it as volume 8 of his Mexican Antiquities in 1848. Since then there have been numerous other Spanish-language editions. A portion has been published in English.*]

Concerning the origin of these peoples, the report the old men [of central Mexico—where Sahagun lived many years] give is that they came by sea from the north [i.e., down the Gulf Coast of Mexico], and true it is that they came in some wooden boats but it is not known how they [the boats] were hewn, but it is conjectured by a report found among all these natives that they came from seven caves,[VIII] and that these seven caves are the seven ships or galleys in which the first settlers of this land came, as gathered from likely conjectures.

The people first came to settle this land from the direction of Florida, and came coasting along

EXTRACTS—BOOK OF MORMON:

Barges, ocean voyage, arrival in promised land

13. And now I proceed with my record; for behold, it came to pass that the Lord did bring Jared and his brethren forth even to that great sea which divideth the lands. And as they came to the sea they pitched their tents; and they called the name of the place Moriancumer; and they dwelt in tents, and dwelt in tents upon the seashore for the space of four years.

14. And it came to pass at the end of four years that the Lord came again unto the brother of Jared, and stood in a cloud and talked with him, and for the space of three hours did the Lord talk with the brother of Jared, and chastened him because he remembered not to call upon the name of the Lord.

15. And the brother of Jared repented of the evil which he had done, and did call upon the name of the Lord for his brethren who were with him. And the Lord said unto him: I will forgive thee and thy brethren of their sins; but thou shalt not sin any more, for ye shall remember that my Spirit will not always strive with man; wherefore, if ye will sin until ye are fully ripe ye shall be cut off from the presence of the Lord. And these are my thoughts upon *the land which I shall give you for your inheritance; for it shall be a land choice above all other lands.*[X]

16. And the Lord said: Go to work and build, after the manner of barges[VIII] which ye have hitherto built. And it came to pass that the brother of Jared did go to work, and also his brethren, and built barges after the manner which they had built, according to the instructions of the Lord. And they were small, and they were light upon the water, even like unto the lightness of a fowl upon the water.

17. And they were built after a manner that they were exceeding tight, even that they would hold water like unto a dish; and the bottom thereof was tight like unto a dish; and the sides thereof were tight like unto a dish; and the ends thereof were peaked; and the top thereof was tight like unto a dish; and the length thereof was the length of a tree; and the door thereof, when it was shut, was tight like unto a dish.

the coast disembarking in the port of Panuco, which they call *Panco,* which means "place where those arrived who crossed the water."[VIII] This people came in search of the terrestrial paradise,[X] and they had as a family name Tamoanchan, which means "we are looking for our home."

Introduccion al Primer Libro.

18. And it came to pass that the brother of Jared cried unto the Lord, saying: O Lord, I have performed the work which thou hast commanded me, and I have made the barges according as thou has directed me. . . .

20. And the Lord said unto the brother of Jared: Behold, thou shalt make a hole in the top, and also in the bottom; and when thou shalt suffer for air thou shalt unstop the hole and receive air. And if it be so that the water come in upon thee, behold, ye shall stop the hole, that ye may not perish in the flood.

21. And it came to pass that the brother of Jared did so, according as the Lord commanded.

22. And he cried again unto the Lord saying: O Lord, behold I have done even as thou hast commanded me; and I have prepared the vessels for my people, and behold there is no light in them. Behold, O Lord, wilt thou suffer that we shall cross this great water in darkness?

23. And the Lord said unto the brother of Jared: What will ye that I should do that ye may have light in your vessels? For behold, ye cannot have windows, for they will be dashed in pieces; neither shall ye take fire with you, for ye shall not go by the light of fire.

24. For behold, ye shall be as a whale in the midst of the sea; for the mountain waves shall dash upon you. Nevertheless, I will bring you up again out of the depths of the sea; for the winds have gone forth out of my mouth, and also the rains and the floods have I sent forth.

1. And it came to pass that the brother of Jared, (now the number of the vessels which had been prepared was eight) went forth unto the mount, which they called the mount Shelem, because of its exceeding height, and did molten out of a rock sixteen small stones; and they were white and clear, even as transparent glass; and he did carry them in his hands upon the top of the mount, and cried again unto the Lord, saying . . .

6. And it came to pass that when the brother of Jared had said these words, behold, the Lord stretched forth his hand and touched the stones one by one with his finger. And the veil was taken from off the eyes of the brother of Jared, and he saw the finger of the Lord; and it was as the finger of a man, like unto flesh and blood; and the brother of Jared fell down before the Lord, for he was struck with fear. . . .

2. For it came to pass after the Lord had prepared the stones which the brother of Jared had carried up into the mount, the brother of Jared came down out of the mount, and he did put forth the stones into the vessels which were prepared, one in each end thereof; and behold they did give light unto the vessels.

Ether 2:1-7, 13-18, 20-24; 3:1, 6; 6:2.

4. And it came to pass that when they had prepared all manner of food, that thereby they might subsist upon the water, and also food for their flocks and herds, and whatsoever beast or animal or fowl that they should carry with them —and it came to pass that when they had done all these things they got aboard of their vessels or barges, and set forth into the sea, commending themselves unto the Lord their God.

5. And it came to pass that the Lord God caused that there should be a furious wind blow upon the face of the waters, *towards the promised land;* and thus they were tossed upon the waves of the sea before the wind.

6. And it came to pass that they were many times buried in the depths of the sea, because of the mountain waves which broke upon them, and also the great and terrible tempests which were caused by the fierceness of the wind.

7. And it came to pass that when they were buried in the deep there was no water that could hurt them, their vessels being tight like unto a dish, and also they were tight like unto the ark of Noah; therefore when they were encompassed about by many waters they did cry unto the Lord, and he did bring them forth again upon the top of the waters.

8. *And it came to pass that the wind did never cease to blow towards the promised land* while they were upon the waters; and thus they were driven forth before the wind.

9. And they did sing praises unto the Lord; yea, the brother of Jared did sing praises unto the Lord, and he did thank and praise the Lord all the day long; and when the night came, they did not cease to praise the Lord.

10. And thus they were driven forth; and no monster of the sea could break them, neither whale that could mar them; and they did have light continually, whether it was above the water or under the water.

11. And thus they were driven forth, three hundred and forty and four days upon the water.

12. *And they did land upon the shore of the promised land.*[x] And when they had set their feet upon the shores of the promised land they bowed themselves down upon the face of the land, and did shed tears of joy before the Lord, because of the multitude of his tender mercies over them.

13. And it came to-pass that they went forth upon the face of the land, and began to till the earth.

18. . . . and they did wax strong in the land.

Ether 6:4-13, 18.

18. And it came to pass that they began to spread upon the face of the land, and to multiply and to till the earth; and they did wax strong in the land. . . .

6. Now the land of Moron, where the king dwelt, was near the land which is called Desolation by the Nephites.[XLIII]   Ether 6:18; 7:6.

30. [Regarding the land which had been inhabited by the Jaredites, a Nephite historian wrote:] And it [Bountiful, the Nephite land] bordered upon the land which they called Desolation, it being so far northward that it came into the land which had been peopled and been destroyed, of whose bones we have spoken, which was discovered by the people of Zarahemla, it being the place of their first landing.

31. And they came from there up into the south wilderness. Thus the land on the northward was called Desolation, and the land on the southward was called Bountiful, it being the wilderness which is filled with all manner of wild animals of every kind, a part of which had come from the land northward for food.

32. And now, it was only the distance of a day and a half's journey for a Nephite, on the line Bountiful and the land Desolation, from the east to the *west sea;* and thus the land of Nephi and the land of Zarahemla were nearly surrounded by water, there being a small neck of land between the land northward and the land southward.   Alma 22:30-32.

VIII. "CAVES" OR "BARGES" AND PLACE OF LANDING

Ixtlilxochitl's statement that the people, "having crossed large lands and seas, living in caves," closely resembles *The Book of Mormon* account wherein it is reported that the Jaredites journeyed over extensive lands from Babel, crossed a sea in the wilderness, crossed further lands to the ocean and then traversed the ocean (thus justifying the use of the plural "seas") living in boats they called "barges" during the transoceanic journey to the New World.[7] Note how significantly the word "caves" used by *Ixtlilxochitl* suggests the more detailed description of the "barges" as given in *The Book of Mormon.*

According to *The Book of Mormon* the first settlers of the territory northward from the "narrow neck of land" were the people of Jared who came in eight boats. They would seem to correspond closely to the "Giants" or "Ancient Ones" of *Ixtlilxochitl's* account. It is likely that the "Ancient Ones" and the Ulmecs (the latter probably identical with the Mulekites of *The Book of Mormon*), both arrived in the Panuco area on the Gulf Coast of Mexico. According to *Ixtlilxochitl,* the Ulmecs encountered a remnant of the "Ancient Ones" between Panuco and the

---

[7] *The Book of Mormon,* pp. 480-481 (Ether 2:6-7, 13).

Isthmus of Tehuantepec. The Nephite history expressly declares that the last of the Jaredites came in contact with the Mulekites. This encounter is the subject of Chapter 12 herein.

The Book of Mormon makes it clear that the ancient people of Jared never moved far from the area called by them "the land of Moron" which was located just north of the "narrow neck of land."[8] Sahagun may, therefore, have given us the landing point of both the Jaredites and the Mulekites. Panuco meets all the requirements of the landing point of both peoples.

It is noted there is a difference of one boat between the report of Sahagun and that of The Book of Mormon. A possible explanation for this is that in the ancient Near East from whence came the colonizers, as well as in Middle America, seven was regarded as a sacred number.[9] The early Babylonian astronomers and astrologers discovered the seven planets in the night sky. There were seven "days" involved in the Old Testament creation account. Among the ancient Hebrews seven was the most im-portant sacred number of all. Besides the sacredness of the sev-enth day of the week, the seventh month, the Sabbatical year and the Jubilee year were determined by the number seven. Seven priests blew the horn at the siege of Jericho. There were seven pillars of wisdom, seven princes of Persia, and a man was required to forgive his brother seven times seven. Also, the Nephite record states that the second colonizers were comprised of seven subdivisions or "tribes" and these may have become confused with the First settlers from Babel who came in eight barges.

In view of the sacred significance of the number seven, it is quite possible that during the many centuries that intervened between the arrival of the "Ancient Ones," stretching from the early Tower of Babel period down to the time of Sahagun in the sixteenth century A. D., the original "eight barges" could easily have been reduced to seven. The Book of Mormon account was taken from an eye-witness source; therefore, it can be relied upon to be more accurate and dependable than Sahagun's state-ment.

It should also be observed that The Book of Mormon account gives the most detailed and reasonable explanation yet

---

[8] Moron was the Jaredite center from the beginning of Jaredite history to the end. It was in territory immediately north of the "narrow neck of land." (Ether 7:6, 16-17; 14:6; Alma 22:30.)

[9] See an excellent discussion by le comte H. de Charencey, Les Cites Votanides, Valeur Symbolique des Nombres, dans la Nouvelle Espagne, 1885, pp. 44-48.

found of the famous seven-caves origin tradition of the Mayas and Mexicans, and it is in close accord with Sahagun.

The Book of Mormon states this colony from Babel was expecting to find a "promised land," a land "choice above all other lands of the earth." Sahagun agrees, saying "This people came in search of the terrestrial paradise." The nature of the place where they settled in the New World is discussed in the next chapter.

The analogy between the boats and caves is readily understood in view of The Book of Mormon description of the barges. They were completely enclosed and dark—cavern-like.

In view of the fact that the vessels were without sails, a period of 344 days would seem to be a reasonable time for the crossing of the ocean, probably the Atlantic. If the landing took place at Panuco, near Tampico, Mexico, on the Gulf Coast, it would necessarily have been the Atlantic that was crossed.

IX. Ixtlilxochitl's Dates

Ixtlilxochitl dates the great flood, it being the first great calamity, at 3513 B. C. (1,716 years after his creation date, 5229 B. C.) The date of the arrival of the first artisans, whom he refers to elsewhere as "the Ancient Ones," in Hue-hue Tlapallan (ancient bountiful land) in the New World is placed by him at 2993 B. C. Since it had been 104 years earlier that they departed from "the very great tower," the departure date would be 3097 B. C., according to his chronology. The exact date of the building of the Tower of Babel has not been arrived at by the archæologists. This date given by Ixtlil-xochitl would seem to be reasonable in the light of modern archæology. Babel antedated the temple tower of Ur in the same general Mesopotamian area by a considerable period and Ur dates from 2300 B. C.[10] Thus, we may have help from the New-World historian, Ixtlilxochitl, in arriving at the true date for the Tower of Babel.

Summary Statement

The Book of Mormon and Ixtlilxochitl corroborate each other on the matter of the origin of the earliest civilized settlers of Middle America. In turn, they are supported by Sahagun, a reputable writer of high integrity, as well as by other important documentary sources.

[10] C. L. Wooley, The Ziggurat and its Surroundings (1938); Seton Lloyd, Ruined Cities of Iraq (1945) p. 51.

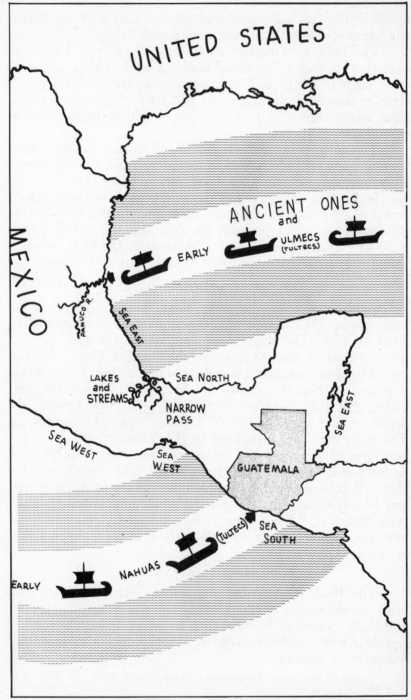

Fig. 5: Map—Landing Places of Ancient Ones,
Ulmecs and Nahuas

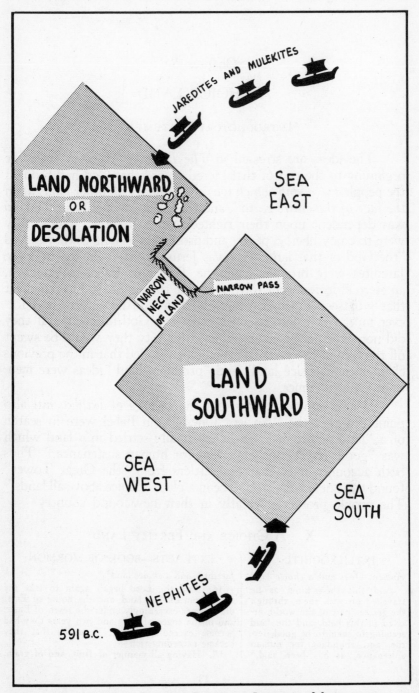

Fig. 6: MAP—LANDING PLACES OF JAREDITES, MULEKITES, AND NEPHITES

Chapter 5

A CHOICE LAND

INTRODUCTORY STATEMENT

The ideas are stressed in *The Book of Mormon* from the beginning to the end of that sacred record that God had brought the people to "*a land which was choice above all other lands upon the face of the entire earth*"; and that their prosperity in the land was dependent upon their righteousness. In other words, they were to enjoy liberty, peace, and prosperity as long as they served "the God of that land who was Jesus Christ." At the time the Jaredites were brought from the Tower of Babel to America, an eternal decree went forth from the throne of God to the effect that whatsoever people possessed that land henceforth and forever must live righteous lives and serve God faithfully. If they did not, when they became ripe in iniquity they would be swept off the face of the earth. It should be recalled that in the previous chapter the "choice land" and "promised land" ideas were mentioned several times.

It is a significant fact that the *Works of Ixtlilxochitl* also point out that the "Ancient Ones" from Babel were in search of a "land of promise" and they finally settled in a land which was "good, fertile, and abundant for human sustenance." Thus both accounts state that the settlers from "the Great Tower" found their new homeland to be in a place "choice above all lands." The people prospered greatly in their new-found country.

X. A CHOICE AND FERTILE LAND

IXTLILXOCHITL:

Ancient Ones and a choice land

And this their king, as he travelled on with them, through the greater part of the world, arrived in this land, and the land seeming to them to be good, fertile, and abundant for human sustenance, as has been said,[x]

EXTRACTS—BOOK OF MORMON:

Jaredites and a choice land[x]

16. And the Lord began again to take the curse from off the land, and the house of Emer did prosper exceedingly under the reign of Emer; and in the space of sixty and two years they had become exceeding strong, insomuch that they became exceeding rich—

17. Having all manner of fruit, and of grain,

they settled the greater part of it [Mexico], especially that toward the north [i.e., north of the capital of Mexico], then *Chichimecatl* called it all by his own name. Later his descendants gradually settled the rest, and each kingdom or province kept the name, according as to who was the lord or king who first settled it, as can be seen in the lands, kingdoms, and provinces of the Tultecas, which were generally called *Tullan*, because the first king they had was so called.XLIII

Just so, the same thing happens with the rest of the large regions and provinces which are in this land; but notwithstanding the fact that some are called Tultecas, others *Aculhuas, Tepanecas* or *Otomites*, all of them take pride in the fact that they are of the lineage of the *Chichimecas*, because all of them descend from them, although it is true that there is a difference from some *Chichimecas* to others, in that some took more culture than others, like the *Tultecas*; and others look more to being great barbarians(savages), like the *Otomites* and others of their kind. Those who are purely *Chichimecas*, whose kings descend in direct line from their first king and settler, *Chichimecatl*, have been warlike men, warriors, and fond of power and having the rest in subjection; and because some lead a courteous (cultured, polite) life, and others are very harsh and of evil thoughts, or haughty and arrogant, fond of killing, it has come about that there are virtuous and evil rulers; and finally, as they themselves say and confess, besides being in their histories, all are of the lineage of *Chichimecas*, and all their ancestors came, as has been said, from Occidental parts.

and of silks, and of fine linen, and of gold, and of silver, and of precious things;

18. And also all manner of cattle, of oxen, and cows, and of sheep, and of swine, and of goats, and also many other kinds of animals which were useful for the food of man.

19. And they also had horses, and asses, and there were elephants and cureloms and cummoms; all of which were useful unto man, and more especially the elephants and cureloms and cummoms.LXIV

20. And thus the Lord did pour out his blessings upon this land, which was choice above all other lands; and he commanded that whoso should possess the land should possess it unto the Lord, or they should be destroyed when they were ripened in iniquity; for upon such, saith the Lord: I will pour out the fulness of my wrath. . . .

20. And they built a great city by the narrow neck of land, by the place where the sea divides the land.

21. And they did preserve the land southward for a wilderness, to get game. And the whole face of the land northward was covered with inhabitants.

22. And they were exceedingly industrious, and they did buy and sell and traffic one with another, that they might get gain.

23. And they did work in all manner of ore, and they did make gold, and silver, and iron, and brass, and all manner of metals; and they did dig it out of the earth; wherefore, they did cast up mighty heaps of earth to get ore, of gold, and of silver, and of iron, and of copper. And they did work all manner of fine work.

24. And they did have silks, and fine-twined linen; and they did work all manner of cloth, that they might clothe themselves from their nakedness.

25. And they did make all manner of tools to till the earth, both to plow and to sow, to reap and to hoe, and also to thrash.

26. And they did make all manner of tools with which they did work their beasts.

27. And they did make all manner of weapons of war. And they did work all manner of work of exceedingly curious workmanship.

28. And never could be a people more blessed than were they, and more prospered by the hand of the Lord. And they were in a land that was choice above all lands, for the Lord had spoken it.

Ether 9:16-20; 10:20-28.

In numerous passages in *The Book of Mormon*, the writers of that ancient record described the productivity of the land in which they lived. During the days of King Lib the Jaredites reached a great peak in prosperity and culture. The Nephite prophet, Moroni, abridged the Jaredite record. In doing so, he described the gold, silver, brass, iron, and other precious metals that those ancient Americans were expert in working. He also mentioned the "silks and fine-twined linen" that they made. He then pointed out the fact that the Jaredites "did make all manner of tools to till the earth, both to plow and to sow, to reap and to hoe, and also to thrash. And they did make all manner of tools with which they did work their beasts." Then Moroni summarized this great period by saying: "And never could be a people more blessed than were they, and more prospered by the hand of the Lord. *And they were in the land that was choice above all lands, for the Lord had spoken it.*"

Both accounts refer to the occupied area as a northerly region. *Ixtlilxochitl* says it was "especially that toward the north." *The Book of Mormon* says it was "the land northward." The area was northward in relation to the "narrow neck of land."

The statement made by *Ixtlilxochitl* regarding the "good and fertile land" which was settled by the first Tultecas, the "Ancient Ones," is sustained by the foregoing information given in *The Book of Mormon* in its version of the productive land colonized by the first settlers of ancient Middle America following the flood.

Chapter 6

SECOND GREAT CALAMITY

INTRODUCTORY STATEMENT

Ixtlilxochitl and *The Book of Mormon* both report that a series of calamities came to these early settlers of ancient Mexico. The first great calamity experienced by the people from Babel was the flood; and the second great calamity is described in this chapter. There were long intervals, covering several generations, between each of the reported calamities. Our two primary sources differ in some of the details concerning these calamities, but there is accord on the more general aspects of these various disasters. *Ixtlilxochitl,* who had the benefit of the European chronology, which he correlated with the ancient calendar of Mexico, says the second calamity occurred 1,715 years after the first. Both accounts agree that after the second great destruction prosperity was restored and the kingdom renewed.

XI. SECOND GREAT CALAMITY

ITLILXOCHITL:

A terrible destruction

And 1,715 years after the deluge they [the "Ancient Ones"] *were destroyed* by a very great hurricane[XI] which took with it trees, rocks, houses, and people and large buildings, although many men and women escaped, especially those who could escape in caves and parts where this great hurricane could not reach them; and after some days or some time, they came out of them [the caves] to see what the world (land) had come to, and they found it all populated and covered with monkeys, which the wind had brought [from the jungles] and they were in darkness all this time without seeing the sun and the moon; and from

EXTRACTS—BOOK OF MORMON:

A terrible destruction[XI]

6. For so great had been the spreading of this wicked and secret society that it had corrupted the hearts of all the people; therefore Jared was murdered upon his throne, and Akish reigned in his stead.

7. And it came to pass that Akish began to be jealous of his son, therefore he shut him up in prison, and kept him upon little or no food until he had suffered death.

8. And now the brother of him that suffered death, (and his name was Nimrah) was angry with his father because of that which his father had done unto his brother.

9. And it came to pass that Nimrah gathered together a small number of men, and fled out of the land, and came over and dwelt with Omer.

10. And it came to pass that Akish begat other sons, and they won the hearts of the people notwithstanding they had sworn unto him to do

this the Indians invented a fable: they say that men turned into monkeys, and they called this age, or second world, *Ehecatona-tiuh,* which means *Sun of wind,* and after having escaped [this second calamity] *they began to rebuild anew and to multiply.*[XII]

all manner of iniquity according to that which he desired.

11. Now the people of Akish were desirous for gain, even as Akish was desirous for power; wherefore, the sons of Akish did offer them money, by which means they drew away the more part of the people after them.

12. And there began to be a war between the sons of Akish and Akish, which lasted for the space of many years, yea, unto *the destruction of nearly all the people of the kingdom,* yea, even all, save it were thirty souls, and they who fled with the house of Omer.

13. Wherefore, Omer was restored again to the land of his inheritance.

14. And it came to pass that Omer began to be old; nevertheless, in his old age he begat Emer; and he anointed Emer to be king to reign in his stead.

15. And after that he had anointed Emer to be king he saw peace in the land for the space of two years, and he died, having seen exceeding many days, which were full of sorrow. And it came to pass that Emer did reign in his stead, and did fill the steps of his father.

16. *And the Lord began again to take the curse from off the land, and the house of Emer did prosper exceedingly under the reign of Emer; and in the space of sixty and two years they had become exceeding strong insomuch that they be-came exceeding rich*—[XII]   Ether 9:6-16.

According to *Ixtlilxochitl,* this second great catastrophe occurred about 1798 B. C., that is, 1,715 years from his date for the Deluge. The two accounts agree generally on the time period when the destruction occurred and on the extent of the destruction. However, they differ in the causes they give for the calamity. *Ixtlilxochitl* gives as the cause "a very great hurricane." On the other hand, *The Book of Mormon* mentions that the underlying cause of destruction was brought about by the wicked-ness of the people. Elsewhere *Ixtlilxochitl* says that all the calami-ties came as punishments from heaven. Civil war broke out, according to *The Book of Mormon,* with the result that all of the inhabitants of the kingdom were killed except King Omer and his household and thirty other people.

It should be remembered that the Jaredite record in *The Book of Mormon* is a very brief account. In fact, Moroni, the Nephite abridger, made an extremely brief digest in only fifteen short chapters of more than 2,000 years of history of that people. Therefore it could be possible that the Ancient Ones may have experienced "a very great hurricane," as *Ixtlilxochitl* pointed out,

and the abridger of the Book of Ether (Jaredite record) considered that it was not important enough to mention in his brief
account. He was more inclined to describe throughout the entire
record the troubles and the destructions which the people inflicted
on each other, especially when they became wicked. Being a
prophet of God, Moroni doubtless had in mind the promise made
by the Lord to this ancient people. He reported the following:

> And the Lord . . . would that they should come forth even unto the
> land of promise, which was choice above all other lands, which the Lord
> God had preserved for a righteous people. And he had sworn in his
> wrath unto the brother of Jared, that whoso should possess this land of
> promise, from that time henceforth and forever, should serve him, the
> true and only living God, or they should be swept off when the fulness
> of his wrath should come upon them.[1]

XII. POPULATION INCREASED AND PROSPERITY RENEWED

Both *Ixtlilxochitl* and *The Book of Mormon* state that following the second great destruction which took place among the
Ancient Ones from Babel the people again multiplied and built
up their kingdom. In fact, they enjoyed bounteous prosperity
once more. The statement regarding this renewed prosperity is
given much more briefly in *Ixtlilxochitl* than in *The Book of
Mormon*. It should be so since the latter is derived from first-
hand eyewitness sources.

---

[1] *The Book of Mormon*, p. 481, verses 7-9 (Ether 2:7-9).

Chapter 7

THIRD GREAT CALAMITY

Introductory Statement

The third great calamity followed the second catastrophe rather closely, 158 years intervening, according to *Ixtlilxochitl*. The ancient system of dating events by reigns-of-kings is followed in the Jaredite record. However, even with that cumbersome system, sufficient data is given in *The Book of Mormon* to enable us to calculate the interval between the second and third calamities at between 150 and 200 years. Thus, there is accord as to the duration of the interval. Both accounts indicate that some of the colonizers survived this third calamity, *Ixtlilxochitl* stating that the escapees were those "who were more inland."

XIII. The Quinametzin

In this chapter, as will be seen, *Ixtlilxochitl* calls the "Ancient Ones," or the settlers who came from the Tower of Babel, *"Quinametzin"*; and he also refers to them as *"Giants."* The first half of this name, *Quina-metzin,* means "house of the sun." In the Maya *Quin* or *Kin* means "sun," and *na* means "house." It is a name used in Chiapas.[1] As used here, the name *Quinametzin* refers to the earliest Tultecas or civilized colonizers of Middle America.

XIV. Giants

Since *Ixtlilxochitl* makes his first mention of "Giants" in this chapter, the writers thought it advisable to give a brief explanation at this point. However, in the next chapter, the Mexican historian refers to the "Giants" again and gives a much more detailed discussion of them.

---

[1] Marcos E. Becerra, *Nombres Geographicos Indigenas del Estado de Chiapas* (1930), p. 273.

Fig. 7: FIGURINE FROM JAREDITE ERA

The turban headdress of woven cloth tells much. The figure is from a site near Mexico City. It is classified as El Arbolillo I, it being from the earliest strata of the site known as El Arbolillo. It dates from about 1600 B. C.—well within the period of the Ancient Ones from Babel.

Ixtlilxochitl's use of the term "Giants" is interesting in the light of *Book of Mormon* statements that indicate the Jaredites were large of stature. When Limhi's men discovered the Jaredite remains, they observed that the Jaredite breastplates ". . . are large."[2] Jimenez Moreno, a Mexican scholar, points out that the people may have been "intellectual giants," makers of gigantic monuments.[3] When the word "giant" is used to describe the size of men it is a relative term—for what may be a giant in one age or place might be an average man in another time or place.

IXTLILXOCHITL:

Quinametzin, giants, third calamity

One hundred fifty-eight years after the great hurricane and 1,964 [3,589 years] since the creation of the world, those of this land had another destruction, who were the *Quinametzin,*[XIII] Giants,[XIV] who lived in this corner which is now called New Spain, which destruction consisted of a great earthquake which swallowed and killed them, volcanoes bursting the high mountains, so that all [sic] were destroyed without anyone escaping [sic] and if anyone did escape, he was of those who were more inland;[XV] and likewise many of the Tultecas died, and the Chichimecas and their neighbors, which (this) was in the year of *ce Tecpatl;* the age they called *Tlacchitonatiuh,* which means *sun of earth.*

EXTRACTS—BOOK OF MORMON:

Third great calamity

21. And Emer did execute judgment in righteousness all his days, and he begat many sons and daughters; and he begat Coriantum, and he appointed Coriantum to reign in his stead.

22. And after he had anointed Coriantum to reign in his stead he lived four years, and he saw peace in the land; yea, and he even saw the Son of Righteousness, and did rejoice and glory in his day; and he died in peace.

23. And it came to pass that Coriantum did walk in the steps of his father, and did build many mighty cities, and did administer that which was good unto his people in all his days. And it came to pass that he had no children even until he was exceeding old.

24. And it came to pass that his wife died, being an hundred and two years old. And it came to pass that Coriantum took to wife, in his old age, a young maid, and begat sons and daughters; wherefore he lived until he was an hundred and forty and two years old.

25. And it came to pass that he begat Com, and Com reigned in his stead; and he reigned forty and nine years, and he begat Heth; and he also begat other sons and daughters.

26. And the people had spread again over all the face of the land, and there began again to be an exceeding great wickedness upon the face of the land, and Heth began to embrace the secret plans again of old, to destroy his father.

27. And it came to pass that he did dethrone his father, for he slew him with his own sword; and he did reign in his stead.

28. And there came prophets in the land again, crying repentance unto them—that they must prepare the way of the Lord or there should come a curse upon the face of the land; yea, even there should be a great famine, in which they should be destroyed if they did not repent.

---

[2] *The Book of Mormon,* p. 151 (Mosiah 8:10).
[3] W. Jimenez Moreno, "El Enigma de los Olmecas," *Cuadernos Americanos,* vol. 2, p. 5, 1942; cited by Miguel Covarrubias, *Mexico South, The Isthmus of Tehuantepec,* 1946, p. 116.

30. And it came to pass that there began to be a great dearth upon the land, and the inhabitants began to be destroyed exceeding fast because of the dearth, for there was no rain upon the face of the earth.

31. And there came forth poisonous serpents also upon the face of the land, and did poison many people. And it came to pass that their flocks began to flee before the poisonous serpents, towards the land southward. which was called by the Nephites Zarahemla.[XLIII, XCI]

32. And it came to pass that there were many of them [flocks] which did perish by the way; nevertheless, there were some which fled into the land southward

34. And it came to pass that the people did follow the course of the beasts, and did devour the carcasses of them which fell by the way, until they had devoured them all. Now when the people saw that they must perish they began to repent of their iniquities and cry unto the Lord.

35. And it came to pass that when they had humbled themselves sufficiently before the Lord he did send rain upon the face of the earth; and the people began to revive again, and there began to be fruit in the north countries round about. And the Lord did show forth his power unto them in preserving them from famine.

Ether 9:21-35.

XV. The Third Calamity

Ixtlilxochitl tells that 158 years after the great hurricane a third calamity occurred which took many lives. In fact, he indicates only those who were more inland—and, apparently away from the center of population—escaped this destruction. One hundred fifty-eight years after the hurricane of 1798 B. C. would place this "third calamity" at about 1640 B. C. His correlation with the creation date is an obvious error here. *Ixtlilxochitl* says this destruction was the work of an earthquake and volcanoes.

The Book of Mormon indicates that the "third great calamity" came to the settlers from Babel between 150 and 200 years after the "second calamity." This time interval can be calculated from the reign of kings. Following the second Jaredite calamity, Emer reigned 62 years. His son, Coriantum, lived 142 years, some of which years were lived during the reign of his father, Emer. It is safe to assume that Coriantum reigned about 40 to 80 years of his long lifetime. Com succeeded to the throne and reigned 49 years and at the end of his reign the third calamity began. Thus, by adding the reigns of Emer (62 years), Cori-

antum (40 to 80 years) and Com (49 years) the total is somewhere between 151 to 191 years as the interval between the
second and third calamities. This *Book of Mormon* time interval
is in close accord with *Ixtlilxochitl's* 158 years.

A difference is noted as to the nature of the "third calamity"—*Ixtlilxochitl* specifying earthquake and volcanic eruption
while *The Book of Mormon* designates drought.

Later it will be pointed out that *The Book of Mormon*
mentions certain animals, such as horses, which were in ancient
America in Jaredite and Nephite times. It should be observed
in the foregoing extract from that record that the "flocks" were
eaten, the people devouring them "until they had devoured them
all." Thus these droughts may have resulted in the extermination of certain animal species in ancient America and it
may give a clue as to why some of the domestic animals mentioned in *The Book of Mormon* were not found in Middle
America at the time of the Spanish Conquest. There were other
severe droughts in Middle America between the early period
covered by *The Book of Mormon*—which records the history
down only to 421 A. D.—and the Spanish Conquest. *Ixtlilxochitl* is very explicit in that regard, as will be seen later on.

Chapter 8

COMPLETE DESTRUCTION OF THOSE FROM BABEL

Introductory Statement

The emphasis in this chapter will be on the complete destruction which came to the ancient Americans who had come originally from the Tower of Babel, pointing out the causes and date of that destruction. Since a discussion of the "Giants" was given in the previous chapter, that topic need not be repeated here.

One of the most precise parallels between *Ixtlilxochitl* and *The Book of Mormon* occurs with regard to the destruction of the descendants of the original settlers from the Great Tower. Both accounts agree that the destruction was *complete*. *Ixtlilxochitl* fixes the date of the destruction at 299 B. C.-236 B. C. *The Book of Mormon* indicates the destruction occurred sometime between 300 B. C. and 222 B. C. There is a remarkable consistency in this dating.

Jaredites or "Ancient Ones" Destroyed

IXTLILXOCHITL:

Complete destruction, causes, date

In this New Spain there were *giants*. Besides the demonstration (proof) of their bones, which are found in many parts, the ancient Tultec historians say that they were called *Quinametzin* and that they got to know them and had many wars and dissensions with them, especially in all the land that is now called New Spain.

They were destroyed and exterminated by great calamities and punishments from heaven, for some grave sins that they had committed;[XVI] and there is

EXTRACTS—BOOK OF MORMON:

Complete destruction of Jaredites

1. And it came to pass that the days of Ether were in the days of Coriantumr; and Coriantumr was king over all the land.

2. And Ether was a prophet of the Lord; wherefore Ether came forth in the days of Coriantumr, and began to prophesy unto the people, for he could not be restrained because of the Spirit of the Lord which was in him.

3. For he did cry from the morning, even until the going down of the sun, exhorting the people to believe in God unto repentance lest they should be destroyed, saying unto them that by faith all things are fulfilled.[XVI] Ether 12:1-3.

13. And I [Moroni, the Nephite historian] was about to write more, but I am forbidden; but great and marvelous were the prophecies of Ether; but they esteemed him as naught, and

even opinion of some of these ancient histories that these giants descend from the Chichimecas themselves, and they say that in these northern lands [of Mexico] where the ancient empire of the Chichimecas stood, there are provinces where men of more than thirty spans in height live; and it is not to be wondered at, for even our Spaniards, notwithstanding the fact that they have not yet entered into the interior, except through these coasts, like the lands of *Chicoranos* and *Duharezases,* have found men in these parts eleven and twelve spans in height, and accounts of there being others taller.

The greatest destruction that these *Quinametzin* had was in the year and figure (picture) that the natives call *ce Toxtli,* which means *rabbit number first,* 299 years before the incarnation of Jesus Christ;[XVII] and with them ended the third age which was called *Ecatonatiuh,* on account of the great winds and earthquakes, and nearly all of them were destroyed.

cast him out; and he hid himself in the cavity of a rock by day, and by night he went forth viewing *the things which should come*[1] upon the people.

14. And as he dwelt in the cavity of a rock he made the remainder of this record, viewing the destructions which *came* upon the people, by night.

15. And it came to pass that in that same year in which he was cast out from among the people there began to be a great war among the people, for *there were many who rose up, who were mighty men,* and sought to destroy Coriantumr by their secret plans of wickedness, of which hath been spoken.

16. And now Coriantumr, having studied, himself, in all the arts of war and all the cunning of the world, wherefore he gave battle unto them who sought to destroy him.

17. But he repented not, neither his fair sons nor daughters; neither the fair sons and daughters of Cohor; neither the fair sons and daughters of Corihor; and in fine, there were none of the fair sons and daughters upon the face of the whole earth who repented of their sins.

18. Wherefore, it came to pass that in the first year that Ether dwelt in the cavity of a rock, there were many people who were slain by the sword of those secret combinations, fighting against Coriantumr that they might obtain the kingdom.

19. And it came to pass that the sons of Coriantumr fought much and bled much.

20. And in the second year the word of the Lord came to Ether, that he should go and prophesy unto Coriantumr that, if he would repent, and all his household, the Lord would give unto him his kingdom and spare the people—

21. Otherwise they should be destroyed, and all his household save it were himself. And he should only live to see the fulfilling of the prophecies which had been spoken concerning another people receiving the land for their inheritance; and Coriantumr should receive a burial by them; and every soul should be destroyed save it were Coriantumr.

22. And it came to pass that Coriantumr repented not, neither his household, neither the people; and the wars ceased not; and they sought to kill Ether, but he fled from before them and hid again in the cavity of the rock. . . .

25. Now there began to be a war upon all the face of the land, every man with his band fighting for that which he desired.

26. And there were robbers, and in fine, all manner of wickedness upon all the face of the land.   Ether 13:13-22, 25-26.

---

[1] Moroni corrects this error in the next verse. He could not erase since he was engraving this account on metal tablets.

1. And now there began to be a great curse upon all the land because of the iniquity of the people, in which, if a man should lay his tool or his sword upon his shelf, or upon the place whither he would keep it, behold, upon the morrow, he could not find it, so great was the curse upon the land.

2. Wherefore every man did cleave unto that which was his own, with his hands, and would not borrow neither would he lend; and every man kept the hilt of his sword in his right hand, in the defence of his property and his own life and of his wives and children.

21. And so great and lasting had been the war, and so long had been the scene of bloodshed and carnage, that the whole face of the land was covered with the bodies of the dead.

22. And so swift and speedy was the war that there was none left to bury the dead, but they did march forth from the shedding of blood to the shedding of blood, leaving the bodies of both men, women, and children strewed upon the face of the land, to become a prey to the worms of the flesh.

23. And the scent thereof went forth upon the face of the land, even upon all the face of the land; wherefore the people became troubled by day and by night, because of the scent thereof.

24. Nevertheless, Shiz did not cease to pursue Coriantumr; for he had sworn to avenge himself upon Coriantumr of the blood of his brother, who had been slain, and the word of the Lord which came to Ether that Coriantumr should not fall by the sword.

25. And thus we see that the Lord did visit them in the fulness of his wrath, and their wickedness and abominations had prepared a way for their everlasting destruction.

Ether 14:1-2, 21-25.

2. He saw that there had been slain by the sword already nearly two million of his people, and he began to sorrow in his heart; yea, there had been slain two millions of *mighty men,* and also their wives and their children.

13. And it came to pass that Ether did behold all the doings of the people; and he beheld that the people who were for Coriantumr were gathered together to the army of Coriantumr; and the people who were for Shiz were gathered together to the army of Shiz.

14. Wherefore, they were for the space of four years gathering together the people, that they might get all who were upon the face of the land, and that they might receive all the strength which it was possible that they could receive.

15. And it came to pass that when they were all gathered together, every one to the army which he would, with their wives and their children—both men, women and children being armed with

weapons of war, having shields, and breastplates, and head-plates, and being clothed after the manner of war—they did march forth one against another to battle; and they fought all that day, and conquered not.

16. And it came to pass that when it was night they were weary, and retired to their camps; and after they had retired to their camps they took up a howling and a lamentation for the loss of the slain of their people; and so great were their cries, their howlings and lamentations, that they did rend the air exceedingly.

17. And it came to pass that on the morrow they did go again to battle, and great and terrible was that day; nevertheless, they conquered not, and when the night came again they did rend the air with their cries, and their howlings, and their mournings, for the loss of the slain of their people. . . .

20. And it came to pass that they fought all that day, and when the night came they slept upon their swords.

21. And on the morrow they fought even until the night came.

22. And when the night came they were drunken with anger, even as a man who is drunken with wine; and they slept again upon their swords.

29. Wherefore, he did pursue them, and on the morrow he did overtake them; and they fought again with the sword. And it came to pass that when they had all fallen by the sword, save it were Coriantumr and Shiz, behold Shiz had fainted with the loss of blood.

30. And it came to pass that when Coriantumr had leaned upon his sword, that he rested a little, he smote off the head of Shiz.[XVI]

31. And it came to pass that after he had smitten off the head of Shiz, that Shiz raised upon his hands and fell; and after that he had struggled for breath, he died.

32. And it came to pass that Coriantumr fell to the earth, and became as if he had no life.

33. And the Lord spake unto Ether, and said unto him: Go forth. And he went forth, and beheld that the words of the Lord had all been fulfilled: and he finished his record; (and the hundredth part I have not written) and he hid them in a manner that the people of Limhi did find them.[XVII, XCII]

Ether 15:2, 13-17, 20-22, 29-33.

XVI. Fourth Calamity and Complete Destruction

As is very evident in the foregoing quotations, both *Ixtlilxochitl* and *The Book of Mormon* refer to the "total destruction" of the Ancient Ones from Babel. They are in close agreement on this fourth calamity and complete destruction. Also, they are in accord as to the nature of this calamity—war! To quote the exact words of *Ixtlilxochitl*: "[They] had many wars and dissensions." As is observed from the quoted text, *The Book of Mormon* discusses this great war in detail. *Ixtlilxochitl*, like *The Book of Mormon*, states it was a final, total, and complete destruction and that God was behind it all because of the wickedness of the people. To quote from the Mexican historian: *"They were destroyed and exterminated by great calamities and punishments from heaven, for some grave sins that they had committed."* That statement is marvelous in light of the more detailed accounts of the causes of the destruction of the Ancient Ones or Jaredites, as reported in *The Book of Mormon*.

XVII. DATE OF THE DESTRUCTION

The reader probably observed that *Ixtlilxochitl* places the date of the destruction of the "Ancient Ones (Quinametzin)" at 299 B. C. He later states that this destruction took place 270 years prior to the eclipse of the sun and the moon, which eclipse he clearly fixed "at the time Christ suffered."[2] This would date the destruction of the Ancient Ones at 236 B. C. Thus, it took place some time between 299 B. C. and 236 B. C., according to *Ixtlilxochitl*.

The Book of Mormon is in very close agreement with *Ixtlilxochitl's* calculations. Chapter 12 herein will show that about 122 B. C. a party of Nephite (*Nahuale*) explorers found the battleground where the final destruction of the Ancient Ones occurred. At that time (122 B. C.) the battle area was still "covered with bones of men, and of beasts, and was also covered with ruins of buildings of every kind . . . a land which was covered with dry bones . . ."[3] Weapons and armor were found on the battleground by the exploring party, for they returned home with "breastplates . . . and they are of brass and of copper, and are perfectly sound. And again, they have brought swords, the hilts thereof have perished, and the blades thereof were cankered with rust . . ."[4] From this detailed description of things found at the scene of the destruction, it would appear that the battle must have occurred within a hundred, or perhaps two hundred

---

[2] See page 189.
[3] *The Book of Mormon*, p. 150 (Mosiah 8:8); p. 176 (Mosiah 21:26).
[4] *Ibid.*, p. 151 (Mosiah 8:10-11).

years prior to 122 B. C.—or between about 300 B. C. and 222 B. C., dating very close to *Ixtlilxochitl's* 299-236 B. C.

SUMMARY STATEMENT

There is a remarkable consistency between *Ixtlilxochitl* and *The Book of Mormon* on the matter of the cause and date of the destruction of the descendants of the Ancient Ones from Babel, and in other particulars, including the completeness of this fourth and final calamity to befall that people.

Chapter 9

SECOND SETTLERS OF MIDDLE AMERICA
(Tultecas, Nephites, Nahuales)

Introductory Statement

Both *Ixtlilxochitl* and *The Book of Mormon* make mention
of the fact that there were three separate and distinct groups
of people who migrated across the ocean to ancient America. As
has been pointed out and discussed, the first of these was known
in the *Works of Ixtlilxochitl* as "the Ancient Ones," "Giants,"
or "the first Tulteca" settlers, while *The Book of Mormon*
designates them as "Jaredites." The second group of colonists
were called by *Ixtlilxochitl* "Tultecas" or the "People of Bountiful." *The Book of Mormon* refers to them as "Nephites" and
to a branch or faction that split from them as "Lamanites."

The Mexican historian tells nothing of where these people
came from but Guatemalan accounts do. Nephite historians not
only declare that these second colonizers came from Jerusalem
and were a branch of the "House of Israel" but the major portion of *The Book of Mormon* is devoted to a discusssion of their
history and religious teachings. The Nephite record also gives
the exact date of their departure from Jerusalem as "the first
year of the reign of Zedekiah"—i.e., 600 years before the birth
of Christ. This latter record also points out that the second
group of cultured settlers set sail for America from a spot in
Arabia which they called "Bountiful." Their principal homeland in the New World was also called by the same name,
Bountiful-plant-land (*Zarahemla* in Hebrew). It shall be pointed
out later that numerous American sixteenth-century documentary sources confirm the fact that these people lived in the land
of Bountiful in America.

Both the Nephite record and other documentary sources
maintain that these second colonizers of ancient America were

of Israel and were directed from their home in the East to the New World by the Lord, which is significant.

Since the *Works of Ixtlilxochitl* tell nothing of where these second Tultec settlers lived prior to their coming to America and since other sixteenth-century documentary sources give that information, the writers quote some of these other accounts in addition to the *Works of Ixtlilxochitl*.

One of these sixteenth-century documentary accounts is called *Titulo de los Señores de Totonicapan* or "*Genealogical Claims of the Lords of Totonicapan.*" For the sake of brevity, it will be referred to as "*Totonicapan.*" This record comes from the Quiché-Mayas of ancient Guatemala. It was written in 1554 A. D., and subscribed by those responsible for it on September 28 of that year. It was first published in French and Spanish in Paris in 1885. Dr. M. Wells Jakeman published the extracts quoted in this book in 1945, and that was the first time that they had been published in English. A new Spanish edition of the entire paper appeared in Mexico in 1950. It was the work of the able Adrian Recinos.

Another sixteenth-century work of importance is the *Popol Vuh*. It is the sacred book of the ancient Quiché-Maya of the highlands of Guatemala. It was first transcribed in the Maya language, but in our letters, about 1550 A. D., by a highly literate Mayan. The manuscript of the latter was found in Chichicas-tenango in Guatemala by Father Francisco Ximenez at the close of the seventeenth century. It was published for the first time in Spanish in Vienna in 1857. A French edition was published in Paris in 1861. The first complete English version appeared in 1950. The latter work, done by Delia Goetz and the late Mayan expert, Sylvanus G. Morley, is the one quoted from in this book.

The *Popul Vuh* could well be considered as the Lamanite (Maya) version of many of the things covered in the Nephite *Book of Mormon*. It speaks of the people of the land of Bounti-ful with the same contempt that the Nephite account uses in referring to the people of the highlands of the land of Nephi, the Lamanites. In every way, the *Popol Vuh*, excellent as it is, is far inferior to *The Book of Mormon*. However, the scholastic world has made much "to-do" over the *Popul Vuh*, and, on the other hand, has ignored the Nephite record.

SECOND SETTLERS OF ANCIENT AMERICA

IXTLILXOCHITL:	EXTRACTS—BOOK OF MORMON:
Second settlers, Tultecas (People of Bountiful)—Teotihuacan, Tula and Cholula	*Second settlers of ancient America (Nephites)*
The Tultecas[XVII] were the second settlers of this land after the decline of the giants. . . .	14. . . . those who are friendly to Nephi I shall call Nephites, or the people of Nephi, according to the reign of the kings.
	Jacob 1:14b.
Tulteca means *artisan* and *wise man*,[XVII] because the people of this nation were great artisans, as is seen . . . in the ruins of their buildings, in this town of *Teotihuacan, Tula* and *Cholula*.[XVIII]	11. And it came to pass that whosoever would not believe in the traditions of the Lamanites, but believed those records which were brought out of the land of Jerusalem, and also in the traditions of their fathers, which were correct, who believed in the commandments of God and kept them, were called Nephites, or the people of Nephi.
	Alma 3:11.

XVII. TULTECAS—NAHUALES—NEPHITES

As has been mentioned, according to *Ixtlilxochitl,* the name of the second settlers of ancient America and the ones who followed the "Ancient Ones" or "Giants" to this land were known as Tultecas. *The Book of Mormon* calls the second settlers "Nephites." The sixteenth-century Guatemalan accounts refer to them as "Nahuales." All of these accounts, including the Nephite record, when translated into English designate the central homeland of these people as "Bountiful" or "Bountiful-land." We shall speak, therefore, of the second settlers as "the people of Bountiful-land." Later this terminology shall be developed more completely.

When *Ixtlilxochitl* says that *"Tulteca* means *artisan* and *wise men,"* he is not giving a literal translation of the term, as will be shown later. He is merely saying that the people of Bountiful were such great artisans and craftsmen that to be called a person of Bountiful was a tribute. It was like a nickname.

Totonicapan speaks of these people as "sages" which is in accord with *Ixtlilxochitl's* statement that they were "wise men." *The Book of Mormon* describes them as men of great wisdom and culture, acting under direct revelation from God.

The name "Nahuales" from *Totonicapan* has a resemblance to the name "Nephites" from *The Book of Mormon.* It seems, therefore, that the name "Nephites" carried on in a slightly altered form in Guatemala until the sixteenth century A. D. which was more than 1,000 years after the extermination of this people. Tultec remnants (Lamanites) in central Mexico also kept an altered form of the name "Nephites" alive until the Spanish Conquest, for the name *Nahuas* was in common use in the Valley of Mexico when Cortez arrived. Descendants, some of them degenerated to rather low levels, of the once-cultured Nephites, claimed that ancient name. Even some aliens who had infiltrated Mexico from the north claimed to be *Nahuas*.

The *Totonicapan* states that the Nahuales came "from the Orient"; but that statement does not mean the Far East or China. It merely means that they came from the East; and later the same record makes its meaning clear by stating that they came *"from the other side of the sea, from Civan-Tulan [Bountiful] at the confines of Babylonia."* That statement agrees perfectly with *The Book of Mormon* account wherein it points out that the Nephites came from a place named Bountiful which was located on the southeastern shores of Arabia.

XVIII. Teotihuacan, Tula, and Cholula

Ixtlilxochitl mentions the ruins of three cities, *Teotihuacan* (pronounced Tay-o-tee-wah-ca'n), *Tula* and *Cholula* (pronounced Chol-oo'-lah). The *Tula* referred to by him here is not the ancient and original *Tulan,* to be discussed later. Rather, it is a later one in Hidalgo, Mexico, not more than about seventy miles from *Ixtlilxochitl's* home. All are great archæological centers of Mexico. The first two, *Teotihuacan* and *Tula,* are at the northwestern rim or frontier of the zone of high civilizations. They are situated north of Mexico City and can be reached by auto travel over good roads. The *Tula* referred to here was established long after the close of the Nephite record (421 A. D.), but it, like other Tulas, was named after the far earlier and more ancient *Tulan* located several hundred miles to the south in the Tabasco-Chiapas country. *Teotihuacan,* here mentioned by *Ixtlilxochitl,* was founded by the Tultecs after their expulsion from ancient Bountiful-land (*Tulan*) in the south-of-Tehuantepec country. In fact, *Teotihuacan* was also originally called *Tula.* It was the surviving remnant of the Tultecs which built these later centers in "the land northward." It will be seen later on in this book that *Ixtlilxochitl* gives the year 556 A. D. for the founding of the new Tula in the north country. This, of course, places the founding of Tula in the post-*Book of Mormon* period.

Vaillant, archæological authority on the early civilizations of the central-plateau region of Mexico, says that archæological research dates the earliest discovered Teotihuacan culture close to 500 A. D.[1] In his summary of the history of the Teotihuacan Tultecs, Vaillant dates the history from 510 A. D. through 1122 A. D.[2]

Torquemada (1723) says that Cholula was occupied continuously for five hundred years prior to 1168 A. D., when it was evacuated.[3] Some technicians date the beginning of the Teotihuacan around 300 A. D.[4] At any rate, the archæologists are in rather close agreement with *Ixtlilxochitl* on this matter. *Cholula,* the third example of Tultec antiquities mentioned by *Ixtlilxochitl,* is an important and somewhat earlier archæological center than either *Teotihuacan* or *Tula* (Hidalgo). Cholula is located about eighty miles southeast of Mexico City. It too is accessible by good roads. Reports on this location are incomplete, but it appears that the innermost structure within the great temple-tower of Cholula is very early, possibly dating as early as the fourth century A. D. The pyramid is the largest in the world, measuring approximately 800 feet on each side. One of the writers has explored the miles of tunnels which have been excavated within this immense structure. The pyramids at *Cholula* and *Teotihuacan* are the two greatest in America. *Cholula* was a great Tultec market center, like *Tula* and *Teotihuacan.*[5]

XIX. Date of Departure from Jerusalem and Migration to America

EXTRACTS—TITULO DE LOS SENORES DE TOTONICAPAN OR "GENEALOGICAL CLAIMS OF THE LORDS OF TOTONICAPAN":

Nahuales—sages of Israel, came from East (Orient)

Voyage of the Quiché nations and of the other peoples united with them.

The sages, the *Nahuales* [Nephites],[XVII] the chiefs and leaders of the three great tribes, and

EXTRACTS—BOOK OF MORMON:

Nephites and Lamanite, of House of Israel, leave Jerusalem in ancient East 600 B. C.

4. [Nephi writes:] For it came to pass in the commencement of the first year of the reign of Zedekiah, king of Judah,[XIX] (my father, Lehi, having dwelt at Jerusalem in all his days); and in that same year there came many prophets, prophesying unto the people that they must repent, or the great city Jerusalem must be destroyed. 1 Nephi 1:4.

1. For behold, it came to pass that the Lord spake unto my father, yea, even in a dream, and

---

[1] George C. Vaillant, *Aztecs of Mexico* (1944), Table I, pp. 26-27.
[2] *Ibid.,* Table V, p. 67.
[3] Miguel Covarrubias, *Mexico South* (1946), p. 115.
[4] *Ibid.,* chart p. 123. Covarrubias says the artifacts of Teotihuacan came from the south, i.e., from the Tehuantepec area.
[5] Vaillant, *op. cit.,* Table I, pp. 26-27, 52-55.

of still others called *U Mamae* [the Ancients] who joined them, having extended their gaze over the four quarters of the world and over all that which is under heaven — without having encountered any obstacles—they came from the other side of the sea,[XIX] from there where the sun comes up, from the place called Pa Tulan, Pa Civan. The principal chieftains were four in number . . .

These factions came together from the other side of the sea, from the Orient,[XIX] from *Pa Tulan, Pa Civan.*

said unto him: Blessed art thou, Lehi, because of the things which thou hast done; and because thou hast been faithful and declared unto this people the things which I commanded thee, behold, they seek to take away thy life.

2. And it came to pass that the Lord commanded my father, even in a dream, that he should take his family and depart into the wilderness.

3. And it came to pass that he was obedient unto the word of the Lord, wherefore he did as the Lord commanded him.[XXII]

4. And it came to pass that he departed into the wilderness. And he left his house, and the land of his inheritance, and his gold, and his silver, and his precious things, and took nothing with him, save it were his family, and provisions, and tent, and departed into the wilderness.

1 Nephi 2:1-4.

The Book of Mormon is very explicit in fixing the date of the departure of "the sages" (Nephites) from Jerusalem at "the commencement of the first year of the reign of Zedekiah, king of Judah." (The reign-of-kings dating system was in vogue in the Near East at the time.) Bible chronologists now say that the first year of the reign of Zedekiah was 599 B. C.[6] The Lachish letters date from the eleventh or last year of the reign of King Zedekiah, now fixed at 589 or 588 B. C. This would place the first year of the reign of Zedekiah at 600 or 599 B. C. *The Book of Mormon*, it is seen, is in perfect agreement with the latest dating of Zedekiah's reign.

Neither *Ixtlilxochitl* nor the Guatemalan-Maya accounts date the departure from the Old World center. However, as will be seen later, *Ixtlilxochitl* has this people well established in the Bountiful-land center by 132 B. C., the date he gives for an important astronomical-calendar meeting which was held by the people of that land.

With regard to the time when the colonizers of Bountiful-land first arrived in the New World, a scholarly Spanish Padre, Sahagun, makes a very significant statement. He wrote:

Touching on the antiquity of this people, I learn from investigating that they have inhabited this land which now [sixteenth century] is called New Spain more than 2,000 years, because by their ancient writings it is learned that the famous city, which was called Tula, had already existed about 1,000 years when it was destroyed. . . . It is sound and true that

---

[6] If 597 B. C. is the correct Gregorian date for the first year of the reign of Zedekiah, then Christ was born in 3 A. D. (Gregorian date), according to *The Book of Mormon* chronology—for he was born 600 solar years after Lehi left Jerusalem. William Foxwell Albright, *Archaeology of Palestine* (1949), p. 136.

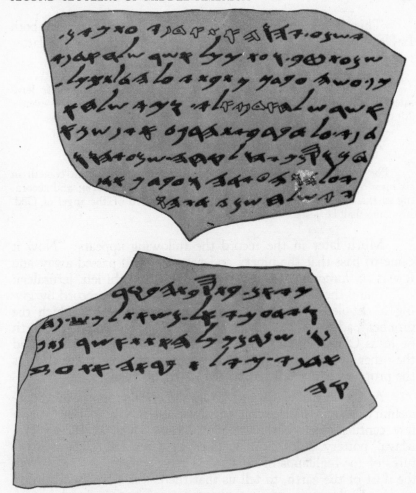

Fig. 8: Hebrew Script Written in 589 B. C.

This was the year the Mulekites left Jerusalem. This is one of the famous Lachish Letters written in the Hebrew cursive script of Lehi's time. The Lachish letters were written on broken pieces of pottery (ostraca) during Nebuchadnezzar's attack on Israel. Lachish was a fortress about thirty miles southwest of Jerusalem. The Lachish letters were sensational when discovered in 1935 and 1938.

more than a thousand years had passed, by which it follows that *for about 500 years before the birth of Christ our Redeemer, this land was populated.*[7]

[7] Bernardino de Sahagun, *op. cit., Introduction al Primer Libro de la Histoira.* The Spanish, from which the quotation was translated, is as follows: "En lo que toca a la antiguedad de esta gente tienese por averiguado que ha mas de dos mil años que havitan en esta tierra que ahora se llama la Nueva España, porque por sus pinturas antiguas hay noticiá que aquella, famosa ciudad que se llamo Tula, ha ya mil anos o muy cerca de ellos, que fué destruida, y antes que se edificase, los que la edificaron estuvieron muchos poblados en Tulanzinco, donde dejaron muchos edificios muy notibles, pues en lo que alli estuvieron, y en lo que tardaron an edificar la ciudad de Tula, y en lo que duro en su prosperidad antest que fuese destruida, es consono a verdad que pasaron mas de mil años, de lo cual resulta, que por lo menos quinientos años antes de la Encarnacion de Nuestro Redentor, esta tierra era poblada."

This dating by Sahagun is in remarkable accord with both *Ixtlilxochitl* and *The Book of Mormon.* In fact, in the latter record Nephi recorded the following:

> Yea, *even six hundred years* from the time that my father left Jerusalem, a prophet would the Lord God raise up among the Jews—even a Messiah, or in other words, a Savior of the world.[8]

And on another occasion the same author wrote:

> For according to the words of the prophets, the Messiah cometh in *six hundred years from the time that my father left Jerusalem;* and according to the words of the prophets, and also the word of the angel of God, his name shall be Jesus Christ, the Son of God.[9]

Much later in the record the following appears: "Now it came to pass that the ninety and first year had passed away and it was *six hundred years* from the time that Lehi left Jerusalem; . . ."[10] and then the writer continues his historical record by giving a detailed account of the signs being fulfilled which the prophet had predicted would take place at the time of the birth of Jesus Christ. In fact, the record keeper testified that he and the other people knew that Jesus Christ came into the world, as the prophets had predicted, at that particular time.

Archæological work in Middle America supports the documentary sources in locating an advanced people in that area a few centuries before the time of Christ. The excellent "preMaya" pottery, jades, stone metates, figurines and religious structures of the highlands of Guatemala have spoken, as voices from the dust of the earth, to tell us that there was a highly advanced people in the very area at about the very time fixed in our written sources.

The earliest history in the Guatemala highlands is represented by such archæological sites as Kaminaljuyu (near Guatemala City), Chukumuk (at Lake Atitlan, Guatemala) and Alta Verapaz. The artifacts from these sites antedate the Classic Maya remains which date from about 320 A. D. In several Middle American sites the types of artifacts that characterize the early "Nahuale-Nephite" period are found to underlie remains of the Classic Maya Period. This early Middle American

---

[8] *The Book of Mormon*, p. 16 (1 Nephi 10:4); p. 41 (*Ibid.*, 19:8).
[9] *Ibid.*, p. 91 (2 Nephi 25:19).
[10] *Ibid.*, p. 399 (3 Nephi 1:1).

culture is *"on a level with,* and *extraordinarily like,* those of our own cultural ancestors of the ancient Near East, or Palestine."[11]

In the words of the late Sylvanus G. Morley, an eminent scholar in this field: ". . . the Maya civilization—or, better, *those cultural elements which led up to it*—had their beginnings between two and three thousand years ago, roughly some time during the first millenium before Christ, probably nearer the later than the earlier limit."[12]

We turn now to the *Totonicapan, Popol Vuh,* and *Book of Mormon* accounts concerning the coming of the second settlers to ancient America. Many remarkable details are found in the Nephite account, especially with regard to the journey across the Arabian peninsula. These details will be discussed later, for they demonstrate that the account is in authentic Hebrew-Arabic terminology. Many of the points are confirmed by the *Totonicapan* and *Popol Vuh* reports.

LEHI'S PARTY LEAVES JERUSALEM AND RECEIVES LIAHONA

EXTRACTS—TOTONI-
CAPAN:

Descendants of Israel; Giron-Gagal (Liahona) received from Nacxit (God); crossing the ocean and arrival in America

These then were the three nations of Quiche, *descendants of Israel.*[XX] They came from there where the sun comes up, speaking the same tongue and having the same customs.

When they left there, from *Pa Tulan, Pa Civan* [Old-World "Bountiful"],[XXIV] their first chief was Balam Quitze, named by the unanimity of voices, and the Grandfather *Nacxit* [God] gave them a gift called *Giron-Gagal.*[XXII]

When they reached the shores of the sea, *Balam-Quitze* struck it with his staff[13] and instantly a

EXTRACTS—BOOK OF MORMON:

Lehi's small party camped by Red Sea; joined by Ishmael's family; marriages; sorrow on leaving homeland; brass ball or Liahona received from God

5. And he came down by the borders near the shore of the Red Sea; and he traveled in the wilderness in the borders which are nearer the Red Sea; and he did travel in the wilderness with his family, which consisted of my mother, Sariah, and my elder brothers, who are Laman, Lemuel, and Sam.[XXIII, XXVI]

6. And it came to pass that when he had traveled three days in the wilderness, he pitched his tent in a valley by the side of a *river of water.*[XXIII]

7. And it came to pass that *he built an altar of stones,*[XXIII] and made an offering unto the Lord, and gave thanks unto the Lord our God.

8. And it came to pass that he called the name of the river, Laman, and it emptied into the Red Sea; and the valley was in the borders near the mouth thereof.

---

[11] The Miraflores, Mamon-Chicanel and Playa de Muertos underlie Classic Maya artifacts. They appear to belong to the early "Nahuale-Nephite-Lamanite" people of the documentary sources. Alfred V. Kidder, et al, *Kaminaljuyu,* Guatemala (1946), publication 561, Carnegie Institution of Washington, D. C., pp. 241-244, 260.

[12] Sylvanus G. Morley, *The Ancient Maya* (1946), p. 40.

[13] Lehi probably did carry a staff—but it is doubtful, from the account of Nephi, that he used his staff on the divine instrument. There are many references to "staffs" in the Old Testament, and in *The Book of Mormon,* see p. 6 (1 Nephi 3:28). The present-day Chorti-Mayas use "tall staffs" in religious ceremonies.

passage opened [a way was opened for them, or shown to them] which closed shortly after. The Sovereign Lord[XXII] did this for them because they were the sons of Abraham and of Jacob.[XX]

It was thus that the three nations passed [to the New World] and with them thirteen others called Vuh-Amag. Once arrived [here] from the other side of the sea,[XXV] the absence of nourishment obliged them to nourish themselves from roots; nevertheless, the immigrants proceeded gay and content. Finally they arrived at the shore of a small lake and there they found a great abundance of small game.

* * *

. . . our ancestors . . . had come from the other side of the sea,[XIX] from Civan-Tulan at the confines of Babylonia.

EXTRACTS—POPOL VUH:

Second settlers came to America from "other side of the sea;" descendants of Llocab (Jacob?); original in East; led to America by Tohil (God); departed to America from Tulan (Bountiful); sorrow on leaving homeland

This we shall write now under the Law of God and Christianity; we shall bring it to light because now the *Popol Vuh* ["Book of the Community"], as it is called, cannot be seen any more,[14] in which was clearly seen the coming from the other side of the sea.[XIX] The original book, written long ago, existed, but its sight is hidden to the searcher and to the thinker.
Preamble, pp. 79-80.

The beginning is known, too, of those of Tamub [a Quiche tribe] and those of Llocab [Jacob?][15] who came together from there in the East.[XIX]

* * *

Three groups of families existed; but they did not forget the name of their grandfather and

9. And when my father saw that the waters of the river emptied into the fountain of the Red Sea, he spake unto Laman, saying: O that thou mightest be like unto this river, continually running into the fountain of righteousness!

10. And he also spake unto Lemuel: O that thou mightest be like unto this valley, firm and steadfast, and immovable in keeping the commandments of the Lord!

15. And my father dwelt in a tent [in the valley of Lemuel].   1 Nephi 2:1-10, 15.

1. And now I would that ye might know, that after my father, Lehi, had made an end of prophesying concerning his seed, it came to pass that the Lord spake upon him again, saying that it was not meet for him, Lehi, that he should take his family into the wilderness alone; but that his sons should take daughters to wife, that they might raise up seed unto the Lord in the land of promise.

2. And it came to pass that the Lord commanded him that I, Nephi, and my brethren, should again return unto the land of Jerusalem, and bring down Ishmael and his family into the wilderness.

3. And it came to pass that I, Nephi, did again, with my brethren, go forth into the wilderness to go up to Jerusalem.

4. And it came to pass that we went up unto the house of Ishmael, and we did gain favor in the sight of Ishmael, insomuch that we did speak unto him the words of the Lord.

5. And it came to pass that the Lord did soften the heart of Ishmael, and also his household, insomuch that they took their journey with us down into the wilderness to the tent of our father.   1 Nephi 7:1-5.

6. And it came to pass that as we journeyed in the wilderness, behold Laman and Lemuel, and two of the daughters of Ishmael, and the two sons of Ishmael and their families, did rebel against us; yea, against me, Nephi, and Sam, and their father, Ishmael, and his wife, and his three other daughters.[XXIII, XXVI]

7. And it came to pass in the which rebellion, they were desirous to return unto the land of Jerusalem.[XXI]   1 Nephi 7:1-7.

6. Now, all these things were said and done as my father dwelt in a tent in the valley which he called Lemuel.

7. And it came to pass that I, Nephi, took one of the daughters of Ishmael to wife; and also, my brethren took of the daughters of Ishmael to wife; and also Zoram took the eldest daughter of Ishmael to wife.[XXVI]

[14] Like the original plates of *The Book of Mormon*, the original manuscript of the *Popol Vuh* cannot now be seen. We do not know where it is. This does not mean, however, that a certified translation copy is not of great value.

[15] The Ll in *Llocab* is pronounced "Y." Llocab is pronounced exactly like the Hebrews pronounced Jacob—Yah-ak-obe'. James Strong, *Dictionary of the Hebrew Bible* (1890), word 3290.

father, those who propagated and multiplied there in the East.[XVII]

* * *

Many men were made and in the darkness they multiplied. Neither the sun nor the light had yet been made when they multiplied. All lived together, they existed in great number and walked there in the East.

Nevertheless, they did not sustain nor maintain [their God]; they only raised their faces to the sky, and they did not know why they had come so far as they did.

There they were then, in great number, the black men and the white men, men of many classes, men of many tongues, that it was wonderful to hear them.

* * *

The speech of all was the same. They did not invoke wood or stone [idols], and they remembered the word of the Creator and the Maker, the Heart of Heaven, the Heart of Earth.

Part III, Ch. 3, pp. 170-173.

In *Tulan* power came instantly to them; great was their wisdom in the darkness and in the night.

Then they came, they pulled up stakes there and left the East. "This is not our home; let us go and see where we should settle," Tohil [God] said then.

In truth, he [God] was accustomed to talking to Balam-Quitze, Balam Acab, Mahucutah, and Iqui-Balam: "Give thanks before setting out; do what is necessary to bleed your ears, prick your elbows, and make your sacrifices,[16] this shall be your thanks to God."

"Very well," they said, and took blood from their ears. And they wept in their chants because of their departure from *Tulan;* their hearts mourned when they left *Tulan.*[XXI]

"Pity us! We shall not see the dawn here [in the East] when the sun rises and lights the face

8. And thus my father had fulfilled all the commandments of the Lord which had been given unto him. And also, I, Nephi, had been blessed of the Lord exceedingly.

9. *And it came to pass that the voice of the Lord spake unto my father by night, and commanded him that on the morrow he should take his journey into the wilderness.*[XXIII]

10. *And it came to pass that as my father arose in the morning, and went forth to the tent door, to his great astonishment he beheld upon the ground a round ball of curious workmanship; and it was of fine brass. And within the ball were two spindles; and the one pointed the way whither we should go into the wilderness.*[XXII]

1 Nephi 16:6-10.

---

[16] Self-mutilation was an ancient practice among Semitic peoples. It was a way of demonstrating humility, sorrow or thanksgiving. Deuteronomic law forbade such practices. Regarding the practice, see *Jeremiah* 16:6; *Leviticus* 19:28; *Deuteronomy* 16:1. For a discussion of the subject, see Maurice H. Farbridge, *Studies in Biblical and Semitic Symbolism,* 1923, pp. 226-239.

of the earth," they said at leaving. But they left some people
on the road which they followed
so that they would keep watch.

Each of the tribes kept getting
up to see the star [Morning
Star], which was the herald of
the sun. This sign of the dawn
they carried in their hearts when
they came from the East [the
Morning Star, Venus, was a symbol of Quetzalcoatl-Christ in
Middle America] and with the
same hope [i.e., faith in God]
they left there, *from that great
distance,*[XXV] according to what
their songs now say.

XX. A Branch of House of Israel

The Book of Mormon and the *Totonicapan* accounts each
credit the colonizers with being of Israel and with having been
led to the New World directly by God or Jehovah. The *Popol
Vuh* accords with the latter point. *Ixtlilxochitl* and the *Popol
Vuh,* by implication, say these people were of Israel for they
both state they had knowledge of the creation, the deluge and
other matters contained in Hebrew history, thereby being in
accord with the other two reports.

The *Totonicapan* account states that the Lord supplied the
Giron-Gagal (director) and led the colony across the sea
". . . because they were the sons of Abraham and of Jacob."
The Book of Mormon declares in a number of places that the
Lord was interested in leading the colony to the New World
as a part of his great plan in dealing with the House of Israel.
One extract on the point will suffice:

Yea, even my father spake much concerning the Gentiles, and also
concerning the house of Israel, that they should be compared like unto
an olive-tree, whose branches should be broken off and should be scattered
upon all the face of the earth. Wherefore, he said *it must needs be that
we should be led with one accord into the land of promise, unto the fulfilling of the word of the Lord, that we* [Israel] *should be scattered upon
all the face of the earth.* And after the house of Israel should be scattered
they should be gathered together again; or, in fine, after the Gentiles had
received the fulness of the Gospel, the natural branches of the olive-tree,
or *the remnants of the house of Israel, should be grafted in, or come to
the knowledge of the true Messiah, their Lord and their Redeemer.*"[19]

[19] *Book of Mormon,* pp. 16-17 (1 Nephi 10:12-14).

Thus, to summarize the thought, the colony was led to America in anticipation of the denial of Jesus by the Jews in Palestine. Through their records which have come down to us, the ancient colonizers of Middle America are to be responsible for convincing the House of Israel that Jesus was the true Messiah. As the *Totonicapan* record says, the Lord led the original colony to America because it was comprised of the sons of Abraham and Jacob.

The fact that "they did not invoke wood or stone [idols]" (*Popol Vuh*) is noteworthy. We recall Jehovah's precept in this regard: "Thou shalt not make unto thee any graven image . . . Thou shalt not bow down thyself to them, nor serve them: for I the Lord thy God am a jealous God. . . ."[20] The *Popol Vuh* and the Nephite record are corroborated with respect to this matter of idols by the famous sixteenth-century Maya historian of Yucatan, Gaspar Antonio Chi. Concerning the early Itza-"Christians" who colonized Yucatan from the Bountiful-land area (Tutulxiu or Tulan), he wrote:

The ancients say that those who anciently came to people this land [of Yucatan] were those who founded Chichen Itza, a very ancient city, and they were very simple [in their worship] and did not worship idols or make any sacrifice.[21]

Another sixteenth-century Maya account is in accord:

It is said that the first founders of Chichen Yza were not idolators until Kukulcan, a Mexican captain [of the tenth century A. D.], entered these provinces. He it was who showed (them) idolatry as they said.[22]

Christ was alluding to the New World branch of the House of Israel when he said: "And *other sheep I have,* which are not of this fold [Palestine]: them also I must bring, and they shall hear my voice; and there shall be one fold and one shepherd." It appears that Christ was also referring to the eventual unity of the House of Israel—in the above-quoted *Book of Mormon* language, when "the remnants of the house of Israel should be grafted in or come to the knowledge of the true Messiah, their Lord and their Redeemer." That Christ did visit Middle America will be shown later on in this book. The "grafting in" is yet to take place.

[20] Exodus 20:5.
[21] Gaspar Antonio Chi, *Historical Recollections* (1577). Translation by M. Wells Jakeman, *Origins and History of the Mayas* (1945), p. 95.
[22] *Relaciones de Yucatan,* translated by Alfred M. Tozzer and quoted by Tozzer in his *Landa's Relacion de las Cosas de Yucatan* (1941), note 124.

The great German historian, Edward Meyer, observed the complete harmony of the Nephite account with the Judæo-Christian writings of the Old World. To quote:

A Bible for America, in absolute harmony with the Old and New Testaments, but at the same time *an explanation and fulfillment of their teachings* which restore the primitive purity of revelation or the Gospel, that is the thought which runs through the entire *Book of Mormon,* and in which it is rooted.[23]

Confirming the foregoing accounts is a fourth by Diego de Landa (1524-1579 A. D.). In writing his great work, *Relacion de las cosas de Yucatan (Account of the things of Yucatan),* he said:

Some of the old people of Yucatan say that they have heard from their ancestors that this land was occupied by a race of people who came from the East and whom God had delivered by opening twelve paths through the sea. If this were true, it necessarily follows that all the inhabitants of the Indies are descendants of the Jews.[24]

Landa's deduction that all the inhabitants of the New World are descendants of the Jews if the ancestors of the Mayas came from the East by sea with the aid of God is, of course, far too sweeping and is an unfounded conclusion. What went on between northeastern Siberia and Alaska, for example, would have had no relation to the colonization of Middle America by transoceanic people from the Near East.

It will be shown later from other Maya sources that the first cultured settlers of Yucatan, the Itzan-Mayas, followers of the bearded white God, Itzamna [Christ] were descendants of the people of Bountiful-land, *Tulan,* who had originally come from the Near East. Further, it will be shown later that they left Bountiful-land during *The Book of Mormon* period, that is, about 238-239 A. D. Thus, the tradition reported by Landa accords with all the other reliable and early native accounts, as well as with *The Book of Mormon.*

The Nephite account gives details of conversations between Lehi and the Lord, Nephi and the Lord, and between Jacob and the Lord. The text makes it clear that there was a very close and personal relationship between the leaders of the Nephites and Jehovah. They even used the term "Christ" in the sixth

---

[23] Edward Meyer (1912), p. 41. English translation by Franklin S. Harris, Jr.
[24] Diego de Landa, *Relacion de las cosas de Yucatan,* written about 1566, English translation by Alfred M. Tozzer, Harvard University (1941), p. 16. See also translation by William Gates, *Maya Society* (1937), p. 8. Italics added for emphasis.

century B. C.—centuries before the birth of Jesus. The record shows that God had such a personal interest in the colony that he told them to leave Jerusalem, that he furnished them the direc- tor—that he even instructed Nephi concerning the building of the ship that was to transport them across the ocean. Thus there is complete accord between the various accounts quoted. The *Popol Vuh* states: ". . . they remembered the word of the Creator and the Maker . . ." Also, "In truth, he [God] was accustomed to talking to Balam-Quitze . . ."!

XXI. SORROW ON LEAVING ANCIENT HOMELAND

The *Popol Vuh* is in close parallel with *The Book of Mor- mon* in stating that the company left the ancient homeland with great sorrow and reluctance. The Maya report, we note, contains this observation: "And they wept in their chants be- cause of their departure from Tulan; their hearts mourned when they left Tulan. Pity us! . . . they said at leaving." The Nephite record states that the reluctance of some of the party to leave Jerusalem was so great "that as we journeyed in the wilderness, behold Laman and Lemuel, and two of the daughters of Ishmael, and the two sons of Ishmael and their families, did rebel against us . . . in the which rebellion, they were desirous to return unto the land of Jerusalem." The disappointment of the rebellious members of the company turned into bitter hatred and those feelings were passed on to their children and descendants for gen- erations. As late as 178 B. C. it was written of that faction:

Now, the Lamanites knew nothing concerning the Lord, nor the strength of the Lord, therefore they depended upon their own strength. Yet they were a strong people, as to the strength of men. They were a wild, and ferocious, and a blood-thirsty people, believing in *the tradition of their fathers, which is this*—Believing that they were driven out of the land of Jerusalem because of the iniquities of their fathers, and that they were wronged in the wilderness by their brethren, and they were also wronged while crossing the sea; and again, that they were wronged while in the land of their first inheritance, after they had crossed the sea, and all this because that Nephi was more faithful in keeping the command- ments of the Lord—therefore he was favored of the Lord, for the Lord heard his prayers and answered them, and he took the lead of their journey in the wilderness.[25]

Again it is written in the *Popol Vuh*, " 'Oh, we have come without joy! If only we could see the rising of the sun [the

[25] *Book of Mormon*, pp. 154-155 (Mosiah 10:11-14).

East]! What shall we do now? If we lived in harmony in our country, why did we leave it?' they said to each other, in the midst of their sadness and affliction, and with mournful voices."

This calls to mind a sadly eloquent statement, which statement was written about eighty years after the arrival in the New World by an aged Nephite who was born during the great trek to the western hemisphere:

... I, Jacob, began to be old ... I conclude this record ... by saying that the time passed away with us, and also our lives passed away like as it were unto us a dream, we being a lonesome and a solemn people, wanderers, cast out from Jerusalem, born in tribulation, in a wilderness, and hated of our brethren, which caused wars and contentions; wherefore, we did mourn out our days.[26]

XXII. "GIRON-GAGAL" OR "LIAHONA"

It has been pointed out that three accounts, The Book of Mormon, Totonicapan, and the Popol Vuh, refer to a sacred device which opened the way, that is—showed the way, across the ocean to the New World. The accounts agree that it was provided by God. They agree that it worked as though by magic —by the power of the Lord. Clearly, it was an instrument that, for the day and age involved, was "supernatural"—and for that reason some readers may have difficulty accepting the reality of it. There are a few facts and observations concerning those facts that can be pointed out that may have some convincing power.

First, our accounts (Ixtlilxochitl, Popol Vuh, Totonicapan, and The Book of Mormon) come down to us from independent sources. Ultimately, those sources go back to the very same events —artisan colonizers departing for the New World from Bible lands several centuries before Christ. They claimed to be of Israel and in intimate contact with Jehovah. It is unthinkable that Joseph Smith could have fabricated such a peculiar and unique story and have it match up with recorded traditions and histories from Middle America. It is doubly absurd that this portion of The Book of Mormon could have been a fictional concoction. It appears

---

[26] Ibid., p. 125 (Jacob 7:26).

that the Nephite name for the divine instrument, *Liahona*,[27] may possibly be a composite of the two Hebrew words which describe the functioning of the instrument, *"Lahab-hennah."*[28] These words mean "point" and "whither."

It can not be stated with certainty that *Liahona* is derived from the foregoing Hebrew words, but it appears possible. The Nephites and Mulekites modified the Hebrew tongue as they did the Egyptian tongue. Also, when Joseph Smith sounded out ancient names to his scribes, those names were written the way they sounded to the scribes; and they were not necessarily written the way the ancients themselves would have done so.

It should be recalled that Nephi made the following observation:

And it came to pass that as my father arose in the morning, and went forth to the tent door, to his great astonishment he beheld upon the ground a round ball of curious workmanship; and it was of fine brass. And within the ball were two spindles; and the one pointed the way whither we should go into the wilderness.[28a]

According to *The Book of Mormon* extract quoted above, the functioning of the director is described as follows: ". . . And within the ball were two spindles; and the one *pointed the way whither* we should go into the wilderness." The name *Liahona* appears in the Nephite text in this statement:

And now, my son, I [Alma] have somewhat to say concerning the thing which our fathers call a ball, or director—or our fathers called it *Liahona,* which is, being interpreted, a compass; and the Lord prepared it. And behold, there cannot any man work after the manner of so curious a workmanship. And behold, it was prepared to show unto our fathers the course which they should travel in the wilderness. And it did work for them according to their faith in God; therefore, if they had faith to believe that God could cause that those spindles would point the way they should go, behold, it was done; . . . surely . . . this director [Liahona] did bring our fathers, by following its course, to the promised land. . . .[29]

---

[27] Mormon students have heretofore groped for the meaning of *Liahona*. See J. M. Sjodahl, *An Introduction to the Study of The Book of Mormon* (1927), p. 127.

[28] James Strong, *A Concise Dictionary of the Words in the Hebrew Bible,* appendage to his *Exhaustive Concordance of the Bible* (1890), words 3851-3852 and 2008. This is a scholarly work that has gone through 15 printings since 1890.

[28a] *The Book of Mormon,* p. 31 (1 Nephi 16:10).

[29] *The Book of Mormon,* p. 291 (Alma 37:38-40, 45).

According to both the *Popol Vuh* and *The Book of Mormon*, Lehi left this sacred instrument with his heirs when he died. As indicated by the *Popol Vuh,* it was symbolic of the power of God which power was possessed by these early colonizers. They were on more intimate terms with God than were their kindred left behind in the Old World. Concerning the deathbed statement of the original head of the colony, the *Popol Vuh* says:

> Then Balam-Quitze left the symbol of his being: "This is a remembrance which I leave for you. This shall be your power. I take my leave filled with sorrow," he added. Then he left the symbol of his being, the Pizom-Gagal, as it was called . . .

Therefore, when the twenty-four-years-old Joseph Smith published *The Book of Mormon* 120 years ago in the little country town of Palmyra, New York, he gave to the world a description of the Liahona which was completely in accord with references made to a sacred director in Middle American documentary sources brought to light since Joseph's day.

JOURNEY TO BOUNTIFUL IN ARABIA

EXTRACTS—POPOL VUH:

Second settlers' hunger, sorrow and difficulties; crossing ocean to America; few immigrants; came from Tulan in Zuyva (Bountiful in Arabia)

There they were come together to await the dawn and to watch for the coming of the star, which comes just before the sun, when it is about to rise. "We came from there [the East], but we have separated," they said to each other.

And their hearts were troubled; they were suffering greatly; they did not have food; they did not have sustenance; they only smelled the ends of their staffs and thus they imagined they were eating; but they did not eat when they came.[XXIII]

It is not quite clear, however, how they crossed the sea; they crossed to this side, as if there were no sea; they crossed on stones, placed in a row over the sand. For this reason they were called Stones in a Row, Sand Under the Sea, names given to them when they (the tribes) crossed the sea, the waters hav-

EXTRACTS—BOOK OF MORMON:

Arabian desert crossed; hunger, sorrow and difficulties; Bountiful in Arabia

11. And it came to pass that we did gather together whatsoever things we should carry into the wilderness, and all the remainder of our provisions which the Lord had given unto us; and we did take seed of every kind that we might carry into the wilderness.

12. And it came to pass that we did take our tents and depart into the wilderness, across the river Laman.

13. And it came to pass that we traveled for the space of four days, nearly a south-southeast direction, and we did pitch our tents again; and we did call the name of the place Shazer.[XXIII]

14. And it came to pass that we did take our bows and arrows, and go forth in the wilderness to slay food for our families; and after we had slain food for our families we did return again to our families in the wilderness, to the place of Shazer. And we did go forth again in the wilderness, following the same direction, keeping in the most fertile parts of the wilderness, which were in the borders near the Red Sea.

15. And we did follow the directions of the ball, which led us in the more fertile parts of the wilderness.

25. And it came to pass that the voice of the Lord came unto my father; and he was truly chastened because of his murmuring against the Lord,[XXI] insomuch that he was brought down

ing parted when they passed.[xxv]
Part III, Ch. 7, pp. 182-183.

* * *

They had come that far. "Oh, we have come without joy! If only we could see the rising of the sun! What shall we do now? If we lived in harmony in our country, why did we leave it?"[xxi] they said to each other, in the midst of their sadness and affliction, and with mournful voices."
Part III, Ch. 8, p. 185.

* * *

When the sun arose, the hearts of Balam-Quitze, Balam-Acab, Mahucutah. and Iqui-Balam were filled with joy. Great was their joy when it dawned. And there were not many men at that place [of first settlement in the New World]; only a few were there on the mountain Hac-avitz [in Guatemala]. There dawn came to them, there they burned their incense and danced, turning their gaze toward the East, whence they had come.[xx] There were their mountains and their valleys, whence had come Balam Quitze, Balam-Acab, Mahucutah, and Iqui-Balam, as they were called.

But it was here where they multiplied, on the mountain, and this was their town; here they were, too, when the sun, the moon, and the stars appeared, when it dawned and the face of the earth and the whole world was lighted. Here, too, began their song, which they call ca-mucu, they sang it, but only the pain in their hearts and their innermost selves they expressed in their song. "Oh pity us! In Tulan [in Old World] we were lost, we were separated, and there our older and younger brothers stayed.[xx] Ah, we have seen the sun! but where are they now, that it has dawned?" so said the priests and the sacrific-ers of the Yaqui [Tultecas].

Because, in truth, the so-called Tohil is the same God of the Yaqui, the one called Yolcuat-

into the depths of sorrow.

26. And it came to pass that the voice of the Lord said unto him: Look upon the ball, and behold the things which are written.

3. And it came to pass that we did again take our journey, traveling nearly the same course as in the beginning; and after we had traveled for the space of many days we did pitch our tents again, that we might tarry for the space of a time.

34. And it came to pass that Ishmael died, and was buried in the place which was called *Nahom*.

35. And it came to pass that *the daughters of Ishmael did mourn exceedingly, because of the loss of their father*, and because of their afflic-tions in the wilderness; and they did murmur against my father, because he had brought them out of the land of Jerusalem, . . .[xxi]
1 Nephi 16:11-15, 20, 25-26, 33-35.

17. And after we had traveled for the space of many days, we did pitch our tents for the space of a time, that we might again rest our-selves and obtain food for our families.

18. And it came to pass that as I, Nephi, went forth to slay food, behold, I did break my bow, which was made of fine steel; and after I did break my bow, behold, my brethren were angry with me because of the loss of my bow, for we did obtain no food.

19. And it came to pass that we did return without food to our families, and being much fatigued, because of their journeying they did suffer much for the want of food.[xxiii]

20. And it came to pass that Laman and Lemuel and the sons of Ishmael did begin to murmur exceedingly, because of their sufferings and afflictions in the wilderness; and also my father began to murmur against the Lord his God; yea, and they were all exceeding sorrowful, even that they did murmur against the Lord.

21. Now it came to pass that I, Nephi, having been afflicted with my brethren because of the loss of my bow, and their bows having lost their springs, it began to be exceedingly difficult, yea, insomuch that we could obtain no food.[xxiii]

22. And it came to pass that I, Nephi, did speak much unto my brethren, because they had hardened their hearts again, even unto complain-ing against the Lord their God.

23. And it came to pass that I, Nephi, did make out of wood a bow, and out of a straight stick, an arrow; wherefore, I did arm myself with a bow and an arrow, with a sling and with stones. And I said unto my father: Whither shall I go to obtain food?

74   ANCIENT AMERICA AND THE BOOK OF MORMON

Quitzalcuat [Quetzalcoat—Quetzal bird serpent—the Fair God.]
XLVII

"We became separated there
in Tulan, in Zuyva, from there
we went out together,LIV, LV and
there our race was created when
we came," they said to each
other.
     Part III, Ch. 9, pp. 188-189.
* * *

30. And it came to pass that I, Nephi, did go
forth up into the top of the mountain, according
to the directions which were given upon the ball.

31. And it came to pass that I did slay wild
beasts, insomuch that I did obtain food for our
families.

32. And it came to pass that I did return to
our tents, bearing the beasts which I had slain;
and now when they beheld that I had obtained
food, how great was their joy!XXIII And it came
to pass that they did humble themselves before
the Lord, and did give thanks unto him.
                           1 Nephi 16:17-23, 30-32.

1. And it came to pass that we did again
take our journey in the wilderness; and we did
travel nearly eastward from that time forth. And
we did travel and wade through much affliction
in the wilderness; and our women did bear children in the wilderness.XXVI

2. And so great were the blessings of the Lord
upon us, that while *we did live upon raw meat
in the wilderness,*XXIII our women did give plenty
of suck for their children, and were strong, yea,
even like unto men; and they began to bear their
journeyings without murmurings.

4. And we did sojourn for the space of many
years, yea, even eight years in the wilderness.XXIII

5. And we did come to the land which we
called Bountiful,XXIV because of its much fruit
and also wild honey; and all these things were
prepared of the Lord that we might not perish.
And we *beheld the sea,* which we called *Irreantum,* which, being interpreted, is many waters.
[Note: *Irreantum* may be from the Hebrew words
meaning "behold the deep." They are very
similar.]

6. And it came to pass that we did pitch our
tents by the seashore; and notwithstanding we
had suffered many afflictions and much difficulty,
yea, even so much that we cannot write them all,
we were exceedingly rejoiced when we came to
the seashore; and we called the place Bountiful,
because of its much fruit.   1 Nephi 17:1-2, 4-6.

11. I [Nephi] *did smite two stones together
that might make a fire* [at the end of the journey
across Arabia].

12. *For the Lord had not hitherto suffered
that we should make much fire, as we journeyed
in the wilderness;*XXIII for he said: I will make
thy food sweet, that ye cook it not;

13. And I will also be your light in the wilderness; and I will prepare the way before you, if it
so be that ye shall keep my commandments;
wherefore, inasmuch as ye shall keep my commandments ye shall be led towards the promised
land; and ye shall know that it is by me that ye
are led.XXII   1 Nephi 17:11-13.

XXIII. ARABIAN DESERT CROSSED

The first seventeen chapters of *The Book of Mormon* report the journey of Lehi, an Israelite with some Egyptian background, and Ishmael, an Arab-Israelite, and their families, out of Jerusa-lem, along the Red Sea and across the Arabian desert. As the extracts from Nephi's account show, many details of that journey are provided. Professor Hugh Nibley of the Brigham Young University has recently examined the details of this entire account with great care with an eye to ascertaining whether they reflect the true local color of the time and of the desert. We are indebted to him for most of the observations made herein concerning the journey.[30]

The personal names of the members of the expedition are true Hebrew, Arabic and Egyptian, and they were names in use in the Near Eastern world of Lehi's time. The very name *Lehi* was discovered on a piece of broken pottery that was found in 1940 at the site of King Solomon's copper refineries near the northern end of the Red Sea. The vowels are not present and the name appears, when transliterated, as *Lhy,* vocalized by Professor Nelson Glueck as "Lahai." It dates from the fifth or fourth century B. C.[31]

The expedition going out from the "land of Jerusalem" under the leadership of Lehi included the following personnel: Lehi; Sariah; Ishmael; Laman; Lemuel; Nephi; Sam; the wife of Ishmael; the daughters of Ishmael (5); the sons of Ishmael (2); and Zoram. This totals sixteen persons. Children were born during the eight years spent in Arabia before the company embarked for the New World.

The name *Sariah* was, of course, common to the ancient Hebrews and it need not be discussed. The name *Ishmael* is an ancient Arabic name that was also found among the kindred Hebrew. "The proverbial ancestor of the Arabs is Ishmael. His is one of the few Old Testament names which is also at home in ancient Arabia. His traditional homeland was the Tih, the desert between Palestine and Egypt, and his people were hunters of the 'borders' between the desert and the town; he was regarded

---

[30] Hugh Nibley, "Lehi in the Desert," *The Improvement Era* (1950), vol. 53, pp. 14, 102, 200, 276, 382, 486.

[31] *Ibid.,* p. 104. Nibley cites Nelson Glueck, "Ostraca from Elath," *Bulletin of the American Schools of Oriental Research,* No. 80 (Dec., 1940), p. 5. See also P. Haupt, "Heb, Lehi, cheek and lo-a', jaw," Jul. Bibl. Lit. XXXIII (1914), 290-5.

as the legitimate offspring of Abraham by an Egyptian mother. . . . Lehi, faced with the prospect of a long journey in the wilderness, sent back for Ishmael, who promptly followed into the desert with a large party. . . ."

Since Lehi spoke Egyptian and knew how to write a form of Egyptian shorthand, and since he was a travelling merchant and since his political leanings were toward Egypt, and since his genealogy was recorded in the Egyptian language on the brass plates which he took along to America, it is apparent that he had had considerable contact with Egyptian culture, or that he and his ancestry may have lived in Egypt or in its borders at one time. This explains the presence in *The Book of Mormon* of such authentic Egyptian names as Pacumeni, Pahoran and Paanchi.[32]

The name *Lamon,* rendered *Leimun* (the vowels must be supplied by guesswork) has been found in ancient Palestine.[33] It might be noted also that the name *Alma,* so common in the Nephite record, was likewise popular among the ancient Arabs.[34] *Lemuel* is an Arabic name that appears but twice in the Old Testament.[35] It is likewise found in the desert area to the south of Jerusalem in the direction of Egypt. It appears in an Edomite text from an area where the Jewish religion prevailed in ancient times.[36]

The names of Lehi's younger sons, *Nephi* and *Sam,* are true Egyptian personal names.[37] The names of the youngest sons, those born during the eight years in the Arabian desert, *Jacob* and *Joseph,* are, of course, Hebrew. Dr. Nibley makes this interesting observation concerning the names of the six sons of Lehi: "It should be noted here that archæology has fully demonstrated that the Israelites, then as now, had not the slightest aversion to giving their children non-Jewish names, even when those names smacked of a pagan background. One might, in a speculative mood, even detect something of Lehi's personal history in

[32] In a personal letter to one of the writers, Professor Wm. Foxwell Albright, outstanding American authority of the ancient languages of the Near East, verified some of *The Book of Mormon* names as true Egyptian names of the period in question.

[33] Nibley, *op. cit.,* p. 157. He cites C. Clermont-Ganneau, "Moslem Mukams," in *Survey of Western Palestine, Special Papers,* p. 325; C. R. Conder, in same vol., p. 272.

[34] Nibley, *op. cit.,* p. 157, citing *Survey of Western Palestine, Name Lists* (E. H. Palmer, Comment., London, 1881), pp. 40, 17, 66.

[35] Proverbs 31:1, 4.

[36] Nibley, *ibid.,* pp. 156-157, citing E. ben Yehuda, "The Edomite Language," *Journal of Palestine Oriental Society,* vol. 1 (1921), pp. 113-115.

[37] *Nfy* was the name of an Egyptian captain. Nibley, *op. cit.,* note 48, p. 72. He cites S. K. R. Glanville, "The Letters of Ahmose of Peniate," *Journal of Egyptian Archaeology,* vol. 14, p. 304, line 10. See also Hugh Nibley, "The Book of Mormon as a Mirror of the East," *The Improvement Era,* p. 51 (Apr., 1948).

the names he gave his sons. The first two have Arabic names— do they recall his early days in the caravan trade? The second two have Egyptian names, and indeed they were born in the days of his prosperity. The last two, born amid tribulations in the desert, were called with fitting humility, Jacob and Joseph. Whether the names of the first four were meant, as those of the last two sons certainly were (2 Nephi 2:1, 3:1), to call to mind the circumstances under which they were born, the names are certainly a striking indication of their triple [Arabic, Egyptian, Hebrew] heritage."[38]

Lehi's departure from Jerusalem took place in the spring of the year. This fact is known because Nephi states that it was "in the commencement of the first year of the reign of Zedekiah, king of Judah." Nibley says: "Since, 'in the Bible throughout the first month always refers to the first spring month,' Nephi's 'commencement of the year' would fall in the springtime, regard-less of when Zedekiah began to reign, since the Jews, like the Egyptians, dated a king's rule from the beginning of the real year, the ritual time of coronation."[39] This explains the presence of water in the intermittent stream, *the river of water,*" in the valley where Lehi's company first pitched tents. It is only in the springtime that most of the stream beds in Palestine and the desert by the Gulf of Agaba contain water. In fact, the writers note that the Hebrew language has one word, *nahar,* for "river of water" and another for the dry stream bed, *nachal.*[40] Thus, the odd expression of Nephi, "river of water," was in harmony with a common Hebrew practice.

That Lehi "built an altar of stones" is also in true local color. He was at the river where he could obtain washed river stones for constructing the altar. The law of Moses required that if an altar were built of stones that they be unhewn stones. "And if thou wilt make me an altar of stone, thou shalt not build it of hewn stone; for if thou lift up thy tool upon it, thou hast polluted it."[41] An example of such an altar in the New World is the one at the early site of Cuicuilco just south of Mexico City. It is a well-fashioned altar of river stones.

[38] Nibley, *ibid.,* p. 157.
[39] *Ibid.,* note 248, p. 518.
[40] Smith, *Bible Dictionary* (1884 ed.).), p. 566.
[41] Exodus 20:24-25. Regarding the custom in Lehi's land of erecting such altars of unhewn stones, see Nibley, *op. cit.,* p. 322.

It has recently been pointed out that the naming of the river by Lehi and the naming of the valley also, after his two eldest sons, was quite in keeping with the best traditions of Lehi's time and place.[42]

After leaving the camp by the stream, the caravan "traveled for the space of four days, nearly a south-southeast direction, and we did pitch our tents again; and we did call the name of the place *Shazer*." The name, strange as it seems, was most appropriate and descriptive—it means ". . . a weak but reliable water supply—or a clump of trees." It is a term found in Arabic. As *shajer* it is quite a commonplace name in Palestine.[43]

After traveling for a considerable time in Arabia, Ishmael died, at which time and place "the daughters of Ishmael did *mourn* exceedingly, because of the loss of their father, and because of their afflictions in the wilderness. . . ." Strange as it seems, the Mormons have lately learned that *Nahom* is from the Arabic root *NHM* meaning "to sigh or *moan*," to "sigh or *moan* with another." In this connection, Nibley points out "that among the desert Arabs mourning rites for the dead are a strict monopoly of the women, related Hebrew rites being less exclusively female. Ishmael here seems more of an Arab than ever, while Nephi (the historian-recorder) continues to display unerring accuracy on every point."[44]

The only place in Arabia where suitable timber could be found for the building of a transoceanic boat was in southeastern Arabia. It took Lehi and his camel caravan eight years to reach that area. It was a long but a necessary journey under the circumstances. That there was no timber available along the Red Sea is evident from the fact that King Solomon had to bring all his timber by land from Palestine to the Red Sea in order to build ships at the Red Sea. Lehi could not remain in Palestine to build his ship. The eight years is about the right amount of time that would have been required for the traversing of the extensive Arabian peninsula.[45]

The fact that special mention is made on various occasions in Nephi's account of his father's tent shows that the record was written by a true Bedouin desert-traveler. The head of a desert

[42] Nibley, *op. cit.*, p. 486, where he cites numerous authorities.
[43] *Ibid.*, p. 487. Authorities are cited by Nibley.
[44] *Ibid.*, p. 517. Authorities are cited by Nibley.
[45] *Ibid.*, p. 277. He points out that the Arabs would camp for many days at a time, sometimes stopping long enough to gather a crop. They have been known to stay at a single encampment as long as five or six months. W. E. Jennings-Bramley, "The Bedouin of the Sinaitic Peninsula," *Palestine Expedition Fund Quarterly* (1907), p. 284.

caravan made his tent his headquarters and it figured prominently in the desert life. Lehi took the customary step of carrying
a large supply of grain for his camels, "all manner of seeds of
every kind." No express reference is made to the camel—it was
simply taken for granted. The camel caravans usually carry
large bags of grain for the camels, two 150 to 180 pound bags
to a camel.

The genuineness of Nephi's account is again demonstrated
in his statement that Lehi's company had very few fires and that
they had to eat raw food much of the time because it was not safe
to light fires. At the end of the trans-Arabian desert journey,
Nephi wrote: "I did smite two stones together that I might make
a fire. For the Lord had not hitherto suffered that we should make
much fire, as we journeyed in the wilderness; for he said: I will
make thy food sweet, that ye cook it not; and I will also be your
light in the wilderness. . . ." A remarkable parallel is found in an
account of a journey made through central and eastern Arabia
in 1862-1863:

> Then an insufficient halt for rest or sleep, at most two or three hours,
> soon interrupted by the oft-repeated admonition, "If we linger here, we
> all die of thirst," sounded in our ears, and then to remount our jaded
> beasts and push them on through the dark night with the constant proba-
> bility of attack or plunder from roving marauders . . . at about an hour
> before sunset we would stagger off our camels as best we might, to prepare
> an evening feast of precisely the same description as that of the forenoon,
> no more often, lest the smoke of our fire should give notice of some distant
> rover, to content ourselves with dry dates and half an hour's rest on
> the sand.[46]

Another traveler familiar with conditions in the Arabian
desert says: "I well remember taking part in a discussion upon
the unhealthfulness of campfires by night; we discontinued them
forthwith in spite of the bitter cold."[47] Major Cheesman's guide
would not even let him light a tiny lamp, and they never dared
build a fire on the open plain when it "would attract the attention of a prowling raiding party over long distances and invite
a night attack."[48]

Nibley shows that even the family life, quarrels and dreams
of Lehi's company are in true Jewish-Arabic style and color.
He points out that shortly after Lehi left Jerusalem, many other

[46] Ibid., p. 276, quoting William G. Palgrave, Narrative of a Year's Journey Through Central and
Eastern Arabia (1862-3) (London, 1866), vol. 1. Other authorities are set out by Nibley.
[47] Bertram Thomas, Arabia Felix, p. 137; cited by Nibley, op. cit., p. 382.
[48] Cheesman, Unknown Arabia, pp. 228f, 234,, 240f, 280; cited by Nibley, p. 382.

Jews took flight from the city heading for Egypt as a place of refuge from the wrath of the conquering Babylonian, Nebuchad-nezzar. Some of the descendants of those Jews who fled from Jerusalem lived in Egypt for many generations—and those descendants of Lehi's contemporaries are found to have borne some of the same personal names as are encountered in *The Book of Mormon*.[49]

We need only call attention to the close agreement between the *Popol Vuh* and *The Book of Mormon* concerning the great hardships of the journey from the original homeland in the East and regarding the endless complainings of some members of the party. *The Book of Mormon* mentions occasions when "they did suffer much for the want of food." The *Popol Vuh* says "they were suffering greatly; they did not have food; they did not have sustenance. . . ." Also, just prior to the death in the New World of the original leader (*Lehi* in the case of Nephi's account, *Balam Quitze* in the case of the Maya account), sane advice and wise counsel were given by the venerable prophet.

The story of Lehi meets the test. It correctly reflects the cultural horizon, the religious ideas, the social and family customs, the practices and even the language requirements of the time and place involved. Only recent scholarship has made even the test itself possible.

BUILDING SHIP AT TULAN (BOUNTIFUL)

EXTRACTS—TOTONI-CAPAN:

Nahuales came to America from Tulan, from the other side of ocean

. . . they came from the other side of the sea, from there where the sun comes up, from the place called Pa Tulan, Pa Civin.

. . . our ancestors . . . had come from the other side of the sea, from Civan-Tulan at the confines of Babylonia.

EXTRACTS—BOOK OF MORMON:

Building a ship; set sail at Bountiful and crossed ocean to promised land (America)

7. And it came to pass that after I, Nephi, had been in the land of Bountiful[XXIV] for the space of many days, the voice of the Lord came unto me, saying: Arise, and get thee into the mountain. And it came to pass that I arose and went up into the mountain, and cried unto the Lord.

8. And it came to pass that the Lord spake unto me, saying: Thou shalt construct a ship, after the manner which I shall show thee, that I may carry thy people across these waters.

1 Nephi 17:7-8.

1. And it came to pass that they did worship the Lord, and did go forth with me; and we did work timbers of curious workmanship. And the Lord did show me from time to time after what manner I should work the timbers of the ship.

---

[49] *Ibid.*, p. 202. He cites William Foxwell Albright, in *The Biblical Archaeologist*, IX (1946), p. 5f.

EXTRACTS—POPOL VUH:

Second settlers came to America from Tulan, from other side of the sea

. . . in which [the original *Popol Vuh*] was clearly seen the coming from the other side of the sea. . . .

Then they came, they pulled up stakes and left the East. . . . and they wept in their chants because of their departure from Tulan; their hearts mourned when they left Tulan. . . .

. . . they left there, from that great distance. . .

It is not quite clear, however, how they crossed the sea; they crossed to this side. . . .

2. Now I, Nephi, did not work the timbers after the manner which was learned by men, neither did I build the ship after the manner of men; but I did build it after the manner which the Lord had shown unto me; wherefore, it was not after the manner of men.

4. And it came to pass that after I had finished the ship, according to the word of the Lord, my brethren beheld that it was good, and that the workmanship thereof was exceeding fine; wherefore, they did humble themselves again before the Lord.

5. And it came to pass that the voice of the Lord came unto my father, that we should arise and go down into the ship.

6. And it came to pass that on the morrow, after we had prepared all things, much fruits and meat from the wilderness, and honey in abundance, and provisions according to that which the Lord had commanded us, we did go down into the ship, with all our loading and our seeds,[LXIII] and whatsoever thing we had brought with us, every one according to his age; wherefore, we did all go down into the ship, with our wives and our children.

7. And now, my father had begat two sons in the wilderness; the elder was called *Jacob* and the younger *Joseph*.[XXIII]

8. And it came to pass after we had all gone down into the ship, and had taken with us our provisions and things which had been commanded us, we did put forth into the sea and were driven forth before the wind towards the promised land. . . .[XXV].

28. And it came to pass that I, Nephi, did guide the ship, that we sailed again towards the promised land.

23. And it came to pass that after we had sailed for the space of many days we did arrive at the promised land; and we went forth upon the land, and did pitch our tents; and we did call it the promised land.[XXV]

24. And it came to pass that we did begin to till the earth, and we began to plant seeds; yea, we did put all our seeds into the earth, which we had brought from the land of Jerusalem.[LXIII] And it came to pass that they did grow exceedingly; wherefore, we were blessed in abundance.

1 Nephi 18:1-8, 22-24.

XXIV. BOUNTIFUL—POINT OF EMBARKATION

The Book of Mormon states that the point of departure in the Near East was a place they "called *Bountiful,* because of its much fruit and also wild honey. . . ."[50] The *Totonicapan* account and the *Popol Vuh* say the point of departure was

---
[50] *The Book of Mormon.* p. 34 (1 Nephi 17:5-7).

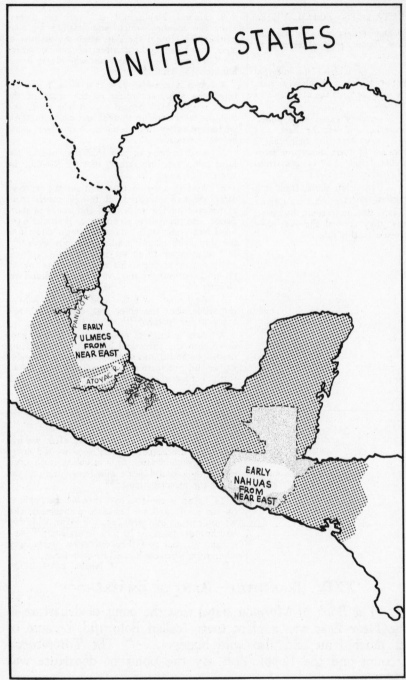

Fig. 9: MAP—EARLY AMERICAN HOMELAND OF
ULMECS AND NAHUAS

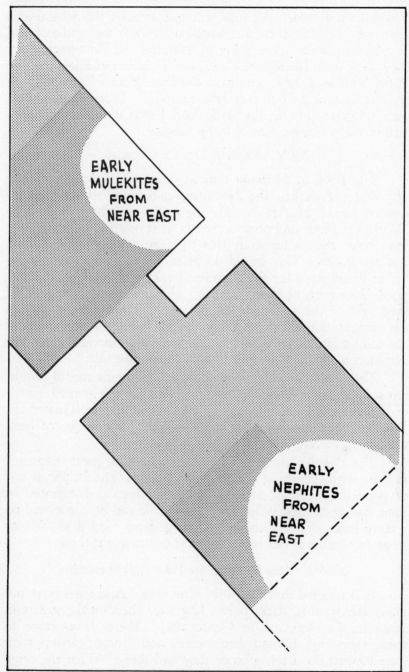

Fig. 10: MAP—EARLY HOMELAND
OF MULEKITES AND
NEPHITES

Tulan-in-the-Ravine. All four accounts indicate the general area from whence came these artisan-colonizers was the cradle of Old World civilization. *The Book of Mormon* and *Totonicapan* say they were from Israelite territory, and *Ixtlilxochitl* infers it. The *Popol Vuh* says they came from the East, from a "distant country" from where "our race was created." There existed there men "in great number, the black [dark] men and the white men, men of many classes, men of many tongues. . . ."

XXV. Pacific Ocean Crossed

The Book of Mormon indicates that the second colonizers of ancient America, the Nephites, embarked from the southeastern corner of Arabia. Having been brought to the New World by winds and ocean currents, it is believed by those who have given the matter study that they crossed the Indian Ocean and the Pacific. This would doubtless have necessitated a number of island stops for the purpose of taking on water and provisions. However, neither *The Book of Mormon* nor *Ixtlilxochitl* shed light on the particulars of the trans-oceanic journey. When the geographical data in *The Book of Mormon* is analyzed and charted, it establishes that the "land of first inheritance" of the Nephites in the New World was on the Pacific side.

That these second colonizers, the Nephite-Bountiful people, crossed the Pacific Ocean finds support in the quoted annals of the ancient Quiche-Mayas of the Pacific nation, Guatemala. Another, the *Annals of Xahila,* is in accord and is quoted hereafter in topic XXVII.

The *Popol Vuh* says they came "from that great distance." It goes without saying that a journey across the Pacific is one of great distance. However, it has lately been demonstrated by some daring Scandinavians that the Pacific can be negotiated on a mere balsa raft. With personal help from God it would not be as impossible as our more skeptical critics might think.

XXVI. Few Persons in First Settlement

It is recalled that the *Popol Vuh* says, "And there were not many men at that place; only a few were there on the mountain Hacavitz [a mountain in Guatemala]. There dawn came to them, there they burned their incense and danced, turning their gaze toward the East, whence they had come." That the original colony was small is borne out by the data from *The Book of Mormon.* There were but sixteen persons in the company that left Jerusalem. Children were born during the journey across Arabia and possibly more during the transoceanic voyage. But the total number arriving in the New World was relatively small.

EXTRACTS—POPOL VUH:	EXTRACTS—BOOK OF MORMON:

EXTRACTS—POPOL VUH:

Leaders' premonition of death; their farewell exhortations; leaving of Pizom-Gagal with descendants

And now we shall tell of the death of Balam-Quitze, Balam Acab, Mahucutah, and Iqui-Balam, as they were called.

And as they had had a presentiment of their death,[xxvi] they counseled their children. They were not ill, they had neither pain nor agony when they gave their advice to their children.

* * *

"Oh, our sons! we are going, we are going away; sane advice and wise counsel we leave you. And you, also, who came from our *distant country,* oh our wives!"[51] they said to their women, and they bade farewell to each one. . . .

These words they said when they bade them farewell.[xxvi] Then Balam-Quitze left the symbol of his being: "This is a remembrance which I leave for you. This shall be your power. I take my leave filled with sorrow," he added. Then he left the symbol of his being, the *Pizom-Gagal*[xxii] [Giron-Gagal of the Totonicapan account—*Liahona,* "Point-Whither," of the Nephite account], as it was called, whose form was invisible because it was wrapped up and could not be unwrapped; the seam did not show because it was not seen when they wrapped it up. Part IV, Ch. 4-5, pp. 204-205.

EXTRACTS—BOOK OF MORMON:

Lehi's and Nephi's premonitions of death; their farewell exhortations; their deaths; seven subdivisions or tribes

[Lehi's exhortation—and death.]

1. And now it came to pass that after I, Nephi, had made an end of teaching my brethren, our father, Lehi, also spake many things unto them—how great things the Lord had done for them in bringing them out of the land of Jerusalem.[xx]

2. And he spake unto them concerning their rebellions upon the waters, and the mercies of God in sparing their lives, that they were not swallowed up in the sea.

9. [Said he:] Wherefore, I, Lehi, have obtained a promise, that inasmuch as those whom the Lord God shall bring out of the land of Jerusalem shall keep his commandments, they shall prosper upon the face of this land; and they shall be kept from all other nations, that they may possess this land unto themselves. . . .

10. But behold, when the time cometh that they shall dwindle in unbelief, after they have received so great blessings from the hand of the Lord—having a knowledge of the creation of the earth, and all men, knowing the great and marvelous works of the Lord from the creation of the world; having *power* given them to do all things by faith; having all the commandments from the beginning, and having been brought by his infinite goodness into this precious land of promise—behold, I say, if the day shall come that they will reject the Holy One of Israel,[xx] the true Messiah, their Redeemer and their God, behold the judgments of him that is just shall rest upon them.

11. Yea, *he will bring other nations unto them,*[52] and he will give unto them power, and will take away from them the *lands of their possessions,* and he will cause them to be scattered and smitten. 2 Nephi 1:2, 9-11.

14. [Lehi quoted:] Awake! and arise from the dust, and hear the words of a trembling parent, whose limbs ye must soon lay down in the

---

[51] This refutes Harold Gladwin's notion that there were no women among the early colonists who came by sea from the Levant to Middle America. See his lively book, *Men Out of Asia,* 1947, p. 204.

[52] The reader would profit by reading the full account in *The Book of Mormon,* 2 Nephi, Chapters 1-4. Other nations did enter Middle America in the post-Book-of-Mormon period and prior to the coming of the Europeans. Strong Mongoloid elements were present among some of the nations. See, for example, figure 33, at page 253. The Aztecs were late comers from the north, apparently having no connection with Book-of-Mormon peoples.

cold and silent grave, from whence no traveler can return; a few more days and I go the way of all the earth.

15. But behold, the Lord hath redeemed my soul from hell; I have beheld his glory, and I am encircled about eternally in the arms of his love.   2 Nephi 1:14-15.

12. And it came to pass after my father, Lehi, had spoken unto all his household, according to the feelings of his heart and the Spirit of the Lord which was in him, he waxed old. And it came to pass that he died, and was buried.[XXVI]
                    2 Nephi 4:12.

9. Now Nephi began to be old, and he saw that he must soon die;[XXVI] wherefore, he anointed a man to be a king and a ruler over his people now, according to the reigns of the kings.

10. The people having loved Nephi exceedingly, he having been a great protector for them, having wielded the sword of Laban in their defence, and having labored in all his days for their welfare——

11. Wherefore, the people were desirous to retain in remembrance his name. And whoso should reign in his stead were called by the people, second Nephi, third Nephi,[XVII] and so forth, according to the reigns of the kings; and thus they were called by the people, let them be of whatever name they would.

12. And it came to pass that Nephi died.[XXVI]

13. Now the people which were not Lamanites were Nephites; nevertheless, they were called [1] Nephites, [2] Jacobites, [3] Josephites, [4] Zoramites, [5] Lamanites, [6] Lemuelites, and [7] Ishmaelites.[XXVII, LV]

14. But I, Jacob, shall not hereafter distinguish them by these names, but I shall call them Lamanites that seek to destroy the people of Nephi, and those who are friendly to Nephi I shall call Nephites,[XVII] or the people of Nephi, according to the reigns of the kings.   Jacob 1:9-14.

DEATH OF FIRST LEADERS

Special mention is made of the deaths of the original leaders of the Second Settlers—in both the *Popol Vuh* and *The Book of Mormon*. Balam-Quitze, Balam Acab, Mahucutah, and Iqui-Balam each having "had a presentiment of their death, they counseled their children." Contrast that with the following from the Nephite account: ". . . after my father, Lehi, had spoken unto all his household, according to the feelings of his heart and the Spirit of the Lord which was in him, he waxed old. And it came to pass that he died, and was buried." Nephi also had "a presentiment" of his death: "Now I, Nephi, began to be old . . . and he saw that he must soon die; wherefore, he anointed a man to be a king and a ruler over his people . . . And it came to pass that Nephi died."

It is amazing to find confirmation concerning such details. The farewell statements of the first leaders are set forth in both the *Popol Vuh* and the Nephite record. *The Book of Mormon* and the *Popol Vuh* refer to the fatherly or patriarchal blessings bestowed by the leader before his death. The Nephite account gives some of these blessings verbatim.

XXVII. SEVEN SUBDIVISIONS OR TRIBES

The *Totonicapan* record refers to the division into Seven Tribes. *The Book of Mormon* refers to a division of the Bountiful-artisans into seven tribes: *Nephites, Jacobites, Josephites, Zoramites, Lamanites, Lemuelites* and *Ishmaelites*. These tribes retained their identity from the beginning of Nephite history until the end. The earliest reference is set out in *The Book of Mormon* column.[53]

Another pre-Conquest Quiche-Mayan source contains additional corroborating data. The *Xahila* family, one of the royal lines of the Quiches of the highlands of Guatemala, left an account in the Maya tongue entitled *Annals* of *Xahila*. It is stated therein:

> We were brought forth, coming we were begotten by our mothers and our fathers, as they say. . . . They say that the *seven tribes* arrived first at Tullan, and we the warriors followed, having taken up the tributes of all the *seven tribes* when the gate of Tullan was opened.[54]

It is observed that the *Xahila* record likewise indicates a departure from an Old World *Tullan* (Bountiful) and the settlement of seven tribes in a principal homeland, *Tullan* (Bountiful), in the New World. It is anticipating, somewhat, things to be discussed later, but it should be noted that the *Xahila* account indicates that the seven tribes, whose center was *Tullan*, were required to pay tribute to the Quiche warriors of the Guatemala highlands. It will be seen that the *Nephites* of lowland-Bountiful, according to *The Book of Mormon*, paid tribute to the *Lamanites* of the highlands to the south of Bountiful before the gates

---

[53] *The Book of Mormon*, p. 459 (4 Nephi, 1:37-38), shows the Seven Tribes still intact in 245 A. D.
[54] Daniel G. Brinton, editor and translator, *The Annals of the Cakchiquels*, 1885, secs. 4 and 8, cited in Jakeman, *op. cit.*, pp. 70-72.

were opened by the warring *Lamanites* who finally drove the Nephites into exile from their ancient Bountiful home-land. For a further discussion of this same subject, see Chapter 27.

SUMMARY STATEMENT

The Second Settlers were a branch of the House of Israel. *The Book of Mormon* gives the precise time of their departure from the Old World. The sorrows of members of the company on leaving the home of their fathers, Jerusalem, are detailed in the *Popol Vuh* and *The Book of Mormon*. The colony was directed by God and assisted by a divine instrument that *pointed the way whither* they should go. That instrument, the *Liahona,* is referred to in *The Book of Mormon* and in the *Totonicapan* account, as well as in the *Popol Vuh*.

The Nephite account of the journey across the Arabian desert is in the true local color of the ancient Near East in all particulars. The personal names and place names in the account are authentic Semitic names as far as we were able to determine.

The colony arrived in the New World in the 6th century B. C.—according to *The Book of Mormon*. General support for this date comes from the reliable Sahagun, from *Ixtlilxochitl* (who has them in their permanent "seat of the kingdom" by 132 B. C.) and from the archæology of Guatemala. There were "not many men" in the original company. However, their descendants were divided into seven tribes bearing the names of the seven original colonizers.

In view of the fact that *The Book of Mormon* is confirmed by all of the earliest and best documentary sources—and by archæology where data from that source exists—it cannot be said that believers in that book are unduly credulous.

Chapter 10

RELIGIOUS KNOWLEDGE OF SECOND SETTLERS

Introductory Statement

In addition to the other documentary materials which have been referred to in the previous chapters, extracts from the writings of *Juan de Torquemada* are also quoted in this chapter. He was a Catholic Padre who spent many years in Mexico during the latter part of the sixteenth and early part of the seventeenth centuries. His book, entitled *Monarquia Indiana,* was first published in Spain in 1613 A. D. His writings, which contain the traditions which he received from the Indians in Mexico, also confirm the other primary accounts, including *The Book of Mormon.*

According to *Ixtlilxochitl, Juan de Torquemada,* the *Popol Vuh,* the *Totonicapan* account and *The Book of Mormon,* as well as other early authoritative sources, the Second Settlers, or Nephites, like the Ancient Ones, or Jaredites, brought to America from the ancient East a knowledge of God, the creation, the flood and the prophecy concerning the ultimate ending of the world by fire. Some of these writings refer to the ancient records themselves which allegedly contained such information.

XXIX. Knowledge of Creation and Flood

IXTLILXOCHITL:

Tultec knowledge of creation and flood

. . . and they [the Tultecas] had knowledge of the creation of the world, and how it was destroyed by the deluge,[XXIX] and many other things they had in picture and in history . . .

EXTRACT—TORQUE-MADA:

Knowledge of creation and flood

The Tultecs (according to ancient histories) were the second settlers of these lands, after the

EXTRACTS—BOOK OF MORMON:

Nephite knowledge of creation and flood

10. And after they had given thanks unto the God of Israel, my father, Lehi, took the records which were engraven upon the plates of brass, and he did search them from the beginning.

11. And he beheld that they did contain the five books of Moses,[XXXI] which gave an account of the creation of the world, and also of Adam and Eve, who were our first parents;[XXIX]

12. And also a record of the Jews from the beginning, even down to the commencement of the reign of Zedekiah, king of Judah;

13. And also the prophecies of the holy prophets, from the beginning, even down to the

giants, especially in this corner and part which is called New Spain [Mexico]. These Tultecs occupied these Provinces as lords and proprietors of them. They say of them that they had knowledge of the creation of the world, and how the people of it were destroyed by the Deluge,[XXIX] and many other things which they had in painting and history.

EXTRACTS—POPOL VUH, SACRED BOOK OF THE ANCIENT QUICHÉ MAYA OF GUATEMALA:

Knowledge of creation and flood[XXIX]

. . . the original book[XXXI] written long ago, existed, but its sight' is hidden to the searcher and to the thinker. Great were the descriptions and the account of how all the sky and earth were formed, how it was formed and divided into four parts; how it was partitioned, and how the sky was divided; and the measuring-cord was brought, and it was stretched in the sky and over the earth, on the four angles, on the four corners, as was told by the Creator and the Maker, the Mother and the Father of Life, of all created things, he who gives breath and thought, she who gives birth to the children, he who watches over the happiness of the people, the happiness of the human race, the wise man, he who meditates on the goodnesss of all that exists in the sky, on the earth, in the lakes and in the sea.

Popol Vuh pp. 77-80.

A flood was brought about by the Heart of Heaven; a great flood was formed which fell on the heads of the wooden creatures.

Of *tzité* the flesh of man was made, but when woman was fashioned by the Creator and the Maker, her flesh was made of rushes. These were the materials the Creator and the Maker wanted to use in making them.

But those that they had made, that they had created, did not think, did not speak with their Creator, their Maker. And for this reason they were killed, they were deluged. A heavy resin

commencement of the reign of Zedekiah; and also many prophecies which have been spoken by the mouth of Jeremiah.   1 Nephi 5:10-13.

22. Yea, and I say unto you that if it were not for the prayers of the righteous, who are now in the land, that ye would even now be visited with utter destruction; yet it would not be by flood,[XXIX] as were the people in the days of Noah, but it would be by famine, and by pestilence, and the sword.   Alma 10:22.

9. . . . for as I have sworn that the waters of Noah should no more go over the earth, so have I sworn that I would not be wroth with thee.

10. For the mountains shall depart and the hills be removed, but my kindness shall not depart from thee, neither shall the covenant of my people be removed, saith the Lord that hath mercy on thee.   3 Nephi 22:9-10.

fell from the sky.
        Popol Vuh, p. 90.

The statement made by *Ixtlilxochitl* that the second Tultecas colonizers of ancient America *"had a knowledge of the
creation of the world, and how it was destroyed by a deluge, and
many other things that they had in picture and in history"* is very
significant when one compares that statement with the vast
amount of religious teachings contained in *The Book of Mormon.*

Torquemada and the *Popol Vuh* are in strong confirmation
of our two primary accounts. Only the first portion of the creation story, as found in the *Popol Vuh,* is set forth above. *Tepeu,*
one of the Quiché-Mayan names for the Creator, means "King"
or "Sovereign."[1] He was co-creator with Gucumatz. The latter
means "green-feathered serpent,"[2] being identical with *Quetzalcoatl,* the Messiah of ancient Mexico, *Itzamna* of Yucatan and
the resurrected *Christ* of the Old World.[3]

The *Popol Vuh* lends further credence to our two primary
accounts on another point. *Vucub-Caquix* ("seven macaws")
who plays a role identical to that of Lucifer,[4] is mentioned in the
Quiché "Bible." He is referred to in connection with the flood.
To quote:

> His [Vucub-Caquix's] only ambition was to exalt himself and to domi-
> nate. And all this happened when the flood came because of the wooden
> people. Now we shall tell how Vucub-Caquix was overthrown and died,
> and how man was made by the Creator and the Maker.[5]

Bishop Landa, writing in about 1556 of the Mayas of Yucatan with whom he lived, says that "the world was destroyed by
the deluge," according to the Yucatecans. In fact the Maya word
for flood is *haiyokocab,* meaning "water over the earth."[6]

Another Quiché account from Guatemala, written in 1554,
states that the Quiché people were "descendant of Israel . . . speaking the same tongue [at the outset] and having the same customs."[7] Surely the Quichés of the sixteenth century had nothing
to gain by fabricating a claim that they were of Israel. The Jews
were plagued by persecutions then as now by the European
gentiles.

[1] Delia Goetz and Sylvanus G. Morley, *Popol Vuh* (1950), p. 78.
[2] *Ibid.*
[3] This matter is discussed in more detail in chapter 16.
[4] Father Francisco Ximenez, Dominican Friar, who discovered the Quiché manuscript in Guatemala near
   the beginning of the eighteenth century, believed *Vucub-Caquix* to be identical with Lucifer. See
   Goetz and Morley, *ibid.,* p. 93.
[5] *Ibid.,* p. 94.
[6] Alfred M. Tozzer, *Landa's Relacion de las Cosas de Yucatan* (1941), note 633.
[7] A. Recinos, *Titulo de los señores de Totonicapan* (1950), p. 216.

As has been mentioned, the Nephites possessed the Hebrew account of the creation of the world; therefore, throughout the entire course of their history a knowledge of the creation was commonly held throughout the entire land. Thus, to a certain degree, the Lamanites would have had an understanding of that creation story but perhaps in an altered form. The account that will be quoted following this paragraph is the version of the creation story which existed at the time of the Spanish Conquest among the descendants of the ancient Americans, the Quiché-Mayas of Guatemala. It is interesting to read this account and compare it with the one found in the Bible for the purpose of ascertaining to what extent alterations have occurred during the period of over one thousand years' time from the date of the destruction of the Nephites (421 A. D.) to the writing of the *Popol Vuh,* following the arrival of the Spaniards in Guatemala. This much is obvious: Although the true Gospel of Jesus Christ and the Priesthood had been taken from the earth as early as the closing years of Nephite history, yet a portion of the divine truths remained from age to age like a golden thread. Following is the creation story as it appears in the *Popol Vuh:*

EXTRACTS—*POPOL VUH:*

Quiché-Maya creation story [7a]

This is the account of how all was in suspense, all calm, in silence; all motionless, still, and the expanse of the sky was empty.

This is the first account, the first narrative. There was neither man, nor animal, birds, fishes, crabs, trees, stones, caves, ravines, grasses, nor forests; there was only the sky.

The surface of the earth had not appeared. There was only the calm sea and the great expanse of sky.

There was nothing brought together, nothing which could make a noise, or tremble, or could make noise in the sky.

There was nothing standing; only the calm water, the placid sea, alone and tranquil. Nothing existed.

There was only immobility and silence in the darkness, in the night. Only the Creator, the Maker, Tepeu, Gucumatz [the Fair God], the Forefathers, were in the water surrounded with light. They were hidden under green and blue feathers, and were therefore called Gucumatz. XLVIII By nature they were great sages and thinkers. In this manner the sky existed and also the Heart of Heaven, which is the name of God and thus He is called.

Then came the word. Tepeu [God] and Gucumatz [the Fair God—Quetzalcoatl—Christ] came together in the darkness, in the night, and Tepeu and Gucumatz talked together. They talked then, discussing and deliberating; they agreed, they united their words and their thoughts.

Then while they meditated, it became clear to them that when Dawn would break, man must appear. Then they planned the creation, and the growth of the trees and the thickets and the birth of life and the creation of man. Thus it was arranged in the darkness and in the night by the Heart of Heaven who is called Huracán.

[7a] Compare the *Popol Vuh* account of the creation with the one in the "Book of Abraham"; and also compare the statement: "Then came the *word*" with "in the beginning the *Word was*" (D. & C. 93:8); and "In the beginning was the *Word*" (John 1:1).

The first is called Caculhá Huracán. The second is Chipi-Caculhá. The third is Raxa-Caculhá. And these three are the Heart of Heaven [Godhead].

Then Tepeu and Gucumatz came together; then they conferred about life and light, what they would do so that there would be light and dawn, who it would be who would provide food and sustenance.

Thus let it be done! Let the emptiness be filled! Let the water recede and make a void, let the earth appear and become solid; let it be done. Thus they spoke. Let there be light, let there be dawn in the sky and on the earth! There shall be neither glory nor grandeur in our creation and formation until the human being is made, man is formed. So they spoke.

Then the earth was created by them. So it was, in truth, that they created the earth. Earth! they said, and instantly it was made.

Like the mist, like a cloud, and like a cloud of dust was the creation, when the mountains appeared from the water; and instantly the mountains grew.

Only by a miracle, only by magic art were the mountains and valleys formed; and instantly the groves of cypresses and pines put forth shoots together on the surface of the earth.

And thus Gucumatz was filled with joy, and exclaimed: "Your coming has been fruitful, Heart of Heaven; and you, Huracán, and you, Chipi-Caculhá, Raxa-Caculhá!"

"Our work, our creation shall be finished," they answered.

First the earth was formed, the mountains and the valleys; the currents of water were divided, the rivulets were running freely between the hills, and the water was separated when the high mountains appeared.

Thus was the earth created, when it was formed by the Heart of Heaven, the Heart of Earth, as they are called who first made it fruitful, when the sky was in suspense, and the earth was submerged in the water.

So it was that they made perfect the work, when they did it after thinking and meditating upon it.

Popol Vuh, pp. 81-84.

By way of summary, it has been shown that all of the foregoing sixteenth-century Indian and Spanish documents are in agreement with the Nephite record in proclaiming that the ancient Americans had knowledge of the creation of the world and of the flood. Thus they bear witness to the fact that *The Book of Mormon* is a true history of ancient America.

XXX. World to Be Destroyed by Fire

EXTRACTS—BOOK OF MORMON:

IXTLILXOCHITL:

Destruction by fire

This [third] age having passed, from this time on, the fourth age entered, which they said was called *Tletonatiuh* which means *sun of fire,* because *they said that this fourth and last age was to end with fire.*[xxx]

Destruction by Fire

77. And when the time cometh that evil fruit shall again come into my vineyard, then will I [the Lord] cause the good and the bad to be gathered; and the good will I preserve unto myself, and the bad will I cast away into its own place. And then cometh the season and the end; and my vineyard will I cause to be burned with fire.[xxx]   Jacob 5:77.

3. And how blessed are they who have labored diligently in his vineyard; and how cursed are they who shall be cast out into their own place! And the world shall be burned with fire.[xxx]
                    Jacob 6:3.

14. And behold, according to the words of the prophet, the Messiah will set himself again the second time to recover them; wherefore, he will manifest himself unto them in power and great glory, unto the destruction of their enemies,

EXTRACT—TORQUE-
MADA:

Destruction by fire

. . . And they also say that
they had knowledge of how the
world is to end again, by con-
summation by fire.XXX

when that day cometh when they shall believe in
him; and none will he destroy that believe in him.

15. And they that believe not in him shall
be destroyed, both by fire, and by tempest, and
by earthquake, and by bloodsheds, and by pestilence, and by famine. And they shall know that
the Lord is God, the Holy One of Israel.

2 Nephi 6:14-15.

10. For the time speedily cometh that the
Lord God shall cause a great division among the
people, and the wicked will he destroy; and he
will spare his people, yea, even if it so be that
he must destroy the wicked by fire.XXX

2 Nephi 30:10.

1. For behold, the day cometh that shall burn
as an oven; and all the proud, yea, and all that
do wickedly, shall be stubble; and the day that
cometh shall burn them up, saith the Lord of
Hosts, that it shall leave them neither root nor
branch.XXX   3 Nephi 25:1.

9. And at my command the heavens are
opened and are shut; and at my word the earth
shall shake; and at my command the inhabitants
thereof shall pass away, even so as by fire.XXX

Ether 4:9 (see also 3 Nephi 26:3).

A significant point in both *Ixtlilxochitl* and *The Book of
Mormon* is that each predicts that the last age of this earth shall
end by fire. In other words, they both agree that this earth
shall be cleansed with fire and that that cleansing has not taken
place yet but shall take place at some future date.

Professor Tozzer of Harvard University found existing
among the present-day Mayas in Yucatan the belief that the
world is now in the fourth period of its existence.[8]

Bishop Bartolomé de Las Casas, writing in 1552-1553, said
of the natives of Guatemala: "They had among them information of the flood and of the end of the world, and called it *Butic,*
which is the word which means flood of many waters and means
[the final] judgment, and so they believe that another *Butic* is
about to come which is another flood and judgment, not of water,
but of fire which they say would be the end of the world . . ."[9]

Ixtlilxochitl, The Book of Mormon, Torquemada, the *Popol
Vuh, Las Casas* and the *Bible*[10] are all in agreement on this
matter of a final destruction by fire. Herein is another example
in which all of our sources bear testimony to the fact that the

8 Alfred M, Tozzer, *op. cit.* (1941), note 633.
9 Bartolomé de Las Casas, *Apologética Historia de las Indias,* Cap. CCXXXV. Cited in Goetz and Morley,
  op. cit., p. 92.
10 Malachi 4:1; 2 Thessalonians 1:7-8; Revelation 20:7-15.

doctrines taught by the holy Nephite prophets persisted throughout the ages and were encountered among the Indians by the
earliest Christian missionaries in the New World.

METALLIC RECORDS OR PLATES

EXTRACT—TORQUE-
MADA:

Metallic records
. . . the ancients . . . put [i.e.,
wrote or inscribed] many things
in two columns, one of metal,[XXXI]
and another of brick or stones, so
that in case of fire, the column of
brick would remain; but since I
am not in possession of complete
certainty on this I do not care to
go deeply into this idea. I only
say that Tultec means artisan,
for those of this nation were
great artisans, as is seen today in
many parts of this New Spain.

EXTRACTS—BOOK OF MORMON:

Metallic records or "plates"[XXXI]

1. And it came to pass that the Lord commanded me [Nephi] wherefore I did make plates
of ore that I might engraven upon them the record of my people. And upon the plates which I
made I did engraven the record of my father, and
also our journeyings in the wilderness, and the
prophecies of my father; and also many of mine
own prophecies have I engraven upon them.

2. And I knew not at the time when I made
them that I should be commanded of the Lord
to make these plates; wherefore, the record of my
father, and the genealogy of his fathers, and the
more part of all our proceedings in the wilderness
are engraven upon those plates of which I have
spoken; wherefore, the things which transpired
before I made these plates are, of a truth, more
particularly made mention upon the first plates.

3. And after I had made these plates by way
of commandment, I, Nephi, received a commandment that the ministry and the prophecies, the
more plain and precious parts of them, should be
written upon these plates; and that the things
which were written should be kept for the instruction of my people, who should possess the land,
and also for other wise purposes, which purposes
are known unto the Lord.

4. Wherefore, I, Nephi, did make a record
upon the other plates, which gives an account, or
which gives a greater account of the wars and
contentions and destructions of my people. And
this I have done, and commanded my people
what they should do after I was gone, and that
these plates should be handed down from one
generation to another, or from one prophet to
another, until further commandments of the Lord.

5. And an account of my making these plates
shall be given hereafter; and then, behold, I proceed according to that which I have spoken; and
this I do that the more sacred things may be kept
for the knowledge of my people.
1 Nephi 19:1-5.

1. I, Nephi, having been born of goodly parents, therefore I was taught somewhat in all the
learning of my father; and having seen many
afflictions in the course of my days, nevertheless,
having been highly favored of the Lord in all my
days; yea, having had a great knowledge of the

goodnesss and the mysteries of God, therefore I make a record of my proceedings in my days.

2. Yea, I make a record in the language of my father, which consists of the learning of the Jews and the language of the Egyptians.

3. And I know that the record which I make is true; and I make it with mine own hand; and I make it according to my knowledge.

1 Nephi 1:1-3.

1. And all these things did my father see, and hear, and speak, as he dwelt in a tent, in the valley of Lemuel, and also a great many more things, which cannot be written upon these plates.

2. And now, as I have spoken concerning these plates, behold they are not the plates upon which I make a full account of the history of my people; for the plates upon which I make a full account of my peope I have given the name of Nephi; wherefore, they are called the plates of Nephi, after mine own name; and these plates also are called the plates of Nephi.

3. Nevertheless, I have received a command- ment of the Lord that I should make these plates, for the special purpose that there should be an account engraven of the ministry of my people.

4. Upon the other plates should be engraven an account of the reign of the kings, and the wars and contentions of my people; wherefore these plates are for the more part of the ministry; and the other plates are for the more part of the reign of kings and the wars and contentions of my people.

5. Wherefore, the Lord hath commanded me to make these plates for a wise purpose in him, which purpose I know not.

6. But the Lord knoweth all things from the beginning; wherefore, he prepareth a way to ac- complish all his works among the children of men; for behold, he hath all power unto the fulfilling of all his words. And thus it is. Amen.

1 Nephi 9:1-6.

28. And thirty years had passed away from the time we left Jerusalem.

29. And I, Nephi, had kept the records upon my plates, which I had made, of my people thus far.

30. And it came to pass that the Lord God said unto me: Make other plates; and thou shalt engraven many things upon them which are good in my sight, for the profit of thy people.

31. Wherefore, I, Nephi, to be obedient to the commandments of the Lord, went and made these plates upon which I have engraven these things.

32. And I engraved that which is pleasing unto God. And if my people are pleased with the things of God they will be pleased with mine engravings which are upon these plates.

33. And if my people desire to know the more particular part of the history of my people they must search mine other plates.

2 Nephi 5:28-33.

1. For behold, it came to pass that fifty and five years had passed away from the time that Lehi left Jerusalem; wherefore, Nephi gave me, Jacob, a commandment concerning the small plates, upon which these things are engraven.

2. And he gave me, Jacob, a commandment that I should write upon these plates a few of the things which I considered to be most precious; that I should not touch, save it were lightly, concerning the history of this people which are called the people of Nephi.

3. For he said that the history of his people should be engraven upon his other plates, and that I should preserve these plates and hand them down unto my seed.

4. And if there were preaching which was sacred, or revelation which was great, or prophesying, that I should engraven the heads of them upon these plates, and touch upon them as much as it were possible, for Christ's sake, and for the sake of our people.   Jacob 1:1-4.

9. And for a testimony that the things that they [King Lemhi's 43 scouts] had said are true they have brought twenty-four plates which are filled with engravings, and they are of pure gold.

27. And they brought a record with them, even a record of the people [Jaredites] whose bones they found; and it was engraven on plates of ore.

10. Now king Mosiah had no one to confer the kingdom upon, for there was not any of his sons who would accept of the kingdom.

11. Therefore he took the records which were engraven on the plates of brass, and also the plates of Nephi, and all the things which he had kept and preserved according to the commandments of God, after having translated and caused to be written the records which were on the plates of gold which had been found by the people of Limhi, which were delivered to him by the hand of Limhi;

12. And this he did because of the great anxiety of his people; for they were desirous beyond measure to know concerning those people who had been destroyed.

Mosiah 8:9, 21:27; 28:10-12.

(See also: Alma 8:21-31; Ether 1:1-5; 15:33-34.)

XXXI. Metallic Records or "Plates"—Scriptures Brought to New World—Languages of Nephites and Mulekites

Torquemada states that "the ancients . . . put many things on two mediums, one of metal, and the other of brick or stones . . ." Many hieroglyphs on stone have been found which were left by the ancients of Middle America. None have yet been found on metallic plates except those Joseph Smith claimed to have possessed. The fact that no other plates inscribed with hieroglyphs have come to light does not disprove the declarations of Torquemada or the claims of the Nephite record in that regard. For a full discussion of the Tultecas' use of metals, see pages 276-283. The literary evidence strongly supports the use of metallic plates in ancient Middle America. In the *Popol Vuh,* at a point where various craftsmen are listed, we find a reference to "the maker of beautiful plates."[11] This may refer, of course, to a ceramic expert—but it may also refer to a worker of metallic plates.

The ancients, like modern men, were much more apt to bury and hide away their works of gold than they were their works of stone. Plates of gold or other metal may yet be discovered in the countless unexplored archæological sites of Middle America.

Before leaving the vicinity of Jerusalem, Lehi was instructed by the Lord to bring to the Promised Land (the New World) a copy of the Hebrew scriptures which were engraven on "brass plates." After experiencing some difficulties, his son Nephi secured those records from a Jew named Laban. The "brass plates" contained the teachings of Israel down to the Prophet Jeremiah. The writings on that record were in "the language of the Egyptians," the adopted language of Lehi's immediate ancestors.[12] From 700 B. C. to 470 A. D. the Egyptians were using a shorthand form of their *hieratic* script which was known as *demotic*. From the dates given it is apparent that Lehi and Nephi (who left Jerusalem approximately 600 B. C.) probably knew how to read and write the Egyptian demotic and it seems quite possible that the copy of Hebrew scriptures engraved on the "brass plates" was written in the demotic script and Egyptian tongue. As time passed during the 1,000 years of Nephite his-

---

[11] Goetz and Morley edition (1950), p. 87.
[12] *The Book of Mormon*, p. 37 (Mosiah 1:4); p. 6 (1 Nephi 3'19); p. 1 (1 Nephi 1:1).

tory, the Egyptian language known and used by Nephite leaders underwent further modification and finally the last historian called it "reformed Egyptian." (See Fig. 11.) About 400 A. D. Moroni wrote:

. . . we have written . . . in the characters which are called reformed Egyptian, being handed down and *altered by us, according to our manner of speech.*[13]

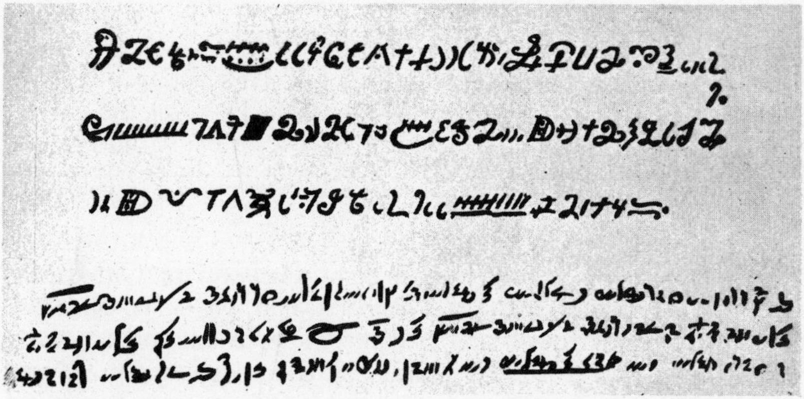

Fig. 11: THREE LINES OF DEMOTIC *(bottom)* COMPARE WITH CHARACTERS TAKEN FROM THE PLATES OF THE BOOK OF MORMON *(top)*

The manner of speech of the Nephites was originally Hebrew, but it too was greatly modified, according to the record, as the centuries rolled by.[14] It was apparently the intent of the Lord that the Nephite record should be written in a language which would be a dead tongue and script—a language that no man could translate in 1830 without divine aid. Moroni said: "But the Lord knoweth the things which we have written, and also that none other people knoweth our language; therefore he hath prepared means for the interpretation thereof."[15]

This viewpoint is sustained when one considers that the Prophet Lehi considered it of the utmost importance that the Egyptian language and Egyptian script be preserved among his descendants. This was one of the principal reasons for his taking the "brass plates" along to the New World.

---

[13] *Ibid.*, p. 478 (Moroni 9:32).
[14] When the Nephites encountered the Third Settlers, the *Mulekites,* the latter outnumbered the Nephites and the original Hebrew tongue of the *Mulekites* had been so altered by 400 years of illiteracy that the Nephites could not even understand them. *The Book of Mormon,* p. 130 (Omni 17); p. 182 (Mosiah 25:2); p. 478 (Mormon 9:33).
[15] *Ibid.*, p. 478 (Mormon 9:34).

The "brass plates" served to preserve the modified Egyptian language and also to preserve the Hebrew scriptures. Those scriptures, as is seen from the quotations, contained the "five books of Moses" and the teachings of the prophets of Israel down to 600 B. C., or down to the Prophet Jeremiah. Nephi quoted at length from the writings of Isaiah, a prophet who lived about one hundred years before Nephi's time.

In 1946 Dr. Sidney B. Sperry wrote of the "Isaiah Problem" in The Book of Mormon:

> The Book of Mormon quotes twenty-one complete chapters of Isaiah and parts of others. In the light of modern Biblical criticism these quotations raise problems that have a serious bearing on the integrity of the Nephite record as a whole. It is believed, therefore, that a presentation of the literary problem of Isaiah and its bearing on The Book of Mormon will be of general interest.[16]

The problem arises because certain schools of Old Testament scholars doubt that the Prophet Isaiah was responsible for much of the Book that bears his name. They think portions were written long after 700 B. C.—and that such portions were therefore not in existence when Lehi left Jerusalem at the beginning of the sixth century B. C. The all-important discovery in 1947 in Palestine of the entire Book of Isaiah on an immense parchment scroll excited, and continues to excite, all Biblical scholars. Professor William Foxwell Albright and other experts who have begun the study of this Isaiah scroll are of the opinion that the Hebrew script found on the scroll dates the manuscript from about the second century B. C. It is the oldest original Old Testament manuscript known today. If the Book of Isaiah was intact as early as 200 B. C., many of the reasons given by those who think it was not the product of the one man, Isaiah, fail. There is a strong possibility it was a single unit four centuries earlier—in the time of Lehi and "the brass plates."

It is quite certain that Joseph Smith did not depend on the writings of Isaiah in the King James version or the Greek Septuagint version but rather that he worked directly with the transcript contained on the "gold plates." In certain respects Joseph Smith's translation is more complete than either of the two. For example, The Book of Mormon is the only account containing the full and complete three lines of the following verse:

---

[16] Sidney B. Sperry, Our Book of Mormon (1947), p. 155. See his excellent discussion of the problem, pp. 155-177.

And upon all the ships of the sea,
And upon all the ships of Tarshish,
And upon all pleasant pictures.[17]

The first line of the foregoing verse is entirely missing from the King James version of Isaiah.[18] How did Joseph Smith supply it then? He knew no Greek and had no access to the Greek version where the first line is also found. Joseph Smith gave the

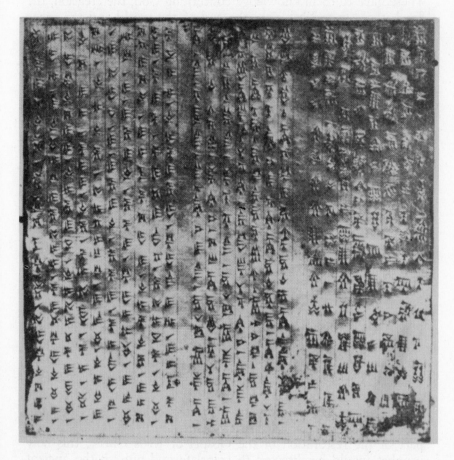

Fig. 12: GOLD TABLETS FROM PALACE OF DARIUS

One of the gold tablets from the Palace of Darius discovered in Iran in 1933. They date from about 500 B. C.—near the time of Nephi. The Empire of Darius included Nephi's homeland.

[17] *The Book of Mormon*, p. 75 (2 Nephi 12:16).
[18] King James version, *The Bible*, Isaiah 2:16.

complete rendering.[19] *The Book of Mormon* is also even more complete than the Greek version for—oddly enough—the *third* line of the verse is missing from the Greek, but the Nephite record has it! Other such evidences have been found.[20]

Thus, it appears that the Nephites, Second Settlers, actually possessed ancient Hebrew scriptures, which included the writ-ings of Moses, of Isaiah, and others of the earlier prophets. These gave to them knowledge concerning God, the creation, the flood, the awaited Messiah, the end of the world and the other teachings of the prophets. The Middle American literary sources support this view. Further, the Nephite record stands well in the light of close literary scrutiny. The discovery of the Jerusa-lem scroll of Isaiah in 1947 near the Dead Sea only strengthened the position of *The Book of Mormon* regarding the "brass plates."

PLATES OF THE BOOK OF MORMON

Did anyone in our modern world, other than Joseph Smith, see the "gold tablets" which he claimed comprised the Nephite records? Eleven persons testified that they saw the plates and they gave their testimony in writing.

The background of the matter, the testimonials themselves, and the lives and reputations for truthfulness and veracity of these witnesses will now be briefly dealt with.

PREDICTIONS REGARDING THREE WITNESSES

The ancient prophet Lehi, writing in the sixth century B. C., predicted that his descendants would keep a record on which their history and also the Gospel of Jesus Christ would be re-corded. This record would be preserved by the power of God and would be brought forth in the latter days through the same power. It would be given to a great prophet whom the Lord should direct to establish His church again upon the earth. As part of the restoration of the Gospel of Jesus Christ, this holy prophet would be directed to translate and publish the ancient Nephite record. Lehi also declared that this prophet would be a descendant of Joseph who was sold into Egyptian bondage; and his name would be Joseph and his father's name would be

19 Sperry, op. cit., pp. 172-173.
20 Ibid., pp. 155-198.

Joseph.[21] Speaking prophetically of the time when *The Book of Mormon* should be brought forth, Nephi, Lehi's son, said:

> Wherefore, at that day when the book shall be delivered unto the man of whom I have spoken, the book shall be hid from the eyes of the world, that the eyes of none shall behold it save it be that three witnesses shall behold it, by the power of God, besides him to whom the book shall be delivered; and they shall testify to the truth of the book and the things therein.

> And there is none other which shall view it, save it be a few according to the will of God, to bear testimony of his word unto the children of men: for the Lord God hath said that the words of the faithful should speak as if it were from the dead. Wherefore, the Lord God will proceed to bring forth the words of the book; and in the mouth of as many witnesses as seemeth him good, will he establish his word; and wo be unto him that rejecteth the word of God.[22]

About 400 A. D. Moroni, the last writer on the Nephite records, predicted that the one who should translate the records in the latter days would be privileged to "show the plates unto those who shall assist to bring forth this work."[23] Also he wrote:

> And unto three shall they be shown by the power of God; wherefore they shall know of a surety that these things are true. And in the mouth of three witnesses shall these things be established; and the testimony of three, and this work, in the which shall be shown forth the power of God, and also his word, of which the Father, and the Son, and the Holy Ghost bear record; and all this shall stand as a testimony against the world at the last day.[24]

Shortly after Martin Harris had lost the first 116 pages of manuscript translated from the tablets the voice of God came to the Prophet Joseph Smith in which the predictions of the ancient prophets were confirmed. The Lord made clear to Joseph His will and purposes in the following words:

> Behold, verily I say unto you, I have reserved these things which I have entrusted unto you, my servant Joseph, for a wise purpose in me, and it shall be made known unto future generations; but this generation shall have my word through you;

> And in addition to your testimony, the testimony of three of my servants, whom I shall call and ordain, unto whom I will show these things, and they shall go forth with my words that are given through you.

---

[21] *Book of Mormon*, p. 56 (2 Nephi 3:6-8).
[22] *Ibid.*, p. 96 (2 Nephi 27:12-14).
[23] *Book of Mormon*, p. 487 (Ether 5:2).
[24] *Ibid.*, p. 487 (Ether 5:3-4).

Yea, they shall know of a surety that these things are true, for from heaven will I declare it unto them.

I will give them power that they may behold and view these things as they are; and to none else will I grant this power, to receive this same testimony among this generation, in this the beginning of the rising up and the coming forth of my church out of the wilderness; clear as the moon, and fair as the sun, and terrible as an army with banners.

And the testimony of three witnesses will I send forth of my word; . . . And their testimony shall also go forth unto the condemnation of this generation if they harden their hearts against them.[25]

THE THREE WITNESSES

According to the predictions of the ancient prophets and also the word of the Lord to Joseph Smith in modern revelation, "three" special witnesses would be shown the plates "by the power of God." In addition to these, a "few" others, "according to the will of God," would behold them, "that they may bear testimony to the word of God unto the children of men." The word of the Lord was definite to the effect that the "three witnesses" were to see the plates under some circumstances attended by a demonstration of the power of God. However, no promise of such divine demonstration was given to the "few" others who were to have the privilege of viewing the sacred relics.

According to the word of the Lord, these three special witnesses were to be chosen from among those who assisted in bringing forth The Book of Mormon. Since Joseph had received more assistance while translating the records from three young men—Oliver Cowdery, David Whitmer, and Martin Harris— than from anyone else, it is not surprising to learn that when the fact became known to them that three special witnesses would have the privilege of viewing the holy records that they should desire to be the ones. They asked the Prophet, therefore, to inquire of the Lord if they might receive this great honor. In answer to their solicitations, the following revelation from the Lord was received for them:

Behold, I say unto you, that you must rely upon my word, which, if you do, with full purpose of heart, you shall have a view of the plates, and also the breastplate, the sword of Laban, and Urim and Thummim, which were given to the brother of Jared upon the mount when he talked with the Lord face to face, and the miraculous directors [Liahona] which were given to Lehi while in the wilderness on the border of the Red Sea;

---

[25] Doctrine and Covenants 5:9-15, 18.

and it is by your faith that you shall obtain a view of them, even by that faith which was had by the prophets of old. And after you have obtained faith, and have seen them with your eyes, you shall testify of them by the power of God. . . .

And ye shall testify that you have seen them, even as my servant Joseph Smith, Jun., has seen them, for it is by my power that he has seen them, and it is because of his faith; And he has translated the book, even that part which I have commanded him, and as your Lord and Your God liveth it is true.[26]

The exact date when the translation of The Book of Mormon was completed is not known, but it was some time during the summer of 1829. As soon as the work was completed, however, the Prophet wrote a letter to his parents, who were still living near Palmyra, informing them that the translation was completed and asking them to come to him at the Whitmer home. They immediately notified Martin Harris and invited him to accompany them to Fayette. According to a statement of Lucy Smith, it was the day following their arrival at the home of the Whitmers that the three witnesses obtained their view of the plates. Her interesting account gives the following detail connected with Martin Harris' becoming one of the three special witnesses:

The next morning [i.e., following the arrival of the party from Palmyra], after attending to the usual services, namely, reading from the scriptures, singing, and praying, Joseph arose from his knees, and approaching Martin Harris with a solemnity that thrills through my veins to this day, when it occurs to my recollection, said:

"Martin Harris, you have got to humble yourself before your God this day, that you may obtain a forgiveness of your sins. If you do, it is the will of God that you should look upon the plates, in company with Oliver Cowdery and David Whitmer."[27]

The Prophet's own account of what happened on that day is very important and so we shall quote it. After he had made reference to the revelation already quoted which promised Cowdery, Whitmer, and Harris that they should view the ancient relics, Joseph Smith recorded in his journal the following:

Not many days after the above commandment was given, we four, viz., Martin Harris, David Whitmer, Oliver Cowdery, and myself agreed to retire into the woods and try to obtain by fervent and humble prayer, the fulfillment of the promise given in the revelation, that they should have a view of the plates, etc. We accordingly made choice of a piece of woods convenient to Mr. Whitmer's house, to which we retired, and having

---

[26] Ibid., 17:1-3, 5-6.
[27] Lucy Mack Smith, History of Joseph Smith, pp. 151-152.

knelt down we began to pray in much faith to Almighty God to bestow upon us a realization of these promises. According to previous arrangements, I commenced by vocal prayer to our heavenly Father, and was followed by each of the rest in succession. We did not, however, obtain any answer or manifestation of the divine favor in our behalf. We again observed the same order of prayer, each calling on and praying fervently to God in rotation, but with the same result as before. Upon this, our second failure, Martin Harris proposed that he should withdraw himself from us, believing, as he expressed himself, that his presence was the cause of our not obtaining what we wished for; he accordingly withdrew from us, and we knelt down again, and had not been many minutes engaged in prayer, when presently we beheld a light above us in the air of exceeding brightness; and, behold, an angel stood before us; in his hands he held the plates which we had been praying for these to have a view of. He turned over the leaves one by one, so that we could see them and discover the engravings thereon distinctly. He then addressed himself to David Whitmer and said, "David, blessed is the Lord, and he that keeps his commandments."

When immediately afterwards, we heard a voice from out of the bright light above us, saying: "These plates have been revealed by the power of God, and they have been translated by the power of God. The translation of them which you have seen is correct, and I command you to bear record of what you now see and hear."

I now left David and Oliver, and went in pursuit of Martin Harris, whom I found at a considerable distance fervently engaged in prayer. He soon told me, however, that he had not yet prevailed with the Lord, and earnestly requested me to join him in prayer, that he also might realize the same blessing which we had just received. We accordingly joined in prayer, and ultimately obtained our desries, for before we had finished, the same vision was opened to our view, at least it was again for me, and I once more beheld and heard the same things whilst at the same moment Martin Harris cried out, apparently in ecstasy of joy, "'Tis enough; mine eyes have beheld!" and jumping up, he shouted hosanna, blessing God and otherwise rejoiced exceedingly.[28]

David Whitmer's account of the viewing of the ancient relics by the three witnesses contains some interesting details not present in the Prophet's account; therefore, part of his account is presented as follows:

Martin Harris was not with us at this time; he obtained a view of them afterwards (the same day). Joseph, Oliver and myself were together when I saw them. We not only saw the plates of *The Book of Mormon* but also the brass plates, the plates of the *Book of Ether,* the plates containing the records of the wickedness and secret abominations of the people of the world down to the time of their being engraved, and many other plates.

---

[28] Joseph Smith, *History of the Church,* Period I, vol. 1, pp. 54-55.

The fact is, it was just as though Joseph, Oliver and I were just sitting here on a log, when we were overshadowed by a light. It was not like the light of the sun nor like that of a fire, but more glorious and beautiful. It extended away around us, I cannot tell how far, but in the midst of this light about as far off as he sits (pointing to John C. Whitmer, sitting a few feet from him), there appeared as it were, a table with many records or plates upon it, besides the plates of The Book of Mormon, also the Sword of Laban, the Directors—i.e., the ball which Lehi had [Liahona]— and the Interpreters [Urim and Thummim]. I saw them just as plain as I see this bed (striking the bed beside him with his hand), and I heard the voice of the Lord, as distinctly as I ever heard anything in my life, declaring that the records of the plates of The Book of Mormon were translated by the gift and power of God.[29]

The Prophet's mother described the events of the memorable day in the following words:

Joseph, Martin, Oliver, and David, repaired to a grove, a short distance from the house, where they commenced calling upon the Lord, and continued in earnest supplication, until he permitted an angel to come down from his presence, and declare to them, that all which Joseph had testified of concerning the plates was true.

When they returned to the house it was between three and four o'clock p.m. Mrs. Whitmer, Mr. Smith and myself were sitting in a bedroom at the time. On coming in Joseph threw himself down beside me, and exclaimed: "Father, mother, you do not know how happy I am; the Lord has now caused the plates to be shown to three more besides myself. They have seen an angel, who has testified to them, and they will have to bear witness to the truth of what I have said, for now they know for themselves that I do not go about to deceive the people, and I feel as if I was relieved of a burden which was almost too heavy for me to bear, and it rejoices my soul, that I am not any longer to be entirely alone in the work." Upon this Martin Harris came in: He seemed almost overcome with joy, and testified boldly to what he had both seen and heard. And so did David and Oliver, adding, that no tongue could express the joy of their hearts, and the greatness of the things which they had both seen and heard.[30]

As a result of the commandment of God for the three witnesses to bear record to the world of what they had seen and heard, they published the following statement in The Book of Mormon, and it has appeared in every edition of that book to the present day:

---

[29] David Whitmer, "Interview between David Whitmer, Orson Pratt and Joseph F. Smith, at Richmond, Missouri, Sept. 7, 1878," cited in Preston Nibley, The Witnesses of the Book of Mormon, p. 68.
[30] Lucy Mack Smith, op. cit., pp. 152-153.

THE TESTIMONY OF THE THREE WITNESSES

Be it known unto all nations, kindreds, tongues, and people unto whom this work shall come, that we, through the grace of God the Father, and our Lord Jesus Christ, have seen the plates which contain this record, which is a record of the people of Nephi, and also of the Lamanites, their brethren, and also of the people of Jared, who came from the tower of which hath been spoken; and we also know that they have been translated by the gift and power of God, for his voice hath declared it unto us; wherefore we know of a surety that the work is true. And we also testify that we have seen the engravings which are upon the plates; and they have been shewn unto us by the power of God, and not of men. And we declare with words of soberness, that an angel of God came down from heaven, and he brought and laid before our eyes, that we beheld and saw the plates, and the engravings thereon; and we know that it is by the grace of God the Father, and our Lord Jesus Christ, that we beheld and bear record that these things are true; and it is marvelous in our eyes, nevertheless the voice of the Lord commanded us that we should bear record of it; wherefore, to be obedient unto the commandments of God, we bear testimony of these things. And we know that if we are faithful in Christ, we shall rid our garments of the blood of all men, and be found spotless before the judgment-seat of Christ, and shall dwell with him eternally in the heavens. And the honor be to the Father, and to the Son, and to the Holy Ghost, which is one God. Amen.

OLIVER COWDERY
DAVID WHITMER
MARTIN HARRIS

VALIDITY OF THE TESTIMONY OF THE THREE WITNESSES

It is a significant fact of great importance that all three of those men for many years were outside the Church, with feelings of bitterness toward it and toward its leaders, and yet they clung tenaciously to their testimony. Oliver Cowdery and David Whitmer were excommunicated in April, 1838. Martin Harris stayed with the Church until the Saints left Kirtland, Ohio, about the time of the excommunication of the other special witnesses, but he failed to move West with his people. However, he was never excommunicated; and later he made the claim that he did not leave the Church but that the Church left him. Therefore, one of the strongest evidences of the validity of the testimony of the three witnesses is the fact that, although one of them never again affiliated himself with the Church while the other two came back just prior to their deaths, yet at no time throughout the entire course of their lives did any of them deny their testimony as to the divine authenticity of *The Book of Mormon*.

If the testimony of the three witnesses was not valid—if they along with the Prophet had not had the experience that they claimed to have had—Joseph Smith, as president of the Church, would never have allowed them to be excommunicated. He would have been afraid that they would accuse him of instigating a fraud and enticing them to enter into a collusion to deceive the world. But each of these four men knew that they had seen an angel and had heard the voice of God and they dared not deny that which they had experienced lest they lose their salvation.

SUBSEQUENT TESTIMONIES OF THE SPECIAL WITNESSES

For ten years after being excommunicated from the Church in 1838, Oliver Cowdery practiced law in Ohio, Wisconsin, and Michigan. The following incident is indicative of Oliver's attitude while he was not affiliated with the Church. During the course of a murder trial, the attorney for the defendant arose and, with taunting sarcasm, challenged Oliver Cowdery in the following words:

May it please the court and gentlemen of the jury, I see one Oliver Cowdery is going to reply to my argument. I wish he would tell us something about that golden Bible that Joe Smith dug out of the hill; something about the great fraud he perpetrated upon the American people whereby he gained thousands of dollars. Now he seems to know so much about this poor prisoner, I wonder if he has forgotten all about Joe Smith and his connection with him.[31]

Finally it came Oliver Cowdery's turn to reply. He arose and was as calm as a summer morning. There was no hesitation, fear, or anger in his voice. He replied:

May it please the court and gentlemen of the jury, my brother attorney on the other side has charged me with connection with Joseph Smith and the golden Bible. The responsibility has been placed upon me, and I cannot escape reply. Before God and man I dare not deny what I have said, and what my testimony contains as written and printed on the front page of The Book of Mormon. May it please your honor and gentlemen of the jury, this I say, I saw the angel and heard his voice—how can I deny it? It happened in the daytime when the sun was shining bright in the firmament; not at night when I was asleep. That glorious messenger from heaven, dressed in white, standing above the ground, in a glory I have never seen anything to compare with—the sun insignificant in comparison—told us if we denied that testimony there is no forgiveness in this life nor in the world to come. Now how can I deny it—I dare not; I will not![32]

[31] Statement of Judge C. M. Nielsen, cited in Preston Nibley, op. cit., p. 44.
[32] Ibid., p. 45.

In October, 1848, the year following the arrival of the Latter-day Saints in the desert region of the Great Basin, Oliver Cowdery returned to the Church. Certainly there was nothing of earthly value to gain in joining with the Mormons at that time. Many of the Saints were camped at Winter Quarters and Council Bluffs on the banks of the Missouri River. A conference was being held on October 21, presided over by Orson Hyde. A man in his early forties, with an intelligent appearing, beardless face, arose to speak. A deep hush fell over the congregation, for many of them knew who he was. Following is part of the touching sermon which he gave:

> Friends and Brethren: My name is Cowdery, Oliver Cowdery. In the early history of this church I stood identified with her, and one in her councils. True it is that the gifts and callings of God are without repentance; not because I was better than the rest of mankind was I called; but, to fulfill the purposes of God, He called me to a high and holy calling.

> I wrote, with my own pen, the entire *Book of Mormon* (save a few pages) as it fell from the lips of the Prophet Joseph Smith, as he translated it by the gift and power of God, by the means of the Urim and Thummim, or, as it is called by that book, "Holy Interpreters." I beheld with my eyes and handled with my hands the gold plates from which it was translated. I also saw with my eyes and handled with my hands the "Holy Interpreters." That book is true. Sidney Rigdon did not write it; Mr. Spaulding did not write it; I wrote it myself as it fell from the lips of the Prophet. It contains the Everlasting Gospel, and came forth to the children of men in fulfillment of the revelations of John, where he says he saw an angel come with the Everlasting Gospel to preach to every nation, kindred, tongue and people. It contains the principles of salvation; and if you, my hearers, will walk by its light and obey its precepts, you will be saved with an everlasting salvation in the kingdom of God on high.[33]

After being baptized, Oliver intended to come to Utah and join the Latter-day Saints in their new "Zion." Before doing so, however, he went to Richmond, Missouri, to see his brother-in-law, David Whitmer. His wish to join the Saints in Utah was never fulfilled. Shortly after arriving at the Whitmer home, he died. He was at this time a few months past his forty-third birthday. On his death-bed he bore his last testimony to the divine origin of *The Book of Mormon*. Lucy P. Young, his half-sister, relates the circumstances of Oliver's death as follows:

---

[33] *Deseret News*, April 13, 1859; *Millenial Star*, vol. 11, p. 43.

Just before breathing his last, he asked his attendants to raise him up in bed that he might talk to the family and his friends who were present. He then told them to live according to the teachings contained in *The Book of Mormon,* and promised them if they would do this that they would meet him in heaven. He then said, "Lay me down and let me fall asleep." A few moments later he died, without a struggle.[34]

There is little likelihood that a man who is contemplating death will falsify. Even our strict legal rules of evidence admit such statements under certain circumstances, even though they are hearsay (the decedent not being present in court for cross-examination).

David Whitmer, who was also present on this occasion, adds the following statement:

Oliver died the happiest man I ever saw. After shaking hands with the family and kissing his wife and daughter, he said: "Now I lay me down for the last time: I am going to my Savior"; and he died immediately with a smile on his face.[35]

Since Martin Harris was the second of the three witnesses to die, we shall now present a few of the many testimonies that he bore regarding *The Book of Mormon.* In 1831 Martin made his home at Kirtland, Ohio, and he remained there until 1870. It was his greatest joy throughout those years to show visitors through the Kirtland Temple, tell them of events connected with the early rise of the Church of Jesus Christ, and bear testimony to the divine origin of *The Book of Mormon.* At no time in his life did he deny this testimony. Elder Edward Stevenson, who was instrumental in later years in bringing Martin to Utah, related the following experience of Martin Harris:

On one occasion several of his old acquaintances made an effort to get him tipsy by treating him to some wine. When they thought he was in a good mood for talk they put the question very carefully to him, "Well, now, Martin, we want you to be frank and candid with us in regard to this story of your seeing an angel and the golden plates of *The Book of Mormon* that are so much talked about. We have always taken you to be an honest good farmer and neighbor of ours but could not believe that you ever did see an angel. Now, Martin, do you really believe that you did see an angel, when you were awake?"

"No," said Martin, "I do not believe it."

The crowd was delighted, but soon a different feeling prevailed, as Martin, true to his trust, said, "Gentlemen, what I have said is true, from the fact that my belief is swallowed up in knowledge; for I want to say

---

[34] Statement of Lucy P. Young, cited in Preston Nibley, *op. cit.,* p. 57.
[35] Statement of David Whitmer, cited in *ibid.,* p. 41.

to you that as the Lord lives I do know that I stood with the Prophet Joseph Smith in the presence of an angel, and it was in the brightness of day."[36]

As the years rolled by, Martin Harris became very bitter toward the leadership of the Church of Jesus Christ. He felt that he had been slighted by them. In December, 1869, William H. Homer, on his return from a mission to England, stopped off at Kirtland, Ohio, to visit him. He introduced himself as a brother-in-law of Martin Harris Jr., as he had married Harris' eldest sister, and also as an elder of the Church who was returning to Utah. Quoting Elder Homer:

> The effect of the introduction was electric. But the fact of relationship was overwhelmed by the fact of Utah citizenship. The old man bristled with vindictiveness. "One of these Brighamite Mormons, are you?" he snapped. Then he railed impatiently against Utah and the founders of the Mormon commonwealth.[37]

Mr. Homer changed the subject as soon as possible. Then Martin showed him through the Kirtland Temple, explained many things relative to the rise of the Church, and expressed the happiness he enjoyed in those days when he associated with the Prophet Joseph Smith. As they were nearing the end of that experience, Elder Homer said to Martin Harris:

> "What about your testimony to *The Book of Mormon?* Do you still believe that *The Book of Mormon* is true and that Joseph Smith was a prophet?" Again the effect was electric. A changed old man stood before me. He was no longer a man with an imagined grievance. He was a man with a message.
>
> "Young man," answered Martin Harris with impressiveness, "Do I believe it? Do I see the sun shining? Just as surely as the sun is shining on us and gives us light, and the moon and stars give us light by night, just as surely as the breath of life sustains us, so surely do I know that Joseph Smith was a true prophet of God, chosen of God to open the last dispensation of the fulness of times; so surely do I know that *The Book of Mormon* was divinely translated. I saw the plates; I saw the angel; I heard the voice of God. I know that *The Book of Mormon* is true and that Joseph Smith was a true Prophet of God. I might as well doubt my own existence as to doubt the divine authenticity of *The Book of Mormon,* or the divine calling of Joseph Smith."[38]

Then Elder Homer asked Martin Harris how he could bear such a wonderful testimony after having left the Church. Martin replied: "Young man, I never did leave the Church; the Church

[36] Statement of Edward Stevenson, cited in Edward E. Berrett, *The Restored Church,* pp. 70-71.
[37] Statement of William H. Homer, cited in Preston Nibley, *op. cit.,* p. 116.
[38] *Ibid.,* pp. 117-118.

left me." Then Martin was approached on the possibility of going to Utah to see his children who lived there. Finally he consented to permit Elder Homer to speak to Brigham Young regarding sending money to pay for his conveyance to the Great Basin on condition that enough be sent for a round trip. Upon arriving in Salt Lake City, Elder Homer presented his story to President Young. The Mormon leader beamed with pleasure and replied:

"I want to say this: I was never more gratified over any message in my life. Send for him? Yes, even if it were to take the last dollar of my own. Martin Harris spent his time and money freely, when one dollar was worth more than one thousand dollars are now. Send for him? Yes, indeed, I shall send! Rest assured Martin Harris will be here in time. It was Martin Harris who gave the Prophet Joseph Smith the first money to assist in the translation of *The Book of Mormon*. Martin Harris was the first scribe to assist in the translation of the *Book* from the original plates, as dictated by the Prophet, who was led by the Holy Ghost. . . . It was true that Martin Harris did not apostatize; he was never tried for his fellowship; he was never excommunicated."[39]

Edward Stevenson also visited Martin Harris in 1869 and approached him regarding his coming to Utah. After returning to Salt Lake City and reporting to the First Presidency, Elder Stevenson was assigned to collect enough money by subscription to bring Martin to "Zion." The following summer (1870) Elder Stevenson journeyed to Kirtland and brought Brother Harris to Salt Lake. Soon after his arrival, Martin applied for baptism, saying "that the Spirit had made known to him that it was his duty to renew his covenant before the Lord." Thereupon he was baptized by Elder Stevenson. Martin remained in Salt Lake a few days visiting old acquaintances, and then he went to Clarkston, Utah. There he made his home with his son, Martin Harris, Jr., remaining with him until he died on July 10, 1875. His death occurred a few months after his ninety-second birthday. William H. Homer was standing beside his deathbed just before his spirit passed to the eternal world beyond the veil. Martin opened his eyes and, recognizing Elder Homer, said:

"I know you, you are my friend. . . . Yes, I did see the plates on which *The Book of Mormon* was written; I did see the angel; I did hear the voice of God; and I do know that Joseph Smith is a Prophet of God, holding the keys of the Holy Priesthood."[40]

[39] *Ibid.*, pp. 120-121.
[40] *Ibid.*, p. 122.

Then he closed his eyes in sleep and the spirit of the second witness to die passed into the other world to meet his God. Today a granite pillar, designating him as one of the three wit- nesses of *The Book of Mormon,* marks the site of his grave in the Clarkston cemetery.

David Whitmer, the last of the three witnesses to leave this mortal realm, was excommunicated from the Church in 1838 and never again affiliated himself with Mormonism. Shortly after leaving the Church he purchased a farm at Richmond, Missouri, and there he spent the balance of his life. Many published testi- monies exist signed by his acquaintances and neighbors which declare him always to have been an honest and reliable citizen. On every occasion that presented itself, he affirmed his testimony, as printed in *The Book of Mormon,* concerning the great vision had by the three witnesses and the validity of their testimony.

In 1881 the editor of the Kansas City *Journal,* knowing that David Whitmer was the last surviving witness to *The Book of Mormon,* sent a reporter to Mr. Whitmer to receive his first- hand story regarding the coming forth of the ancient records. At first David was reluctant to talk, because he had been misquoted so many times. Finally the reporter won his confidence and David Whitmer gave the story similar to that which has been recorded in this history. The story received was published in the *Journal* on June 5, 1881. We shall quote only the portion here which reaffirms David's testimony to *The Book of Mormon.* He said:

"Joseph, Oliver Cowdery and myself were together, and the angel showed them to us. We not only saw the plates of *The Book of Mormon,* but he also showed us the brass plates [and the plates] of the *Book of Ether* and many others. They were shown to us in this way: Joseph and Oliver and I were sitting on a log when we were over-shadowed by a light more glorious than that of the sun. In the midst of this light, but a few feet from us, appeared a table upon which were many golden plates, also the sword of Laban and the directors. I saw them as plain as I see you now and distinctly heard the voice of the Lord declaring that the records of the plates of *The Book of Mormon* were translated by the gift and the power of God."[41]

About the same time that the foregoing was published at Kansas City in the *Journal,* a report had been circulated by a man named John Murphy to the effect that David Whitmer had denied his testimony to *The Book of Mormon.* In a strong state-

41 Kansas City *Journal,* cited in *ibid.,* pp. 81-82.

ment, David Whitmer denied Murphy's report. His signed statement was published in his home-town paper, the Richmond, Missouri, *Conservator,* on March 24, 1881. Part of Whitmer's statement is as follows:

Unto all Nations, Kindreds, Tongues and People, unto whom these presents shall come: It having beeen represented by one John Murphy, of Polo, Caldwell County, Missouri, that I, in a conversation with him last summer, denied my testimony as one of the three witnesses of *The Book of Mormon* . . .

I have never at any time denied that testimony or any part thereof, which has so long since been published with that book, as one of the three witnesses. Those who know me best well know that I have always adhered to that testimony. And that no man may be misled or doubt my present views in regard to the same I do again affirm the truth of all my statements as then made and published.[42]

Five years after the foregoing testimony had been published by David Whitmer, he was visited by Elder Edward Stevenson. Reporting that visit in a letter addressed to President Daniel H. Wells under date of February 16, 1886, Elder Stevenson quoted David Whitmer as saying:

"As sure as the sun shines and I live, just so sure did the angel appear unto me and Joseph Smith, and I heard his voice and did see the angel standing before us, and on a table were the plates, the sword of Laban, and the ball or compass."[43]

In his advanced age in 1887, just one year before his death, to refute all claims that he had denied his original testimony, David Whitmer wrote a remarkable pamphlet under the title of *Address to All Believers in Christ.* From this pamphlet, the following is quoted:

It is recorded in the *American Encyclopedia* and *Encyclopedia Britannica* that I, David Whitmer, have denied my testimony as one of the Three Witnesses of *The Book of Mormon,* and that the other two witnesses, Oliver Cowdery and Martin Harris, denied their testimony to that book.

I will say once more to all mankind, that I have never at any time denied that testimony or any part thereof. I also testify to the world that neither Oliver Cowdery nor Martin Harris ever at any time denied their testimony. They both died reaffirming the truth of the divine authenticity of *The Book of Mormon.*[44]

---

[42] Richmond *Conservator,* cited in *ibid.,* pp. 88-89.
[43] Edward Stevenson to Daniel H. Wells, cited in *ibid.,* p. 99.
[44] David Whitmer, *Address to All Believers in Christ,* p. 8.

On January 25, 1888, David Whitmer died. He was at that time eighty-three years of age. An article appeared in his home-town paper describing his last hours of mortality. In the article the following report is given:

On Sunday evening at 5:30 (Jan. 22, 1888) Mr. Whitmer called his family and some friends to his bedside, and addressing himself to the at-tending physician, said:

"Dr. Buchanan, I want you to say whether or not I am in my right mind, before I give my dying testimonay."

The doctor answered: "Yes, you are in your right mind, for I have just had a conversation with you."

David Whitmer then addressed himself to all around his bedside in these words: "Now you must all be faithful in Christ. I want to say to you all, the Bible and the Record of the Nephites (*Book of Mormon*) are true, so you can say you have heard me bear my testimony on my death-bed. All be faithful in Christ, and your reward will be according to your works. God bless you all. My trust is in Christ forever, worlds without end. Amen."[45]

Friends, who were constantly at his bedside during those last few days, claim that he had many manifestations of the truths of the great beyond. In fact, the day after he bore his last testimony, after awaking from a short slumber, he declared that he had seen beyond the veil and there he saw Christ. Two days later he passed on to the eternal world where the immortal beings dwell. With his death, the last of the special witnesses went to meet his God.

Today an unusual monument stands on Temple Square in Salt Lake City, erected in memory of the three special witnesses. Their testimony is engraved on plaques which are set into the granite shaft. Thus their testimony will be perpetuated on their monument and in *The Book of Mormon*.

THE EIGHT WITNESSES

A few days after the three witnesses were shown *The Book of Mormon* plates by the angel, the ancient records were shown to the eight witnesses by the Prophet Joseph himself. The Proph-et's mother gives the most detailed account of the circumstances incident to this historical event. She points out that she, her husband, and Martin Harris returned to Palmyra the day follow-ing the one on which the angel showed the three witnesses the plates. To continue her account:

In a few days we were followed by Joseph, Oliver, and the Whit-mers, who came to make us a visit, and make some arrangements about

---

[45] Richmond *Democrat*, February 2, 1888. It is important to note that all three of the special witnesses reaffirmed their testimony of *The Book of Mormon* when at death's door. It is highly improbable that all three would falsify or seek to perpetuate a hoax and fraud at such a time!

getting the book printed. Soon after they came, all the male part of the company, with my husband, Samuel and Hyrum, retired to a place where the family were in the habit of offering up devotions to God. They went to this place because it had been revealed to Joseph that the plates would be carried thither by one of the ancient Nephites. Here it was that those eight witnesses, whose names are recorded in *The Book of Mormon,* looked upon them and handled them. . . . After these witnesses returned to the house, the angel again made his appearance to Joseph, at which time Joseph delivered up the plates into the angel's hands.[46]

Lucy Smith's statement regarding the return of the plates to the angel is confirmed by a statement made by Joseph Smith in his history. When the angel Moroni first gave the plates to the Prophet he informed Joseph that when the assignment was completed he would call for them. After giving an account of the efforts made by evil-designing men to wrest the plates from him, Joseph states:

But by the wisdom of God they remained safe in my hands, until I had accomplished by them what was required at my hand. When, according to arrangements, the "messenger" [the angel Moroni] called for them, I delivered them up to him; and he has them in his charge until this day, being the second of May, 1838.[47]

The very evening that the eight witnesses examined the plates a meeting was held at the Smith residence near Palmyra "in which all the witnesses bore testimony" to having been shown the ancient Nephite records. Then they wrote their testimony as here given and it has been printed, following the testimony of the three witnesses, in every edition of *The Book of Mormon* to the present day.

TESTIMONY OF THE EIGHT WITNESSES

Be it known unto all nations, kindreds, tongues, and people unto whom this work shall come, that Joseph Smith, Jun., the translator of this work, has shown unto us the plates of which hath been spoken, which have the appearance of gold; and as many of the leaves as the said Smith has translated, we did handle with our hands; and we also saw the engravings thereon, all of which has the appearance of ancient work, and of curious workmanship. And this we bear record with words of soberness, that the said Smith has shown unto us, for we have seen and hefted, and know of a surety that the said Smith has got the plates of which we have spoken. And we give our names unto the world, to witness unto the world that which we have seen; and we lie not, God bearing witness of it.

CHRISTIAN WHITMER	HIRAM PAGE
JACOB WHITMER	JOSEPH SMITH, SEN.
PETER WHITMER, JUN.	HYRUM SMITH
JOHN WHITMER	SAMUEL H. SMITH

46 Lucy Mack Smith, *op. cit.*, pp. 154-155.
47 Joseph Smith, "The Wentworth Letter," *History of the Church,* Period I, vol. 4, pp. 537-538.

VALIDITY OF THE TESTIMONY OF THE THREE
AND EIGHT WITNESSES

Now the Lord has fulfilled his word (previously quoted) which he spoke through the mouth of His ancient prophet Nephi wherein that Prophet declared that "the book shall be hid from the eyes of the world, that the eyes of none shall behold it save it be that three witnesses shall behold it by the power of God, besides him to whom the book shall be delivered; and they shall testify to the truth of the book and the things therein. And there is none other which shall view it, save it be a few according to the will of God, to bear testimony of his word unto the children of men."[48]

Two kinds of testimony to the truth of *The Book of Mormon* are found in the testimonies of the three and the eight witnesses respectively. One could be regarded as divine and the other human. The testimony of the three witnesses was attended by a remarkable display of the glory and power of God, and the ministration of an angel. The testimony of the eight witnesses, on the other hand, was attended by a plain, matter-of-fact exhibition of the plates by Joseph Smith to his friends. They saw the plates; they handled them; they examined the curious workmanship of the characters engraved upon them; and they turned the leaves one by one. In fact, they could pass the plates from one to another, guess at their weight, make remarks regarding the curious workmanship which had the appearance of being ancient, and make the following expression to each other: "We have seen and hefted, and know of a surety, that the said Smith has got the plates." Thus, by the Lord furnishing both miraculous and ordinary testimonies, objectors and scoffers are left with evidence which has proven irrefutable.

It is a fact of significance that the experiences related by both sets of witnesses occurred in the bright light of day when reality is most pronounced in the minds of men. Every man in the group was a practical, intelligent, honest, God-fearing American frontiersman, and was so recognized by his neighbors and acquaintances. Of the eight witnesses, all of them joined the Church of Jesus Christ of Latter-day Saints. Only five of them, however, remained true to the faith until their deaths. They were Christian Whitmer, Peter Whitmer, Joseph Smith, Sr., Hyrum

---
[48] *Book of Mormon*, p. 96 (2 Nephi 27:12-14).

Smith, and Samuel H. Smith. The other three, Jacob Whitmer, John Whitmer, and Hiram Page, left the Church and were ex-communicated from it in 1838. The latter three, like the three witnesses after their estrangement from the Church, were bitter against the Latter-day Saint leaders. In fact, at times they sought to bring Joseph Smith into disrepute. But never at any time did they deny the testimony which was printed in *The Book of Mormon* with their signatures attached.

More than one hundred years have now passed since the three and the eight men saw the ancient Nephite records and bore their testimonies, and these testimonies stand unrefuted and unchanged in spite of all the attacks which have been launched against them by men and women desirous of destroying the work established through the Prophet of God.

Oliver Cowdery (himself a lawyer), Martin Harris, and David Whitmer each had a reputation for truthfulness and veracity which, from the legal point of view, could not be impeached. Each outlived Joseph Smith—Oliver Cowdery out-lived him by six years, Martin Harris by thirty-five years and David Whitmer by forty-four years.

There is no evidence that they ever made statements incon-sistent with their original testimony—although they were ques-tioned on countless occasions. Nor is there any evidence to im-peach their reputations for truthfulness and veracity. On the contrary, the following list of citizens of Richmond, Missouri, certified to David Whitmer's integrity and honesty as follows:

We, the undersigned citizens of Richmond, Ray County, Mo., where David Whitmer, Sen., has resided since the year A. D. 1838, certify that we have been long and intimately acquainted with him and know him to be a man of the highest integrity, and of undoubted truth and veracity.

Given at Richmond, Mo., this March 20, A. D. 1881.

Signed: A. W. DONIPHAN
GEO. W. DUNN, *Judge of the Fifth Judicial Circuit*
T. D. WOODSON, *President of Ray Co. Savings Bank*
J. T. CHILD, *Editor of Conservator*
H. C. GARNER, *Cashier of Ray Co. Savings Bank*
W. A. HOLMAN, *County Treasurer*
J. S. HUGHES, *Banker, Richmond*
D. P. WHITMER, *Attorney-at-Law*
J. W. BLACK, *Attorney-at-Law*
L. C. CANTWELL, *Postmaster, Richmond*
GEO. I. WASSON, *Mayor*
JAMES A. DAVIS, *County Collector*

C. J. Hughes, *Probate Judge and Presiding Judge
of Ray County Court*
Geo. W. Trigg, *County Clerk*
W. W. Mosby, M. D.
Thos. McGinnis, *Ex-Sheriff, Ray County*
J. P. Quesenberry, *Merchant*
W. R. Holman, *Furniture Merchant*
Lewis Slaughter, *Recorder of Deeds*
Geo. W. Buchanan, M. D.
A. K. Reyburn[49]

Any lawyer would rejoice if the reputation for truthfulness and veracity of one of his star witnesses were supported by such an array of citizens from the community in which the man had lived for many years.

Summary Statement

The evidence presented in the foregoing chapter clearly shows that the Second Settlers, the Nephites (*Nahuales*), had a knowledge of the God of ancient Israel. The facts further establish that those colonizers had records on which they recorded sacred and religious matters. There was no scarcity of gold in the centers of high culture in ancient America and the evidence shows that the people of Bountiful-land were capable of making tablets of gold—did make tablets of gold—and that a set of those tablets was seen in the nineteenth century in the presence of Joseph Smith by reputable witnesses who gave testimony in writing and on their deathbeds that they had seen the plates. Those witnesses never denied that testimony though some had lived for many, many years after the manifestation.

If those witnesses were all perjurers (and the undisputed facts show they were not) and did not see the plates—where, then, did the 522 pages of data come from that were published in the little village of Palmyra, New York, March 26, 1830, as announced in the Palmyra *Reflector* of that date? Surely the data did not come from the mind of Joseph Smith or from the mind of any of his contemporaries (nor could any man in 1950 produce such a book) anywhere in the world! The only reasonable conclusion is that Joseph Smith did possess the tablets—that the witnesses did see them—that from those tablets came *The Book of Mormon* as we have it to scrutinize today. Joseph Smith's translation is still the book's best witness.

---

49 Preston Nibley, *op cit.*, pp. 89-90.

Chapter 11

THIRD SETTLERS OF MIDDLE AMERICA
(Ulmecas—Mulekites—People of Zarahemla)

Introductory Statement

Ixtlilxochitl and *The Book of Mormon* both report on a third colony of settlers which came to Middle America. Each states that this people came from the ancient East—the Nephite record again being the more precise in declaring that the point of departure in the Old World was the land of Jerusalem. *The Book of Mormon* dates the departure from the Holy City "at the time that Zedekiah, king of Judah, was carried away captive into Babylon." That event occurred about 589 B. C. *Ixtlilxochitl* gives no precise date.

Strong support for this migration comes from the sixteenth century writings of the distinguished Spanish priests, Sahagun and Torquemada, both of whom lived in Mexico following the Spanish Conquest. Inasmuch as *Ixtlilxochitl* is very brief in dealing with this early colony, statements from both Sahagun and Torquemada are added to the double-column quotations. The third group of settlers of ancient America landed on the Gulf Coast of Mexico near the mouth of the Panuco River, the same area at which the First Settlers or Jaredites landed, this being made clear by Sahagun and Torquemada. This accords with *The Book of Mormon,* the Nephite record indicating that the landfall was in the same region as that of the Jaredites at a point north of the isthmus or "Narrow Neck of Land."

Sahagun, Torquemada and *The Book of Mormon* each declare that from the place of first landing the Third settlers migrated southward across an isthmus to a veritable paradise, Bountiful-land. The precise date of the arrival in the Bountiful-land area is not given in any of the histories. However, it occurred some time between 589 B. C. (approximate year of the landing) and 200 B. C. (approximate year the Mulekites were discovered in Bountiful-Zarahemla by the Nephites). *Ixtlilxochitl* has the settlers in Bountiful-land before 132 B. C.

It is clear from Sahagun's account that the Third Settlers crossed the Isthmus of Tehuantepec in this southward trek. This conclusion follows by reason of the fact that Panuco, on the one hand—the starting point—is on the north side of that isthmus and Tamoanchan-Tullan (Bountiful-land), on the other hand—the terminus—is on the south side of that isthmus.

It is likewise clear from *The Book of Mormon* account that the Third Settlers crossed the Narrow-Neck-of-Land of the Nephite record in this southward trek. This conclusion follows since the "place of first landing," on the one hand—the starting point—was on the north side of that isthmus and Bountiful-Zarahemla, on the other hand—the terminus—was on the south side of that isthmus.

Thus, the two accounts are in exact agreement on the fundamental problem of geography that is involved. The location of the paradise-land, Bountiful (Tullan) and the various names by which it was known, are discussed in Chapter 13.

A significant parallel exists between Torquemada and *The Book of Mormon* in this respect: both say there was a meeting or merging of the Third Settlers with another people in the new homeland, Bountiful, below the isthmus. *Torquemada* states that the Third Settlers, on arriving in *Tullan* (Bountiful-land), "were hospitably received by the natives of that province, being much regaled there . . ." *The Book of Mormon* is in agreement on the "regaling"—"Now there was great rejoicing among the people of Zarahemla (Mulekites); and also Zarahemla did rejoice exceedingly . . ." However, there is one variance between the two accounts. The Nephite record states that the Mulekites were the first to settle Bountiful-Zarahemla, whereas Torquemada has the Third Settlers being received by the "natives." The Nephites arrived down in Bountiful-Zarahemla where they found the Mulekites already occupying the region.

Ixtlilxochitl says nothing at this point about the merging of the Second and Third Settlers. However, such a merger is strongly implied by him, for hereafter he refers to both groups, *Ulmecas* and *Tultecas,* collectively, as *Tultecas* (Bountiful-land people), as does the Nephite record. "And it came to pass that the people of Zarahemla [Mulekites], and of Mosiah [Nephites], did unite together; and Mosiah [Nephite leader] was appointed to be their king."

Bountiful-Zarahemla, according to both Ixtlilxochitl and The Book of Mormon, remained the "seat of the kingdom" until about 320 A. D. Thus, Bountiful-land was the capital of the combined nations for a period in excess of 500 years—200 B.C.- 320 A. D.

IXTLILXOCHITL:

The Ulmecas or Third Settlers

Those who possessed this new world in this third age were the Ulmecas[XXXIII] and Xicalancas; and according as is found in their histories, they came in ships or boats from the part of the Orient to the land of Potonchan,[XXXII] at which point they began to settle it;

EXTRACTS—BOOK OF MORMON:

The Mulekites (People of Zarahemla) or Third Settlers

15. . . . the people of Zarahemla[XXXIII] came out from Jerusalem at the time that Zedekiah, king of Judah, was carried captive into Babylon.

16. And they journeyed in the wilderness, and were brought by the hand of the Lord[XXXIV] across the great waters, into the land where Mosiah [Nephite leader] discovered them,[XXXII] and they had dwelt there from that time forth.

Omni 1:15-16.

EXPLANATION

Both of the foregoing quotations, equally brief, make possible the same misleading inference. One could infer from Ixtlilxochitl's statement that the first landing place of these settlers was at Potonchan. One could deduce from The Book of Mormon statement that the settlers first landed in the area "where Mosiah discovered them"—Bountiful-Zarahemla. As will be seen, they landed on the Gulf Coast of Mexico at the mouth of the Panuco River, later migrating southward below the Isthmus of Tehuantepec—i.e., to Bountiful-Zarahemla. Jose Fernando Ramirez, Mexican scholar, says of Potonchan:

[It was an] ancient town of Tabasco, situated on the banks of the river of the same name, and of which no other remembrance or relic is preserved, according to Herrera, than the town called Tabasquillo. At Potonchan, Francisco Hernandez de Cordova landed, first navigator that set foot on the shore of the Mexican territory, receiving there the wounds of which he died a few days later. At the same point landed later, with better success, Juan de Grijalva and Hernan Cortes, conquering over the natives. The gift of slave women made to Cortes, among which was found the celebrated doña Marina, also took place at Potonchan. It is singular that this should have been the general point of landfall of the ancient navigators.[1]

[1] José Fernando Ramirez, cited in Spanish in Alfredo Chavero's edition of Obras Históricas de Don Fernando de Alva Ixtlilxochitl (1891 edition), note 3, p. 19.

Potonchan in Tabasco, Mexico, may have been the place of *second* landing, i.e., the place where they landed after migrating southward from the Panuco River area of first occupation. *The Book of Mormon* quotations which follow, as well as those from Sahagun and Torquemada, show that the place of "first landing" was north of the Isthmus of Tehuantepec at Panuco near the present city of Tampico, Mexico.

LANDING PLACE OF JAREDITES AND MIGRATION SOUTHWARD

EXTRACTS—SAHAGUN:

Landing and migration southward, guided by God's prophets

Concerning those who are *Cuextecas*,[2] and the *Toueyome* and the *Panteca* or *Panoteca*: the same are called *Panteca* or *Panoteca*, which means "men of the passage place," who were thus called because they lived in the province of *Panuco*, which is properly called *Pantlan* or *Panotlan*, almost identical with Panoayan, which means "the place through which they pass," which is by the seashore; and they said that the reason why the place is called *Panoayan* is because it is said that the first settlers that came to settle this land of Mexico, which is now called East India, arrived at that port on ships with which they crossed the sea. . . .[XXXII]

Libro Noveno, Capitulo 29, Seccion 8.

Countless years ago the first settlers arrived in *these parts of New Spain* [Mexico, where Sahagun lived] which is almost *another world*, and they came in ships by sea approaching this northern port; and because they disembarked there it was called *Panutla,* or *Panoayan*, "place where they arrived who came by sea," now corruptly called *Pantlan (Panuco)*.[XXXII] And from this port they began to travel [southward] along the coast, beholding the snowy sierras and the volcanoes [doubtless Popocatepetl, Ixtaccihuatl and Orizaba], until they reached the province of Guatemala [which included the present Gulf Coast states of Tabasco and Campeche]; being guided by a priest who himself was guided by their God, with whom he continually took counsel respecting what they ought to do.[XXXIV]

Seccion 12.

EXTRACTS—BOOK OF MORMON:

Land of Mulek (Desolation) and Land of Bountiful-Zarahemla

21. And now will you dispute that Jerusalem was destroyed? Will ye say that the sons of Zedekiah were not slain, all except it were Mulek? Yea, and do ye not behold that the seed of Zedekiah are with us, and they were driven out of the land of Jerusalem? But behold, this is not all—

Helaman 8:21.

10. Now the land south was called Lehi, and the land north was called Mulek, which was after the son of Zedekiah; for the Lord did bring Mulek into the land north [of the isthmus] and Lehi into the land south [of the isthmus].

Helaman 6:10.

29-30. Bountiful . . . bordered upon the land which they called Desolation, it [Desolation] being so far northward that it came into the land which had been peopled and [which people had] been destroyed, of whose bones we have spoken [Jaredites or First Settlers], which was discovered by the people of Zarahemla, it being the place of their first landing.[XXXII]

31. *And they came from there* [Desolation] *up into the south wilderness* [Bountiful-Zarahemla]. Thus the land on the northward was called Desolation, and the land on the southward was called Bountiful. . . .

Alma 22:29-31.

---

[2] The *Cuextecas,* better known as the *Huastecas,* are a people of the Maya linguistic stock, having the unique distinction of being the only Maya-speaking people living outside of the confines of the Maya area to the south of the Isthmus of Tehuantepec. The *Huastecas* still live in the northern Vera Cruz area on the Gulf Coast oof Mexico.

EXTRACTS—TORQUEMADA:
(1723 edition)

Landing place of Third Settlers

Some years after the origin and beginning of *Tulla*, there came from the
northern part [of Mexico] a certain
people that landed in the vicinity of
*Panuco.*XXXII . . .

Concerning this nation, it is not
known where they originated, because
there is no data on the subject other
than that given above which says that
they landed at the province of *Panuco.*
XXXII

Tomo I, pp. 254-255.

XXXII. Landing Place and Location of Permanent Settlement

As is seen, *Torquemada* and *Sahagun* give us the exact
location of the original landing point of the *Ulmecas* on the east,
i.e., Gulf Coast, of Mexico. It was at Panuco, near the present
city of Tampico, Mexico. From the place of first landing, these
immigrants travelled southward to a land of abundance just
south of the Isthmus of Tehuantepec, the first narrow-neck-of-
land encountered to the south. This region to which they went
was in *Sahagun's* day in the sixteenth century, a part of Guatemala—as he states. Today it is comprised of the Mexican states
of Tabasco, Chiapas and Vera Cruz (south portion only of the
latter). Sahagun here calls the region *Tamoanchan, Torquemada*
calls it *Tullan* and *The Book of Mormon* calls it Bountiful-Zarahemla. All three names refer to the same area, as will be seen
in Chapter 13.

The parallels between *Ixtlilxochitl, Sahagun* and *Torquemada* on the one hand, and *The Book of Mormon* on the other,
with regard to this northern landing on the Gulf Coast are very
close. Each lends credibility to the other. The four accounts are
in accord in having the settlers arrive by boat from across the
sea. *Sahagun,* like the Nephite account, indicates it was a voyage from one hemisphere or "world" to another: ". . . the first
settlers arrived in these parts of New Spain which is almost
another world . . ." Three of the accounts designate the landing
place at a point north of an isthmus or "narrow neck of land."
Sahagun and *Torquemada* place the landing point about 400 miles
north of the Isthmus of Tehuantepec, "at Panuco." *Ixtlilxochitl,*

as will be seen in Chapter 12 hereafter, says that these colonizers encountered some of the giants ("Ancient Ones") "on the banks of the Atoyac river, which is the one that passes between Puebla and Cholula . . ." thus indicating early exploration by the Third Settlers of the area 150-300 miles north of the Isthmus of Tehuantepec.

The Book of Mormon quite properly, in the light of its claim of having been compiled in the fourth century A. D., does not refer to the landing point in terms of fifteenth and sixteenth century place-names, but rather, says the landing of Mulek took place north of the "narrow neck of land." To quote: ". . . and the land north [of the narrow neck of land] was called Mulek, which was after the son of Zedekiah; for the Lord did bring Mulek into the land north, and Lehi into the land south."[3] The landing place is definitely placed in the region north of the "narrow neck of land," it having been on the coast of the general region formerly inhabited by the *Jaredites,* "the Ancient Ones": ". . . it being so far northward that it came into the land which had been peopled and [which people had] been destroyed, of whose bones we have spoken, which [land] was discovered by the people of Zarahemla [Mulekites], it being the place of their [the Mulekites] first landing."[4]

Thus, *Sahagun, Torquemada, Ixtlilxochitl* and *The Book of Mormon* are in close agreement on "the place of their first landing." The identification of the landing place of the Mulekites aids greatly the task of determining other important places, such as the Narrow Neck of Land to the south, and Bountiful-Zarahemla just below the isthmus.

All four accounts have these transoceanic immigrants later migrating southward from the place of landing to a land of abundance (Bountiful-land) below the key location, the narrow neck of land. There they "remained a long time," as *Sahagun* puts it. *The Book of Mormon* and *Ixtlilxochitl* maintain that they remained there until about 320 A. D., or more than 500 years. *Ixtlilxochitl* refers to the area as "the seat of the kingdom," as will be seen hereafter.

---

[3] *The Book of Mormon,* p. 373 (Helaman 6:10).

[4] *Ibid.,* p. 254 (Alma 22:30). All of the statements contained in *The Book of Mormon* concerning the lands occupied north of the isthmus, or narrow neck of land, are collected in Ferguson's book *Cumorah—Where?* pp. 16-35. That collected data indicated this landfall to have been within a very few hundred miles north of the narrow neck of land.

Nephites and Mulekites Unite

EXTRACT—TORQUEMADA:

Ulmecas and Second Settlers unite and become one people

These people, departing from *Panuco,* made their way with fine diligence, not being delayed by war or conflicts; and it was by chance that they arrived at *Tullan*[XXXIII, XLII] where, on arriving, they were hospitably received by the natives of that province. . . .

Tomo I, p. 254.

EXTRACTS—BOOK OF MORMON:

Nephites and Mulekites unite and become one people

12. Behold, I am Amaleki, the son of Abinadom. Behold, I will speak unto you somewhat concerning Mosiah, who was made king over the land of Zarahemla; for behold, he being warned of the Lord that he should flee out of the land of Nephi, and as many as would hearken unto the voice of the Lord should depart out of the land with him, into the wilderness——

13. And it came to pass that he did according as the Lord had commanded him. And they departed out of the land into the wilderness, as many as would hearken unto the voice of the Lord; and they were led by many preachings and prophesyings. And they were admonished continually by the word of God; and they were led by the power of his arm, through the wilderness, until they came down into the land which is called the land of Zarahemla.

14 And they discovered [about 200 B. C.] a people, who were called the people of Zarahemla.[XXXIII] Now, there was great rejoicing among the people of Zarahemla; and also Zarahemla did rejoice exceedingly. . . .

17. And at the time that Mosiah discovered them, they had become exceeding numerous. Nevertheless, they had had many wars and serious contentions, and had fallen by the sword from time to time; and their language had become corrupted; and they had brought no records with them; and they denied the being of their Creator; and Mosiah, nor the people of Mosiah, could understand them.[XXXI]

18. But it came to pass that Mosiah caused that they should be taught in his language. And it came to pass that after they were taught in the language of Mosiah, Zarahemla gave a genealogy of his fathers, according to his memory; and they are written, but not in these plates.

19. And it came to pass that the people of Zarahemla, and of Mosiah, did unite together; and Mosiah was appointed to be their king.   Omni 1:12-14, 17-19.

2. Now there were not so many of the children of Nephi, or so many of those who were descendants of Nephi, as there were of the people of Zarahemla, who was a descendant of Mulek, and those who

came with him into the wilderness.[XXXIII]

3. And there were not so many of the people of Nephi and of the people of Zarahemla as there were of the Lamanites; yea, they were not half so numerous.

4. And now all the people of Nephi were assembled together, and also all the people of Zarahemla, and they were gathered in two bodies.   Mosiah 25:2-4.

XXXIII. Ulmecas or Mulekites and Their Merger with Nephites

As has been mentioned, according to the *Works of Ixtlil-xochitl* the people who composed the third group of colonizers of ancient America were known as "Ulmecas"; and *The Book of Mormon* speaks of the third group as "Mulekites," or as "the people of Zarahemla." They were known by the name of *Mulek-ites* because *Mulek,* one of King Zedekiah's sons, was a member of the original company that migrated to America from Jerusalem. Since Mulek was a member of Israel's royal family, it was the proper thing for his associates to call themselves *Mulek-ites.* In fact, Mulek (MLK) is a true Hebrew name meaning "royal" or "king"![5] Also, they received the appellation "the people of Zarahemla" which name was the same as that of their king at the time the Nephites discovered them (about 200 B. C.) and also, the city in which they lived.

The Bible states that at the time when Nebuchadnezzar, the king of Babylon, captured Jerusalem, he had all of King Zedekiah's sons put to death. To quote the words of the Hebrew scriptures: "And they slew the sons of Zedekiah before his eyes, and put out the eyes of Zedekiah, and bound him with fetters of brass, and carried him to Babylon."[6] *The Book of Mormon,* on the other hand, informs us that all of King Zedekiah's sons were slain except Mulek,[7] and that he and a party of associates fled from Jerusalem and came to America at the time of Nebuchadnezzar's conquest of the Holy City.

The Nephite history also reports that the people of Zarahemla were descendants of Mulek and his associates[8] and that approximately 400 years following their arrival in America the Mulekites and the Nephites merged together and became one

---

[5] James Strong, *Dictionary of Words in The Hebrew Bible* (1890), words 4429-4432.
[6] 2 Kings 25:7.
[7] *The Book of Mormon,* p. 380 (Helaman 8:21), quoted previously.
[8] *Ibid.,* p. 182, verse 2 (Mosiah 25:2).

people. This merging took place approximately 200 B. C. From that date forward the combined peoples are usually referred to in *The Book of Mormon* as *Nephites* and in *Ixtlilxochitl* as *Tul-tecas* (people of Bountiful).

The *Book of Mormon* tells the details of the first union of the two divisions of Bountiful-people (Mulekites and Nephites). It came about in the following manner: About the year 200 B. C. the Lord commanded Mosiah I, king of the Nephites, to take with him all of his people who were righteous and migrate north-ward from the city of Nephi which city had been the homeland of his people for many years. The purpose of the exodus was to get away from their perennial enemies, the Lamanites. Mosiah and those of his people who would obey the commandment of the Lord did as they had been directed and migrated northward. As has been pointed out, these migrating Nephites suddenly came upon the Mulekites who, at that time, were illiterate and without records. Thereupon the two peoples, Nephites and Mulekites, merged together, thereafter living unitedly as one people.

As was pointed out in the Introductory Statement of this chapter, *Torquemada* also refers to the memorable and historic meeting and merging of the Third Settlers with another people in *Tullan* (Bountiful-land), the newcomers being "hospitably received . . . being much regaled." *The Book of Mormon* con-firms the statement that the merger took place in Bountiful-land.

XXXIV. God Guided the Third Settlers

Sahagun and *The Book of Mormon* are very explicit in stating that God directed these settlers. The Nephite record says that the Mulekites "were brought by the hand of the Lord across the great waters." *Sahagun* states that the colony was "guided by a priest who himself was guided by their God, with whom he continually took counsel respecting what they ought to do." He quotes one of the ancient prophets of the colony: "Know that our God commands you to remain here in these lands of which he makes you masters and gives possession . . . you will await him in these lands . . . since for this purpose you came hither . . ." *The Book of Mormon* makes it clear that the Lord led the Ne-phites and Mulekites to the New World in anticipation of the rejection of Christ by Old-World Israel—the history and doctrines of the Nephite-Mulekite people of the New World to be instrumental in ultimately convincing the Jews that Jesus was and is their Messiah.

Both *Sahagun* and *The Book of Mormon* declare that the Lord of these settlers was to return a second time. In *Sahagun's* language, "when it shall be time for the world to come to an end," he would return. There are several statements in *The Book of Mormon* on the identical point. To quote some of them:

> And behold, according to the words of the prophet, the Messiah will set himself again the second time to recover them; wherefore, he will mani-fest himself unto them in power and great glory, unto the destruction of their enemies, when that day cometh when they shall believe in him; and none will he destroy that believe in him.[9]
>   . . . when I [Christ] shall come in my glory with the powers of heaven.[10]

XXXV. KNOWLEDGE AND SKILLS OF THE THIRD SETTLERS

The crafts and learning of the cultured settlers will be dealt with in detail in chapters 18 to 25. Here, however, a few points may be noted in that regard. *Sahagun, Ixtlilxochitl, The Book of Mormon* and *Torquemada* all credit the people with mechani-cal arts and skills. They were "learned men, or prophets"; "men learned in the ancient paintings [writings]"; people with "paint-ings [records] which they had brought [*The Book of Mormon* shows the Third Settlers did not have records until they met the Nephites] relating to the religious rites and mechanical arts"; "men of good carriage, well dressed in long robes of black linen"; "a very wise people"; "skilled in working gold and silver"; "very great artisans," "great lapidaries . . . skilled in many delicate things . . . in tilling and plowing land"; "noted for their good government and great industries," and "men of great capacity."

EXTRACTS—SAHAGUN:	EXTRACTS—BOOK OF MORMON:
Ulmecas directed by prophets of God; sacred records carried away	*Mulekites directed by the Lord; sacred records hidden*
They came to settle in *Tamoanchan,* [XLIII] where they remained a long time, and they never ceased to have their learned men, or prophets, called *amox-oaque,* which means "men learned in the ancient paintings,"[XXXI, XXXV] who, although they came at the same time,	10. . . . for the Lord did bring Mulek into the land north, and Lehi into the land south. Helaman 6:10b.
	6. And it came to pass that when we had gathered in all our people in one to the land of Cumorah, behold I, Mormon, began to be old; and knowing it to be the

9 *Ibid.,* p. 63 (2 Nephi 6:14).
10 *Ibid.,* p. 452 (3 Nephi 28:7).

did not remain with the rest in *Tamoan-chan*. After leaving them, there, they reembarked and carried away with them all the paintings [records] which they had brought relating to the religious rites and mechanical arts.XXXVI

Before their departure they discoursed as follows: "Know that our God commands you to remain here in these lands of which he makes you masters and gives you possession.XXXIV He returns to the place whence he and we came but he will come back to visit you when it shall be time for the world to come to an end; in the meantime you will await him in these lands, expectantly and possessing them and all contained in them, since for this purpose you came hither; remain therefore, for we go with our God.

Seccion 12.

EXTRACTS—TORQUEMADA:
Culture, arts, industries of Third Settlers; ship-building

[The Ulmecas were] much regaled there because they were a very wise people, and skilled in ship building XXXVII [the Spanish word is *tracas*, meaning "strakes"], industries, and in working gold and silver, and they were very great artisans in whatsoever art [you might mention]; they were great lapidaries and they were skilled in delicate things, and in other industries for human sustenance; and in tilling and plowing land; and they were strong people noted for their good government and great industries and skills, and they were men of great capacity. XXXV When they arrived they were greatly esteemed and honored.XXXIII

Tomo I, p. 255.

last struggle of my people. and having been commanded of the Lord that I should not suffer the records which had been handed down by our fathers, which were sacred, to fall into the hands of the Lamanites, (for the Lamanites would destroy them) therefore I made this record out of the plates of Nephi, and hid up in the hill Cumorah all the records which had been entrusted to me by the hand of the Lord, save it were these few plates which I gave unto my son Moroni.

Mormon 6:6.

11. And it came to pass that the army of Coriantumr did pitch their tents by the hill Ramah; and it was that same hill where my father Mormon did hide up the records unto the Lord, which were sacred.

Ether 15:11.

XXXVI. Sacred Records Hidden or "Carried Away"

Sahagun says that the learned men or prophets of the Settlers, the "men learned in the ancient paintings," did not remain in the homeland—and that they "carried away with them all the paintings [records] which they had brought relating to the religious rites and mechanical arts." There is a very similar statement in *The Book of Mormon*. The latter record reports that in 385 A. D., after the Nephite-Mulekite people were exiled from their ancient homeland in Bountiful-Zarahemla, one of their great prophet-leaders, Mormon, hid up all but one of the sacred records of the nation. A great battle was about to be fought when he cached away the records. He left a written statement on the matter for he was the compiler of *The Book of Mormon:*

> . . . I, Mormon, began to be old; and knowing this to be the last struggle of my people, and having been commanded of the Lord that I should not suffer the records which had been handed down by our fathers, which were sacred, to fall into the hands of the Lamanites, (for the Laman-ites would destroy them) therefore I made this record [*The Book of Mormon*] out of the plates of Nephi, and hid up in the hill Cumorah all the records which had been entrusted to me by the hand of the Lord, save it were these few plates which I gave unto my son Moroni.[11]

As far as is known, the original records of the Nephites are still hidden where Mormon placed them.

XXXVII. SHIP BUILDING

Torquemada says these colonizers were "skilled in ship build-ing." *The Book of Mormon* relates that after the Nephites and Mulekites united in Bountiful-land rather extensive ship-building activities were engaged in by that people. To quote the latter record:

> And it came to pass that Hagoth, he being an exceedingly curious man, therefore he went forth and built him an exceedingly large ship, on the borders of the land Bountiful, by the land Desolation, and launched it forth into the west sea, by the narrow neck which led into the land northward.

> And behold, there were many of the Nephites who did enter therein and did sail forth with much provisions, and also many women and chil-dren; and they took their course northward. And thus ended the thirty and seventh year.

> And in the thirty and eighth year, this man built other ships. And the first ship did also return, and many more people did enter into it; and they also took much provisions, and set out again to the land northward.

> And it came to pass that they were never heard of more. And we suppose that they were drowned in the depth of the sea. And it came to pass that one other ship also did sail forth; and whither she did go we know not.[12]

---

[11] *The Book of Mormon*, p. 469 (Mormon 6:6).
[12] *The Book of Mormon*, p. 358 (Alma 63:5-8). See also the quotations frcm the Nephite record herein at p. 80 ff., concerning the ship built by Nephi. The Mulekites also must have brought with them some knowledge of ships, for they had a vessel good enough to cross the Atlantic ocean. It may have been of Phœnecian design.

XXXVIII. Dress of Third Settlers

EXTRACT—TORQUEMADA:
Clothing of the Ulmecas

These people [the Ulmecas or the Third Settlers] were men of good carriage, well-dressed in long robes of black linen, like Turks, the robes being like the cassocks of the [Catholic] clergy, open in front, and without capes, low-cut at the neck, and with short wide sleeves which did not reach the elbow—the natives of today use such robes in their dances in imitation of those [ancient] people.[XXXVII]

The "long robes" mentioned by *Torquemada* were, of course, characteristic of the dress of the ancient Near East. That such were worn by these early settlers in Middle America is confirmed by archæological discoveries in stone and pottery. Archæology even supplies us with a description of the footgear of the bearded white men from the Near East. In describing the shoes of "Uncle Sam," the bearded man and his companion, as carved in relief on the fourteen-foot monument at La Venta, Tabasco (on the southern Gulf Coast of Mexico), Matthew V. Stirling, who discovered the stone in 1939-1940, says: "Both figures wear shoes with odd pointed, upturned toes."[13] See Fig. 13 at page 133. Neither the shoes nor the face and flowing beard of "Uncle Sam" belong to a red-skinned Indian.

For a more complete discussion of the dress of the Second and Third Settlers, see Chapter 24 hereafter.

Fig. 13: "Uncle Sam" Figurine from La Venta Stela

This picture is an artist's representation of the "Uncle Sam" aristocratic figurine on the La Venta stele. The clothing and shoes are the type worn by the ancients of America and also of the Near East.

Such archæological discoveries in the Gulf Coast region confirm *The Book of Mormon, Ixtlilxochitl, Sahagun* and *Torque-*

---

[13] Matthew W. Stirling, *National Geographic Magazine* (Sept., 1940), p. 327.

mada in remarkable fashion. The documentary sources confirm each other completely and are in turn corroborated by stone and ceramic evidence from the ground.

(c) N.G.S. COURTESY OF NATIONAL GEOGRAPHIC MAGAZINE

Fig. 14: LA VENTA MONUMENT AND "UNCLE SAM" FIGURINE

This fourteen-feet-high monument was discovered by Matthew W. Stirling at La Venta, Tabasco (southern Gulf Coast of Mexico), in 1939-1940. The picture was taken from the *National Geographic Magazine*, September, 1940, p. 327. The following was printed under the picture:

WORTH DIGGING FOR WAS THE FACE OF THE LARGEST STELA

The lower figure with flowing beard was nicknamed "Uncle Sam" by the staff. His aquiline nose and aristocratic features were different from all other faces depicted at the site. The monument was found in the center of a large stone enclosure at La Venta. . . . The face of one of the standing figures has unfortunately been broken off, but that of the other shows a remarkably handsome individual with an aristocratic aquiline nose and a curious long flowing beard. Both figures wear shoes with odd pointed, upturned toes. Over these two figures, apparently floating through the air, are a number of others in human form, which may represent deities.

It is quite likely that the figure nicknamed "Uncle Sam" was a representation of one of the early colonizers of ancient Tulan from the Near East, or at least one of his descendants. It is to be noted that he wears the same type of shoes that were worn by the ancient inhabitants of the Mediterranean world.

Summary Statement

It may be concluded that *Ixtlilxochitl, Sahagun, Torque-mada* and *The Book of Mormon* are all in close accord with each other concerning the Third Settlers who came by sea from the Near East, landing at the mouth of the Panuco River on Mexico's Gulf Coast. They, like the Ancient Ones and like the Nephites (Nahuales), were led by God. They were a cultured people who brought with them some of the knowledge and skills of the Near Eastern world of the time. Their dress conformed to that of the ancient Israelites, "from head to toe"—literally. They united with the Second Settlers, the Nephites (Nahuales) in Bountiful-land. The sacred records of the united Nephite-Mulekite (Na-huale-Ulmeca) peoples were taken away and were seen no more.

The harmony between the several accounts is too perfect to be the result of chance. No one of the histories quoted can be said to have been a fabrication of someone's imagination when all four corroborate each other on numerous peculiar techni-calities. Furthermore, all of these sixteenth-century writers con-firm the more ancient record of the Nephites—*The Book of Mormon.*

Richard MacNeish of the University of Michigan, a pro-fessional and trained archæologist, has recently been excavating near the mouth of the Panuco River. His reports on discoveries being made there will be awaited with much interest.

Chapter 12

THIRD SETTLERS ENCOUNTER REMNANT
OF FIRST SETTLERS

INTRODUCTORY STATEMENT

It is recalled from Chapter 8 that the Ancient Ones, the Jaredites, the First Settlers, were exterminated. There is a sequel to that chapter and it is reported here.

Our two primary accounts state that a remnant of the Ancient ones from Babel survived the last great calamity of that people, and this remnant was discovered by the Third Settlers (Ulmecas-Mulekites). Both accounts agree that the "finding" was done by the Third Settlers rather than by the remnant of the Ancient Ones. However, the Nephite account makes reference to but one lone Jaredite having survived the carnage of the last Jaredite war. That lone survivor lived long enough to carve inscriptions on a stela, giving an account of himself and "the slain of his people." *Ixtlilxochitl* indicates several of the Ancient Ones were involved in the encounter of the two peoples.

Ixtlilxochitl tells us where the meeting took place—"on the banks of the Atoyac River." The Atoyac River empties into the Gulf of Mexico about ten miles south of the city of Vera Cruz. This is an important contribution to Jaredite geography.

XXXIX. A JAREDITE DISCOVERED BY MULEKITES

IXTLILXOCHITL:

Ulmecas and the Giants meet

. . . on the banks of the Atoyac river, which is the one that passes between *Puebla* and *Cholula,* they [the Ulmecas] found some of the giants[XXXIX] that had escaped the calamity and extermination of the second age.

EXTRACTS—BOOK OF MORMON:

Mulekites and a Jaredite meet

20. And it came to pass in the days of Mosiah, there was a large stone brought unto him with engravings on it; and he did interpret the engravings by the gift and power of God.

21. And they gave an account of one Coriantumr, and the slain of his people. *And Coriantumr was discovered by the people of Zarahemla;*[XXXIX] and he dwelt with them for the space of nine moons.

22. It also spake a few words concerning his fathers. And his first parents came out from the tower, at the time the Lord confounded the language of the people; and the severity of the Lord fell upon them according to his judgments, which are just; and their bones lay scattered in the land northward.

Omni 1:20-22.

Ixtlilxochitl points out that the *Ulmecas* "found some of the giants who had escaped the calamity and the extermination of the second age." When one compares that statement with that quoted from *The Book of Mormon,* he is led to marvel over the accuracy of the details reported in the history of *Ixtlilxochitl.*

As the extract from the Nephite record indicates, following the destruction of his people, Coriantumr, the last survivor of the Jaredites (the Ancient Ones) was discovered by the Mulekites. He wrote on a stone a brief account of the destruction of his people, making reference to the fact that his ancestors had come from the Tower of Babel. He stayed with them nine months before he died. Naturally, at the outset he could not understand the language of the Mulekites nor could they understand his language. Later, however, after the Nephites had joined with the Mulekites, Mosiah I, the king and prophet of the Nephites, through the power of the Lord, translated the inscription that Coriantumr had engraved on the stone. Two generations later, the Nephites and Mulekites obtained a more complete knowledge of their predecessors—the Jaredites. Mosiah II translated from "twenty-four gold plates" a rather detailed history of the Jaredites which had been written by their last prophet, Ether, and found about 122 B. C. on the battlegrounds by some Nephite explorers. Thus these people who inhabited ancient America not only saw the last Jaredite but they also learned much about his people.

Both accounts indicate that the finding or discovering was done by the Third Settlers (Ulmecas-Mulekites).

Although *Ixtlilxochitl's* account of the discovery of a remnant of the Giants and *The Book of Mormon* story of the finding of Coriantumr by the Mulekites do not agree in every detail, it is significant to note that each account claims that two ancient peoples met and that the accounts are in agreement regarding the identity of these people. *Ixtlilxochitl* calls them the "Ancient Ones," "Giants" or "First Settlers from Babel," on the one hand, and the "Ulmecs" on the other hand. *The Book of Mormon* designates them as the "Jaredites" or first settlers, on the one hand, and the "Mulekites" on the other.

TIME AND PLACE

In Chapter 8 it was pointed out that the last great battle of the Jaredites occurred some time between about 300 B. C. and 222 B. C. It is quite likely that Coriantumr was found by the

Mulekites in that same era where the last battle occurred. He had been sorely wounded more than once during the war and it is not likely that he lived long after the Mulekites found him.

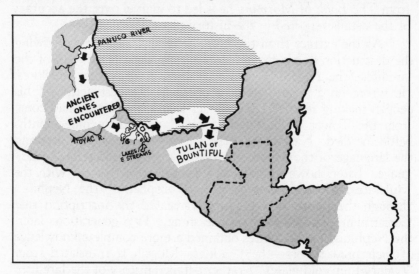

Fig. 15: MAP—ULMECAS DISCOVER REMNANT OF ANCIENT ONES

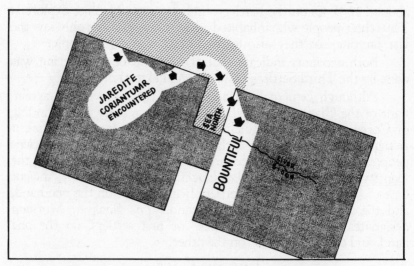

Fig. 16: MAP—MULEKITES DISCOVER CORIANTUMR

Although *The Book of Mormon* does not name the locale where the encounter took place, sufficient geographical data is supplied in that record to make possible a general check against *Ixtlilxochitl's* claim that the meeting occurred "on the banks of the Atoyac River."

The Atoyac, as has been said, runs into the Gulf of Mexico at a point ten miles below the present city of Veracruz, Mexico, in the State of Veracruz. The mouth of the Atoyac is at a point between the Panuco River (where both the Jaredites and the Mulekites landed) and the Isthmus of Tehauntepec, southern boundary of Jaredite occupation. By the same token, the Atoyac lies about midway between the Ulmec-Mulekite place-of-first-landing and their southern capital, Bountiful-Zarahemla, below Tehuantepec. (See Chapter 13.) Thus, it would be reasonable to suppose from the data presented in *The Book of Mormon* that the discovering of the remnant of the First Settlers would have occurred in the general area now comprising the State of Vera-cruz, Mexico, the very zone designated by *Ixtlilxochitl!*

The general area in which Coriantumr fought and bled and in which his people were destroyed was known as the land of Desolation. It lay directly northward from the "narrow neck of land." Desolation was described by the Nephite expedition sent out from the land of Nephi in search of Bountiful-Zarahemla; the party found the Jaredite battleground, "a land among *many waters* . . . a land which was covered with the bones of men, and of beasts, and was also covered with ruins of buildings of every kind . . ."[1]

Thirty miles south of the mouth of the Atoyac River is a land honeycombed with many rivers and lakes—the *Tlacotalpan* area of Vera Cruz. Rio Papalopan, Rio Tesechoacan and Rio San Juan are only three of many streams in the area. The many lakes and streams of the region were photographed from an airplane by W. Glenn Harmon and Thomas Stuart Ferguson in 1948.

It therefore appears that *The Book of Mormon* is in close accord with *Ixtlilxochitl* when the latter designates the Atoyac-River locale as a place where the remnant of the Ancient Ones was found.

[1] *The Book of Mormon*, p. 150 (Mosiah 8:8). See also p. 363 (Helaman 3:3-7).

XL. Freedom Gained Through Getting Enemies Drunk

IXTLILXOCHITL:

Ulmecas obtained freedom by getting giants drunk

The giants, taking advantage of their strength and corpulence to oppress and enslave their neighbors, (who were) the principal leaders of the new settlers, made up their minds to free themselves from them, and the means employed was a feast they made for them, very solemn. After they (the giants) were replete and drunk,^{XL} with their own arms they finished and destroyed them, with which deed they were freed and exempt from their subjection, and the power and command of these Xicalancas and Ulmecas kept on increasing.

EXTRACTS—BOOK OF MORMON:

Nephites obtained freedom through getting Lamanites drunk

3. Now it came to pass that Gideon went forth and stood before the king, and said unto him: Now O king, thou hast hitherto hearkened unto my words many times when we have been contending with our brethren, the Lamanites.

4. And now O king, if thou hast not found me to be an unprofitable servant, or if thou hast hitherto listened to my words in any degree, and they have been of service to thee, even so I desire that thou wouldst listen to my words at this time, and I will be thy servant and deliver this people out of bondage.

5. And the king granted unto him that he might speak. And Gideon said unto him:

6. Behold the back pass, through the back wall, on the back side of the city. The Lamanites, or the guards of the Lamanites, by night are drunken; therefore let us send a proclamation among all this people that they gather together their flocks and herds, that they may drive them into the wilderness by night.

7. And I will go according to thy command and pay the last tribute of wine to the Lamanites, and they will be drunken; and we will pass through the secret pass on the left of the camp when they are drunken and asleep.

8. Thus we will depart with our women and our children, our flocks, and our herds into the wilderness; and we will travel around the land of Shilom.

9. And it came to pass that the king hearkened unto the words of Gideon.

10. And king Limhi caused that his people should gather their flocks together; and he sent the tribute of wine to the Lamanites; and he also sent more wine, as a present unto them; and they did drink freely of the wine which king Limhi did send unto them.

11. And it came to pass that the people of king Limhi did depart by night into the wilderness with their flocks and their herds, and they went round about the land of Shilom in the wilderness, and bent their course towards the land of Zarahemla, being led by Ammon and his brethren.

12. And they had taken all their gold, and silver, and their precious things, which they could carry, and also their provisions with them, into the wilderness; and they pursued their journey.

13. And after being many days in the wilderness they arrived in the land of Zarahemla, and joined Mosiah's people, and became his subjects.

14. And it came to pass that Mosiah received them with joy; and he also received their records, and also the records which had been found by the people of Limhi.   Mosiah 22:3-14.

Ixtlilxochitl reports that finally the Ulmecas freed them-, selves from the "Giants" by getting them drunk and exterminat- ing them. Although the story told in *The Book of Mormon* does not deal with the same group of ancient Americans but with their contemporaries, the Nephites and Lamanites, yet it is so similar to *Ixtlilxochitl's* account that it deserves special notice.

According to *The Book of Mormon,* a group of Nephites had been in bondage for a number of years to their brethren the Lamanites.

The story told in *The Book of Mormon* about these Ne- phites obtaining their freedom from the Lamanites by getting them drunk and then escaping while they were drunk, is so similar to the incident reported by *Ixtlilxochitl* that it is quite probable that the latter account came as tradition from the original historical incident as recorded in the Nephites' record. Since in the one account it is the Ulmecas (Mulekites) and the Giants (Jaredites) that are involved and in the other record it is the Nephites and the Lamanites, and since the Mulekites and Nephites merged together and become one people, therefore, it was natural for the tradition to come down to *Ixtlilxochitl's* time through the descendants of the Nephite-Mulekite people.

Chapter 13

BOUNTIFUL-LAND

INTRODUCTORY STATEMENT

Ixtlilxochitl declares that a great council meeting was held in *Huehuetlapallan,* or the "seat of the kingdom," at a time which would fall at 132 B. C. This was a council of "wise men." *The Book of Mormon* states that Benjamin, king over ancient Bountiful-Zarahemla (which names, it will be shown, mean "Bountiful-plant-land"), held a council meeting with his "holy men" at about 132 B. C. The Nephite record also reports on two other great meetings that were held within the succeeding twelve-year period.

The meaning and location of *Ixtlilxochitl's "Huehuetlapallan"* will be discussed in this chapter. Likewise, the meaning and location of the Nephite "*Zarahemla*" will be discussed. It will be seen that *Huehuetlapallan* seems to be identical to *Zarahemla.* This land was the "seat of the kingdom," according to both of our primary accounts, from the time of the council meeting in 132 B. C. until 322 A. D. This was the all-important central homeland of the ancient artisans—the original and ancient *Tullan* (Bountiful) of the Tultec and Maya histories and traditions.

All of the earliest and most reliable Spanish and Indian documentary sources point to the Tabasco-Chiapas-southern Vera Cruz region of southern Mexico as the location of this important and very ancient center.

A variance of opinion exists among members of the Church of Jesus Christ of Latter-day Saints, as will be shown, as to where the land of Bountiful and the land of Zarahemla were located. Evidence seems to indicate that the Prophet Joseph Smith, in about the only instance where he expressed any opinion concerning *Book of Mormon* geography, pointed to this same general locale as the place where *Zarahemla* was most probably located. His statement indicates he was merely expressing an opinion. Joseph Smith suggested the ruins of Quirigua as the possible site of Zarahemla. Quirigua lies only 250 miles southeast of the region suggested herein for the location of ancient Bountiful-plant-land.

The authors have devoted much diligence to the study of the sixteenth-century sources, archæological data and geographical comments in *The Book of Mormon*. From all this, plus support from the opinion of the Prophet Joseph Smith, a suggested location of Bountiful-Zarahemla is given in this chapter. However, it is to be clearly understood that this suggestion does not constitute the official view of the Church of Jesus Christ of Latter-day Saints on this matter but it merely represents the private opinion of the authors as to where the center of Nephite civilization might have been located, according to the best and most complete evidences that we have been able to assemble up to the present time. If any new evidence bearing on the problem is brought to light in the future, the writers will be happy to receive it.

By the way of introducing the opinion of Joseph Smith and the status of knowledge concerning *Book of Mormon* geography as it has existed heretofore, we can do nothing better than to quote Dr. John A. Widtsoe of the Council of the Twelve Apostles of the Church of Jesus Christ of Latter-day Saints. This statement by Dr. Widtsoe appears in the July, 1950, issue of *The Improvement Era:*

IS BOOK OF MORMON GEOGRAPHY KNOWN?
By JOHN A. WIDTSOE, *of the Council of the Twelve*

The actual geographical locations of Book of Mormon events and places have always intrigued students of the book. Several volumes and many articles on the subject have been published.[1] The various writers so far have failed to agree. Often the suggested locations vary, with different authors, thousands of miles. An earnest, honest search is being continued by enthusiastic Book of Mormon students.

The Book of Mormon was written centuries ago. Consequently, it makes no direct reference to modern, easily identifiable locations. Students must depend, chiefly, upon existing natural monuments, such as mountains, rivers, lakes, or ocean beaches, and try to identify them with similar places mentioned in *The Book of Mormon*. Ruins of early cities are also used as clues by the investigator. Usually, an ideal map is drawn based upon geographical facts mentioned in the book. Then a search is made

---

[1] Among them: J. A. and J. N. Washburn, *An Approach to the Study of Book of Mormon Geography* (Provo, Utah, 1939); T. S. Ferguson, *Cumorah—Where?* (Independence, Mo., 1947); Joel Ricks, *Geography of Book of Mormon Lands* (1940); Orrin G. Wilde, *Landmarks of Ancient American People* (1947); Lynn C. Layton, "An 'Ideal' Book of Mormon Geography" (*The Improvement Era*, 41:394, July, 1938).

for existing areas complying with the map. All such studies are legitimate, but the conclusions drawn from them, though they may be correct,
must at the best be held as intelligent conjectures.

As far as can be learned, the Prophet Joseph Smith, translator of the
book, did not say where, on the American continent, *Book of Mormon*
activities occurred. Perhaps he did not know. However, certain facts and
traditions of varying reliability are used as foundation guides by students
of *Book of Mormon* geography.

First, it is known by revelation that Adam, the father of the human
race, lived in or near the territory known as the state of Missouri.[2] This
has no bearing on *Book of Mormon* geography, since it deals with a period
long before the coming of *Book of Mormon* people to America.

Second, on the journey into northwestern Missouri, led by the Prophet,
the skeleton of a large man was uncovered near the Illinois River. Joseph
Smith said it was the remains of a white Lamanite named Zelph, a leader
among this people.[3] This is not of much value in *Book of Mormon* geographical studies, since Zelph probably dated from a later time when Nephites and Lamanites had been somewhat dispersed and had wandered over
the country.

Third, the hill from which the *Book of Mormon* plates were obtained
by Joseph Smith is definitely known. In the days of the Prophet this hill
was known among the people as Cumorah.[4] This is a fixed point in *Book
of Mormon* later history. There is a controversy, however, about the Hill
Cumorah—not about the location where *The Book of Mormon* plates
were found, but whether it is the hill under that name near which Nephite
events took place.[5] A name, says one, may be applied to more than one
hill; and plates containing the records of a people, sacred things, could
be moved from place to place by divine help.

However, the hill known today as Cumorah in northern New York is
a fixed, known point.

Fourth, a statement in the *Compendium* has been very generally
accepted by the Church. This book, published in 1882, dealing with the
doctrines of the gospel, was compiled by Franklin D. Richards and James
A. Little. Elder Richards was a member of the Council of the Twelve,
and James A. Little, a prominent and trusted elder in the Church. In
the book is a section devoted to "Gems from the History of the Prophet
Joseph Smith." The last of these "gems" reads as follows:

"Lehi's Travels.—*Revelation to Joseph the Seer.* The course that
Lehi and his company traveled from Jerusalem to the place of their destination: They traveled nearly a south-southeast direction until they came
to the nineteenth degree of north latitude; then nearly east to the sea of
Arabia, then sailed in a southeast direction, and landed on the continent
of South America, in Chile, thirty degrees, south latitude."[6]

[2] *The Improvement Era*, 53:42 (January, 1950).
[3] *History of the Church* (Salt Lake City, Utah, 1902-1932), 2:79.
[4] *Ibid.*, 1:15.
[5] Mormon 6:2, 6; 8:2; Ether 15:11.
[6] *Compendium* (Salt Lake City, Utah, 1886), 289.

This, if correctly quoted would be another fixed, certain point in the study of. *Book of Mormon* geography. Curiously enough, however, this statement is not found in the history of Joseph. Investigation points to a slip of paper in possession of the Church Historian said to have been the property of President Frederick G. Williams, one of Joseph's counselors. On the paper are notes pertaining to the doctrine and history of the Church. There also is found the above item relating to "Lehi's Travels." Much doubt has been cast upon the reliability of this statement, since diligent search has failed to trace it to the Prophet. It came into the possession of the Church Historian as a gift from Ezra G. Williams, son of Frederick G. Williams, in 1864, twenty years after the Prophet's death, and was not published until thirty-eight years after the Prophet's death.

Fifth, a statement from the days of Joseph Smith, seldom quoted, bears on this subject. In the *Times and Seasons,* 1842, Zarahemla, a great *Book of Mormon* city, is tentatively identified with the ruins of Quirigua, spoken of in Stephens' great book *Incidents of Travel in Central America, Chiapas and Yucatan.*[7] The article in the *Times and Seasons* positively stated that Zarahemla, while not necessarily where the Quirigua ruins now stands, was in "this land." This seems to place many *Book of Mormon* activities in this region. The interesting fact in this connection is that the Prophet Joseph Smith at this time was editor of the *Times and Seasons,* and had announced his full editorial responsibility for the paper.[8] This seems to give the subjoined article an authority it might not otherwise possess. The following is an excerpt from the editorial.

"Since our 'Extract' was published from Mr. Stephens' 'Incidents of Travel,' &c., we have found another important fact relating to the truth of *The Book of Mormon.* Central America, or Guatemala, is situated north of the Isthmus of Darien and once embraced several hundred miles of territory from north to south—the city of Zarahemla, burnt at the crucifixion of the Savior, and rebuilt afterwards, stood upon this land, as will be seen from the following words in the book of Alma:—'And now it was only the distance of a day and a half's journey for a Nephite, on the line Bountiful, and the land Desolation, from the east to the west sea; and thus the land of Nephi, and the land of Zarahemla was nearly surrounded by water: there being a small neck of land between the land northward and the land southward.'" [See *Book of Mormon* 3rd edition 280-81.]

"It is certainly a good thing for the excellency and veracity, of the divine authenticity of *The Book of Mormon,* that the ruins of Zarahemla have been found where the Nephites left them: and that a large stone with engravings upon it, as Mosiah said: and a *'large round stone, with the sides sculptured in hieroglyphics,'* as Mr. Stephens has published, is also among the left remembrances of the (to him), *lost and unknown. We are not going to declare positively that the ruins of Quiri-gua are those of Zarahemla,* but when the land and the stones and the

---

[7] John L. Stephens, *Incidents of Travel in Central America, Chiapas, and Yucatan* (New York, 1841), vol. 2, p. 118,ch. VII.
[8] *Times and Seasons* (Nauvoo, Ill., 1839-1846); 3:710. See also *History of the Church* (March 2, 1842), 4:524.

books tell the story so plain, we are of the opinion, that it would require more proof than the Jews could bring, to prove the disciples stole the body of Jesus from the tomb, to prove that the ruins of the city in question, are not one of those referred to in *The Book of Mormon*."[9]

They who work on the geography of *The Book of Mormon* have little else than the preceding approaches with which to work, viz: that Nephites found their way into what is now the state of Illinois; that the plates of *The Book of Mormon* were found in a hill in northwestern New York state; that a statement exists of doubtful authenticity that Lehi and his party landed on the shore of the land now known as Chile; and that under the Prophet's editorship Central America was denominated the region of *Book of Mormon* activities.

Out of diligent, prayerful study, we may be led to a better understanding of times and places in the history of the people who move a cross the pages of the divinely given *Book of Mormon*.

The foregoing statement by Dr. Widtsoe, one of the foremost scholars in the councils of the Mormon Church, is an accurate declaration concerning the status of knowledge regarding *Book of Mormon* geography.

The important sixteenth-century sources cited herein, which have proven so helpful, have not been utilized in writings previously published concerning *Book-of-Mormon* geography. Another important aid utilized by the writers which was not available to former students of *Book of Mormon* geography is the Aeronautical Chart Service, U. S. Air Force, Washington, D. C. The splendid maps of the western hemisphere, published lately by the Air Force, are based on partial coverage by aerial photography. They have been most helpful in making a study of terrain. The authors have worked with maps which were revised to February, 1948. Almost every detail of terrain is shown. Archæological discoveries made since 1938 have also proven of great assistance.

It should be clearly understood that the views expressed in this chapter are those of the writers and are not the official views of the Church of Jesus Christ of Latter-day Saints.

---

[9] *Times and Seasons*, 3:927 (No. 23, October 1, 1842); *Cumorah Where?* p. 60.

XLI. Great Council Meeting of Tultecs (Nephites-Mulekites) 132 B. C.

IXTLILXOCHITL:

Tultecas' great council meeting, 132 B. C.

In the year 5097 since the creation of the world, which was *ce Tecpatl, and* 104 years after the total destruction of the *Quinametzin* Philistines, all the land of this New World being in peace, all the Tulteca *wisemen,*[XLI] astrologers as well as men of other arts, got together[XLI] in *Huehuetlapallan,*[XXLII] *seat of their kingdom,*[XLIII] *where* they discussed many things, happenings and calamities that they had, and movements of the heavens since the creation of the world, as well as many other things which, because their histories were burned, have not been able to be known nor understand more than what has here been written. Among other things, they added the leap year in order to make the solar year agree with the equinox,[XLI] and many other curiosities, as will be seen in their tables and rules for their years, months, weeks, and days, signs and planets, according as they understood them, and many other curiosities.

EXTRACTS—BOOK OF MORMON:

Nephite-Mulekite council of holy men about 132 B. C.

16. And after there had been false prophets, and false preachers and teachers among the people, and all these having been punished according to their crimes; and after there having been much contention and many dissensions away unto the Lamanites, behold, it came to pass that king Benjamin, with the assistance of the holy prophets who were among his people—

17. For behold, king Benjamin was a holy man, and he did reign over his people in righteousness; and there were many holy men[XLI] in the land, and they did speak the word of God with power and with authority; and they did use much sharpness because of the stiffneckedness of the people—

18. Wherefore, *with the help of these, king Benjamin, by laboring with all the might of his body and the faculty of his whole soul, and also the prophets, did once more establish peace in the land.*

Words of Mormon 16, 17, 18.

Great Nephite-Mulekite council meeting 124 B. C.

1. And now there was no more contention in *all the land of Zarahemla,* among all the people who belonged to king Benjamin, so that king Benjamin had continual peace all the remainder of his days.

10. Therefore, he had Mosiah brought before him; and these are the words which he spake unto him saying: My son, I would that he should make a proclamation throughout all this and among all this people, or the people of Mosiah who dwell in the land, that thereby they may be gathered together; for on the morrow I shall proclaim unto this my people out of mine own mouth that thou art a king and a ruler over this people, whom the Lord our God hath given us.

18. And now, it came to pass that Mosiah went and did as his father had commanded him, and proclaimed unto all the people who were in the *land of Zarahemla* that thereby they might gather themselves together, to go up to the temple to hear the words which his father should speak unto them.

Mosiah 1:1, 10, 18.

1. And it came to pass that after Mosiah had done as his father had commanded him, and had made a proclamation throughout all the land, that the people gathered themselves together throughout all the land, that they might go up to the temple to hear the words which king Benjamin should speak unto them.

2. And there were a great number, even so many that they did not number them; for they had multiplied exceedingly and waxed great in the land.

6. And they pitched their tents round about the temple, every man having his tent with the door thereof towards the temple, that thereby they might remain in their tents and hear the words which king Benjamin should speak unto them;

8. And it came to pass that he began to speak to his people from the tower; and they could not all hear his words because of the greatness of the multitude; therefore he caused that the words which he spake should be written and sent forth among those that were not under the sound of his voice, that they might also receive his words.

Mosiah 2:1-2, 5, 8.

Another Nephite-Mulekite meeting, about 121 B. C.

1. And now king Mosiah caused that all the people should be gathered together [at Zarahemla].[XL]

4. And now all the people of Nephi [Nephites] were assembled together,[XLI] and also all the people of Zarahemla [Mulekites] and they were gathered together in two bodies.

5. And it came to pass that Mosiah did read, and caused to be read, the records of Zeniff to his people; yea, he read the records of the people of Zeniff, from the time they left the land of Zarahemla until they returned again.[XLIII]

6. And he also read the account of Alma and his brethren, and all their afflictions, from the time they left the land of Zarahemla until the time they returned again.

7. And now when Mosiah had made an end of reading the records, his people who tarried in the land were struck with wonder and amazement.

8. For they knew not what to think; for when they beheld those that had been delivered out of bondage they were filled with exceeding great joy.

14. And now it came to pass that when Mosiah had made an end of speaking and reading to the people, he desired that Alma should also speak to the people.

15. And Alma did speak unto them, when they were assembled together in large bodies, and he went from one body to another, preaching unto the people repentance and faith on the Lord.

19. And it came to pass that king Mosiah granted unto Alma that he might establish churches *throughout all the land of Zarahemla;* and gave him power to ordain priests and teachers over every church.

Mosiah 25: 1-19.

As is evident from the foregoing quotations, both *Ixtlilxochitl* and *The Book of Mormon* give an account of famous meetings which were held by the people of ancient America. The Mexican historian points out that the principal things discussed at this important gathering were (1) historical events, i.e., "happenings" and "calamities," (2) astronomical-calendrical matters and (3) "many other things." *The Book of Mormon* account, on the other hand, mentions that about 132 B. C. king Benjamin had a council of "holy men" whom he called upon to establish peace in the land. Nothing is said of astronomy. However, in the two later meetings of the Nephite-Mulekite nation many important things were discussed.

According to *The Book of Mormon,* these meetings were held in Zarahemla (Bountiful-plant-land), the seat of the kingdom of the united Nephite-Mulekite nations, after the complete destruction of the Jaredites. *Ixtlilxochitl* is in complete agreement on that point, stating that the meeting was held at ancient Bountiful (Huehuetlapallan) by the Tultec "wisemen" at a time when the people of the New World were at peace one with another, it being 104 years after the complete destruction of the Quinametzin Philistines (Giants) or "Ancient Ones." According to *Ixtlilxochitl's* chronology, the Ancient Ones were destroyed in 236 B. C., so the date of the great council meeting mentioned by him would be 132 B. C., or 104 years after the extermination of the Jaredites.

XLII. HUEHUE TLAPALLAN

Ixtlilxochitl states that the name for "the seat of the kingdom" as of 132 B. C. was *Huehuetlapallan,* which means "ancient Bountiful land." *Hue-hue* is from the Nahua (Mexican) tongue and means "old, old" or "ancient."[10] *Tlapallan (Tula-pallan)* is derived from the primary Maya root *Tul,* meaning "bountiful or abundance."[11] Professor Marcos E. Bercerra of the Mexican Society of Geography, in his book on the native geographical names of the state of Chiapas, says that *Huehue-tlan* means "bountiful place of the ancients." He locates it in the state of Chiapas, Mexico.[12]

Bercerra shows that many of the place names of Chiapas include this important name, *Tula* or *Tulan* or *Tlan,* meaning "bountiful" or "abounding." He uses the Spanish word *abundancia* to define it. *Abundancia* is defined "abundance, opulence, fertility, plenty."[13] The following are some of the forms in which *tula* appears in Bercerra's work:

Ama*tan* (where the fig trees abound)
Ama*stlan* (*tlan* meaning "abundancia")

[10] Brasseur de Bourbourg, *Histoire des Nations Civilisees Du Mexique et de L'Amerique-Centrale* (1857), p. 95; Hubert Howe Bancroft, *Native Races* (1876), vol. 5, p. 214.
[11] Martinez Hermandez, *Diccionario de Motul* (Merida, Yucan, 1930), p. 874.
[12] Marcos E. Bercerra, *Nombres Geograficos Indigenas del Estado de Chiapas* (1930), p. 140.
[13] Velazquez, *Dictionary of Spanish and English Languages* (1900), p. 5.

Cacahoatan (where the cacao trees abound)
Coapiltan (where the serpent-people prisoners abound)
Coaton (serpent-people bountiful)
Guitatan (Gods of the Bountiful ancestors)
Hixtan (where thorns abound)
Ishuatan (where the green corn stalks abound)
Istacomitan (where white bones abound)
Ocotitlan (where black smoke abounds)
Ostitan (where caves abound)
Pinolan (where foreigners abound)
Sinacantan (Bountiful of the bat-people)
Sitala (from Sitla-lan) (abounding in rabbits)
Soyatitan (where palm trees abound)
Shuchitan (where flowers abound)
Tecpatan (where flint abounds)
Tenacantlan (where the lime reeds abound)
Tuxtla (where rabbits abound)

To this list from Bercerra may be added the ancient Maya term, *Tutul-xiu,* meaning "abounding in plants," the equivalent in Hebrew of *Zara-hamullah* or *Zarahemla.*

The famous Spanish-born Bernardino de Sahagun (1499-1590), able Catholic priest who lived in Mexico from 1529 until his death in 1590 and who wrote much concerning the ancient people of Middle America, says of the ancient *Tulan:* "This city they called *Tullan,* which means *place of fertility and abundance.*"[14]

Juan de Torquemada (1613 A. D.) was of the belief that the Tultecas prefixed the term *HueHue,* meaning "old" or "ancient" to *Tlapallan* to distinguish their ancient homeland from later and newer regions bearing the same name, *Tula-pallan.* He says they wished to perpetuate their attachment to their ancient country and their grief at being expelled from it.[15]

The French savant, H. de Charencey, points out that the root *Tul* means "abundance, excess," and that the Maya term *Tutul* (as used in *Tutul-xiu*) is a doubled "Tul": *Tul-tul.* The double use of the term makes it plural—this plural form being used for emphasis in the same fashion that *Hue-hue,* "old-old," means "very old" or "ancient." *Tutul* means "very Bountiful."[16]

---

[14] Bernardino de Sahagun, *Historia General de las Cosas de Nueva Espana* (written about 1560-1570), Prologo, Libro Octavo. "Tulla que quiere decir: lugar de fertilidad y abundancia . . ."
[15] Juan de Torquemada, *Los Viente i un Libros Rituales i Monarchia Indiana* (3 vols., Madrid, 1723).
[16] Le comte H. de Charencey, *Les Cites Votanides, Valeur Symbolique des Nombres,* etc. (1885), pp. 52-56.

The term *Tlapallan* sometimes appears in the old accounts as *Tulapan*,[17] meaning "Bountiful-land capital." *Pan* is Maya for center or capital, as pointed out by Charencey.[18]

Thus, the name of the "seat of the kingdom," *Huehue Tla-pallan*, means "Ancient Bountiful-land Capital." It was the capital or "seat of the kingdom" of the Tulteca-Ulmeca settlers at the time of the council meeting of 132 B. C. *Tultecas (Tul-tecas)* means "Bountiful-people" or "People of Bountiful-land."

Another very similar name was applied to the ancient "seat of the kingdom" of the "holy men." That name is *Tutul-xiu*. The new element here is the last part of the term "xiu," meaning "herbs" or "plants." The Maya-Spanish dictionary of Martinez Hernandez so defines it. *Tutul-xiu* means, then, as a place name, "Bountiful-plantland" or "Abounding in Herbs."

The French scholar of Middle American antiquities, Bras-seur de Bourbourg, makes a point which confirms this meaning. He points out that the cultured colonizers, "the petticoat men," of the Tabasco-Chiapas region of southern Mexico, also called *Tula*, their capital city, "Great City of Herbs." He gives the name in the Mexican or *Nahua* tongue as *Hue-Zacatlan*. His authority was the learned priest, Ordoñez y Aguiar, who lived in Chiapas, Mexico, in the eighteenth century.[19]

Professor M. Wells Jakeman wrote in 1945 that *Tutulxiu* means "land of abundance" or "Bountiful."[20]

XLIII. Bountiful-Zarahemla

The Book of Mormon refers to the "seat of the kingdom" of the Nephite-Mulekite people by two names, "Bountiful-land," a translated name, and *"Zarahemla,"* an untranslated name. *Zara-hemla* is Hebrew and it means "Bountiful plant (seed) land" or "abounding, overflowing, with seed plants or grain." Thus, *The Book of Mormon* place-names for the Capital or Seat of the Kingdom of the United Second and Third Settlers are in perfect and complete agreement with the various other documentary sources, Spanish, Mayan and Nahuatl!

It is readily shown that *Zarahemla* means "Bountiful-plant-land." Joseph Smith said that when he translated *The Book of Mormon* script, he sounded out the words to his scribe. The

---

[17] The sixteenth century Maya book from Yucatan, *Chilam Balam de Mani*, contains this usage, *Tulapan*
[18] Charencey, *op. cit.*, pp. 52-56.
[19] Brasseur de Bourbourg, *op. cit.*, pp. 74-75.
[20] M. Wells Jakeman, *The Origins and History of the Mayas* (1945), p. 186.

scribe would then set down in our English script what he had heard. *Zarahemla,* like all other proper names, with two exceptions, was left untranslated. It was merely transliterated or transferred to our script by a scribe unskilled in ancient tongues. The principal scribe, Oliver Cowdery, said he wrote "as it fell from the lips of the Prophet Joseph Smith, as he translated it by the gift and power of God. . . ."

Zarahemla is comprised of two Hebrew words *Zara* and *hemla.* Zara means "grain" or "seed" or "plant."[21] Garcilasso de la Vega (1506-1616), son of an Inca royal mother and a titled Spanish father, and foremost of the sixteenth century writers on the ancient Incas, says the Incas called maize *sara.*[22] Thus, the original Hebrew term *Zara* or *sara* survived not only in *The Book of Mormon,* but elsewhere in New World literature. See figure 17. *Hemla* is a short form of the Hebrew word *Hamullah.* It means "fully," "overflowing," "abundance" or "bountiful."[23]

2232. זָרַע zâraʻ, *zaw-rah';* **a prim. root; to** *sow;* **fig. to** *disseminate, plant, fructify:—* **bear, conceive seed, set with, sow (-er), yield.**

1999. הֲמֻלָּה hămullâh, *ham-ool-law';* **or (too fully)**

Fig. 17: MEANING OF ZARAHEMLA

The Mulekite name *Zarahemla* is from two Hebrew words, *Zara* and *hamulla* or *hamullah.* The Hebrew script for each of these words is shown, together with the meanings—as given by James Strong.

Whether there is a direct connection between the *ullah* (of the Hebrew *hamullah*) and *ulla* (of the Maya *tulla*) is not known. However each constitutes an integral part of the respective Hebrew and Maya words meaning "bountiful."

In *The Book of Mormon* there are references to a "city of Zarahemla" and a "land *Zarahemla,*" and to a "city Bountiful"

---

21 James Strong, *Dictionary of the Words in the Hebrew Bible* (1890), words 2232-2233, as shown in figure 17.
22 Ynca, Garcillaso de la Vega, *Royal Commentaries of the Yncas* (1600), 1869 edition, edited and translated by Sir Clements R. Markham, vol. 1, pp. 49, 189. There is evidence that the earliest cultured settlers of Peru were from Middle America. They were probably Nephite or Lamanite (Nahuale or Maya) adventurers.
23 James Strong, op. cit., words 1998-1999. In accord is J. M. Sjodahl, *An Introduction to the Study of The Book of Mormon* (1927), p. 153.

and a "land Bountiful." The "land Zarahemla" might be called "greater Bountiful-plant-land" for it included the others.[24] *Zarahemla* was the "heart" and "center" of Nephite-Mulekite territory.[25]

CITIES AND LANDS NAMED AFTER PEOPLE

According to *The Book of Mormon,* the king or leader to colonize the Zarahemla-Bountiful area was Zarahemla. The region was named after him in true Nephite-Tulteca fashion. The naming of *Zarahemla* (Huehue-tula-pallan) is an excellent illustration of the custom referred to in both *Ixtlilxochitl* and *The Book of Mormon,* as shown in the following:

IXTLILXOCHITL:	EXTRACT—THE BOOK OF MORMON:
Custom respecting place names	*Custom respecting place names*
. . . each kingdom or province kept the name, according as to who was the lord or king who first settled it, as can be seen in the lands, kingdoms, and provinces of the *Tultecas,* which were generally called *Tullan,* because the first king they had was so called.	Now it was the custom of the people of Nephi to call their lands, and their cities, and their villages, after the name of him who first possessed them; and thus it was with the land of Ammonihah. Alma 8:7.

Not only do the two foregoing quotations corroborate each other as to the general custom, but *Ixtlilxochitl's* observation corroborates the Nephite record in the matter of the actual naming of *Bountiful.* It was named after Zarahemla, the colonizer and "lord" who first settled it!

Further, the foregoing custom conforms to ancient Hebrew-Arabic practice in the Near East.[26]

VARIOUS NAMES APPLIED TO THE "SEAT OF THE KINGDOM"

Ixtlilxochitl and *The Book of Mormon* are in complete and exact agreement on the various and numerous other names applied to the ancient "seat of the kingdom" of the Nephites *(Nahuales—Tultecas—Ulmecas—Tzendales.)* In English, the basic name was "Bountiful-plant-land"—whether translated from the Hebrew, Maya or Nahuatl-Mexican tongues. The following table may clarify this somewhat involved matter.

[24] *The Book of Mormon,* p. 254 (Alma 22:29-32); p. 323 (Alma 50:29-34).
[25] *Ibid.,* p. 350 (Alma 60:19); p. 361 (Helaman 1:18, 25, 26, 27).
[26] T. Canaan, "Studies in the Topography and Folklore of Petra," in *Journal Palest. Or. Soc.,* vol. 9 (1929), pp.138-218; E. H. Palmer, *The Desert of the Exodus* (1871), vol. 1, p. 20. These authorities cited by Hugh Nibley, "Lehi in the Desert," *The Improvement Era,* June, 1950, p. 486.

English translation of the *ancient names* used in *referring to* the "seat of the kingdom," as found in 9 sources.	Ancient *names* used in *referring to* the "Seat of the Kingdom," as found in 9 sources claiming antiquity.	Account where ancient name is found; year account written; year published; whether account was available to Joseph Smith in 1830.
Ancient Bountiful-land	Huehue-Tlapallan (Nahua-Maya tongues)	*Ixtlilxochitl* [circa 1600 A. D.], 1848 (Kingsborough ed.). In Spanish only. Not available to Joseph Smith.
Bountiful	[Not available. May have been *Hamullah,* Hebrew term meaning "overflowing or bountiful."]	*The Book of Mormon* [circa 380 A. D.] 1830 (first edition). English translation by Joseph Smith, with divine assistance.
Bountiful	Tulla (Nahua-Maya tongues)	*Sahagun* [circa 1575 A. D.], 1829 (Mexican edition), in small, rare edition. In Spanish only. Not available to Joseph Smith.
Bountiful Bountiful-Seven	Tullan (Maya tongue) Tollan " " Tulan " " Tulan- Zuiua " "	*Xahila, Totonicapan. Popol Vuh* and *Chronicle of Mani,* all written in 16th century from earlier hieroglyphic sources. First published 1860-1885, in Spanish. Not available to Joseph Smith. First published in English in 1950.
Bountiful-capital Land-of-nine-rivers	Tulapan Chico- nautlan " "	*Chronicle of Mani* [16th century], 1882 (English-Maya ed., U. S.). Not available to Joseph Smith.
Bountiful-land	Tulapallan, Tlapallan (Nahua-Maya tongues)	*Torquemada* [circa 1613 A. D.], 1723 (Spanish edition). Not available to Joseph Smith.
Bountiful-herb-land	Zarahemla (Hebrew tongue) Zara-hamullah (Hebrew tongue)	*The Book of Mormon* [circa 380 A. D.], op. cit.
Bountiful-plant-land	Tutul-xiu (Maya tongue) Hue-Zacatlau (Nahua-Maya tongue)	*Chronicle of Mani, op. cit.*
Serpent land; land of the serpent people	Nachan (Tzendal-Maya tongue)	*Ordoñez y Aguiar,* after Brasseur de Bourbourg [1857]. Not available to Joseph Smith.
		Ordoñez y Aguiar, written from *Probanza de Votan,* a pre-Conquest hieroglyphic source. Extracts published in French in 1857; brief references appeared in Spanish in 1702 in Rome. Not available to Joseph Smith.
Land-of-lineage-of-heaven	Tamoanchan (Nahua tongue)	*Sahagun, op. cit.* Not available to Joseph Smith.

From the foregoing chart it is readily seen that the *Works of Ixtlilxochitl* and *the Book of Mormon* are in accord with other leading, authoritative, documentary sources.

NACHAN OR "SERPENT LAND"

The name "Nachan" appears in the chart as one of the names applied to the seat of the kingdom. It is easily explained. *Chan* is the Maya word for "serpent." *Nachan* means "serpent-land."[27] *The Book of Mormon* makes it very clear that the Bountiful region was "the land of the Serpent-people." The inhabitants of the region Bountiful, land of the "serpents," were the *Christians* of ancient Middle America, worshippers of Jehovah, the God of ancient Israel—the Messiah. As will be shown later, the serpent, according to *The Book of Mormon,* was adopted by the *Nephites,* people of Bountiful, as the symbol of the resurrected Lord. The "Serpent" was symbolic of the Lord; the Serpent-people were "the people of the Lord." In fact, not only in the ancient Bountiful area was the serpent the dominant motif, but this was likewise true in Yucatan and the central plateau region of Mexico to which the "Bountiful-people" immigrated from Bountiful.

TAMOANCHAN OR "LAND OF THE LINEAGE OF HEAVEN"

The name *Tamoanchan,* by which the Bountiful region was also known, is explained by Sahagun as the "land-of-the-lineage-of-heaven."[28] It was the land settled by the colonizers led to the New World by the Lord (Naxcit). Those colonizers were of Israel and considered themselves "children of God." In *The Book of Mormon* the following noteworthy statement appears regarding the early colonizers:

And it came to pass that Alma [a Nephite leader], having authority from God, ordained priests; even one priest to every fifty of their number did he ordain to preach unto them, and to teach them concerning the things pertaining to the kingdom of God. . . . And he commanded them that there should be no contention one with another, but that they should look forward with one eye, having one faith and one baptism, having their hearts knit together in unity and in love one towards another. And thus he commanded them to preach. And thus they became the *children of God.*[29]

---

[27] Brasseur de Bourbourg, *op. cit.,* p. 69. Brasseur says: "This name [Na-Chan] is found in Ordonez. *Na-Chan,* word for word means 'city or habitation of the serpent'." Brasseur also says that the people of *Na-Chan* "were called by Ordoñez *Chan* meaning 'serpent'. . . . These foreigners had large boats, and were dressed in full long vestments, which gave them the name *Tzequil,* 'men with female skirts! . . .' " *Ibid.,* p. 70. (Translated from the French.)

[28] Edward Seler, as cited in article entitled "*Tamoanchan,*" by Paul Henning, Francisco Plancarte, Cecilio A. Robelo and Paul Gonzalez,, in the *Anales del Museo Nacional de Arqueologia,* etc., Mexico, vol. 4, pp. 433-462.

[29] *The Book of Mormon,* p. 169 (Mosiah 18:18-26).

Both the Maya chronicles and *The Book of Mormon* refer to the Bountiful-land followers of the Fair God as the "Holy Men." That expression is used in the Maya chronicle of Mani, in referring to the ancient *Itzas* who went out from *Tutulxiu,* "Bountiful-plant-land," and into Yucatan. In *The Book of Mormon* the statement is made: ". . . and there were many *holy men* in the land, and they did speak the word of God with power and with authority."[30]

Tamoan-chan, "land-of-those-claiming-descent-from-heaven," can be understood as a place-name for the seat-of-the-kingdom in the light of the foregoing factors. It is observed that the name, like *Nachan,* included *chan,* meaning "serpent."

One of the most significant statements made by Sahagun relates to this matter:

According as the old men affirmed, in whose possession were the writings and memories of ancient things, those who first came to settle this land of New Spain came [down the coast] from the north [from Panuco] in search of the earthly paradise which they referred to as *Tamoanchan.* . . . Some of the highly esteemed settlers fortunately had received and divulged a revelation that the earthly paradise [*Tamoanchan*] is toward the south [of the Valley of Mexico], it being true, according to almost all who write, that it was below the equinoxial line; and they settled near the highest mountains they found, because they had [with them] an account that it [the earthly paradise] is a very high mountain; and it is true that way.

These first settlers, according as it is manifested by the very ancient buildings that are now seen, were very energetic and very wise and bellicose people. Among other very notable things they accomplished was the building of a very strong city, *in a very opulent land,* of whose happiness and riches there are signs today even in the ruined buildings. This city they called *Tullan,* which means *place of fertility and abundance.* . . . In this city reigned for many years a king called *Quetzalcoatl.* . . . And they say that he is alive and that he is to return to reign and to rebuild that city that was destroyed, and thus today [about the year 1575] they await him. And when Don Fernando Cortez came they thought it was He, and they received him as such, until his conversation and that of those who came with Cortez undeceived them.[31]

JESUS CHRIST VISITED THE PEOPLE IN BOUNTIFUL

Further, according to *The Book of Mormon* and the other principal documentary sources, Bountiful was the very region where the Fair God descended to earth out of the sky, demon-

[30] *The Book of Mormon,* p. 133 ("Words of Mormon" 1:17;) see Alma 3:6, 13:26.
[31] Sahagun, *op. cit., Libro Octavo, Prologo.*

strating his power to pass through the air, even as the beautiful
Quetzal bird. The *Quetzal* bird, native to *Tullan,* "seat of the
kingdom," thus became a symbol of the Fair God. Sahagun
refers to *Tullan* as the "city of *Quetzalcoatl.*"[32] As is well known,
Quetzalcoatl is the Mexican name for the Fair God who, in the
form of man, descended from the sky. The name is made up of
the Mexican terms for the two principal symbols of the "Fair
God," the *Quetzal* and the serpent. *Coatl* means "serpent."
When Sahagun refers to the "city of *Quetzalcoatl,*" he is speaking of the city of the "Fair God" who was symbolized by the
Quetzal bird and by the *serpent,* to wit: Bountiful, also known as
Tullan, Tamoanchan, Nachan, etc. As is well known, *The Book
of Mormon* gives an elaborate account of the appearance of Jesus
Christ in Bountiful here in the New World after His resurrection.[33] Later in this book Christ's appearance to the Nephites and
the gospel doctrines He taught them will be discussed more or
less in detail.

The evidence appears quite definite that "the seat of the
kingdom" was the land of luxuriant vegetation, "Bountiful,"
where the early settlers were visited by the "bearded Fair God."
There is further evidence connecting *Tamoanchan, Nachan,* or
ancient *Tulan,* "the seat of the kingdom," with the locale visited
by the Fair God who descended from the sky.

SUMMARY STATEMENT

The Book of Mormon and the *Works of Ixtlilxochitl* are
in accord with each other and with the other early documentary
sources in identifying the Bountiful region as "the seat of the
the kingdom" of the early civilized transoceanic immigrants. Further, it is clear from all the accounts that Bountiful was a virtual
earthly paradise, a land of plenty, the home of the "holy men"
or "children of God," land of the worshippers of the Fair God
who was symbolized by the *Quetzal* bird and the serpent, the
tree of life and the cross.[34] In short, Bountiful-land was the seat
of the kingdom (from about 200 B. C. to 350 A. D.) of the
colonizers who came from the Near East to the New World by
boat. It was the early center of the worshippers of the ancient

[32] Sahagun, *op. cit., Libro Octavo, Prologo.*
[33] *The Book of Mormon,* p. 421 ff. (3 Nephi 11).
[34] More will appear later identifying Quetzalcoatl with the resurrected Christ. See Chapters 15 and 16.

God of Israel and His Son, the Fair God of Middle America, Jesus the Christ.

When Joseph Smith called the name in English, "Bountiful," he was in harmony with *Ixtlilxochitl, Sahagun,* and the various terms by which the capital was known among the ancient Mayas. Likewise when the strange-sounding name *Zara-hemla* "fell from the lips of the Prophet Joseph Smith," as the scribe, Oliver Cowdery, put it, the twenty-four-year-old translator again gave us exactly the right name for the seat of the kingdom— this time in Hebrew, one of the tongues known by these early settlers whom the Totonicapan account says were descendants of Abraham. Oliver Cowdery must have known what he was talking about when he testified that as he wrote, the youthful Prophet translated "by the gift and power of God." There is no other explanation for the data in this chapter alone, much less the entirety of the work of Joseph Smith.

SUGGESTED LOCATION OF THE LAND OF BOUNTIFUL

To any student of *The Book of Mormon,* the problem naturally arises as to where the land of Bountiful could have been

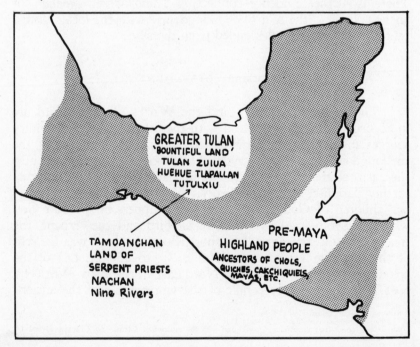

Fig. 18: MAP—HUEHUE TLAPALLAN AND HIGHLAND REGION

located. First, the answer to that problem is not definitely known. Second, a number of *Book of Mormon* students have believed that it was located in the northern part of South America. Third, probably an equal number of competent students feel that that particular region does not meet the requirements set forth in the record itself; nor do they believe that it is sustained by early documentary sources; therefore, they suggest various locations in Central America, Guatemala, or Mexico as being regions more in conformity with all evidence available concerning the location of Zarahemla and Bountiful.

Much help has been obtained by the writers from a number of reliable documentary sources, as well as from *The Book of Mormon* itself, which has resulted in their selecting a region which seems to them to best meet all the requirements for the lands of Bountiful and Zarahemla. The suggestions that are offered are merely given as possible locations and not as known and definitely established facts. As previously stated, the opinions stated herein are the individual views of the authors, there being as yet no officially accepted or endorsed interpretation of *Book-of-Mormon* geography on the part of the Church of Jesus Christ of Latter-day Saints.

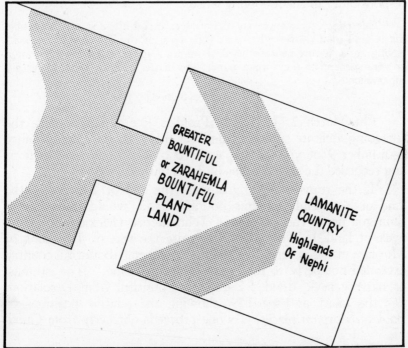

Fig. 19: MAP—LANDS OF BOUNTIFUL AND NEPHI

It is suggested that Bountiful-land, "the seat of the king-dom," could have been located in the area shown on the map, page 158. This area is comprised of parts or all of the following states of the present Republic of Mexico: Chiapas, Tabasco, southern-most part of Vera Cruz, western Campeche, and the southernmost part of Oaxaca. It is the area lying between the Isthmus of Tehuantepec and the Usumacinta River. In the sixteenth cen-tury this area was regarded as part of Guatemala. The suggested area meets all the requirements of all the primary documentary sources (including *The Book of Mormon*), and finds greater sup-port from the findings of the "dirt archæologists" than does any other candidate zone.

JOSEPH SMITH'S OPINION

The statement from the *Times and Seasons,* as set forth by Dr. John A. Widtsoe and quoted in the Introductory State-ment of this chapter, was that the ruins of Quirigua might well be those of the city of Zarahemla. That statement seems to rep-resent Joseph Smith's opinion, since he was the editor of the *Times and Seasons* at that time and had declared his editorial responsibility in the following words:

This paper commences my editorial career; I alone stand responsible for it, and shall do for all papers (i.e., Nos. of the *Times and Seasons.*) having my signature henceforward. I am not responsible for the publication or arrangement of the former paper; the matter did not come under my supervision.

[Signed]   JOSEPH SMITH

On March 2, 1842, the Prophet Joseph Smith made the foregoing definite announcement of his editorial responsibility in number 9 of volume 3, page 710 of the *Times and Seasons* and recorded the same statement in his journal.

If the ruins of Quirigua were the city of Zarahemla, the *land* of Zarahemla, greater Bountiful-land, would extend from Quirigua up to the Isthmus of Tehuantepec (Mexico's "narrow neck of land"). This follows because the text of *The Book of Mormon* makes it very clear that the Zarahemla-Bountiful country extended northerly to the "narrow neck of land." The isthmus, or narrow neck, divided Zarahemla-Bountiful from Desolation. See the chart at page 159, showing the relative positions of *Book-of-Mormon* places. As one proceeds northerly from Quirigua the first (and only) isthmus encountered is Tehuantepec. Working from the Prophet's suggested location for the *city* of Zarahemla and from the text of the Nephite record, it is seen that the *lands* of Zarahemla and Bountiful would be the zone between Quirigua and Tehuantepec—the *very locale designated by all the reliable sixteenth-century histories, and by archaeology as well.* See the map at page 158.

SAHAGUN'S STATEMENT

Sahagun points directly to this suggested area as being the "seat of the kingdom," *Tamoanchan.* According to that learned prelate, when the settlers left Panuco, the region of their first landing, they traveled southward down the east coast of Mexico ". . . until they arrived at the province of Guatemala. . . . And they went to settle in *Tamoanchan,* where they remained for a long time. . . ."[35] This information could indicate no region other than the Chiapas-Tabasco area below Tehuantepec. The scholarly French student of American antiquities, Abbe Brasseur de Bourbourg, looked upon the above-quoted statement of Sahagun in the same light:

Sahagun says expressly that they entered the kingdom of Guatemala. In the period in which he wrote, the province of Chiapas [now part of Mexico] was a part of this kingdom of Guatemala. His account elsewhere is perfectly clear. In regard to the word *Tamoanchan,* it is difficult to give the exact meaning of it. This information, together with traditions which we have concerning the landing of the *Nahoas* [*Nephites?*], adequately proves that the settlement was in the vicinity of the territories neighboring in the vicinity of the coast of Xicalanco.[36]

Xicalanco is readily identified as the area bordering on the western end of the Laguna de Terminos in the western part of the state of Campeche. A small settlement on the western side of the Laguna de Terminos still bears the name *Xicalanco.* One of the writers participated in a cursory exploration of the Xicalanco area in 1948. It is noted that *Ixtlilxochitl* refers to these first settlers of Bountiful-land as the *Ulmecas* and *Xicalancas.* So we have the location of Xicalanco to assist in the correlation problem, along with Sahagun's important state-

---

[35] Sahagun, *op. cit.,* Libro 10, Capitulo XXIX, Sec. 12.
[36] Abbe Brasseur de Bourbourg, *History of the Civilized Nations of Mexico and Central America During the Centuries Prior to Christopher Columbus, Written from Original and Entirely Unedited Documents,* etc. . . ., Paris, 1857, in French, p. 110.
Bancroft, *op. cit.,* vol. 5, pp. 214-218, is in accord, citing Brasseur and others.

ment quoted above. Sahagun further says that the people who lived in the Tabasco-Chiapas area were called *Olmecs, Uixtotin, Nonualco.*"[37] Torquemada corroborates this.

TORQUEMADA'S EVIDENCE

Torquemada describes the journey of a tenth century Tul-tec king from central Mexico (it is believed the starting point was Teotihuacan, also known in the tenth century A. D. as Tula, the latter being named after the more ancient center in the Chiapas region) which took the king to a point south of the Isthmus of Tehuantepec—to the ancient *Tlapallan,* home of his ancestors. The king is variously referred to as Topiltzin and Quetzalcoatl (after the ancient Fair God, he claiming to have been a priest of the Fair God). The journey took the king southward through *Cholula* and on to *Coatzalcoalco*[38] (now known as *Puerto Mexico*) on the gulf coast of the Isthmus of Tehuantepec. The ancient Bountiful-land lay between *Coatzal-coalco* and Yucatan. Also, the *Itzas* who colonized Yucatan traveled easterly from the Tabasco-Chiapas area to get into the peninsula after departing from Bountiful-land. See the map, page 163. Topiltzin continued on through the ancient "seat of the kingdom" of his *Tultec* ancestors to arrive in Yucatan. There he became known as Kukulcan[39] (Maya translation of Quetzal-coatl). The region between Tehuantepec and Yucatan is the area suggested for the location of the ancient Bountiful-land. Torquemada clearly points to the suggested area as "the seat of the kingdom":

> He [Topiltzin, Tultec prince of the tenth century central Mexico] determined to leave the country [Teotihuacan is approximately thirty miles northeast of Mexico City], and thus he did and went away with a very large part of his people, giving as the cause of his going away that he went to visit other provinces and peoples whom he had sent to populate the lands of *Onohualco* [identical with *Nonoual-Tulapan*], which are near the sea and those which we call Yucatan, Tabasco, Campeche, since all these provinces were called by these natives in their heathendom, Onohualco.[40]

It is certainly reasonable to suggest that the tenth century *Quetzalcoatl-Kukulcan,* referred to by Torquemada, was heading for the ancient Bountiful-land which had been occupied by his

[37] Alfred M. Tozzer, 1941, *op. cit.,* note 159.
[38] *Coatzalcoalco* is on the gulf side of the Isthmus of Tehuantepec, Mexico's narrow neck of land. The name *Coatzalcoalco* means "in the sanctuary of the serpent."
      Miguel Covarrubias, *Mexico South,* 1946, p. 38.
[39] Juan de Torquemada, *op. cit.,* vol. 2, p. 50.
[40] Torquemada, *op. cit.,* vol. 3, ch. VII; cited and translated by Tozzer, 1941, note 128.

Nephite-Mulekite ancestors from about 200 B. C. to about 350 A. D. He was going back to that land originally settled by the people who landed from ships at Panuco, which people migrated from Panuco to settle the Tabasco-Chiapas country to the southeast.

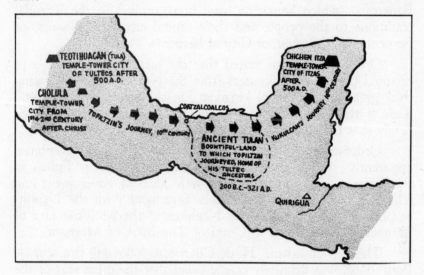

Fig. 20: MAP—TOPILTZIN'S JOURNEY

ORDOÑEZ Y AGUIAR'S VIEW

The foregoing description is in close accord with that given by another early writer to the settlers he too claimed were the first to colonize the said Chiapas-Tabasco country . Ordoñez y Aguiar, who obtained his data from a hieroglyphic manuscript obtained by him in the Chiapas area, described the colonizers as "men with petticoats," because of their peculiar dress. They were the "serpent people" whose original homeland on the other side of the sea had been in the land where Solomon's temple was located, for they knew of that edifice.[41] This accounts for their

---

[41] Because they knew of Solomon's temple, Ordonez made the mistake of dating their arrival in the New World at "about 1000 B. C.," or about contemporary with Solomon himself. *The Book of Mormon* makes it clear that the Nephites had historical knowledge of Solomon when they arrived in America about 600 B. C. Solomon reigned 960-925 B. C., approximately.

Thirty years after leaving Jerusalem or about 570 B. C., Nephi, one of the prophet leaders of the colonizers of ancient America, built a temple in the New World. In the record of his people, the following is recorded: "And I, Nephi, did build a temple; and I did construct it after the manner of Solomon save it were not built of so many precious things; for they were not to be found upon the land, wherefore, it could not be like unto Solomon's temple. But after the manner of the construction was like unto the temple of Solomon; and the workmanship thereof was exceedingly fine." *The Book of Mormon*, p. 61 (2 Nephi 5:16).

From the foregoing quotation and from many others that could be cited from the ancient Nephite record, it is very definite that these people not only knew of Solomon but patterned some of their buildings after the ones the ancient Hebrew king erected.

ancient Near-Eastern garb. The hieroglyphic manuscript from which Ordoñez y Aguiar obtained his information was, in fact, a genealogical record written to prove that the people were of the "serpent lineage." A nickname for these serpent people was *Tzendal*, meaning "men with petticoats." "The only name," says Bancroft, "which seems to have been applied in the Tzendal traditions to the people and their capital city were *Chanes*, or Serpents, and *Nachan*, or City of Serpents."[42]

Ordoñez y Aguiar stated that the hieroglyphic manuscript credited these early colonizers from the Near East with creating their great and powerful kingdom "*in the Usumacinta region*." This is the Chiapas-Tabasco-Campeche territory. He believed firmly that the ancient capital city was located in Chiapas.[43]

Ordoñez stated that the "men with petticoats [Nephites, apparently] found another people already settled in *Tullan* in the Chiapas area and gave them new ideas of government and religion."[44] This is in remarkable agreement with the Nephite account of the arrival of the Nephites in the Mulekite city of Zarahemla, as reported in Omni of *The Book of Mormon*.

The French savant, H. de Charency, following Brasseur de Bourbourg, was definitely of the belief that the great seat of the Tultec kingdom was in the Chiapas area. He devoted a sixty-two-page treatise to the subject.[45] He points out that it was the center of the original serpent-men, the *Chans*, whose principal city was *Nachan*, "city of the Serpents." Like Brasseur, he cites Ordoñez y Aguiar for the point that the Serpent Men of Quetzalcoatl came in by sea by way of the Gulf of Mexico and that they disembarked upon the banks of the Usumacinta River. These were the men dressed in garb like long petticoats. These were the people of the first Quetzalcoatl. Charencey even cites *Ixtlilxochitl* to the effect that the first appearance of Quetzalcoatl occurred toward the beginning of the Christian era. He also mentions that the age of civilization of the Serpent-Men began in 68 A. D. with the appearance of the first Quetzalcoatl.[46]

42 Hubert Howe Bancroft, *Native Races*, vol. 5, pp. 161-165.

43 *Ibid.*, p. 165; Ordoñez y Aguiar, *Historia del Cielo y del Mundo*, etc., pp. 9-10, where Ordoñez says the "seat of the kingdom" of the Serpents was located in the Palenque region of Chiapas. The great ruins near the present village of Palenque were visited by Ordoñez. Those ruins were among the first to be discovered in modern times. However, they are too far west of the river to be the ruins of Zarahemla, original capital of Bountiful-land. It is easy enough to understand his great interest in Palenque.

44 Hubert Howe Bancroft, *Native Races* (1883), vol. 5, p. 187.

45 Le comte H. and de Charencey, *Les Cites Votanides, Valeur Symbolique des nombres*, etc. (1885).

46 *Ibid.*, p. 57.

If Ordoñez y Augiar was correct in placing the appearance of the Fair God in the Chiapas area, the suggested location of "the seat of the kingdom," he is in accord with *The Book of Mormon* in that the latter record says that Christ appeared in Bountiful. Thus, if He did appear in the Chiapas area, as Ordoñez indicated, that would constitute further evidence that "Bountiful-land" was in the Chiapas region.

EVIDENCE FROM CHILAM BALAM OF MANI

The Maya Book of Chilam Balam of Mani (an important sixteenth-century record from Yucatan) also indicates that Bountiful-land was in the Tabasco-Chiapas region to the west of Yucatan. The chronicle summarizes Maya history from 150 A. D. down to 1611 A. D., covering about 1,400 years. This sixteenth-century record was derived from reliable and authentic hieroglyphic sources. It has been translated from the Maya tongue into English. At the very outset the chronicle says, in substance, that the *Itzas,* "holy men," left their homeland, *Tulapan Chiconautlan* (*Bountiful*-land-of-nine-rivers), which was to the west of the peninsula of Yucatan.

The name *Tutulxiu* (Bountiful-plant-land) is also used in the opening statement of the Chronicle of Mani and likewise refers to the ancient homeland. Two other names are applied to the Itzan-serpent-people's ancient home, *Nonoual* and *Zuiua.* Zuiua means "seven," as previously shown. There were seven tribes of the people of Lehi. The *Itzas* arrived in Yucatan, it is said, from Tulapan (Bountiful-land) to the *west of Yucatan.*

The *Itzan* leader of the retinue was a serpent-prince, *Holon-Chan,* "Bee-serpent," being identified by this name as a priest of the "Fair God" and as having come from *Na-chan,* "land of the Serpents." The chronicle says, in part:

> . . . they [the *Itzas*] departed from their home *Nonoual* . . . at the west *Zuiua.* The land from whence they came was *Tulapan Chiconautlan.*
> . . . they arrived here with prince *Holon Chan* and his retinue of subjects.
> . . . six score years they ruled Chichen Itza. Then Chichen Itza was abandoned, and they went to live in Chanputan.[47] There they had their homes, the Itzas, holy men.[48]

---

[47] Chanputun is identical with the present-day Champoton on the Campeche coast.
[48] Daniel Brinton, *The Maya Chronicles* (1882), pp. 95-99; M. Wells Jakeman, *op. cit.,* pp. 64-65; Sylvanus G. Morley (1946), p. 86. Deletions are made here for the sake of clarity.

Nine Rivers

A look at the map of the peninsula of Yucatan reveals that the region immediately to the west of the peninsula is the Ta-basco-Chiapas country. That is the zone of *Tulapan Chiconautlan* "Bountiful land-of-nine-rivers." The nine rivers which empty into the Gulf of Mexico from that region are: Rio Chacalapa, Rio Coatzalcoalcos, Rio Tonala, Rio Grijalva, Rio Usumacinta, Rio S. Pedro y S. Pablo, Rio Palizada, Rio Chumpan and the Rio Candelaria. Morley of Carnegie Institution of Washington, D. C. (until his death in 1947), was in accord in placing *Tulapan* in the said region. He definitely stated that it "lay somewhere to the southwest of the northern half of the Yucatan peninsula."[49] American research also is in agreement in placing Tulapan-No-noual, seat of the Serpent-kingdom, in the lowlands of the Usu-macinta basin. Speaking of *Tulapan,* also known as *Nonoual,* Professor Tozzer of Harvard says, "This place is usually located near *Xicalango.*"[50] *Xicalango* (identical with *Xicalanco*) is on the western side of the Laguna de Terminos in the state of Campeche. It is in the very center of the nine-rivers country.

Herrera

Tozzer lends further help by translating and quoting An-tonio de Herrera y Tordesillas (1598 A. D.), who wrote of extensive post-*Book-of-Mormon* migrations from this Chiapas-Tabasco center:

> While the Cocoms [of northern Yucatan] were living in this good order, great companies of people, who, they were sure were from Chiapas, entered [Yucatan] from the south-[west] from the slopes of the sierras of Lacandon; . . . The *Tutulxius,* for thus foreigners were called, in view of this civility [invitation from the lords of Mayapan in northern Yuca-tan] went to the city and built."[51]

The hills of the Lacandon Maya are in the Chiapas country lying just to the west of the Usumacinta River. A small remnant of Maya-speaking Lacandons still survives in that area. From there came the Tutulxius. Thus, those "foreigners," those Tutu-lxius, were people who came into Yucatan from the land of Zara-hemla in Chiapas.

49 Morley, 1946, *op. cit.,* p. 87.
50 Alfred M. Tozzer, *op. cit.,* note 159.
51 Herrera, *Historia General de los Hechos de los Castellanos en las Islas y Tierra Firme del Mar Oceano* (1598 or 1601 A. D.), translated by Tozzer, 1941, p. 215, and note 159.

PEDRO DE ALVARADO

Pedro de Alvarado was the Spanish conqueror of Guatemala. In 1524 he wrote from Santiago, Guatemala [not far
from Quirigua], to Cortez, announcing his intention to explore
the country of "Tlapallan . . . which is in the interior fifteen days'
march[52] from here. It is pretended that the capital is as large
as Mexico." Bancroft says, in connection with Alvarado's statement: "This indicates that at the time of the Conquest the name
[Tlapallan] was still applied to the region that may correspond
very well with Honduras, Peten, or *Tabasco*. *Ixtlilxochitl* himself, in relating the expeditions on which his ancestor of the same
name (Ixtlilxochitl) accompanied Cortes, mentions one '*Tlapalan*,
a province which lies toward *Ihueras* [Honduras].' "[53] This information clearly suggests the Tabasco-Chiapas-Campeche country which lay in the path of Cortez as he proceeded from the
central mesa of Mexico to Honduras in his great march.[54]

IXTLILXOCHITL'S VIEWPOINT

Ixtlilxochitl directs attention to the Chiapas-Tabasco region
as the probable location of the "seat of the kingdom." In covering the history of Mexico for the tenth and eleventh centuries
A. D., he discussed the flight from Mexico's central mesa of
the great Topiltzin, Tultec king. After suffering a series of
defeats and disasters, Topiltzin decided to flee to *Tlapallan*,
ancient home of his Tultec ancestors. Where did he go? He
went south and east to the Chiapas-Tabasco country, part of Guatemala at the time of the Spanish Conquest. To quote *Ixtlilxochitl*:

Topiltzin left . . . seeing the land [Mexico's central mesa] totally
destroyed, he went to *Tlapallan,* a province that reaches down to the South
Sea [Pacific Ocean], a land very prosperous, rich and well-settled. On
departing for Tlapallan he told his vassals that he was going toward the
rising sun [i.e., eastward from the central mesa], to some kingdoms and
possessions of his ancestors, very prosperous and rich. . . .

Likewise, those *Tultecas* who escaped went down the coasts of the
sea of the South [Pacific] and the sea of the North [Gulf of Mexico] to
Guatemala, Coatzalcoalco, Campeche Tacolotlan, and to the islands and
coasts of the two seas. . . .

---

[52] See *The Book of Mormon*. p. 188 (Mosiah 27:3-4); p. 182 (Mosiah 23:3-4, 24:24-25). From the
highlands of Nephi to the very city of *Zarahemla* was a 21 days' journey.

[53] Bancroft, *op. cit.*, vol. 5, p. 214.

[54] Regarding the march of Cortez to Honduras, and the route traveled, see Sylvanus G. Morley, *Inscrip-
tions of Peten* (1937-1938), vol. 1, Carnegie Institution of Washington, D. C., pub. No. 437;
E. Wylls Andrews, *The Archaeology of Southwestern Campeche* (1943), Carnegie Institution of
Washington, D. C., pub. No. 546.

THE BOOK OF MORMON INDICATES LANDS OF BOUNTIFUL AND ZARAHEMLA WERE JUST SUCH REGIONS AS CHIAPAS-TABASCO COUNTRY

Guatemala and Southern Mexico seem to meet the require-ments of the reconstruction of *Book of Mormon* geography. The South Vera Cruz-Tabasco-Chiapas-Campeche country meets all the requirements of the lands of Bountiful and Zarahemla of *The Book of Mormon*. It is lowland country. It lies adja-cent to an isthmus (Tehuantepec) which has a narrow coastal pass leading into a land of many waters (lakes and streams of Vera Cruz) to the north. It has two great rivers running through it, which rivers have headwaters in highlands to the south (highlands of Guatemala), the latter running east and west, the river running from south to north and emptying into a sea on the north (Gulf of Mexico). Either the Usumacinta or the Grijalva rivers might qualify as the Sidon River of the Nephite record. It has mountains on the south and seas to the north, east and west. It is a very fertile region and a land of abundant and exuberant plantlife and vegetation. And it has the proper dimen-sions, its center being about 200 to 300 miles from the central portion of the highlands to the south. See the map of the area, pages 158-159.

Further, it even has the *seasonal* fevers required by *The Book of Mormon*.[57] Approximately twelve per cent of the deaths in the area are caused by malaria.[58] The region has more rainfall than any other area of Mexico. There is a variation of from 31 to 118 inches of rainfall per year in the region.[59] Because of malaria and other tropical fevers the zone is not heavily popu-lated at the present time.[60] Heat and humidity also tend to keep people from resettling what anciently was the greatest center of population in the New World. "The several rivers which flow northward through the state of Tabasco overflow their banks during the rainy seasons, creating stagnant pools, which serve as breeding grounds for mosquitoes, thus resulting in widespread malaria among the inhabitants."[61]

[57] *The Book of Mormon*, p. 312 (Alma 46:40).
[58] Nathan L. Whetten, *Rural Mexico*, 1948, p. 334.
[59] *Ibid.*, p. 7.
[60] *Ibid.*, pp. 17, 30-31. Population averages about 27 per square mile.
[61] *Ibid.*, p. 17.

Thus in every respect the region seems to meet the requirements of the text of *The Book of Mormon* as regards elevation,
seas, the principal river, mountains to the south, the narrow pass
and seasonal fevers. The extent of the area is just right in terms
of travel times given in Nephite history. Therefore, it may be
said that the geographical data presented in *The Book of Mormon*,
along with the documentary sources, point to the South Vera
Cruz-Tabasco-Chiapas-Campeche area as the locale of ancient
Bountiful-land.

ARCHÆOLOGICAL EVIDENCES

What evidence has been brought forth from the ground?
What has archæology to say on the problem? Have objects of pottery, jade, stone or other materials that could withstand the damp,
humid climate for over 2,000 years been found in the southern
Gulf Coast region and neighboring Chiapas? Have objects signify-
ing high culture and ties with the ancient Near East been found
there? Is there evidence out of the ground of such a culture and
people back as far as 200 B. C. to 350 A. D.,[62] the period of early
Nephite occupation?

The answer to each of the questions is "yes."

Although comparatively little deep digging has been done in
the area, sufficient objects have been found to convince the leading archæologists of Mexico that it was in this very area that
the "mother culture" of ancient Middle America was centered.
They regard it as the center of distribution. Alfonso Caso speaks
for the leaders of the Mexican school of archæology when he says:

. . . a most ancient mother culture . . . is found . . . which spread
from a place, so it appears, that we must locate in the southern part of
Veracruz and in the near-by sections of Tabasco, Oaxaco and Chiapas.[63]

At Tres Zapotes in southern Vera Cruz a monument was
found within the present decade bearing the bar-dot date (i.e., the

---

[62] *The Book of Mormon* has the Mulekites and Nephites in Zarahemla-Bountiful about 200 B. C. Ixtlil-
xochitl has the Tultecs and Ulmecs in there in time for the astronomical conference in 132 B. C.
The Book of Mormon has them in Zarahemla-Bountiful proper until 327-328 A. D. (*The Book of
Mormon*, p. 461, 2:2-3.) The final defeat and banishment occurred 386 A. D., as will be seen.

[63] See Sylvanus G. Morley, *The Ancient Maya*, 1946, p. 42; Matthew W. Stirling, "Discovering the
New World's Oldest Dated Work of Man," *National Geographic*, August, 1939, p. 183 ff. The
Goodman-Thompson-Martinez correlation is now conceded to be correct by virtually all experts.

system the ancient Americans used in writing dates) of 7.16. 6.16.18 or 21 B. C. The first numeral •• (7) is missing and the date is therefore somewhat speculative. However, it is generally regarded as 21 B. C. The Tuxtla jade statuette bears the "Maya" date 8.6.4.2.17 or 162 A. D. It, like the last-mentioned monument, was found in southern Vera Cruz and the date is questioned by some scholars and accepted by others as having been carved on the designated date.

Whatever differences of opinion there are regarding the authenticity and contemporary dating of the aforesaid Tuxtla discoveries, the fact remains that all the experts agree that the system of hieroglyphic writing and dating were in full bloom in 320 A. D., the date appearing on the Leyden Plate found in near-by Guatemala. Thus, even the conservative Morley, who made mounmental contributions to Middle American research, says that the Maya time system must have been devised and in use by the third or fourth century before Christ.[64] He feels, however, that the start was made at Tikal or Uaxactun, about 150 miles to the east of the Usumacinta River and 150 miles north of Quirigua. The distance is not great enough to be very significant. Much digging is yet to be done. The documentary sources are in complete accord with the Mexican archæologists who place the ancient seat of empire in the southern Vera Cruz and Tabasco-Chiapas-Campeche region.

One of the writers participated in excavations in the vicinity of Carmen, Mexico,

Fig. 21: TUXTLA STATUETTE

The man represented in this jade object has his head tilted back. Beneath his nose is what may be a well-groomed beard. This ancient jade piece bears the bar-dot date equal to 162 A. D. It is from San Andres Tuxtla, Vera Cruz, Mexico—not far northwest of the narrow pass on the north side of the Isthmus of Tehuantepec. The date falls within the great era of peace.

[64] Morley, op. cit., p. 44.

on the western side of the Laguna de Terminos in the state of Campeche in the winter of 1948. Pottery, dating about the time of Christ, was found. Chicanel-type pottery, found in the area under general discussion, dates from about 300 B. C. to 317 A. D.[65] Morley lists six dated objects falling within the time span *Ixtlilxochitl* and *The Book of Mormon* allot to the ancient Bountiful-land empire area:

Maya Long Count	Gregorian Equivalent
8.14.0.0.0	317 A. D., September 1
8.14.3.1.12	320 A. D., September 17
8.14.10.13.15	328 A. D., April 11
8.15.0.0.0	337 A. D., May 19
8.16.0.0.0	357 A. D., February 3
8.17.0.0.0	376 A. D., October 21

It is observed that all of these dates occur during the period when, according to *The Book of Mormon,* the Lamanites from the highlands were dominant and had pushed the Nephites from the border lands, which would include the Tikal-Uaxactun area 150 miles to the east of the Usumacinta River. The particular style of hieroglyphic dates and inscriptions found in the typical Old Empire Maya art, beginning with the six mentioned above, are Lamanite if our correlations are correct. (The Goodman-Thompson-Martinez Hernandez correlation is now accepted as correct.) It is suggested that the earlier Tuxtla dates found in the southern Vera Cruz area are authentic Nephite inscriptions. It is further suggested that there is a strong possibility that more deep digging in the territory west of the Usumacinta River will throw support to the views of the Mexican archæologists and to the documentary sources, including *The Book of Mormon,* all of which indicate that the very center and heart of the ancient kingdom of the early settlers extended westerly from the Usumacinta or Grijalva rivers to the Isthmus. The late Sylvannus G. Morley, dean of Maya scholars, wrote shortly before his death that the ancient *Ulmecas* (Olmeca-Xicalanca) "lived at the south of Vera Cruz."[66] Southern Vera Cruz lies between the Grijalva River and the Isthmus of Tehuantepec. The writers have identified the *Ulmec* people as the people of *Mulek.*

65 *Ibid.*, Table IX, opposite p. 392, dates Chicanel from 353 B. C. to 317 A. D.
66 Sylvanus G. Morley and Delia Goetz, *Popol Vuh* (1950), p. 64.

Fig. 22: LEYDEN PLATE

This figure shows both sides of the Leyden Plate, an art object bearing the bar-dot date equivalent to 320 A. D. It was found in Maya-Lamanite territory—Puerto Barrios, Guatemala, in 1864. It is in the typical flamboyant Lamanite style which characterized the art of the era of Lamanite dominance which began about 320 A. D., the very year this object was fashioned.

Covarrubias, speaking the views of the Mexican archæologists, places the LaVenta (Tabasco) site within the period from
200 B. C. to 300 A. D., thus corroborating the documentary
sources which proclaim the same early occupation of the southern
Gulf Coast region. At La Venta was found the carving of a
statue of a man which reminds one of the usual portrayal of
"Uncle Sam." This figure had a full beard and aquiline nose and
represented a person that Covarrubias described as having "sur-
prisingly pronounced Semitic features."[67] See pages 133-134. Also
found at the site was a distinctly different physical type: baby-
faced, of Mongoloid appearance.

The present state of archæological knowledge regarding the
area suggested as the "seat of the kingdom" for the period from
200 B. C. to 328 A. D. may be summarized by quoting Covarrubias:

As a result of somewhat feverish investigation and research, central
Mexico on the one hand and the Yucatan Peninsula on the other have
been rather thoroughly studied by the scientists, artists, sociologists, and
plain tourists. But in this mass of information and interpretation there is
virtually nothing · about the immensely important narrow strip of land
that is the bridge between these two regions: the Isthmus of Tehuantepec.[68]

Everywhere there are archæological treasures that lie hidden in the
jungles and under the rich soil of southern Vera Cruz, burial mounds and
pyramids, masterfully carved colossal monuments of basalt, splendid statuettes of precious jade, and sensitively modeled figurines of clay, all of an
unprecedented, high artistic quality. The tantalizing presence of a great
and remote past in what is now uninhabited, impenetrable jungle is all the
more puzzling because most archæologists now agree that many of these
artistic masterpieces date back to the beginnings of the Christian era.
Appearing suddenly out of nowhere in a state of full development, they
constitute a culture that seems to have been the root, the mother culture,
from which the later and better-known (Maya, Totonac, Zapotec, etc.)
cultures sprang.

This oldest of native American high cultures is also the newest, since
it was "discovered" only a few years ago and still awaits exhaustive scientific study.[69]

What a lot is said in those short paragraphs!

[67] Covarrubias, op. cit., p. 90.
[68] Covarrubias, ibid., p. xxii.
[69] Ibid., pp. 79-80.

Conclusions

It may be safely said that numerous reliable documentary sources,[70] including *Ixtlilxochitl* and *The Book of Mormon,* are in close accord in placing the seat of the ancient Bountiful-land kingdom and culture in the lowlands of the southern Gulf Coast region of Mexico. The region may be more particularly described as including southern Vera Cruz, all of Tabasco, western Campeche, the northeastern half of Chiapas and the most southerly corner of Oaxaca. Further, although but very little digging has been done in the area, the latest archæological findings support the documentary sources, both as to locale and as to time. The early period of occupation, 200 B. C. to 350 A. D., is also confirmed.

The principal occupants of the region in early time are variously identified: *Chans* "serpents"; early *Nahuas* "Nephites"; *Tultecs* "Bountiful people"; early *Tutulxius* "Zarahemla people"; *Itzas* "Disciples of *Itzamna,*" "Christians, holy men"; *Tzequils* "people who wore long robes or petticoats like the ancient Semites" and shoes with "odd pointed upturned toes" (see Figure 14). They were a white people with Semitic noses, and the men were bearded. The physical characteristics of these people will be dealt with later on.

---

[70] It is clear that both Tultec and Maya documentary sources came down from other older literary works. They are historical and not merely traditional. Generally speaking, the transmitters were competent and had good historical sense. As more and more work is done with the documentary sources, it becomes more and more apparent that they are consistent with each other, regardless of completely independent origin in many cases. Also, they are being confirmed by dirt archæology. For a scholarly discussion of the authenticity and reliability of Maya accounts, see M. Wells Jakeman, *The Origins and History of the Mayas,* 1945, Chapters 5 and 6.

Chapter 14

COLONIZATION OF AREA NORTH OF ISTHMUS— LAND NORTHWARD—55 B. C.-17 A. D.

INTRODUCTORY STATEMENT

The Book of Mormon contains some very specific statements concerning colonists who are said to have gone out from the lands of Bountiful and Zarahemla to settle territory to the north. The land route was by way of a "narrow pass which led by the sea into the land northward, yea, by the sea, on the west and on the east." This movement began in 55 B. C. Sixty-two years later the colonists were all called back to Bountiful-Zarahemla.

The story told in this chapter of colonizing the land north-ward is based on the geography suggested in Chapter 13, which geography was presented merely as a possible answer to the problems involved in that study. Since a possible location of the lands of Bountiful and Zarahemla, as pointed out in the previous chap-ter, could have been in Chiapas-Tabasco country adjacent to the Isthmus of Tehuantepec, a problem arises with respect to certain claims made in *The Book of Mormon.* If one proceeds northerly from the region identified as ancient Tullan or Bountiful, does he find a "narrow pass which led *by the sea* into the land northward"? And beyond that pass does he find a "land of many waters" bearing evidence of occupation between 55 B. C. and 17 A. D., and is that "land of many waters" relatively near the Isthmus—for there was shipping and traffic between "the seat of the kingdom" and the newly colonized zone, and the colonizers were called back to Zarahemla in 17 A. D.? And is there any archæological evidence in the vicinity of the "land of many waters" of remains left by the Ancient Ones—Jaredites, who allegedly lived in the general region in very, very early times?

Ixtlilxochitl has nothing to say concerning land settling in the region north of the Isthmus of Tehauntepec during the half-century immediately preceding the birth of Christ. However, the Nephite record gives some interesting details on the matter which are supported by recent archæological discoveries. There-fore, a brief discussion of the colonizing of this region is given herein.

From the time of the arrival of the Nephites in the lands of Bountiful and Zarahemla, about 200 B. C., down to 55 B. C., no settlements were established in the territory north of the "narrow neck of land." Of course the Jaredites were living in their land of Moron, probably located somewhere between the Panuco River on the north and Tehuantepec on the south, for many centuries prior to their destruction about 300 B. C. And the Mulekites may have lived for a time between Panuco and Tehuantepec (for how long The Book of Mormon does not state), but in a state of illiteracy. The literate Nephite-Mulekite nation began colonizing north (actually west and north or north-west) of the Isthmus in 55 B. C. The colonial program came to an abrupt halt in 17 B. C.

The following extracts from The Book of Mormon contain the pertinent statements regarding the colonial work carried on during the period under discussion:

And it came to pass that in the thirty and seventh year of the reign of the judges, there was a large company of men, even to the amount of five thousand and four hundred men with their wives and their children, departed out of the land of Zarahemla into the land which was northward. [About 55 B. C.][1]

On page 132 a quotation appears from The Book of Mormon in which Hagoth's activities as a ship builder and the migration of many people by ship to the land northward are presented.[2] These events took place in 55 and 54 B. C. The Nephite record also states:

And it came to pass that in this year there were many people who went forth into the land northward. And thus ended the thirty and eighth year [54 B. C.][3]

[1] The Book of Mormon, p. 358 (Alma 63:4). Apparently a land journey by way of the Narrow Pass by the sea (Gulf of Mexico).
[2] Ibid., p. 358 (Alma 63:5-6). Apparently a journey up the Pacific side.
[3] Ibid., p. 358 (Alma 63:7-9). It has been suggested that these vessels may have wound up in some island or islands in the Pacific Ocean—possibly Hawaii.

And it came to pass in the thirty and ninth year of the reign of the judges . . . Corianton had gone forth to the land northward in a ship, to carry forth provisions unto the people who had gone forth into that land. [53 B. C.][4]

And it came to pass in the forty and sixth year [of the reign of Judges], there was much contention and many dissensions in the which there were an exceeding great many who departed out of the land of Zarahemla, and went forth unto the land northward to inherit the land. And they did travel to an exceeding great distance, insomuch that they came to large bodies of water and many rivers. Yea, and even they did spread forth into all parts of the land, into whatever parts it had not been rendered desolate and without timber, because of the many inhabitants who had before inherited the land. And now no part of the land was desolate, save it were for timber; but because of the greatness of the destruction of the people who had before inhabited the land it was called desolate. [Thus, the land "Desolation" was named.] And there being but little timber upon the face of the land, nevertheless the people who went forth became exceeding expert in the work of cement; therefore they did build houses of cement, in the which to dwell. [46 B. C.][5]

And it came to pass that they did multiply and spread, and did go forth from the land southward to the land northward, and did spread insomuch that they began to cover the face of the whole earth, from the sea south to the sea north, from the sea west to the sea east. And the people who were in the land northward did dwell in tents, and in houses of cement, and they did suffer whatsoever tree should spring up upon the face of the land that it should grow up, that in time they might have timber to build their houses, yea their cities, and their temples, and their synagogues, and their sanctuaries, and all manner of buildings. [About· 46 B. C.][6]

And it came to pass as timber was exceedingly scarce in the land northward, they did send forth much by way of shipping. And thus they did enable the people in the land northward that they might build many cities, both of wood and of cement. And it came to pass that there were many people of Ammon, who were Lamanites by birth, did also go forth into this land. [About 46 B. C.][7]

And the Nephites and the armies of Moronihah were driven even into the land of Bountiful; And there they did fortify against the Lamanites, *from the west sea, even unto the east* [Note: No reference is made to an east "sea."]; it became a day's journey for a Nephite, on the line which they had fortified and stationed their armies to defend their north country. And thus those dissenters of the Nephites, with the help of a numerous army of the Lamanites, had obtained all the possessions of the Nephites which was in the land southward. [About 34 B. C.][8]

[4] *Ibid.*, p. 358 (Alma 63:10).
[5] *Ibid.*, pp. 363-364 (Helaman 3:3-7). The area referred to may well be central Vera Cruz.
[6] *Ibid.*, p. 364 (Helaman 3:8-9).
[7] *Ibid.*, p. 364 (Helaman 3:10-12).
[8] *Ibid.*, p. 367 (Helaman 4:6-8).

And it came to pass that many of the Lamanites did go into the land northward; and also Nephi and Lehi went into the land northward, to preach unto the people. [About 28 B. C.][9]

. . . they became exceeding rich, both the Lamanites and the Nephites; and they did have an exceeding plenty of gold, and of silver, and of all manner of precious metals, both in the land south and in the land north. Now the land south was called Lehi, and the land north was called Mulek, which was after the son of Zedekiah; for the Lord did bring Mulek into the land north; and Lehi into the land south. And behold, there was all manner of gold in both these lands, and of silver, and of precious ore of every kind; and there were also curious workmen, who did raise grain in abundance, both in the north and in the south; and they did flourish exceedingly, both in the north and in the south. [About 27 B. C.][10]

Behold, now it came to pass in the sixty and ninth year of the reign of judges over the Nephites, that Nephi, the son of Helaman, returned to the land of Zarahemla from the land northward. For he had been forth among the people who were in the land northward, and did preach the work of God unto them. . . . And they did reject all his words, insomuch that he could not stay among them, but returned again unto the land of his nativity. [23 B. C.][11]

[The Nephites] had all gone forth to the place which had been appointed that they should gather themselves together, to defend them-selves against their enemies. And the land which was appointed was the land of Zarahemla and the land Bountiful, yea, to the line which was between the land Bountiful and the land Desolation. And there were a great many thousand people who were called Nephites, who did gather themselves together in this land. *Now Lachoneus did cause that they should gather themselves together in the land southward, because of the great curse which was upon the land northward. And they did fortify themselves against their enemies; and they did dwell in one land, and in one body.* . . . [About 17 A. D.][12]

LINE OF NEPHITE FORTIFICATIONS

In the Book of Alma a description is given of the division line between the Nephites' Bountiful-land and Desolation, the latter having been the ancient Jaredite homeland. To quote:

And now, it was only the distance of a day and a half's journey for a Nephite, on the line Bountiful and the land Desolation *from the east to the west sea;* and thus the land of Nephi and the Land of Zara-hemla were nearly surrounded by water, there being a small neck of land between the land northward and the land southward.[13]

[9] *Ibid.*, p. 373 (Helaman 6:6).
[10] *Ibid.*, p. 373 (Helaman 6:9-12).
[11] *Ibid.*, p. 376 (Helaman 7:1-3).
[12] *Ibid.*, p. 405 (3 Nephi 3:22-25). All colonizers return to Zarahemla-Bountiful.
[13] *Ibid.*, p. 254 (Alma 22:32).

The "line" referred to here was a fortified line—a line of fortified posts. This line extended from the Pacific Ocean at the Isthmus of Tehuantepec in a general easterly direction a distance of probably ten to thirty miles. That the line did not extend completely across the Isthmus is apparent from the foregoing quotation and also from the reference to this "line" in the Book of Helaman, also recently quoted. To repeat the latter statement: "And the Nephites and the armies of Moronihah were driven even into the land of Bountiful; and there they did fortify against the Lamanites *from the west sea, even unto the east;* it being day's journey for a Nephite, on the line which they had fortified and stationed their armies to defend their north country."

There is nothing in the record to indicate that the line extended easterly to "an east sea." The western terminus, however, was at the "west sea." Support for this view comes not only from careful reading of the text but from the physical facts—it would be physically impossible to cross from the Pacific to the Atlantic in a day or a day and a half at either Tehuantepec or Panama. The former is 125 miles wide and the latter is 50 miles wide. A line of forts extending easterly from the Pacific at Tehuantepec would serve as a barrier to an enemy trying to proceed northward across Tehuantepec from the Guatemala highlands of the early "Nahua-Mayas." See one of the maps.

COLONIES WERE NOT FAR NORTH OF THE NARROW NECK OF LAND

In 17 A. D., the governor, Lachoneus, called all of the colonists back into the Bountiful-land region. This would seem to indicate that the area that had been colonized during the preceding seventy-two years was relatively near the Bountiful-land zone, being northward and in close proximity to the Narrow Neck of Land.

With regard to the new colonies to the north, Helaman, a Nephite historian, reported about 29 B. C., that the Nephites in the land north had found plenty of gold and silver. He also made the following statement:

Now the land south [of narrow neck of land] was called Lehi, and the land north was called Mulek, which was after the son of Zedekiah;

for the Lord did bring Mulek into the land north, and Lehi into the land south. And behold, there was all manner of gold in *both* these lands, and of silver, and of precious ore of every kind; and there were also curious workmen, who did work all kinds of ore and did refine it; and thus they did become rich. They did raise grain in abundance, both in *the north* and in the south; and they did flourish exceedingly, both in the *north* and in the south. And they did multiply and wax exceedingly strong in the land. And they did raise many flocks and herds, yea, many fatlings. Behold, their women did toil and spin, and did make all manner of cloth, of fine-twined linen and cloth of every kind, to clothe their nakedness.[14]

Prior Nephite-Mulekite Knowledge of Land Northward

The Nephites not only referred to the "land north" as Mulek but they also often called it "the land of Desolation." As an example, the following is quoted from *The Book of Mormon:*

> Bountiful [located just south of the narrow neck of land] bordered upon the land which they called Desolation, it [Desolation] being so far northward [from Bountiful-land] that it came into the land which had been peopled and [which people had] been destroyed, of whose bones we have spoken, which was discovered by the people of Zarahemla [Mulekites], it being the place of their first landing. And they [the Mulekites] came from there up into the south wilderness [Bountiful-land].[15]

It is recalled from Chapter 12 that somewhere in the land northwest, resettled from 55 B. C.-17 A. D., the Mulekites had discovered Coriantumr, a surviving Jaredite leader, some time around 300 B. C. He lived for nine months with them after they had discovered him.[16] Inasmuch as the Mulekites were a comparatively illiterate people prior to their association with the Nephites in Bountiful-Zarahemla, the Nephites probably learned but little from them concerning Jaredite history in the northern area.[17]

In addition to what the Mulekites were able to tell the Nephites concerning the northern lands, the latter people may have learned something on the subject from the large stela, or inscribed stone, that was left by Coriantumr.

[14] *Ibid.*, p. 373 (Helaman 6:9-13).
[15] *Ibid.*, p. 254 (Alma 22:30-31).
[16] *Ibid.*, p. 131 (Omni 21); p. 504 (Ether 13:21).
[17] *Ibid.*, p. 130 (Omni 17).

The additional source of information possessed by the Nephites concerning the northern outpost country prior to the colonizations of 55 B. C. was, apparently, the Book of Ether which was discovered by a party of scouts about 121 B. C. The Book of Ether is a summation of the history of the Jaredites, "Ancient Ones," who occupied a region north of the "narrow neck of land" for many centuries. This occupation lasted for approximately 2,500 years to a date prior to 200 B. C. It gives some information concerning the northern region into which the Nephites expanded, commencing in 55 B. C.

EXPEDITION OF LIMHI'S SCOUTS, 122 B. C.-121 B. C.

A brief discussion of the travels of Limhi's scouts will be pertinent at this point in connection with the discussion of the Nephites' northern land-settlement program, because those travels assist in locating the area colonized during the period commencing in 55 B. C.

In 122 B. C.-121 B. C. King Limhi, a just man, was king of a small Nephite colony located in the southern highlands— that is, in the land of Nephi. His domain was confined to the city or town of Nephi and a suburb, Shilom, and its environs. His was really a city-state, isolated in hostile Lamanite territory. He and his followers were virtual prisoners and the oppression had become unbearable. Limhi longed to lead his people back to the city of Zarahemla. However, there had been no communication with the land of Zarahemla for over two generations and Limhi knew only that the city of Zarahemla lay to the north. He therefore sent a party of forty-three men northward in search of said city.

The destination of the party, Zarahemla, actually lay approximately 200 miles north of the starting point. It was a twenty-one days' journey for a party of men, women and children, together with their gear.[18]

The important thing about this expedition, as regards the northern colonizations of the Nephites, is that the party traveled northward—by-passing the city of Zarahemla, crossed the "narrow neck of land," and went into the land northward to the very region colonized in 55 B. C. When the members of the

---

[18] *Ibid.*, p. 178 (Mosiah 23:1-4, 19); p. 185 (Mosiah 24:24-25). Forty-nine days were required by the sixteen "strong men" of Mosiah II. See *Ibid.*, p. 147 (Mosiah 7:2-6, 13-14).

expedition arrived in the locale, they mistakenly supposed it to be Zarahemla. They found the bleak ruins of the Jaredites in the "land of many waters" and supposed that Zarahemla had been destroyed.[19] This gives some idea of how close the Jaredite land of many waters was to the "narrow neck of land." All of this tends to show that these northern colonies, which were settled by Nephites from Bountiful-land (commencing in 55 B. C.), were in close proximity to the "narrow neck of land."

It stands to reason that in the seventy-two years, from 55 B. C. to 17 A. D., during which the northern colonies were first settled and then abandoned, no very extensive territory could be colonized. The extent of the territory actually settled during that period becomes important when one begins checking against what has come from the ground as a result of the diggings of archæologists. It must be admitted, however, that compara-tively little digging has been done by archæologists in the area immediately north and west of ancient Bountiful-land. Covar-rubias makes that point clear in the statement quoted heretofore in Chapter 13.

The Book of Mormon furnishes other clues indicating the nearness of the northern colonies to the Isthmus. Some of them are as follows: the Jaredite homeland, resettled by the colonists from Bountiful-land, was so near the "narrow neck" that their flocks fled "towards the land southward, which was called by the Nephites Zarahemla";[20] Jaredites hunted for game in Boun-tiful-land;[21] and it was shown in the quotations set forth above that the colonists in the "land northward" received provisions, lumber and missionaries from Bountiful-land. All of these factors indicate nearness of the two lands to each other. Later on it will be shown that Mormon, abridger of the Nephite records, was born in these northern colonies (the colonies having been reoccupied after 17 A. D.) and traveled from there to Zara-hemla when but a child of eleven years of age.[22]

THE NARROW PASS

Still further help is given in the Nephite record in deter-mining the approximate location of the northern colonies. The region to the north was most accessible by way of a "narrow

[19] Ibid, pp. 174-176 (Mosiah, ch. 21), and pp. 150-151 Mosiah 8:7-11).
[20] Ibid., p. 495 (Ether 9:31-33); p. 489 (Ether 7:5-6).
[21] Ibid., p. 497 (Ether 10:19-21).
[22] Ibid., p. 460 (Mormon 1:1-6); p. 493 (Ether 9:3) locates Shim near the land-of-many-waters.

pass" running east and west along a seashore at the narrow neck of land. This narrow pass is mentioned four times in the record as follows:

... the *narrow pass* which led by the sea into the land northward, yea, by the sea, on the west and on the east, ...[23]
... the *narrow pass* which led into the land northward....[24]
... the *narrow passage* which led into the land southward....[25]
... the *narrow pass* which led into the land southward ...[26]

At the Isthmus of Tehuantepec, adjacent to ancient Hue-hue-Tlapallan (ancient Bountiful-land), is a narrow pass meeting all the requirements of the pass referred to by the Nephite historians. It is on the Gulf of Mexico side of Tehuantepec. One of the writers studied and photographed it from a Cub airplane in 1948.[27] It runs by the sea for about seventy miles in a general northwesterly-southeasterly direction. The seashore pass is between the Gulf on the one hand and the high Tuxtla Mountains on the other. The pass is but a few yards wide in some places. The dense vegetation that covers the mountains extends to the narrow beach which constitutes the pass. It is described as a "narrow coastal plain" by Oliver G. Ricketsen Jr., in one of his reports in the Carnegie Institution of Washington, D. C. series. His statement clearly explains the significance of the "narrow pass"—the only land avenue of migration open to the north from the ancient "Seat of the Kingdom":

The ancient Maya [and this would apply equally well to the pre-Maya Nephite-Tultec-Ulmec peoples of greater Bountiful-land], therefore, would seem to have enjoyed a location as nearly free from foreign attack as is ever given to any people, the only two migration avenues to threaten them being *the narrow coastal plain along the north side of the Isthmus of Tehuantepec* or the still more narrow Ulua Valley to the south [in Honduras]. Their kinsfolk in the highlands probably regarded the lowland heat as intolerable. Forests and swamps would further discourage concerted movements in that direction. But if migrations did flow down, en masse, the invaders differed only as Spartans differed from Athenians. Once the ancient Maya [and the pre-Maya beforehand] were securely settled in the lowlands, acclimated, and peaceably established (at least within large tribal units scattered over a fertile plain and no longer hemmed into small valleys by abrupt mountains), it is not astound-

---

[23] *Ibid.*, p. 323 (Alma 50:34). This indicates the shoreline ran east-west at the pass, as does the shoreline at Coatzalcoalcos, Tehuantepec.
[24] *Ibid.*, p. 328 (Alma 52:9).
[25] *Ibid.*, p. 463 (Mormon 2:29).
[26] *Ibid.*, p. 464 (Mormon 3:5).
[27] The pass or narrow coastal plain is clearly shown on the Millionth Maps of the American Geographical Society and on the Air Force maps mentioned in Chapter 13.

ing that they, free from foreign attack, should have relegated war to a position of secondary importance and have devoted their efforts to the development of art and architecture. Only a people in harmony with their environment and at peace with their neighbors could leave behind them monuments such as those found on the Yucatan peninsula.[28]

In the same paragraph and immediately preceding the foregoing quotation, Ricketson refers to the "ring of belligerent highland peoples at the base of the Yucatan peninsula." His terminology and descriptions are intended to refer to the period of Maya dominance—that is, the Lamanite era or post-Book-of-Mormon epoch that followed the proto-Maya or Nephite-Tultec-Ulmec period dealt with here. During much of the period of Nephite dominance in the land of Bountiful, from 200 B. C. to 322 A. D., the highland peoples of the base of the Bountiful-land area formed a belligerent crescent on the south and on the east and west. That crescent-ring is described in *The Book of Mormon* as follows:

And it came to pass that the king [of the Lamanites] sent a proclamation throughout all the land, amongst all his people who were in all his land, who were in all the regions round about, which was bordering even to the sea, on the east and on the west, and which was divided from the land of Zarahemla by a narrow strip of wilderness, which ran from the sea east even to the sea west, and round about on the borders of the seashore, and the borders of the wilderness which was on the north by the land of Zarahemla, through the borders of Manti, by the head of the river Sidon, running from the east towards the west—and thus were the Lamanites and the Nephites divided.

Now, the more idle part of the Lamanites lived in the wilderness, and dwelt in tents; and they were spread through the wilderness on the west, in the land of Nephi; yea, and also on the west of the land of Zarahemla, in the borders by the seashore, and on the west in the land of Nephi, in the place of their fathers' first inheritance, and thus bordering along by the seashore.

And also there were many Lamanites on the east by the seashore, whither the Nephites had driven them. And thus the Nephites were nearly surrounded by the Lamanites; . . .[29]

Thus, it is seen that the narrow pass at Tehuantepec meets all the requirements of the Nephite account, being at the sea-shore and running in a somewhat east-west direction. The area to the east of the pass, the Tabasco-Chiapas-Peten area meets all the topographical requirements of Bountiful-Zarahemla, a low-

---

[28] Oliver G. Ricketson Jr., *Uaxactun, Guatemala, Group E, 1926-1931*, Publication 447, Carnegie Institution of Washington, D. C., 1937, pp. 14-15.
[29] *The Book of Mormon*, pp. 253-254 (Alma 22:27-29), The quotation dates from about 90 B. C.

land area surrounded by seas on the north, east and west and by a ring of highlands. What could be said of the country to the north of the Tehuantepec pass? According to the Nephite account, as one proceeded northward from the narrow pass a land was encountered variously described as follows:

... *a land among many waters;*[30]
... *a land covered with large bodies of water;*[31]
... *a land of large bodies of water and many rivers;*[32]
... *a land of many waters, rivers and fountains;*[33]

Fig. 23: LAKES, RIVERS, AND LAGOONS OF VERA CRUZ, MEXICO

An air photo by Thomas S. Ferguson of the lakes, rivers and lagoons near the coast of central Vera Cruz—ancient Anahuac, a "land of many waters."

As one proceeds northward beyond the narrow pass on the Gulf Coast of Mexico, the coastline takes a swing westward just beyond the Tuxtla Mountains. The coastline runs in an east-west line for about thirty-five miles and then takes a swing northward. In that area is a region of lakes, rivers, lagoons and rivulets. Alvarado and Tlatocalpan are the principal towns in the area. The region has been described by Miguel Covarrubias in these words:

Alvarado is a sleepy, decaying port of fishermen out on the very tip of one of the two narrow tongues of land that close off the sea from the intricate system of lagoons, rivulets, and marshes where many great rivers

---

[30] *Ibid.*, p. 150 (Mosiah 8:8).
[31] *Ibid.*, p. 323 (Alma 50:29).
[32] *Ibid.*, p. 363 (Helaman 3:4).
[33] *Ibid.*, p. 469 (Mormon 6:4).

empty their waters—the Papaloapan, "River of Butterflies," the Tesechoacan, Rio de San Juan, Rio Hondo, Rio Blanco, and many others. These
rivers descend from the high sierras of Oaxaca and Puebla, far from each
other, beginning as ordinary mountain streams that worm their way down
the slopes, growing constantly, all toward a single objective, into the vast
jungle plains of southern Vera Cruz, winding and twisting, forming
islands and lagoons, overflowing into great swamps filled with white
herons. This swampy region, known as La Mixtequilla or Sotavento, "Lee-
ward," rich in cattle and agricultural land—growing the minute black
beans that make Vera Cruz famous, corn, chili peppers, and sugar cane—
is a definite unit, with a fascinating character and personality of its own.[34]

The Tuxtla mountains rise out of the plains containing the
"large bodies of water and many rivers" just described. There

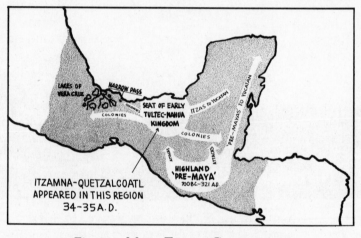

Fig. 24: Map—Tultec Colonization

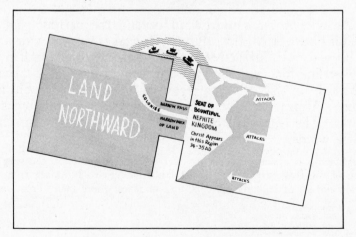

Fig. 25: Nephite Colonization

are two prominent peaks in these mountains, San Martin (4,920 feet) and Santa Maria (4,800 feet). The description given by Covarrubias of the mountain area is also noteworthy:

Out of the plains of southern Vera Cruz rises the range of Los Tuxtlas, an imposing cluster of volcanoes forming a gigantic bowl of rich, dark earth blanketed with luscious tropical vegetation, crisscrossed by rushing rivers and studded with waterfalls [fountains] and calm volcanic lakes.[35] . . . the town[San Andres Tuxtla, population 24,000] is perched up high in a deep valley in a ring of velvety green mountains—a land of unprecedented fertility, watered in all directions by streams, waterfalls and lakes.[36]

Evidence seems to indicate that the foregoing described area is a region which meets all the geographical requirements of the Nephites' "land northward," including the narrow pass by the seashore to the south, which pass divided the land northward from the "ancient Seat of the Kingdom."

ARCHÆOLOGY OF THE AREA

A check will now be made against the discoveries of archæologists in the area suggested as the territory colonized from 55 B. C. to 17 A. D. Is there any evidence of settlement that early by the highly cultured early Semitic Nephite people?

The earliest dated work of man yet discovered in the New World was found January 16, 1939, in this "land of many waters" very near Tuxtla Mountains. It bears an Ulmec (Olmec-Nahuale) jaguar mask and a very early date believed to be 31 B. C., almost directly in the middle of the period under discussion. Apparently the monument was carved a few years after the colonizers settled "the land northward." It would be pointed out that if the monument bore a Maya inscription date earlier than 55 B. C. we would have a real problem on our hands, for according to the Nephite account, there were no Nephite-Lamanite settlers from Bountiful-land in the area north of the narrow pass prior to 55 B. C. The Mulekites had been in the area earlier, but they were illiterate until they were joined by the Nephites in Zarahemla below Tehuantepec. No dated Jaredite monuments have been found—i.e., none bearing calendrical dates.[37]

---

[34] Miguel Covarrubias, Mexico South—The Isthmus of Tehuantepec, 1946, pp. 10-11.
[35] Ibid., p. 22.
[36] Ibid., p. 27.
[37] However, figurines and other ceramics having a resemblance to ceramics from lower Mesopotamian Early Dynastic period have been found at Zacatenco, near Mexico City. Charcoal from this site has recently been dated well within the Jaredite-Quinametzin period—having been dated at 1450 B. C. by the newly discovered Radio-Carbon-14 dating system. Another important archæological site near Mexico City, El Arbolillo, dates from the same Jaredite era. See M. Wells Jakeman, "The XXIXth International Congress of Americanists," in Bulletin of the University Archaeological Society (Brigham Young University, May, 1950), pp. 26-33.

SUMMARY STATEMENT

The Nephite record declares that between 55 B. C. and 17 A. D. the cultured Nephite-Mulekite people sent out colonizers from Bountiful-Zarahemla into the area northerly from the "seat of the kingdom." Some went by sea up the west coast. Others went by land, crossing the "narrow neck of land" by way of a narrow pass that led into the land northward where there were many streams and lakes.

Southern Vera Cruz meets all the requirements of *The Book of Mormon* as regards those colonists who went by way of land. The archæological remains are in the right place for the very period involved. A "narrow neck of land" lies between ancient Bountiful-Zarahemla (Tulan-Tutulxiu) and a land of lakes and rivers. A narrow pass by the sea, said pass running in a general east-west direction, leads directly into a land of many waters. See map at page 186. Within 200 miles of the Tuxtla-land-of-waters country of southern Vera Cruz have been found artifacts dating at 1450 B. C. which are surely those of "the Ancient Ones," or Jaredites, a people whom our two primary accounts state had once lived in the "land northward" to which the colonizers of 55 B. C. journeyed.[38]

Again it appears that technical and detailed statements found in the Nephite record receive equally technical corroboration from facts learned only recently through scholastic research.

Fig. 26: TRES ZAPOTE DATED STELA

This stone bears a bar-dot date falling very shortly after the birth of Jesus Christ. Stela was recently discovered at Tres Zapotes in the land of lakes, streams and lagoons of Vera Cruz, Mexico.

[38] See the last preceding note, 37.

Chapter 15

AT THE TIME OF THE CRUCIFIXION

INTRODUCTORY STATEMENT

The quotations from the *Works of Ixtlilxochitl* and *The Book of Mormon* used in this brief chapter are remarkably similar. *Ixtlilxochitl* and *The Book of Mormon* agree—almost to the very day—upon the calendar time of the crucifixion of Jesus. Further, they are in close accord on the events which took place in the Bountiful-land country of the Ulmecas-Nahuales—Mulekites-Nephites at the time of the crucifixion in Palestine. Among other things, *Ixtlilxochitl* refers to the eclipse of "the *sun* and the *moon*"—*The Book of Mormon* says the people saw "neither the *sun*, nor the *moon*, nor the *stars*."

Ixtlilxochitl says "*and the earth trembled, and the rocks broke*"—*The Book of Mormon* says "*it did shake the whole earth as if it was about to divide asunder . . . And behold, the rocks were rent in twain; they were broken* up upon the face of the whole earth, insomuch that they were found in broken fragments, and in seams and in cracks, upon all the face of the land."

The reader is to be reminded that, since the Catholic missionaries knew nothing regarding the calamities that occurred in America at the time of Christ's crucifixion, *Ixtlilxochitl* would necessarily have obtained the information for his history through the channels he claimed, i.e., from the tradition of his people—Indian descendants of the ancient Lamanites.

The only variance between the two accounts is in regard to human casualties. *Ixtlilxochitl* says there were none. *The Book of Mormon* says there were many who perished.

XLIV. WHEN CHRIST OUR LORD SUFFERED

Ixtlilxochitl is here correlating the ancient Mexican calendar with New Testament history, having learned the latter from the Catholic missionaries and soldiers in Mexico. The correlations and parallels between his account and *The Book of Mormon* on the events which occurred on the fourth day of the month in 34 A. D., *"when Christ our Lord suffered,"* are very striking, to say the least. *Ixtlilxochitl* double checks his date, stating it was 166 years since the calendar was corrected and adjusted at the great council meeting. That meeting was held in 132 B. C., as has been shown. Thus 166 years after 132 B. C. is the year 34 A. D. His other check, "270 years since the *Ancient Ones* had been destroyed," also conforms. *Ixtlilxochitl's* chronology indicates that the descendants of the settlers from the Great Tower met their fourth and final calamity in 236 B. C., and 270 years thereafter falls at 34 A. D.

IXTLILXOCHITL:

Calamities at time of crucifixion of Christ

It was 166 years since they had adjusted their years and times with the equinox, and 270 since the ancient ones had been destroyed, when *the sun and the moon eclipsed,* and the earth trembled, and the rocks broke, and many other things and signs took place, although there was no calamity whatever toward men. This happened in the year of *ce Calli,* which, adjusting this count with ours, comes to be *at the same time when Christ our Lord suffered,*[XLIV &XLV] and they say it happened during the first days of the year.[XLVI] These and many other things the Tultecas comprehended, from the creation of the world up to our times. As I have said, in order to avoid prolixity all things they knew are not set out according as they appear in their histories and pictures, especially the original, I mean all the things which can be found in pictures and history, for everything is abridgment (contraction) in comparison with the histories that the first archbishop of Mexico ordered burned.

* * *

A few days after he [Quetzalcoatl] went from there, *the destruction and desolation*[XLV] related of the third age of the world took place, and then was destroyed that memorable and

EXTRACTS—BOOK OF MORMON:

Calamities at the time of Christ's crucifixion[1]

5. And it came to pass in the thirty and fourth year, in the first month, on the fourth day of the month [from the time of the sign of the birth of Christ], there arose a great storm, such an one as never had been known in all the land.[XLVI]

6. And there was also a great and terrible tempest; and there was terrible thunder, insomuch that it did shake the whole earth as if it was about to divide asunder.

7. And there were exceeding sharp lightnings, such as never had been known in all the land.

8. And the city of Zarahemla did take fire.

9. And the city of Moroni did sink into the depths of the sea, and the inhabitants thereof were drowned.

10. And the earth was carried up upon the city of Moronihah, that in the place of the city there became a great mountain.

11. And there was a great and terrible destruction in the land southward.

12. But behold, there was a more great and terrible destruction in the land northward; for behold, the whole face of the land was changed, because of the tempest and the whirlwinds, and the thunderings and the lightnings, and the exceeding great quaking of the whole earth;

13. And the highways were broken up, and the level roads were spoiled, and many smooth places became rough.

14. And many great and notable cities were sunk, and many were burned, and many were shaken till the buildings thereof had fallen to the earth, and the inhabitants thereof were slain, and the places were left desolate.

15. And there were some cities which remained; but the damage thereof was exceeding

sumptuous building and tower in the city of *Cholula,* which was like another tower of Babel, which these people were building almost with the same designs, it being destroyed by the wind. And later those who escaped the extermination of the third age built a temple on its ruins to *Quetzalcoatl,* whom they placed as *god of wind,* because the wind was the cause of its destruction, they understanding that this calamity was sent by his hand; and they likewise called it *ce Acatl,* which was the name of the year of his coming. *And, as it seems through the mentioned histories and annals, the aforementioned happened some years after the Incarnation of Christ our Lord.*[XLV]

great, and there were many in them who were slain.

16. And there were some who were carried away in the whirlwind; and whither they went no man knoweth, save they know that they were carried away.

17. And thus the face of the whole earth became deformed, because of the tempests, and the thunderings, and the lightnings, and the quaking of the earth.

18. And behold, the rocks were rent in twain; they were broken up upon the face of the whole earth, insomuch that they were found in broken fragments, and in seams and in cracks, upon all the face of the land.

19. And it came to pass that when the thunderings, and the lightnings, and the storm, and the tempest, and the quakings of the earth did cease—for behold, they did last for about the space of three hours; and it was said by some that the time was greater; nevertheless, all these great and terrible things were done in about the space of three hours—and then behold, there was darkness upon the face of the land.

20. And it came to pass that there was thick darkness upon all the face of the land, insomuch that the inhabitants thereof who had not fallen could feel the vapor of darkness;

21. And there could be no light, because of the darkness, neither candles, neither torches, neither could there be fire kindled with their fine and exceedingly dry wood, so that there could not be any light at all;

22. And there was not any light seen, neither fire, nor glimmer, neither the sun, nor the moon, nor the stars, for so great were the mists of darkness which were upon the face of the land.

23. And it came to pass that it did last for the space of three days that there was no light seen; and there was great mourning and howling and weeping among all the people continually; yea, great were the groanings of the people, because of the darkness and the great destruction which had come upon them.

                                                    3 Nephi 8:523.

1. And it came to pass that there was a voice heard among all the inhabitants of the earth, upon all the face of this land, crying:

2. Wo, wo, wo unto this people; wo unto the inhabitants of the whole earth except they shall repent; for the devil laugheth, and his angels rejoice, because of the slain of the fair sons and daughters of my people; and it is because of their iniquity and abominations that they are fallen! . . .

12. And many great destructions have I caused to come upon this land, and upon this

---

[1] For prophecies on this subject see 1 Nephi 19:812; Helaman 14:12, 14, 2027.

people, because of their wickedness and their abominations.

13. O all ye that are spared because ye were more righteous than they, will ye not now return unto me, and repent of your sins, and be converted, that I may heal you?

14. Yea, verily, I say unto you, if ye will come unto me ye shall have eternal life. Behold, mine arm of mercy is extended towards you, and whosoever will come, him will I receive; and blessed are those who come unto me.

15. Behold, I am Jesus Christ the Son of God. I created the heavens and the earth, and all things that in them are. I was with the Father from the beginning. I am in the Father, and the Father in me; and in me hath the Father glorified his name.

16. I came unto my own, and my own received me not. And the scriptures concerning my coming are fulfilled.

17. And as many as have received me, to them have I given to become the sons of God; and even so will I to as many as shall believe on my name, for behold, by me redemption cometh, and in me is the law of Moses fulfilled.

18. I am the light and the life of the world. I am Alpha and Omega,[2] the beginning and the end.   3 Nephi 9:1-2, 12-18.

XLV. DESTRUCTION AT TIME OF CHRIST'S CRUCIFIXION

The Works of Ixtlilxochitl make reference to a great "destruction and desolation" which took place among the inhabitants of ancient America, and then the significant statement appears that the destruction took place *"at the same time when Christ our Lord suffered."* That statement is in complete accord with the account given in *The Book of Mormon*. Ixtlilxochitl also said: "And, as it seems through the mentioned histories and annals, the afore-mentioned happened *some years after the incarnation of Christ our Lord." The Book of Mormon*, on the other hand, tells in detail about the great "destruction and desolation" which occurred on the western hemisphere and places the event exactly at the time of the crucifixion of Jesus Christ. Note that the datings of the event in the two records are identical with each other.

---

[2] It is not surprising that Christ should use this simple Greek expression in talking to the New World branch of Israel. It is possible that some of the intelligentsia of the Nephite-Mulekite nation knew the expression. Archæological discoveries in Palestine have recently revealed that there was a close relationship between the Greeks and Israel of 600 B. C. when Lehi and Mulek left Palestine for the New World. W. F. Albright, *The Archaeology of Palestine* (1949), pp. 143, 193.

As early as 600 years B. C., the prophet Nephi looked down through the stream of time and saw the coming of Jesus Christ into mortality. He saw in vision the history of the ancient Americans following his day, and it was made known to him that exactly at the time that Jesus Christ was crucified in Palestine, a great destruction would take place on the American continent. One of the prime purposes of that destruction was to destroy the wicked people prior to the visitation that Christ would make among the more righteous people here on this continent.

In 3 Nephi *The Book of Mormon* gives a very vivid and rather full account of this destruction, the record being made very soon after the destruction had occurred on this continent. Only a few short extracts from the Nephite record are quoted in this book. For more detailed information one should go directly to *The Book of Mormon*.

XLVI. TIME OF CRUCIFIXION OF CHRIST

Another very significant point is made by both *Ixtlilxochitl* and the Nephite account—that Christ was crucified during the early part of the year. *Ixtlilxochitl* states, *"and they say it happened during the first days of the year";* and *The Book of Mormon* reported the event as occurring *"in the first month [and] on the fourth day of the month."*

The Nephites changed their point of reckoning time when the signs of the birth of Christ were fulfilled in harmony with Samuel the Lamanite's predictions. From that time forward they dated from that point. It is a well-known fact that Jesus Christ was crucified during the period of the Jewish Feast of the Passover. That feast was held during the first month of the Jewish lunar year (March-April).

The Nephite record reports that the Man of Galilee was thirty-three years and four days old when He was crucified; therefore, He was born in March or April, according to our calendar, and died during the same month thirty-three years later. Also, He was crucified during the first month of the Jewish (Nephite) year. Thus *The Book of Mormon* establishes the approximate time of the birthday of our Lord and Master and its testimony is confirmed by *Ixtlilxochitl* to the effect that Christ was crucified "during the first days of the year."

Summary Statement

The parallels between our two accounts regarding events as of the time of the crucifixion of Jesus, and the time of year when those events took place, are remarkable, to say the least. Both agree that these things happened at the very beginning of the year. This indicates that the ancients of Mexico held in remembrance the Jewish-Nephite dating of the event or, perhaps, even retained a knowledge of that system down to *Ixtlilxochitl's* time.

Therefore, accurate historical data, recorded in *The Book of Mormon* at the time the events occurred, was handed down from age to age even from the time of Christ's crucifixion to the Spanish Conquest of Mexico.

Both agree that the sun and the moon were darkened and that the earth trembled and rocks broke.

Ixtlilxochitl says that many "signs took place." Signs of what? Everything in the two accounts shows that Jesus was the Messiah who, with His Father, is the God and Creator and Controller of our universe—and that He lives.

Chapter 16

JESUS CHRIST IN ANCIENT AMERICA

INTRODUCTORY STATEMENT

One of the important problems of research is this: Was Jesus of Nazareth the Fair God of Middle America? Did the man Jesus visit and minister in the New World after His crucifixion in Palestine? If Jesus did appear in the New World in 34 A. D., it necessarily follows that He is a true God, immortal, resurrected from the dead, divine, the very light and life of the world. If that is true, then we may know that what was said by Him concerning the immortality and eternal life of man can be counted true.

In view of the infinite importance attached to the problem of the identity of Quetzalcoatl, the "Fair God" of Middle America, all available evidence should be assembled and carefully weighed. Prejudices and preconceived conclusions should be cast aside. This calls for an honest and true evaluation of *The Book of Mormon* and *Ixtlilxochitl,* for they contain the most specific claims regarding the problem. The data concerning the "Fair God" form an integral part of the writings of *Ixtlilxochitl* and of *The Book of Mormon.* It is quite reasonable, therefore, especially with regard to the latter book, that if the particulars in the entire record which lend themselves to testing and checking against scientific data (archæological and historical-documentary data) are found to be authentic, that the portion concerning the alleged visit of Christ to the New World is true. As stated, the appearance and ministry of Christ in Bountiful-land is an integral and component part of the Nephite record.

If, tested by scientific methods, *The Book of Mormon* is found to be true, then we can really know God, for *The Book of Mormon* claims to set forth facts (knowledge) concerning the nature of God. *The Book of Mormon* holds itself out as a work compiled under the direct instruction and supervision of God. Though a history, it is in the nature of a great revelation or series of revelations from God to the ancient cultured colonizers of Middle America. They received special privileges and special punishments directly from the hand of God.

If Joseph Smith fabricated part of the Nephite account, the whole is false. On the other hand, if any portion of *The Book of Mormon* came from the original eye-witness sources, then it is highly probable, or virtually certain, that the entire *Book of Mormon* is derived from original authentic sources. If the First Book of Nephi is true, then certainly Third Nephi is true. If Lehi possessed the Liahona and came to Middle America in the sixth century B. C. from the Near East, then that part of the record which states that the resurrected Christ appeared in Bountiful-land in the New World is likewise true.

If divine agents assisted Joseph Smith in discovering and translating ancient American records, it is absurd to think so favored a man would wilfully add fabrication to the work by inserting a conjured-up appearance of Christ in America.

In view of the importance to all mankind of the problem of the identity of Quetzalcoatl, and in view of the remarkable claims of *The Book of Mormon* and *Ixtlilxochitl* with respect to that problem, it follows that our two accounts deserve the utmost consideration.

The importance of the question can be summarized by saying that the opportunity presents itself to prove, through certain branches of science which supply known facts in regard to the history and culture of ancient America (anthropology, archæology, documentary research, etc.), the physical resurrection of Christ, the immortality of the soul of man, and the true nature of God! *The Book of Mormon* may be that long-hoped-for revelation that lends itself to scientific proof. About seventy years before the first printing of *The Book of Mormon,* David Hume, distinguished English philosopher, after examining into the then hopelessly confused state of knowledge concerning the nature of God, wrote:

The most natural sentiment which a well-disposed mind will feel on this occasion, is a longing desire and expectation, that heaven would be pleased to dissipate, or at least alleviate, this profound ignorance, by affording some more particular *revelation* to mankind, and making discoveries of the nature, attributes, and operations of the divine object of our faith. A person seasoned with a just sense of the imperfections of natural reason, will fly to *revealed truth*.[1]

Of the relatively few persons who have read *The Book of Mormon,* a substantial percentage have concluded it was re' vealed truth and have clung to it, come what might. However, not all persons "fly to revealed truth" when exposed to it. And, of course, those who do the disclosing and disseminating of revealed truth are not always gifted in the best techniques and methods of circulating the truths which have come to them— so that their auditors are not always to blame if they fail to "fly to revealed truth."

Atomic research has made possible and probable the com' plete destruction of mankind. The identification of Quetzalcoatl with Jesus Christ and the acceptance by the human family of the doctrines He revealed to the ancient Americans would assist immeasurably in saving mankind from annihilating itself. It would give Christianity that impetus or stimulus that will cause it to prevail over the forces of darkness, death and destruction. If a revitalized Christianity is not widespread enough to keep the peace of nations it will nonetheless bring salvation and happiness to the individuals who embrace it.

Not Incredible that Christ and Quetzalcoatal Were Identical.

If Christ were literally resurrected from the tomb in Pales' tine, as Christianity proclaims, there would appear to be nothing inherently illogical or unsound in *The Book of Mormon* position that He appeared thereafter in the New World. In fact, it is consistent with a certain statement in the New Testament which is not otherwise explained. That statement, which appears in the Book of John, calls for a personal ministry by the Christ to a branch of Israel in a place other than Palestine. Now if Middle America were colonized by hook'nosed, bearded, white' skinned settlers from the eastern end of the Mediterranean, as the documentary and archæological sources indicate it was, what is more probable than that Christ would want to visit such a branch of Israel?

Is it not reasonable to suppose that while He was contem' plating His crucifixion and departure from Palestine He would

---

[1] David Hume (1711-1776), "Concerning Natural Religion," in *Hume Selections* (edited by Charles W. Hendel, 1927), pp. 400-401.

consider visiting an isolated branch of Israel? It has already been shown that He led the Nephite-Mulekite people to the New World in order that their story might, in our day, convince the House of Israel that Jesus was the Messiah. That such was the case appears evident from the comment He inserted into the parable of the sheep:

> I am the good shepherd, and know *my* sheep, and am known of mine. As the Father knoweth me, even so know I the Father: and I lay down my life for the sheep. And *other sheep I have which are not of this fold:* them also I must bring, and *they shall hear my voice;* and there shall be one fold, and one shepherd.[1a]

Those of the Palestinian fold did not understand the parable or the comments of Christ. John wrote in the same chapter:

> This parable spake Jesus unto them: but they understood not what things they were which he spake unto them. . . . There was a division therefore again among the Jews for these sayings. And many of them said, He hath a devil, and is mad; why hear ye him? Others said, These are not the words of him that hath a devil. Can a devil open the eyes of the blind?[2]

It was a part of God's plan that Christ should minister personally to the House of Israel and its branches.

As will be seen by the quotations from *The Book of Mormon* and *Ixtlilxochitl,* the "Fair God" appeared in Bountiful ("Tlapallan" or "Tulapan"), seat of the kingdom, shortly after the crucifixion and resurrection in Palestine. In corroboration of this dating of his New World ministry is that statement of Motolinia (Toribio de Benovente) that the first Quetzalcoatl was responsible for establishing civilization in the year 68 A. D. Thus, Motolinia differs with our parallel texts by exactly 34 years.[3] Benaduci Boturini, whose writings were published in Madrid in 1746, states that the Tultecs noted in their ancient records that a solar eclipse occurred in the Tultec kingdom in the year VII *tochtli.* That year, he says, was the year of the crucifixion of our Redeemer.[4]

[1a] Book of John, 10:14-16.
[2] *Ibid.,* 10:6, 19-23.
[3] Motolinia, author of *Historia de los Indios de la Nueva Espanzo,* dates it thirty-four years later, i.e., at 68 A. D.
[4] Benaduci Boturini, *Idea de Una Nueva Historia General de la America Septentrional* (1746). Francisco Javier Clavigero, *Historia Antigua de Mexico* (1780), refers to Boturni: Añade el citado caballero que los toltecas teñian notado en sus pinturas el eclipse solar, acaeido en la muerte de nuestro Redentor, en el año VII *tochtli.* 1945 Mexican edition of Clavigero, Tomo I, Capitulo II, p. 179. Boturini is also quoted on the point by Ordoñez y Augiar, *Historia de la Creacion,* etc. (1907 edition), p. 2.

Christ made the following comment while visiting in the New World concerning the parable of the sheep as related by him to the Israelites in Jerusalem:

This much did the Father command me that I should tell unto them [in Jerusalem]: That other sheep I have which are not of this fold; them also I must bring, and they shall hear my voice; and there shall be one fold, and one shepherd. And now because of stiffneckedness and unbelief they understood not my word; therefore I was commanded [of the Father] to say no more concerning this thing unto them. . . . it is because of their iniquity that they do not know of you.[5]

This explains why the "Fair God" singled out the colonizers of ancient Bountiful-land in the New World for a visit, and why such an important event was not called forcibly to the attention of the Israelites or others in the Near East.

XLVII. Quetzalcoatl

In Mexico's great central mesa where *Ixtlilxochitl* lived, the name by which the Fair God was generally known was *Quetzalcoatl*. "Quetzal" was the name of the beautiful bird with the resplendent long green feathers and the dainty crest.[6] See Fig. 27. "Coatl" is the ancient Mexican word for *serpent*.[7] Thus, the name *Quetzalcoatl* means literally "Quetzal-bird serpent."

If *Quetzalcoatl* were identical with Christ, how can the use of such a symbol-name be explained? *The Book of Mormon* answers the question and explains better than any other single source why the name was applied to the New World God who was in the form of a man, bearded, white-robed, and a great teacher of moral principles. The Nephite account makes it clear that though a man He descended out of the sky. He had the power to pass through the air. He did pass through the air,

---

[5] *The Book of Mormon*, p. 430 (3 Nephi 15:16-19).
[6] Sahagun gives an excellent description of the Quetzal bird: "There is a bird in this land that is called Quetzaltototl; it has very rich and colorful plumage; the bill is sharp and yellow, and the feet are yellow. It has a feather tuft on its head, like a rooster's comb. It is . . . the size of a magpie of Spain. . . . The tail feathers are called Quezalli and they are very green and shiny. They are wide like the leaves of reeds and they bend when the wind hits them and they shine very beautifully. These birds have some black feathers in the tail with which it covers ·these rich [green] ones which are in the midst of the black ones. The black feathers are very black on the outside, and on the inside are the rich dark green feathers, they being not very long nor wide. The tuft this bird has on its head is very beautiful and glossy . . . and the bird has a red and glossy neck. . . . The neck, on the back, and the entire back of the bird has resplendent green feathers. Under the tail and between its legs it has a delicate feather of clear green color, soft and resplendent; on the veins or elbows of the wings are green feathers, and black ones under the wings. . . . These birds inhabit the province that is called Tocolotlan, which is toward Honduras, or near. They live in groves. They make their nests in trees to rear their young." Sahagun, *Libro* 11, *Cap.* 2, *Sec.* 1.
[7] George C. Vaillant, *Aztecs of Mexico*, p. 52; Bancroft, *Native Races*, vol. 2, p. 511 ff.

(c) N.G.S. COURTESY OF NATIONAL GEOGRAPHIC MAGAZINE

Fig. 27: THE QUETZAL BIRD

Ancient symbol of Quetzalcoatl, God of the Air, the bearded white man who was seen by a multitude as he descended from the sky as though a bird. *Finlay Photograph by Luis Marden, courtesy of National Geographic Magazine.*

and in a manner that only birds had been seen to do. To an age lacking airplanes, blimps, jets and rockets, this "miracle" must have impressed itself greatly upon the settlers. After the Nephites and Lamanites had apostatized from the true Gospel of Jesus Christ and the former people had been exterminated, the Lamanites still retained in their traditions a memory of the appearance of the resurrected Savior to their forefathers. Thus, they added a pagan touch to that memorable event by selecting a symbol in its commemoration. But what more fitting symbol of the appearance of the Christ could have been selected by the people in the New World than the most beautiful and highly prized bird, the Quetzal!

The *coatl*, or "serpent," was an ancient symbol of Israel's Messiah, "the Anointed One." In the Old Testament we read:

Make thee a fiery serpent, and set it upon a pole: and it shall come to pass, that everyone that is bitten, when he looketh upon it, shall live. And Moses made a serpent of brass, and put it upon a pole, and it came to pass, that if a serpent had bitten any man, when he beheld the serpent of brass, he lived.[8]

The serpent was the principal symbol of the hopedfor Messiah from the time of Moses (about 1200 B. C.) until about 700 B. C. A brass serpent on a pole or beam was maintained as a representation of the Messiah in the chief temple of the Israelite nation from the time of Moses until about 700 B. C., i.e., for about 500 years.[9] Christ clearly identified the serpent symbol with His own crucifixion, according to John in the New Testament:

And as Moses lifted up the serpent in the wilderness, even so must the Son of Man be lifted up: that whosoever believeth in him should not perish, but have eternal life.[10]

In *The Book of Mormon* we read further of the serpent symbolism:

Did Moses not bear record, that the Son of God should come? And as he lifted up the brazen serpent in the wilderness, even so shall be lifted up who should come. And as many as should look upon that serpent

---

[8] Old Testament, Numbers 21:8-9. The serpent symbol apparently was in common use in ancient Palestine. A stela of a serpent entwined about a personage was discovered at Tell Beit Mirsim, about thirty-five miles southwest of Jerusalem. W. F. Albright dates the stela in the sixteenth century B. C. during the Canaanite period. See Albright, *The Archaeology of Palestine* (1949), Figure 20, p. 97. Rowe made a similar discovery at Bethahan, near the Jordan river and about fifteen miles south of the Sea of Galilee.
[9] Maurice H. Farbridge, *Studies in Biblical and Semitic Symbolism* (1923), p. 75; H. P. Smith, *Old Testament History*, p. 240.
[10] New Testament, John 3:14-15.

should live. Even as many as should look upon the Son of God, with faith, having a contrite spirit, might live, even unto that life which is eternal.[11]

The quetzal-serpent symbolism is encountered in the ancient artifacts of Middle America. Feathered serpents appear on the facades of temples and palaces, on ceramics, in stone sculptured works and in gold representations. Lord Kingsborough reports: "Representations of the lifting up of serpents frequently occur in Mexican paintings."[12]

Again, as the generations passed following the extermination of the Nephites, the Lamanites degenerated the serpent-symbol into the pagan forms that were found in Mexico, Guatemala, and Yucatan by the European missionaries following the Spanish Conquest. Thus, these quetzal-serpent symbols are degenerated pagan reminders of the true Christ and Lord who had once visited ancient America and had given his gospel to its inhabitants.

Other symbols of the Fair God appear, including the cross; however, none dominated the art of the ancient New World as did the quetzal-serpent motif. The dominance of the quetzal symbol over the cross symbol is understandable when it is realized that the thing observed by a multitude of eyewitnesses in Bountiful-land was the descent from heaven. None of the inhabitants of the New World was an eyewitness to the crucifixion. Therefore, the cross did not figure so prominently in their thinking. On the other hand, a great multitude saw Christ descend through the sky as if He were a bird—a thing so marvelous that if repeated even now in the middle of the twentieth century it would amaze and astound its most sophisticated witnesses. Such mastery of physical laws still belongs, in man's own scale of progress, to a forecasted age such as that of Buck Rogers. Of course the quetzal-bird symbol, coupled with the more ancient serpent symbol of Israel, dominated over the cross, under the circumstances; but each of these symbols became adulterated with a degenerated paganism. Christ was "god of the air and winds" to the early settlers and to their descendants.

---

[11] *The Book of Mormon*, p. 379 (Helaman 8:14-15); p. 281 (Alma 33:18-19.
[12] Lord Kingsborough, *Mexican Antiquities*, vol. 8, p. 208.

Jesus Christ (Quetzalcoatl) in Ancient America

IXTLILXOCHITL:

Quetzalcoatl (Jesus Christ) visited ancient America—His teachings

And when they were in the height of their power, there arrived in this land a man whom they called Quetzalcoatl[XLVII] and others Huemac on account of his great virtues, considering him as just, saintly [holy], and good; teaching them by deeds and words the path of virtue and *forbidding them their vices and sins, giving laws and good doctrine.* And in order to refrain them from their pleasures and dishonesties, he *instituted (established) fasting* for them and [he was] the first who worshiped and placed the cross[XLIX] which they called Quiahuiteotl-chicahualizteotl and others Tona-caquahuitl, which means: God of rains and of health and tree of sustenance or of life.[L]

Quetzalcoatl[XLVII] through literal interpretation means serpent of *precious plumage;* in an allegorical sense it means *very wise man;* and as for the name *Huemac,* some say he [Quetzalcoatl] was so called because he imprinted and stamped his hands on a rock, as if it were on very soft wax, as a testimony that all he had told them would come true; others would have it mean *he of the large or powerful hand.*

EXTRACTS—BOOK OF MORMON:

Jesus Christ (Quetzalcoatl) visited ancient America—His teachings[13]

4. And they began to prosper and to wax great; and the twenty and sixth and seventh years passed away, and there was great order in the land; and they had formed their laws according to equity and justice.   3 Nephi 6:4.

1. And now it came to pass that according to our record, and we know our record to be true, for behold, it was a just man who did keep the record; for he truly did many miracles in the name of Jesus....

2. And now it came to pass, if there was no mistake made by this man in the reckoning of our time, the thirty and third year had passed away....

5. And it came to pass in the thirty and fourth year, in the first month, on the fourth day of the month,...

9:1b. ... there was a voice heard among all the inhabitants of the earth, upon all the face of the land, crying:...

15a. Behold, I am Jesus Christ the Son of God.   3 Nephi 8:1-2, 5a; 9:1b, 15a.

1. And it came to pass that there were a great multitude gathered together, of the people of Nephi, round about the temple which was in the land Bountiful; and they were marveling and wondering one with another, and were showing one to another the great and marvelous change which had taken place.

2. And they were also conversing about this Jesus Christ, of whom the sign had been given concerning his death.

3. And it came to pass that while they were thus conversing one with another, they heard a voice as if it came out of heaven; and they cast their eyes round about, for they understood not the voice which they heard; and it was not a harsh voice, neither was it a loud voice; nevertheless, and notwithstanding it being a small voice it did pierce them that did hear to the center, insomuch that there was no part of their frame that it did not cause to quake; yea, it did pierce them to the very soul, and did cause their hearts to burn.

4. And it came to pass that again they heard the voice, and they understood it not.

5. And again the third time they did hear the voice, and did open their ears to hear it; and their eyes were towards the sound thereof; and

---

[13] Only a meager portion of Jesus' voluminous doctrinal teachings to the Nephites will be quoted here. It is suggested that 3 Nephi be read completely through at this point.

they did look steadfastly towards heaven, from whence the sound came.

6. And behold, the third time they did understand the voice which they heard; and it said unto them:

7. Behold my Beloved Son, in whom I am well pleased, in whom I have glorified my name —hear ye him.

8. And it came to pass, as they understood they cast their eyes up again towards heaven; and behold they saw a Man descending out of heaven; and he was clothed in a white robe;[XLVIII] and he came down and stood in the midst of them; and the eyes of the whole multitude were turned upon him, and they durst not open their mouths, even one to another, and wist not what it meant, for they thought it was an angel that had appeared unto them.

9. And it came to pass that he stretched forth his hand and spake unto the people, saying:

10. *Behold, I am Jesus Christ, whom the prophets testified shall come into the world.*

11. *And behold, I am the light and the life of the world; and I have drunk out of that bitter cup which the Father hath given me, and have glorified the Father in taking upon me the sins of the world, in the which I have suffered the will of the Father in all things from the beginning.*

12. And it came to pass that when Jesus had spoken these words the whole multitude fell to the earth; for they remembered that it had been prophesied among them that Christ should show himself unto them after his ascension into heaven.

13. And it came to pass that the Lord spake unto them saying:

14. Arise and come forth unto me, that ye may thrust your hands into my side, and also that ye may feel the prints of the nails in my hands and in my feet, that ye may know that I am the God of Israel, and the God of the whole earth, and have been slain for the sins of the world.

15. And it came to pass that the multitude went forth, and thrust their hands into his side, and did feel the prints of the nails in his hands and in his feet; and this they did do, going forth one by one until they had all gone forth, and did see with their eyes and did feel with their hands, and did know of a surety and did bear record, that it was he, of whom it was written by the prophets, that should come.

16. And when they had all gone forth and had witnessed for themselves, they did cry out with one accord, saying:

17. Hosanna! Blessed be the name of the Most High God! And they did fall down at the feet of Jesus, and did worship him.

18. And it came to pass that he spake unto Nephi (for Nephi was among the multitude) and he commanded him that he should come forth.

19. And Nephi arose and went forth and bowed himself before the Lord and did kiss his feet.

20. And the Lord commanded him that he should arise. And he arose and stood before him.

21. And the Lord said unto him: I give unto you power that ye shall baptize this people when I am again ascended into heaven.

22. And again the Lord called others, and said unto them likewise; and he gave unto them power to baptize. And he said unto them: On this wise shall ye baptize; and there shall be no disputations among you.

23. Verily I say unto you, that whoso repent- eth of his sins through your words, and desireth to be baptized in my name, on this wise shall ye baptize them—Behold, ye shall go down and stand in the water, and in my name shall ye baptize them.

24. And now behold, these are the words which ye shall say, calling them by name, saying:

25. Having authority given me of Jesus Christ, I baptize you in the name of the Father, and of the Son, and of the Holy Ghost. Amen.

26. And then shall ye immerse them in the water, and come forth again out of the water.

27. And after this manner shall ye baptize in my name; for behold, verily I say unto you, that the Father, and the Son, and the Holy Ghost are one; and I am in the Father, and the Father in me, and the Father and I are one.

28. And according as I have commanded you thus shall ye baptize. And there shall be no disputations among you, as there have hitherto been; neither shall there be disputation among you concerning the points of my doctrine, as there have hitherto been.

29. For verily, verily I say unto you, he that hath the spirit of contention is not of me, but is of the devil, who is the father of contention, and he stirreth up the hearts of men to contend with anger, one with another.

30. Behold, this is not my doctrine, to stir up the hearts of men with anger, one against another; but this is my doctrine, that such things should be done away.

31. Behold, verily, verily, I say unto you, I will declare unto you my doctrine.

32. And this is my doctrine, and it is the doctrine which the Father hath given unto me;

and I bear record of the Father, and the Father beareth record of me, and the Holy Ghost beareth record of the Father and me; and I bear record that the Father commandeth all men, everywhere, to repent and believe in me.

33. And whoso believeth in me, and is baptized, the same shall be saved; and they are they who shall inherit the kingdom of God.

34. And whoso believeth not in me, and is not baptized, shall be damned.

35. Verily, verily, I say unto you, that this is my doctrine, and I bear record of it from the Father; and whoso believeth in me believeth in the Father also; and unto him will the Father bear record of me, for he will visit him with fire and with the Holy Ghost.

36. And thus will the Father bear record of me, and the Holy Ghost will bear record unto him of the Father and me; for the Father, and I, and the Holy Ghost are one.

37. *And again I say unto you, ye must repent, and become as a little child, and be baptized in my name,* or ye can in nowise receive these things.

38. And again I say unto you, ye must repent, and be baptized in my name, and become as a little child, or ye can in nowise inherit the kingdom of God.

39. Verily, verily, I say unto you, that this is my doctrine, and whoso buildeth upon this buildeth upon my rock, and the gates of hell shall not prevail against them.

40. And whoso shall declare more or less than this, and establish it for my doctrine, the same cometh of evil, and is not built upon my rock; but he buildeth upon a sandy foundation, and the gates of hell stand open to receive such when the floods come and the winds beat upon them.   3 Nephi 11:1-40.

16. Moreover, *when ye fast* be not as the hypocrites, of a sad countenance, for they disfigure their faces that they may appear unto men to fast. Verily I say unto you, they have their reward.

17. But thou, when thou fastest, anoint thy head, and wash thy face;   3 Nephi 13:16-17.

41. Therefore, go forth unto this people, and declare the words which I have spoken, unto the ends of the earth.   3 Nephi 11:41.

1. And it came to pass that as the disciples of Jesus were journeying and were preaching the things which they had both heard and seen, and were baptizing in the name of Jesus, it came to pass that the disciples were gathered together and were *united in mighty prayer and fasting.*   3 Nephi 27:1.

9. And it came to pass that when he had thus spoken, all the multitude, with one accord,

did go forth with their sick and afflicted, and their lame, and with their blind, and with their dumb, and with all them that were afflicted in any manner; and he did heal them every one as they were brought forth unto him.

10. And they did all, both they who had been healed and they who were whole, bow down at his feet, and did worship him; and as many as could come for the multitude did kiss his feet, insomuch that they did bathe his feet with their tears.   3 Nephi 17:9-10.

THE BOOK OF MORMON AND JESUS CHRIST

Beyond a shadow of a doubt, the white God of ancient America was none other than Jesus of Nazareth, the Only Begotten son of God, the Savior of the world, known in the Old Testament as Jehovah.

Of the New World accounts concerning the Christ, *Ixtlilxochitl* comes nearer to giving an accurate report than does any other source, excluding *The Book of Mormon*. Even the Popol Vuh is vague and unintelligible in comparison to the lucid Nephite history. Traditions of a white God were very prevalent in the Americas when the Europeans began to arrive; especially was this so in the vicinity of the ancient centers of high culture— Middle America and Peru. Those traditions and memories, some of them recorded, are a far cry from the detailed eyewitness reports in *The Book of Mormon*. However, where the histories and traditions of Middle America and Peru do contribute something it is in corroboration of the Nephite account. Bancroft summarizes the status of the knowledge of the Fair God as it existed generally in New World traditions at the time of the Spanish Conquest:

Although bearing various names and appearing in different countries, the American culture-heroes all present the same general characteristics. They are all described as white, bearded men, generally clad in long robes; appearing suddenly and mysteriously upon the scene of their labors; they at once set about improving the people by instructing them in useful and ornamental arts; giving them laws, exorting them to practice brotherly love and other *Christian* virtues, and introducing a milder and better form of religion; having accomplished their mission, they disappeared as mysteriously and unexpectedly as they came.[14]

On the other hand, *The Book of Mormon* contains more specific and more accurate information concerning the personality and role of Jesus Christ—universal Creator, Savior and Messiah of mankind, and his plan for the redemption and exaltation of

the people of the earth—than can be found in the literature of the
ancient pagan cults, in the Old Testament, in the New Testament and in the New World traditions combined. Certain things
are lacking in all of them that are found in the Nephite record
in clear and simple language.

No other book in the world gives so complete nor so clear a
picture of the mission of Christ, both preceding and following his
advent on earth, as does The Book of Mormon. The Son of God
was foreordained to come into the world to redeem man from
temporal death and to save him from the retrograding forces of
evil.[15]

Shortly after Nephi left Jerusalem Christ revealed to him
that he and his people were to keep a record of the revelations
from the Lord and of the religious instructions of their prophets
and seers. This they did with much precision and accuracy.
When Jesus visited the Nephites after His resurrection, He commanded them to be very careful in recording in their scripture
the sacred information. In fact, He even reprimanded them for
having neglected to write one particular item which had been
revealed to them.[16] The fact that the revelations were written on
the Nephite record shortly after their reception means that The
Book of Mormon is a more accurate portrayal of the mission of
Christ than is the New Testament.

The revealed purpose of the Nephite record is to be another
witness to the divinity and mission of Jesus the Christ. It sustains
and amplifies the testimony of the Bible, and even confirms the
hopes which arose in the breasts of the ancient pagans relative
to the reality of God, the efficacy of the Savior, and an assurance
of eternal life. The reader who will peruse diligently the contents
of this extraordinary book will find that it is a powerful witness
that Jesus is the Christ, the light of the world, and the author of
eternal salvation.

The very heart of this unique book is the information which
it contains relative to the gospel plan as taught by our Lord and
Master. From Nephi to Moroni, the avowed purpose of each of
the writers was to produce a work "to the convincing of the
Jew and the Gentile that Jesus is the Christ, the Eternal God,
manifesting Himself unto all nations."[17]

14 Hubert H. Bancroft, Native Races, vol. 5, pp. 23-24.
15 The Book of Mormon, p. 483 (Ether 3:4); ibid., pp. 208, 212, 252-253 (Alma 5:49, 7:14-16;
        22:13-18).
16 Ibid., pp. 445-446 (3 Nephi 23:6-14).
17 "Preface," The Book of Mormon.

Schooled as they were in Jewish knowledge of the plan of redemption as understood by the holy prophets, Lehi and his successors kept open the paths of communion with God. One Nephite prophet after another received direct revelation from the divine fountain of truth, even the Christ. Beginning with their first prophet, Lehi, the Redeemer revealed to them portions of His gospel. The Nephite leaders were righteous prophets and seers. Nephi recorded the Lord's intentions regarding revelations:

> Thus saith the Lord God; I will give unto the children of men line upon line, precept upon precept, here a little and there a little; and blessed are those who hearken unto my precepts, and lend an ear unto my counsel, for they shall learn wisdom; for unto him that receiveth, I will give more; and from them that shall say, we have enough, from them shall be taken away even that which they have.[18]

The climax of God's program for revealing the purpose of man's existence to the Nephites is recorded in 3 Nephi, wherein Jesus the Christ appeared to the people on this western hemis-phere after his crucifixion in Palestine. The gospel of Christ, as set forth in 3 Nephi, is more clearly presented than it is in the New Testament.

As a result of the close relationship between God and the Nephite prophets for over a thousand years, the Nephites possessed a very comprehensive and thorough knowledge of the plan of redemption. They knew that Jesus had been selected before the foundation of this earth to perform a very important work, that of making possible the immortality and eternal life of mankind. They also had a keen insight into the part that man plays in bring-ing about his own atonement. As far as we know from the scriptures now in existence, the Nephites possessed a greater amount of foreknowledge of Christ than did their Israelitish ancestors. One is not surprised, therefore, to find that the traditions of a bearded white God visiting ancient America were so numerous and widespread among the natives when one considers the fact that the ancient cultured settlers of America were a select branch of Israel. The knowledge of Christ's visit to ancient America had carried on for many generations to the time of the Conquest.

One of the strongest desires of mankind is to find God and to live eternally with him in a future existence. No people has

---

[18] *Ibid.*, p. 160 (2 Nephi 28:30). This might also be said to apply to students of the Nephite record itself. Some seem to say "we have enough." Actually we are only at the threshold of *Book of Mormon* research. Wonderful developments seem to lie ahead.

left us a book containing so complete an explanation of the way of life eternal as did the Nephites in the unusual record—*The Book of Mormon*. The reader is invited to study carefully the extensive information contained therein relative to the mission of the Messiah.

XLVIII. Quetzalcoatl—or Jesus—Described

EXTRACTS—BOOK OF MORMON:

Quetzalcoatl described

Quetzalcoatl was a favorably disposed man, of a grave aspect, white, and bearded. His dress was a long tunic.XLVIII

Whiteness of countenance of Jesus

25. And it came to pass that Jesus blessed them [the twelve Nephite disciples chosen by him] as they did pray unto him; and his countenance did smile upon them, and the light of his countenance did shine upon them, and behold they were as *white* as the countenance and also the garments of Jesus; and behold the whiteness thereof did exceed all the whiteness, yea, even there could be nothing upon earth so white as the whiteness thereof.

3 Nephi 19:25.

Ixtlilxochitl's description of the Fair God is brief but it is very significant. His statement that Quetzalcoatl "was a favorably disposed man, of grave aspect, white and bearded" contains one descriptive item, viz., the beard, which is not mentioned in the Nephite narrative. Neither does the New Testament mention the beard of Jesus. Both of our primary accounts refer to the Fair God as a "man" of white countenance. *The Book of Mormon* dwells at length on the "whiteness" of the countenance of the resurrected Lord. Both sources state he wore a robe or tunic. The Nephite account adds that the robe was white.

XLIX. Jesus Christ and Symbol of the Cross

According to the *Works of Ixtlilxochitl* the symbol of the cross was given to the ancient inhabitants of America by Quetzalcoatl. *The Book of Mormon* is in complete accord with that teaching, making the claim that the symbol of the cross was given to the inhabitants of ancient America by Jesus Christ. In fact, Christ revealed to the ancient Nephite prophets prior to his coming into the world that He would be lifted upon the Cross and crucified. Helaman compared the lifting of the brazen serpent in the wilderness by Moses to the lifting of Christ upon the cross.

The Book of Mormon says that Christ himself spoke to the ancient inhabitants of Bountiful-land concerning the cross as follows "And *my Father sent me that I might be lifted up upon the cross;* and after that I had been lifted up upon the cross; that I might draw all men unto me. . . ."

Thus again we find that the ancient Mexican history and the Nephite record are in complete accord. And archæology supports them in this connection. Ancient pre-Spanish-Conquest crosses have been found in southern Mexico in ancient Bountiful-land territory. A beautiful example is the famous cross on the stone altar in the Maya temple at Palenque. Atop that cross sits the quetzal bird, another symbol of the resurrected Lord. That the cross and the quetzal bird appear together is noteworthy. Another beautiful cross was found by archæologists at Yachilan on the Guatemala side of the Usumacinta River. It too is an ancient Mayan (Lamanite) city of the post-*Book-of-Mormon* period of Lamanite dominance. The Lamanites and their descend-ants retained many of the teachings and symbols of Jesus. The cross was known and used in Yucatan right down to the time of the coming of the Spaniards.

Symbol of cross and tree of life

[He was] the first who wor-shiped and placed the Cross,[XLIX] which some called *Quiauhtzte-otlchicahualizteotl,* and others called Tonacaquahuitl, which means *god of rains and health, and tree of sustenance or of life.*[L]

Symbol of Cross[XLIX]

13. But, behold, ye not only deny my words, but ye also deny all the words which have been spoken by our fathers, and also the words which were spoken by this man, Moses, who had such great power given unto him, yea, the words which he hath spoken concerning the coming of the Messiah.

14. Yea, did he not bear record that the Son of God should come; And as he lifted up the brazen serpent in the wilderness, even so shall he be lifted up who should come.

15. And as many as should look upon that serpent should live, even so as many as should look upon the Son of God with faith, having a contrite spirit, might live, even unto that life which is eternal.

16. And now behold, Moses did not only testify of these things, but also all the holy prophets, from his days even to the days of Abraham.   Helaman 8:13-16.

14. *And my Father sent me that I might be lifted up upon the cross;*[XLIX] *and after that I had been lifted up upon the cross, that I might draw all men unto me, that as I have been lifted up by men even so should men be lifted up by the Father, to stand before me, to be judged of their works, whether they be good or whether they be evil—*   3 Nephi 27:14.

"Tree of Life".

25. And it came to pass that I beheld that the rod of iron, which my father had seen, was the word of God, which led to the fountain of living waters, or to the tree of life; which waters are a representation of the love of God; and *I also beheld that the tree of life was a representation of the love of God.*[L]

1 Nephi 11:25.

21. And it came to pass that they did speak unto me again, saying: What meaneth this thing which our father saw in a dream? What mean- eth the tree which he saw?

22. And I said unto them: It was a repre- sentation of the tree of life. . . .

27. And I said unto them that the water which my father saw was filthiness; and so much was his mind swallowed up in other things that he beheld not the filthiness of the water.

28. And I said unto them that it was an awful gulf, which separated the wicked from the *tree of life*,[L] and also from the saints of God. . . .

36. Wherefore, the wicked are rejected from the righteous, and also from that tree of life, whose fruit is most precious and most desirable above all other fruits; yea, and it is the greatest of all the gifts of God. And thus I spake unto my brethren. Amen.

1 Nephi 15:21-22, 27-28, 36.

33. Behold, he sendeth an invitation unto all men, for the arms of mercy are extended towards them, and he saith: Repent, and I will receive you.

34. Yea, he saith: Come unto me and ye shall partake of *the fruit of the tree of life;* yea, ye shall eat and drink of the bread and the waters of life freely.

35. Yea, come unto me and bring forth works of righteousness, and ye shall not be hewn down and cast into the fire——. . .

62. I speak by way of command unto you that belong to the church; and unto those who do not belong to the church I speak by way of invitation, saying: Come and be baptized unto repentance, that ye also may be partakers of *the fruit of the tree of life.* Alma 5:33-35, 62.

40. And thus, if ye will not nourish the word, looking forward with an eye of faith to the fruit thereof, ye can never pluck of *the fruit of the tree of life.*

41. But if ye will nourish the word, yea, nourish the tree as it beginneth to grow, by your faith with great diligence, and with pa- tience, looking forward to the fruit thereof, it shall take root; and behold *it shall be a tree springing up unto everlasting life.*

Alma 32:40-41.

L. "Tree of Life"

Of particular interest is data which shows that the symbolic *"tree of life"* had its New World "roots" in *Tamoanchan,* "seat of the kingdom." It was an important symbol in the religion of *Itzamna* (Christ). The tree of life was used as a symbol by the early colonizers of southern Mexico and Guatemala, according to many sources. The *tree of life* is connected with the *cross,* the two having somewhat the same significance. Both relate to the resurrection, eternal life, the Lord and the "love of God." The symbolism may be summarized by saying that the tree of life is representative of eternal life, to be obtained by those who love God. Before the crucifixion of Christ, the *tree of life* symbol was used extensively. After the crucifixion the cross seems to have replaced it to a degree.

Ixtlilxochitl and *The Book of Mormon* mention the *tree of life* as a symbol used by the ancients of Bountiful. It is interesting to note that the tree of life is mentioned sixteen times in *The Book of Mormon,* six times in the Old Testament and three times in the New Testament.[19] It is mentioned many times in early Maya and Tultec accounts. In the Old World the "tree of life" was used by the earliest civilized people of the world, in the Tigris-Euphrates country and later in the kingdom of Israel.[20]

By the time the Spaniards arrived in Mexico and Yucatan, the Indians had degenerated the ancient Nephite doctrine of "the tree of life" into a ritual wherein they worshipped a symbolic tree of life. When Padre Andres de Avendaño y Loyola first visited the Itzas in Yucatan in 1696 A. D., he found them worshipping the said tree. He stated that the object ". . . is called in the name by which they worship it, *Yax cheel cab,* which means in their (Maya) language, 'the first tree in the world,' and, as is understood in their old songs (which few people understand) they wish to have it known they worship it because it was the tree of whose fruit our first father Adam ate, who in their language is called *Ixanom.*"[21]

---

[19] James Strong, *Exhaustive Concordance of the Bible,* pp. 1074-1075; George Reynolds, *Concordance of The Book of Mormon,* p. 419.

[20] Hugo Gressman, *The Tower of Babel,* 1928, Fig. 3, and discussion relating thereto; Old Testament, Genesis 2:9; 3:22-24; Proverbs 11:30; 13:12; 15:4.

[21] Andres de Avendaño y Loyola, *Relacion de las dos Entrades que hize a Peten Ytza* (1697), English translation by Philip Ainsworth Means, cited in *History of the Conquest of Yucatan and of the Itzas* (1917), p. 135. The *anom,* of *Ix-anom,* is not far from our "Adam."

In a paper entitled "*Tamoanchan,*" which appeared in the *Annals of the National Museum of Mexico,* it is clearly pointed out that *Tamoanchan* was identical with Tulan; and further, that "the ancient Americans symbolized *Tamoanchan,* the natal land, by means of the first original tree, *Chichihualquauitl.* . . . The *Chichihaulquauitl* [Nahua tongue] being the same as *Tutul Xiu* in Maya . . .; the identical interdependence is noticed between the tree of life, the first tree, the original, and many other names of the ancient civilized nations."

The authors of the paper go on to point out that the name *Zapotec,* the name of a tribe that resided on the westerly side of Tehuantepac, is derived from *zapote,* "symbol of the tree of life of this tribe. . . ." The next-succeeding paragraph of the article begins: "Another tribe, which without any doubt belonged to the worshippers of the tree of life, and from it derived its origin, was that of the *Ulmeca-Xicalanca*"! The authors go on to observe: "Another tribe-name which is an evident proof that those who bore it considered themselves children of the tree of life is that of the *Itzas.* They were forerunners of the Mayas and there seems to be no traditions respecting their origin; but the relation of their name with the term *Itzahte* 'tree of liquid amber,' *Itzamat* the ceiba 'God tree,' the sacred tree . . . 'and *Itzamna,* the God of the *Itzas,* that no special traditions are necessary to clarify the origin and filiation of this tribe.' Further, 'The Cakchikeles [of Guatemala], close relatives of the Mayas, likewise call themselves descendants of the tree of life'."[22] All of these people, the *Ulmeca-Xicalanca* [Mulekites, first colonizers of Zarahemla-Bountiful], the Tultecs, the *Itzas* and the *Zapotecs,* were identified with the "Fair God," the "tree of life" and the land Bountiful.

LI. SECOND COMING OF JESUS CHRIST

Quetzalcoatl predicts that He shall return and that His people shall possess the land

And at the time he went about taking leave of these people, *he told them that in time to come, in a year which would be called ce Atatl, he would re-*

Jesus Christ predicts His second coming and His people shall possess the land

3. And he did expound all things, even from the beginning until the time that *he should come in his glory*—yea, even all things which should come upon the face of the earth, even until the elements should melt with a fervent heat, and the earth should be wrapt together as a scroll,

---

22 Paul Henning, Francisco Plancarte, Cecilio A. Robelo, and Paul Gonzalez, "Tamoanchan, Estudio Arqueologico e Historico," *Anales del Museo Nacional de Arqueologic,* etc., vol. 4, pp. 433-462. See also Morley, 1946, *op cit.,* pp. 8, 221.

turn,[LI] and then his doctrine would be received, *and his children would be masters and possess the land.* ...

and the heavens and the earth should pass away; 3 Nephi 26:3.

22. And behold, this people will I establish in this land, unto the fulfilling of the covenant which I made with your father Jacob; and it shall be a New Jerusalem. And the powers of heaven shall be in the midst of this people; yea, even I will be in the midst of you.

23. Behold, I am he of whom Moses spake, saying: A prophet shall the Lord your God raise up unto you of your brethren, like unto me; him shall ye hear in all things whatsoever he shall say unto you. And it shall come to pass that every soul who will not hear that prophet shall be cut off from among the people.

24. Verily I say unto you, yea, and all the prophets from Samuel and those that follow after, as many as have spoken, have testified of me.

25. And behold, ye are the children of the prophets; and ye are of the house of Israel; and ye are of the covenant which the Father made with your fathers, saying unto Abraham: And in thy seed shall all the kindreds of the earth be blessed.

26. The Father having raised me up unto you first, and sent me to blesss you in turning away every one of you from his iniquities; and this because ye are the children of the covenant——   3 Nephi 20:22-26.

Both the *Works of Ixtlilxochitl* and *The Book of Mormon* are in perfect accord in the claim they make that Quetzalcoatl, or Jesus Christ, told the people that He would return and that "His children," or the people who accepted Him and practiced His teachings, would "be masters and possess the land."

In fact, the people of Mexico so strongly retained the tradition of the second coming of Quetzalcoatl that when Cortez and his Spanish conquistadors came to Mexico, they were received very kindly by Montezuma. The Mexican monarch and his people believed that Cortez was the bearded white God for whom they had been waiting for so long a time to return in conformity with His promise.

There is no tradition so prevalent among the American Indians in both North and South America as the one that their ancestors had been visited by a bearded white God and that after that marvelous visitor had done many things of importance for them He departed from their presence. Before leaving, however, He promised them that He would return. A. Hyatt Verrill has made the following statement:

Among the Mexicans, the Mayas, and the pre-Incan and Incan people of Peru there was a persistent, universally believed tradition of a bearded white man who visited their lands, taught them their civilizations and religions and then mysteriously disappeared. The tradition tells of this bearded God having reached Mexico and Yucatan in a "magic ship" and the tradition of the first Inca-"Manko Kapak"—having appeared from Lake Titicaca and having declared himself the "Son of the Sun."[23]

Evidence could be multiplied which proves that Jesus Christ visited ancient America. The source material on the subject is so extensive that to include it all here would be to make this book unduly long.

LII. QUETZALCOATL (CHRIST) PREDICTED THAT THE PEOPLE WOULD PASS THROUGH MANY CALAMITIES

IXTLILXOCHITL:

Quetzalcoatl (Jesus Christ) predicted calamities

And [Quetzalcoatl predicted] that *they and their descendants would pass through many calamities and persecutions;*[LI] and many other prophecies [were made by him] which later were very clearly seen.

EXTRACTS—BOOK OF MORMON:

Predictions that Nephites would pass through many calamities and destruction

9. But the Son of righteousness shall appear unto them; and he shall heal them, and they shall have peace with him, until three generations shall have passed away, and many of the fourth generation shall have passed away in righteousness.

10. And when these things have passed away a speedy destruction cometh unto my people; for, notwithstanding the pains of my soul, I have seen it; wherefore, I know that it shall come to pass; and they sell themselves for naught; for, for the reward of their pride and their foolishness they shall reap destruction; for because they yield unto the devil and choose the works of darkness rather than light, therefore they must go down to hell.

11. For the Spirit of the Lord will not always strive with man. And when the Spirit ceaseth to strive with man *then cometh speedy destruction,* and this grieveth my soul.[LII]

2 Nephi 26:9-11.

32. [Jesus Christ declared:] But behold, it sorroweth me because of the fourth generation from this generation, for they are led away captive by him even as was the son of perdition; for they will sell me for silver and for gold, and for that which moth doth corrupt and which thieves can break through and steal. And in that day will I visit them, even in turning their works upon their own heads.[LII] 3 Nephi 27:32.

---

[23] A. Hyatt Verrill, *Old Civilizations of the New World,* New Home Library, p. 28.

It is important and interesting to note that *Ixtlilxochitl* recorded in his history the fact that when Quetzalcoatl visited the people in ancient America he told them that "their descend- ants would pass through many calamities and persecutions."

In numerous places in *The Book of Mormon,* predictions, and the reports of actual historical events happening after the time of Christ's ministry, sustain *Ixtlilxochitl's* statement. For example, as early as 600 B.C. the Prophet Nephi had a vision in which he looked down through the stream of time and saw that following the resurrection of Jesus Christ that He would visit the descendants of the colony of Lehi. And after this visitation would take place, Nephi was informed, three generations would live in righteousness, peace, and happiness, but in the fourth gen- eration the people would turn against Jesus Christ and the gospel which He had proclaimed to them. Thereupon they would become very wicked. Then Nephi saw that as a result of their wickedness, God would send great calamities upon them and one faction (Nephites) would be destroyed by the other (Lamanites).

When Jesus Christ appeared to the inhabitants of ancient America following his resurrection, He re-affirmed Nephi's pre- diction and lamented because almost all of the people of the nation, Nephites as well as Lamanites, during the fourth gen- eration, would turn against righteousness and truth and would reject Him as their Savior and Lord. Thereupon He made the prediction that *Ixtlilxochitl* refers to, viz., "that great calamities and punishments would come upon the people."

In the days of Mormon and Moroni, the prophet-leaders of the fourth century A. D., gross wickedness prevailed among the inhabitants of Middle America and the calamities which had been foreseen came upon them because of their ungodliness, as will be shown in detail later on. These calamities came in the form of wars, bloodshed, and the final and complete de- struction of the Nephite nation and priesthood. As Nephi and Jesus Christ had predicted they were destroyed by their brethren, the Lamanites. *The Book of Mormon* tells a rather complete story of these calamities and thereby confirms the statement made by *Ixtlilxochitl.*

LIII. Quetzalcoatl's (Christ's) Departure

FROM IXTLILXOCHITL:

Departure of Quetzalcoatl (Jesus Christ)

He [Quetzalcoatl] having preached the said things in the majority of the cities of the Ulmecas and Xicalancas and in particular in that of Cholula, where he most visited, and seeing the little fruit brought about by his doctrine, he returned through the same part from whence he had come, which was by the Orient [Jerusalem?] disappearing through Coatzalcoalco.^LIII

FROM THE BOOK OF MORMON

Ascension of Jesus Christ (Quetzalcoatl)

38. And it came to pass that when Jesus had touched them all, there came a cloud and overshadowed the multitude that they could not see Jesus.
39. And while they were overshadowed *he departed from them, and ascended into heaven.* And the disciples saw and did bear record that he ascended again into heaven.^LIII

3 Nephi 18:38-39.

1. And now it came to pass that *when Jesus had ascended into heaven,* the multitude did disperse, and every man did take his wife and his children and did return to his own home.

3 Nephi 19:1.

Both *Ixtlilxochitl* and *The Book of Mormon* proclaim that Jesus Christ, or Quetzalcoatl, worked among the people of the land of Bountiful for a time, establishing his doctrines and teaching the people the way they should live to be happy. Then He departed from them. The two accounts are in agreement in that they have Him departing by the way that He came.[24]

Parallels Between Ixtlilxochitl and Nephite Accounts

The clear-cut parallels concerning Jesus Christ in ancient America given in our two leading sources are quite amazing. In order that they may be easily seen they are set out in chart form.

FROM IXTLILXOCHITL:

Great earthquakes, winds and darkness occurred in the area occupied by settlers ". . . at the time when Christ our Lord suffered, and they say it happened *during the first days of the year.*"

He appeared in ancient Bountifulland *(Huehue-tlapallan)* ". . . *some years after the incarnation of Christ our Lord.*"

"They were in the height of *their prosperity,* when in this land arrived a man whom some called Quetzalcoatl. . . ."

FROM THE BOOK OF MORMON:

Great earthquakes, winds and darkness occurred in the area occupied by settlers at the time of the Crucifixion, ". . . in the thirty and fourth year [since signs of birth of Christ] *in the first month, on the fourth day of the month,*"[25]

He descended from the sky in Bountiful-land thirty-three years after his birth.

He appeared at the beginning of their period of greatest prosperity and happiness: "And the *Lord did prosper them* exceedingly in the land. . . . they had become exceeding *rich.*"

---

[24] *The Book of Mormon,* p. 421 (3 Nephi 11:7-10).
[25] Up to this time the Nephites were apparently following the ancient calendar system of the Israelites. Under that system, the year began on the day of the first new moon after the Spring equinox.

"Quetzalcoatl was a favorably disposed man, of grave aspect, *white* and *bearded.* . . ."

"His countenance did shine upon them, and the light of his countenance did shine upon them, and behold they were as *white as the countenance* . . . *of Jesus;* and behold the whiteness thereof did exceed all the whiteness, yea, even there could be nothing upon earth so white as the whiteness thereof."

"His dress was a *long tunic.*"

". . . he was clothed in a white robe. . . ."

He was ". . . just, saintly and good." He taught them ". . . by deeds and words the path of virtue . . . forbidding them their vices and sins, giving laws and good doctrines."

He was just, saintly and good. He said of himself: "Behold, I am Jesus Christ, whom the prophets testified shall come into the world. . . . I am the light and the life of the world. . . ." He delivered to them the beatitudes, commandments on virtue, etc.

". . . he established *fasting* among them . . ."

Christ taught them to fast and pray. ". . . continue in *fasting* and *praying.* . . ."

He was a god of ". . . *health.*"

". . . he did *heal* them every one as they were brought forth unto him."

He was ". . . *god of rain.* . . ."

He had the power to cause it to rain. "For the earth was smitten that it was dry, and did not yield forth grain. . . . therefore *cry unto the Lord our God that he turn away from us this famine.* . . ."

". . . He was the first who worshipped and placed the *cross* among them. . . ."

He was symbolized by the *cross.* He said to the people in Bountiful-land "And my Father sent me that I might be lifted up upon the *cross.* . . ."

He was the first "who worshipped and placed . . . [among them] . . . the tree of sustenance or the *tree of life.* . . ."

The tree of life was symbolic of him and of love of him. ". . . I also beheld that *the tree of life* was a representation of the love of God."

"Quetzalcoatl . . . means *serpent of precious plumage.* . . . Quetzalcoatl was a . . . *man.*"

He was symbolized by the *serpent* and he had *power to pass through the air.* ". . . they saw a *Man* descending out of heaven . . ."

". . . he told them that in time to come, in the year which would be called Ce Acatl, *he would return, and then his doctrine would be received.* . . ."

He promised to return. "And he did expound all things, even from the beginning until the time that *he should come in his glory.* . . ."

He told them ". . . that they [the colonizers] and their descendants would pass through many calamities and per-

He said the colonizers would meet with calamities: "But behold, it sorroweth me because of the fourth generation from

secutions; and many other prophecies, which later were very clearly seen."

this generation, for they are led away captive by him even as was the son of perdition. . . . They shall reap destruction."

". . . the fourth age . . . was called Tletonatiuh, which means sun of fire, because they said that *this fourth and last age was to end with fire.*"

He predicted that the last age of the world will end with destruction by fire. ". . . *and when that day shall come they shall be visited of the Lord of Hosts, . . and with the flame of devouring fire.*" "*And the world shall be burned with fire.*"

He told them ". . . *his children would be masters and possess the land. . . .*"

He prophesied that his people would ultimately possess this land of the settlers: "*. . . this people will I establish in this land, unto the fulfilling of the covenant which I made with your father Jacob; and it shall be a New Jerusalem.*"

Even the most sceptical minds must admit that the foregoing parallels between *Ixtlilxochitl* and *The Book of Mormon* are remarkable. The number is considerable. On the other hand, there are no conflicts between the two reports. It must be said that the Nephite account is far longer and more detailed. That too is consistent with the claims made for *The Book of Mormon,* that it was derived directly from original eyewit-ness records. It should be the more detailed and the more precise, and so it is. The perfect accord between these two independent records is in itself rather strong evidence that the resurrected Christ was the Quetzalcoatl of Huehuetlapallan or ancient Bountiful-land.

The signs of the death of the Master, i.e., the engulfing of the Nephite country in darkness with the accompanying storm and earthquakes, as reported by both *Ixtlilxochitl* and *The Book of Mormon,* symbolized very aptly the life of Jesus and his imme-diate going out of the world, thereby leaving the world tempor-arily in darkness. As previously mentioned, this condition lasted. during the three days while the Lord's body was in the tomb, but when he was resurrected the darkness gave way to the light of another beautiful day. Then, as pointed out in the extracts pre-viously quoted from *The Book of Mormon,* Jesus Christ appeared to the Nephite-Mulekite people. He descended from heaven to them and taught them the gospel for a number of days and then He ascended back into heaven. When Christ was born in Pales-tine, possibly the same new star which was seen by the Magi[26]

---

[26] Matthew 2:1-11; *The Book of Mormon,* p. 400 (3 Nephi 1:21).

in the East was hailed by the Nephites on the opposite side of the world as an appropriate sign of that great event. Shortly after the signs of Christ's birth had been fulfilled, the Nephites added to their calendar system that event,[27] using it as a new and additional starting point from which to count the years. The people on the eastern hemisphere did not adopt the birth of Jesus as the time point from which to date events until many years later.[28]

SUMMARY STATEMENT

It is not incredible that Jesus Christ appeared personally to the ancient inhabitants of Bountiful-land in the New World following his crucifixion and resurrection in Palestine. The people of Bountiful-land were of His own house of Israel—they were sheep of His fold. He had led their ancestors to the New World six hundred and thirty-three years earlier for His own special purposes, that is, to the end that through the history of the Nephite nation (which was to include Christ's ministry in Bountiful-land) the Jews, Gentiles and the remnants of the Nephite-Lamanite people might have a special witness of the Messiahship of Jesus. Why then, is it not reasonable to suppose that the resurrected Lord should visit his New World sheep?

Among the ways in which Quetzalcoatl resembled Jesus was that He was a bearded white man, favorably disposed, of grave aspect and dressed in a long tunic. Shortly before Jesus' debut in Bountiful-land in 34 A. D. there occurred a period of darkness accompanied by earthquakes and a breaking of rocks—and this at the very time Christ was crucified across the sea; He taught the same things that Jesus had taught in Palestine; He was symbolized by the raised-up serpent, the same symbol that ancient Israel had used for hundreds of years to represent the long-awaited Messiah of Moses and the other Jewish prophets; He was also symbolized by the cross—the same type or representation that stood for the crucified Jesus; and He left the same lasting impression in the New World that Jesus left in the Old World. Therefore, Quetzalcoatl could have been none other than the resurrected Jesus of Nazareth, the Only Begotten Son of God and the Savior of the world.

---

[27] Ibid., p. 402 (3 Nephi 2:7-8).
[28] "Chronology," Encyclopedia Britannica.

The fact should be emphasized again that, although the account of Quetzalcoatl's visit to ancient America is beautifully told in the *Works of Ixtlilxochitl,* it is in *The Book of Mormon* that one finds the most complete and true picture of the life and mission of Jesus Christ to be found in any existing book. The New Testament is not excluded from that list.

Since the Nephites had such a thorough knowledge of the Son of God and the gospel plan of salvation, it is not surprising to find that numerous teachings resembling true gospel doctrines were found in great abundance among the Indians by the early Christian missionaries. Thus, Las Casas (1474-1566 A. D.), a prominent Spanish Catholic missionary, concluded that the devil had arrived in America ahead of the Christians and implanted in the minds and hearts of the natives many teachings closely akin to Christianity. The true answer is that Jesus the Christ visited ancient America and gave the people His true plan of salvation; and His visit was attested to on every hand by the prevalence of the tradition that a bearded white God had visited the ancient inhabitants of Middle America and had promised to return in the latter days.

Chapter 17

"MANY YEARS OF QUIET PEACE"

INTRODUCTORY STATEMENT

Many years of quiet peace followed the ministry of Christ in Bountiful-land. Ixtlilxochitl dates the interruption at 305 years after the crucifixion—that is, 305 years after the eclipse of the sun and the moon that occurred in 34 A. D. Thus, the peace lasted until 339 A. D., according to him. *The Book of Mormon* is consistent, reporting this long era as an epoch of peace, prosperity, righteousness and happiness. The first signs of war in 300 years flared up in 322 A. D. By 339 A. D., *Ixtlilxochitl's* date for the disruption of the peace, war was in full progress again. Where did the trouble start? Both accounts point to the ancient "seat of the kingdom." *Ixtlilxochitl,* like *The Book of Mormon,* refers to the absolute banishment of the Bountiful artisans from ancient Bountiful.

What was the cause of all the trouble? Both of our primary accounts give the same explanation—selfish men usurping power and wealth from others, apostasy from the rules of human conduct as laid down by the Lord for the welfare and happiness of mankind.

MANY YEARS OF PEACE

IXTLILXOCHITL:

Peace for 305 years from eclipse of 34 A.D., i.e. to 339 A.D.

It was 305 years since the sun and moon had eclipsed,[LIV] and 438 since the destruction of the Philistines, *Quinemetzin,* and 5,486 since the creation of the world, when *Chalcatzin* and *Tlacamhtzin,* very great gentlemen descendants of the royal house of the Tultecas, began to usurp the kingdom, wanting to take it away from the legitimate

EXTRACTS—BOOK OF MORMON:

Peace for 300 years from ministry of Christ in 34 A.D., i.e., to 339 A.D.

1. And it came to pass that the thirty and fourth year passed away, and also the thirty and fifth, and behold the disciples of Jesus had formed a church of Christ in all the lands round about. And as many as did come unto them, and did truly repent of their sins, were baptized in the name of Jesus; and they did also receive the Holy Ghost.

2. And it came to pass in the thirty and sixth year, the people were all converted unto the Lord, upon all the face of the land, both

successor, *after having had many years of quiet peace,*[LIV] which [disruption of the peace] happened in the year 13 *Acatl:* They were exiled and had some wars, until they drove them out of the city of *Tlachicalzincan,*[1] in the region of *Hueytlapallan,* their country, with all their allies and families, men as well as women, which was a great number of them.

They [Tultecas, the people of Bountiful-land] left the year following *ce Tecpatl,* banished from all the land, as will be seen in what follows, and in our count (way of figuring) at 439 [339] years from (since) the incarnation of Christ our Lord.[LIV]

Nephites and Lamanites, and *there were no contentions and disputations among them,*[LIV] and every man did deal justly one with another.

3. And they had all things common among them; therefore there were not rich and poor, bond and free, but they were all made free, and partakers of the heavenly gift.

4. And it came to pass that the thirty and seventh year passed away also, and there still continued to be *peace in the land.*[LIV]

5. And there were great and marvelous works wrought by the disciples of Jesus, insomuch that they did heal the sick, and raise the dead, and cause the lame to walk, and the blind to receive their sight, and the deaf to hear; and all manner of miracles did they work among the children of men; and in nothing did they work miracles save it were in the name of Jesus.

6. And thus did the thirty and eighth year pass away, and also the thirty and ninth, and forty and first, and the forty and second, yea, even until forty and nine years had passed away, and also the fifty and first, and the fifty and second; yea, and even until fifty and nine years had passed away.

7. And the Lord did prosper them exceedingly in the land; yea, insomuch that they did build cities again where there had been cities burned.

8. Yea, even that great city Zarahemla did they cause to be built again.

9. But there were many cities which had been sunk, and waters came up in the stead thereof; therefore these cities could not be renewed.

10. And now, behold, it came to pass that the people of Nephi did wax strong, and did multiply exceedingly fast, and became an exceedingly fair and delightsome people.

11. And they were married, and given in marriage, and were blessed according to the multitude of the promises which the Lord had made unto them.

12. And they did not walk any more after the performances and ordinances of the law of Moses; but they did walk after the commandments which they had received from their Lord and their God, continuing in fasting and prayer, and in meeting together oft both to pray and to hear the word of the Lord.

13. And it came to pass that *there was no contention among all the people, in all the*

---

[1] The name *Tlachiclazincan* is made up of at least three words, *Tla* (*Tula,* meaning "bountiful"), *chical* (possibly meaning "savanna") and *zincan* (*Tsinakan,* meaning "bats"). Thus, the name may mean "savanna abounding with bats." Professor Marcos E. Becerra, in his book, *Nombres Geograficos Indigenas del Estado de Chiapas* (1930), word 208, page 108, includes the name *Tsinakan-tlan,* stating that it means "place where bats abound." He indicates the name "bat" was applied to a certain people. Note that *Ixtlilxochitl* states that this city was in *Huehuetlapallan,* ancient Bountiful-land. Thus *Ixtlilxochitl* is in agreement with the Nephite record in identifying Bountiful-land as a region—a "country"—just as was Bountiful-Zarahemla.

land;[LIV] but there were mighty miracles wrought among the disciples of Jesus.

14. And it came to pass that the seventy and first year passed away, and also the seventy and second year, yea, and in fine, till the seventy and ninth year had passed away; yea, *even an hundred years had passed away,* and the disciples of Jesus, whom he had chosen, had all gone to the paradise of God, save it were the three who would tarry; and there were other disciples ordained in their stead; and also many of that generation had passed away.

15. And it came to pass that *there was no contention in the land,*[LIV] *because of the love of God which did dwell in the hearts of the people.*

16. And *there were no envyings, nor strifes, nor tumults, nor whoredoms, nor lyings, nor murders, nor any manner of lasciviousness; and surely there could not be a happier people among all the people who had been created by the hand of God.*

17. There were no robbers, nor murderers, neither were there Lamanites, nor any manner of ·ites; but they were in one, the children of Christ, and heirs to the kingdom of God.

18. And how blessed were they! For the Lord did bless them in all their doings; yea, even :hey were blessed and prospered until *an hundred and ten years had passed away; and the first generation from Christ had passed away, and there was no contention in all the land.*

19. And it came to pass that Nephi, he that kept this last record, (and he kept it upon the plates of Nephi) died, and his son Amos kept it in his stead; and he kept it upon the plates of Nephi also.

20. And he kept it eighty and four years, and *there was still peace in the land, save it were a small part of the people who had revolted from the church and taken upon them the name of Lamanites;* therefore there began to be La-manites again in the land.

21. And it came to pass that Amos died also, (and it was an hundred and ninety and four years from the coming of Christ) and his son Amos kept the record in his stead; and he also kept it upon the plates of Nephi; and it was also written in the book of Nephi, which is this book.

22. And it came to pass that *two hundred years had passed away;* and the second genera-tion had all passed away save it were a few.

23. And now I, Mormon, would that ye should know that the people had multiplied, in-somuch that they were spread upon all the face of the land, and that they had become exceed-ing rich, because of their prosperity in Christ.

24. And now, in this two hundred and first year there began to be among them those who were lifted up in pride, such as the wearing of costly apparel, and all manner of fine pearls, and of the fine things of the world.

25. And from that time forth they did have their goods and their substances no more common among them.

26. And they began to be divided into classes; and they began to build up churches unto themselves to get gain, and began to deny the true church of Christ.

27. And it came to pass that when two hundred and ten years had passed away there were many churches in the land; yea, there were many churches which professed to know the Christ, and yet they did deny the more parts of his gospel, insomuch that they did receive all manner of wickedness, and did administer that which was sacred unto him to whom it had been forbidden because of unworthiness....

45. And it came to pass that *when three hundred years had passed away, both the people of Nephi and the Lamanites had become exceeding wicked one like unto another.*

46. And *it came to pass that the robbers of Gadianton did spread over all the face of the land;* and there were none that were righteous save it were the disciples of Jesus. And gold and silver did they lay up in store in abundance, and did traffic in all manner of traffic.

47. And it came to pass that after *three hundred and five years had passed away,* (and the people did still remain in wickedness) Amos died; and his brother, Ammaron, did keep the record in his stead.

48. And it came to pass that when *three hundred and twenty years had passed away,* Ammaron, being constrained by the Holy Ghost, did hide up the records which were sacred—....

4 Nephi 1:1-27, 45-48a.

LIV. THREE HUNDRED YEARS OF PEACE

Ixtlilxochitl and *The Book of Mormon* are in close agreement in crediting the people of Bountiful-land with an era of peace which lasted almost 300 years immediately following the ministry of thee Messiah. The Nephite record gives the dates of continuous peace from 34 A. D. to 322 A. D., a total of 288 years, while *Ixtlilochitl* states that peace continued until 339 A. D., a period of 305 years. This long epoch of peace constitutes one of the longest periods of continuous peace ever enjoyed by any important nation, ancient or modern. In contrast consider the brief intervals of peace experi-

enced by the United States of America since the American
Revolution: American Revolution 1775-1783; *29 years interval*—War of 1812; *36 years interval*—Mexican War 1846; *13
years interval*—Civil War 1861-1865; *33 years interval*—Span-
ish-American War 1898; *19 years interval*—World War I
1917-1918; *23 years interval*—World War II 1941-1945; *?
years interval*—WorldWar III ——.

The foregoing figures show an average interval of twenty-
five years of peace between wars—and the people of the United
States are a peace-loving population compared with many other
peoples of the world.

Some people complain when they read the entire *Book of
Mormon* about the fact that so many wars were engaged in by
those ancient Americans; but when one looks carefully into the
matter, he finds that in comparison with our country, the Nephites
had more years of peace and fewer wars throughout their history
than we have had in the United States up to the present time.

The point is this—we can take a lesson from the book of
the ancients of Middle America. How did they achieve approximately 300 years of continuous peace between wars? Were we
to enter such an epoch of peace, the next mass murder of men
by their fellowmen would be deferred to the year 2250 A. D.
Imagine what could be accomplished in that interval with no war!

Ixtlilxochitl refers to the golden age of peace and the
wind-up of it by saying: "It was 305 years since the sun and
the moon eclipsed . . . when Chalcatzin and Tlacamihtzin, very
great gentlemen descendants of the royal house of the Tultecs,
began to desire to usurp the kingdom, wanting to take it away
from the legitimate successor, *after having been many years in
quiet peace. . . .*" He does not attempt to explain how it happened that the Tultecs experienced those "many years of quiet
peace."

The Book of Mormon, as should be expected, gives us more
details and more insight into the causes of peace and also of war.

Jesus Christ, with His pure and undefiled principles of
living, based on love of God and fellowman, is the hope of the
world. Christianity has not failed the modern world. It hasn't
been tried. There is a vast difference between the true gospel
and the doctrines taught by churches that have been established
for personal gain by those who modify fundamentals to suit
themselves.

If the ministry of Christ in the New World was followed by 200 years of righteous adherence to what He taught and by 300 years of peace, why was it not so in the Mediterranean world where His Church was also established? We can only speculate as to the answer. In Middle America the society was more compact, homogeneous and smaller. There were no out- side pagan influences and barbaric invasions as there were in the case of the early Roman Church. In the New World no emperors played politics with the Church and its doctrines as was done in the Old World. The entire background of the Nephite-Lamanite people had been Israelitish and there was never a time from 600 B. C. until after 400 A. D. when the Middle Americans were without inspired leadership. At no time was the entire Roman world converted to Christianity—but in the case of Middle America, all the people, both Nephite and Lamanite, were converted for a time. It is also quite likely that during the first two or three centuries after the time of Christ a higher percentage of the Middle Americans were literate than was the case among the people subjected to Christianity in the Mediterranean World.[2] From the time the Nephites left Jeru- salem under the leadership of Lehi, they were under inspired leadership that was possessed of an intimate knowledge of God. The Middle Americans attained greater spiritual heights and had closer contact with Jehovah-Christ in the six centuries im- mediately preceding His earthly ministry than did the people of the Old World.[3] They were far more ready to receive Him and accept Him than were their brothers in the Old World.

Our modern world has several things in common with the ancient Middle Americans which might mean real success if its inhabitants endeavored to try out Christ's program. Trans- portation, communication and educational facilities have made us compact. The world is small now. Ours is, relatively speak- ing, a very literate world. Universal education exists in most countries, making it possible to enlighten everyone concerning truth. Thus universal coverage is possible as was the case with the Middle Americans of the first century A. D. All this is

---

[2] The Book of Mormon, p. 136, verses 6-8 (Mosiah 2:6-8).

[3] It has been pointed out in this book that several Middle American accounts, including the Popol Vuh, Totonicapan, Annals of Xahila and The Book of Mormon, indicate that God led the Bountiful-land people to the New World and that close contact with Jehovah-Christ continued until the close of the fourth century A. D. See in The Book of Mormon the following: 1 Nephi 11:26-29;12:4-10; Helaman 14:2-8, 20-28; 2 Nephi 25:16-29, 30:7; 33:10; Jacob 1:8; 4:5; Mosiah 3:13; Alma 5:27; 11:42-44; 15:6-8; 21:9; 22:14; 27:27-29; 31:17, 38; 46:14, 27; 48:13; Mosiah 18:17.

encouraging and a blessed day awaits the inhabitants of the earth
if they will turn to God, accept the Gospel of Jesus Christ, and
live righteous lives.

DISRUPTION OF PEACE AND DIVISION INTO SEVEN TRIBES

IXTLILXOCHITL:

Disruption of peace

[It is suggested that the readers refer back to *Ixtlilxochitl's*
last discussion.]

EXTRACTS—BOOK OF MORMON:

Disruption of the Peace—Seven Tribes

8. And it came to pass in this year [322
A. D.] *there began to be a war between the
Nephites, who consisted of the* ①*Nephites and
the* ②*Jacobites and the* ③*Josephites and the*
④*Zoramites; and this war was between the Nephites, and the* ⑤*Lamanites and the* ⑥*Lemuelites and the* ⑦*Ishmaelites.*XXVII, LV

12. And it came to pass that the Lamanites
withdrew their design, and there was peace settled in the land; and *peace did remain for the
space of about four years,* that there was no
bloodshed.

18. And these Gadianton robbers, who were
among the Lamanites, did infest the land, insomuch that the inhabitants thereof began to hide
up their treasures in the earth; and they became
slippery, because the Lord had cursed the land,
that they could not hold them, nor retain them
again.

19. And it came to pass that there were sorceries, and witchcrafts, and magics; and the
power of the evil one was wrought upon all the
face of the land, even unto the fulfilling of all
the words of Abinadi, and also Samuel the Lamanite.

1. And it came to pass in that same year
there began to be a war again between the Nephites and the Lamanites. And notwithstanding
I [Mormon] being young, was large in stature;
therefore the people of Nephi appointed me that
I should be their leader, or the leader of their
armies.

2. Therefore it came to pass that in my sixteenth year I did go forth at the head of an
army of the Nephites, against the Lamanites;
therefore three hundred and twenty and six
years had passed away.

3. And it came to pass that in the three hundred and twenty and seventh year the Lamanites did come upon us with exceeding great
power, insomuch that they did frighten my armies; therefore they would not fight, and they
began to retreat towards the north countries.

4. And it came to pass that we did come to
the city of Angola, and we did take possession
of the city, and make preparations to defend
ourselves against the Lamanites. And it came to

pass that we did fortify the city with our might; but notwithstanding all our fortifications the Lamanites did come upon us and did drive us out of the city.

5. And they did also drive us forth out of the land of David.

6. And we marched forth and came to the land of Joshua, which was in the borders west by the seashore.

7. And it came to pass that we did gather in our people as fast as possible, that we might get them together in one body.

Mormon 1:8, 12, 18-19; 2:1-3, 4-7.

8. But behold, the land was filled with robbers and with Lamanites, and notwithstanding the great destruction which hung over my people, they did not repent of their evil doings; therefore there was blood and carnage spread throughout all the face of the land, both on the part of the Nephites and also on the part of the Lamanites; and it was one complete revolution throughout all the face of the land.

9. And now the Lamanites had a king, and his name was Aaron; and he came against us with an army of forty and four thousand. And behold, I withstood him with forty and two thousand. And it came to pass that I beat him with my army that he fled before me. And behold all this was done, and three hundred and thirty years had passed away.[LIV]   Mormon 2:8-9.

28. And the three hundred and forty and ninth year had passed away. And in the three hundred and fiftieth year we made a treaty with the Lamanites and the robbers of Gadianton, in which we did get the lands of our inheritance divided.[XLIII, LV]

29. And the Lamanites did give unto us the land northward, yea, even to the narrow passage which led into the land southward. And we did give unto the Lamanites all the land southward.   Mormon 2:28-29.

LV. DATE OF DISRUPTION OF THE PEACE

Ixtlilxochitl dates the disruption of the long era of peace in relation to three other events. He first relates it back 305 years to the great eclipse of the sun and the moon which was accurately fixed by him and the Nephite record as having happened at the time of the crucifixion of Christ in 34 A. D. The date he is talking about would be, therefore, 339 A. D.—305 years subsequent to 34 A. D. At the end of the paragraph he inadvertently added one hundred years, stating it was "439" years from the birth of Christ. When he dates the event in relation to the destruction of the Ancient Ones (Jaredites) and the Creation, he also errs. Three hundred thirty-nine A. D. would be 575 years after his date for the destruction of the Ancient Ones (Quinametzin) and 5,568 from his date for the Creation.

According to *The Book of Mormon,* "there began to be a war" in 322 A. D. This was of short duration, the peace era continuing for four more years. In 326 A. D. armies were again on the march, and in 327 A. D. the Nephites retreated north-ward, presumably by way of the narrow pass by the seashore. The war was going at full tempo by 339 A. D., *Ixtlilxochitl's* date for the end of the long epoch of peace.

In 350 A. D. the Great Treaty was signed by which the Nephites lost to the Lamanites their entire Bountiful-homeland region below the Isthmus. They retained only the northern colonies which had been first settled in 55 B. C. "... we did get the lands of our inheritance divided. And the Lamanites did give unto us the land northward, yea, even to the narrow passage which led into the land southward. And we did give unto the Lamanites all the land southward."

LVI. Division into Seven Tribes

Attention is called to the statement in *The Book of Mormon* concerning the restoration of the original seven divisions or tribes of the colony of Lehi: Nephites, Jacobites, Josephites, Zoramites, Lamanites, Lemuelites and Ishmaelites. These seven tribes are mentioned elsewhere in the Nephite record.[4] This matter of seven subdivisions of the early cultured colonizers of Middle America is significant. Several of the early writings, including Fray Sahagun, make reference to the original seven tribes. In fact, the seven tribes are associated with Bountiful-land, *Tulan-Zuiva* being a term that appears in several of the native accounts. It means "Bountiful-seven" and was one of the names applied to "the seat of the kingdom." Legend from central Mexico has reference to the ancient Bountiful coun-try by the term *Chicomoztoc* which word means "Seven Caves" or Seven Ravines. Sometimes ancient Bountiful-land just east of Tehuantepec is referred to simply as *Zuiva* or *Zuyva* (Seven).[5] This is understandable in the light of *The Book of Mormon* declarations that it was the capital of the seven united tribes from the time of Christ's ministry until about 322 A. D. when

---

[4] *The Book of Mormon,* p. 108 (Jacob 1:12-14); pp. 458-459 (4 Nephi 35-38).
[5] Delia Goetz and Sylvanus G. Morley, *Popol Vuh* (1950), pp. 62-67.

the division again occurred. These same seven tribes existed as of about 500 B. C.—almost from the beginning of Nephite-Lamanite history.[6]

In the *Popol Vuh* it is said: "Now then, the name of the place where Balam-Quitze, Balam Acab, Mahucutah, and Iqui-Balam and those of Tamub and Llocab went was *Tulan-Zuiva*."[7] The foregoing are names of six tribes as listed in the Guatemalan account. In the manuscript of Sahagun from the *Academia de la Historia* this statement, directly in point, is found: "Our fathers had news that from Chicomoztoc they had come, as they themselves said, *the seven tribes who proceeded from there,* [were] born there." In the *Popol Vuh* this important statement also is found: "We became separated there in Tulan, in Zuyva, from there went out together and there our race was created when we came."[8]

CONCLUDING THOUGHT

It would have been impossible for *Ixtlilxochitl* to have known that his ancestors experienced a long period of peace following the visitation of Jesus Christ to the western hemisphere except through the authentic traditions and records which came to him from his predecessors. The Catholic missionaries were not informed on that matter and could have had no influence on his thinking. Therefore, the *Works of Ixtlilxochitl* once again bear witness to the fact that *The Book of Mormon* is a true historical record of certain of the inhabitants of ancient America.

---

[6] *The Book of Mormon*, p. 108 (Jacob 1:12-14). The divisions were not based on family or blood lines alone, but rather "they did separate one from another into tribes, every man according to his family and his kindred *and friends.*" *The Book of Mormon*, p. 413 (3 Nephi 7:2).
[7] Delia Goetz and Sylvanus G. Morley, *op. cit.*, p. 174.
[8] *Ibid.*, note 4, p. 174; pp. 188-189.

Chapter 18

KNOWLEDGE CONCERNING GOD

INTRODUCTORY STATEMENT

The following seven chapters, with the exception of Chapter 19, deal with the knowledge and culture of the people of Bountiful-land. Chapter 19 is concerned with the physical characteristics of the settlers. The documentary sources again confirm each other to a remarkable degree. They are corroborated by archæological findings. *Ixtlilxochitl* is used as a guide in these chapters, topics discussed being suggested by what he has to say. Not all aspects of the culture of the ancients are covered in these chapters, nor is any attempt made to designate with particularity the time period when the various elements of culture appeared or disappeared. *The Book of Mormon,* however, maintains that the Nephites arrived in America shortly after 600 B. C. and brought with them a high degree of culture which they retained down to the time of their final disintegration and destruction during the fourth century A. D. The cultural summit was doubtless reached during "the many years of quiet peace"discussed in Chapter 17.

The chapter at hand shows that the Second and Third Settlers (Nephites-Mulekites—Nahuales-Ulmecas), generally referred to by *Ixtlilxochitl* as the Tultecas, had a knowledge of God as Creator of all things, a universal God, Lord of heaven and earth. Their knowledge of God was virtually identical with that of the Ancient Ones who had disregarded that knowledge and exterminated themselves like wild unintelligent beasts in fierce combat.

233

LVII. God the Creator of All Things

IXTLILXOCHITL:

Universal God and creator of all things

The most weighty authors and historians that there were in the paganism of the ancients ... declare through their histories that the god *Teotloquenahuaque, Tlachihihualcipal nemoanulhuicahua Tlaltipacque,* which means, according to the true sense, *the universal God of all things, creator of them (the things)*[LVI] *and by whose will all creatures live, Lord of heaven and earth, etc., after having created all things, created the first parents of men,*[LVII] *from whence descended all the others,*[LVII] *and the mansion and habitation that He gave them was the world.*

* * *

This [world] they say has four ages.[1] The first which was, after its origin, called *Atonatiuh,* which means *sun of water,* because the world ended by a deluge.

The second, called *Tlachitonatiuh,* means *sun of earth,* because the world ended by earthquakes, so that nearly all men perished; in which age and time lived the giants that are called *Quinametintzocuilhicxime.*

The third are called *Ecatonatiuh,* which means *sun of wind,* because this age ended with wind, which was so much that it uprooted all the buildings and trees, and even broke the rocks, and the majority of men perished; and those who escaped this calamity found a great number of monkeys that the wind must have brought from other parts, they said that men turned into monkeys.

EXTRACTS—BOOK OF MORMON:

Universal God and creator of all things

14. And now, my sons, I [Lehi] speak unto you these things for your profit and learning; for there is a God, *and he hath created all things,*[LVI] both the heavens and the earth, and all things that in them are, both things to act and things to be acted upon.

15. And to bring about his eternal purposes in the end of man, after he had created our first parents,[LVII] and the beasts of the field and fowls of the air, and in fine, all things which are created, it must needs be that there was an opposition; even the forbidden fruit in opposition to the tree of life; the one being sweet and the other bitter.[LVII]

16. Wherefore, the Lord God gave unto man that he should act for himself. Wherefore, man could not act for himself save it should be that he was enticed by the one or the other.

17. And I, Lehi, according to the things which I have read, must needs suppose that an angel of God, according to that which is written, had fallen from heaven; wherefore, he became a devil, having sought that which was evil before God.

18. And because he had fallen from heaven, and had become miserable forever, he sought also the misery of all mankind. Wherefore, he said unto Eve, yea, even that old serpent, who is the devil, who is the father of all lies, wherefore he said: Partake of the forbidden fruit, and ye shall not die, but ye shall be as God, knowing good and evil.[LVII]

19. And after Adam and Eve had partaken of the forbidden fruit they were driven out of the garden of Eden, to till the earth.

20. And they have brought forth children; yea, even the family of all the earth.[LVII]

2 Nephi 2:14-20.

17. Now after Mosiah had finished translating these records, behold, it gave an account of the people who were destroyed, from the time that they were destroyed back to the building of the great tower, at the time the Lord confounded the language of the people and they were scattered abroad upon the face of all the earth, yea, and even from that time back until the creation of Adam. Mosiah 28:17.

36. Now when Ammon had said these words, he began at the creation of the world, and also the creation of Adam,[LVI] and told him all the

---

[1] *Ixtlilxochitl's* statement of the four ages of the earth, as given here, is a restatement of things he has said before.

things concerning the fall of man, and rehearsed and laid before him the records and the holy scriptures of the people, which had been spoken by the prophets, even down to the time that their father, Lehi, left Jerusalem.   Alma 18:36.

12.   And it came to pass that when Aaron saw that the king would believe his words, he began from the creation of Adam, reading the scriptures unto the king—how God created man after his own image,[LVI] and that God gave him commandments, and that because of transgres-sion, man had fallen.

13.   And Aaron did expound unto him the scriptures from the creation of Adam, laying the fall of man before him, and their carnal state and also the plan of redemption, which was prepared from the foundation of the world, through Christ, for all whosoever would believe on his name.   Alma 22:12-13.

11.   But behold, I will show unto you a God of miracles, even the God of Abraham, and the God of Isaac, and the God of Jacob; and it is that same God who created the heavens and the earth, and all things that in them are.[LVI]

12.   Behold, he created Adam, and by Adam came the fall of man. And because of the fall of man came Jesus Christ, even the Father and the Son; and because of Jesus Christ came the redemption of man.   Mormon 9:11-12.

On almost every page in *The Book of Mormon* one meets God, in His might, in His majesty, His compassion, His love, His mercy, His justice, and in His eternal purposes. He led the various *Book of Mormon* peoples to the New World and after doing so He had a special interest in them. The God of the ancient Nephites was not merely a tribal or national deity. He was a cosmological, infinite God in the full sense of the word. He was a Creator of the heavens and the earth and of all things which they contain. His creative activities included the creation of man, the stars, and the whole universe.

In *The Book of Mormon,* God was known by a variety of names. He is referred to as "God the Eternal Father," or "the Very Eternal Father," and again, "Father of the Only Begotten Son," "Eternal Father of heaven and earth."

He was the Supreme Being unto whom "the children of God"[2] turned for inspiration, help, and guidance. According to the Nephite writers, under His direction all things pertaining to the administration of the affairs of the universe were accom-plished. He was not only the Supreme Being, but He was the

---

[2] This expression appears in the Nephite record. *The Book of Mormon,* p. 169 (Mosiah 18:22); p. 272 (Alma 30:42); p. 424 (3 Nephi 12:9); p. 459 (4 Nephi 1:39).

Father of all. He created the first man and the first woman and placed them upon this earth, and from them the human family has come.

Now, it would be well to note that the Tulteca teachings regarding God, as set out by *Ixtlilxochitl,* are very similar to those of *The Book of Mormon.* The Mexican history states that "they declare through their histories that the God *Teotloquenahuaque* ...universal God of all things, creator of them [all things] and by whose will all creatures live, Lord of heaven and earth, etc., after having created all things, created the first parents of men." Doctrines of this kind are almost an exact duplicate of ones appearing time and time again in the Nephite record. Certainly these parallel statements furnish substantial evidence that *Ixtlilxochitl's* ancestors stem from the House of Israel, as all the leading sources indicate.

OPPOSITION IN ALL THINGS

One of the basic ideas running through the religious philosophy of *The Book of Mormon* is this—that "it must needs be that there was an opposition." Earlier in the same chapter of the Nephite record is a similar statement, "For it must needs be that there is an opposition in all things."[3] The idea of opposition and opposites is one of the uppermost factors in Nephite religious thought. From the extracts quoted in the double column it is seen that a number of opposites are mentioned: the tree of forbidden fruit in opposition to the tree of life; the sweet and the bitter; even God has opposition: the devil is in opposition to Him; the good is in opposition to the evil. Near the end of *The Book of Mormon* this statement appears:

Wherefore, all things which are good cometh of God; and that which is evil cometh from the devil; for the devil is an enemy unto God, and fighteth against him continually, and inviteth and enticeth to sin, and to do that which is evil continually. But behold, that which is of God inviteth and enticeth to do good continually; wherefore, every thing which inviteth and enticeth to do good, and to love God, and to serve him, is inspired of God. Wherefore, take heed, my beloved brethren, that ye do not judge that which is evil to be of God, or that which is good and of God to be of the devil. For behold, my brethren, *it is given unto you to judge,* that ye may know good from evil; and the way to judge is as plain, that ye may know with a perfect knowledge, as the daylight is from the dark night. For behold, *the Spirit of Christ is given to every man, that he may*

---

[3] *Ibid.*, p. 53 (2 Nephi 2:11).

know good from evil; wherefore, I show unto you the way to judge; for everything which inviteth to do good, and to persuade to believe in Christ, is sent forth by the power and gift of Christ; wherefore ye may know with a perfect knowledge it is of God."[4]

This Nephite philosophy also penetrated the thinking of the enemy which crushed the Nephite-Mulekite nation in the fourth century after Christ, for it continued to pervade the religious thinking of the ancient Mexicans for many centuries and it still persists. This matter is beautifully summarized in the recent book of a scholarly Mexican of the present day, Miguel Covarrubias:

> The legends of the struggle between Quetzalcoatl [Christ] and Tez-catlipoca [the devil] are probably a Toltec rationalization to correlate his-torical events with an older myth, the eternal war between good and evil, black and white, war and peace, darkness and light, which is *the basic undercurrent in Mexican religious philosophy.* An old Indian legend claims that the feud dated back to the beginning of the world, when Tezcatlipoca ruled over the earth as the sun that lit and fed an incipient world.[5]

Lehi, the original colonizer who came out from Jerusalem, explains in simple, clear-cut language the reason behind the idea that "there must needs be opposition in all things." Said Lehi:

> Wherefore, the Lord God gave unto man that he should act for him-self [make choices]. Wherefore, man could not act for himself save it should be that he was enticed by the one or the other. . . . they [men and women] have become free forever, knowing good from evil; to act for themselves and not to be acted upon, save it be by the punishment of the law . . . Wherefore, men are free according to the flesh; and all things are given them which are expedient unto man. And they are free to choose liberty and eternal life, through the great mediation of all men, or to choose captivity and death, according to the captivity and power of the devil; for he seeketh that all men might be miserable like unto himself.[6]

Lehi goes on to explain that man must have freedom to be happy and to experience joy and progress. He points out that if there were no opposition things would stand still and there would be no joy for man. The purpose of man's existence, as far as God is concerned, is that he might make progress and have joy. "This is my work and my glory—to bring to pass the immor-tality and eternal life of man." Lehi said this:

---

[4] *Ibid.,* p. 513 (Moroni 7:12-16).
[5] Miguel Covarrubias, *Mexico South, The Isthmus of Tehuantepec* (1946), p. 136.
[6] *The Book of Mormon,* pp. 54-55 (2 Nephi 2).

And now, behold, if Adam had not transgressed he would not have fallen, but he would have remained in the garden of Eden [in an unprogressive status]. And all things which were created must have *remained in the same state* in which they were after they were created; and they must have remained forever, and had no end. And they would have had no children; wherefore they would have remained in a state of innocence, *having no joy, for they knew no misery;* doing no good, for they knew no sin. But behold, all things have been done in the wisdom of him who knoweth all things. Adam fell that men might be; and men are, that they might have joy.[7]

These ideas which Lehi passed on to his sons and to his posterity explain a great many things. They explain the origin of what Covarrubius calls "the basic undercurrent in Mexican religious philosophy." Thus the doctrine of opposites in all things was proclaimed to the inhabitants of ancient America by the holy prophets of God as early as the sixth century, B. C.; and those same teachings persisted from age to age among the descendants of the Nephites even until after the time of the Spanish Conquest and probably on to the present day. In other words, even after the ancient Lamanites had lost the true Gospel certain truths persisted.

---

[7] *Ibid.*

Chapter 19

RACES OF ANCIENT AMERICA

INTRODUCTORY STATEMENT

Both *Ixtlilxochitl* and *The Book of Mormon* state that there were white people in ancient Middle America. Strong support for such claims is at hand and will be presented hereafter. That other racial types were present in pre-Columbian America goes without saying. The sixteenth-century soldiers, clergy and adventurers found a variety of physical types of people in the New World. Since 1492, students of the native races of America have learned that the Eskimo of Alaska and northern Canada has the same slant eye and eye fold, the same low-bridged nose, the same hair and same general stature as the native of northeastern Asia. Some of the Indian peoples of Canada and parts of the United States are very similar to the natives of northeastern Asia.

In the southern tip of South America, in the "land of fire," the first European explorers found the most backward and primitive type of man to be found in America—a man whose physical characteristics reveal that he is entirely unrelated to the cultured settlers of ancient Middle America.

Thus, in this great hemisphere of millions of square miles, there were varying physical types of men, different races being represented. *Ixtlilxochitl* and *The Book of Mormon* contain declarations concerning racial types that allegedly occupied the middle portion of the New World in ancient times. Those declarations do not conflict with the facts established by present-day experts; in fact, the claims are supported by recent archæological and anthropological evidences. And very early in Nephite history Lehi said: ". . . behold, I say, if the day shall come that they [the Nephites] will reject the Holy One of Israel, the true Messiah, their Redeemer and their God . . . he will bring *other nations* unto them, and he will give unto them power, and he will take away from them the lands of their possessions, and he will cause them to be scattered and smitten." The fulfillment of this prophecy did not wait until the coming of the Europeans in the fifteenth century, as will be shown.

WHITE PEOPLE

IXTLILXOCHITL:

Kings of Bountiful-land were white and bearded

These kings were high of stature, and white, and bearded like the Spaniards,[LVIII] and for this reason the Indians, when the Marquis [Hernando Cortez] came, thought it was Topiltzin,[1] since he had told them that he was to return at a certain time with his old vassals of his ancestors; and they were with this uncertain hope up to the coming of the Spaniards. I mean the simple people and those who were of the Tulteca nation, for the Lords of this land well knew that he went to die in the province of Tlapallan, and he ordered that certain laws be kept which later the kings of this land agreed to (granted), and their vassals kept.

EXTRACTS—BOOK OF MORMON:

Nephites and Mulekites of Bountiful-land were white and bearded; Lamanites were dark

20. Wherefore, the word of the Lord was fulfilled which he spake unto me, saying that: Inasmuch as they will not hearken unto thy words they shall be cut off from the presence of the Lord. And behold, they were cut off from his presence.

21. And he caused the cursing to come upon them [Lamanites], yea, even a sore cursing, because of their iniquity. For behold, they had hardened their hearts against him, that they had become like unto a flint; wherefore, as *they were white, and exceeding fair and delight-some,*[LVIII] that they might not be enticing unto my people *the Lord God did cause a skin of blackness to come upon them.*
2 Nephi 5:20-21.

5. Behold, the Lamanites your brethren, whom ye hate because of their filthiness and the cursing which hath come upon their skins, are more righteous than you; . . .

8. O my brethren I fear that unless ye shall repent of your sins that their skins will be whiter than yours, when ye shall be brought before the throne of God.   Jacob 3:5, 8.

14. And it came to pass that those Lamanites who had united with the Nephites were numbered among the Nephites.

15. And *their skins became white like unto the Nephites.*[LVIII]

16. And their young men and their daughters became exceedingly fair, and they were numbered among the Nephites and were called Nephites. And thus ended the thirteenth year.
3 Nephi 2:14-16.

15. And I beheld the Spirit of the Lord, that it was upon the Gentiles, and they did prosper and obtain the land for their inheritance; *and I beheld that they were white, and exceeding fair and beautiful, like unto my people before they were slain.*[LVIII]   1 Nephi 13:15.

---
[1] Topiltzin was a tenth century Tultec. See discussions concerning him hereafter on pages 384, 390-394, 405-407.

LVIII. Appearance of the Kings and People of Bountiful-Land

As previously mentioned, when Christopher Columbus discovered America, he found a bronze-colored people living in the New World who received the name "Indians"; however, as has been shown, Ixtlilxochitl and The Book of Mormon both make the claim that there were white people in ancient times in Middle America. The references to white people heretofore in this book have been given primarily for the purpose of showing that Quetzalcoatl (Jesus Christ) was a white person when He visited ancient America and that the Nephites were "a white and delightsome people." In this chapter, an additional fact is presented and that fact is that there were white Indians living in America following the destruction of the Nephites. References to white people persisted in the traditions and histories of Mexico and Guatemala even down to and following the colonial period. In fact, after the Spaniards arrived in America, they discovered some very light-complexioned Americans, descendants of the ancient cultured inhabitants, living in Guatemala, Yucatan, Mexico and Peru, ancient seats of high culture.

Fig. 28: Ceramic Head from "Miraflores" Period

This masterful ceramic head was uncovered in the Guatemala highlands at Kaminaljuyu near Guatemala City. It dates from the "Miraflores" period—this meaning it was likely contemporaneous with the early Nahuas or Nephites. From Rafael Girard, Los Chortis Ante el Problema Maya Historia de los Culturas Indigenas de America, Desda su origen hosta hoy, Mexico, 1949, 5 vols., vol. 5, plate 78, following p. 1738.

As is evident from the quotations cited from The Book of Mormon, the people who colonized ancient America in 600 B. C. came directly from Jerusalem. These original settlers were white people and were of Semitic origin. Shortly after the arrival in the western hemisphere of the colony of Lehi, one faction (the Lamanites, Lemuelites and the Ishmaelites combined) became distinguished by dark skins. The ancient Nephite record gives the reasons why this faction of the original colonists became dark-skinned while the others remained white. It points out that when Lehi and Sariah left Jerusalem they had four sons. The two older sons, Laman and Lemuel, were rebellious and failed to keep the commandments of the Lord, as was shown in the chapter on the journey to America. Because of their rebellious and wicked lives, God cursed them, their wives, and those associated with them—all of whom were wicked—with dark skins. Only thirty years had passed away from the time

Fig. 29: BEARDED MAN OF ANCIENT VERA CRUZ, MEXICO

This unusual work of art shows two important things: (1) the physical characteristics of the early settlers of Vera Cruz, Mexico; (2) the high artistic sense and skills of the ancients. Note the aquiline nose, the eye form and the beard. This portrays a white man and it was fashioned by a highly skilled artisan—the type described in our documentary sources—and not by an ordinary North American or South American Indian.

that Lehi's colony left Jerusalem when Nephi declared in the ancient records that this cursing of "*a skin of blackness*" had already come upon them. The date was only 570 B. C. It stands to reason that God, the Creator of mankind and of our universe, had the power to change the skin-color of those people and endow them with that particular skin pigment which perpetuated itself through their posterity from generation to generation.[2] Thus their descendants were called Lamanites; and the curse carried on to the present day.

The younger sons, Sam and Nephi, and other members of the original settlers, continued faithful to the commandments of God; therefore, their descendants remained "*white, exceedingly fair, and delightsome.*"

There was little intermarriage between the white settlers (Nephites and Mulekites) and the darker people (the Lamanites) down to the birth of Christ. At that time there began a period of unity with the dark-skinned neighbors in the highlands to the south. Political, religious and social unity existed with the darker people until about 231 A. D. It is apparent from the record that during that period of time there was intermarriage and close social, religious and political ties. Little if any distinction appears to have been made thereafter on the basis of skin color. In fact, the record states:

And it came to pass that those Lamanites who had united with the Nephites were numbered among the Nephites. And their curse was taken away from them, and their skins became white like unto the Nephites, and their young men and their daughters became exceedingly fair, and they were numbered among the Nephites and were called Nephites, and thus ended the thirteenth year [13 A. D.].[3]

In the year 231 A. D., there arose a division among the people. The true believers in Jesus Christ called themselves Nephites after their ancestral name, and those who rejected the gospel were designated as Lamanites. Of the latter group, *The Book of Mormon* states:

... they did not dwindle in unbelief, but they did willfully rebel against the gospel of Christ; and they did teach their children that they should not believe, even as their fathers, from the beginning, did dwindle.[4]

---

[2] Hugh Nibley, in "Lehi in the Desert," *Improvement Era* (May, 1950), note 227, p. 449, discusses the matter of skin color of the settlers from Jerusalem.
[3] *The Book of Mormon*, pp. 402-403 (3 Nephi 2:14-16).
[4] *Ibid.*, p. 459 (4 Nephi 1:38).

Thus for about two hundred years there must have been considerable blending of the two physical types. This blending continued, insofar as can be learned from the Nephite record, until the close of *The Book of Mormon* period in 421 A. D. Important political and religious divisions and differences existed which divided the people again into ancient factions; but the record is silent concerning skin colors after the period of unity. However, in 385 A. D., Mormon, the historian-poet-soldier, prophesied that the unbelieving and adulterous enemy political-religious faction, the Lamanites—doubtless comprised at that time of whites, darks and blends—would ultimately become "a dark, a filthy, and a loathsome people, beyond the description of that which ever hath been amongst us, yea, even [more so than] that which hath been among the Lamanites, and this because of their unbelief and idolatry. For behold, the Spirit of the Lord hath already ceased to strive with their fathers; and they are without Christ and God in the world; and they are driven about as chaff before the wind. They [Lamanite faction] were once a delightsome people, and they had Christ for their shepherd; yea, they were led even by God the Father."[5] This prophecy seems to refer to a degeneration that was to occur gradually following the collapse of the Nephites in 385 A. D. It also suggests that the "skin of blackness" which had come upon the Lamanites by 570 B. C. was not a negroid blackness; and that there was still a possibility of further shading. In other words, Mormon's statement was a prediction to the effect that following the destruction of the Nephites, the surviving Lamanites would eventually become a more savage people, possessing darker skins than they had had at any given time during the *Book of Mormon* period.

Thus, it would appear from the meager facts available from *The Book of Mormon* on the matter that at the time the record closed in 421 A. D. there were both white-skinned and dark-skinned people in the victorious Lamanite political ranks.[6] It is therefore not surprising to find *Ixtlilxochitl* talking about "white" Tultec kings as late as the tenth century A. D. He points out that Topiltzin, ruler of Teotihuacan (Tula of Mexico's central plateau) in the tenth century, was white and bearded and so much like Cortez, the Spanish conqueror, that when Cortez arrived

---

[5] *Ibid.*, p. 468 (Mormon 5:15-16).
[6] Moroni makes it clear that as of about 400-421 A. D. not all of the Nephite religious-political faction had yet been killed off. *The Book of Mormon*, p. 510 (Moroni 1:2-3).

in the Valley of Mexico approximately 500 years after the time of Topiltzin, the natives "thought he was Topiltzin, since Topiltzin had prophesied that he was to return at a certain time."

Strong strains of white blood still remained in Tultec remnants as late as the tenth century. The white blood was, apparently, diluted gradually and continuously until the arrival of the Europeans in the sixteenth century. By then the descendants of the original settlers from the Near East had lost their identity as a white race and other non-Book-of-Mormon peoples and racial types had long since appeared on the Middle American scene. Since the Spanish Conquest, the process has been reversed to a degree, with the blood of the white Europeans being blended somewhat with that of the darker New World types.

Ixtlilxochitl, in speaking of events of the tenth century, says that at that time "there was a law that whenever a child was born that was very white and blond, when it was five years of age, it was right away sacrificed, and it [the law] lasted until the coming of the Spaniards." This barbaric law, we note, existed during the dominance of the Aztecs, the warlike Algonquin immigrants from the north. It appears, however, that by the tenth century blond children were somewhat of a rarity.

The fifteenth century Mexican account concerning Tezozomoic (1343-1427 A. D.) makes frequent mention of the sacrifice of white children.[7]

Sahagun's description of the physical characteristics of the Tultecs is very brief, no mention being made of skin color. "And they were tall, of greater bodies than those now living, and because they were so tall they ran and strided a great deal, for which reason they were called tlanquacemilhuiqu, which means, 'they ran a whole day without resting'."[8] However, the great priest-historian, Sahagun, is more precise in his description of the Huastecas of the lowlands of northern Vera Cruz and the adjacent foothills of San Luis Potosi. The Huastecas came from the same stock as the ancient Bountiful-land settlers below Tehuantepec, for they spoke the Maya language of that Guatemala-southern-Mexico region. Their separation from the main body of Maya-speaking people and their migration to northern Vera Cruz took place very early for they did not have the unique culture of the Mayas of the post-Book-of-Mormon period.[9] For

[7] Alfredo Chavero, Obras Historicas de Ixtlilxochitl (1891), Tomo 1, footnote 2, pp. 49-50.
[8] Sahagun, Historia de las Cosas de Nueva Espana, Libro Noveno, Capitulo 29, Sec. 1.
[9] Sylvanus G. Morley, The Ancient Maya (1947), pp. 39-40.

Fig. 30: BEARDED MAN ON VASE

This bearded man of ancient America is represented on a vase discovered at Quirigua. Guatemala. The original specimen is in the St. Louis Art Museum. The beard and the eyes distinguish him from the Mongoloid type.

a discussion on the identity of the Mayas see Chapter 33 herein. Sahagun describes the Huasteca-Mayas as a white people:

These *Totonaques* are settled in the northern part and they say they are "Guastecas" [*Huastecas*]. They have long faces and flat heads. . . .

All of them, men and women, are *white* and of good and well-proportioned faces and good features; their language is very different from the others [of the central mesa and northern gulf-coast of Mexico], although some of them spoke the language of the *Otomies* and others that of the Nahuas or Mexicans; and others there are that understand the *Guastecas* language. And they are very expert and good officers of song; they dance gracefully and with beautiful movements.[10]

Sahagun's description of dress and textiles of these Huasteca people is interesting and worth inserting at this point for it further-demonstrates their ties with the original people of Bountiful-land.

These lived in good breeding, because the men wore good clothes and mantles; they wear shoes, jewels and beads around the neck and feathers and they have fans and amulets and they are curiously shaved. They look at themselves in mirrors and their women put on painted and elegant skirts and blouses. They are polished and expert in everything because they said they were *Guastecas;* they used to wear skirts and blouses of many colors and some of them dressed in what they called *camitl,* which is a *huipil* [tunic] like a net; and it is said that it was all of this that the principal ones and their wives wore, and all the rest of the people wore a different kind of dress, the plebeian women wearing blue and white skirts. And the braids they used to fix in their hair were of different colors, and twisted with feathers. When they went to market they would dress very elegantly. And they were great weavers of handwork.[11]

The Ulmec colonizers of Bountiful-land are said to have been a white people. Mixed with them was a darker or yellow-skinned people.[12] The early Tultecs, that is, the founders of the ancient Tullan of the Vera Cruz-Tabasco-Chiapas-Campeche country, were white people, according to Mexican accounts.[13]

The *Popol Vuh* of the highland Mayas of Guatemala makes reference to the "white men" among the Old-World inhabitants from whence came the *Nahuales:* "There were then, in great number, the black men and the *white men,* men of many classes, men of many tongues, that it was wonderful to hear them."[14]

[10] Bernardino de Sahagun, *op. cit.,* Capitulo 29.
[11] Sahagun, *op. cit.,* Libro Noveno, Capitulo 29, Sec. 7.
[12] Desire Charnay, *Native Races,* vol. 5, note 62, pp. 202-203.
[13] Harold I. Velt, *America's Lost Civilizations,* 1949, p. 84.
[14] Brasseur de Bourbourg quotes this from the manuscript of *Chichicastenango,* the *Popol Vuh,* in his *Histoire des Nations Civilisees Du Mexique* (1857), p. 106. The instant translation is from Goetz and Morley, *The Popol Vuh* (1950), p. 172.

The original Itzas, priest-rulers, who emigrated from Bountiful-land to the Yucatan peninsula during the Nephite period, were of the white race. Evidence of this is found in the facial characteristics, head form, and also in carefully reported observations of surviving remnants. In 1696-1697 A. D. Padre Andres de Avendaño y Loyola, a truly noble Catholic priest, visited the only surviving remnant of the Itzas (the "holy men" of the Fair God) in Tayasal, Peten, Guatemala. The skin color, as described by him, is the same as that of the ancients (and present-day natives) of the ancient Near East—a dusky white or mestizo: "These Ytzaes are well-featured and, like mestizos, nearly all of a *light complexion* and of very perfect stature and of natural gifts."[15]

Another Spaniard, Villagutierre Sotomayor, visited the Itzas remnants shortly after Avendaño, describing them as "well-featured, their color brownish but lighter than that of [Mayas] of [northern] Yucatan."[17]

The founder of the ancient Maya city of *Mutul* in Yucatan was one *Zac Mutul*, his name meaning "white man."[18] Since the city was founded centuries before the coming of Europeans, it is apparent that the name was descriptive of the man. *Zac* is the Maya word for "white." Amazing enough the Hebrew word for "white" is identical to the Maya—*Zac!*

How Races Are Classified

Anthropology (science of man) classifies mankind, generally speaking, into three primary races: Caucasians, Mongoloid and Negroid. Sometimes the natives of Australia are regarded as a fourth primary race. The Caucasian race is sometimes referred to as the white race, the Mongoloid as the yellow race and the Negroid as the black race. A large percentage of the people of the world are of mixed descent, having some of the characteristics of one race and some of another. Skin color is merely one factor that helps determine racial type. Hair texture, the shape of the nose, the shape of the head (particularly the outline of the head when viewed from above), and the shape and

---

[15] Andres de Avendano y Loycla, *Relacion de las dos Entradas que hize a Peten Ytza* (1697), English translation by Philip Ainsworth Means, cited in *History of the Conquest of Yucatan and of the Itzas* (1917), p. 22.
[17] Juan de Villagutierre Sotomayor, *Historia de la Conquista de el Itza* (1701); translation by M. Wells Jakeman, *Origins and History of the Mayas* (1950), p. 181.
[18] Jakeman, *op. cit.*, p. 182, citing Martin de Palomar, *Relacion de Motul* (1898 edition), p. 77; Tozzer (1941), note 128.

angle of the eye are helpful in determining the race to which one belongs. Also, the amount of hair on the body and facial hair are of some value in classifying types.

Most of the ancients of the Near East, including those of Israel, fall into one or more subdivisions of the Caucasian Race. They are characterized generally by a white skin (shaded darker than the skin of the Nordic subdivision of the race), long heads, slender bodies, horizontal eyes which sometimes have an outer fold, receding foreheads, lips that are full and curved, noses that are long, high-bridged, narrow and generally convex. The adult males usually have heavy beards.

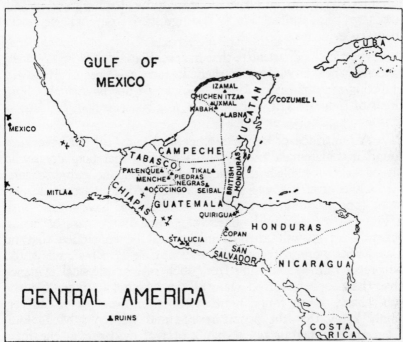

Fig. 31: Map Showing the Distribution of the Bearded Figures
The crosses indicate the locations in which the bearded figures have been found.

If *The Book of Mormon*, *Ixtlilxochitl*, the *Totonicapan* paper and the *Popol Vuh* are correct in bringing the early colonizers of Middle America out from the Near East,[19] then cer-

---

[19] There is a possibility that some of the *Mulekites*, who landed on the Gulf Coast, were Phœnecians from Sidon. They may well have set sail from Sidon in Phœnecia. In 608-596 B. C. the Phœnecians of Sidon were such great sailors that Necho II of Egypt called on them to man his ships. They are known to have sailed westward to Tarshish, Spain, that early. Nebuchadnezzar also conquered Sidon and other Phœnecian towns. The child, Mulek, son of Zedekiah, may have fled with Phœnecians. This is entirely speculative because the Mulekite migration account is very brief and very general.

tainly there should be some evidence of the existence of members
of the Mediterranean subdivision of the Caucasian race in ancient
Middle America. We have already seen documentary and eyewitness evidence that such was the case, particularly with reference to skin color.

REAL EVIDENCE

Departing now from documentary and eyewitness evidence,
we turn to what lawyers call "real or physical" evidence—i.e.,
tangible things found at the scene where certain events are alleged to have occurred. Real evidence speaks for itself and merely
needs to be identified. It is distinguished from oral or documentary evidence.

Practically all artifacts that the archæologist digs up are "real
evidence" of one kind or another. In fact, it is necessarily a very
enduring type of real evidence or it would not be available hundreds or thousands of years after having been fashioned. Usually
it is ceramic, stone, or bone.

A multitude of ceramic, stone and bone objects have been
found in Guatemala and southern Mexico that help greatly in
an effort to establish the racial identity of the early settlers.

Of course, if every ancient Middle American ceramic and
stone representation of a person was found to have a nose with
a low bridge, eyes with inner folds and, in the case of males,
scant beard growth, then it might well be concluded that no
Caucasians were in the area in ancient times. In fact, we would
be pretty safe in deducing from such real or physical evidence
that the people involved were of the Mongoloid race. On the
other hand, if we found none of those features, we would certainly know that the people represented were not Mongoloid.
The more numerous our exhibits of real evidence in the form
of bearded persons with high-bridged convex noses and horizontal eyes (minus the Mongoloid fold), the stronger the case
for the Caucasian. If both types are found, then it would appear
that somehow both Caucasian and Mongoloid people made their
way to Middle America some time or other before the Conquest. If both types are found in the same strata it would
tend to indicate they were contemporary. If only one type is
found in the lower and earliest strata, it would appear that the
type so found probably arrived in the area first.

It should be pointed out that there is nothing in *The Book* *of Mormon* to indicate the presence of persons of the Mongoloid race in Bountiful-land (or any other region occupied by the Nephite-Mulekite-Lamanite people) during the period covered

Fig. 32: BEARDED "MEPHISTOPHELES"

This bearded "Mephistopheles" of ancient Mexico is from Libertad, Chiapas, Mexico. The original specimen is in the American Museum of Natural History.

by the Nephite record, 600 B. C. to 421 A. D. However, it does indicate that some of the colonizers were dark-skinned.[20] On the other hand, *The Book of Mormon* does not deal with events after 421 A. D., and it is entirely possible that Mongoloid-type people or Negroids entered Bountiful after that date. In fact, Nephite prophets predicted that other people would enter *Book-of-Mormon* lands.[21] Certainly, we are sure that long before the Spanish Conquest nomadic Mongoloids and Algonquins of Asiatic descent[22] began arriving from the north. South of the Rio Grande in central Mexico, these late immigrants into Middle America found the cultured "Tultecs" and "Mayas" and related peoples who had survived the earlier calamities related in the *Works of Ixtlilxochitl* and *The Book of Mormon*.

Some of the "real" or physical evidence that has been turned up in Guatemala and southern Mexico is shown in the photographs on pages 241, 242, 245, 251, 253 and 254. The reader can draw his own conclusions.

The evidence regarding the physical characteristics of the ancient *Itzas*, who colonized Yucatan from Bountiful-land to the southwest during *The Book of Mormon* era, has been summarized by an able scholar. His statement may be considered as applying to all the peoples identified with ancient Bountiful-land, including Nephites, early Nahuas, Mulekites, early Ulmecs, Lamanites, Quiches, Tultecs, Tzendals, and proto-Mayas:

> These .[documentary] descriptions, at least as to their features, are confirmed and also established for ancient times by the evidence of the sculptured, modeled and painted representations of Itzan priest-rulers at the various ruined temple-cities of the Old Empire and at Chichen Itza. For according to these representations the Itzas had the orthognathic faces and narrow, high-bridged noses of Caucasians. In fact their noses—their most distinctive feature—are exclusively Caucasian in type: long, relatively narrow and high-bridged, and either convex (that is, "Hebrew" or Armenoid Caucasian), or straight or slightly aquiline (that is Mediterranoid and Nordic Caucasian).
>
> Also Caucasian in type are their receding foreheads (extreme cases due to artificial compression), full, curved lips, and somewhat recessive but firm chins.
>
> Moreover, a close study of these representations reveals additional Caucasian-like facial traits, in mixture with some "Mongoloid" more char-

[20] *The Book of Mormon*, p. 61 (2 Nephi 5:21-23); p. 201 (Alma 3:6-10).
[21] For a discussion on the various migrations from Asia, read Harold Gladwin's *Men Out of Asia* (1947).
[22] The regions occupied by the colonizers from the Near East were to be preserved for them only so long as the commandments of God were adhered to faithfully. See e.g., *The Book of Mormon*, p. 50 (2 Nephi 1:9).

acteristics of the native.[23] In some figures the face is relatively long or narrow, presenting an entirely Caucasian appearance, while in others it is broad, especially at the cheek-bones, giving a distinctly Mongoloid cast. Again, the eyes may be depicted in a horizontal line like those of Caucasians, or they may be shown with a decidedly Mongoloid slant.

Finally, as noted previously, some of the Itzan priest-rulers are depicted with long chin-beards like the ancient Caucasian priest-rulers of Egypt and Babylonia, while others are shown without beards like most Mongoloids.[24]

Skeletal remains are another form of "real" evidence supplying help in solving the problem of the racial type or types of the early colonizers. Actually, little work along this line has been done in Middle America. Few skeletons of great antiquity have been found, because of the nature of the climate. All those that have been studied appear to date after 400 A. D.

Fig. 33: MAYAN MONGOLOID TYPE
A Maya head of the post-Book-of-Mormon period. Not all Mayas had the same physical characteristics. This one had the nose and eyes of the Mongoloid type. Contrast these features with the convex nose, the beard and the eye of Figure 30.

However, those found and studied should and do, in part, reflect the racial type or types of the earlier people.

One of the most important results of recent work in the field of racial anthropology is the finding that all of the "Indian" people of the western hemisphere do not stem from one physical type. The "Indians" are not one homogeneous type. Diverse types are represented. Included in the strains found are elements from both the Mongoloids and the Caucasians.[25] Even the Austroloids are represented, but there is nothing indicating their presence in Book-of-Mormon lands in Book-of-Mormon epochs. This means there is accord between the documentary sources and the "real evidence" on the point.

[23] The stone representations from northern Yucatan are all dated in the post-Book of Mormon period, that is, after Mongoloid infiltration.
[24] M. Wells Jakeman, op. cit., pp. 181-182.
[25] W. W. Howells, Univ. of Wisconsin, "The Origins of American Indian Race Types," The Maya and Their Neighbors, a compilation, D. Appleton-Century Company (1940), pp. 3-9.

Attention is called to the fact that the bones of the ancient Mayas of northern Yucatan (the "hooked, beaky noses" helping the work of classifying them) resemble those of the people of the Near East. Professor Earnest A. Hooton, one of the few men who have applied the principles of somatology (comparative

Fig. 34: Mayan Semitic Type

Observe the Semitic-type nose and lips of this ancient inhabitant of Mexico. Also, note the interesting hat. This fine ceramic may be seen in the National Museum in Mexico City. *Photo by Glen Harmon.*

study of the structure and development of the human body) to ancient Maya skeletal remains, says:

It is of considerable interest to ponder the fact that intentional artificial deformation of the skull in a people with *hooked, beaky noses* is associated with the development of high civilizations in two widely separated areas—the Near East and the Western cordillera of the Americas. . . . I am inclined to think that the ancestors of the classical Mayas were not very different from the white hybridized type which we call Armenoid—hook noses from . . . the Iranian Plateau race, round heads from the good old Alpines—and inspired with similar æsthetic ambitions to improve their head form. Eventually they picked up some Mongoloid features—hair, pigmentation, cheek-bones, *et cetera*. These may have been fairly recent accretions, because Mongolization is a late racial phenomenon in the Old World and probably still later in the New. It's a long, long way to Chichen-Itza [Yucatan], but the Roman-nosed god and the Long-nosed god both made it.[26]

All-or-None Theory

Elsewhere, in discussing the Mayas, Professor Hooton has said that the Mayas seem farther removed from the ideal Mongoloid types than the Indians of our Southwest and our great plains.[27] He disagrees with the view taken by some students of the "natives" of America, that all are from the same stock, that all are of the same race. This view, it seems, can safely be classified as a "sweeping all-or-none, black-or-white judgment, characteristic of totalitarian attitudes, and having no place in science, whose very nature is judicial."[28] Certainly there was room in the great western hemisphere in ancient times for some Near Easterners, especially if they confined themselves for many centuries to the territory below the Rio Grande. The sweeping claim that all of the ancients of the New World came by way of northeastern Siberia and Alaska is entitled to no less harsh condemnation than the all-Mongoloid race generality. These two unscientific theories, adhered to by some scientists, the *all-Mongoloid-or-none* and the *all-by-way-of-Siberia-Bering-Straits-or-none,* flies directly into the face of fundamental somatological laws and completely disregards highly reliable documentary

---

[26] Ernest A. Hooton, prof. of Anthropology, Harvard University, in article, "Skeletons from the Cenote of Sacrifice at Chichen Itza, in *The Maya and Their Neighbors* (1940), pp. 279-280. Howells, *op. cit.,* indicates that in some of the natives of the New World there are Caucasian elements. In the United States the Caucasian features are particularly pronounced in the Indians of the eastern part of the country. See also M. Wells Jakeman, *A Map of the New World at the Close of the Native or Pre-Columbian Age, showing . . . racial types* (1944).

[27] Ernest F. Hooton, *Apes, Men and Morons* (1937), p. 178.

[28] After the language of the distinguished anthropologist, A. L. Kroeber, in *American Anthropologist* (April-June, 1949), p. 320.

and archæological sources. Further, to claim that such bearded, convex-nosed characters as "Uncle Sam" of La Venta, "Mephistopheles" of Tres Zapotes and "Kukulcan" of the Castillo at Chichen Itza are representations of Mongoloids is to ignore clearcut "real evidence" to the contrary. They are representations of Caucasians and all the dodging and ignoring that is going on with respect to such evidence will not change the truth. It is to the credit of a few experts like Hooton of Harvard and Harold Gladwin that they are brave enough to face the facts.

Those who persist in following the "all-or-none" theories must accuse *Ixtlilxochitl*, Sahagun, Torquemada, the Señores of Totonicapan and Xahila, and Joseph Smith of ignorance or deliberate misstatements for saying that the colonizers came to America by boat from across the sea. These remarkable people are dead and cannot speak for themselves; however, the stone and ceramic figures of the ancient colonizers are speaking quite eloquently out of the ground. They are "voices from the dust" which constitute real evidence that will not easily be overcome; and, to a marked degree, it seems that this "real evidence" points to the fact that the original settlers of Bountiful-land were very much like the ancient Near Easterners, both in mien and dress.

NOTE: The following material is taken from the book *Fusang or the Discovery of America by Chinese Buddhist Priests in the Fifth Century*. by Charles C. Leland, published by Trubner & Company, Ludgate Hill, London, 1875:

In one of the regularly entered reports in the *Year Books* or *Annals* of the Chinese Empire, the claim is made that a Buddhist monk or missionary named Hoei-shin "returned to China in the year 499 A. D. from a long journey to the East." It is believed by many historians and scholars that the part of the world visited by Hoei-shin was Mexico.

In 1761 A. D., the French sinologist Deguignes set forth in a very ably written paper in the *Memoirs de L'Academie des Inscriptions et Belles Lettres* (vol. 28) the fact that he had "found in the works of early Chinese historians a statement that in the fifth century of our era certain Buddhist priests had discovered a country which they called Fusang, and which from the direction and distance as described by them appeared to be Western America, and in all probability Mexico."

In 1841 Carl Frederick Neumann, Professor of Oriental Languages and History at the University of Munich, published the original narrative of Hoei-shin from the *Annals*. Part of Dr. Neumann's comments regarding this event is as follows:

I am far from claiming that it has been absolutely proved that Hoei-shin was in Mexico, or that he was preceded thither by "five" beggar-monks from the Kingdom of Kipin. But all that Hoei-shin declares he saw is not only probable, but is confirmed, almost to the minute details, by what is now known of Old and New Mexico.

Among the objects which were seen and described by the Buddhist priest was the maguey plant, or great cactus which he also called Fusang, naming it after a Chinese plant slightly resembling it. He reported:

Many Fusang trees grow there, whose leaves resemble the Dryanda Cordifolia. The sprouts on the contrary resemble those of the bamboo-tree, and are eaten by the inhabitants of the land. The fruit is like a pear in form but is red. From the bark they prepare a sort of linen which they use for clothing, and also a sort of ornamented stuff. . . . They have written characters in this land, and prepare paper from bark of the Fusang. (P. 27.)

Certainly the maguey plant of Mexico fits this description.

Chapter 20

ARTS AND CRAFTS

INTRODUCTORY STATEMENT

Ixtlilxochitl and several other sixteenth century writers claim that the Tultecas of ancient Bountiful-land were highly skilled in the various arts and crafts. *Ixtlilxochitl's* statement is short but directly to the point. The writers of *The Book of Mormon* described in much detail the skills of the Nephite-Mulekite people, claiming that they were highly civilized. They pointed out time and time again that those ancient Americans were workers of gold, silver, and other precious metals, as well as skilled architects, mechanics, carpenters, and great masters of many arts and crafts, as will be shown in this chapter. Thus again, numerous sources are in agreement in regards to the skills and achievements of the people of ancient Bountiful-land.

IXTLILXOCHITL:	EXTRACTS—BOOK OF MORMON:
Arts and crafts of the Tultecas[LIX]	*Arts and crafts of the Nephites*[LIX]

Arts and crafts of the Tultecas[LIX]

The Tultecas were great architects and carpenters and were skilled in the mechanical arts, like silversmiths. They took out [mined] gold and silver and smelted it, and carved precious stones; they did the best thing of what there is in the world.

Arts and crafts of the Nephites[LIX]

25b. And we did find all manner of ore, both of gold, and of silver, and of copper.
1 Nephi 18:25b.

13. And it came to pass that we began to prosper exceedingly, and to multiply in the land.

14. And I, Nephi, did take the sword of Laban, and after the manner of it did make many swords, lest by any means the people who were now called Lamanites should come upon us and destroy us; for I know their hatred towards me and my children and those who were called my people.

15. And I did teach my people to build buildings, and to work in all manner of wood, and of iron, and of copper, and of brass, and of steel, and of gold, and of silver, and of precious ores, which were in great abundance.

16. And I, Nephi, did build a temple; and I did construct it after the manner of the temple of Solomon save it were not built of so many precious things; for they were not to be found upon the land, wherefore, it could not be built like unto Solomon's temple. But the manner of the construction

was like unto the temple of Solomon; and the workmanship thereof was exceeding fine.

17. And it came to pass that I, Nephi, did cause
my people to be industrious, and to labor with their
hands.   2 Nephi 5:14-17.

8. And we multiplied exceedingly, and spread
upon the face of the land, and became exceeding
rich in gold, and in silver, and in precious things,
and in fine workmanship of wood, in buildings, and
in machinery, and also in iron and copper, and brass
and steel, making all manner of tools of every kind
to till the ground, and weapons of war—yea, the
sharp pointed arrow, and the quiver, and the dart,
and the javelin, and all preparations for war.

                                              Jarom 1:8.

9. And it came to pass that they became exceeding rich, both the Lamanites and the Nephites; and
they did have an exceeding plenty of gold, and of
silver, and of all manner of precious metals, both in
the land south and in the land north.

11. And behold, there was all manner of gold in
both these lands, and of silver, and of precious ore
of every kind; and there were also curious workmen,
who did work all kinds of ore and did refine it; and
thus they did become rich.   Helaman 6:9, 11.

4. And they [the Nephites] began again to prosper and to wax great; . . .

8. And there were many highways cast up, and
many roads made, which led from city to city, and
from land to land, and from place to place.

11. For there were many merchants in the land,
and also many lawyers, and many officers.

                                           3 Nephi 6:4, 8, 11.

LIX. Arts and Crafts of People of Bountiful-Land

If *The Book of Mormon* and the other accounts which state
that the early artisan-colonizers arrived in the New World from
the Near East are true, a simple deduction follows: the arts and
crafts of Middle America and Peru should mirror the arts and
crafts of the Near East of 600 B. C. There should be many
parallels.

Perfect accord in all details of every craft or art should not
be expected, however. Allowance must be made for the fact
that the original colonizers who arrived by boat directly from
the eastern Mediterranean world were relatively few in number. Further, there was no regular influx of population for many
centuries. Manpower was limited for several generations. *The
Book of Mormon* indicates that less than fifty persons were in
the original Nephite colony. Not all of the skills of the artisans
of the ancient Near East may have been represented. Manpower was so limited during the first 400 years, according to

the data contained in *The Book of Mormon,* that no great build-ing program was possible. Some of the skills and some of the knowledge of the original company may have been lost because of not having been put to use by succeeding generations. Such losses may have occurred both during the period of Nephite history covered in *The Book of Mormon* (600 B.C. to 421 A.D.) and the period between the close of *Book of Mormon* history and the coming of the Europeans in the sixteenth century.

Actually the parallels far outnumber the differences, even at the present date when archæological work in the Tehuantepec region in Middle America is still in its infancy. In the Near East, archæology has gone a long way, but important new dis-coveries are still being made. What now seem to be differences between the arts and crafts of the two zones may yet disappear.

WHEELS

The wheel was known, of course, in the ancient Near East. It is mentioned in *The Book of Mormon* in several connections. Only in recent years has sufficient archæological data come to

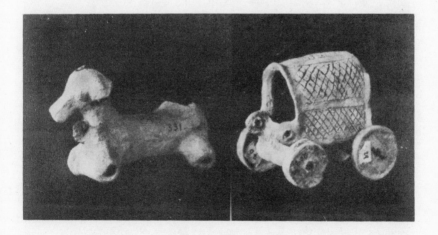

Fig. 35: WHEELED TOY FOUND IN THE OLD WORLD

This ancient toy with wheels was found in the upper Tigris River country, the general area from whence came the Ancient Ones—the Jaredites. It was found at an archæo-logical site known as Tepe Gawra in 1926. It dates from about 3000 B. C. Taken from E. A. Speiser's article, "The Historical Significance of Tepe Gawra," *Annual Report, Smithsonian Institution,* 1933, p. 428. Other wheeled toy dogs have been found in the Babylonian country, as mentioned by Gordon Ekholm's article "Wheeled Toys in Mexico," *American Antiquity* (April, 1946), pp. 222-228.

light to definitely establish, from evidence out of the ground, the fact that the ancient Americans had the wheel. The evidence consists of ceramic toys having wheels, ceramic wheels being the only kind of wheels that would have survived the interven' ing centuries.[1] It is to be noted that some of these ceramic wheels come from very early Olmec strata, and are to be dated within *The-Book-of-Mormon* period. In fact, some of these toys are so similar to those found in the Babylonian country—the toys

Fig. 36: WHEELED TOYS FOUND IN THE NEW WORLD

These ancient New World toys with wheels were all found in Mexico. In fact, all were found between Panuco and the Isthmus of Tehuantepec—the very area in which the Ancient Ones from Babel lived. Toys *a* and *b* were found at Panuco, the very place where the Jaredites from Babel landed. Toy *c* was found near Popocatepetl southeast of Mexico City. Toy *d* is from Tres Zapotes, Vera Cruz, not far from the narrow pass by the sea and near the Tuxtla mountains. Toy *e* is from the Valley of Oaxaca. These may be of Jaredite-Quinametzin origin, having turned up in exactly the right locale and having their counterpart in the Babylonia world of 3000 B. C. Taken from Gordon Ekholm's article in *American Antiquity*, vol. XI, plate xxvi.

---

[1] Gordon F. Ekholm, "Wheeled Toys in Mexico," *American Antiquity*, April, 1946, pp. 222-228. Ekholm says: "In my opinion, the evidence to be presented [in the article] indicates that the Indians of Mexico had some knowledge of the principle of the wheel in pre-conquest times. This will come as a surprise to many, because the supposed absence of any knowledge of this principle in the New World has often been stressed in discussions concerning the origin of the American Indian and his cultures." See also Thomas Stuart Ferguson, "The Wheel in Ancient America."

that date from 3000 B. C.—it seems quite reasonable to suggest that the comparable New World toys may date to the Jaredites who migrated to America from Babel. The area where they have been found is right. Before the Conquest the knowledge of the wheel was lost, probably going out of use in a period of retrogression along with roads and a number of other things, including certain scripts of the ancients.

ROADS IN ANCIENT AMERICA

Archæological evidences sustain *The Book of Mormon* claim that the inhabitants of ancient America not only had wheels but they had excellent roads also upon which to use those wheels. In speaking of conditions among the Nephites in 27 A. D., the following pertinent comment appears in their records: "*And there were many highways cast up, and many roads made, which led from city to city, and from land to land, and from place to place.*"[1a]

The foregoing statement is in complete accord with the evidences that have been discovered by the archæologists in the land of the Mayas; and the Mayas were the successors of the Nephites. For example, Mr. Thompson described the Mayan roads as follows:

> The Mayas, like the Romans, were finished builders of roads. In the days of their greatness, macadamized roads, raised from six to eight feet above the ordinary level of the country and surfaced with hard, smooth cement, led from palace terrace to temple, from temple centre to temple centre. Such highways radiated from Chichen Itza toward all the other great centres of population. From Coba a road led all the way across the peninsula to the Coast of Cozumel which was a sacred place with the ancients and contained many shrines. Pilgrimages thither were conducted from all parts of Yucatan. I have described these as macadamized roads, and the term is appropriate for the Mayas a thousand years ago built their highways on practically the same principle as McAdam adopted in the nineteenth century.[2]

It seems from available evidence that the ancient Mayan people were among the greatest road builders that the world has known. They made their roads to endure for ages. Note the following quotation:

> Roman roads, proverbial for their permanence, have disappeared, and can be traced today only with difficulty, or not at all. Our modern roads will, if left to the forces of nature, have completely disappeared, without leaving a trace in 500 years, but this great Maya road has withstood the

---

[1a] *The Book of Mormon*, p. 411 (3 Nephi 6:8).
[2] Thompson, *People of the Serpent*, pp. 173-174.

passage of centuries, in a country of heavy rainfall and luxuriant vegetation, and with the exception of its cement facing, is almost the same now
as it was the day when the last Maya trod its smooth level surface.[2a]

HORSES AND CHARIOTS

It is not known just what kind of traffic passed over the
Mayan highways, but a certain amount of details are available
regarding the uses which the Nephites made of their roads.
The fact is evident from their own records that they used horses
and chariots. In fact, horses are mentioned fourteen times in *The
Book of Mormon;* and from that record it is very evident that
those animals were domesticated and were used for purposes similar to the uses that we make of them today. For example, the
following appears in the Nephite records in connection with an
experience had by Lamoni, a Lamanite king, and his servant
Ammon, a Nephite, about 90 B. C.:

And it came to pass that king Lamoni inquired of his servants, saying:
Where is this man that has such great power?

And they said unto him: Behold, he is feeding thy horses. Now the
king had commanded his servants, previous to the time of the watering of
their flocks, that they should prepare his *horses and chariots,* and conduct
him forth to the land of Nephi; for there had been a great feast appointed
at the land of Nephi, by the father of Lamoni, who was king over all the land.

Now when king Lamoni heard that Ammon was preparing his horses
and his chariots he was more astonished, because of the faithfulness of
Ammon.[3]

The use of horses and chariots is also mentioned in connection with a war between the Nephites and the Lamanites, which
occurred 17 years A. D. Observe the following extract from
The Book of Mormon:

And it came to pass in the seventeenth year, in the latter end of the
year, the proclamation of the Lachoneus had gone forth throughout all
the face of the land, and they had taken *their horses, and their chariots,*
and their cattle, and all their flocks, and their herds, and their grain, and
all their substance, and did march forth by thousands and by tens of thousands, until they had all gone forth to the place which had been appointed
that they should gather themselves together, to defend themselves against
their enemies.[3a]

[2a] Gann, *Ancient Cities and Modern Tribes,* p. 114.
[3] *The Book of Mormon,* p. 241 (Alma 18:8-10a).
[3a] *The Book of Mormon,* p. 405 (3 Nephi 3:22).

CEMENT

A significant point in the quotations from Mr. Thompson and Mr. Gann is the fact that the ancient Mayas surfaced their roads with cement. Archæologists have found also that those people set rock work together in many of their buildings with an excellent grade of cement; and they also used that material in numerous other ways in construction work. In fact, archæologists have found that these people became expert in its use. The presence today of that substance in various archæological remains is too numerous to warrant presenting much more evidence.

It is a fact of much importance that The Book of Mormon claims that the Nephites and Lamanites (ancestors of the Mayas) used cement extensively in building their towns and cities. According to their own written record, these people ". . . became exceedingly expert in the working of cement; therefore they did build houses of cement in the which they did dwell." Other statements similar to this one are found also in the Nephite records. For example, we read: "And thus, they did enable the people in the land northward that they might build many cities both of wood and of cement."

Thus again we find that The Book of Mormon is sustained by numerous evidences unearthed by the archæologists.

IRON

Iron presents a problem. Iron was in use in Palestine from 1200 B. C.[4] The Book of Mormon, therefore, necessarily credited the Nephite emigrants to the New World with a knowledge of it. Ixtlilxochitl, like The Book of Mormon, says the Tultecas (Bountiful people) used it. He says that when the Tultecas fought they used, among other things mentioned by him, ". . . long lances, and others [javelins] which are thrown, and clubs garnished [nailed] with iron." The full text in which this appears is set forth below.

However, the American archæologists have found but one or two small pieces of iron. At Uxactun, Guatemala, within an ancient pyramid, were found some jars containing oxide of iron and iron (hematite) crystals.[4a] An iron object that becomes com-

[4] William Foxwell Albright, From the Stone Age to Christianity, 1940, pp. 12, 26, 32, 41, 193; I Samuel 13:19-21.
[4a] This discovery was made during the excavation of pyramid E-VII at Uxactun, 1927-1931, by personnel of Carnegie Institution of Washington, D. C. The jars were found in cist. 12, about 12 feet from the top of the outer pyramid. Oliver G. Ricketson Jr., Uxactun, Guatemala, Carnegie Institution of Washington, D. C., publication No. 447 (1937), pp. 71-72.

pletely corroded becomes iron oxide. It is still the consensus of opinion among the archæologists that the ancient Americans did not work with iron. It should be borne in mind, of course, that iron is one of the most perishable of metals. It would have been particularly subject to rapid corrosion in the damp tropical regions where the principal center of early American cultures were located, of southern México and the Peten country of Guatemala. Even at the present time, in the middle of the twentieth century, ornamental iron is used very little in the gulf coast region of Mexico. Covarrubias points out that the ornamental balconies of the homes in the city of Vera Cruz are of "turned wood (because iron rusts too quickly in the tropical sea air)."[5] Since both *Ixtlolxochitl* and *The Book of Mormon* are in accord on the matter of iron, it is probable that more of it will be found in the future.

ARCH—TEMPLE OF SOLOMON

The keystone arch was also known to the Near East prior to 600 B. C.[5a] It has not been found in the discovered archæological ruins of the New World. *The Book of Mormon* makes no mention of it one way or the other.

The first building erected by the Nephites of which mention is made was a temple. It was patterned after the temple of Solomon and the "workmanship thereof was exceeding fine."[6] This contruction took place, it is reported, between twenty and thirty years after the colonists arrived in the New World. Thus, lack of manpower was probably the principal factor in causing them to build this temple as they did. However, it should be noted that the roof of the temple of Solomon was flat . The suggested plans indicate there were no true arches used in the structure.[7]

In the temple of Solomon were two main rooms or chambers. The inner chamber was the Holy of Holies where the copy of the ancient covenant between God and Abraham was kept in the Ark or Chest. Most temples of ancient Middle America have but the two chambers, the innermost being inaccessible except by passage through the outer chamber. Some have two columns at the entrance, having a correspondence to the famous pillars, *Boaz* and *Jachin*, at the entrance of Solomon's

---

[5] Covarrubias, *Mexico South, The Isthmus of Tehuantepec* (1946), p. 5.
[5a] It has been found in very early ruins in the Bible lands.
[6] *The Book of Mormon*, p. 61, verse 16 (2 Nephi 5:16).
[7] Nowack, *Hebrew Arch* (1894), vol. 2, pp. 71-86; Funk and Wagnalls, *op. cit.*, 890-900, and authorities cited there.

temple. An example is the temple atop the inner temple-tower at Uxmal in Yucatan. There the two pillars stand at the entrance which faces in an easterly direction, as in Solomon's temple.

Fig. 37: MAYA ARCHITECTURE AT UXMAL IN YUCATAN, MEXICO
This magnificent building forms part of a great square. It dates from the tenth century.

Fig. 38: MAYA TEMPLE-TOWER AT UXMAL
This structure is 125 feet high. It was erected to the Fair God and some of His symbols are found on the exterior. *Photos by Ferguson.*

TEMPLE TOWERS

The temple-towers (ziggurats) of Palestine, Mesopotamia and early Egypt are identical in design and purpose to those of Mexico and Guatemala. Figure 39 shows temple-towers of the ancient Near East. Figures 37, 38, and 40 show ziggurats of Mexico and Guatemala. In all instances the purpose was to

a. Egyptian   b. Babylonian

c. Assyrian   d. Babylonian

Fig. 39: TEMPLE-TOWERS OF THE OLD WORLD

Pictures of temple-towers from the general area from whence the early artisan settlers of Middle America claim to have come. The reconstructions are identifiable. The New-World temple-towers were identical in design and purpose to these Old-World prototypes.

(c) N.G.S. COURTESY OF NATIONAL GEOGRAPHIC MAGAZINE

Fig. 40: TEMPLE-TOWERS OF THE NEW WORLD

These were of the same design and function as the Old-World temple-towers shown in Fig. 39. The top structure is in Vera Cruz, Mexico. The bottom tower is the famous "Castillo" at Chichen Itza, Yucatan, Mexico.

furnish a "high place" for worship. These structures are trun-
cated at the top to provide space for a temple. The slopes
are generally terraced, providing symmetrical design. Some are
filled with rubble and surfaced with cut stone. In some instances
sun-dried brick were used in building these towers in both the
Old and New worlds. For example, the temple-tower at Ur
(2300 B. C.) on the Euphrates and the temple-tower at Teotihuacan in Mexico are examples of sun-dried bricks.[8] The pointed
pyramids of Egypt are to be distinguished from the temple-
towers.

The Hebrew term for "house of God" is *bethel*.[9] This name
appears to have been applied anciently to tower or mountain
altars. Abraham built an altar unto the Lord on a mountain
and the place was called *Bethel*.[10] The term *Babel* is from *Babilu*,
meaning "gate of God."[11] The general Babylonian term for the
temple-tower was *ekur*, meaning "mountain home."[12] In Middle
America the Maya name for the temple-tower is *Ku*, meaning
"God." *Hunab Ku* was the great unseen father-God of the universe, head of the Maya godhead.[13] Therefore, it is evidence that
the name of the Mayan temple *(Ku)* stems back directly to
its Hebrew predecessor *(bethel)*.

Thus, not only are the temple-towers of Middle America
identical in design and purpose to those of the Near East, but
in both of these high centers of civilization the names applied
to them are identical in meaning. Perhaps Isaiah (about 730
B. C.) had in mind the temple-tower design of his ancient homeland when he spoke of "mountain of the Lord's house":

> And it shall come to pass in the last days, that the mountain of the
> Lord's house shall be established in the top of the mountains, and shall be
> exalted above the hills, and all nations shall flow unto it; and many people
> shall go and say, Come ye, and let us go up to the mountain of the Lord,
> to the house of the God of Jacob; and he will teach us of his ways, and
> we will walk in his paths....[14]

That prophecy has been fulfilled during the past one hundred
years by the Mormons, or members of The Church of Jesus Christ
of Latter-day Saints, who have erected marvelous temples in the
tops of the Rocky Mountains in the western part of free America.

---

[8] Seton Lloyed, *Ruined Cities of Iraq* (1945), p. 50; Vaillant, *Aztecs of Mexico*, p. 56.
[9] James Strong, *Dictionary of Hebrew Bible* (1890), word 1008; Funk and Wagnalls, *Bible Dictionary* (1936), p. 104; Albright, *op. cit.*, 188.
[10] Genesis 13:1-6; Joseph Smith, translator, *The Book of Abraham*, 2:20; 1:20.
[11] Hugo Gressman, *The Tower of Babel* (1928), pp. 5-8, 14.
[12] *Ibid.*
[13] Sylvanus G. Morley, *The Ancient Maya* (1946), p. 213.
[14] Isaiah 2:2-4. See also Micah 4:1-3).

LIME, PLASTER AND ROCK MASONRY

The Israelites were dwelling in stone houses and were using lime plaster in Palestine very shortly after being led to the Promised Land by Moses about 1290 B. C.[16] There are numerous Old Testament references to lime, plaster and mortar.[17] Excavations at Meggiddo in Palestine, conducted since 1929, have revealed among other things one of the chariot centers of Solomon. His great stables, built about 960-925 B. C., were found to have had cement floors.

Lime plaster and cement were in common use in ancient Middle America. Many of the rooms of the Maya temples of both the Old Empire (317 A. D. - 987 A. D.) and the New Empire (987 A. D. - 1441 A. D.) have been found with stucco walls. Bishop Landa (1566 A. D.) speaks of a New Empire Yucatan Maya building at Tihoo. In doing so he mentions the use of lime plaster: "The top was in the form of a flat roof, very heavily plastered, in the way it is done there with a certain juice from the bark of a tree."[18] Professor Tozzer of Harvard University gives authority for his statement that the Mayas soaked the bark of the *chocom* tree to get the soluble chemical for making lime plaster. "Lime, moistened with it, takes a magnificent polish under the trowel and is practically impervious to water."[19] Landa also described the cement plaza at Chichen Itza.

Many of Maya Old and New Empire interior stucco walls were beautifully painted by skilled artists. The best preserved stucco murals from the Maya Old Empire are those discovered at Bonampak, Chiapas, by Carlos Fry (now deceased) in 1946. Fry told one of the writers of using a manual-type phonograph as inducement to get a Lacandone chief to lead him to the ruins.

Sylvanus G. Morley places the beginnings of stone architecture in the Maya area in the period called by him Pre-Maya III, dating from 353 B. C. to 317 A. D.[20] This corresponds to the ceramic period known as Chicanel. This era is the very period in which the Nephite-Mulekite-Lamanite people of *The Book of Mormon* first had sufficient manpower to do serious

---

[16] Albright, *op cit.*, pp. 195, 217.
[17] Genesis 11:3; Leviticus 14:42, 45; Isaiah 41:25; Ezekiel 13:10, 11, 14, 15; Deuteronomy 27:2; Strong, *Hebrew and Chaldee Dictionary, op. cit.*, word 7875.
[18] Alfred M. Tozzer, *Historia de las cosas de Yucatan* (an English translation of Landa, with extensive notes) (1941), pp. 175-176.
[19] *Ibid.*, note 917.
[20] Sylvanus G. Morley, *The Ancient Maya* (1946), Table III, opposite p. 40.

work in stone architecture. In fact, the first work in cement and stone mentioned specifically in the Nephite period is about 46 B. C., and this only because timber was unavailable in the zone involved.[21]

One of the earliest masonry structures yet discovered in the New World dates from between 100 A. D. and 200 A. D., squarely within the Nephite period. It is the beautifully pre-served stucco-covered pyramid found at Uaxactun in the Peten-Maya country. It is identified by the archæologists as structure number E-VII-sub. Observe carefully photograph below. On the

Fig. 41: EARLIEST ARCHITECTURAL CONSTRUCTION YET DISCOVERED IN
THE MAYA AREA

This temple-tower at Uaxactun, Guatemala—E-VII-sub, is stucco covered. Post holes in the lime-plaster flooring on top of the pyramid indicate there was a religious shrine or temple there. It dates from about 200 B. C. and is very possibly a Nephite (early Nahuale) structure.

platform at the top of this temple-tower, in the lime-plaster floor, were found the post holes for the wooden temple which once stood there. Sylvanus G. Morley, who died in 1947, one of the most distinguished Mayan scholars, says of this important edifice:

This stucco-covered pyramid, ascended by four stairways, one on each side, and decorated with sixteen heroic-sized stucco masks each eight feet square, is a marvel of early Maya architecture. It was never painted, and its lime-stucco finish when first uncovered glistened like silver in the

---

[21] *The Book of Mormon*, p. 364, verses 6-10.

sunlight. Its style is so early as to be proto-Maya, rather than pure Maya in character. However, though built of masonry, it is only a substructure, and clearly antedates the first stone buildings proper. It is in fact, barring the low walls of the early Chicanel ceramic period . . . the oldest Maya stone construction that has come down to us and probably dates from the second century of the Christian era.[22]

In January, 1948, at Aguacatal, not far from the city of Carmen, on the Campeche Gulf Coast region of southern Mexico, one of the writers assisted in the partial excavation of a lime-plaster covered pyramid. Pottery excavated at the base of the pyramid was largely monochrome. Similar pottery was recovered at a site on the eastern end of the island of Carmen by the Laguna de Terminos. The pottery dates close to the beginning of the Christian era.

ALTARS

The fact has already been mentioned that Ancient Israel erected its altars of uncut, unhewn stones. Washed river stones were ideal for the purpose. In Exodus is recorded: "And if thou wilt make me an altar of stone, thou shalt not build it of hewn stone: for if thou lift up thy tool upon it thou hast polluted it."[23]

The American descendants of the ancient Israelites also erected altars of uncut stones. A very early example of such an altar of uncut river stones in Middle America is that uncovered on top of the inner temple-tower at Cuicuilco, located on the outskirts of Mexico City. It is the work of Tultecs who pushed up from the Tehuantepec area (Mexico's narrow neck of land) not long after the close of *The Book of Mormon* period which ended 421 A. D. It represents, along with the great ceremonial center, Teotihuacan, a northern outpost of the Tultec-people-of-Bountiful, dating from about 500 A. D.[24]

DOORJAMBS

In ancient Bible lands it was not an uncommon practice to decorate doorjambs and lintels with inscriptions.[25] This was done in Egypt as well as in Palestine. In the Maya country of Middle America this was also done. Examples include the temple of Secret Writing and the hieroglyphic lintel on the altantean figures at Chichen Itza.

---

[22] Morley, *op. cit.*, pp. 344-345.
[23] Exodus 20:24-25.
[24] Vaillant, *op. cit.*, pp. 42-47.
[25] Wilkinson, *Manners and Customs*, etc., vol. 2, pp. 102, 123; Deuteronomy 6:4 ff.

TYPES OF STRUCTURES

The following architectural structures have been discovered in the Old Empire Maya period (317 A. D. - 987 A. D.), which includes the closing century of *The Book of Mormon* era: temple-towers, temples, palaces, astronomical observatories, ball courts, colonnades, dance platforms, vapor baths, monumental stairways, reviewing stands, square stadiums for public spectacles, city walls and moats, causeways, bridges and aqueducts.[26]

The Book of Mormon mentions for the early colonial period, 200 B. C.-421 A. D.: temples, towers, palaces, city walls and moats, houses of cement, markets, highways, roads and prisons.[27]

In 600 B. C. the Israelites and others of the Near East had all of the foregoing types of construction, except possibly ball courts. The latter are not mentioned in *The Book of Mormon* and may have been conceived in the post-*Book of Mormon* period. Temple-towers, temples, palaces, and cement work have already been discussed above. In a brief summary of Bible-land architecture, it is said:

> Aggregations of houses in towns were regularly encircled by protecting walls . . . and towers for defense. A city like Jerusalem might contain . . . stairways or bridges . . . pools or reservoirs . . . porticos or colonnades. . . . In the palaces of Jerusalem and Samaria there was some use of halls whose roofs were supported by columns. In these buildings precious materials like ivory, gold, silver, and brass and imported woods, like cedar, were used. To columns and walls, color and carving were somewhat applied.[28]

Bernardino Sahagun, Spanish-born priest who lived in Mexico from 1529 to 1590 A. D., wrote of Tultec buildings as follows:

> These said Toltecs . . . were fine and excellent in whatever they set their hand to; the houses they built were very excellent, some being decorated inside with precious green stones and others were finished with whitewash; the stones of which the houses were made were so well cut and so well joined that they appeared as mosaic; and thus, with reason, they [the buildings] were called works of the fine and excellent artisans because they were so beautiful and excellent in workmanship.
>
> There was also a temple which by its priests was called Quetzalcoatl, much more polished and precious than their houses, the said temple having

---

[26] Morley, *op. cit.,* Table VIII, pp. 354-355. Vaillant, *op. cit.,* p. 52, states that the Tultecs used the *temascal* or "vapor bath," and built houses and palaces of stone and mortar.
[27] Verla Birrell, *The Book of Mormon Guide Book* (1948), pp. 266-276. This work contains classified lists of every aspect of culture of the peoples of *The Book of Mormon,* giving full quotations from the record itself.
[28] Funk and Wagnalls, *op. cit.,* pp. 62-63.

four rooms; one was toward the east and was of gold and they called it the golden room or golden house because it had instead of whitewash, sheets of gold covering the walls, these being finely joined together. And another room was to the west, this being a room of emeralds and turquoise, these being joined like a mosaic work, which was very admirable. Towards the south, was another room, this one having divers sea shells, the walls being of silver, the silver so finely placed that the junctures did not appear. And the fourth room was toward the north and this room was of red stone and jasper and shells, being very decorative.[29]

FORTIFICATIONS

According to *The Book of Mormon*, as early as 72 B. C. the lowland Bountiful-Zarahemla country had fortified towns. Some of their defenses are described as follows:

And now it came to pass that Moroni did not stop making prepara-tions for war, or to defend his people against the Lamanites; for he caused that his armies should commence in the commencement of the twentieth year of the reign of the judges, that they should commence in digging up heaps of earth round about all the cities, throughout all the land which was possessed by the Nephites. And upon the top of these ridges of earth he caused that there should be timbers, yea, works of timbers built up to the height of a man, round about the cities. And he caused that upon those works of timbers there should be a frame of pickets built upon the timbers round about; and they were strong and high. And he caused towers to be erected that overlooked those works of pickets, and he caused places of security to be built upon those towers, that the stones and the arrows of the Lamanites could not hurt them. And they were prepared that they could cast stones from the top thereof, according to their pleasure and their strength, and slay him who should attempt to approach near the walls of the city.[30]

Even hundreds of years later the Maya people were using this identical type of fortification. On his famous journey from Mexico City to Honduras in 1524-1525 A. D., Cortez passed through certain towns in what is now the state of Campeche of the Gulf Coast Maya area. In what was then the province of Mazatlan were the towns of Tiac and Yasuncabil and a third which Cortez did not name. Speaking of these towns, the follow-ing was written: "All villages mentioned were surrounded by a deep moat, a high stockade of cut poles, and defensive towers of wood."[31]

[29] Fr. Bernardino de Sahagan (1499-1590), *Historia de las Cosas de Nueva Espana*, *Libro Decimo*, Capitulo XXIX, English translation made from 1946 Mexican edition.
[30] *The Book of Mormon*, p. 321 (Alma 50:1-5).
[31] E. Wyllys Andrews, *The Archaeology of Southwestern Campeche*, Carnegie Institution of Washing-ton, D. C., Pub. No. 546 (1943), p. 25.

Armor and Weapons of the Tultecas (Nephites)

The *Book of Mormon* also gives a description of the armor and weapons of the Nephite soldiers during the same period that they fortified their towns and cities. *Ixtlilxochitl's* description of armor and weapons of the Tultecas is in close accord with the Nephite account, as will be seen.

Fig. 42 : Pottery Figure of Bearded Warrior

This bearded warrior is a pottery figure from the ancient archæological site of Quen Santo in the highlands of western Guatemala. The original can be seen in the Museum of the American Indian, Heye Foundation, New York City. He has the "earmarks" of a cultured white man.

IXTLILXOCHITL:	EXTRACTS—BOOK OF MORMON:
Tultecas' armour and weapons	*Nephites' and Lamanites' armor and weapons*
When the Tultecas fought they would put on some sort of	19. . . . Moroni had prepared his people [Nephites] with breastplates and with arm-

long tunics down to the heels, of a thousand colors, embroidered, and very closely woven and *thick*, so that no matter how hard they would hit each other with the lances — for these [lances] were what they most used—they could not pass them (cut them through); and they used long lances, and others which were thrown, and clubs garnished with iron. They wore morions and helmets of brass and gold, and some used the rodelas, particularly those who had clubs.

shields, yea and also shields to defend their heads, and also they were dressed with *thick clothing—*

20. Now the army of Zerahemnah was not prepared with any such thing; they had only their swords and their cimeters, their bows and their arrows, their stones and their slings; and they were naked, save it were a skin which was girded about their loins; yea, all [those in the Lamanite army as of about 74 B. C.] were naked, save it were the Zoramites and the Amalekites [both dissenters from the Nephite ranks];

21. But they were not armed with breast-plates, nor shields—therefore, they were exceedingly afraid of the armies of the Nephites because of their armor . . .

Fig. 43: ARMOR—QUILTED CLOTHING

Heavily armed spearman of ancient Chichen Itza, Yucatan. Note the thick quilted clothing, spear and shield. In his headdress are feathers of the sacred Quetzal bird, one of the symbols of the Messiah.

The reference to the protective "thick clothing" is particularly significant. Bishop Landa, writing in the sixteenth century, described the armor of the ancient Mayas and we learn from him and other early writers that they wore thick quilted cotton clothing into battle.[19] Landa and *The Book of Mormon* find confirmation from archæology, for representations of the thick and quilted clothing have been found. See Figs. 43 and 44. Landa also lists some of the weapons used in ancient Middle America:

And the Yucatecans . . . learned from the Mexicans the use of arms, and they soon became masters of the bow and arrow, the lance and the axe; their shields and jackets were made *strong with twisted cord and cotton,* as well as other instruments of war. . . .[32]

The archæologist, Vaillant, reports that *Ixtlilxochitl* spoke of helmets of copper worn by the Tultec soldiers.[33] *The Book*

[32] Alfred Tozzer's translation, *Landa's Relacion de las Cosas de Yucatan* (1941 edition), p. 35. See also Tozzer's note 174 where quilted cotton armor "so strong that the arrows did not go thru" is mentioned.
[33] Vaillant, *op. cit.,* p. 51.

of Mormon mentions the use of iron, copper and brass, and thick clothing worn by the Nephite soldiers as has been shown. There are six references to *head plates* in *The Book of Mormon*.[34] These

appear between the years 74 B. C. and 19 A. D. Father Sahagun (1499-1590 A. D.), speaking of the Tultecs, says some of the noble lords of that nation "used to wear in war a kind of gold helmet. . . . They also used another kind of silver helmet."[35] Many of the ancient Maya warriors de- picted on the stone shafts of Chichen Itza, Yucatan, are seen to wear breastplates. A gold breastplate was recovered from Tomb 7 at Monte Alban in Oaxaca. The parallel from the ancient Near East is clearly drawn: "And Saul armed David with his armour, and he put *an helmet* of brass upon his head.[36] Thus, further evidence is given of *The Book of Mormon's* claim that the Nephites came to America from Palestine.

Fig. 44: ARMOR—
QUILTED CAP
Quilted cap with chin-
guard. From the ancient
Maya ruins near the pres-
ent town of Palenque in
Chiapas, Mexico.

METAL WORK

It is seen that both *Ixtlilxochitl* and *The Book of Mormon* credit the Tultec-Bountiful people with expertness in the work- ing of metals. The use of copper, iron, gold and silver are men- tioned by both accounts. To be consistent and in accord with truth, both accounts necessarily had to credit the Bountiful- colonizers with knowledge of working those metals, since these people has migrated from the former home in the Near East. In 600 B. C. the Near East had skilled artisans in metallurgy, and metal crafts had existed for many centuries prior thereto.

The Bronze Age in Palestine, Mesopotamia and Egypt began about 3000 B. C. Bronze is an alloy of copper and tin, while brass is an alloy of copper and zinc. It is claimed that the Iron Age began in those lands about the time Moses led the Israelites from Egypt into Palestine, around 1200 B. C.[37] Gold and silver

---

[34] *The Book of Mormon*, p. 302; p. 304 (Alma 43:44); p. 320 (Alma 50:24); p. 360 (Helaman 1:14);
[35] Sahagun, *op. cit.*, *Libro* 8, *Capitulo* 12.
   p. 406 (3 Nephi 3:26).
[36] Samuel 18:38; 2 Chronicles 26:14.
[37] Albright, *op. cit.*, pp. 105-123.

had been worked from verly early times. References to gold, silver, and brass are very numerous in Israelite history prior to 600 B. C. One need only consult any concordance of the Old Testament in this regard. Many of the tools and instruments of the metalsmith are mentioned in the Old Testament, including bellows, crucible, melting-oven, hammer, anvil, tongs and graving tools.[38]

It should be noted that references in the Old Testament to "steel" were, apparently, to the metal we now refer to as bronze. Prior to the eighteenth century there was no such word in English as "bronze." That copper-tin alloy was anciently referred to as "steel" to distinguish it from brass. Not until the eighteenth century did the English word "bronze" come into use. Thus, the King James translators necessarily rendered the Hebrew word nechushah (pronounced nekh-oo-shaw) as "steel," distinguishing it from nechosheth which is generally rendered "brass."[39]

The word "steel" is also used in The Book of Mormon on four occasions.[40] It could be that these references are to what we know as bronze, the latter being suitable for making bows with which to shoot arrows. Joseph Smith would have been modernizing had he translated the script of the record to read "bronze." He followed the same course taken by the sages of King James.[41]

The Book of Mormon credits the Israelites of 600 B. C. with using brass and gold as a medium on which to write sacred or important records for long preservation. After arriving in the New World, the Nephites, it is claimed, for special reasons engraved the original of The Book of Mormon itself on gold tablets. It would be a gold alloy. That original record, like the original manuscripts of the Bible and the Popol Vuh, is not available at the present day. However, some of the twelve eyewitnesses who saw and examined the original plates have given us a detailed description of them. Further, we have the verbatim translation plus several lines of the hieroglyphic script copied directly from the plates. Joseph Smith described the original record as follows:

[38] Exodus 28:11; 32:4; Isaiah 41:7; Jeremiah 6:29; also, Funk and Wagnalls, op. cit., p. 576.
[39] James Strong, Hebrew Chaldee Dictionary (1944 ed.), words 5154 and 5178; Funk and Wagnalls, op. cit., p. 576.
[40] The Book of Mormon, p. 7, 1 Nephi 4:9; p. 32, 1 Nephi 16:18; p. 61, 2 Nephi 5:15; p.490, Ether 7:9.
[41] 2 Samuel 22:35; Job 20:24; Psalms 18:34; Jeremiah 15:12.

These records were engraven on plates which had the appearance of gold: each plate was six inches wide and eight inches long, and not quite so thick as common tin. They were filled with engravings in Egyptian characters and bound together in a volume as the leaves of a book, with three rings running through the whole. The volume was something over six inches in thickness, part of which was sealed. The characters on the unsealed part were small and beautifully engraved. The whole book exhibited many marks of antiquity in its construction, and much skill in the art of engraving.[42]

There is evidence external to *The Book of Mormon* that the ancients of both the Near East and the culture-centers of the New World made tablets of gold and less precious metals.

Dating from 3000 B. C. is a thin gold bar on which is engraven the name *Menes,* Egyptian ruler of the time. This can be seen in the Haskell Museum.[43]

Dating from about 1700 B. C. are a number of copper plates discovered in Palestine in the early 1930's by M. Dunard. (Since copper plates have been found, "Brass Plates" sound reasonable.) Engraven on them is a very early script believed to have been Canaanite (Hebrew). They were described by Dunard in 1935 at the International Congress of Orientalists held in Rome.[44]

In about 1254 B. C. the Egyptians entered into a treaty with the Hittites of Asia Minor, the terms of which were entered on a silver tablet. A copy of the treaty makes reference to the original silver tablet. The copy has been translated by A. H. Sayce, part of it reading as follows:

> This is a copy of the contents of the *silver tablet,* which the great king of the Hittites, *Khattu-sil,* had caused to be made and which was presented to the Pharoah by the hand of his ambassador Re-mes, to propose friendship with the king Ramessu-Miamum.[45]

Dating from about 1200 B. C., from the time of the Egyptian Pharoah Rameses III, is this clear-cut historical statement making reference to writings on tablets of gold and silver:

> I made for thee *great tablets of gold* in beaten work, engraved with the great name of thy majesty, bearing my praises—I made for thee *great tablets of silver* in beaten work, carved with the graver's tool, bearing the decrees and the inventions of the houses and temples which I made [in] Egypt.[46]

---

42 Joseph Smith, *Times and Seasons,* Nauvoo, Illinois, March 1, 1842; Francis W. Kirkham, *A New Witness for Christ in America* (1942), p. 191.
43 James Henry Breasted, *A History of Egypt* (1999), Fig. 13, opposite p. 34.
44 *Bull. Am. Sch. Or. Research,* No. 60, pp. 3 ff., cited in Albright, *op. cit.,* p. 13.
45 A. H. Sayce, *The Hittites,* p. 41; quoted by Franklin S. Harris Jr., address delivered Sept. 1, 1946, radio station KSL.
46 James Henry Breasted, *Ancient Records,* par. 202; quoted by Harris, *ibid.*

These statements, found in Israelite records, date from Moses' time (c. 1200 B. C.):

And thou shalt make a *plate of pure gold,* and grave upon it, like engravings of a signet, HOLINESS TO THE LORD.''[47]

And they made *the plate of the holy crown of pure gold,* and wrote upon it a writing like to the engravings of a signet, HOLINESS TO THE LORD.[48]

In the first part of the seventh century B. C. lived Jeremiah, one of the prophets of the decline and fall of the Israelite monarchy. He was a contemporary of Lehi. In the book of Jeremiah is recorded this significant statement: "The sin of Judah is written with a *pen of iron,* and the *point of a diamond: it is graven upon the table of their heart.*[49] Also, "Silver spread into plates is brought up from Tarshish, and gold up from Uphaz, the work of workmen. . . .''[50]

From 521 B. C. to 485 B. C. Darius reigned in Persia (Iran). In 1933, in the ruins of the palace of Darius at Persepolis, Iran, were discovered two silver tablets and two gold tablets, each covered with cuneiform inscriptions, and each tablet being approximately 13x13 inches square. They can be seen in the Museum of Archæology, Teheran. The discovery was made by Professor Herzfeld of the Oriental Institute of the University of Chicago. The inscriptions relate to the building of certain palaces in the city of Darius.[51]

Some of the mining and smelting works of the Israelites prior to 600 B. C. were operated on a large scale. The modern world knew nothing of the great copper mining and refining activities of Solomon (about 960 B. C.-925 B. C.) until 1938. Near the Red Sea, at Ezion-geber, Nelson Glueck, archæologist, discovered a great copper refinery of Solomon's covering one and one-half acres and surrounded by a brick wall.[52]

Not only were the people of the Near East and their descendants, the Nephites, expert goldsmiths, but the Indians in Mexico, even after the Conquest, were still skilled workmen. From sixteenth-century Mexico we have an interesting statement by Sahagun. It comes from his chapter entitled "Concerning the Craftsmen Who Worked Gold." Under this heading he says:

[47] Exodus 28:36.
[48] Ibid., 39:30.
[49] Jeremiah 14:1.
[50] Ibid., 10:9.
[51] Franklin S. Harris, "Gold Plates in Persia," *The Improvement Era,* Dec., 1940, p. 714.
[52] Albright, *op. cit.,* p. 223.

This chapter begins the subject of craftsmen who worked gold and silver. The craftsmen or officers who worked gold are of two kinds, some that are called "hammerers" or "pounders" because these work wrought gold, pounding the gold with rocks and with hammers, in order to make it as *thin as paper;* others were called *Tlatlalianine,* which means that they settle the gold or something in the gold or in the silver, and these are the real craftsmen who are called by name *Tolteca;* but they are divided into two groups because they work gold in different ways.[53]

From Mexico comes the report that certain natives of the state of Oaxaca, south of Mexico City, sold a few ancient and very thin gold plates to some Europeans.[54a]

In the deYoung Museum in Golden Gate Park in San Francisco, California, two thin plates of gold from ancient Colombia, South America, are on exhibit. Each plate is approximately five inches wide, twelve inches long and about one-fifteenth inch thick.

Among the many wonderful objects of gold dredged from the famous cenote (well) at Chichen Itza in the State of Yucatan, Mexico, by Edward Thompson not so many years ago were the following:

> seventeen gold discs, embossed or beaten, six inches in diameter;
>
> eight gold discs, embossed or beaten, about eight inches in diameter;
>
> seven gold discs, embossed or beaten, about eight inches in diameter;
>
> ten gold discs, embossed or beaten, small sizes;
>
> one basin of fine gold, twelve inches in diameter, perfectly preserved;
>
> eleven animal figures and reptiles, used as ornaments, most of them cast (not beaten work), of pure gold;
>
> one solid-gold mask seven inches in diameter;
>
> one tiara or forehead band of gold, four inches wide and eight inches long, with a design of entwined serpents and with quetzal feathers, symbolic of the Christ in Middle America, one of the most excellent works in gold ever found in Middle America;
>
> one hundred gold bells, with clappers, of various sizes;
>
> ten human and monkey-like figures of gold;
>
> one throwing stick, *hul-che,* of entwined serpents;
>
> fourteen objects of gold shaped like candlesticks;

[53] Sahagun, *op. cit., Libro Noveno, Capitulo* XV. Translated here from Spanish.
[54a] Padre Gay, *Historia de Oaxaca,* vol. 1, Cap. 4, p. 62; cited by Franklin S. Harris Jr., *op. cit.* An excellent article by Levi Edgar Young regarding the use of metal plates as a writing medium in ancient times was published in *The Improvement Era,* April, 1949.

> forty objects of gold or of gold and bronze, including
>   sandals and various ornaments;
> twenty gold rings;
> forty gold washers or weights [or coin weights].[54]

In 1932, Alfonso Caso, Mexican archæologist, discovered at Monte Alban, in the state of Oaxaca, Mexico, the famous Tomb Seven. Therein he found, among other beautiful things, the following:

> one great breast piece of gold, attached to which were
>   feathers of gold thread;
> one gold crown or diadem with a plume of gold;
> one gold mask.

In addition there were necklaces, earrings and armlets of gold found in Tomb Seven. These and the other treasures from the tomb can be seen at the local museum in the town of Oaxaca.[55]

At Guaytun, Guatemala, in the Motagua River valley was found in an ancient Maya tomb a thin sheet of copper-gold alloy of seven square centimeters and about one-tenth centimeter in thickness. It is 87 per cent copper and 13 per cent gold. The gold was on the surface, thus giving the piece the appearance of being entirely gold. It is believed that the guilding of gold was produced by treating the original gold-copper plate with an acid which removed the copper from the surface, leaving the gold for a final burnishing. This is known as the *mise-en-couleur process,*[56] a technical method in use in ancient Middle America.

It is undisputed that the ancients of Middle America melted down gold, silver and copper, using molds to cast works of art into preconceived designs. Even the technical lost-wax process of casting was used. It was identical to the *cire-perdue* (lost-wax process) used in the ancient Bible lands.[57] Vaillant describes the process briefly:

> The desired shape was modeled in clay, over which was dusted finely ground charcoal, followed by an even layer of wax. This coating was also dusted with charcoal and the whole enclosed in clay, which was perforated at the top and bottom. The molten metal was poured in at the upper hole after the wax was melted and the lower orifice plugged. When the metal cooled the case was broken and the finished object removed.[58]

---

[54] T. A. Willard, *The City of the Sacred Well* (1926), pp. 285-286. *The Book of Mormon* speaks of gold and silver coin weights.
[55] Edgar L. Hewitt, *Ancient Life in Mexico and Central America* (1936), pp. 125-126.
[56] A. L. Smith and A. V. Kidder, *Exploration in the Motagua Valley, Guatemala*, Carnegie Inst. of Washington, D. C., pub. No. 546 (1943), p. 170.
[57] Vaillant, *op. cit.*, p. 147.
[58] *Ibid.*

Another advanced metallurgical process, plating, was known to the ancients of the New World cultural centers. Some of the items found in the well at Chichen Itza were gold-plated. Further, some were bronze, being alloys of copper and tin.[59] It should be noted that the metals from which the items found in Chichen Itza came were from other cultural centers such as Chiapas and Oaxaca in Mexico, and from Guatemala, Honduras, and possibly from as far away as Colombia and Panama. Yucatan itself is a great limestone peninsula with no native metals. Many of the items of metal came into the peninsula from Usumacinta River country, the headwaters of that river being in the highlands of Guatemala and the stream running down through the Chiapas country, the ancient region of the Tultec and Ulmec artisans.

It might be observed that gold bells and copper helmets were common to both Bible lands and *Book of Mormon* lands. In the Old Testament, from Exodus, we read: "And they made bells of pure gold, and put the bells between the pomegranates upon the hem of the robe, round about between the pomegranates; a bell and a pomegranate, a bell and a pomegranate, round about the hem of the robe to minister in; as the Lord commanded Moses."[60]

One of the Incas of Peru, Garcilasso de la Vega (1540-1616 A. D.), says of the ancient Peruvians:

In many of the palaces and temples of the Sun, they used molten lead, silver, and gold instead of mortar. . . . They plated the temples of the Sun and royal palaces with gold, and put in them many figures of men and women; of birds of the air and water; of wild animals, such as tigers, bears, lions, foxes, dogs, cats, deer, huanacus, and vicunas, and of domestic llamas, all of gold and silver, worked in imitation of nature. . . . They did not have tapestry for the walls [of the king's palace], because they were covered with gold and silver. They also had . . . a vast store of *cloaks and belts interwoven with gold wire.*[62]

Compare the preceding statement of the Inca of Peru with that from an early Israelite record: "And they did beat the gold into thin plates, and cut it into wires, to work it in the blue, and in the purple, and in the scarlet, and in the fine linen, with cunning work."[63]

Harold Gladwin, who has recently dared to brave the wrath and scorn of his fellow-archæologists, contends that metallurgical

---

[59] Morley, *op. cit.,* p. 434.
[60] Exodus 39:25-26.
[62] Garcilasso de la Vega, *op. cit.,* vol. 2, pp. 99-102.

skills of the high culture centers of the New World must have been brought there by immigrants from the Middle East.[64]

It does seem absurd for some people to credit the typical backward "Indian" of the New World with having invented for himself in a relatively short space of time such things as gold castings by the lost wax-process, smelting and combining of copper and tin to make bronze, the making of gold wire for weaving into cloth, gilding with gold by the *mise-en-couleur* process and gold and silver plating. Under the surface of the ground in Middle America, Peru, and Colombia nothing has been found indicating that there were any long ages of development and progress leading up to the age of the skilled artisans.[65]   It took from about 5000 B. C. until about 1200 B. C. for the Sumerians, Canaanites, Egyptians and the Semites to attain the skills found in Mexico and Peru from the first occupations of certain colonizers not arriving earlier than 600 B. C.

A curious problem presents itself to those who contend that virtually all of the original colonizers of the New World came here, in a state of ignorance, by way of Bering Straits from northeastern Asia. The oldest zone of occupation, according to such a theory, would have been the most northerly parts of the continent, and yet, in those northern regions where men are supposed to have gotten their start in the New World, nothing evidencing advanced cultures has been discovered. Nothing really advanced has been found north of the Rio Grande. The "Moundbuilders" date from about 400 A. D. and thereafter.[66] And oddly enough, an almost inexhaustible volume of material has been found, and is being found at an ever increasing rate, in Middle America.

WORKING OF PRECIOUS STONES

Ixtlilxochitl and *The Book of Mormon* both comment on the use of precious stones by the Tultecs or Bountiful-people. *Ixtlilxochitl's* comment is brief and to the point: "The Tultecas . . . carved *precious stones*. . . ." *The Book of Mormon* says the "gold and silver, and *precious stones*" of the people of Bountiful-Zarahemla were sought after by their envious neighbors in

[64] Harold Gladwin, *Men Out of Asia* (1947).
[65] Of Middle America, George C. Vaillant says: "No evidence of truly primitive communities have been discovered as yet," *op. cit.*, p. 14.
[66] Vaillant, *op. cit.*, p. 15. Artifacts from Mexico have been found in the United States, in the Moundbuilder country. The "Mounds" date from about 400 A. D. See Ross T. Christensen, "Ancient Diffusion from Mesoamerica to the 'Mound Area' of Eastern United States, an Annotated Bibliography," *Bulletin of the University Archaeological Society, Brigham Young Univ.*, May, 1950, pp. 13-20.

the highlands to the south.[67] The expression generally used in
The Book of Mormon in referring to gems is "precious things."
The term "gem" appears in neither The Book of Mormon nor
in the Old Testament.[68]

Fr. Bernardino de Sahagun makes the following interesting
statement concerning the pre-Conquest lapidaries of Mexico:

> The lapidaries who worked precious stones, in the time of their idolatry
> worshipped four gods . . . They said that to these gods was attributed the art of
> carving precious stones, including the making of beavers for war helmets and
> black stone earrings and crystal earrings and amber earrings, and other
> white earrings; to these they also attributed the carving of beads and brace-
> lets, and strings that they wore around their wrists, and all carving of
> stones and chalchihuites, and the boring and polishing of all stones.[69]

Thus, it is evident that the carving of precious stones and
making use of them was continued from the Nephite period down
to the coming of the Spaniards. In fact, that the lapidary art was
fully developed as early as the Bountiful-Zarahemla occupation
(200 B. C.-350 A. D.) of The Book of Mormon period has been
confirmed by archæology. A carved and polished jade pendant,
the famous Leyden plate, bears a hieroglyphic date which, correlated with our calendar, falls at 320 A. D.[70] See figure 22.

It is believed that the Leyden Plate was made at the great
archæological center now known as Tikal, situated on the eastern
frontier of the ancient Tulan (bountiful) region.[71] It is illustra-
tive of the numerous jade pieces dating from very early times
which have been found between the Guatemala highlands and
the Valley of Mexico. Jade is extremely hard and difficult to
work and yet in some of these jade objects from this ancient
cultural region holes were drilled that they might be worn as
neck pieces.

An even earlier jade object in Olmec (Ulmec) style has
been found at Tuxtla in southern Vera Cruz, Mexico, just on
the northerly side of Mexico's narrow-neck-of-land. It bears the

[67] The Book of Mormon, p. 238 (Alma 17:14).
[68] George Reynolds, Concordance of The Book of Mormon (1900); James Strong, Exhaustive Con-
     cordance of the Bible (1890).
[69] Sahagun (1499-1590 A. D.), op. cit., Libro 8, Capítulo 17.
[70] Eleven miles north of where the Leyden Plate was made in 320 A. D., was discovered a monument
     dated 8.14.10.13.15, or April 11, 328 A. D. The latter is identified by archæologists as Stela 9,
     found at Uaxactun, about one hundred miles east of the Usumacinta River. Jakeman, The Origins
     and History of the Mayas (1945), pp. 57-58.
[71] Morley, op. cit., pp. 435-426.

hieroglyphic date in bars and dots, equal to 162 A. D. It appears to be of Nephite origin. The bar equals our numeral 5 and each dot is 1.

• • •	[8]	8 units of 144,000 days each
•	[6]	6 units of 7,200 days each
• • • •	[4]	4 units of 360 days each
• •	[2]	2 units of 20 days each
	[17]	17 units of 1 day each

The foregoing adds up to 1,196,657 days. In other words, this date 8.6.4.2.17 is the 1,196,657th day from the starting day of this particular calendar system in use in ancient Middle America. That starting point was, in our system of time reckoning, August 13, 3114 B. C. In the example given, the data on the Tuxtla Statuette, the date falls within our year 162 A. D.[72] This date is 259 years before the close of *The Book of Mormon* era (421 A. D.) Virtually all scholars of the Maya calendar are now agreed on the correlation used above.[73]

Beautifully worked jade earplugs, pendants and ornaments have been discovered in the Valley of Mexico. Since jade is not found in that region, these ornaments were brought there from some other section of the country. It is believed that they came from the ancient *Tulan* (Bountiful) area and the highland region of Guatemala where the early Nahuales settled after their transoceanic journey. Some of these finds have been made in deep excavations dating back to about 100-300 A. D. They clearly indicate lapidary skills and also colonization work (or at least trade) from the ancient *Tulan area to the south*.

As has been previously discussed, the earliest trade and colonization work mentioned in *The Book of Mormon* as between *Bountiful-Zarahemla* and the country northward from the narrow-neck-of-land occurred about 55 B. C.[74] It is doubtful if these earliest colonizations in the "land northward" extended as far as the Valley of Mexico, however. It should be recalled that in 17 B. C. all the colonists in the northern lands were called back to Bountiful-Zarahemla below the narrow-neck-of-land.[75] This indicates the early movement northward had not extended

---

[72] Morley, *op. cit.*, p. 42. For an excellent discussion of the Maya calendar and its correlation with the Gregorian calendar, see M. Wells Jakeman, *The Origins and History of the Mayas* (1945), Ch. 3.
[73] The correlation used here was worked out by three individuals working severally and it is generally known as the Goodman-Thompson-Martinez Hernandez correlation.
[74] *The Book of Mormon*, p. 358 (Alma 63:4, 9-10).
[75] *Ibid.*, pp. 404-405 (verses 12-13, 21, 23-25).

very far. The jade objects mentioned were apparently carried to the Valley of Mexico between 100-300 A. D., as
indicated by the archæologists in their dating of the Copilco-
Zacatenco culture.[76]

That skilled lapidaries practiced their trade in southern
Mexico in the centuries immediately following the close of the
era encompassed in The Book of Mormon is very evident. From
the famous Tomb Seven at Monte Alban, Oaxaca, came necklaces of pearl, turquoise and jade. Jet, amber, and shell objects
also were discovered. Hundreds of beads were used in making
some of the necklaces. Also a remarkable cup or chalice, cut
and hollowed from a single block of hard white rock crystal,
was found.[77]

Among the objects found in the sacred cenote at Chichen
Itza, Yucatan, were hundreds of jade beads and pendants. These
are described as "artistically carved and shaped."[78] Within the
last ten years beautiful statuettes of jade and many great stone
heads of basalt have been discovered in the vicinity of the
narrow-neck-of-land of southern Mexico, Tehuantepec. These
"Olmec"[79] masterpieces date close to the time of Christ, well
within the time of Tultec-Nephite occupation of Bountiful-land.
A Mexican scholar has recently suggested that they may have
been the work of "the mother culture, from which the later
and better-known (Maya, Totonac, Zapotac, etc.) cultures
sprang."[80]

The art of carving stones was fully developed in the Near
East in 600 B. C. when the Bountiful people reportedly left
there for the New World. The term, "precious stones," found
in The Book of Mormon, was used many times in early Old Testament times.[81] Stones were engraved for signet rings from early
times.[82] Solomon (about 960-925 B. C.) decorated his temple
with "precious stones."[83] Rock-crystal, emeralds, topaz, sapphires,

[76] Vaillant, op. cit., pp. 26-27 (Table I), 32.

[77] Hewett, op. cit., p. 125. An excellent description of the treasures is also found in Covarrubias, op. cit., pp. 178-179.
     The earliest culture at Monte Alban, i.e., Monte Alban I, dates within The Book of Mormon period. That is, it is prior to 421 A. D. See Covarrubias, p. 123.

[78] Willard, op. cit., p. 286.

[79] The term "Olmec" is applied to the early colonizers who came by sea to the east or Gulf Coast of Mexico prior to the time of Christ.

[80] Miguel Covarrubias, Mexico South, The Isthmus of Tehuantepec (1946), pp. 79-81.

[81] 2 Samuel 12:30; 1 Kings 10:2, 10, 11; 1 Chronicles 20:2; 29:2, 8; 2 Chronicles 32:27; Proverbs 17:8.

[82] Exodus 28:11; Genesis 38:18; 1 Kings 21:8.

[83] 2 Chronicles 3:6; 1 Chronicles 29:2, 8.

diamonds, agates, jacinth, onyx, coral and jasper are among the stones mentioned in the Old Testament.[84]

Thus, the data set forth in *Ixtlilxochitl* and *The Book of Mormon* regarding architecture, metallurgy and the lapidary art of the Bountiful people, credited with coming from beyond the sea, are confirmed by both Near Eastern antiquities and Middle American archæology and history.

CERAMICS

Excellent pottery of fine craftsmanship has been found on both sides of the Isthmus of Tehuantepec, and in close prox' imity to that narrow-neck-of-land, dating within the very period designated by both *Ixtlilxochitl* and *The Book of Mormon* for the occupancy of that zone. Five "Olmec" sites have been dis' covered within the past few years in this Bountiful-land region and the area adjacent to it on the northwest: (1) *San Lorenzo,* Vera Cruz; (2) *La Venta,* Tabasco; (3) *Tres Zapotes,* Vera Cruz; (4) *Monte Alban,* strata I and II, Oaxaca; (5) *Tonala,* Chiapas.[85] Pottery from all of these important sites is of a high order and dates within the period of Nephite-Mulekite—Tultec- Ulmec occupancy of Bountiful-land and the areas allegedly colo' nized from the capital zone. That period, as was shown here' tofore, was from about 200 B. C. to about 350 A. D.

The Chicanel pottery of northern Guatemala also dates within this period. The region where it is found lies to the east of Bountiful-land proper. That area was colonized some time prior to 90 B. C. About that year the Nephites sent a colony of con' verted Lamanites (Ammonites), whose home had formerly been in the highlands of Nephi to the south, over southeast of Bountiful' land to what they called the land of Jershon. A Nephite historian wrote, "Behold, we will give up the land of Jershon, which is on the east by the sea, which joins the land Bountiful, which is on the south of the land Bountiful; and this land Jershon is the land which we will give unto our brethren for an inheritance." Chicanel pottery, found in the area southeast of ancient Boun' tiful-land and over near the Caribbean Sea on the east, dates within the 200 B. C.-350 A. D. period given by *Ixtlilxochitl* and *The Book of Mormon.*

---

[84] Funk and Wagnalls, "Precious Stones," *op. cit.*, pp. 866-867.
[85] M. Wells Jakeman, "Some Recent Discoveries," *Bulletin, University Archaeological Society,* Brig' ham Young Univ., May, 1950, p. 24; Covarrubias, *op. cit.*, Ch. IV.

Both the "Olmec" ware and the Chicanel ware are of a good quality and do credit to the descendants of Jacob from the Near East who colonized ancient America.

At Lachish have been found ceramics dating from the very time Lehi and Mulek left Palestine for the New World. Ceramics were recently found at Sacatepequez and Las Charcas[86] in the highlands of Guatemala which date very close to the time of Christ and may be early Lamanite wares, well within the period of Nephite dominance. If Bountiful-land is properly located, the land of Nephi (Lamanite homeland) would have been in the very area where these recent discoveries have been made.

SUMMARY STATEMENT

It is undisputed, by reason of important archæological discoveries made in recent years, that in the Tehuantepec narrow-neck-of-land area there lived a people of high culture, a people possessed of many arts and crafts—just as described in *The Book of Mormon* and in the writings of *Ixtlilxochitl*—and in the very time period designated by those two histories. Later peoples, Maya-Lamanites, late "Tultecs," Mixtecs and even Aztecs, perpetuated many of the skills of the wonderful "people of Bountiful-land." Many important discoveries are anticipated from the region in the next few years. The Mexican archæologists have already singled the zone out as the home of the "mother" culture.

The arts and crafts of ancient Middle America are about what one would expect to find there if the region were colonized from the eastern Mediterranean world in the sixth century B. C., as indicated by the Totonicapan history, the *Popol Vuh,* the Annals of Xahila, *Ixtlilxochitl* and *The Book of Mormon.* They all say the culture was imported with a culturally advanced people who came by sea. This explains why nothing primitive is found beneath the civilizations mentioned in the written sources.

In view of facts that have come to light in recent years from both the Near East and the two cultural centers of the ancient New World concerning metallurgical skills—and particularly the use of plates and tablets of precious and semi-precious metals as writing mediums—the idea that the heads of church and state in ancient Bountiful-land may have fashioned some golden tablets for their sacred writings is no longer incredible. Nor is it taxing one's credulity to believe that the voyagers could have brought with them the sacred writings of early Jewish prophets on "Brass Plates."

---

[86] *Ibid.,* p. 27.

Chapter 21

BLACK MAGIC AND GOOD ARTS

INTRODUCTION

As usual, all of the documentary sources, including *The Book of Mormon,* are in substantial agreement regarding the abilities of the ancient inhabitants of Bountiful-land in the fine arts, claiming that they were excellent orators, poets, and philosophers. In fact, they practiced black magic as well as the good arts. *The Book of Mormon* testifies that the ancient American holy prophets were continuously exerting efforts to counteract the practice of "sorceries, and witchcrafts, and magics" which now and then were practiced by portions of the populace. There was a continuous effort made throughout the entire history of the Nephite nation to fight the powers of "evil and darkness."

BLACK MAGIC PRACTICED

IXTLILXOCHITL:

Bad arts practiced by Tultecas

To a certain extent they [the Tultecas] were necromancers, enchanters, sorcerers, astrologers.[LX] . . .

EXTRACTS—BOOK OF MORMON:

Bad arts practiced by Nephites and Lamanites
Sorceries, witchcrafts, magics[LX]

32. For those who did not belong to their church, [Nephite church of Christ] did *indulge themselves in sorceries* . . .   Alma 1:32.

19. And it came to pass that *there were sorceries, and witchcrafts, and magics;* and the power of the evil one was wrought upon all the face of the land, even unto the fulfilling of all the words of Abinadi, and also Samuel the Lamanite.   Mormon 1:19.

16. And I will cut off *witchcrafts* out of thy land, and thou shalt have no *more soothsayers;*

19. And it shall come to pass that all lyings, and deceivings, and envyings, and strifes, and *priestcrafts,* and whoredoms, shall be done away.
        3 Nephi 21:16, 19.

LX. Necromancers, Enchanters, Sorcerers, Astrologers

Necromancers are those who pretend to forecast events by alleged communication with the dead. Necromancy is generally regarded as one of the black arts, along with sorcery. The latter is related to magic or witchery. Astrology, too, is a false "science" by which the destinies of men are allegedly told by study of the stars. So, we see that *Ixtlilxochitl* has grouped together four of the pseudo-arts practiced by the Tultecas prior to the Conquest: necromancy, enchantment, sorcery and astrology.

Like idolatry, they blossomed from time to time, even during the Nephite (Nahuale-Ulmec) dominance. *The Book of Mormon* makes it clear that with the defeat and virtual destruction of the righteous priesthood leadership at the beginning of the fourth century A. D., many black arts were practiced. During the 1,000 years that intervened between the fourth century and the Conquest, the black arts made great headway in Mexico and Middle America. They were in common use at the time of the Conquest.[4]

All four of the black arts mentioned by *Ixtlilxochitl* were practiced anciently in the Near East before the colonizers of America arrived from that land. In fact, prior to the time of the departure of Lehi and Mulek from Palestine at the outset of the sixth century B. C., the true prophets of Israel had spoken out strongly against the black arts of the pseudo-prophets. The ancient and fully developed systems of magic and divination of Egypt and Babylon were thriving in the lands neighboring on Israel. For example, the Bible states: "Then Pharaoh also called the wise men and the sorcerers; now the magicians of Egypt, they also did in like manner with their enchantments."[5] We read that when the Babylonian king, Nebuchadnezzar, brought four young Israelites before him ". . . in all matters of wisdom and understanding . . . he found them ten times better than all the magicians and astrologers that were in his realm."[6]

Usually those who sought or practiced the black arts were endeavoring to obtain some unfair advantage over their fellows. The practices were condemned under ancient Israelite law but were never wholly eradicated. The law is given in Deuteronomy as follows:

---

[4] Hubert Howe Bancroft, *Native Races*, vol. 2, pp. 253, 271, 462; vol. 5, pp. 450, 469. Bancroft cites several excellent authorities, including *Ixtlilxochitl* and *Torquemada*.
[5] Exodus 7:11.
[6] Daniel 1:20.

There shall not be found among you anyone that maketh his son or his daughter to pass through the fire, or that useth divination, or an observer of time, or an enchanter, or a witch, or a charmer, or a consulter with familiar spirits, or a wizard, or a necromancer. For all that do these things are an abomination unto the Lord: and because of these abominations the Lord thy God doth drive them out from before thee.[7]

Virtually the same law existed in Middle America, even as late as the Conquest period. Sorcery and witchcraft were illegal if employed to injure the community or the individual.[8]

In striking confirmation of *Ixtlilxochitl's* statement on the black arts is *The Book of Mormon* report of happenings in Bountiful-Zarahemla just prior to the expulsion of the Nephites from that ancient center. To quote:

And it came to pass that there were sorceries, and witchcrafts, and magics; and the power of the evil one was wrought upon all the face of the land.[9]

... no man could keep that which was his own, for the thieves, and the robbers, and the murderers, and the magic art, and the witchcraft which was in the land. Thus there began to be a mourning and a lamentation in all the land because of these things, and more especially among the people of Nephi.[10]

Sahagun wrote of the astronomy and astrology of the ancients of Bountiful:

They were so capable at natural astrology, the said *Toltecs*, that they were the first that had counted and calculated the days of the year and the night and its hours and the difference of time. They knew very well those [days] that were helpful and those that were harmful, which they left identified by 20 figures or characters. They also invented the art of interpreting dreams and they were so able and wise that they knew the movements of the heavens. . . .[11]

LXI. Poets, Philosophers, Orators

IXTLILXOCHITL:	EXTRACTS—BOOK OF MORMON:
Poets, philosophers, orators[LXI] [The Tultecs were] poets, philosophers, and orators, so that they used all the arts, the good as well as the bad.	*Examples of Nephite poetry and the people's ability as orators will be given later*

[7] Deuteronomy 18:10-12; Isaiah 8:19; Ezekiel 21:21; Jeremiah 27:9; I Samuel 15:23. The Babylonian Code of Hammurabi (about 2100 B. C.) forbids witchcraft.
[8] Torquemada, *op. cit.*, tomo 2, *libro doce, capitulo* 7, p. 386. In his marginal note Torquemada cites Deuteronomy, Ch. 18. Several authorities, including *Ixtlilxochitl*, Torquemada and Las Cases are cited by Bancroft, *op. cit.*, vol. 2, p. 462, note 71.
[9] *The Book of Mormon*, p. 461 (Mormon 1:19).
[10] *Ibid.*, p. 462 (Mormon 2:10-11).
[11] Sahagun, *op. cit.*, Libro Noveno, Capitulo 29, Sec. 1.

There are many evidences in *The Book of Mormon* showing that the ancients of Bountiful-Zarahemla were "poets, philosophers and orators," possessors of the "good arts," as *Ixtlilxochitl* puts its. These extracts which follow this discussion from the Nephite record are given only as examples. Sahagun says of the Tultecas:

> They were good singers and while they sang or danced they used drums and wooden jingles . . .; they played and composed and arranged curious songs. They were great orators and very devout.

> And these said *Toltecs* were apt in the Mexican language for they were not barbaric, although they did not speak it [the Mexican "Nahua" tongue] as perfectly as it is now used. They were rich, and because they were intelligent and capable, in a brief time, with their diligence, they had riches that they said their God and Lord, *Quetzalcoatl*, gave them. And thus it was said among them that he who in a brief time became rich was the son of *Quetzalcoatl*.[12]

A high percentage of the natives of Mexico today are very musical. Many have excellent singing voices. Countless tourists have been delighted on hearing the lovely music produced by the little troupes of musicians, the *mariachis*. And it should be recalled that these people trace their ancestry to the early Tultecas or Nephites.

The only examples of poetry and oratory available to us at this time from the very early period of settlement come to us from *The Book of Mormon*. However, there are a number of references indicating that the ancients were thoroughly familiar with these arts. Antonio Chi, able historian of the Mayas of Yucatan, writing in 1582, said in his report on some of the customs: ". . . [They had written records of] important things which had occurred in [the past] . . . [the prognostications] of their prophets and the lives . . . of their lords; and for the [common] people . . . certain songs in meter . . . according to the history they contained."[13] Cogolludo (1688) said of the Mayas, "They sing their fables and their ancient lore."[14]

As shall be shown, examples of Mexican poetry from the Aztec period preceding the Conquest have come down to us. These appear to reflect the more ancient thought of the refined Tultecs. Bancroft wrote:

---

[12] Sahagun, *Historia de las Cosas de Nueva Espana.*
[13] Translation by Alfred M. Tozzer, *Historia de las Cosas de Yucatan* (Landa's) (1946), note 154.
[14] Cited in *ibid.*, note 403. Diego Lopez Cogolludo, *Historia de Yucatan* (1688).

Poets, if somewhat less numerous, were no less honored than orators. Their compositions were also recited, or sung, before the Council of Music in *Tezcuco* [province not far from what is today Mexico City], and the most talented bards were honored with prizes. The heroic deeds of war-like ancestors, national annals and traditions, praise of the gods, moral lessons drawn from actual events, allegorical productions with illustrations drawn from the beauties of nature, and even love and the charms of women were the common themes. The emperor Nezahualcoyotl, the protector and promoter of all the arts and sciences, was himself a poet of great renown. Several of his compositions, or fragments of such, have been preserved; that is, the poems were written from memory in Aztec with Roman letters after the Conquest, and translated into Spanish by *Ixtlilxochitl,* a lineal descendant of the royal poet. They have also been translated into other languages by various authors.[15]

Nezahualcoyotl took a deep interest in religion and the arts. He worshipped a single God and left sixty hymns com-posed in honor of the great Creator.[16] It is claimed that he was a wise ruler.[17] José Maria Vigil has translated some of the ex-quisite songs or poems of this same fifteenth century ruler.

EXAMPLES OF NEPHITE AND AZTEC POETRY

Examples of Mexican poetry of the Aztec period preceding Span-ish conquest[LXI]

NEZHUALCOYOTL'S SONGS
Translated by Ixtlilxochitl

[Nezhualcoyotl was the ruler of the Province of Texcoco, lo-cated near the present City of Mexico, from 1418 A. D. to 1472 A. D.][17]

Now will I sing for a moment,
Since time and occasion offer
And I trust to be heard with favor
If my effort proveth deserving;
Wherefore thus I begin my sing-ing,
Or rather my lamentation.

O thou, my friend, and beloved,
Enjoy the sweet flowers I bring thee;
Let us be joyful together
And banish each care and each sorrow;
For although life's pleasures are fleeting,
Life's bitterness also must leave us.

Examples of Nephite poetry[LXI]

NEPHI'S PSALM—"REJOICE, O MY HEART"

Behold, my soul delighteth in the things of the Lord;
And my heart pondereth continually upon the things which I have seen and heard.
Nevertheless, nowithstanding the great goodness of the Lord in showing me His great and mar-velous works, my heart exclaimeth:
"O wretched man that I am!"
Yea, my heart sorroweth because of my flesh;
My soul grieveth because of mine iniquities.

I am encompassed about,
Because of the temptations and the sins which do so easily beset me.
And when I desire to rejoice, my heart groan-eth because of my sins.
Nevertheless, I know in whom I have trusted;
My God hath been my support.
He hath led me through mine afflictions in the wilderness;
And He hath preserved me upon the waters of the great deep.
He hath filled me with His love,
Even unto the consuming of my flesh.
He hath confounded mine enemies,
Unto the causing of them to quake before me.

[15] Bancroft, *op. cit.,* vol. 2, p. 497, note 32.
[16] Vaillant, *op. cit.,* p. 102.
[17] Vaillant, *Aztecs of Mexico,* table p. 95.

I will strike, to help me in singing,
The instrument deep and sonor-
ous;
Dance thou, while enjoying these
flowers,
Before the great Lord who is
mighty;
Let us grasp the sweet things of
the present,
For the life of a man is soon
over.

But yet thou shalt not be for-
gotten,
Nor the good thou has ever ac-
complished;
For, is not the throne that thou
fillest
The gift of the God without
equal,
The mighty Creator of all things,
The maker of Kings and
Princes?[18]

*   *   *   *   *   *

There is, indeed, another life
beyond.
Would that I could go there;
There the birds are singing;
There I would learn to know
Those fair flowers, those sweet
flowers,
The only ones which appease
And mildly intoxicate.[19]

Behold, He hath heard my cry by day
And He hath given me knowledge by visions
in the night-time.
And by day have I waxed bold in mighty prayer
before Him.
Yea, my voice have I sent up on high,
And angels came down and ministered unto me.
And upon the wings of His Spirit hath my body
been carried away upon exceeding high moun-
tains,
And mine eyes have beheld great things, yea,
even too great for man;
Therefore, I was bidden that I should not write
them.

O, then, if I have seen so great things,
If the Lord in His condescension unto the children of men hath visited men in so much
mercy;
Why should my heart weep and my soul linger
in the valley of sorrow,
And my flesh waste away, and my strength
slacken because of mine afflictions?
And why should I yield to sin because of my
flesh:
Yea, why should I give way to temptations, that
the evil one have place in my heart, to destroy
my peace and afflict my soul?
Why am I angry because of mine enemy?

Awake, my soul! No longer droop in sin,
Rejoice, O my heart, and give place no more for
the enemy of my soul.
Do not anger again because of mine enemies.
Do not slacken my strength because of mine
afflictions.
Rejoice, O my heart, and cry unto the Lord
and say:
"O Lord, I will praise Thee forever;
Yea, my soul will rejoice in Thee, my God and
the Rock of my salvation."

OH LORD, REDEEM MY SOUL

"O Lord, wilt Thou redeem my soul?
Wilt Thou deliver me out of the hands of mine
enemies?
Wilt Thou make me that I may shake at the
appearance of sin?
May the gates of hell be shut continually before me,
Because that my heart is broken and my spirit
is contrite!
O Lord, wilt Thou not shut the gates of Thy
righteousness before me, that I may walk in
the path of the low valley,
That I may be strict in the plain road.

---

[18] Only four of the sixteen verses quoted by Hubert Howe Bancroft in *Native Races*, are reprinted here.
[19] Cited in Edgar L. Hewett, *Ancient Life in Mexico and Central America* (1941), p. 250, pp. 245-250.

O Lord, wilt Thou encircle me around in the
robe of Thy righteousness!
O Lord, wilt Thou make a way for mine escape
before mine enemies!
Wilt Thou make my path straight before me!
Wilt Thou not place a stumbling block in my
way—but that Thou wouldst clear my way before me, and hedge not up my way, but the
ways of mine enemy.

O Lord, I have trusted in Thee, and I will trust
in Thee forver.....
I will not trust in the arm of flesh; for I know
that cursed is he that putteth his trust in the
arm of flesh.
Yea, cursed is he that putteth his trust in man
or maketh flesh his arm.
Yea, I know that God will give liberally to
him that asketh,
Yea, my God will give me, if I ask not amiss.
Therefore I will lift up my voice unto Thee;
Yea, I will cry unto Thee, my God, the Rock of
my Righteousness.
Behold my voice shall forever ascend up unto
Thee,
My Rock and mine everlasting God. Amen.

2 Nephi 4:16-35.

Mormon's Lamentation

And my soul was rent with anguish because
of the slain of my people, and I cried:
O ye fair ones, how could ye
have departed from the
ways of the Lord!
O ye fair ones, how could ye
have rejected that Jesus,
who stood with open
arms to receive you!
Behold, if ye had not done this,
ye would not have fallen.
But behold, ye are fallen,
and I mourn your loss.

O ye fair sons and daughters,
ye fathers and mothers,
ye husbands and wives,
ye fair ones, how is it
that ye could have fallen!
But behold, ye are gone,
and my sorrows cannot
bring your return. . . .

O that ye had repented before
this great destruction had
come upon you.
But behold, ye are gone, and
the Father, yea, the Eternal
Father of heaven, knoweth
your state; and he doeth
with you according to his
justice and mercy.

Mormon 6:16-20, 22.

ABILITY OF NEPHITES AS ORATORS

Nephite skills in speech and oratory—Nephi's statements[LXI]

1. And now I, Nephi, cannot write all the things which were taught among my people; neither am I mighty in writing, like unto speaking; for when a man speaketh by the power of the Holy Ghost the power of the Holy Ghost carrieth it unto the hearts of the children of men.

2 Nephi 33:1.

Examples of speaking with power and results of Benjamin's sermon[LXI]

45. And behold, the Holy Spirit of God did come down from heaven, and did enter into their hearts, and they were filled as if with fire, and they could speak forth marvelous words.

46. And it came to pass that there came a voice unto them, yea, a pleasant voice, as if it were a whisper, saying:

47. Peace, peace be unto you, because of your faith in my Well Beloved, who was from the foundation of the world.

Helaman 5:45-47.

1. And now, it came to pass than when king Benjamin had made an end of speaking the words which had been delivered unto him by the angel of the Lord, that he cast his eyes round about on the multitude, and behold they had fallen to the earth, for the fear of the Lord had come upon them.

2. And they had viewed themselves in their own carnal state, even less than the dust of the earth. And they all cried aloud with one voice, saying: O have mercy, and apply the atoning blood of Christ that we may receive forgiveness of our sins, and our hearts may be purified; for we believe in Jesus Christ, the Son of God, who created heaven and earth, and all things; who shall come down among the children of men.

3. And it came to pass that after they had spoken these words the Spirit of the Lord came upon them, and they were filled with joy, having received all remission of their sins, and having peace of conscience, because of the exceeding faith which they had in Jesus Christ who should come, according to the words which king Benjamin had spoken unto them.

Mosiah 4:1-3.

Moroni's statement concerning Nephite language skills[LXI]

23. And I said unto him: Lord, the Gentiles will mock at these things, because of our weakness in writing; for Lord thou hast made us

mighty in word by faith, but thou hast not made us mighty in writing; for thou hast made all this people that they could speak much, because of the Holy Ghost which thou hast given them;

24. And thou hast made us that we could write but little, because of the awkwardness of our hands. Behold, thou hast not made us mighty in writing like unto the brother of Jared, for thou madest him that the things which he wrote were mighty even as thou art, unto the overpowering of man to read them.

25. Thou hast also made our words powerful and great, even that we cannot write them; wherefore, when we write we behold our weakness, and stumble because of the placing of our words; and I fear lest the Gentiles shall mock at our words.

26. And when I had said this, the Lord spake unto me, saying: Fools mock, but they shall mourn; and my grace is sufficient for the meek, that they shall take no advantage of your weakness;   Ether 12:23-26.

Concluding Thought

It is quite evident from what has been presented in this chapter that both *The Book of Mormon* and *Ixtlilxochitl* were correct in ascribing to the transoceanic colonizers the finer arts of poetry, oratory, and philosophy, together with the black arts of necromancy, sorcery, and astrology.

Chapter 22

"THE SUN STOOD STILL"

INTRODUCTION

Recently Dr. Immanuel Velikovsky wrote a book entitled *Worlds in Collision,* in which he discussed the numerous traditions which have persisted from ancient times in both the Old and New worlds, showing that "the sun stood still." The following statement appeared in *The Readers' Digest* in March, 1950, announcing Dr. Velikovsky's new book:

> Nations and tribes in many other places have traditions about a cosmic catastrophe during which the sun did not shine; the long darkness is remembered in Finland, Babylonia and Peru, by the American Indians, by peoples all over the world. Hundreds of thousands of men and animals were killed during an upheaval that shook the earth.[1]

It is the opinion of the authors that none of the numerous references to the sun standing still cited by Dr. Velikovsky from the various countries of the world, with the possible exception of the one found in the Bible, are as outstanding and explicit on this subject as the account given in *The Book of Mormon* and sustained by the *Works of Ixtlilxochitl.* We shall now devote our attention to an examination of these early American sources.

IXTLILXOCHITL:	EXTRACTS—BOOK OF MORMON:
Sun stood still	*Sun stood still*
And in the year 8 *Tochtli,* which was 1,347 years after the second calamity, and 4,779 since the creation of the world, they have in their history[LXII] that the sun stood [still] for a natural day without moving from one spot (place), and they add a fable saying that as the mosquito saw the sun so suspensive and pensive, he said to him: Lord of the world, why are you so suspensive and pensive and not do your work as it has been ordered	7. O how great is the nothingness of the children of men; yea, even they are less than the dust of the earth.
	8. For behold, the dust of the earth moveth hither and thither, to the dividing asunder, at the command of our great and everlasting God.
	9. Yea, behold at his voice do the hills and the mountains tremble and quake.
	13. Yea, and if he say unto the earth—Move —it is moved.
	14. Yea, if he say unto the earth—Thou shalt go back, that it lengthen out the day for many hours—it is done;

[1] Preview by Fulton Oursler of Dr. Immanuel Velikovsky, "Worlds in Collision," in *Readers' Digest* (March, 1950), pp. 139-148.

you to do? Do you want to destroy the world as you are
wont?

15. And thus, according to his word the
earth goeth back, and it appeareth unto man that
the sun standeth still;[LXII] yea, and behold, this
is so [i.e., that the earth goes back] for surely
it is the earth that moveth and not the sun.

Helaman 12:7-15.

Continuous light during a day, night, and day

1. And now it came to pass that Samuel, the
Lamanite, did prophesy a great many more things
which cannot be written.

2. And behold, he said unto them: Behold,
I give unto you a sign; for five years more cometh, and behold, then cometh the son of God to
redeem all those who shall believe on his name.

3. And behold, this will I give unto you for
a sign at the time of his coming; for behold,
there shall be great lights in heaven, insomuch
that in the night before he cometh there shall
be no darkness, insomuch that it shall appear
unto man as if it were day.

4. Therefore, there shall be one day and a
night and a day, as if it were one day and there
were no night; and this shall be unto you for a
sign; for ye shall know of the rising of the sun
and also of its setting; therefore they shall know
of a surety that there shall be two days and a
night; nevertheless the night shall not be darkened; and it shall be the night before he is born.
[LXII]

Helaman 14:1-4.

8. But behold, they did watch steadfastly for
that day and that night and that day which
should be as one day as if there were no night,
that they might know that their faith had not
been in vain. . . .[LXII]

12. And it came to pass that he cried might-
ily unto the Lord, all the day; and behold, the
voice of the Lord came unto him, saying:

13. Lift up your head and be of good cheer;
for behold, the time is at hand, and on this
night shall the sign be given, and on the morrow
come I into the world, to show unto the world
that I will fulfill all that which I have caused to
be spoken by the mouth of my holy prophets. . . .

15. And it came to pass that the words which
came unto Nephi were fulfilled, according as
they had been spoken; for behold, at the going
down of the sun there was no darkness; and the
people began to be astonished because there was
no darkness when the night came. . . .

19. And it came to pass that there was no
darkness in all that night, but it was as light as
though it was mid-day. And it came to pass
that the sun did rise in the morning again, according to its proper order; and they knew that
it was the day that the Lord should be born,
because of the sign which had been given.[LXII]

3 Nephi 1:8, 12-13, 15, 19.

LXII. "THE SUN STOOD STILL"

Ixtlilxochitl's statement that the sun stood still for a natural day has its counterpart in *The Book of Mormon*. This statement would appear to refer to a period of thirty-six hours of continuous daylight. According to *Ixtlilxochitl's* count of 4,779 years from the creation and 1,347 years from the great hurricane (the Second Calamity), this incident of "the sun standing still" would have occurred about 450 B. C. No such event is reported in *The Book of Mormon* for that year. However, the quoted statement from Helaman was originally written about 7 B. C. and it doubtless refers back to some specific astronomical event or demonstration of an earlier date.

There is also another possible answer to this problem. As the extract from 3 Nephi shows, at the time of the birth of Christ in Bethlehem it is reported by the Nephites in the New World that ". . .*there was no darkness in all that night, but it was as light as though it was midday. And it came to pass that the sun did rise in the morning again, according to its proper order; and they knew that it was the day that the Lord should be born, because of the sign which had been given.*"[2] The memory of this event may have come down as tradition to *Ixtlilxochitl* in a slightly altered form.

There is a third source which should receive due consideration in regards to *Ixtlilxochitl's* statement "that the sun stood [still] for a natural day." It should be remembered that the inhabitants of ancient America brought with them from the land of Canaan the Hebrew scriptures (the Brass Plates), containing the history and doctrine of the Jews down to the time of the Prophet Jeremiah. It is recorded in that scripture that Joshua commanded the sun to stand still and he was obeyed. To quote:

And the sun stood still, and the moon stayed, until the people had avenged themselves upon their enemies. Is not this written in the Book of Jasher? So the sun stood still in the midst of heaven, and has not to go down about a whole day.

It could be that the foregoing event which was recorded in the Hebrew scripture found a place in the traditions of the inhabitants of ancient America and *Ixtlilxochitl* recorded it in connection with the early settlers of America.

2 *The Book of Mormon*, p. 400 (3 Nephi 1:19b).
3 Joshua 10:13.

At least this much can be said, the statement found in the *Works of Ixtlilxochitl* that the sun stood still for a natural day has its counterpart both in *The Book of Mormon* and in the Old Testament and, as has been pointed out, corroboration for such a cosmic event in ancient times comes from various quarters of the world. In fact, the conclusion in *The Readers' Digest* condensation of Dr. Velikovsky's sensational new book is that ". . . familiar tales of wonder emerge not as myths but as accurate reporting of actual events."[4]

---

[4] Fulton Oursler, *op. cit.*

Chapter 23

AGRICULTURE AND DOMESTIC ANIMALS

Introductory Statement

Each of our primary accounts declares that the Bountiful-land settlers were skilled agriculturists—sedentary people who raised particular crops. The statements in *The Book of Mormon* are very explicit in this regard and have caused some persons to question the authenticity of the record. The problems presented by the statements of the Nephite historians as to both crops and domestic animals will be discussed. *Ixtlilxochitl* wrote little concerning these matters, but what he did say is helpful. Even now the facts are not all in from the archæologists, botanists and others, and further developments will be awaited with interest. As things stand, the claims of *The Book of Mormon* concerning a number of plants and animals are neither proven nor disproven by direct evidence. It might be said that the claims of the Nephite record have been established indirectly—for the Nephite record is corroborated and sustained on innumerable other technicalities, and so there would seem to be justification for accepting the declarations regarding plants and animals, especially since the experts are lately upsetting some of the older notions which conflicted with *Book of Mormon* assertions respecting certain plants.

Nephite (Tulteca) Agriculture

IXTLILXOCHITL:

Crops produced by the Tultecs

They [the Tultecs] had maize [corn], cotton, chili beans, and other seeds[LXIII] that there are in the land.
* * *

EXTRACTS—BOOK OF MORMON:

Nephite agriculture

24. And it came to pass that we did begin to till the earth, yea, we began to plant seeds; yea, we did put all our seeds[LXIII] into the earth, which we had brought from the land of Jerusalem. And it came to pass that they did grow exceedingly; wherefore, we were blessed in abundance. 1 Nephi 18:24.

8. And my people would that we should call the name of the place Nephi; wherefore we did call it Nephi.

11. And the Lord was with us; and we did prosper exceedingly; for we did sow seed, and we did reap again in abundance. . . .   2 Nephi 5:8, 11.

22. And all this he did, for the sole purpose of bringing this people into subjection or into bondage. And behold, we at this time do pay tribute to the king of the Lamanites, to the amount of one half of our corn,[LV] and our barley, and even all our grain of every kind, and one half of the increase of our flocks and our herds; and even one half of all we have or possess the king of the Lamanites doth exact of us, or our lives.   Mosiah 7:22.

9. And we began to till the ground, yea, even with all manner of seeds, with seeds of corn, and of wheat, and of barley, and with neas, and with sheum, and with seeds of all manner of fruits; and we did begin to multiply and prosper in the land.   Mosiah 9:9.

12. They did raise grain in abundance, both in the north and in the south; and they did flourish exceedingly, both in the north and in the south. And they did multiply and wax exceedingly strong in the land. And they did raise many flocks and herds, yea, many fatlings.   Helaman 6:12.

LXIII. Maize and Other Agricultural Products

Indian corn, that is *maize,* or "corn-on-the-cob," did not exist in the Old World in ancient times. It was native to the New World. Not until after the discovery by Columbus did people in Europe, Asia, and Africa have corn in their diet or as a food for stock. Today it is the greatest food crop in the world. More bushels of corn are raised than wheat. Of course, much of the output is consumed by swine and cattle, thus being converted into another form of food for man.

Bible references to "corn" are actually to grain, including barley, wheat and rye,[1] and not to what we in America call corn.

It appears certain that the people of Bountiful-Zarahemla included *maize* as an important food item. Indications are that it was domesticated by the "Ancient Ones" (Jaredites).[2] It is clear from the documentary and archæological sources that *maize* was being raised during the early *Tultec* or Nephite period.

When the Jaredites, Nephites or Mulekites arrived by boat from the Near East maize was doubtless found in a wild state. Inasmuch as it thrives well in the tropical parts of Middle America, it soon assumed an important role. Of course it was neces-

---

[1] Funk and Wagnalls, "Corn," *New Standard Bible Dictionary* (1936 ed.), p. 151.
[2] Herbert W. Dick has shown that specimens of primitive maize found in Bat Cave, New Mexico, date from about 2000 B. C. M. Wells Jakeman, "XXIX International Congress of Americanists," *Bulletin of the University Archaeological Society,* Brigham Young Univ., May, 1950, p. 33.

sary to give the newly discovered grain a name. It appears that
the name given to that grain may have been translated by
Joseph Smith as "corn." Two unfamiliar crops are listed in *The
Book of Mormon,* one of which might possibly be the original
Nephite term for corn or the other important staple, beans. As
of about 200 B. C. a Nephite historian recorded the following
important statement:

> And we began to till the ground, yea, even with all manner of seeds,
> with seeds of *corn,* and of wheat, and of barley, and with *neas,* and with
> *sheum,* and with seeds of all manner of fruits.[3]

It is the present view of a number of scholars that both maize
and several varieties of beans were first domesticated in Middle
America.[4] The foregoing quotation from *The Book of Mormon*
indicates that *neas* and *sheum,* whatever they may have been,
were not brought from the Old World, for the people had no
Old World names for them.

In his chapter on the *Tultecs,* Bernardino de Sahagun says:

> Their food was the same sustenance that is now [sixteenth century]
> used, that of maize, and *they* planted it and *developed it,* the white as well
> as the other colors of maize with which they sustained themselves; and
> they bought and dealt with it as coins.[5]

By the sixteenth century, and perhaps several centuries earlier, maize had become the principal food in the diet of the people
of Middle America. Seventy-five to eighty-five per cent of the
food eaten by the present-day Maya is maize in one form or
another.[6] When the Europeans arrived in the New World, the
familiar Old World grains (wheat, rye, barley and oats) were
not to be found in America, in any form, wild or otherwise.
Further, no evidence outside *The Book of Mormon* has as yet
come to light indicating the existence of those grains in ancient
America.

The only explanation that can be given at the present time
for the quotation from *The Book of Mormon,* as set forth above,
is that Lehi brought these grains from the Old World and that
some time between 200 B. C. and the Conquest they were abandoned and died out of existence in the tropical regions where
they were not well adapted. This is, of course, somewhat speculative. That they were brought to the New World by Lehi

---

[3] *The Book of Mormon,* p. 152 (Mosiah 9:9).
[4] Ralph Linton, "Crops, Soils, and Culture in America," *The Maya and Their Neighbors* (1940),
    p. 33 ff.
[5] Sahagun, *Historia General de las Cosas de Nueva Espana,* Libro Noveno, Capitulo 29, Sec. 1.
[6] Sylvanus G. Morley, *The Ancient Maya* (1946), p. 142.

seems clear from two statements that appear early in the Nephite record, the first relating to the gathering of seeds in preparation for the departure from the Near East, and the second relating to planting and harvesting shortly after the arrival in the New World:

And it came to pass that we had gathered together all manner of seeds of every kind, both of *grain of every kind,* and also of the seeds of fruit of every kind.[7]

And it came to pass that we did begin to till the earth, and we began to plant seeds; yea, we did put all our seeds into the earth, *which we had brought from the land of Jerusalem.* And it came to pass that they did grow exceedingly; wherefore, we were blessed in abundance.[8]

With the coming of Europeans, wheat and barley were again brought from the Old World to America. It is interesting to observe the production figures of Mexico for these grains and contrast the figures with those for the production of maize. These figures of present-day production seem to give some help in connection with the problem under discussion:[9]

Crops:	Production in Metric Tons, average per year, 1940-1944:
Maize	2,067,138
Wheat	429,621
Barley	90,106

In modern times, and as it probably was anciently, maize is the great crop of Mexico. It may have been the main crop to survive the desolating wars and droughts experienced by the people of the land of Bountiful in ancient times.[10a]

As of the time of the Conquest (and some people think this applies to the entire pre-Conquest time span), certain crops appear to have been grown only in the New World and certain others appear to have been produced only in the Old World:[10]

---

[7] *The Book of Mormon,* p. 13 (Nephi 8:1).

[8] *The Book of Mormon,* p. 40 (1 Nephi 19:24), p. 60 (2 Nephi 5:11); p. 127 (Enos 1:21); p. 149 (Mosiah 7:22); p. 152 (Mosiah 9:9); p. 373 (Helaman 6:12). The Nephites were en route for about nine years before reaching the New World. Seeds brought from Jerusalem could still germinate. Wheat seed has germinated after twenty years, where precautions were taken. See Harold Gladwin (1947) *Men Out of Asia,* pp. 354-356.

[9] Nathan L. Whetten, *Rural Mexico* (1948), p. 253.

[10a] Some botanists have suggested that maize was first domesticated in the highlands of Guatemala—for in that locale are found the only two native grasses that will cross with maize, *teosinte* and *tripsacum* (Morley, *op. cit.,* pp. 137-141). There is good reason for believing that the highland region of Guatemala constituted the land of Nephi in *The Book of Mormon.* If this is so it would be the area occupied by the Nephites during the first 400 years after the arrival of Lehi in the New World, i.e., from about 580 B. C. to about 200 B. C. But see footnote 2 herein.

[10] Elmer D. Merrill, "Crops and Civilizations," *Journal of American Museum of Natural History* (May-June, 1933), vol. 33. Merrill considers this list evidence for the view that the early American civilizations had no contacts with the Old World or with "the lost tribes of Israel." We have removed cotton from his New World list because it has been shown to have also existed in the Old World.

Old World and New World Products

New World Crops Exclusively	Old World Crops Exclusively	
1. maize or Indian corn	1. wheat	44. yam
2. potato	2. rye	[also in the
3. sweet potato[11]	3. barley	new world]
4. cassava	4. oats	45. sugar cane
5. lima bean	5. millet	46. sesame
6. common garden beans	6. Italian millet	(and others)
7. runner bean (scarlet	7. pearl millet	47. apple
runner bean)	8. sorghum	48. pear
8. tepari bean	9. rice	49. plum
9. yam	10. coix	50. cherry
10. tomato	11. buckwheat	51. wine grape
11. pepper	12. turnip	52. apricot
12. Jerusalem artichokes	13. cabbage	53. peach
13. sunflower	14. rutabaga	54. prune
14. squash	15. grape	55. olive
15. pumpkin	16. chard	56. fig
16. fig-leaved pumpkin	17. mustard	57. almond
17. musky pumpkin	18. radish	58. persimmon
18. peanut	19. beet	59. quince
19. chayote	20. parsnip	60. pomegranate
20. papaya	21. carrot	61. jujube
21. avocado	22. onion	62. melon
22. pineapple	23. leek	63. watermelon
23. custard apple	24. garlic	64. cucumber
24. sour-sop	25. shallot	65. banana
25. cherimoya	26. spinach	66. coconut
26. guava	27. eggplant	67. orange
27. cacao	28. lettuce	68. pomelo
28. cashew	29. endive	69. lemon
29. sapote	30. salsify	70. lime
30. white sapote	31. celery	71. date
31. sapodilla	32. asparagus	72. mango
32. mammei	33. globe artichoke	73. breadfruit
33. Mexican plum	34. pea	74. jak-fruit
(and others)	35. soy bean	75. rambutan
	36. cowpea	76. litchi
	37. chick-pea	77. longan
	38. pigeon-pea	78. mangosteen
	39. lentil	(and others)
	40. broad bean	79. alfalfa
	41. hyacinth bean	80. clover
	42. asparagus bean	(and most of
	43. taro	hay grasses)

---

[11] These plants were also found in the Pacific islands and they were doubtless taken there by boats from America. They will not live in salt water and, therefore, could not have reached the islands without man's aid. The name for yam in ancient America and Polynesia is similar. The sweet potato is called *kumar* in Peru and *kumara* in Polynesia.

The imposing list of New World crops is such that only an agricultural, sedentary, advanced people would have developed them. The early colonizers of America must be given credit for agricultural genius.[12] Regardless of what seeds may have been brought from Jerusalem, and what may ultimately have come of those crops in America, it can safely be said that the early settlers found many new forms of plants here and that they had the ability to develop and utilize the edible and useful ones, to the lasting benefit of our modern world.

COTTON

Cotton is of special interest. There is some very recent evidence that the plant was imported into ancient America from the Old World. It was cultivated in early times in both hemispheres. At the twenty-ninth meeting of the International Congress of Americanists held at New York City in September, 1949, an important paper was read by a botanist, George Carter.[14] He notes that three groups of this plant are known. The first has thirteen large chromosomes. The second type has thirteen small chromosomes. The third type has thirteen small and thirteen large chromosomes. Old World domesticated cotton has only the large chromosomes. New World wild cotton has only the small chromosomes. The cotton of the cultured settlers of ancient Middle America is a blend of Old World cotton and New World wild cotton because it alone has both the thirteen large chromosomes and the thirteen small chromosomes. It appears that the ancient sedentary settlers of either Middle America or Peru brought Old World cotton to the New World and blended it with the wild species native to this hemisphere.

Dr. M. Wells Jakeman suggests further that the New World twenty-six-chromosome domesticated cotton appears to have been carried back part way across the ocean to the Polynesian Islands, where the twenty-six-chromosome cotton was also cultivated in pre-European times.

This evidence is very powerful in defense of *Book of Mormon* declarations that seeds were brought to the New World in the boats of both the Jaredites and the Nephites. Cotton alone appears to make out a very strong case in support of *Book of Mormon* position. If one single plant, such as cotton, were

---

[12] Harold Sterling Gladwin, *Men Out of Asia* (1947), p. 73.
[14] The data presented here comes from a brief report of the highlights of the 1949 meeting: M. Wells Jakeman, *op. cit.*, pp. 31-33.

brought to America by sea from the Old World, it is enough to sustain the claim put forth in *The Book of Mormon*. That book speaks of seeds having been brought to America by only two groups of agriculturists, Jaredites and Nephites. The fact that cotton was brought to the western hemisphere from the Old World and that an American variety was developed by crossing it with a wild cotton found here proves definitely that at least one boatload of colonizers did make the transoceanic trip (as the Nephite record claims) and those passengers who came by boat were agriculturally minded. Furthermore, they were intelligent enough to know how to crossbreed plants of the same family. These facts in regard to cotton show that whoever the people were who accomplished the foregoing, they must have brought the cotton from somewhere in that section of the world from whence the ancestors of the Nephites and Jaredites emigrated; i.e., from somewhere in the area between India and Egypt, because that section of the Old World was the original home of Old World cotton. Furthermore, those colonists had knowledge concerning the same things that the ancient records claim that the Jaredites and Nephites knew regarding agricultural matters.

Concerning the recent information coming from the field of botany, one archæologist recently wrote as follows:

The botanical evidence, it should be noted, is against any of these Old World plants (cotton, sorghum, bottle gourd and the yam) possibly having drifted across the ocean to America by itself. The only alternative is that, if they actually did originate in the Old World as now indicated, they must have been carried across in ships in early transoceanic migra- tions from the Old World long before the supposed beginnings of oceanic navigation. This conclusion brings surprising new support to the "extreme migrationist" or "direct Old World colonization" theory of the origin of the ancient American agricultural civilization.[15]

LXIV. Animals and Fowls

IXTLILXOCHITL:

Tultecas' animals and fowls

...likewise they [Tultecas] had chickens and turkeys,[LXIV] and many seeds and vegetables [LXIII] for their sustenance— and many other things they had and used, which to relate all would take very long.

* * *

. . . they had . . . trees

EXTRACTS—BOOK OF MORMON:

Nephites' animals and fowls

25. And it came to pass that we did find upon the land of promise, as we journeyed in the wilder- ness, that there were beasts in the forests of every kind, both the cow and the ox, and the ass and the horse,[LXIV] and the wild goat, and all manner of wild animals, which were for the use of man.
                                        1 Nephi 18:25.
. . . And we began to raise flocks, and herds, and animals of every kind.   2 Nephi 5:116.

[15] Jakeman, *op. cit.*, p. 33.

and plants and animals[LXIV] and fowls[LXIV] of all kinds ...

29. And now, because of the steadiness of the church they began to be exceeding rich, having abundance of all things whatsoever they stood in need—and abundance of flocks and herds, and fatlings of every kind, and also abundance of grain. ...
Alma 1:29.

1. And now it came to pass that the people of the Nephites did all return to their own lands in the twenty and sixth year, every man, with his family, his flocks and his herds, his horses and his cattle, and all things whatsoever did belong unto them.
3 Nephi 6:1.

The Book of Mormon is far more specific than *Ixtlilxochitl* with regard to animals possessed by the ancients of Bountiful-land. Difficult problems are presented. The answer to these problems may come from future archæological discoveries as work progresses in southern Mexico as well as in the Guatemala highlands.

The Nephite account names certain domestic animals. Whether these animals, some of which bore the names of Old World animals, were merely named after the Old World species is uncertain. It has been suggested by some writers that the animal referred to in *The Book of Mormon* as the "horse" was actually some other species, possibly the much smaller tapir. The tapir is native to Middle America and has a long, narrow face and head like the horse. The writers do not subscribe to this view. However, it is a well-established rule that when strange animals or other things are first encountered by a people, such animals or things are called by the names of other animals or things within the previous experience of that people. When the Spaniards first saw the vicunas they called the animals "sheep." Pedro de Cieza de Leon, who traveled in the New World from 1532 to 1550, wrote: "Before the Spaniards arrived there were great flocks of *sheep* in the province of Huamachuco, and in the lofty and uninhabited mountains [of Peru] there were other wild kinds called guanaco and vicunas, which resemble those which are domesticated."[16]

Both *Ixtlilxochitl* and *The Book of Mormon* mention fowls and chickens as having been known to the ancients of Bountiful-land. *Ixtlilxochitl* speaks of "turkeys," a word which was not in the Nephite vocabulary—nor could it have been, for the bird was unknown in the Old World. The Nephites and Jaredites doubtless had a name for the bird, but it would have been a name invented by them. The wild turkey was a new species to

---

[16] Clements R. Markham, *Travels of Pedro de Cieza de Leon* (London, 1864), vol. 33.

the sixteenth-century Europeans, as has been pointed out. Perhaps it was one of the wild fowl enjoyed in the New World as far back as Jaredite times. The Jaredites knew the art of snaring fowls. To quote: "And they did also lay snares and catch fowls of the air. . . .

Twenty-one hundred years after the Nephites arrived in the New World the Spanish conquistadores arrived in the same New World. On encountering new animals and birds which were unknown in Europe, the Spaniards gave those animals and birds names. The names given were sometimes the names of similar Old World animals or birds. The strange turkey was called "hen"; the strange llama and alpaca were called "sheep." Bishop Landa referred to the American cougars as "small lions," to jaguars as "tigers," and to armadillos as "pigs." The Nephites may have done likewise in some instances. The Mayas of the sixteenth century did this very thing when they reversed the process on the Spaniards by referring to the horses of the Europeans as *Tzimin,* the Maya name for *tapir.*

Bishop Landa, in reporting on conditions in Yucatan at the time of the Conquest, comments as follows:

The Indians [of Yucatan] have been without many animals and especially have they lacked those which are most necessary for the service of man; but they had others, most of which they made use of for their sustenance and none of them was domesticated except the dogs, who do not know how to bark nor do harm to men, but in hunting it is otherwise for they raise partridges and other birds, follow deer a great deal and some of them are great trackers. . . . There are tapirs in only one corner in the region which lies back of the mountains of Campeche and there are many of them and the Indians have told me that they are of many colors for there are silver gray, blossom colored, bay and chestnut and very white and black. . . . It is an animal of the size of medium mules, very fleet, and has a cloven hoof like the ox and a small proboscis on its snout in which it holds water. . . . They call it *tzimin* and from these they have given their name to horses.[17]

On the other hand, the animals mentioned in the Nephite record may actually have existed in Nephite lands for a time, becoming extinct before the Conquest. However, neither the art works nor the documentary materials from ancient Middle America as yet support this position. There are two references in the Nephite account supporting the view that the animal referred to therein as the "horse" was actually the horse as we

---

[17] Diego de Landa (cir. 1556), *Relacion de las Cosas de Yucatan* (1941 ed.), p. 203.

know it and that it was used as a draft animal. In about the
year 90 B. C. the following occurred, according to *The Book
of Mormon:*

> King Lamoni [Lamanite king in highlands] inquired of his servants,
> saying, Where is this man that has such great power? And they said unto
> him: Behold, he is feeding thy *horses.* Now the king had commanded his
> servants, previous to the time of the watering of their flocks that they should
> prepare his *horses* and *chariots,* and conduct him forth to the land of
> Nephi; for there had been a great feast appointed in the land of Nephi,
> by the father of Lamoni, who was king over all the land.[18]

On arriving in the New World the Nephites ". . . did find
upon the land of promise, as we journeyed in the wilderness, that
there were beasts in the forests of every kind, both the cow and
the ox, and the ass and the horse, and the goat and the wild
goat, and all manner of wild animals, which were for the use
of men."[19] Elsewhere the dog is mentioned.[20]

When the Europeans arrived only two of the animals mentioned in the Nephite record were found in America—dogs and
wild goats. When the Spanish brought in horses, pigs, sheep,
mules and cows they may have actually been re-introducing them
to Middle America. There is rather good evidence in *The Book
of Mormon* that whole species were exterminated during the many
long eras of continuous and wholesale warfare. In the following
quotation dating from about 18 A. D., the fact is apparent
that the animal referred to as the "horse" was being used for food:

> But behold, there were no wild beasts nor game in those lands which
> had been deserted by the Nephites, and there was no game for the robbers
> save it were in the wilderness.
>
> And the robbers could not exist save it were in the wilderness, for
> the want of food; for the Nephites had left their lands desolate, and had
> gathered their flocks and their herds and all their substance, and they
> were in one body.
>
> Therefore, there was no chance for the robbers to plunder and to
> obtain food, save it were to come up in open battle against the Nephites;
> and the Nephites being in one body, and having so great a number, and
> having reserved for themselves provisions, and horses and cattle, and flocks
> of every kind, that they might subsist for the space of seven years, in the
> which time they did hope to destroy the robbers from off the face of the
> land; and thus the eighteenth year did pass away.

---

[18] *The Book of Mormon,* p. 241 (Alma 18:8-9), and see also the further reference to the same
"horses and chariots" at p. 247 (Alma 20.6).
[19] *The Book of Mormon.* p. 40 (1 Nephi 18:25).
[20] *Ibid.,* p. 235 (Alma 16:10); p. 377 (Helaman 7:19); p. 158 (Mosiah 12:2). These are typical
Hebrew expressions using the term "dog." See similar expressions in Old Testament.

And it came to pass that in the nineteenth year Giddianhi found that it was expedient that he should go up to battle against the Nephites, for there was no way that they could subsist save it were to plunder and rob and murder.[21]

Very few works of art have been found to date by the archæologists which can be dated within the early colonial period covered by *The Book of Mormon*. The fact that representations of the domestic animals mentioned in the Nephite account have not yet been found does not prove that such animals did not exist. No representations of the bow and arrow have been found in the Maya country for either the pre-Maya, the Old Empire or the New Empire, and yet it is well known that the ancient Mayas used the bow and arrow.[22] Likewise, the wheel has not yet been found depicted in Middle American art, and yet it has been clearly established by archæologists that the wheel existed anciently in the area with which we are concerned.[23] See figures 35 and 36 on pages 259 and 260.

In our own time, during World War II, the Japanese invaders of the Philippines ate all the cattle of those islands. Not a single bull remained at the close of hostilities. The Nephite account clearly indicates that the Lamanites were after the cattle and horses of the Nephites that they might have them for food. The last great Nephite-Lamanite war lasted from 322 A. D. until 385 A. D., a period of sixty-three years. Agriculture and animal husbandry must had reached a low ebb by the end of that period. Such is indicated by the last-quoted statement. It is quite possible that those animal species mentioned in the Nephite records, which animals were extinct when the Europeans arrived, may have been exterminated about the same time the Nephite-Mulekite nation itself was destroyed. This much is known for certain, at least they had become extinct before the arrival of the Spaniards.

Horses and Rancho La Brea Asphalt Deposits

The claim made by *The Book of Mormon* that horses were on this continent and used in ancient America for purpose similar to the uses we make of them today finds strong support in the numerous fossil remains of horses that have been obtained from

---

[21] *The Book of Mormon*, p. 406 (Nephi 4:2-5).
[22] Alfred M. Tozzer, *Landa's Relacion de las Cosas de Yucatan* (1941), Note 551.
[23] Gordon F. Ekholm, "Wheeled Toys in Mexico," *American Antiquity* (April, 1946), p. 222; Matthew Stirling, *National Geographic Magazine* (Sept., 1940), p. 314; *Cuadernos Americanos*, 25, No. 1 (Jan.-Feb., 1946), pp. 193-207; Thomas Stuart Ferguson, "The Wheel in Ancient America," *The Improvement Era* (Dec., 1946).

the asphalt deposits of Rancho La Brea in southern California. Of course, it is claimed that those fossil remains pre-date *Book of Mormon* times. However, there is no logical reason for believing, since horses were here prior to the arrival of the Jaredites and the Nephites, that horses could not have still been in America during the period in which those ancient civilizations flourished. Certainly such was the case.

We could do no better at this point in dealing with this subject than to quote from an official publication of the Los Angeles County Museum on the subject of the existence of horses in early times in America:

The presence of herds of horses in the vicinity of the asphalt deposits during the period of accumulation is clearly testified to by the numerous remains of these mammals found at Rancho La Brea. While many individuals are recorded in the collections, all of them belong to a single species, the extinct western horse (*Equus occidentalis* Leidy). In stage of evolution and in general body structure this type resembles the modern horse, although differing from it in a number of specific details. Standing on the average about 14½ hands (4 feet, 10 inches) at the withers, this animal was of the height of a modern Arab horse. It was, however, of considerably heavier build. . . .

These horses, like their living relatives, were one-toed animals. Limb and body are supported wholly by the enlarged third toe, while slender splintlike bones represent the elements which during an earlier history of

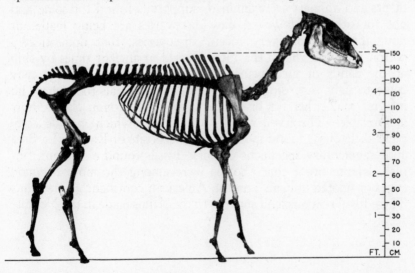

Fig. 45: SKELETON OF WESTERN HORSE (*Equus occidentalis* LEIDY)
Los Angeles County Museum collection; Rancho La Brea Pleistocene. *Courtesy of Chester Stock*

the horse group were more fully developed and carried the second and fourth toes. The hoofs in the Rancho La Brea species are distinctly smaller and more slender than in the larger types of existing horses. In this respect again, a greater resemblance is seen to exist with the asses and zebras.

The species, *Equus occidentalis,* has been known heretofore by isolated teeth and fragmentary skull material collected in Pleistocene deposits in Tuolumne County and in the Buena Vista Lake region of Kern County. Following identification of this form on the basis of the complete remains at Rancho La Brea, *Equus occidentalis* has been recorded from several additional Pleistocene locations in California. It is now known by many specimens that have been recovered from the asphalt deposits of McKittrick.

Horses were among the more common types of hoofed mammals on the North American continent during Pleistocene time and several distinct species have been described from fossil remains. The abundance and wide-spread distribution of horses in North America make the apparent disappearance of the group in this region prior to the advent of the white man an added and an unusual feature of their long and eventful career.[24]

Summary Statement

Ixtlilxochitl and *The Book of Mormon* make statements to the effect that the Bountiful-land settlers were skilled agriculturalists. The general position is supported fully from other sources of information. There is no question about it. When the special claims of the Nephite account regarding particular plants and animals are examined, support is found for some and not for others. However, new discoveries are being made. It now appears, from very recent discoveries, that domesticated cotton was brought to the New World in ancient times by ship at the hands of an advanced people. Similar knowledge may come to light regarding other plants, and animals too, where no information, either for or against *Book of Mormon* claims, now is available. The fossil remains of horses (which include complete skeletons), found in the asphalt deposits of Rancho La Brea and fragmentary specimens of horse fossils found elsewhere, furnish definite proof that "horses were among the more common types of hoofed animals" on the American continent at one time. These fossil remains lend support to the claims made in the Nephite record.

---

[24] Chester Stock, *Rancho La Brea, A Record of Pleistocene Life in California,* pp. 42-43.

Chapter 24

TEXTILES AND DRESS

Introductory Statement

Statements in the Old Testament and knowledge gained from more recent archæological discoveries give us a rather clear picture of the garb, and the materials used therein, of the ancients of Bible lands. *Ixtlilxochitl* and *The Book of Mormon* each have much to say about the textiles and wearing apparel of the Bountiful-land people. The comparisons will show that both of our parallel New World accounts are in substantial agreement with each other and with other documentary sources, as well as with late discoveries by archæologists who have been working in southern Mexico. These New World sources show that the ancients made fine textiles and wore the same type of dress as did the ancient peoples of Palestine from whence the cultured American settlers claim to have come.

LXV. Spinning, Weaving, and Dress

IXTLILXOCHITL:

Weaving, and dress of Tultecs

And they [the Tultecs] (were) painters, the best in the land (world); and the women great spinners and weavers, weaving very gallant mantles of a thousand colors and figures—those which they (the men) wanted, and as fine as those of Castile; and they wove the cloth in many different ways, some that looked like velvet, and others like very fine cloth; others like damask and satin; others like thin linen[LXVI] and others like thick linen, just as they (the men) wanted and needed. The Tultecas dressed,[LXVII] the men and civilians in summertime

EXTRACTS—BOOK OF MORMON:

Spinning, weaving and dress of Nephites

5. And I [Zeniff] did cause that the women should spin, and toil, and work, and work all manner of fine linen,[LXVI] yea and cloth of every kind, that we might clothe our nakedness; and thus we did prosper in the land—thus we did have continual peace in the land for the space of twenty and two years.   Mosiah 10:5.

29. And now, because of the steadiness of the church they began to be exceeding rich, having abundance of all things whatsoever they stood in need . . . and abundance of silk and fine-twined linen,[LXVI] and all manner of good homely cloth.   Alma 1:29.

6. And it came to pass in the eighth year of the reign of the judges that the people of the church began to wax proud, because of their exceeding riches, and their fine silks, and their

with their cotton mantles and trunks; and in wintertime they put on some great wide, sleeve-less coats that came down to their knees, with their mantles and trunks; they wore shoes[LXVIII] after their fashions, *henequen cotargas* or *catles* [leather sandals]; women (wore) their *hui-piles* and skirts, and likewise their *cotaras* of the same material; and when they went out they would put on some white mantles[LXVII] worked in many colors, pointed in back, more or less like a friar's hood, although they [the mantles] came down to the bend of the knees: they called this mantle *Toxquemititl:* and the priests wore some [white] tunics[LXVII] and other black ones that came down to the ground, with their hoods with which they covered their heads; their hair long, braided, which came to their shoulders; and their eyes lowered and humble; bare-footed at the time of their fasts and when they were in the temple very seldom did they wear shoes, except when they went out, and on a long journey.[LXVIII]

fine-twined linen, and because of their many flocks and herds, and their gold and their silver, and all manner of precious things, which they had obtained by industry; and in all these things were they lifted up in the pride of their eyes, for they began to wear very costly apparel.[LXVI &] [LXVII]
                                         Alma 4:6.

13. Behold their women did toil and spin, and did make all manner of cloth, of fine-twined linen and cloth of every kind, to clothe their nakedness. And thus the sixty and fourth year did pass away in peace.   Helaman 6:13.

19. . . . I [Nephi I] took the garments of Laban[LXVII] and put them upon mine own body; yea, even every whit; and I did gird on his armor about my loins.   1 Nephi 4:19.

11. And now it came to pass that when Moroni, who was the chief commander of the armies of the Nephites, had heard of these dissensions, he was angry with Amalickiah. And it came to pass that he rent his *coat* . . .[LXVII]
                                         Alma 46:11-12.

33. . . . O Lord, wilt thou encircle me around in the *robe* of thy righteousness!
                                         2 Nephi 4:33.

8. . . . . and he is. mightier than I, whose *shoe's*[LXVIII] latchet I am not worthy to unloose.
                                         1 Nephi 10:8.

LXVI. "Linen"

It is noted that *Ixtlilxochitl* says that the Tultecs had various kinds of fine cloth, including a material "like linen." *The Book of Mormon* makes reference to "linen," without qualifying it. It may be that the early Nephites had flax-linen. On the other hand, flax (like other things mentioned in the preceding chapter) was not found in America at the time of the Conquest. See the list of products, p. 306. The present scientific view is that linen from flax did not exist in ancient America. Cotton, of course, was commonly used in ancient Middle America. However, the word for *linen* would have been in the vocabulary of settlers coming from Jerusalem in 600 B. C. It occurs many times in the Old Testament. However, Bible scholars have suggested that the various Hebrew words that have been translated "linen" in the Old Testament are, for the most part, of uncertain meaning, and in some cases varieties of cotton are meant.[1] In the United States today we sometimes refer to cotton products as "linen." Thus, perhaps the Nephites did not have flax, but rather used their word for "linen" in a broader sense.

The Hebrew expression "fine twined linen" or "fine linen" appears nine times in The Book of Mormon.[2] It appears thirty-two times in Exodus alone in the Old Testament.[3] The Hebrew background of the Nephites is reflected by its use.

LXVII. DRESS OF THE ANCIENT AMERICANS

According to Ixtlilxochitl, the Tultec men wore mantles. A mantle is a long cloak or robe, short-sleeved or sleeveless. This was the outer garb of the ancients of Palestine also.[4] Sometimes the outer garment worn by men was referred to as a "cloak" and sometimes as a "robe." In either case it constituted a mantle. The term "robe" was generally applied to it if it was comprised of fine cloth. This outer garment, variously known as a robe, cloak or mantle, depending on the wealth or position of the owner, was generally removed by the working man when he was laboring.

The undergarment of those of ancient Israel, both in the Near East and Middle America, was a simple tunic, also known as a shirt or coat. It was a sleeveless garment reaching down to the knees, like a long sleeveless shirt. This undergarment, especially the type worn by the well-to-do, was often long enough to reach to the ankles and also had short sleeves.

In the Bible we read: "And Jonathan stripped himself of the robe that was upon him, and gave it to David, and his garments."[5] Reference is made, as is seen, to both the outer and the inner garments in the same sentence.

In The Book of Mormon as in the Old Testament, the term most commonly used in referring to wearing apparel is "garments." The terms clothing, garments, mantles and robes are used in both accounts. Concordances of the respective scriptures show the term "garment" most commonly used in each.

---

[1] Funk and Wagnalls, New Standard Bible Dictionary (1936), p. 517. Where the Hebrew word pishteh was encountered by the Bible translators, there was no question but that the correct rendering was "linen," for that was the word for flax. See Leviticus 13:47-49; Jeremiah 13:1; Ezekiel 44:17.
[2] George Reynolds, A Complete Concordance to The Book of Mormon (1900), p. 422.
[3] Exodus 25:4; 26:1; 27:9, 16, 18, etc. Isaiah 3:23; 19:9.
[4] A discussion of Dress and Ornaments of Bible lands is found in Funk and Wagnalls, op. cit., p. 189. Many citations are included.
[5] 1 Samuel 18:4.

Reference is made in both the Hebrew and Nephite writings to the ancient Hebrew practice of rending or tearing one's clothing as a symbol of a promise or a pledge, or as a sign of remorse on the death of a loved one or on the death of some important person. It was considered a sign of humility.[6]

It appears from *Ixtlilxochitl* that "trunks" may have taken the place of the more ancient tunic (shirt or coat) as an under-garment in Middle America. However, *Ixtlilxochitl* and *The Book of Mormon* are corroborated from other sources in ascribing the garb of the Near East to the early colonizers of Middle America.

Torquemada's description of the settlers who came by sea to Panuco, the founders of *Tulla,* merits repeating: "These people were men of good carriage, well-dressed in long robes of

Fig. 46: KING JEHU OF ISRAEL
DOING HOMAGE TO SHALMANESER

Fig. 47: KING JEHU'S
STOCKING-CAP

This is an artist's drawing of King Jehu of Israel, depicting the type of caps which were worn by the people in Jerusalem about the time that Lehi and his associates migrated to America. Jehu dates approximately 200 years earlier than Lehi. *Drawing by Ralph Harding.*

black linen, like Turks, like the cassocks of the clergy, open in front, and without capes, cut low at the neck, and with short

6 *The Book of Mormon,* p. 311 (Alma 46:21); Old Testament, Numbers 14:6; 1 Samuel 1:11; 2 Chronicles 34:27; Genesis 37:29, 34; 44:13; Leviticus 13:45; Joshua 7:6; Judges 11:35. The practice was carried over to *New Testament* times: Matthew 9:16; 26:65; Mark 14:63.

wide sleeves which did not reach the elbow."[7] Harold Gladwin quotes Torquemada and then comments that the description of the garb reminds one "of the robes of Biblical times in Palestine."[8]

We have also seen above that the Serpent people of *Nachan* (Christians of Bountiful-land) wore "petticoats" and were called *Tzequils* for that reason. One cannot better describe the ancient tunic of Palestine than to refer to it as a "petticoat."

(c) N.G.S. COURTESY OF NATIONAL GEOGRAPHIC MAGAZINE

Fig. 48: An Ancient American's Stocking Cap

Compare the stocking-cap and beard of the man of ancient Middle America, above, with the stocking-cap of King Jehu of ancient Israel, p. 318. This Ulmec piece, dating about the time of Christ, is now in the National Museum, Mexico City. It was uncovered by Matthew W. Stirling in 1939-1940. *National Geographic Magazine*, September, 1940, p. 317. Like a character from *Faust* is this fine clay head with its pointed beard and crafty grin. The small baked figure from a mound near Tres Zapotes, Vera Cruz, is one of the best examples of ceramic art yet found in the New World. Because of its lifelike appearance, it is probably a study of a prominent person.

[7] Juan de Torquemada, *Monarquia Indiana* (first published in Spain in 1615), 1723 ed., *tomo* 1, p. 37.
[8] Harold Sterling Gladwin, *Men Out of Asia* (1947), p. 305.

Las Casas (1552 A. D.) and Oviedo (1535 A. D.) both reported that the natives of Middle America had, at the time of the arrival of Columbus, "clothing of a kind which they weave of cotton in this land, such as cloth woven with many designs and colors, shirts which reached the knees, and some square pieces of cloth which they use for cloaks, calling them *zuyen*."[9]

Herrera, writing in the year 1601 A. D., describes the clothing of the Maya priests of Yucatan as worn at a native baptismal ceremony as follows: "The priest came forth clad in long and heavy vestments and with a hyssop in his hand."[10]

The outer garment of the ancient Maya layman was called the *pati*. Like the cloak or mantle of the ancient Hebrew, it served the poor as a cover at night.[11]

Bible archæologists have found a representation of King Jehu of Israel (in prostrate form, kissing the ground), dressed in a typical mantle of the ancient Hebrews, as shown in figure 46. Note the short sleeves and the length of the mantle. Also, King Jehu ". . . wears a cap like a modern nightcap, which was at that time (842 B. C.) the style among the Hebrews and the Phœnecians as well as in Asia Minor and later in Phrigia."[12] The distinguished Bible-land archæologist and linguist, Professor William Foxwell Albright of Johns Hopkins University, says in his recent (1949) book, *The Archaeology of Palestine*:

"The men of [ancient] Israel wear long fringed tunics, over which are fringed mantles, both presumably of wool; on their heads they wear *short stocking caps which are bound in place like turbans, while on their feet they wear high boots turned up at the toes* in Hittite fashion. A century and a half later, Sennacherib's capture of Lachish in Judah was celebrated by Assyrian artists; here the men of Judah appear with their tunics drawn up to their knees and fastened in place by their girdles, while the women are shown with long tunics and mantles."[13]

Figure 48 shows the "night cap" worn by one of the ancients of Middle America, it being identical in style to that of King Jehu. This Middle American, "Jehu" was found by Matthew W. Stirling's National Geographic-Smithsonian Expedition of 1940 in the "narrow neck of land" country—i.e., on

---

9 Frans Blom, "Commerce, Trade, and Monetary Units of the Maya," (1932), *Middle American Research Series*, No. 4, p. 533, quoted by Alfred M. Tozzer in *Landa's Relacion de las Cosas de Yucatan* (1941), note 416.
10 English translation by Alfred M. Tozzer, *ibid.*, appendix A, p. 218.
11 Sylvanus G. Morley, *The Ancient Maya* (1946), pp. 191-192; Old Testament, Exodus 22:26-27; Deuteronomy 24:12-13.
12 Hugo Gressman, *The Tower of Babel* (1928), pp. 10-11.
13 William Foxwell Albright, *The Archaeology of Palestine* (1949), pp. 211-212.

the Gulf Coast of Mexico at Tres Zapotes in the southern part of the state of Vera Cruz.[14]

LXVIII. SHOES

As has been mentioned, in the Bountiful-land region at La Venta in the state of Tabasco, Mexico, near the Gulf, Matthew Stirling's expedition found a carved stone fourteen feet high with carvings showing an aristocratic-looking man with an aquiline nose and a long flowing beard. He was wearing peculiar shoes—not the kind of shoes an ordinary American redskin wore—but rather "shoes with odd pointed, upturned toes"! It is striking indeed that Jehu's cap, mantle and boots, the latter "turned up at the toes," should all be found in Bountiful-land in the New World! Figure 14 shows this ancient American of Bountiful-land. Figure 13 is a drawing by Ralph Harding, showing cap, nose, beard, tunic, and shoes of "Uncle Sam."

Figure 50 shows the type of sandals worn by the ancient Mayas. Figure 49 shows ancient Israelite footwear. The only mention of footwear in *The Book of Mormon* is found in a philosophical statement, 1 Nephi 10:8. The custom of removing sandals and going barefooted in the temples, as mentioned by

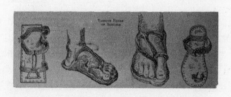

Fig. 49: SANDALS WORN IN THE ANCIENT NEAR EAST

From Funk and Wagnalls *Bible Dictionary*.

Fig. 50: SANDALS WORN IN ANCIENT MIDDLE AMERICA

From S. G. Morley's *The Ancient Maya*. Maya sandals or *xanab* (a, b, c. d. e. f) examples of sandals from the New Empire monuments; (k) ancient method of fastening sandals with two cords, one passing between the first and second toes, the other between the third and fourth toes; (1) modern method of fastening sandals with a single cord passing between the first toe and the second toe.

---

[14] Matthew W. Stirling, "Great Stone Faces of the Mexican Jungle," with photographs by Richard H. Stewart, *National Geographic Magazine* (Sept., 1940), pp. 309-334, at p. 317.

Ixtlilxochitl, was practiced also by the ancient Israelites. In fact it was incumbent on Israelites to remove sandals when in a holy place.[15]

Nothing is said in *The Book of Mormon* regarding hair styles. According to *Ixtlilxochitl* the Tultec priests wore their hair long and in braids. This style also characterized the ancients of Israel, some of whom wore long braids. A reference to braiding is found in Judges:

> And Delilah said unto Samson, . . . tell me wherewith thou mightest be bound. And he said unto her, If thou weavest the seven locks of my head with the web, . . . he told her, There hath not come a razor upon mine head; for I have been a Nazarite unto God from my mother's womb; if I be shaven, then my strength will go from me, and I shall become weak, and be like any other man. . . . And she caused him to shave off the seven locks of his head.[16]

Landa is in accord with *Ixtlilxochitl,* the former saying of the men of the ancient Mayas:

> They wore their hair long like women and on top they burned a space like a great tonsure, and thus the hair grew long below, while that on the top of the head was left short. And they braided it and made a wreath of it around their heads leaving the queue [braids] behind like tassels.[17]

SUMMARY STATEMENT

It is seen from the foregoing that both *Ixtlilxochitl* and *The Book of Mormon* are supported by other reliable sources and also by archæology in their allegations concerning the textiles and garb of the early Bountiful-land settlers (Tultecas-Nephites). This evidence further substantiates the documentary claims that these people came from the ancient Near East—from Israel.

---

[15] Exodus 3:5; Joshua 5:12; 2 Samuel 15:30; Isaiah 20:2-4.
[16] Judges 16:13-19; Funk and Wagnalls, *New Standard Bible Dictionary* (1936), p. 326; 2 Samuel 14:25-26.
[17] Diego de Landa (1524-1579), *Relacion de las Cosas de Yucatan* (1941 English ed.), by Alfred M. Tozzer, p. 88. In note 375 Tozzer cites additional authorities showing Maya men wore the hair in long braids before the Conquest.

Chapter 25

MANNERS AND CUSTOMS

INTRODUCTORY STATEMENT

Only those manners and customs suggested by *Ixtlilxochitl* will be discussed. Were all the manners and customs mentioned in the Nephite record to be discussed, this portion of the book would be unduly long.

From *Ixtlilxochitl's* statements, it will be seen that the ancients of Bountiful-land, the Tultecas, were a highly refined people. They had many commendable customs that characterize a cultured and advanced people. That these settlers were such a people is borne out by the Nephite record and by other documentary and archæological evidence.

Some of the topics dealt with herein include the manner in which the ancients spoke, burial customs, marriage customs, food, miscegenation, or rules or customs regulating intermarriage, and the people's love for jewelry. Close parallels with ancient Jewish customs will be noted in some instances. One of the most surprising is with regard to dowries. The Maya word for "dowry" is identical with the Hebrew word for the same custom.

LXIX. SPEECH OF PEOPLE OF BOUNTIFUL-LAND

EXTRACT—SAHAGUN:

Speech of the Tultecs

These said Tultecs were good men and friends of virtue. They did not tell lies, and their way of speaking and greeting each other was "Sir" and "Sir, brother . . ." and "Sir, older brother" and "Sir, younger brother." Their speech, instead of swearing, was "It is true," "thus it is," "it is ascertained," and "yes" for yea, and "no" for no.

EXTRACTS—BOOK OF MORMON:

Teachings of Jesus to Nephites regarding their speech[LXIX]

33. And again it is written, thou shalt not forswear thyself, but shalt perform unto the Lord thine oaths;

34. But verily, verily, I say unto you, swear not at all; neither by heaven, for it is God's throne;

35. Nor by the earth, for it is his footstool;

36. Neither shalt thou swear by the head, because thou canst not make one hair black or white;

37. But let your communication be Yea, yea; Nay, nay; for whatsoever cometh of more than these is evil.   3 Nephi 12:33-37.

*Regarding speech and teach-
ings of Tultec priests*

. . . they [Tultec priests]
spoke little,[LXIX] they taught
children and young men good
customs and ways of living,
arts good and bad, to whatever they most inclined. . . .
they [the Tultec kings] spoke
little . . .

The Nephite prophets taught the people to guard their
speech. Jesus Christ appeared to the Nephites following His
resurrection and taught them that they should not swear and
that their conversation should be "yea, yea, and Nay, nay."
In other words they must guard their speech and say no evil.

The Prophet Alma proclaimed to the wicked people who
lived in the city of Ammonihah that they should be held account-
able at the judgment seat of God not only for their actions but
for all the words that they spoke and even for their thoughts.
To quote from this great Nephite's discourses:

For our words will condemn us, yea, all our works will condemn us;
and we shall not be found spotless; and our thoughts will also condemn
us; and in this awful state we shall not dare to look up to our God; and
we would fain be glad if we could command the rocks in the mountain to
fall upon us to hide us from his presence.[1]

According to authoritative reports, including the foregoing
statement made by Sahagun, the later Tultecas were careful also
regarding their speech as were their predecessors. In the foregoing discussion, evidence is again presented to sustain the thesis
that the Tultecas were descendants of the ancient Nephites and
Mulekites and that many of the teachings of their predecessors
had carried on from generation to generation even down to the
days of the Conquest.

MANNERS AND CUSTOMS OF BOUNTIFUL-LAND PEOPLE

IXTLILXOCHITL:	EXTRACTS—BOOK OF MORMON:
Manners and customs of the kings and laity	*Manners and customs of kings and laity*
	Wicked King Noah's Temple and Palace:
The kings would always put on some plain white mantles, and other gray ones, with pearls[LXX]	8. And it came to pass that king Noah built many elegant and spacious buildings; and he or- namented them with fine work of wood, and of

---

[1] *The Book of Mormon*, p. 225 (Alma 12:14).

and other carved precious stones, and made into fancywork, and the *Zenefa* all of a thousand colored designs; they would always put on their *Xicole gowns* (long, wide shirts), which came down to their knees, in the same way as their mantles and trunks: they wore their cotton cotaras, with soles of gold: they would put on bracelets of gold and precious stones, and necklaces of the same material . . .

. . . Their buildings were of stone masonry and hewn stones and *tezontli* (porous building stone); they used stone troughs (fountains) and water pipes for drainage like our Spaniards: they had baths to bathe themselves, which the Indians now use, which they called *Tamascalis.*

all manner of precious things, of gold, and of silver, and of iron, and of brass, and of ziff, and of copper;

9. And he also built him a spacious palace, and a throne in the middle thereof, all of which was of fine wood and was ornamented with gold and silver and with precious things.

10. And he also caused that his workmen should work all manner of fine work within the walls of the temple, of fine wood, and of copper, and of brass.

11. And the seats which were set apart for the high priests, which were above all the other seats, he did ornament with pure gold; and he caused a breastwork to be built before them, that they might rest their bodies and their arms upon while they should speak lying and vain words to his people.   Mosiah 11:8-11.

Nephites Wore Pearls[LXXI]

24. And now, in this two hundred and first year there began to be among them those who were lifted up in pride, such as the wearing of costly apparel, and all manner of fine pearls,[LXX] and of the fine things of the world.

4 Nephi 1:24.

LXX. Pearls

Ixtlilxochitl mentions that pearls were used to adorn the mantles of the kings. In *The Book of Mormon* pearls are mentioned but once, and this single reference, as in *Ixtlilxochitl,* is in connection with wearing apparel: ". . . there began to be among them [about 201 A. D.] those who were lifted up in pride, such as the wearing of costly apparel, and all manner of *fine pearls,* and the fine things of the world."[3] Sahagun says of the Tultecs: "they . . . worked . . . with amber and crystal and stones called amethysts and pearls."[4] He also mentions pearl pendants worn by the Aztec kings of the immediate pre-Conquest period. One of the images in the great temple used by Montezuma in Tenochtitlan [Mexico City stands there today], his capital city, was set with seed pearls, along with jade, gold and turquoise.[5]

The priest-rulers of the Quiche-Maya people of Guatemala made use of pearls and other precious gems. The *Popol Vuh,* religious-historical record of that people's pre-Conquest exist-ence, lists pearls and emeralds among the items received as trib-ute: ". . . small and great nations brought considerable tribute:

[3] *The Book of Mormon,* p. 458 (4 Nephi 1:24).
[4] Bernardino de Sahagun, *op. cit., Libro Octavo, Capitulo* 9.
[5] George C. Vaillant, *Aztecs of Mexico,* p. 237.

there arrived precious stones, rich metals, the sweetest honey, sceptres of emeralds and pearls, green and blue feather-work, tributes of all the peoples arrived. . . ."

Pearls are mentioned but once in the Old Testament, as in *The Book of Mormon*. The single Bible reference is a meta-phorical discussion of the worth of wisdom.[6]

Israelite men in ancient times wore ornaments, including bracelets and necklaces. The signet, which served the place of a signature when imprinted on a writing, was generally hung by a cord from the neck. In Genesis we read of a woman asking a man if he would give her his signet and his bracelets.[7] It is believed that in the time of Jeremiah the signet was customarily worn on the hand.[8]

LXXI. BURIAL CUSTOMS

IXTLILXOCHITL:	EXTRACTS—BOOK OF MORMON:
Burial customs[LXXI]	*Burial customs*[LXXI]
. . . they [Tultec kings] were buried shrouded and with their royal insignias, in the temples of their false gods. . . .	1. And it came to pass that after two days and two nights they were about to take his [King Lamoni's] body and lay it in a sepulchre, which they had made for the purpose of burying their dead. Alma 19:1.
	10. And it came to pass that on the morrow the people did assemble themselves together to mourn and to fast, at the burial of the great chief judge who had been slain. Helaman 9:10.

Ixtlilxochitl and *The Book of Mormon* say little concerning the burial customs of the early colonizers. *Ixtlilxochitl* says, it is observed, that the Tultec kings were "buried shrouded and with their royal insignias, in the temples. . . ." *The Book of Mormon* speaks of the burial of a king in a "sepulchre, which they had made for the purpose of burying their dead."[9] The Nephite record goes further, referring to the custom of mourn-ing and fasting for the dead: ". . . the people did assemble themselves together to *mourn* and to *fast,* at the burial of their great chief judge. . . ."[10]

The custom of the ancients of Israel was to mourn and fast at time of death. On the death of Saul, king of Israel, ". . . they

---

[6] Job 28:18. The correct translation of the Hebrew word for "pearl" may be "crystal." See James Strong, *Hebrew and Chaldee Dictionary, op. cit.,* word 1378; Funk and Wagnalls, *New Standard Dictionary, op. cit.*
[7] Genesis 38:18; Proverbs 25:12; Isaiah 3:19-23; Judges 8:26.
[8] Jeremiah 22:24.
[9] *The Book of Mormon,* p. 243 (Alma 19:1).
[10] *Ibid.,* p. 381 (Helaman 9:10).

mourned, and wept and *fasted* until even, for Saul.[11] Also, the body of the decedent was shrouded or wrapped. It was also the practice to bury, with the dead, objects which had been used by the deceased during life and in the case of the kings of Israel this would include royal insignias.[12]

Thus, the burial customs of the early colonizers of Middle America, as briefly set forth in *Ixtlilxochitl* and *The Book of Mormon,* are in accord with ancient Israelite practice. We can further test our two accounts by checking them against other sources dealing with the burial practices of the ancients of Middle America. If *Ixtlilxochitl* and *The Book of Mormon* are based on truth, they should be in general agreement with reliable sources on the subject. Since *Ixtlilxochitl* and *The Book of Mormon* are the only reports furnishing particulars regarding the very early period, we must go to Maya sources to make our check. Bishop Landa says of the Mayas:

> But when in time they came to die, it was indeed a thing to see the the sorrow and the cries which they made for their dead, and the great grief it caused them. During the day they wept for them in silence; and at night with loud and very sad cries, so that it was pitful to hear them. And they passed many days in deep sorrow. They made their abstinences and fasts for the dead, especially the husband or wife; and they said that the devil had taken him away, since they thought that all evils came to them from him,[13] and above all death. Once dead, they put them in a shroud, filling their mouths with ground maize, which is their food and drink which they call *koyem* . . . and with it they placed some of the stone which they use for money, so that they should not be without something to eat in the other life.[14]

Landa then points out that they buried other useful things with the dead, stating that if he was a priest "some of his books" went into the grave with him.

Archæological excavations in the central plateau region of Mexico, where the Tultec remnants settled after the close of *The Book of Mormon* period, reveal similar burial customs. Tools, ornaments, weapons and dishes were often placed in the graves along with the decedents.[15]

---

[11] 2 Samuel 1:12.

[12] Funk and Wagnalls, *op. cit.,* pp. 117-119, 596-597; Old Testament cited therein.

[13] In *The Book of Mormon* we find this: ". . . whatsoever is good cometh from God, and whatsoever is evil cometh from the devil," p. 208 (Alma 5:40).

[14] Diego de Landa (1524-1579), *Relacion de las Cosas de Yucatan* (1941), pp. 129-130.

[15] See Vaillant's description of the burials of what he calls "the Lower Middle Culture." Vaillant, *op. cit.* (1941), pp. 37-39.

Neither the ancient Israelites nor the early Tultecas practiced cremation. Not until the tenth century did the Tultecas
cremate. *Ixtlilxochitl* reports that the last Tultec king, Topiltzin,
was the first to be cremated.[16] Bancroft gives a detailed account
of the burial ceremonies and mourning customs of the Aztecs
and other late New World peoples.[17]

LXXII. MEALS

IXTLILXOCHITL:

Tulteca's meal schedule[LXXII]

... they [the Tultec kings] ate
twice a day, once at noon, and
again at night: they would arise
when the morning star came out,
and slept little: they spoke little,[LXX] and did not allow themselves to be seen many times,
unless it were in very great fes-
tivals.

The Book of Mormon does not report on the meal schedule
of the Nephites. However, if the ancient Israelite custom prevailed their practice would have been to have two regular repasts
a day, one at noon and one after the completion of the day's
work. Biblical references to the midday meal include Genesis
43:16, 25, and Ruth 2:14. The evening meal is spoken of in
Genesis 19:1ff and Judges 19:16-21. *Ixtlilxochitl* states that the
ancient Tultecas of Bountiful-land "ate twice a day, once at
noon and again at night." It has been pointed out that these
people seem to be identical with those of *The Book of Mormon;*
therefore, it appears that the schedule of regular daily meals
was the same for the ancients of Israel and the early colonizers
of Bountiful-land, as is required if our two parallel accounts are
authentic.

The strict dietary regulations of the Israelites have been suggested as one of the factors explaining the exceptional ruggedness
of that people.[18] It may well have been a factor in explanation
of the great achievements of the early colonizers of Middle America. In our own day the dietary rules of the Church of Jesus
Christ of Latter-day Saints are thought to contribute to the
remarkably high health standards and the longevity of that people.

---

[16] Hubert H. Bancroft, *Native Races,* vol. 2, p. 609, citing *Ixtlilxochitl.*

[17] *Ibid.,* 603-623.

[18] William F. Albright, *The Archaeology of Palestine* (1949), p. 254.

LXXIII. GARDENS AND POOLS

IXTLILXOCHITL:

Gardens and pools of Tultec kings[LXIII]

. . . they [the Tultec kings] had gardens and pools within their palaces, which were very large; and trees and plants, animals and fowls of all kinds to amuse themselves.

EXTRACTS—BOOK OF MORMON:

Wicked King Noah's Tower and Vineyards[LXIII]

12. And it came to pass that he built a tower near the temple; yea, a very high tower, even so high that he could stand upon the top thereof and overlook the land of Shilom, and also the land of Shemlon, which was possessed by the Lamanites; and he could even look over all the land round about.

13. And it came to pass that he caused many buildings to be built in the land Shilom; and he caused a great tower to be built on the hill north of the land Shilom, which had been a resort for the children of Nephi at the time they fled out of the land; and thus he did do with the riches which he obtained by the taxation of the people.
* * *
15. And it came to pass that he planted vineyards round about in the land;[LXXIV] and he built winepresses, and made wine in abundance; and therefore he became a wine-bibber, and also his people.   Mosiah 11:12-13, 15.

Nephi's Garden and Tower[LXXIV]

10. And behold, now it came to pass that it was upon a tower, which was in the garden of Nephi, which was by the highway which led to the chief market, which was in the city of Zarahemla; therefore, Nephi had bowed himself upon the tower which was in his garden, which tower was also near unto the garden gate by which led the highway.

11. And it came to pass that there were certain men passing by and saw Nephi as he was pouring out his soul unto God upon the tower; and they ran and told the people what they had seen, and the people came together in multitudes that they might know the cause of so great mourning for the wickedness of the people.
                                                      Helaman 7:10-11.

Gardens are mentioned in connection with the dwellings of the priest-rulers of ancient Bountiful-land. *Ixtlilxochitl* states ". . . they had gardens and pools within their palace, which were very large. . . ." In *The Book of Mormon* reference is made to the garden of Nephi, who dwelt as a priest-ruler in Bountiful-plant-land (Zarahemla) about 20 B. C.[19]

It would appear from this *Book of Mormon* quotation that Nephi's garden was probably on the outskirts of the city near the highway which led into the center of the city. The presence of a tower in the garden is noteworthy. Watchtowers were

---

[19] *The Book of Mormon*, p. 377 (Helaman 7:10); p. 381 (Helaman 9:8).

built in the gardens of the Israelites, and most of such gardens were on the outskirts of the towns.[20] In a parable Christ himself made reference to such a garden: "A certain man planted a vineyard, and set an hedge about it, and digged a place for the winevat, and built a *tower,* and let it out to husbandmen, and went into a far country."[21] The "gardens" of the Israelites were generally planted with fruit trees or vines for domestic use. They were favorite places of devotion.[22] Thus, Nephi's garden is typically Palestinian; *Ixtlilxochitl's* reference to the gardens of the Tultec kings (whose origin took them back to the Old World) was not fantasy.

Pools are mentioned in *The Book of Mormon,* the references going back to the writings of Isaiah.[23] Of the pools mentioned in the Old Testament, those of Solomon were perhaps the most famous. The prophet wrote:

"I made me gardens and orchards, and I planted trees in them of all kinds of fruits: I made me pools of water, to water therewith the wood that bringeth forth trees."[24]

Pools existed in some of the temple enclosures of ancient Mexico. It is known that use was made of the pools or wells in and near the cities of the ancient Mayas of Yucatan. Artificial reservoirs were constructed by the Tultecas of Middle America. A stucco-finished reservoir was found at Uxmal in Yucatan.[25] Of course, such discoveries in Yucatan date much later than the Nephite period of *The Book of Mormon* but they doubtless reflect the cultural attainments of the original and early forebears of Bountiful-land.

LXXIV. Virtue or Chastity

IXTLILXOCHITL:	EXTRACTS—BOOK OF MORMON:
Virtue of Tultec priests[LXXIV]	*Teachings of Nephites regarding virtue and chastity*[LXXIV]
They [the priests] were chaste, they knew no women, they made certain penances every twenty days, when the month and the year entered (began).	11. Wherefore, I [Jacob] must tell you the truth according to the plainness of the work of God. For behold, as I inquired of the Lord, thus came the word unto me, saying: Jacob, get thou up into the temple on the morrow, and declare the word which I shall give thee unto this people. . . . 27. Wherefore, my brethren, hear me, and hearken to the word of the Lord: For there shall

---

[20] William Smith, A Dictionary of the Bible (1884), p. 206.
[21] Mark 12:1.
[22] Jeremiah 29:5; Song of Solomon 6:2, 11; Deuteroromy 11:10; 1 Kings 21:2; Exodus 23:11.
[23] The Book of Mormon, p. 79 (2 Nephi 17:3); p. 88 (2 Nephi 24:23). Isaiah 7:3; 14:23.
[24] Ecclesiastes 2:5-6.
[25] Hubert H. Bancroft, Native Races, vol. 3, pp. 435, 437; vol. 4, pp. 198, 245, 219, 429-430, 525.

not any man among you have save it be one wife; and concubines he shall have none;

28. For I, the Lord God, delight in the chastity of women.[LXIX] And whoredoms are an abomination before me; thus saith the Lord of Hosts.

29. Wherefore, this people shall keep my commandments, saith the Lord of Hosts, or cursed be the land for their sakes.

30. For if I will, saith the Lord of Hosts, raise up seed unto me, I will command my people; otherwise they shall hearken unto these things....

32. And I will not suffer, saith the Lord of Hosts, that the cries of the fair daughters of this people, which I have led out of the land of Jerusalem, shall come up unto me against the men of my people, saith the Lord of Hosts.

33. For they shall not lead away captive the daughters of my people because of their tenderness, save I shall visit them with a sore curse, even into destruction; for they shall not commit whoredoms, like unto them of old, saith the Lord of Hosts....

12. And now I, Jacob, spake many more things unto the people of Nephi, warning them against fornication and lasciviousness, and every kind of sin, telling them the awful consequence of them.
Jacob 2:11, 27-30, 32-33; 3:12.

3. And this is not all, my son. Thou didst do that which was grievous unto me; for thou didst forsake the ministry, and did go over into the land of Siron, among the borders of the Lamanites, after the harlot Isabel.

4. Yea, she did steal away the hearts of many; but this was no excuse for thee, my son. Thou shouldst have tended to the ministry wherewith thou wast entrusted.

5. *Know ye not, my son, that these things* [sex immoralities] *are an abomination in the sight of the Lord; yea, most abominable above all sins save it be the shedding of innocent blood or denying the Holy Ghost?* . . .

7. And now, my son, I would to God that ye had not been guilty of so great a crime. I would not dwell upon your crimes, to harrow up your soul, if it were not for your good.

8. But behold, ye cannot hide your crimes from God; and except ye repent they will stand as a testimony against you at the last day.

9. Now my son, I would that ye should repent and forsake your sins, and go no more after the lusts of your eyes, but cross yourself in all these things; for except ye do this ye can in nowise inherit the kingdom of God. Oh, remember, and take it upon you, and cross yourself in these things.
Alma 39:3-5, 7-9.

27. Behold, it is written by them of old time, that thou shalt not commit adultery;

28. But I [Christ] say unto you, that whosoever looketh on a woman, to lust after her, hath
committed adultery already in his heart.

29. Behold, I give unto you a commandment,
that ye suffer none of these things to enter into
your heart;

30. For it is better that ye should deny yourself
these things, wherein ye will take up your cross,
than that ye should be cast into hell.

                                        3 Nephi 12:27-30.

Throughout the entire course of Nephite history (600 B. C.
to 400 A. D.), the prophets and priests taught the people to
maintain a very high standard of chastity. As the quotations
from *The Book of Mormon* indicate, those ancient American
prophets maintained that in *God's opinion sex immorality was
a sin next in gravity to the shedding of innocent blood or denying the Holy Ghost.* They maintained that those two latter sins
were unforgivable.

In consideraion of the fact that the Nephites during a period
of one thousand years had such high moral standards, it is not
surprising to read in the *Works of Ixtlilxochitl* that the priests
were chaste. They, no doubt, taught the people also to live the
law of chastity. Thus in these respects *The Book of Mormon*
and the *Works of Ixtlilxochitl* are in complete agreement.

There is observable difference, however, in the two records.
Throughout the entire course of Nephite history, the prophets
(priests) married, just as did the laity; however, the law in Nephite
times was for one man to have no more than one wife at a time.
Jacob pointed out that if God wanted a people to practice polygamy, He would give them that commandment. To quote his exact
words: "For if I will, saith the Lord of Hosts, raise up seed unto
me, I will command my people; otherwise they shall hearken unto
these things [the practice of one man having only one wife]."
Thus as far as the Nephites were concerned, the commandment
from the Lord throughout their entire history was that no man
should have more than one wife, and, also, that the prophets and
priests should marry.

It seems in the foregoing quotation from *Ixtlilxochitl* that
the Tultec priests did not marry. If that was the practice before
the Spanish Conquest, the fact is apparent that following the
close of *Book of Mormon* history, the Lamanite priests in ancient
America dropped into the same apostate practice that the Christian church on the eastern hemisphere slipped into, i.e., the prac-

tice of forbidding priests to marry. In modern times God put his
stamp of condemnation on such a wicked and erroneous doctrine.
He said: "And again, I say unto you, that whoso forbiddeth to
marry is not ordained of God, for marriage is ordained of God
unto man."[26]

LXXV. Marriage and Dowry

IXTLILXOCHITL:

Marriage customs of Tultecas
     . . . they [the Tultec kings]
had only one wife,[LXXV] and this
(one) legitimate (lawful), and
when she died, they could not
marry (and) kept chastity until
they died, and the women if
their husbands died before they
did, would inherit the kingdom,
and when they died, their legitimate sons, and just as their husbands, they could not marry
again; it was the same with the
common people, as far as having
one legitimate (lawful) wife,
[LXXV] but they could marry a second and third time.

EXTRACTS—BOOK OF MORMON:

One Wife—Teachings of Jacob
     5. Behold, the Lamanites your brethren, whom
ye hate because of their filthiness and the cursing
which hath come upon their skins, are more
righteous than you; for they have not forgotten
the commandment of the Lord, which was given
unto our fathers—that they should have save it
were one wife,[LXXV] and concubines they should
have none, and there should not be whoredoms
committed among them....

Jacob 3:5.

As has been pointed out, the early priest-rulers and settlers
practiced monogamy, according to our two accounts. Both sources
are very precise on the point. In *The Book of Mormon* polygamy
is forbidden to the Nephites, colonizers of Bountiful-land:

> For there shall not any man among you have save it be one wife; and
> concubines he shall have none . . ."[27]

And, according to the records, the Lamanites continued to
follow the original commandment which had been given to their
ancestors. To quote:

> Behold, the Lamanites . . . have not forgotten the commandment of
> the Lord, which was given unto our fathers—that they should have save
> it were one wife, and concubines they should have none....[28]

Of the Mayas of the post-Nephite period (i.e., after 421
A. D.), Bishop Landa wrote, "There are many who never had
more than one wife." Elsewhere he stated "The Yucatecans never
took more than one wife." There is authority showing that some
of the Mayas practiced polygamy.[29] According to the sacred

---

[26] Joseph Smith, *Doctrine and Covenants*, p. 77 (49:15).
[27] *The Book of Mormon*, p. 111 (Jacob 2:27).
[28] Ibid., p. 112 (Jacob 3:9).
[29] Alfred M. Tozzer, *Landa's Relacion de las Cosas de Yucatan* (1941 ed.), Note 451.

book of the ancient Mayas of the Guatemala highlands, the *Popol Vuh,* the first settlers of that region were monogamous. There were four men at the head of the original colony when it came across the sea from the ancient east, aided by the hand of God (Naxcit) and aided by a divine instrument (Giron Gagal). Each of the four had but one wife. According to the Nephite account, the colonizers arriving in the New World in the sixth century B. C. each had but one wife. *Ixtlilxochitl* sustains the other documentary sources by maintaining that "they had only one wife, and this one legitimate or lawful."

Ancient Maya and Jewish customs were identical as to the manner in which a wife was selected for a prospective bridegroom. The Jewish rule placed a definite responsibility on the father to take a wife to his son: "The father has the same obligation towards his son; he must circumcise him, redeem him, teach him, teach him the Torah, *take a wife* to him, and teach him a trade."[30] The Maya practice is set forth by Landa: "The fathers take great care to seek wives in good time of good quality and position for their sons, and if possible of the same place as themselves. It was considered mean-spirited for men to seek wives for themselves, or for the fathers to seek marriage for their daughters, and for arranging the matter, they employed match-makers to take charge of the business."[31]

After the father had chosen a suitable young lady for his son, the second preparatory step was the arranging of the dowry. In ancient Israel and ancient Maya-land the practice was the same. More significant, the Hebrew and Maya words for the dowry appear to be similar. Dowry was a payment in money or kind which the bridegroom paid to the father of the bride. This price or payment was called the *Mohar* in Hebrew. It is today still called *Mahr* by the natives of Palestine.[32] The Mayas called it Muhul. They still so call the dowry payment.[33] That the Hebrew *Mohar* is similar to the Maya *Muhul* seems evident when attention is called to the fact that it is the consonants of a word that really identify it. Most Hebrew nouns are

[30] Leo Auerbach, *The Babylonian Talmud* (1944), p. 185, quoted by Ph. Karl Eidmann, *Brief Studies of the Life and Times of Lehi* (1947), p. 36.
[31] Diego de Landa, op. cit., pp. 100-101.
[32] James Strong, *Hebrew and Chaldee Dictionary* (1944 ed.), words 4117 and 4119; Funk and Wagnalls, *New Standard Bible Dictionary* (1934), p. 553. Genesis 34:12; Deuteronomy 22:29.
[33] Alfred M. Tozzer, op. cit. (1941), note 456; Robert Redfield and Alfonso R. Villa, *Cham Kom, a Maya Village* (1934), pp. 193-194.

made up of three consonants.[34] Anciently vowel signs were non-existent in Hebrew script. Thus, in the Hebrew word *Mohar*, the three consonants constituting the real written word are M H R. In the Maya word the three consonants are M H L. It is a well-known rule that *R*s and *L*s sound alike (untrained persons learning English sometimes say "vely" for "very") and are interchanged.

Neither *The Book of Mormon* nor *Ixtlilxochitl* discloses the age at which the early colonizers customarily married. The twentieth year was the time for marriage among both the early Mayas and the Israelites, as a general rule. However, earlier marriages were not uncommon. "God utters a curse against those who remain single after twenty years of age; and those who marry at sixteen please Him, and those who do so at fourteen still more." "He who is twenty and is not married lives in sin." The rabbis taught, "'Til the age of twenty, the Lord sits and waits. When will the man take a wife unto himself? But when he reaches twenty and has not taken a wife unto himself, the Lord says: 'Let his bones be swollen'." "Thus the Jewish law declares that on 'reaching the age of eighteen it is the duty of a man to take unto himself a wife in order that he may be fruitful and multiply' [Genesis 1:28]; at any rate he should not pass his twentieth year without having taken a wife."[35]

Landa writes of the Mayas: "In olden times they married when they were twenty years old; but now they marry when they are twelve or fourteen."[36]

The Israelite law and the Maya law are identical in many respects with regard to incestuous marriages. The following marriages were forbidden to a man by both Jewish and Maya law:

> His brother's wife
> His wife's sisters
> His stepmother
> His maternal aunt

[34] A. B. Davidson, *An Introductory Hebrew Grammar* (24th ed.), p. 1: Hebrew roots ". . . are almost entirely triliteral [three lettered] . . ." Concerning the twenty-two letters of the Hebrew alphabet Davidson says: "These twenty-two letters are all consonants. The vowels which were not originally written came, in course of time, to be indicated in the manner which will be explained in sections 2-4. The absence of vowels from the alphabet, and the consequent appearance of no letters but consonants in the original form of the Hebrew text might be regarded as a grave misfortune, and likely to expose interpretation to ambiguity. . . . However . . . the context usually puts the matter beyond doubt, just as, in an English sentence written with consonants alone, it would be tolerably easy to discover whether 'fr' stood for *far, fair, fare, fear, fir, fire, for, fore, four, fur, fray, free, fry,* or *fro*. The proof that vowels are by no means indispensable to a rapid and accurate appreciation of meaning may be found in the fact that Pitman's phonetic shorthand, the reporting style, which practically dispenses with vowels, can be read with perfect ease." (p. 5.)
[35] Karl Eidmann, *op. cit.*, p. 18, citing Gerald Friedlander, tr., *Laws and Customs of Israel* (London, 1915-1916), vol. 4. p. 408; Hermann L. Strack, *Introduction to the Talmud and Midrash* (1945), pp. 12-25; Leo Auerbach, *The Babylonian Talmud* (1944), p. 185.
[36] Diego de Landa, *op. cit.*, p. 100.

Landa states the Maya law in the following words:

> They never took a wife who bore their own name on the father side, as this was a very wicked thing in their opinion, and if any married their sisters-in-law, wives of their brothers, it was considered wicked. They never married their stepmothers nor their sisters-in-law, sisters of their wives, nor their maternal aunts; and if anyone did so, it was thought wicked. They married all their other relations on their mother's side even though they were their own first cousins.[37]

Jewish law will be found in the Old Testament.[38] Both Mayas and Israelites were barred by law from marrying a woman bearing the same family name as the man's father.[39]

Summary Statement

The more one delves into the manners and customs of the ancient inhabitants of Middle America and of Bible lands, the more evident it becomes that there was a close relationship between the two peoples. The same is true with regard to the making of a comparison of the languages of these two widely separated parts of the world. It is suggested that a fruitful field will be found if Arabic, Hebrew and Egyptian vocabularies are compared with vocabularies of the early peoples of Middle America and Peru.

---

[37] Ibid.
[38] Deuteronomy 22:30; 27:20; Leviticus 18:8, 12, 16; 20:11, 19, 21.
[39] Leviticus 18:9, 11, 14, 15; 20:20, 12.

Chapter 26

MORMON (HUEMAN) AND A DIVINE BOOK

INTRODUCTORY STATEMENT

During the period from 339 A. D. to 387 A. D., the out-standing leader, according to *The Book of Mormon,* was the historian-prophet-soldier, Mormon. *Ixtlilxochitl* reports that an identical role was played by Hueman (also referred to as Hue-matzin) of the Tultecas of Bountiful-land. The parallels are so close that one could conclude that Hueman and Mormon are one and the same person. They lived during the same period; each was a prophet; each wrote a sacred book of God (a sacred his-tory); and each led the great exodus from Bountiful-land. Also, Chapter 27 will show that the momentous treaty of 350 A. D. was negotiated by Hueman, according to the Mexican historian, and by Mormon, according to the Nephite record.

The details in *The Book of Mormon* are somewhat more complete than those in *Ixtlilxochitl.* But again, that is to be expected since this portion of the Nephite account is taken directly from the original fourth-century autobiographical writ-ings of Mormon himself. Many details concerning this great leader and historian-prophet are found in *The Book of Mormon* which are lacking in *Ixtlilxochitl.*

The literary achievements of this great man of ancient America will first be dealt with. He was the compiler of a "divine book."

COMPILING OF A DIVINE BOOK

IXTLILXOCHITL:	EXTRACTS—BOOK OF MORMON:
Hueman compiles divine book	*Mormon compiles divine book*
And before going on I want to make an account of *Huemat-zin* [Hueman] the astrologer. . . . Before dying he *(Huemat-zin)* gathered together all the histories the Tultecas had, from	48. And it came to pass that when three hundred and twenty years had passed away, Ammaron, being constrained by the Holy Ghost, did hide up the records which were sacred— yea, even all the sacred records which had been handed down from generation to generation,

the creation of the world up to that time (his time)[LXXVI] and had them pictured in a very large book, where were pictured all their persecutions and hardships, prosperities and good happenings, kings and lords, laws and good government of their ancestors, old sayings and good examples, temples, idols, sacrifices, rites and ceremonies that they had, astrology, philosophy, architecture, and the other arts, good as well as bad, and a resume of all things of science, knowledge, prosperous and adverse battles, and many other things; and he entitled this book calling it *Teoamoxtli*,[LXXVI] which, well interpreted means *Various things of God and divine book:* the natives now call the Holy Scriptures *Teoamoxtli*, because it is almost the same, principally in the persecutions and hardships of men.

which were sacred—even until the three hundred and twentieth year from the coming of Christ.[LXXVI]

49. And he did hide them up unto the Lord, that they might come again unto the remnant of the house of Jacob, according to the prophecies and the promises of the Lord.[LXXVII] And thus is the end of the record of Ammaron.

4 Nephi 1:48-49.

1. And now I, Mormon, make a record of the things which I have both seen and heard, and call it the *Book of Mormon.*[LXXVI]

2. And about the time that Ammaron hid up the records unto the Lord, he came unto me, (I being about ten years of age, and I began to be learned somewhat after the manner of the learning of my people) and Ammaron said unto me: I perceive that thou art a sober child, and art quick to observe;

3. Therefore, when ye are about twenty and four years old I would that ye should remember the things which ye have observed concerning this people; and when ye are of that age go to the land Antum, unto a hill which shall be called Shim; and there have I deposited unto the Lord all the sacred engravings concerning this people.

4. And behold, ye shall take the plates of Nephi unto yourself, and the remainder shall ye leave in the place where they are; and ye shall engrave on the plates of Nephi all the things that ye have observed concerning this people.

5. And I, Mormon, being a descendant of Nephi, (and my father's name was Mormon) I remembered the things which Ammaron commanded me.   Mormon 1:1-5.

17. . . . And behold I had gone according to the word of Ammaron, and taken the plates of Nephi, and did make a record according to the words of Ammaron.

18. And upon the plates of Nephi I did make a full account of all the wickedness and abominations; but upon these plates I did forbear to make a full account of their wickedness and abominations, for behold, a continual scene of wickedness and abominations has been before mine eyes ever since I have been sufficient to behold the ways of man.   Mormon 2:17-18.

3. And now, I speak somewhat concerning that which I have written; for after I had made an abridgment from the plates of Nephi, down to the reign of this king Benjamin [about 130 B. C.], of whom Amaleki spake, I searched among the records which had been delivered into my hands, and I found these plates, which contained this small account [i.e., the small plates comprising I Nephi, II Nephi, Jacob, Enos, Jarom and Omni] of the prophets, from Jacob down to the reign of this king Benjamin, and also many of the words of Nephi.

4. And the things which are upon these plates pleasing me, because of the prophecies of the coming of Christ; and my fathers knowing that many of them have been fulfilled; yea, and I also know that as many things as have been prophesied concerning us down to this day have been fulfilled, and as many as go beyond this day must surely come to pass——

5. Wherefore, I chose these things, to finish my record upon them, which remainder of my record I shall take from the plates of Nephi; and I cannot write the hundredth part of the things of my people.

6. But behold, I shall take these [small] plates, which contain these prophesyings and revelations, and put them with the remainder of my record, for they are choice unto me; and I know they will be choice unto my brethren.

7. And I do this for a wise purpose; for thus it whispereth me, according to the workings of the Spirit of the Lord which is in me. And now, I do not know all things; but the Lord knoweth all things which are to come; where-fore, he worketh in me to do according to his will.

8. And my prayer to God is concerning my brethren, that they may once again come to the knowledge of God, yea, the redemption of Christ; that they may once again be a delight-some people.

9. And now I, Mormon, proceed to finish out my record, which I take from the plates of Nephi; and I made it according to the knowledge and the understanding which God has given me.LXXVI

10. Wherefore, it came to pass that after Amaleki had delivered up these plates into the hands of king Benjamin, he took them and put them with the other plates, which contained rec-ords which had been handed down by the kings, from generation to generation until the days of king Benjamin.

11. And they were handed down from king Benjamin [130 B. C.] from generation to gen-eration until they have fallen into my hands [about 335 A. D.]. And I, Mormon, pray to God that they may be preserved from this time [385 A. D.] henceforth. And I know that they will be preserved; for there are great things written upon them,LXXVI out of which my people and their brethren shall be judged at the great and last day, according to the word of God which is written.   Words of Mormon 1:1-11.

1. And now I, Mormon, being about to de-liver up the record which I have been making into the hands of my son Moroni, behold I have witnessed almost all the destruction of my peo-ple, the Nephites.

2. And it is many hundred years after the coming of Christ that I deliver these records into the hands of my son; and it supposeth me that he will witness the entire desruction of my people.[LXXVII] But may God grant that he may survive them, that he may write somewhat concerning them, and somewhat concerning Christ, that perhaps some day it may profit them.

Words of Mormon 1:1-2.

5. And when three hundred and eighty and four years had passed away, we had gathered in all that remained of our people [the Nephite nation] unto the land Cumorah.[LXXVII]

6. And it came to pass that when we had gathered in all our people in one to the land of Cumorah, I, Mormon, began to be old; and knowing it to be the last struggle of my people, [LXVII] and *having been commanded of the Lord* that I should not suffer the records which had been handed down by our fathers, which were sacred, to fall into the hands of the Lamanites, (for the Lamanites would destroy them) therefore I made this record [*The Book of Mormon*] out of the plates of Nephi, and hid up in the hill Cumorah *all* the records which had been entrusted to me by the hand of the Lord, save it were these few plates [comprising *The Book of Mormon*] *which* I gave unto my son Moroni.

Mormon 6:5-6.

MORONI COMPLETES HIS FATHER'S BOOK

EXTRACTS—BOOK OF MORMON:

Moroni completes his father's record

1. Behold I, Moroni, do finish the record of my father, Mormon. Behold, I have but few things to write, which things I have been commanded by my father.

3. . . . and I even remain alone to write the sad tale of the destruction of my people. But behold, they are gone, and I fulfill the commandment of my father. And whether they will slay me, I know not.

4. Therefore I will write and hide up the records in the earth; and whither I go it mattereth not.

5. Behold, my father hath made this record, and he hath written the intent thereof. And behold, I would write it also if I had room upon the plates, but I have not; and ore I have none, for I am alone. Mormon 8:1, 3-5.

1. And now I, Moroni, proceed to give an account of those ancient inhabitants who were destroyed by the hand of the Lord upon the face of this north country. Ether 1:1.

1. Now I, Moroni, after having made an end of abridging the account of the people of Jared, I had supposed not to have written more. . . .

2. Wherefore, I write a few more things, contrary to what I had supposed; . . .

Moroni 1:1-2.

Moroni's admonition to us regarding The Book of Mormon

4. And when ye shall receive these things, I would exhort you that ye would ask God, the Eternal Father, in the name of Christ, if these things are not true; and if ye shall ask with a sincere heart, with real intent, having faith in Christ, he will manifest the truth of it unto you, by the power of the Holy Ghost.   Moroni 10:4.

LXXVI. DIVINE BOOK

In 384 A. D.-385 A. D., after he had completed his "Divine Book," Mormon deposited the Nephite records in the "hill Cumorah," as is related in the extracts. His own work he delivered to his son, Moroni. The latter, Moroni, ultimately—on September 22, 1823—delivered the record to Joseph Smith at Palmyra, New York.

The Book of Mormon bears the earmarks of a "Book of God." In fact, the first six divisions or "books" were lifted bodily from the "sacred" records of the Nephites—the Small Plates. Nephi had begun that account himself shortly after his departure from Jerusalem, and it had been in the hands of the Nephite prophet-leaders and holders of the holy Priesthood from that early date. Those first six books (First Nephi, Second Nephi, Jacob, Enos, Jarom, and Omni) contain many philosophical and religious quotations, discussions, and allegories. They are quite different from the remaining portion of *The Book of Mormon.* That which follows the first six books is Mormon's digest of the political and economic history; but it also contains much gospel doctrine. In this latter section, Mormon took most of this material from the Larger Plates of Nephi, adding his own eyewitness report on events of his day.

Moroni made a worthwhile contribution in the work that he did in completing his father's records following Mormon's death.

It would be difficult to give a more accurate and concise description of *The Book of Mormon*—Mormon's literary accomplishment—than that given by *Ixtlilxochitl* of the *Book of Hueman,* as quoted above.

Ixtlilxochitl states that Hueman compiled his book "before dying." Mormon compiled *The Book of Mormon* but a few years before his death.

It is noteworthy that *Ixtlilxochitl* declares that Hueman's sacred book was almost the same as the Bible. *The Book of Mormon* does, in fact, contain some of the writings of the Old Testament. For example, many of the teachings of the prophet Isaiah, some of the teachings of Moses, Malachi's predictions and the essential teachings of Jesus Christ were recorded in the Nephite records. The latter teachings were given to the ancient Americans by the Man of Galilee himself following his crucifixion and resurrection. A comparison of the Nephite religious ideas with those of the Bible will show that America's ancient "Divine Book" is, as *Ixtlilxochitl* said it was, "almost the same" as the Bible. Further, *The Book of Mormon* shows that many of the same social and moral rules continued to operate for and against the New World branch of the House of Israel as had operated among the Israelites of the Old World. Adherence to the laws of God brought peace and happiness, willful violations of those laws brought war, misery, and destruction. Those laws were (and are) as relentless as the law of gravity. The Bible and the Divine Book of the Nephites are in close accord.

In conclusion, it may be safely said that the literary accomplishments of Hueman and Mormon appear to be identical. Had *Ixtlilxochitl* stated that the wonderful literary work of Hueman was engraved on tablets of gold, the parellel would have been complete. *Ixtlilxochitl* says nothing of the writing medium used by Hueman. For such an important book, a "divine book" containing "various things of God," surely gold tablets might well have been used—as claimed in the Nephite account and as maintained by Joseph Smith and the eleven witnesses.

LXXVII. LEADERSHIP AND PROPHECIES OF MORMON-HUEMAN[2]

IXTLILXOCHITL:	EXTRACTS—BOOK OF MORMON:
Hueman predicts destruction of his people through war	*Mormon predicts destruction of Nephites through war*
Likewise he [Huematzin] declared that when *five hundred and twelve years* had passed since they left their country, a lord (chief, master, ruler) was	3. And now behold, my son [Moroni], I fear lest the Lamanites shall destroy this people [the Nephites]; for they do not repent, and Satan stirreth them up continually to anger with one another.

[2] The names *Mormon* and *Hueman* are similar to each other, the second syllable of each being identical. It has been shown that *Hue* means "great." The name *Mormon* may possibly be a contraction of certain Hebrew words, possibly *Meorah* (cheerfulness, bright) and *ma'n* (utensil or vessel). See James Strong, *Dictionary of the Hebrew Bible* (1890), words 3974 and 3984.

to inherit the kingdom, with the good-will of some and against the will of others. Further, that he was to have certain marks on his body, and the main one, he was to have curly hair, and of the hair itself nature was to form a tiara on his head, from birth until he died. And during his life time he was to be, at first, very just, wise, and of a good government. In mid-life he was to be foolish and unfortunate (unlucky), for which reason those of his nation were to perish with very great punishments from heaven, and no less than the three destructions they would have—and that the last would be the year of ce Tecpatl (star that so persecuted them). Some men of his own lineage would rise and persecute him [his people] with very great wars, until nearly all of them were exterminated. And he was to escape and return toward where his ancestors had come from. And the latter part of his life he was to be very just, wise, and discreet, as at the beginning. And a few years before their destruction there were to be certain unnatural signs, among them, that the rabbit was to grow horns like the deer, the bird Huetzitzilin was to grow spurs like cocks, and rocks were to give forth fruit, and principal women were to go on pilgrimages, as is the use and custom. They [the women] were to have carnal access with the priests of the temples, the priests breaking the chastity that they professed there in their false religions. And he said Tloque-nahuaque [God], seeing this, would be angry against them; and the other gods (his inferiors) would punish them with lightnings, hails, ice, hunger, vermin, and other persecutions from heaven; and after this with wars with which they would exterminate each other[LXXVII] completely. Further, that so many years from that time, those who escaped this destruction would have another and even some of the Chichimecas too, because that star Tecpatl (which is a flint) would again do its part.

5. . . . and they have lost their love, one toward another; and they thirst after blood and revenge continually. . . .

22. But behold my son, I recommend thee unto God, and I trust in Christ that thou wilt be saved; and I pray unto God that he will spare thy life, to witness the return of his people unto him, or their utter destruction; for I know that they must perish except they repent and return unto him. Moroni 9:3, 5, 22.

2. But behold, I [Mormon] was without hope, for I knew the judgments of the Lord which should come upon them [the Nephites]; for they repented not of their iniquities, but did struggle for their lives without calling upon that Being who created them. Mormon 5:2.

14b. . . . behold the voice of the Lord came unto me [Mormon], saying:

15. Vengeance is mine, and I will repay; and because this people repented not after I had delivered them, behold, they shall be cut off from the face of the earth. Mormon 3:14b-15.

These and other things he declared he understood through
his astrology, and the signs that
planets had in store for them.
And also all these things came
to pass, with God's will, just as
he said.LXXVII

According to *Ixtlilxochitl*, Hueman rose up as a great leader of the people of Bountiful-land in the year they left their ancient homeland (339 A. D.). The date is fixed in Chapter 27.

Mormon's autobiographical sketch from *The Book of Mormon* discloses that he was born in the year 311 A. D. in the Land Northward. (Regarding the area where he was born, see Chapter 14.) In the year 322 A. D., when the war commenced in Zarahemla, he was taken there, to the Seat of the Kingdom, by his father. Mormon was eleven years of age at that time. The remainder of his life was lived during many long, sad, and fateful war years. He experienced few years without the horrors and trials of war. In the year 326 A. D., at the age of fifteen, he had an important spiritual experience. He comments on it as follows:

And I, being fifteen years of age and being somewhat of a sober mind, therefore I was visited of the Lord, and tasted and knew the goodness of Jesus. And I did endeavor to preach unto this people, but my mouth was shut, and I was forbidden that I should preach unto them; for behold they had willfully rebelled against their God.[3]

In 327-328 A. D., at the age of sixteen, Mormon became the leader of the Nephite armies. He wrote of himself:

And notwithstanding I being young, was large of stature; therefore the people of Nephi appointed me that I should be their leader, or the leader of their armies. Therefore it came to pass that in my sixteenth year I did go forth at the head of an army of Nephites, against the Lamanites; therefore three hundred and twenty and six years had passed away [since the birth of Christ].[4]

In 330 A. D., at the age of nineteen years, he was in command of a Nephite army of 42,000 men. In 339 A. D., the year *Ixtlilxochitl* gives for the departure of the Tultecs from the Seat of the Kingdom, Mormon was twenty-eight years of age and was well established as one of the leaders of the disintegrating nation.

[3] *The Book of Mormon*, pp. 460-461 (Mormon 1:17, 15-16).
[4] *Ibid*., pp. 461-462 (Mormon 2:1-2, 9).
    Leland H. Monson has written a good biographical sketch concerning Mormon: *The Improvement Era* (Sept., 1945), p. 412 ff.

Both of our accounts indicate that about the year 339 A. D. —near the time of the beginning of the exodus—Mormon took temporary hope for the welfare of his people. The following per- tinent statement was recorded by Mormon:

Thus there began to be a mourning and a lamentation in all the land because of these things [thieving, robbery, murder, black magic and witch- craft on a large scale], and more especially among the people of Nephi. And it came to pass that when I, Mormon, saw their lamentation and their mourning and their sorrow before the Lord, my heart did begin to rejoice within me, knowing the mercies and the long-suffering of the Lord, therefore supposing that he would be merciful unto them that they would become a righteous people.[5]

· In *Ixtlilxochitl* the temporary hope and optimism of Hueman is mentioned:

There rose among them a great astrologer who called himself Huemat- zin [Hueman], saying to them that he found that since the creation of the world they had always had great persecutions from heaven, and after them their ancestors had enjoyed great well-being, prosperous lands, and long power; and their persecutions always occurred in the year of Ce Tecpatl . . . and this year past, they would then enjoy great well-being.[6]

The details of the military career (including the negotiating of an important treaty) of Hueman and also of Mormon are fully set out in the next chapter. Each is credited with having directed the exodus from Bountiful-land.

LXXVIII. Death of Mormon

EXTRACTS—BOOK OF MORMON:

Death of Mormon reported by Moroni

2. And now it came to pass that after the great and tremendous battle of Cumorah [385- 386 A. D.] behold, the Nephites who had es- caped into the country southward were hunted by the Lamanites, until they were all[7] destroyed.

3. And my father also was killed by them, LXXVIII and I even remain alone to write the sad tale of the destruction of my people. But be- hold, they are gone, and I fulfill the command- ment of my father. And whether they will slay me, I know not.

5. . . . My father hath been slain in battle, LXXVIII and all my kinsfolk, and I have not friends nor whither to go; and how long the Lord will suffer that I may live I know not.

---

[5] *Ibid.*, p. 462 (Mormon 2:10-12).
[6] *Supra*, p.
[7] All the leaders were killed, but Moroni later points out that some of the Nephites escaped. As of 400 A. D., he wrote: ". . . because of their hatred they [the Lamanites] put to death every Nephite that will not deny the Christ." *The Book of Mormon*, p. 510 (Moroni 1:2).

> 6. Behold, four hundred years have passed away since the coming of our Lord and Savior.
>
> 7. And behold, the Lamanites have hunted my people, the Nephites, down from city to city and from place to place, even until they are no more; and great has been their fall; yea, great and marvelous is the destruction of my people, the Nephites.   Mormon 8:2-3, 5-7.

The memory of so great a leader was bound to live in the traditions of the surviving remnants of the nation—and such was the case. Although the Nephite account comes to an abrupt end with the writings of Mormon's son, Moroni, in 421 A. D., *Ixtlilxochitl's* account carries on the history and his report shows how the memory of this great prophet-leader was perpetuated for hundreds of years in Mexico. The exact date of the death of Mormon is not given in the Nephite record; but Moroni reports briefly on his father's death as follows: "And my father also was killed by them . . . My father had been slain in battle . . ." Mormon met his death between 385 A. D. and 400 A. D., the exact year not being given. The date of the death of Hueman was not recorded in the Mexican history, either; but *Ixtlilxochitl* speaks of him as though he were alive for hundreds of years after the normal life span. Obviously, only the memory of the great man was actually alive after the close of the fourth century A. D.

Chapter 27

BANISHMENT AND DESTRUCTION OF
NEPHITE NATION

(Period of Lamanite dominance began 322 A. D., coinciding with Maya Old Empire which began in same year, 322 A. D.)

INTRODUCTORY STATEMENT

Some remarkable parallels are found in this chapter. The period from 322 A. D. was one of wars and migrations, according to both records. As was indicated in Chapter 17, following a long period of peace, a war began in the land of Bountiful in 322 A. D. The war continued intermittently for sixty-four years, as will be shown here, and it culminated in a mighty struggle in 385 A. D. The result of this terrible and prolonged conflict was banishment and then destruction of the Nephite faction of the "Tultecas." *Ixtlilxochitl* identifies the enemy which was responsible for the banishment and defeat of the Tultecas as "fierce kindred" and as "Chichimecs." It is clear from the Nephite account that the enemy was a faction of the once-united people of greater Bountiful-land. The war was in the nature of a rebellion or civil war, according to both histories.

Both *Ixtlilxochitl* and *The Book of Mormon* state that the people of Bountiful-land were forced by the enemy to migrate from place to place during the years from 339 A. D. to 385 A. D., an era of war. The two accounts are in essential agreement concerning the migrations, each helping to clarify the other to a certain extent. *Ixtlilxochitl* gives more details concerning the actual travel time involved, whereas *The Book of Mormon* gives more details on the battles fought during the course of the long war.

Both accounts report on a momentous agreement or treaty that was entered into between the seven tribes in 350 A. D. Each agrees that the negotiations were handled primarily by the two main factions—Nephites on the one hand and Lamanites on the

347

other, according to the Nephite account. For convenience of study, the highlights of the two reports are summarized by the writers in chart form first, and then the details of each account are quoted in narrative form and in the language of our pri-mary histories. Facts brought to light in recent years by the archæ-ologists also will be presented. These facts are in remarkable confirmation of the two primary reports.

COMPARATIVE CHART

SUMMARY OF EVENTS— IXTLILXOCHITL:	SUMMARY OF EVENTS— BOOK OF MORMON:

322 A. D.

	Civil war and revolution begins in greater Bountiful-land (Zarahemla) in 322 A. D. Lamanites (Nephites' kin-dred) begin to dominate. Nephites are on the wane.

322 A. D.—326 A. D.

	Temporary peace prevails in Bounti-ful-land (Zarahemla).

326 A. D.—328 A. D.

War begins in Bountiful-land (Hue-huetlapallan) between Bountiful-land-people (Tultecs) and their own fierce kindred in 326 A. D.	War resumed. Nephite army is de-feated and begins "to retreat towards the north countries." Angola fortified and lost. David fortified and lost. Army moves to Joshua, "which was in the bor-ders west by the seashore"—Nephite people endeavor to gather into one body there.

329 A. D.—330 A. D.

War continues near Bountiful-land. No details given.	War continued in earnest—complete revolution throughout greater Bountiful-land (Zarahemla) and near-by area to the north and west near narrow neck of land. 42,000 Nephites stand firm and defeat Lamanite army of 44,000.

330 A. D.—347 A. D.

War continues. No details given. Kingdom is usurped in 338 A. D.-339 A. D. Bountiful-land people depart from ancient homeland in 339 A. D. They are banished. War continues unabated. Fighting	War continues. Thousands of Ne-phites and Lamanites are hewn down. Details are not given. Fighting from 339 A. D. to 344 A. D. is near Bountiful. In 345 A. D. the Nephites flee north-ward to Jashon, the latter being near the

continues from 339 A. D. to 347 A. D., eight years, near Huehuetlapallan. The Tultecs are forced to leave their ancient homeland, their fierce kindred having compelled them to depart. The contenders are still relatively near Mexico's narrow neck of land, the Isthmus of Tehauntepec, for the fighting during this eight years' period occurs "near their country."

hill Shim where Nephite commander, Mormon, spent his childhood. Fighting is still relatively near the Narrow Neck of Land and Bountiful-land.

In 346 A. D. Nephites flee farther northward to Shim, which town they fortify.

In 346-347 A. D. the Nephites defeat the Lamanites and return southward; they recover Jashon, Joshua, David and Angola and "the lands of our inheritance."

347 A. D.—350 A. D.

Tultecs occupy "Smaller-Bountiful-land," *Tlapallan-Conco* (it probably being a part of their original Bountiful-land) for this three-year period. They had been near this country during the eight years of fighting preceding this occupation.

Nephites reoccupy ancient Bountiful below Narrow Neck of Land for this three years' period. Probably only a portion of greater Bountiful-land is actually reoccupied.

350 A. D.

The seven leaders of the Tultecs enter into an agreement or treaty. There are two main spokesmen. Hueman, great prophet, astrologer and one of the principal leaders of the Tultecs, decides it would be to the best interest of his people if they gave up their ancient homeland— seat of the kingdom — Bountiful-land, which lay immediately to the south of Mexico's narrow neck of land, Tehuantepec. Under this arrangement, the Tultecs were to occupy the region where the Ancient Ones (Giants) once lived, which region had also been occupied for a time by the Ulmecs, second settlers of the area. This means the "Tultecs" are to occupy territory north of Tehuantepec and are abandoning the ancient Bountiful-land to their fierce kindred. The northern lands are considered cursed.

The seven tribes (Nephites, Jacobites, Josephites, Zoramites, Lamanites, Ishmaelites, and Lemuelites) make a treaty. There are spokesmen for the two main divisions, Nephites and Lamanites. Mormon, great Nephite prophet and leader, is the spokesman for the Nephites. The Nephites give up to their fierce kindred, the Lamanites, all of their ancient homeland, which lay immediately to the south of the Narrow Neck of Land. Under the treaty the Nephites are to occupy the land northerly from the Narrow Neck of Land. The Lamanites are to hold the land south of the Narrow Neck of Land. This district includes the ancient Seat of the Kingdom. The northern lands now to be held by the Nephites were those formerly occupied by the Jaredites, and also settled temporarily by Mulekites. The northern lands were considered cursed.

350 A. D.—361 A. D.

Tultecs occupy territory beyond ancient Bountiful-land. New lands are along the seacoast. 'Great Sandy," *Hueyxallan* was colonized 350 A. D.-353 A. D. "Land Near the Sea," *Xalixco,* colonized 353 A. D.-361 A. D.

Nephites occupy the land northward, i.e., territory northerly from Narrow Neck of Land and Narrow Pass. Ten years of peace are spent in saving and storing food and making arms and fortifications. The area occupied is along the coast. The city Desolation, located by the Narrow Pass, is occupied and fortified. The Lamanites attack Desolation near the sea in 361 A. D.

362 A. D.—378 A. D.

Tultecs continue to occupy lands near the seashore beyond the ancient homeland. *Chimalhuacan, Atenco,* "Islands and Seashore," were occupied for five years (about 362 A. D.-367 A. D.) A place called *Tochpan* is settled during five years (about 367 A. D.-371 A. D.). A place called *Quiyahuixtlan Anahuac* "Lands of Coast and Arms of the Sea" is settled during six years from about 371 A. D.-377 A. D.

The Nephites continue to occupy strongholds in the Land Northward near the seashore—particularly Desolation and Teancum. "Teancum lay in the borders by the seashore; and it was also near the city Desolation." Much fighting occurs in that area during this period. Other Nephite cities—Boaz and Jordan—in same general area of Land Northward, are occupied by Nephites. Desolation, Teancum, and Boaz are captured by the Lamanites in 375 A. D. Mormon goes to the hill Shim in 375 A. D. and removes the Nephite archives. Human sacrifice is practiced by the Lamanites. Nephites flee.

378 A. D.—387 A. D.

In 387 A. D., it is 52 years since the wars began in 326 A. D. Tultecs occupy the coastal towns in vicinity of many waters. Zacatlan is occupied for seven years, from about 381 A. D. to about 386 A. D.

Nephites hold Jordan and other northern coastal Nephite towns until 380 A. D. when they again retreat, fleeing to land of lakes, rivers and fountains, "Land of Many Waters"—Cumorah. They occupy the Cumorah area from about 380 A. D. to 385-386 A. D. 230,000 Nephite soldiers are slain at Cumorah. The Nephite government and nation are destroyed. Inspired leadership is no longer in charge. Utter chaos and ruin exist. Lamanites completely dominate Bountiful-land and the "land of many waters." Many Nephites join the Lamanites to preserve their lives.

COMPARATIVE NARRATIVES

The complex historical data found in *Ixtlilxochitl* and *The Book of Mormon* from which the foregoing chart was compiled will now be quoted.

IXTLILXOCHITL: EXTRACTS—BOOK OF MORMON:

322 A. D.

[Mormon is born in 311 A. D. in area immediately north of "narrow neck of land."]

6. And it came to pass that I, [Mormon] being eleven years old [322 A. D.], was carried by my father into the land southward, even to the land of Zarahemla.[XCI]

7. The whole face of the land had become covered with buildings, and the people were as numerous almost, as it were the sand of the sea.

8. And it came to pass in this year there began to be a war[LXXXIV] between the Nephites, who consisted of the Nephites and the Jacobites and the Josephites and the Zoramites; and this war was between the Nephites, and the Lamanites and the Lemuelites and the Ishmaelites.[1]

9. Now the Lamanites and the Lemuelites and the Ishmaelites were called Lamanites, and the two parties were Nephites and Lamanites.[XC]

10. And it came to pass that the war began to be among them in the borders of Zarahemla, by the waters of Sidon.

11. And it came to pass that the Nephites had gathered together a great number of men, even to exceed the number of thirty thousand. And it came to pass that they did have in this same year a number of battles, in which the Nephites did beat the Lamanites and did slay many of them.   Mormon 1:6-11.

322 A. D.—326 A. D.

[As will be seen below, *Ixtlilxochitl* dates the beginning of the war at about 325 A. D.-326 A. D. when he comments to the effect that in the first year the Tultecs were in Zacatlan (which was the year 378 A. D.) it had been 52 years since the wars began with their kindred nation. See page 362 below].

12. And it came to pass that the Lamanites withdrew their design, and there was peace settled in the land; and peace did remain for the space of about four years, that there was no bloodshed. . . .
    Mormon 1:12.

326 A. D.—328 A. D.

1. And it came to pass in that same year [326 A. D.] there began to be a war again between the Nephites and the Lamanites. And notwithstanding I [Mormon] being young, was large in stature; therefore the people of Nephi appointed me that I should be their leader, or the leader of their armies.

2. Therefore it came to pass that in my sixteenth year I did go forth at the head of an army of the Nephites, against the Lamanites; therefore three hundred and twenty and six years had passed away.

3. And it came to pass that in the three hundred and twenty and seventh year the Lamanites did come upon us with exceeding great power, insomuch that they did frighten my armies; there-

---

[1] Note that now, 322 A. D., the once-united people of greater Bountiful-land are again divided into the original seven tribes, and the seven tribes are divided into two great factions—Nephites and Lamanites, These are more politico-religious factions than racial at this date. See topic XC hereafter.

fore they would not fight, and they began to retreat towards the north countries.[2] [XCI]

4. And it came to pass that we did
come to the city of Angola, and we did
take possession of the city, and make
preparations to defend ourselves against
the Lamanites. And it came to pass that
we did fortify the city with our might;
but notwithstanding all our fortifications
the Lamanites did come upon us and did
drive us out of the city.

5. And they did also drive us forth
out of the land of David.

6. And we marched forth and came
to the land of Joshua, which was in the
borders west by the seashore.

7. And it came to pass that we did
gather in our people as fast as it were
possible, that we might get them together
in one body.

Mormon 2:1-7.

329 A. D.—330 A. D.

8. But behold, the land was filled
with robbers and with Lamanites; and
notwithstanding the great destruction
which hung over my people, they did
not repent of their evil doings; therefore
there was blood and carnage spread
throughout all the face of the land, both
on the part of the Nephites and also on
the part of the Lamanites; and it was
one complete revolution throughout all
the face of the land.

9. And now, the Lamanites had a
king, and his name was Aaron; and he
came against us with an army of forty
and four thousand. And behold, I
[Mormon] withstood him with forty and
two thousand. And it came to pass that
I beat him with my army that he fled
before me. And behold, all this was
done, and three hundred and thirty
years had passed away. . . .

Mormon 2:8-9.

330 A. D.—347 A. D.

It was 305 years since the sun and
moon had eclipsed [which occurred in
34 A. D., thereby making the date
339 A. D.], and 438 years since the
destruction of the Philistines, Quinametzin[3] and 5,486 years since the creation

15. And it came to pass that my sorrow did return unto me again, and I
saw that the day of grace was passed
with them, both temporally and spiritually; for I saw thousands of them hewn
down in open rebellion against their

---

[2] Observe that this retreat of the Nephites takes them toward Mormon's childhood homeland, northerly from Zarahemla.

[3] *Ixtlilxochitl* errs here by one hundred years. He should have said 538 years since the destruction of
the Quinametzin, for his chronology dates their destruction at 236 B. C.

of the world, when Chalcatzin and Tla-camihtzin, very great gentlemen descend-ants of the royal house of the Tultecs, began to desire to usurp the kingdom, wanting to take it away from the legiti-mate successor, after having been for many years in quiet peace. This hap-pened in the year 13 Acatl. They [the Tultecs] were exiled[LXXX IX] and had some wars, being driven out of the city of Tlachicalzincan, in the region of Hue-huetlapallan, their country, with all their allies and families, men as well as women, There was a great number of them and they left during the year that followed the year *Ce Tecpatl*—banished from all the land, as will be seen in what follows. In our [Gregorian] count this happened at 439 [339 A. D. no doubt intended since it was 305 years after the eclipse of 34 A. D.] since the birth of Christ our Lord.[4]

In the year *Ce Tecpatl,* as has been said, the Tultecs were banished from their country and nation. They left flee-ing and as they could, while the follow-ers of Tlaxicoliucan, their kindred, came following (harassing) them, until they arrived at a point more than sixty leagues away from their lands, where they stayed—reorganizing themselves and cultivating the land and doing other things for their sustenance. This land they called Tlapallanconco, in memory of their country [ancient Bountiful-land] and the discoverer of this land [Tlapallanconco] was called Cecatzin.[5]
. . . they were near their country[XCI] eight years making war, until they were entirely driven out. . . .[7]

God, and heaped up as dung upon the face of the land. And thus three hun-dred and forty and four years had passed away.

16. And it came to pass that in the three hundred and forty and fifth year the Nephites did begin to flee before the Lamanites; and they were pursued until they came even to the land of Jashon, before it was possible to stop them in their retreat.[6]

20. And it came to pass that in this year the people of Nephi again were hunted and driven. And it came to pass that we were driven forth until we had come northward[XCI] to the land which was called Shem.

21. And it came to pass that we did fortify the city of Shem, and we did gather in our people as much as it were possible, that perhaps we might save them from destruction.

22. And it came to pass in the three hundred and forty and sixth year they began to come upon us again.

23. And it came to pass that I [Mor-mon] did speak unto my people, and did urge them with great energy, that they would stand boldly before the La-manites and fight for their wives, and their children, and their houses, and their homes.

24. And my words did arouse them somewhat to vigor, insomuch that they did not flee from before the Lamanites, but did stand with boldness against them.

25. And it came to pass that we did contend with an army of thirty thousand against an army of fifty thousand. And it came to pass that we did stand before them with such firmness that they did flee from before us.

26. And it came to pass that when they had fled we did pursue them with our armies, and did meet them again, and did beat them; nevertheless the strength of the Lord was not with us; yea, we were left to ourselves, that the Spirit of the Lord did not abide in us; there-fore we had become weak like unto our brethren.

27. And my heart did sorrow because of this the great calamity of my people, because of their wickedness and their

[4] From *Ixtlilxochitl's* "First Account." *Ixtlilxochitl* again makes the same error of one hundred years.
[5] From *Ixtlilxochitl's* "Second Account."
[7] From *Ixtlilxochitl's* "Second Account.'

abominations. But behold, we did go
forth against the Lamanites and the robbers of Gadianton, until we had again
taken possession of the lands of our inheritance.[XCI]   Mormon 2:15-27.

347 A. D.—350 A. D.

28. And the three hundred and forty
and ninth year had passed away.
Mormon 2:28a.

350 A. D.—GREAT TREATY BETWEEN SEVEN TRIBES

And almost in the last of these years
[the eleven-year period following the
departure from their country in 339
A. D.] two principal leaders and five
other minor ones[8] got together to discuss whether they would stay in this
land [Tlapallanconco, near their ancient
homeland] or whether they [the Tul-
tecs] would go on farther.

There arose among the Tultecs a great
astrologer who called himself Huematzin, saying to them that he found that
since the creation of the world they had
always had great persecutions from
heaven, and after persecutions their ancestors had enjoyed great well-being,
prosperity and long power, and that their
persecutions always occurred in the year
Ce Tecpatl . . . and this year Ce Tecpatl once past, they would enjoy great
well-being—that it was a great evil, pre-
lude to greater good. And [Huematzin
went on to tell them] that thus it was
not convenient for them to stay there so
near their enemies. Besides, he found in
his astrology that the land toward the
rising of the sun[9] was extensive and
prosperous, where the Quinametzin had
lived for many years, and it had been
many years since they had been destroyed and it was unsettled. Besides, the
fierce Chichimecas, their neighbors, very
few times went that far and the planet
that governed that land lacked many

28. And in the three hundred and
fiftieth year we made a treaty with the
Lamanites and the robbers of Gadianton, in which we did get the lands of
our inheritance divided.[LXXXIX]

29. And the Lamanites did give unto
us the land northward,[XCI] yea even to
the narrow passage which led into the
land southward. And we did give unto
the Lamanites all the land southward.
Mormon 2:28b-29.

---

[8] Seven leaders are mentioned. This ties in with statements in both records that there were seven
tribes. The two principal tribes were the Nephites and Lamanites. The five mnior ones were the
Jacobites, Josephites, Zoramites, Lemuelites and the Ishmaelites. See above p. 351. According to
The Book of Mormon, this great treaty was entered into between the two major tribes—i.e., the
agreement was entered into by the leader of the Lamanites and the leader of the Nephites.
[9] This reference to the east is error. The migration was west and north. Mariano Veytia, Historia
Antigue de Mexico (1836) properly says "west." See Bancroft, Native Races, vol. 5, p. 212.

years before fulfilling its threats and that in the meantime they could enjoy a golden and happy century—they and all their descendants to the tenth degree, succeeding from children to parents. Besides [the prophet Huematzin said] that planet did not govern over their [Tultec] nation, but rather over the Giants—and that it might be that it would not hurt their descendants very much—and that in this place [Tlapallanconco, 60 leagues from Huehuetlapallan, former seat of the kingdom] they should leave some people to settle it and remain as their vassals—and that as time went on they would return against their enemies and recover their country and nation.

These and many other things Huematzin declared and these two leaders and the other [five] minor ones[LV] thought it good and agreed on it, carrying it [the treaty] all out. And Huematzin told them that if they were different from the others [that is, from the Giants—who had lived wickedly] and were good, they should remain a few days supplying themselves with everything for what was ahead. At the time they left this land [and entered into the said treaty] it had been eleven years since they had left their country [i.e., eleven years after 339 A. D. puts the date at 350 A. D.], because they were near their country eight years making war,[XCI] until they were entirely driven out, and three years in this land which they called Tlapallanconco.

As has been said, they left some of the common people, their women and children, so that they might settle it.

LXXXIX. Great Treaty of 350 A. D.

The parallels between *Ixtlilxochitl* and *The Book of Mormon* concerning the agreement or treaty of 350 A. D. are too striking to pass over without comment. According to *Ixtlilxochitl*, seven leaders held the meeting to discuss terms. Obviously, they were the leaders of the seven original tribal groups into which the Bountiful-land people separated at the end of the long era of peace. *Ixtlilxochitl* mentions that there were "two principal leaders and five other minor ones." This is in close accord with the Nephite record which says that the dominant tribes were the Nephites on the one hand and the Lamanites on the other. Although Mormon is extremely brief concerning the making of this noteworthy treaty, it is strongly implied that there were two principal parties to the treaty-making: ". . . we made a treaty with the Lamanites and the robbers of Gadianton, in which we [the Nephites] did get the lands of our inheritance divided." Although the seven subdivisions of the Nephite and Lamanite peoples were represented, there were two dominant units—Nephites and Lamanites. It is safely inferred from the account of Mormon that there were two chief spokesmen, Mormon speaking for the Nephites and a Lamanite commander speaking for the Lamanites. The five minor spokesmen would have been representing the following subdivisions: Jacobites, Joseph-ites, Zoramites, Lemuelites and Ishmaelites.

Ixtlilxochitl makes it clear that the prophet-historian, Hue-man, spoke for the exiled branch of the original united peoples of Bountiful-land. Mormon, in his own Nephite record, is modest, saying merely that *"we* made a treaty. . . ." Clearly he was the primary or principal spokesman for the exiled Nephites.

Ixtlilxochitl says that the subject under discussion at the treaty conference was "whether they would stay in this land or whether they would go on farther." This appears to have been the same subject discussed at the treaty conference, according to the Nephite record. It was decided, we read, that the Nephites would stay. They wound up with "the land northward," the very territory northerly from the "narrow neck of land" that had formerly been occupied by the Jaredites (Ancient Ones). *Ixtlilxochitl* is in exact agreement with this for he states that Hueman induced his people to agree to settled down in "the land . . . where the Quinametzin had lived for many years, and it had been many years since they had been destroyed and it was unsettled." His observation that this region was one where the enemy "very few times went that far" is in perfect accord with the Nephite data. The idea was for the Nephite faction to stay north of the key location—the isthmus—so that they would be out of the way of their bellicose kinsmen, the Lamanites.

The Book of Mormon dates this treaty at precisely 350 A. D. and *Ixtlilxochitl* does likewise, for he states that the people left their homeland in 339 A. D. and in this section (his Second Account) he states this treaty was made eleven years after "they had left their country"—that is, 350 A. D.

350 A. D.—361 A. D.

IXTLILXOCHITL:

...they [the Tultecs] left Tlapallan-conco and traveled another sixty leagues. And it is to be noted that history says that they traveled 12 days to each journey of new land that they discovered, from which it can be deduced that they traveled six leagues a day,[10] on acount of having with them so many people, women and children, all loaded. And besides, once started on a day's journey they did not stop until night made them stop to sleep and rest—and each day they made six leagues, rather more than less. And 12 days having past, according to the way I figure, they must have traveled about 70 leagues. They arrived at a good and fertile land which was called Hueyxallan [meaning "Great Sandy"[11]], where they stayed four years. There they likewise sowed and did what had been done before where they had been previously—preparing for what was ahead.[12] The discoverer was Ohuatzon, one of the five minor leaders or captains. And on the third year [at Great Sandy], which year was called Ce Calli, they counted a *tlalpilli*, which was a period of thirteen years, since they had left their country [339 A. D. plus 13 years equal 352 A. D.] and they stayed another year [to 353 A. D.]

And then, at that point, they left there [Great Sandy] and went travelling toward the rising of the sun,[13] and more than 100 leagues having been travelled, because they had travelled 20 days[14] uninterruptedly, they arrived in Xalixco, a land which was near the sea —and here they stayed 8 years [353 A. D. + 8 years = 361 A. D.], the discoverer being Xinhcohuatl, also one of the five minor captains. And they did what they had done in other places.

EXTRACTS—BOOK OF MORMON:

1. And it came to pass that the Lamanites did not come to battle again until ten years more had passed away. And behold, I had employed my people, the Nephites, in preparing their lands[XCI] and their arms against the time of battle.

2. And it came to pass that the Lord did say unto me: Cry unto this people —Repent ye, and come unto me, and be ye baptized, and build up again my church, and ye shall be spared.

3. And I did cry unto this people, but it was in vain; and they did not realize that it was the Lord that had spared them, and granted unto them a chance for repentance. And behold they did harden their hearts against the Lord their God.

4. And it came to pass that after this tenth year had passed away, making, in the whole, three hundred and sixty years from the coming of Christ, the king of the Lamanites sent an epistle to me, which gave unto me to know that they were preparing to come again to battle against us.

5. And it came to pass that I did cause my people that they should gather themselves together at the land Desolation, to a city which was in the borders, by the narrow pass which led into the land southward.

6. And there we did place our armies, that we might stop the armies of the Lamanites, that they might not get possession of any of our lands; therefore we did fortify against them with all our force.

7. And it came to pass that in the three hundred and sixty and first year the Lamanites did come down to the city of Desolation to battle against us; and it came to pass that in that year we did beat them, insomuch that they dia return to their own lands again.[XCI]

Mormon 3:1-7.

---

[10] A league is a measure of distance, varying from about 2.42 to 4.6 miles. At the lesser figure, the estimate is 14.52 miles per day of travel, a reasonable distance.[XCI]

[11] So translated by Mariano Veytia in his work, *Historia Antigua de Mexico* (1836). See Bancroft, *Native Races*, vol. 5, p. 212.

[13] The immigration was up the Gulf Coast to west and north.

[12] This infers that a great struggle or calamity was ahead, as proved to be the case.

[14] It has been pointed out that "a day's journey" is used in both *Ixtlilxochitl* and *The Book of Mormon*, on the one hand, and in the ancient Near East, on the other hand, as the measure of distance. This is as it should be if our primary accounts are authentic.

362 A. D.—378 A. D.

. . . they left [Xalixco at the end of the 8 years' period, i.e., in 361-362 A. D.] with all their people, in pursuit of their enterprise, travelling another 20 days, which must have been some 100 leagues, in different parts, as they had done in the other parts. They arrived at some islands and seashore that was called Chimalhuacan Atenco, where they stayed 5 years. And this was the first place where men began to have access with their wives, and here the women began to give birth to children. They had made a vow at the time they left their country [Huehuetlapallan—Bountiful-land] that in 23 years they were not to know their wives and those who broke this vow were to be cruelly punished. And thus the women began to give birth in these islands and seashore.[XCI] On the fourth year [at this place], which was [the year] Tochtli, there having been two tlalpilli [13 years per tlalpilli] of years, it was 27 years since they had left their country [339 A. D., the year they left their country + 27 years = 366 A. D.], which in our [European] count was the year 466 [Ixtlilxochitl missed here an even hundred years, in conformity with his earlier mistake—the date being, as shown, 366 A. D., according to his own figures] from the birth of Christ our Lord.

And the five years having passed, they began the journey, always travelling toward the rising of the sun, going up to Tochpan, where they stopped. And on this road they travelled 18 days, which must have been eighty leagues, and having arrived at this land, they stayed another 5 years [366 A. D.-371 A. D.], doing what they had done in the other parts, and they multiplied in number. The discoverer was Mexotzin, the last of the said five captains.

They took the road again through the same way of the orient. And they travelled 20 days, covering what must have been another hundred leagues, through different parts, and on the last day of them [i.e., of the twenty days of travel], they arrived in Quiyahuixtlan Anahuac,[15] which were lands of the coast and arms of the sea, [XCI, XCII] passing in

8. And in the three hundred and sixty and second year they did come down again to battle. And we did beat them again, and did slay a great number of them, and their dead were cast into the sea. . . .

1. And now it came to pass that in the three hundred and sixty and third year the Nephites did go up with their armies to battle against the Lamanites, out of the land Desolation.[XCI]

2. And it came to pass that the armies of the Nephites were driven back again to the land of Desolation. And while they were yet weary, a fresh army of the Lamanites did come upon them; and they had a sore battle, insomuch that the Lamanites did take possession of the city Desolation, and did slay many of the Nephites, and did take many prisoners.

3. And the remainder did flee and join the inhabitants of the city Teancum. Now the city Teancum lay in the borders by the seashore[XCI] and it was also near the city Desolation.

4. And it was because the armies of the Nephites went up unto the Lamanites that they began to be smitten; for were it not for that, the Lamanites could have had no power over them.

5. But, behold, the judgments of God will overtake the wicked; and it is by the wicked that the wicked are punished; for it is the wicked that stir up the hearts of the children of men unto bloodshed.

6. And it came to pass that the Lamanites did make preparations to come against the city Teancum.

7. And it came to pass in the three hundred and sixty and fourth year the Lamanites did come against the city of Teancum, that they might take possession of the city Teancum also.

8. And it came to pass that they were repulsed and driven back by the Nephites. And when the Nephites saw that they had driven the Lamanites they did again boast of their strength; and they went forth in their own might, and took possession again of the city Desolation.[XCI]

---

[15] Anahuac means "land of waters." Hubert H. Bancroft, Native Races (1875), vol. 2, pp. 87-88; J. M. Sjodahl, An Introduction to the Study of The Book of Mormon (1927), p. 367. The Anahuac or "land of waters" mentioned here by Ixtlilxochitl seems to be identical with the "land of many waters" of the Nephite record. The latter places the area by the seashore on the northerly side of the narrow pass. The Vera Cruz lake-stream area satisfies Ixtlilxochitl and The Book of Mormon.

canoes and boats from one part to another. And the time they stayed there was 6 years [371 A. D.–377 A. D.]. Always they suffered great hardships. The discoverer of them was Acapichtzin, one of the principal leaders.

[Extract from *Ixtlilxochitl,* taken from Chapter 30, relating to the practice of human sacrifice as later carried on by the Tultecas (Mayas) and Aztecs:]

Although it is true that this people were very great idolaters, they did not sacrifice men nor did they do the superstitious sacrifices that the Mexicans [Aztecs] later were accustomed to use, except (to) Tlaloc [the Mexican rain God]. They sacrificed to him five or six maidens of tender age, taking out their hearts and offering them to him, and their bodies they buried, and to Tonacatecuhtli, at certain times of the year they took the greatest evil-doer called Telimonanaiquian, which means meeting place of the stones, and there they placed him in the middle, so the two stones met at the corners and tore him to pieces there with the artifice (device) of these stones. Then they would bury him.

9. And now all these things had been done, and there had been thousands slain on both sides, both the Nephites and the Lamanites.

10. And it came to pass that the three hundred and sixty and sixth year had passed away, and the Lamanites came again upon the Nephites to battle; and yet the Nephites repented not of the evil they had done, but persisted in their wickedness continually.

11. And it is impossible for the tongue to describe, or for man to write a perfect description of the horrible scene of the blood and carnage which was among the people, both of the Nephites and of the Lamanites; and every heart was hardened, so that they delighted in the shedding of blood continually.

12. And there never had been so great wickedness among all the children of Lehi, nor even among all the house of Israel, according to the words of the Lord, as was among this people.

13. And it came to pass that the Lamanites did take possession of the city Desolation, and this because their number did exceed the number of the Nephites.

14. And they did also march forward against the city Teancum, and did drive the inhabitants forth out of her, and did take many prisoners both women and children, and did offer them up as sacrifices unto their idol gods.[XC]

15. And it came to pass that in the three hundred and sixty and seventh year, the Nephites being angry because the Lamanites had sacrificed their women and their children,[XC] that they did go against the Lamanites with exceeding great anger, insomuch that they did beat again the Lamanites, and drive them out of their lands.

Mormon 3:8; 4:1-15.

XC. Human Sacrifices

There is no mention in *The Book of Mormon* of the inhabitants of ancient America practicing human sacrifices until about the time of the destruction of the Nephites by the Lamanites during the fourth century A. D. It seems that during the 1,000 years' time that the Nephites lived on this continent they were free completely from the practice of human sacrifice, but at the time of the last great war between these two peoples, the Lamanites turned to offering sacrifices of their prisoners, as *The Book of Mormon* record indicates.

The foregoing quotations from both records are in perfect accord regarding this matter; therefore, we see that again there is a definite correlation between the teachings of *The Book of Mormon* and those of *Ixtlilxochitl* in regards to the practices of the ancient inhabitants of America.

EXTRACTS—BOOK OF MORMON:

16. And the Lamanites did not come again against the Nephites until the three hundred and seventy and fifth year.

17. And in this year they did come down against the Nephites with all their powers; and they were not numbered because of the greatness of their number.

18. And from this time forth did the Nephites gain no power over the Lamanites, but began to be swept off by them even as a dew before the sun.

19. And it came to pass that the Lamanites did come down against the city Desolation; and there was an exceedingly sore battle fought in the land Desolation,[xci] in the which they did beat the Nephites.

20. And they fled again from before them, and they came to the city Boaz; and there they did stand against the Lamanites with exceeding boldness, insomuch that the Lamanites did not beat them until they had come again the second time.

21. And when they had come the second time, the Nephites were driven and slaughtered with an exceedingly great slaughter; their women and their children were again sacrificed unto idols.

22. And it came to pass that the Nephites did again flee from before them, taking all the inhabitants with them, both in towns and villages.

Mormon 3:8; 4:1-22.

378 A. D.—386 A. D.

And then they took their road and travelled 18 days journey, which must have been some 80 leagues in different parts, until they arrived at Zacatlan. The discoverer was Chacatzin, likewise one of the two principal leaders. And the first year they arrived here was the

1. And it came to pass that I did go forth among the Nephites, and did repent of the oath which I had made that I would no more assist them; and they gave me command again of their armies, for they looked upon me as though I could deliver them from their afflictions.

year Ce Acatl [378 A. D.], at which year they counted a Xiuhtlalpilli [4 units of 13 years each, or 52 years] since they had begun their wars [and counting back 52 years from 378 A. D. we have 326 A. D. for the beginning of the wars] against their kindred nation.

And there was born at this time a son of his [of the leader, Chacatzin, no doubt] and because it was such a significant year they named the son after the land and he was called Zacapant-zin.XCII At that time it was 52 years since they had begun to have wars one with the other. And they stayed here 7 years [378 A. D.-385 A. D.]

[Extract from *Ixtlilxochitl* relating to an event which occurred nearly 500 years later, after Mormon's time:] Topil-tzin, seeing himself so oppressed and that there was no way out, asked for time, for it was a law among them that before a battle they would notify each other some years in advance so that on both sides they would be warned and prepared.XCI

2. But behold, I was without hope, for I knew the judgments of the Lord which should come upon them; for they repented not of their iniquities, but did struggle for their lives without calling upon that Being who created them.

3. And it came to pass that the Lamanites did come against us as we had fled to the city of Jordan; but behold, they were driven back that they did not take the city at that time.

4. And it came to pass that they came against us again, and we did maintain the city. And there were also other cities which were maintained by the Nephites, which strongholds did cut them off that they could not get into the country which lay before us, to destroy the inhabitants of our land.

5. But it came to pass that whatsoever lands we had passed by, and the inhabitants thereof were not gathered in, were destroyed by the Lamanites, and their towns, and villages, and cities were burned with fire; and thus three hundred and seventy and nine years passed away.

6. And it came to pass that in the three hundred and eightieth year the Lamanites did come again against us to battle, and we did stand against them boldly; but it was all in vain, for so great were their numbers that they did tread the people of the Nephites under their feet.

7. And it came to pass that we did again take to flight, and those whose flight was swifter than the Lamanites did escape, and those whose flight did not exceed the Lamanites were swept down and destroyed. . . .

Mormon 5:1-7.

1. And now I finish my record concerning the destruction of my people, the Nephites. And it came to pass that we did march forth against the Lamanites.

2. And I, Mormon, wrote an epistle unto the king of the Lamanites, and desired of him that he would grant unto us that we might gather together our people unto *the land of Cumorah, by a hill which was called Cumorah, and there we could give them battle.*XCI

3. And it came to pass that the king of the Lamanites did grant unto me the thing which I desired.

XCI. Law Regarding Notifying Enemy of Impending War

The foregoing extract from *Ixtlilxochitl* is merely one more incident wherein the Mexican historian corroborates *The Book of Mormon*. It should be recalled that earlier during Mormon's career he recorded the following:

> And it came to pass that the Lamanites did not come to battle again until ten years more had passed away. And behold, I had employed my people, the Nephites, in preparing their lands and their arms against the time of battle. . . .
>
> And it came to pass that after the tenth year had passed away, making, in the whole, three hundred and sixty years from the coming of Christ, the king of the Lamanites sent an epistle to me, which gave unto me to know that they were preparing to come again to battle against us.

Many other similar quotations could be cited from *The Book of Mormon* which definitely show that the ancient Americans did have, as *Ixtlilxochitl* pointed out, "a law among them that before a battle they would notify each other."

Although the event connected with Topiltzin occurred nearly 500 years after Mormon's death, it clearly shows that some of the same laws which were in effect throughout the thousand years' time of Nephite history persisted on from age to age among the descendants of those ancient Americans. Such a statement is strong evidence for the divine authenticity of *The Book of Mormon*.

EXTRACTS—BOOK OF MORMON:

4. *And it came to pass that we did march forth to the land of Cumorah and we did pitch our tents round about the hill Cumorah; and it was in a land of many waters, rivers and fountains;*[15] *and here we had hope to gain advantage over the Lamanites.*

5. *And when three hundred and eighty and four years had passed away, we had gathered in all the remainder of our people unto the land of Cumorah.*

XCII

7. And it came to pass that my people, with their wives and children, did now behold the armies of the La-manites marching towards them; and with that awful fear of death which fills the breasts of all the wicked, did they await to receive them.

8. And it came to pass that they came to battle against us, and every soul was filled with terror because of the greatness of their numbers.

9. And it came to pass that they did fall upon my people with the sword, and with the bow, and with the arrow, and with the ax, and with all manner of weapons of war.

10. And it came to pass that my men were hewn down, yea, even my ten thousand who were with me, and I fell wounded in the midst; and they passed by me that they did not put an end to my life.

11. And when they had gone through and hewn down all my people save it were twenty and four of us, (among whom was my son Moroni) and we having survived the dead of our people, did behold on the morrow, when the Lamanites had returned unto their camps, from the top of the hill Cumorah, [XCII] the ten thousand of my people who were hewn down, being led in the front by me.

12. And we also beheld the ten thousand of my people who were led by my son Moroni.

13. And behold, the ten thousand of Gidgiddonah had fallen, and he also in the midst.

14. And Lamah had fallen with his ten thousand; and Gilgal had fallen with his ten thousand; and Limnah had fallen with his ten thousand; and Joneam had fallen with his ten thousand; and Camenihah, and Moronihah, and Antionum, and Shiblom, and Shem, and Josh, had fallen with their ten thousand each.

15. And it came to pass that there were ten more who did fall by the sword, with their ten thousand each; yea, even all my people, save it were those twenty and four who were with me, and also a few who had escaped into the south countries, and a few who had dissented over unto the Lamanites, had fallen; and their flesh, and bones, and blood lay upon the face of the earth, being left by the hands of those who slew them to molder upon the land, and to crumble and to return to their mother earth.   Mormon 6:1-15.

XCII. Meaning of Cumorah

The name "Cumorah" appears in our script, in the very way in which the scribe wrote it down in 1829 when Joseph Smith sounded it out orally as he translated the ancient hieroglyphs of the "gold tablets." The scribe might just as well have written it out in our script as *Koomorah,* or perhaps as *Qowmahrah.*

The name "Cumorah" appears to be Hebrew. The Hebrew is written out in our script as *komaw* or *Qowmah,* meaning "height, high, tall."[16] The suffix at the end of Cum*orah* may be derived from the Hebrew term sounded out as *rah-*mah, the latter term also meaning "height, high."[17] As has been pointed out, the early Jaredites used the name *Ramah* in referring to the *Cumorah area.*[18] Thus, the two terms, *Ramah* and *Cumorah—*one a Jaredite term for the elevation and the other a Nephite term for the same place—are consistently descriptive of the place. In both instances the meaning is "height" or "high."

Careful study of the Nephite account discloses that Cumorah was a place of considerable elevation. The fact that it was prominent and conspicuous enough to bear a name in both Jaredite and Hebrew-Nephite geographical terminology suggests the idea of a prominent elevation. And as has been said, the very names *Ramah* and *Cumorah* mean "height." Also, the place was known to their historians for many hundreds of years, as has been shown. These factors suggest a prominent elevation. And more important, the details furnished by Mormon concerning events of the morning following the close of the Nephite-Lamanite battle seem to indicate that the elevation must have been quite high. Mormon wrote as follows:

> And when they had gone through and hewn down all my people save it were twenty and four of us [i.e., of the troops of the Nephites], (among whom was my son Moroni) and we having survived the dead of our people, did behold *on the morrow, when the Lamanites had returned unto their camps, from the top of the hill Cumorah,* the ten thousand of my people who were hewn down, being led in the front by me.[19]

He goes on to account for the 230,000 Nephite soldiers slain. He and his companions were able to look out over the great battle area where half a million lay dead—all from "the top of the hill Cumorah." They were able to take that strategic position under some cover, apparently, for they were not seen by the victorious enemy whose camps lay near by.

[16] James Strong, *Concordance of the Bible, Hebrew and Chaldee Dictionary,* words 6966-6967.
[17] Ibid., words 7215 and 7413; Funk and Wagnalls *New Standard Bible Dictionary* (1936 ed.), p. 760; J. M. Sjodahl, *An Introduction to the Study of The Book of Mormon* (1927), p. 317.
[18] *The Book of Mormon,* p. 469 (Mormon 6:6); p. 508 (Ether 15:11).
[19] Ibid., p. 470 (Mormon 6:11-15).

Another factor must be considered. Mormon and his companions made the ascent to the top of the elevation some time between the close of the battle and the next morning. It was such an elevation as could have been ascended by weary warriors overnight, or possibly on a single morning.

The question arises, if Ramah-Cumorah were an elevation of considerable height, as suggested, why then do *The Book of Mormon* writers refer to it as a "hill"? The interesting fact is that all mountains, regardless of size, are referred to as "hills" in *The Book of Mormon*.[20] The Hebrew term *"harar"* is translated "hill or mountain." It is the term used for referring to large elevations. The translators of the Old Testament have sometimes rendered the term "hill" and sometimes as "mountain."[21] Apparently Joseph Smith saw fit to render it "hill" in all instances where an elevation was referred to by name in the Nephite account. In doing so he was doing an excellent job of translating.

Thus, the expression found in the Nephite account, "hill Cumorah" would seem to refer to a mount or mountain of considerable prominence in the area where it was located. It is further recalled that it was near the "hill Shim."

XCIII. MAYA OLD EMPIRE BEGINS IN 320 A. D.-322 A. D.

(Era of Lamanite Dominance)

The year 320 A. D. was the beginning of a very important decade in ancient Middle America. As has been pointed out, according to *The Book of Mormon* the year 322 A. D. marked the beginning of sixty-four years of civil warfare. The seven tribes were again divided into two camps. The war began in Bountiful (ancient Seat of the Kingdom), according to both *Ixtlilxochitl* and *The Book of Mormon*. *Ixtlilxochitl's* sources apparently disregarded the initial outbreak of the war in 322 A. D. and the four years of temporary peace which followed— for according to his reckoning the war began in 326 A. D. (figuring back 52 years from 378 A. D.) In fact, 326 A. D. might, with good reason, be regarded as the year the wars began, accord-

---

[20] *The Book of Mormon*, pp. 147-148, 156 (Mosiah 7:5, 16; 11:13); pp. 196, 199, 303 (Alma 1:15; 2:15, 17; 43:34-35); pp. 460, 467, 469-470 (Mormon 1:3; 4:23; 6:2, 4, 6, 11); pp. 490, 493, 507, 508 (Ether 7:9; 9:3; 14:28: 15:10).

[21] James Strong, *op. cit.*, words 2022 and 2042. Also his main Concordance under "hill" and "mountain."

ing to both of our accounts. The fact that the account given by
Ixtlilxochitl continuously sustains the history as reported in *The
Book of Mormon* is very significant.

For over 500 years immediately preceding 320 A. D., the
lands of Bountiful and Zarahemla had been the heart of the
Nephite-Tultec kingdom. According to the Nephite account,
outposts had been established during that period as far east as
the East Sea.[22]

The entire picture changed abruptly. The Lamanites, whose
center had been to the south in the highlands of Nephi, except
for the period of unity following the ministry of Christ, suddenly became the dominant power. Thereupon the Nephites were
expelled from the Bountiful-land region and the enemy-kindred,
the Lamanites, moved in and in due time took over the land.

Despite the fact that there had been a period of spiritual,
political, commercial and social unity between the Lamanites and
the Nephites, for almost 300 years following the ministry of
Christ-Quetzalcoatl, there were still wide differences between the
two peoples. The Nephites were essentially more refined and
more scholarly. Language differences, no doubt, persisted, including differences in both scripts and tongues. It is quite possible that
there were also differences between the highlanders and the low-
landers in such arts as ceramics, sculpturing, and architecture.
Therefore, one would expect the substitution of the Lamanite
domination in place and stead of Nephite-Mulekite supremacy
to be reflected in the archæological discoveries made in the region.
Such is the case.

The "Maya Old Empire" dates from exactly this period—
almost to the year! The "Mayas" or Lamanites succeeded the
Nephite-early-Nahuas, otherwise known as the Tultecs or People-
of-Bountiful-land, in the occupancy and control of the area between Tehuantepec on the west and the Caribbean Sea on the
east. The Maya Old Empire, the locale of which was in the very
region in question, dates from 320 A. D. Typical "Maya" high-
land-Lamanite hieroglyphic-inscribed monuments began to appear
in 320 A. D. in the area from which the Tultec-Nephite people
were expelled. The famous Leyden Plate, found at Puerto Barrios,
Guatemala, in 1864, and also other monuments which have already

<hr>

[22] *The Book of Mormon*, p. 321 (Alma 50:7-9); J. A. and J. N. Washburn, *Book of Mormon Geography* (1939), pp. 150-161.

been discussed, bear dates as early as 320 A. D., or the date of the beginning of the Maya Old Empire. [22a] See figure 22, page 172.

Maya history has been reconstructed in considerable detail and with accuracy from the beginning of the Old Empire until the present date. The archæologists are entitled to high praise for their excellent work in that respect. In doing the job, both documentary and archæological sources have been utilized and harmonized.

Not only do we find the dated stone monuments of the Maya-Lamanites appearing, but we find a great change occurring in the ceramics of the area at that time. The "pre-Maya" Chicanel ceramic phase (as it is called) ends, and the Maya Old Empire pottery, the Tzakol ceramic phase, begins. The terms "Chicanel" and "Tzakol" are technical terms used by the ceramic specialists to simplify identification of the two types.

Architecture too underwent important changes following the close of the Nephite period. Although *Ixtlilxochitl* tells nothing of the architectural practices of the early Tultecs, some details are given in *The Book of Mormon*. It is made clear in the Nephite account that virtually all buildings in greater Bountiful-land were made of wood during the era of Nephite dominance from 200 B. C. to 322 A. D. These ancient Americans were skilled in wood craftsmanship. They were capable of making ships and boats that would accommodate large numbers of people. They also erected fortresses and walls of wood. In fact, their record states that they engaged in "fine workmanship of wood" . . . doing "fine work of wood.[23] Perhaps the most enlightening statement in *The Book of Mormon* on the building materials used by the Nephites is the one in which the scarcity of timber in the northern colonies is discussed. The Jaredites, who had previously occupied the region had stripped off the timber in the land northward and it had not yet had time to become reforested as of 46 B. C. when the colonists were arriving there from Bountiful-land in large numbers. The inferences are strong to the effect that the people had been accustomed to doing their building in wood. The lack of wood was most disturbing to them and they went so far as to import it by boat from Bountiful-land. These colonists found it necessary to learn skills in

---

working with cement and stone—skills they apparently lacked on departing from Bountiful-land where wood had been the building material in common use. To quote the ancient Nephite record:

And there being but little timber upon the face of the land [the area colonized northward on the Gulf Coast above Tehuantepec], nevertheless the people who went forth became exceeding expert in the working of cement; therefore they did build houses of cement in the which they did dwell. . . . and they did suffer whatsoever tree should spring up upon the face of the land that it should grow up, that in time they might have timber—and it came to pass as timber was exceeding scarce in the land northward, they did send forth much by way of shipping. And thus they did enable the people in the land northward that they might build many cities, both of wood and of cement.[24]

In view of the fact that wood was the primary building material used in greater Bountiful-land during the period of Nephite-Tultec dominance (200 B. C.-320 A. D.), the dirt archæologists have found nothing in the way of impressive stone buildings in the area between Tehuantepec and the Caribbean which dates in that early period. The Nephite record indicates cities and monuments of wood were built prior to 320 A. D. The record is confirmed by the findings of archæologists. Again we turn to Morley:

Chicanel [Nephite-Tultec period] vessels are associated with the earliest masonry constructions at Uaxactun. These constructions were not buildings proper—only low foundation platforms and pyramids upon which perishable houses of saplings and thatch were probably built.[25]

Elsewhere the same expert says:

During the six to seven centuries which elapsed between the invention of Maya chronology on the one hand and the earliest known contemporaneous stone records (the Leyden Plate at Tikal [320 A. D.] and Stela 9 at Uaxactun [328 A. D.]) on the other, the Maya monuments were, in all probability, carved out of wood. . . .

With the first stone records at Tikal and Uaxactun in the early part of the fourth century of the Christian era, the Maya Old Empire may be considered as having formally gotten under way. . . . In those remote times, toward the end of Baktun 8 of Maya chronology (the fourth century of the Christian era), they were still groping clumsily, timidly feeling their way in the sculpture of stone, their hands and stone chisels [sic] as yet unfamiliar with the new medium, so much more difficult to carve than wood. . . .[26]

[24] Ibid., p. 364 (Helaman 3:7-11).
[25] Morley, op. cit., p. 387.
[26] Ibid., pp. 47-49. See LIX herein.

The earliest example of Maya stone architecture that has survived [and yet been discovered] is the stucco-covered under-pyramid, E-VII-sub, at Uaxactun (Fig. 41, p. 270), and the reason for its remarkable state of preservation is simple: Very shortly after it was finished, perhaps some time during the second century of the Christian era, it was completely covered by a rough-rubble, masonry pyramid, E-VII. . . . The top of this later, stucco-covered pyramid was so small that it obviously could never have supported a stone building; there was not enough space for one on its summit. Furthermore, when the rubble-heating of the later E-VII which had completely encased and preserved E-VII-sub was removed, it was found that this earlier pyramid also had never supported a stone superstructure, because in the lime-plaster flooring of the summit of E-VII-sub four filled-in postholes forming a rectangle were found; these undoubtedly had originally held the corner posts of a thatch-and-sapling superstructure. . . . It is in fact, barring the low walls of the early Chicanel ceramic period just mentioned, the oldest Maya stone construction that has come down to us and probably dates from the second century of the Christian era. . . . With the introduction of the stone-stela complex and Tzakol pottery at Uaxactun about 8.14.0.0.0 (317), we meet the earliest example of corbeled-stone roof-vaulting in the Maya area.[27]

In the light of the foregoing, it is readily seen why, even if the original colonists of 600 B. C. brought with them from the Near East a knowledge of the keystone arch, such knowledge would have been lost for lack of use. The absence of the true arch, as an argument against migrations from the Near East to Middle America, loses its force in that regard.

Thus, the Nephite account is in close accord with archæological findings on the matter of architecture in the greater Bountiful-land area during the Nephite-Tultec era of dominance from 200 B. C.-320 A. D. Credit for the spectacular stone temples and palaces discovered in the area must go to the Maya-Lamanites who occupied and controlled the region for many centuries following the banishment of the accomplished and heroic original Bountiful-land people. Present-day explorers vie with each other for the honors that go with the discovery of each new Maya find. Emphasis on the spectacular standing stone ruins is probably one of the major factors explaining the lack of archæological data on the earlier and more important Nephite-Tultec era.

It is anticipated that subsequent to the publication of this book much important data will be uncovered by archæologists in the area between the Isthmus of Tehuantepec and the Usumacinta River. It will be interesting to see whether future dis-

---

[27] *Ibid.*, pp. 344-345.

coveries will further corroborate *Ixtlilxochitl* and *The Book of Mormon*. Existing facts clearly support these two accounts in their claims that beginning about 320 A. D. greater Bountiful-land below the Isthmus was abandoned by the cultured pre-Maya Nephite-Tultec people in favor of the victorious "Mayas" or Lamanites.

SUMMARY STATEMENT

Ixtlilxochitl and *The Book of Mormon* are in very close agreement concerning the highlights of the history of the people of Bountiful-Zarahemla from 320 A. D. to 385 A. D.

Ixtlilxochitl states that as of 378 A. D. "it had been fifty-two years since they began their wars"; and the Nephite record outlines in detail those many years of warfare. What brought on the wars? Both histories agree that it was internal rebellion, civil war, an attempt to "usurp the kingdom," to use *Ixtlilxochitl's* words. The Nephite account shows one attempt after another to usurp power and government. The fight was with "the fierce kindred," according to both accounts.

Both fix the first general exodus of the defensive Tultecas at about 339 A. D. Both place the Great Treaty of Hueman-Mormon—historian-prophet and the captains of the Seven Tribes at exactly 350 A. D. There is remarkable accord concerning the terms of the Treaty, *Ixtlilxochitl* and *The Book of Mormon* agreeing with each other that the exiled faction was allotted that territory formerly inhabited by the "Ancient Ones" (Jaredites-Quinametzin).

The lands occupied by the exiled artisans from 350 A. D. 385 A. D. were northerly from the ancient Seat of the Kingdom, they were near the sea, and they were characterized as "lands of many waters." *The Book of Mormon* mentions a "land of many waters, rivers and fountains"; whereas *Ixtlilxochitl* speaks of *Anahuca*, "land of waters," which, he says, "were lands of the coast and arms of the sea."

Ixtlilxochitl and *The Book of Mormon* each refer to the great hardships suffered by the people during the period. In fact, the Nephite record designates this era as the one in which their fierce kindred, the Lamanite faction, introduced human sacrifice. That human sacrifice was practiced by the ancient Tultecas who survived this particular era is too well established to require further comment.

Ixtlilxochitl indicates that the long war epoch came to an end some time around 378 A. D. He makes no special mention of a terrible last battle between the opposing Tultec factions. As has been pointed out, the Nephite record gives some of the details, including the claim that twenty-three captains died, each with ten thousand troops which also perished, for total military casualties of 230,000 on the Nephite side alone. This indicates a considerable population as having been involved in the great war and exodus from Bountiful-land—a point which finds specific confirmation from *Ixtlilxochitl*. At the very outset of his account concerning the exodus he says: "They were exiled and had some wars, being driven out of . . . the region of Huehuetlapallan, their country, with all their allies and families, men as well as women. *There was a great number of them . . .*"

The Maya Old Empire dates from the exodus of the Nephite faction from ancient Bountiful-land. Thus, the ancient Mayas of the immediate post-*Book-of-Mormon* era appear to be none other than the victorious Lamanites.

Chapter 28

THE TULTECS AFTER 385 A. D.

INTRODUCTORY STATEMENT

Many important events occurred and numerous great things were accomplished in Middle America after the battle at Cumorah in 385 A. D. and before the coming of the Europeans. The Lamanite-Maya empire was just getting a good start by 400 A. D. Although the year 385 marked the terminus of the Nephite priesthood government, it by no means saw the end of all culture and material progress. That a great number of the Lamanites survived 385-386 A. D. is clearly indicated by both *Ixtlilxochitl* and the Nephite record. *Ixtlilxochitl* simply continues his story of the "Tultecas." Also, Moroni, son of Mormon, and a certain number of other Nephites, survived the great battle; Moroni lived on for thirty-six years until 421 A. D. Writing during the year 400 A. D., fifteen years after the Cumorah battle, he made reference to survivors as follows:

> Now I, Moroni . . . had supposed not to have written more, but I have not as yet perished; and I make not myself known to the Lamanites lest they should destroy me. For behold, their wars are exceedingly fierce among themselves; and because of their hatred *they put to death every Nephite that will not deny the Christ.*[1]

The records do not indicate the number of Nephites that survived; however, the prior pendulum-like oscillations in the faith of the Nephites would indicate that the number could have been considerable. Large numbers may have disavowed Christ and been spared. Others, faithful to Christ, may have done as Moroni did. He said to himself: "And I, Moroni, will not deny the Christ; wherefore, I wander whithersoever I can for the safety of mine own life."[2] Also, there was the isolated colony of Itzas (Nephites), worshippers of Christ, who had separated

---

[1] *The Book of Mormon*, p. 510, verses 1-2 (Moroni 1:1-2).
[2] *Ibid.*, verse 3. Dr. Sidney B. Sperry wrote an interesting article, "Moroni the Lonely," which appeared in *The Improvement Era*, February, 1944, p. 83ff.

from the main body of the Nephites prior to the last great wars and settled in northern Yucatan. The existence of that colony may have been unknown to the Nephite historians, Mormon and Moroni. The Itzas actually survived, their religion becoming somewhat degenerated, until long after the coming of the Europeans.

Ixtlilxochitl continues his account of 500 years of Tultec history after the end of the Nephite account. He tells what happened to the victorious Tultecas and to those Nephites who joined them. Many settled in the new Tula in Mexico which is now known as Teotihuacan. There, beginning about 500 A. D., they built a great metropolis of temple towers, palaces and shrines. Their kindred who remained behind in ancient Bountiful-Zarahemla and vicinity caused many cities to be built and a unique culture known as the Maya Old Empire to flower. That story is summarized in Chapter 33.

Hereafter Ixtlilxochitl carries on alone, The Book of Mormon relating little more than the personal experiences of Moroni, son of Mormon, for the period from 385 A. D. until Moroni hid up the sacred record in 421 A. D.

Since we have reached the end of The Book of Mormon account, and since the Works of Ixtlilxochitl heretofore have never (to the knowledge of the writers) been published in English, and also for the sake of those people interested in reading the story of the descendants of the ancient Tultecas down to the Spanish Conquest, the writers are presenting further data from Ixtlilxochitl in each of the two columns without including comments on his presentation, in Chapters 28 to 31. Our discussion will come in Chapters 32 and 33.

As one reads the history of the Tultecas from this point on, he readily observes that the customs, beliefs, and practices of those people were not on as high a level as they had been up to this point. The reason is obvious. The Nephite nation had been destroyed, and there were no more holy prophets of God to teach and lead the people; therefore, an apostasy from the true religion had occurred. However, as has been noted, numerous beliefs and practices resembling the true teachings of Jesus Christ (but in an adulterated form) persisted among the descendants of the Nephites and Lamanites down to the coming of the Spaniards. The Christian Padres expressed great surprise to find so many beliefs held by the Indians resembling Christian doctrine and they speculated regarding the origin of those beliefs.

Before proceeding directly with the *Works of Ixtlilxochitl,* the fact should be mentioned that all places referred to by the ancient historian were located in Mexico.

IXTLILXOCHITL:

They [the Tultecs] traveled another eighteen days [from Zacatlan], which must have been some eighty leagues, when they arrived in *Tutzapan,* and they stayed six years in this land. And on the last of the six (years), which was the year of *ce Tecpatl,* a son of his was born, and because it was such a noted year, and because a *Xiuhtlalpilli* had gone by, which are fifty-two years, since they had left their country, he gave him the name of the land, calling the son Totzapantzin.

And then, the six years having passed, they began to travel, and they traveled twenty-eight days through different parts, at *Tepetla,* which must have been some hundred and forty leagues. They stayed here seven years [402 A. D. to 409 A. D.], the discoverer being *Cohua-tzon,* which was the second time.

And the seven years having passed, they began their road, and they travelled eighteen days, which must have been some eighty leagues, until arriving at *Mazatepec,* the discoverer being *Xuihco-huatl.* And here they stayed eight years [409 A. D. to 417 A. D.] and the sixth, which was *ce Calli,* they counted sixty-six since they had left their country [sixty-six years from 339 A. D. is 415 A. D.].

And eight years having passed, they began to travel, and they travelled another eighteen days, which must have been another eighty leagues, until they arrived at *Xiuhcohuac,* where they stayed another eight years [417 A. D. to 425 A. D.], the discoverer being *Tlapal-metzin,* which was the second time.

And then they began to travel, and they travelled twenty days, which must have been some hundred leagues, in different parts, until arriving at Iztachue-xuca, which is toward the North, where they stayed twenty-six years [425 A. D.-451 A. D.], the discoverer being *Met-zotzin.* And the third year, which was *ce Tochtli,* that they were in this land, they counted seventy-eight years since they had left their country; thirteen years hence, which was *ce Acatl,* they counted ninety-one years since they had left their country.

The twenty-six years having passed, they returned to *Tulantzinco* and they travelled eighteen days through different parts, which must have been some eighty leagues until arriving at the said place of *Tulantzinco,* where they made a very large house of lumber (boards) in which there was room for all the people; and they stayed here almost sixteen years [451 A. D.-467 A. D.], and on the third year they counted an *age* which are hundred and four years, which are two *Xiuhtlalpilli,* since they had left their country, being the year of *ce Tec-patl,* which according to our count was in the year of 543 [443 A. D. is probably correct] of the Incarnation (having suffered very great hardships, and the women giving birth on the roads), the discoverer being Acamapichtzin. This was the third time he discovered new land. And further on we shall give an account of their lives and permanence in this land. In all parts where they arrived they left people so that they may settle these lands, as I have said at the beginning.

Chapter 29

FOUNDING OF TULA (TEOTIHUACAN) AND ITS KINGS

IXTLILXOCHITL:

"Concerning the founding of Tula (Teotihuacan) and the kings it had"

In the year of *ce Calli* (which is a figure of a house, sign of planet which means prosperity and prosperous and abundant power, lucky in all things) the Tultecas, or rather the *Huetlapalanecas,* arrived in Tula, a city which was the seat of their kingdoms and power for many years, and according to our count, it was in the year 556 [443 A. D., as per preceding section] of the Incarnation, . . . And having arrived at this place and land, the Tultecas thought it very good, and especially *Huematzin,* the astrologer that led them, who was already more than a *hundred and eighty* years old [i.e., it was 180 years since the time of Huematzin-Mormon in 363 A. D.]. And seeing the location so good for their purpose and the temperateness of the land, and the other things which he found in his astrology to be good for a city, they began to build it. And for *six years*[1] they were building houses, temples, and other things they used and were accustomed to. And they agreed to swear one of the principal men as king and lord of all of them; and seeing that when they were in *Xiuhcohuac*[2] and *Huexutla* (which is a place of *Panuco* and *Tampico*) the Chichimecas, their competitors, were very near, and that the Chichimecas had bothered them at these two places, and seeing that they had them so near and fearing that they would some day rise against them and take away their lands, town, and places, they agreed to go see the lord who at the time was (ruler) of the Chichimecas, and ask him to give them a son or a very near relative of his lineage so that they would swear him as their king and lord. And with this they were also to ask him upon his word that neither he nor his descendants at any time would bother them. This agreement and opinion was considered good, for the old astrologer Huemac gave [had previously prophesied] it. Besides, he had found in his astrology that in times to come this land was to be settled by the Chichimecas.

And thus, with this determination, some of the principal men, with presents of gold and other things, went to see the lord of the Chichimecas, who, seeing what the Tultecas asked of him, was very pleased and considered it all as good. He gave his word that neither he nor his descendants would bother them; and he gave them a young son he had, whom they brought with great rejoicings all the way to Tula. And it was already the year of *chicome Acatl,* and ours of *five hundred and sixty-two* [the writers correct this to 450 A. D.]; and this same year they swore him as their king and married him to a lady, daughter of the principal Tultecas, who was Acapitzin. And they called him *Chalchiuhtlanetzin,* which means precious

---

[1] Alfred Chavero comments: "In this account *Ixtlilxochitl* sets down the founding of the city in the year 566, and the election of the first monarch six years later, and not seven as he had previously said; so that that event must have taken place in the year 562, while before he had set it as of 510. As the difference is fifty-two years, that is, a Tolteca century, it is evident that the mistake is due to not computing well the number of centuries. Anyway, it is clearly seen that the chronology of the author is mistaken. For that reason I think it appropriate (wise) to continue correcting it in notes, according to the chronology I follow in the mentioned 'Appendix to Father Durar' and in my 'Ancient History'." We shall continue to correct *Ixtlilxochitl* in brackets.

[2] *Huichco huac,* as per Chavero's note.

stone that illuminates, meaning to say that with their new lord they were illuminated (enlightened) and were rested, and were free from worry and persecutions.

And they ordered that their kings were not to reign more than *fifty-two years,* and that when these years passed, if he were still alive, his son, the legitimate successor, was to take charge of the government; and that if he died before the fifty-two years, the republic was to govern until finishing out the term. And thus, this *Chalchiuhtlanetzin* governed for *fifty-two years,* and almost on the last of them (the years) [450 A. D. to 502 A. D.] he died, and he was buried in the principal temple with his royal insignias, different from the way it was later done, which was to burn the bodies, as shall be related in its place.

After his death, his legitimate successor, *Ixtlilcuechahuac,* known also as *Izacatecatl,* succeeded him in the same year, and according to our count it was in the year *six hundred and fourteen* [correction—502 A. D.]. . . . And he governed another fifty-two years [about 502 A. D.-554 A. D.] like his father. At *thirty-two years* of his government, which was in *ce Tecpatl,* the Tultecas counted *two hundred and sixty years* since they had left their country [339

A. D. when they left their country + 260 = 599 A. D. By our reckoning, 502 + 32 = 534 A. D.].

After the death of this lord, his son, legitimate successor, called *Huetzin,* succeeded him in the same year his father died, which was *six Tochtli,* and ours of *six hundred and sixty-six* of the Incarnation.
* * *3

Turning to our history, king *Huetzin,* who was the successor, as we have already said, governed the *fifty-two years* [554 A. D.-606 A. D.], and on the last of them (years) he died, which was the year of *six Tochtli,* and in our count *seven hundred and seventy-eight* [corrected to 606 A. D.] . . .

He (Huetzin) was succeeded by his legitimate son called *Totepeuh,* who governed his kingdoms and possessions in quiet peace as his last parents and ancestors had done, for *fifty-two years* [606 A. D.-658 A. D.]. And on the last he died, being succeeded by his son *Nacaxoc* in the year *five Calli,* which in our count was *seven hundred and seventy* [corrected to 658 A. D.] of the Incarnation, . . . And this *Nacaxoc* governed another fifty-two years [658 A. D.-710 A. D.] with the same order as his ancestors.

---

3 The discussion of Huematzin or Hueman which *Ixtlilxochitl* presented at this point is found in this book in Chapter 36.

Chapter 30

LIFE OF TULTEC KINGS

IXTLILXOCHITL:

"Concerning the life of the Tultec kings"

The *fifty-two years* [658 A. D.-710 A. D.] having passed, king *Nacaxoc* died [i.e., he died some time after completing his fifty-two years' reign] and was succeeded by his son *Mitl*, which was in the year of *five Calli;* and this time adjusted to ours, it was in the year of *eight hundred and twenty-two* [corrected to 710 A. D.] . . . This *Mitl* governed *fifty-nine years* [710 A. D.-769 A. D.] and broke the ancient order (commandment) of the Tultecas of reigning *fifty-two years.* He was a man of great government, made great temples, and other memorable things, and he built among the temples he made, one of the Frog, goddess of water, a very beautiful temple. All its ornaments were of gold and precious stones and the frog was of emerald. The Spaniards who came to this land got to see, and they gave a good account of it (the temple of the Frog).

Almost at the end of the *fifty-nine years,* this lord died, which was in the year of *eleven Acatl,* and in ours of *eight hundred and eighty* [corrected to 769 A. D.] . . . And after his death, his wife, Queen *Xiutlaltzin,* succeeded in the kingdom. She reigned *four years* [769 A. D.-773 A. D.] and died. Her son, legitimate successor, called *Tecpancaltzin,* inherited the kingdom.

And before going on, I want to make an account of the state in which the Tulteca nations were. At this time, for almost a thousand leagues[1] they had settled and built towns and cities, villages and places. Among the most famous was *Teotihucuan,* which means "City and place of God." This city was greater and more powerful than that of Tula, because it was the sanctuary of the Tultecs: it had very large and tall temples, the most terrible (immense) buildings in the world, which even today appear in their ruins, and other great curiosities. In *Toluca* they made some palaces all of stone carved in figures and personages where were all their calamities, wars and persecutions, triumphs, good happenings and prosperities. In *Cuahnahuac,* another city with a famous ancient work, was a palace all built (carved) of large stones, of hewn stones without mud, nor mortar (mixture), nor beams, nor any lumber, but only some large stones placed (stuck) one against the other,[2] and they also founded other great cities like *Cholula,* and *Xalixco, Yototepec* of the South Sea,[3] [Pacific side] and many other cities that were to the South and toward the Orient, *which are now all destroyed,* although in their ruins they show that they were the greatest cities in the world.

---

[1] Alfred Chavero comments at this point as follows: "The little knowledge that the first chroniclers had of the ethnographic characteristics of the ancient people of our territory, made them, sometimes, give their dominions a much greater extension than they really had, and at other times, attribute to them personages and cities belonging to races clearly extinct. Not a thousand leagues, to be sure, did the Toltec nationality embrace. In my 'Appendix to Father Duran' I set its boundaries, in truth, of no great extension, in the strip of land between Tula and Cholula, bounded on the Orient by the Cuexteca and on the East by our Valley."

[2] Chavero suggests that Cuahnahuac is the ruin in Mexico now known as *Xochicalco.*

[3] *The Book of Mormon* and the *Works of Ixtlilxochitl* seem to correlate well in regards to geography. In the *Works of Ixtlilxochitl* reference is made to a South Sea. The Nephite record also makes mention of an *East sea,* a *West sea,* and a *North sea.* For example the following is quoted from *The Book of Mormon:* "And it came to pass that they did multiply and spread, and did go forth from the land southward to the land northward, and did spread insomuch that they began to cover the face of the whole earth, from the sea south to the sea north, from the sea west to the sea east." (Helaman 3:8, p. 364.)

377

The Idols that the Tultecas had of old were the most principal, which were *Tonacatecuhtli*, and today his personage is in the highest Cu (temple of this people), which is dedicated to the Sun. The name means God of sustenance. His wife they regarded as a goddess. They say that this god of sustenance was a figure of the sun, and his wife of the moon. And they had other gods which they called the brothers (and sisters) of the sun and of the moon, *of which there are still pieces in the Cus* (temples). And they had another idol which they have worshipped up to the time the Spaniards came. It was *Tlaloc*. Tlaloc temple was in the highest sierra of *Texcuco*, and pieces of it are still there. And they say that this idol was god of stormy rains, and that he was a very brave king of the *Quinametzin* (who are the Philistines). He did great things and for that reason they set him up as a god. These false gods were the oldest ones and the main ones of more than *two thousand years* of the Tultec history. In addition *Texcatiputla* and *Huitzilopuchtli* were also gods who were over certain very brave gentlemen. It is even found that *Texcatiputla* was a great necromancer (conjurer, magician) and was a great cause of the persecutions of the Tultecas.

Although it is true that this people were very great idolaters, they did not sacrifice men nor did they do the superstitious sacrifices that the Mexicans later were accustomed to use, except (to) *Tlaloc*.[4] They sacrificed to him five or six maidens of tender age,[XCIV] taking out their hearts and offering them to him, and their bodies they buried, and to Tonacatecuhtli, at certain times of the year they took the greatest evil-doer who had committed great crimes, to a certain artifice (device) which they called *Telimonanaiquian*, which means *meeting place of the stones*, and there they placed him in the middle, so that two stones met at the corners and tore him to pieces there with the artifice (device) of these stones. Then they would bury him.

In the feasts they had, all the chiefs would get together. They had a dance that would last nearly all day, and they went through (or did) certain ceremonies which, as I have already related, were not as abominable as those the Mexicans performed when the Marquis del Valle [Cortez] came, and the entrance of Evangelical Law (gospel Rule) into the land . . .

---

[4] Tlaloc was the Mexican name for the Rain-God aspect of Deity.

Chapter 31

TULTEC KINGS AND THEIR DESTRUCTION

IXTLILXOCHITL:

"Concerning the Tultec kings and their destruction"

Tecpancaltzin having inherited the lordship of the Tultecas, after he had governed ten years [773 A. D.-783 A. D.], there came to his palace a maiden, very beautiful, who had come with her parents to bring a certain present for him. And they even say that it is found in history that it was *black honey of maguey* and some *chiancacas*, sugar of this honey. They were the first inventors of this delicacy; and as it was a new thing, they brought it as a gift to the king. These gentlemen (people) being of noble blood and of his own lineage, the king was very pleased to see them and granted them many favors. He thought a great deal of this present, and on account of her beauty, he grew very fond of this maiden who was called *Xochitl* which means *rose flower*. He ordered them to favor him again with this present and he ordered that their daughter bring it alone with some woman servant. And the parents, not thinking of what might happen, were very pleased, and gave him their word that they would do so.

And after a few days the maiden came to the palace with a woman servant loaded with *honey, chiancaca,* and other small gifts newly invented, or rather maguey preserves. As soon as she arrived, they notified the king that the maiden, daughter of the gentleman who invented the maguey honey, called Papantzin, was there. The king was very pleased and ordered her to be brought (admitted) alone with the gift she brought. And the servant, who was an old nurse of hers, was ordered to sit in the room and the king ordered that they give her many mantles and gold, and go entertain her until it was time for her to return with her mistress. And the servants did so, bringing in the maiden alone, and rendering all kinds of service and entertainment to the servant woman, according as the king commanded it.

The king, having seen the gift of the maiden *Xuchitl* and her parents, was very pleased, and told her how he had been fond of her for days, begging her to accede to his wishes, that he would give her his word to do many favors to her parents and to her. Consequently, they were quite a while in the rendezvous until the maiden, seeing there was no way out of it, had to do what the king ordered her to do. His low (infamous) desires having been satisfied, he had her taken to a small place outside the city, placing many guards there. And he sent word to her parents that he had given her to certain ladies to be instructed (taught), because he wanted to marry her to a king, neighbor of his, as a reward for the present she had brought him. He told her parents not to be sad, and to consider her as if she were at their home; and with this he granted them many favors and gave them certain towns and vassals so that they would be lords over the inhabitants and their descendants. Her parents, although they were sorry about it, pretended (not to be), for, as it is said, where there is strength, right is lost.

And the king went often to see the lady *Xuchitl*, his mistress, who was in a very strong, small place, on a hill called *palpan*. She was waited on and feasted to be sure, as something belonging to the king, the Tulteca monarch. In a very short time she became pregnant and gave birth to a son whom his father [King Tepancaltzin] named *Meconetzin*, which means *child of the maguey*, in memory of the invention and virtues of the maguey. The child was born in

379

the year of *ce Acatl*, which according to our count was that of *nine hundred* [this date should be corrected, for according to the count of the years, the king met Xuchitl about 783 A. D.]. . . . This child had nearly all the signs that astronomer *Hueman* said the Tulteca king was to have, in whose time and government the Tultecas were to be destroyed.

The parents of the maiden *Xuchitl*, for they considered her as a maiden, seeing that it was almost three years since they had seen their daughter, were very, very sorry; and they always tried to find out where she might be. Since the city of Tula was so large and there were so many houses of lords (gentlemen), this time (period) of three years passed by without success on their part. Almost at the end of the third year they found out that the king had her in a certain place with many guards, at a place called *Palpan*, as I have already stated, and how no person could see her. The king had ordered particularly that no relative be allowed to enter the place.

And this gentleman (the father) seeing the command of the king, was very worried and sad, and looked for a way to be able to enter without being recognized. Not finding any way, he disguised himself—dressing himself as a farmer, pretending (feigning) he had gone to the city to sell certain things. Since it seemed to the guards he was a simpleton, they let him enter, he having pretended that he wanted to see that place. He gave the guards certain things so that they would let him enter, and thus they gave him permission and he entered looking in all directions.

And entering through some gardens he found his daughter, who held the child in her arms. As he recognized her, he was overjoyed with tenderness on seeing his daughter, and asked her whether the king had put her in that place for her to play with children— not knowing that it was his grandson. The daughter, although with shame, then related to her father all that had happened with the king, and he was very sad. However, he let it be (tolerated it) because it was something that touched his honor.

Then taking leave of his daughter, he started back. The next day he went to see the king, complaining of the affront he had done him. The king consoled him and told him not to be sad—

that since it was a thing of the king, he didn't suffer any affront, and besides, the child would be his heir, for he did not want (wish) to marry any lady. And many other things were said to Xuchitl's father by the king and he granted favors to him and to his relatives. And the king ordered that whenever he and his wife and relatives wanted to see Xuchitl they could do so, provided she did not go out of that place. The king trusted his guards because they were persons of his devotion. And the king did all these things, because they lived at that time with such uprightness, that the Tultecas his vassals considered any small chance or fault on the part of the king as a great evil. And with this, good old *Papantzin* returned to his house somewhat consoled, consoling his wife and relatives: And from then on they often went to see the shut-up daughter—as often as they wanted to.

King *Tecpancaltzin* having governed fifty-two years [773 A. D.-825 A. D.] and, as he was still alive, he decided to have Meconetzin, his natural (illegitimate) son sworn king. His son, known also by the name of Topiltzin, was already a man over forty years old, and very virtuous and a great wise man. And in order that the Tultecas would not invent any novelty (there were three gentlemen (lords) of his lineage very near heirs, who were worthy on account of their great valor and virtue and who were in his kingdom residing far away from the city of Tula more than *two hundred* leagues, near the South Sea in *Xalixco* and other places), he (therefore) called together some friends of his and relatives, particularly those who were devoted to him. Among those called together were two very important leaders who controlled very large lands and many cities and provinces, the one being *Cuauhtli* and the other *Maxtlatzin*. Many other gentlemen (nobles), attended. He told them what he had planned (decided), saying that if they agreed to this, they would be in the city of Tula and they and their children would govern all the kingdoms and possessions, becoming principal heads over all kings and vassals, all three important leaders governing in close accord, although his son was to have the highest (supreme) place, as his heir to be king of kings as he was.

This agreement seemed good to these two kings and they agreed to it, swearing this *Topiltzin* as their king and monarch, with the rites and ceremonies that they were accustomed to use. From then on all three governed in conformity, although *Topiltzin* commanded as a supreme king. This swearing (oath) was in the year *two Acatl*, and ours of 937 [825 A. D., according to the count of years]. . . .

Topiltzin had been governing for forty years [825 A. D.-867 A. D.] when the signs which the astrologer *Hueman* had prognosticated began to appear on earth as well as in the sky (the heavens). *Topiltzin*, almost at the last years of these forty had committed very grave sins, and with his bad example so had all the people of Tula and the rest of the provinces and cities and lands of the Tultecas. And the ladies would go on pilgrimages to the temples, sanctuaries and false gods, in the cities and would get mixed with the priests. And the Tultecs committed other grave and abominable sins. For example, a very important lady from Tula went to Cholula to visit the temples of that city, which were founded seventy-eight years before, and especially a temple dedicated to the god ce Acatl. At the temple were two priests, one called *Ezcoloth* and the other *Texpolcatl*. As I have already said, the false priests of the Tultecas professed chastity, and it was a very great sin if they broke it. And thus, *Texpolcatl*, seeing this lady, who had also professed chastity, made love to her, and had (obtained) her friendship. And a few years later she gave birth to a child who was called *Izcax*. Later he and his descendants continued to inherit the office and dignity of these great false priests or pontiffs. She stayed as a matron in the temple nearly all her life until its destruction.

The inventors of these sins were two brothers, gentlemen of different parts, very brave and great necromancers. The elder brother was called *Tezcatlipuca* and the younger *Tlalkauhquitezcatlipuca*. Later the Tultecas set them up as gods.

The king, all his court and vassals, persisted in great sin, doing things in this evil art they knew, with which they persuaded them easily to (commit) great sins and (do) ugly and abominable deeds.

The king, going one day to certain gardens and forests of his, found a rabbit that was there with deer horns, and he found the bird *Huitzitzilin*, sucking

the liquor (nectar, liquid) of the flowers, with a very long spur. And inasmuch as the king had seen many times in the *Teoamoxtli* that *Hueman* had painted that these were some of the marvels and signs he had prognosticated, he was very sorry. He had the priests of the temples called; and when they were come he showed them what he had seen, (already) now dead, (for) they shot them with a *cervataua*, (and he also showed them) the *Teoamoxtli*, and how these were signs of their total destruction. And so that their god could be appeased, it was necessary to make great feasts and sacrifices, rites and ceremonies to them.

But then in the following year [868 A. D. according to our count of the years] which was that of *ce Calli*, and ours of 984, at the time when wheat and fish rained, God our Lord began to punish these blind, perverse, and idolatrous people, sending them very great heavy showers, hurricanes and toads from heaven that destroyed the greater part of their buildings. It rained almost *a hundred* days without stopping, for which reason they understood that the world seemed as if it were to end with another deluge. But the Lord through his mercy appeased the waters.

And the following year [869 A. D.], which was *ome Tochtli*, a great heat and draught came, (so) that all plants and trees dried up. And on the third year [870 A. D.], which was *ce Acatl*, when they were beginning to be delivered from persecutions, some frosts fell that burned the whole earth, without anything remaining. And on the fourth year [871 A. D.] which was *four Tecpatl*, such large hail and lightnings fell from heaven, and in such abundance, that they totally destroyed all the trees that escaped [the previous calamities] and even the *Magueyes*, were destroyed—without there remaining memory of anything. Even the buildings and strong walls were destroyed.

And this time of calamities having passed, the earth was quiet for nearly *twelve years* [871 A. D.-883 A. D.] and the plants began to produce, which (this) was in that of *four Calli*. Then came many locusts, worms, vermin, and fowls, that destroyed everything. Also there were very great wars with the three near heirs, all on account of the beautiful *Xuchitl*. Her son had inherited the kingdom and she governed the whole land. Although the Tultecas had had great persecutions from heaven, their forces and power were still great.

Likewise in this same year, almost at the last of it, the weevil ate up all the grain in the granaries where the Tultecas kept it. Another *four* years passed [883 A. D.-887 A. D.] with some rest, when on the *fifth* [888 A. D.] (twenty years after the first calamity), which was in the year of *seven Tochtli*, during the first days they found a child on a hill. It was very white and blond and beautiful. It must have been the devil. They took him to the city to show him to the king. When he saw him, he ordered him taken again to (the point) from whence they had brought him, because it didn't seem to him to be a good sign (omen); and the head of this child-devil began to rot on him, and from the bad odor many people would die. The Tultecas tried to kill him, but they could never get to him, because all who approached would die right away. This bad odor caused a great pest throughout the land, so that of every thousand Tultecas, nine hundred died. All these things happened to them, and many other things, but in order to save space, they are not set down here.[1a]

And the three lords, their competitors, did not cease damaging greatly the few Tultecs who had escaped, taking little by little many provinces and cities subject to this great *Topiltzin*. And from that time forth there was a law that wherever a child was born that was very white and blond, when it was five years of age it was right away sacrificed. This law lasted until the coming of the Spaniards.[1]

After a few days the pest relented (was gone), and Topiltzin, seeing that his competitors were little by little taking possession of his lands and provinces, decided to send them a great present of gold, mantles, and precious stones, and jewels, by way of two ambassadors—very brave gentlemen—and a game of ball equipment (for the game being sufficient to fill a medium-sized room) which game is called *Tlachtli*. Included [among the gifts were] four kinds of precious stones, that is to say, emerald, ruby, diamond, and hyacinth; and as a ball, a carbuncle. Topiltzin sent them word that enough of their anger (wrath) had been experienced— that they knew well the hardships he had had, and the persecutions from heaven, and that he was aware of his own ruination and their valor. And he asked that they accept the game of ball, which was the greatest treasure he had, and other precious stones, and other pieces of gold and jewels, and that just as the *Tlachtli* [ball game] had four kinds of precious stones, all four very esteemed and equal, thus, neither more nor less, all four of them would govern their kingdoms and possessions, in very great peace and conformity. And Topiltzin further stated to them that as between the four rulers, that whoever first ordered anything done, that the other three would consider it as very well done, and they would live always in conformity with each other, they and their descendants.

These and many other words the great Topiltzin sent to be told to his three competitors, fearing that they at some time might become lords of all. And Topiltzin told his three competitors that if they did not want his friendship, they ought to desist from invading Tultec lands and cities—which was what worried the Tultecs—because the land was already so demolished that it no longer served any purpose and was very sickly.

It is found in history, besides being in the account old men give, that this present and treasure was the greatest that was ever seen in this land. This Tultec treasure was so large and it weighed so much that *onxi quipili tlacatl* of the Tultecas were counted, which are *eighteen thousand* men and that it took them one hundred and forty days to move the treasure to *Xalixco* in Quiyahuitztlanxalmolan. When *Topiltzin's* ambassadors arrived, they were well received and the treasure pleased the donees—but not even then did the three enemies desist from pursuing their endeavor, although for the moment with feigned words they bade the ambassadors farewell, saying to them that they would not discuss anything at all. However,

---

[1a] When one compares the foregoing story with the beautiful doctrinal teachings of *The Book of Mormon*, he readily sees how much the Maya-Tultec descendants of the ancient Nephites and Lamanites had apostatized from the true Gospel of Jesus Christ.

[1] Chavero comments: "Tezozomoc makes frequent mention in his Chronicle, of the sacrifices of white children that the Mexicans made in the vortex of the lake called *Pantitlan*. Probably this practice came from the Tultecas."

they told *Topiltzin's* ambassadors that they would stop doing them harm by destroying *Topiltzin's* armies, and they said other words, neither very good nor very bad, but all cautious. For this reason the ambassadors returned very sorrowful, and gave their answer to the great *Topiltzin*. Although not very pleased, *Topiltzin* consoled himself because the greater part of the treasure had been taken to the enemy, which was what made them quarrel the most. The enemy already had kingdoms and possessions; and they were very prosperous and free from calamities from heaven.

In the year of *ce Acatl* and in ours of *nine hundred and ninety-eight* [corrected to 882 A. D. by our count of the years], . . . the three competitor kings of the great *Topiltzin* came to the city of Tula with a great army. They made fun of all the Tultecas as a shattered (destroyed) people and they entered into the very city. *Topiltzin*, on learning of their entry, received them and ordered that they and their people be given whatever they needed. And he discussed with them peace and conformity again, just as he had done before by his ambassadors. They did not come for that purpose, but rather to avenge themselves, and so they refused to agree to it. They told him to get his people ready—that they would understand each other with arms. *Topiltzin*, seeing himself so oppressed and that there was no way out, asked for time, for it was a law among them that before a battle they would notify each other some years in advance so that on both sides they would be warned and prepared. The idea was that their descendants, at some future time, could with just reason do the same. This custom was adhered to up to the time the Spaniards came to this land. They answered *Topiltzin*, telling him that they would give him ten years, and on the last of the ten years they would engage in battle at *Tultitlan*. And with this order (plan) and agreement they returned to their lands, because their army was suffering very great hunger, for this land was such (in such a state) that even its inhabitants could hardly support (nourish) themselves. And it is found in the histories that this journey that these three lords (chieftains) made with their army and so useless a journey, was made only for the purpose of seeing the Tultec land and the state of things in it, and to

countermine and see the forces and resistance that *Topiltzin* might have. The pretext was that the soldiers were looking for food for their maintenance. They did not leave the city until they had seen it well.

During the last days of the year *ten Tecpatl*, these three chieftains returned with a greater army than at first, which was, according to our count, the year of 1008 [893 by our count of the years]. . . . Already by this time the great *Topiltzin* had two large armies stationed, one nearly a hundred leagues from Tula, toward the last lands and provinces of the *Tlahuicas*, and the other in *Tultitlan*, where he in person remained with his army and all his vassals. The general in command of the first army was a great captain called *Huihuitenuxcatl*.

Ever since their competitors had left the Tultecs had done nothing but prepare themselves, make many arms, and gather from all the cities, provinces, and places, the people that there were, without omitting any men at all. And even women were loaded with food, for the people were few, although from the many few there came to be made two very great armies, as I have already stated.

The scouts (explorers) notified the first army that the enemy was near. The general went out to meet the enemy at a good place he had selected, and the two armies faced each other.

They engaged in battle, innumerable people dying on both sides. The war lasted three complete years. Those of *Topiltzin* had few reinforcements, while the three chieftains, their competitors, every day received great numbers of people. The Tultecs were vanquished and nearly all the people were killed in this battle. Many Tultec matrons fought very bravely, helping their husbands. Many of them died.

Having been vanquished, the great captain *Huehuetunexcatl*, seeing himself lost, went fleeing from his enemies, and with some of the Tultecas he escaped to Tultitlan where the great *Topiltzin* was. *Topiltzin* was already prepared with his second army to fight with the enemy which was approaching. *Topiltzin*, in the meantime, ordered certain of his men-servants and women-servants to take the children, his sons (the elder called *Pochotl* and the younger *Xiloltzin*) legitimate successors of the kingdoms, to the very high mountains and lands of Toluca, so that the lineage of the Tultec kings might not end with them. The servants immediately carried out the order.

When the enemy arrived, the armies fought cruelly, dying on the one side and the other. They had been fighting forty days, day and night, when those of the great *Topiltzin* began to faint (get discouraged) with the small forces they had. Not being able to resist the great impetus of the enemy, *Topiltzin* in person and his old father and even their wives and other matrons of the city were obliged to go out and fight, plucking up heart, as it is said. And among them were his mother, the beautiful *Xuchitl*, fighting bravely and doing all they could. But finally they were vanquished, and killed, old men and young men, women and children, none being spared. They were all there together, women as well as children, waiting to see how it all would end, for the war had been going on for fifty days.

In the year of *ce Tecpatl*, on the last day of the month of *Totozoztzintli*, on the first day of the week called *Ollin*, which according to our system was in the year 1011 [896 A. D. according to our count of the years] . . . the great *Topiltzin*, seeing himself and his people vanquished, went fleeing toward Tula, their city.[2] But the enemy overtook them in *Chiuhnauhtlan*, although they couldn't overcome them because they defended themselves. Then they went fleeing to *Xaltocan*, and from there to *Teotihuacan*, and then to *Totolapan*. And before they reached a place called *Tultecaxochitlalpan* and the beautiful *Xuchitl* was killed by dagger stabs. *Xiuhtenancatzin* killed the old king who had defended himself bravely, and *Cohuanacoxtzin* killed *Xuchitl* who also had defended herself bravely.

After these two were killed, these two enemy kings went pursuing *Topiltzin*. The two kings who swore allegiance to *Topiltzin*, *Cuauholli* and *Maxtla*, and other Tultec lords, were overtaken and torn to pieces. And in the meantime *Topiltzin* went fleeing and got into *Xico*, a cave that is near *Tlalmanalco*, and thus they could not overtake him. Beyond *Xico* the enemy overtook *Huehue-*

tunexcatl, the great captain, together with those Tultecas who had escaped, and there they had another cruel battle in which *Huehuetunexcatl* and the whole army died. A nurse took *Topiltzin's* younger son, called *Xilotzin*, and with some Tultecas she fled into the wilderness, making an escape. She went ahead with some Tultecas, nobles as well as plebeians, who got into the lakes and sierras with their wives and children. Some whose swift feet saved them were those of *Mallauxiuhcohuac*, *Macatepec*, *Totzatepec*, *Totoepec*, *Quauhquechallan*, *Tepexomacotlazallan*, *Chapoltepec*, *Culhuacan*, and other parts.

The three kings, seeing that they had already killed everybody and that all remained uninhabited then went to the large Tultec cities. From the temples and palaces they took out all the treasures and riches that they found, and returned to their lands with the spoils of their enemies, no person remaining, because the land was very dry and sickly and fruitless.

Then, a few days after that, *Topiltzin* left *Xico* with some of his servants, for his enemies were not to be seen. Seeing the land totally destroyed, he went up to *Atlapallan*, a province that reaches down to the South Sea [Pacific Ocean] —a land very prosperous, rich, and well populated (settled). He said to his vassals, to the few who were in *Culhuacan* (and) who had gone there to escape from the enemy, that he was going toward the rising sun to some kingdoms and possessions of his ancestors, very prosperous and rich and that *five hundred and twelve* years later he would return again to this land, in the year of *ce Acatl*, and would punish the descendants of the kings, his competitors. And many other things he said, and many impossible promises he made to his vassals, which would be too long to relate. He returned once more to *Xico*, and one night, with some Tultecs he left for *Tlapallan* traveling by night through the wilderness until he arrived at that place, where he afterwards lived almost *thirty years*. He was waited upon and entertained (honored, regaled) by the *Tlapaltecas*, and died at the age of *one hundred and four years*, leaving many laws constituted, which later his descendant *Netzahualcoyotzin* confirmed. And he himself ordered his body to be

---

[2] For a discussion of the date of Topiltzin's defeat and flight, see Chapter 32.

burned with the rites and ceremonies that were later used (and he was the first to be burned), and he did and planned many other things.

This king, many Indians say, is still in Xico. They say he did not go to *Tlapallan* with *Netzahualcoyotzin* and *Netzahualpiltzintli*, kings of Texcuco, and his descendants, and *Moquihuitzin* of *Tlatelulco*. Of all the Tultec and Chichimec kings they were the bravest and performed the greatest deeds. There are many fables concerning them, the Indians still believing that they are going to come from there at some time. In this the Indians are like the Portuguese, who still believe that king Sebastian is alive and is going to return, which is to be accepted only as a fable, as I have stated at other times. Likewise the Tultecas who escaped went by the coasts of the sea of the South and North, like Guatemala, *Campeche, Tacolotlan*, and those of the islands and coasts of one and the other sea. Later they multiplied.

When the Tultecas fought they would put on some sort of long tunics that reached down to the heels, of a thousand colors, embroidered, and *very closely woven and thick*, so that no matter how hard they would hit each other with the lances they could not pass them (cut them through): Lances were what they used most. They had long lances and another type which was thrown. Also, they had clubs garnished (nailed) with iron. They wore morions and helmets of brass (copper) and gold, and some used *rodelas*, particularly those who had clubs. Likewise, the Tultecas would put on, besides the dress (clothes) I have mentioned above, tunics like those of the priests. They were white and exactly like the tunics that our religious priests wear underneath. The sleeves are like those of the Oidores, and they wore certain hoods, as I have already stated above.

They also used a certain brass (copper) coin, two fingers long and one thick, like sort of little hatchets and about the thickness of a *real de a ocho*. It hasn't been long since those of *Tultepec* of the South Sea have put this coin aside, because they were of the lineage of the Tultecas.[3] They also bought with *cucao*, which is used even

today in this land, and with mantles, gold and precious stones, and rich plumage. They also had markets (fairs, bazaars) every twenty days on the first day of their twenty-day months. Their year had eighteen months, as shall be related further on. Even now [sixteenth century] this order (plan) of large markets is used in *Tulantzinco*. However, every day in the cities and towns they sold all necessary things. But this great *Tianguis* (market day) was when there were found in the market place many people of different provinces. It was not held in all cities, but (it was held) in *Tula, Tulantzinco Teotihuacan, Cuauhnalmac, Tultitlan, Cholula*, and some five or six other cities or parts.

Before *Topiltzin's* war began, while he was at *Tultitlan* with his army, after having sent *Hueytunexcatl* with the other army a deer entered through the city with its tail dragging on the ground, bellowing. And it passed near *Topiltzin* who was on a very high platform in the middle of the large plaza of the city reviewing his whole army. *Topiltzin* saw it all—and the deer disappeared among the people. We are given to understand that the deer must have been some devil, for they took it as a bad omen. This was the last sign that there was without including many other things and eclipses of the sun and moon, and great comets that there were in the sky.

It is found in the Tultec history that there died of the vassals of *Topiltzin* during the time the wars lasted (as I have said, the war lasted three years and two months, using the Tultec system—and in our system the war lasted three years, one month and ten days) there died, I say, men as well as women. *Zentzon, Xiquilpiltzontli, Oquixolizihuetl*, which are *three million two hundred thousand* men and women: And of the people of the three competitor kings, there were (killed) *caxtolpohual Tzontiquipilzotlitlacatl*, which were *two million, four hundred thousand* men; so that on both sides there were killed *zentzon xiquipiltzontli ihuancaxtolpohualtzontli*, which are *five million six hundred thousand persons*, an incredible thing and which causes admiration.[4] And it is not surprising, for as I have said, men as well as women were included [in the armies] except the very old who, on

---

[4] It appears that in this war there were more casualties than in the battle of Cumorah in 385 A. D. It is recalled there were 230,000 Nephite soldiers killed at Cumorah. See page 364.

acount of their old age, could not stir from one place (spot). The aged and infirm later died, some from hunger and others from cold.

The people were so numerous in this land, particularly in *Topiltzin's* possessions (kingdom) which were almost *one thousand leagues* long and *eight hundred* wide, that even the very high mountains were covered with houses and cultivated lands. There wasn't a span of land that was uncultivated. As can be seen in the ruins of their buildings, which are so large and powerful and with so many curious things, the Tultecs were one of the great and powerful kingdoms of the ancient world.

There escaped from these cruel battles, into caves and deserts and to the lake (without counting those that went fleeing) *nauhtzontli ihuan, nauh pohualli on matlactli ihuan ome oquixtle cihuatl,* which were *one thousand six hundred and twelve* persons, men as well as women. Among them there were twenty gentlemen and illustrious people, who, after their enemies had left and their own king *Topiltzin* had disappeared, as I have in order stated, got together in Culhua-can and there divided themselves into five groups. One division of the gentlemen, it falling to their lot, remained and the other four left toward the four directions later settling on the sea coasts and islands. The fifth part, which were some four hundred odd persons, with the nobles, were the ones who remained in these parts. The nobles divided among themselves the most suitable places in which to live. But, as I have already said, everything was very dry and ruined (destroyed).

The lords who remained in this part were the following: in *Culhuacan*, which is where they got together, there remained *Xiuhtemol*, his wife who was called *Ozalaxuchitl*, together with a son that was born at this time, called *Nauh-yotl;* and *Cuatlix* with his wife *Ilmixuch* and a son called *Acxocuauh:* these, with the people that fell to their lot, stayed at this place making some houses for their habitation. These two were the main families and they were of the house and lineage of the great *Topiltzin.* Later *Nauhyotl* and his descendants were kings of the *Culhuas,* for thus were the surviving Tultecs called later, because *Culhuacan* was their center.

And to *Tlaxcallan* went *Miltitl* and his wife *Cohuaxuchitl* with their family and their two sons, the elder called *Pixahua* and the younger *Accopal.* Later these two small youths, having become grown-up men, went to live at *Quichollan* with some relatives, it being a better place. And they were the ones who again invented anew the working (making designs, cutting, carving), with gold and precious stones, which, by reason of the great hardships of the Tultecas and long years of persecutions, had been forgotten.

And to *Tolzatepec* went *Nacacxoc* and his wife and their son called *Xiupopoca,* with all their family.

And to *Tepexomaco* went *Cohuatl* with his wife and a son called *Quitzalop-poca,* with all his family.

And in Cholula were the priests with the lady (matron) of whom I have already made an account, and some of the Tultecs who had fled and escaped [during the war].

Xitzin settled in Chapultepec with his wife *Oztaxuchitl,* and a son of his, and his family.

And to other remote parts and far from the lake, as I have already stated above, went the rest (remainder, left over) of the fifth part. From all these the Tultecas descended, who later, in the course of time, came to multiply, nobles as well as plebeians. From families there came into being towns and then cities, and from cities, kingdoms and provinces.

This[5] was the end of the great empire of the Tultecas that this New World had, which empire lasted only *five hundred and seventy-two* years.[6] The enemy kings who destroyed it, seeing it so poor and sickly and unappealing (without taste), did not settle it, but returned to their lands with the spoils. Very rich

---

[3] A footnote in the Chavero edition says: "Of this coin Torquemada speaks. I think that in the Museum and in my possession exist samples of it. See what I said about it in my note to the 'History of the Conquest' by Prescott. Cumplido's edition, tenth note.—R."

[5] This paragraph is from the end of a brief digest of Tultec history by Ixtlilxochitl.

[6] Five hundred seventy-two years covers the period from the time the Tultecs settled in the Land Northward, on being banished from their ancient Bountiful-land home, until the flight of *Topiltzin.* It has been pointed out that Ixtlilxochitl erred 100 years in saying the banishment occurred in 439 A. D. He figured 572 years, beginning in 439 A. D. and continuing until 1011 A. D., the year he figured for the flight of *Topiltzin.*

were the treasures they found in the palaces of the lords and temples of their idols. These Tultecas were great wise-men, philosophers, and artisans, as is found in their histories, because they understood and knew the course of the heavens (skies) to a very fine point. They used pictures (paintings) and characters) with which they had recorded all things that had happened from the creation of the world up to their time. They worked (carved, designed, hewed) with gold and precious stones; they built the best cities that the New World has had, as can be seen in the ruins of the towns of *San Juan, Teotihuacan, Cholula, Tula*, and in many other parts. They sowed all the seeds and vegetables that have been found in this land, and were a dressed people and very different from the Chichimecas in everything. They were great idolaters, and had many temples and idols. They had their solar year as well adjusted and with such good reckoning, as we have it; and finally, there has not been in this land a nation more polite and wise.

Chapter 32

LAST DAYS OF THE TULTEC EMPIRE IN CENTRAL MEXICO

Introductory Statement

It would be well at this point to discuss in this chapter some of the more important events connected with the Tultec empire in central Mexico and also the Aztec period. The latter ended with the discovery of America in 1492. Then, in the following chapter, a brief account will be given of the Maya Old and New empires. This story will also close at the time of the Spanish Conquest.

Date of End of Tultec Empire

At the beginning of the last-quoted paragraph from *Ixtlilxochitl* in the preceding chapter, it was stated that this second or new Tultec Empire lasted 572 years. It is apparent that the Mexican historian arrived at that total by figuring the fall of the empire at 1011 A. D. and going back from there to 439 A. D., the date he calculated for the banishment from ancient Bountiful-land. The difference between 1011 A. D. and 439 A. D. is 572 years.

It appears, however, that *Ixtlilxochitl's* calculation is wrong as to the number of years the new Tultec empire endured. In the first place, the banishment from ancient Bountiful-land occurred in 339 A. D. instead of in 439 A. D., as has been shown.[1] Secondly, it has been made clear in the data placed in brackets by the writers in the course of *Ixtlilxochitl's* account of the new Tultec empire that our calculations of the years differ from his. By merely adding the time periods given by *Ixtlilxochitl* for Tultec occupancy periods and events, a total of 557 years elapsed between 339 A. D. and the fall of Topiltzin, making the latter date 896 A. D.[2] This total of 557 years, arrived

---

[1] See pp. 348 ff. and 374 ff.
[2] See pp. 230-231.

at by having added the years of occupancy and events as related by *Ixtlilxochitl*, is not far from his figure of 572 years, it being a difference of only fifteen years.

Apparently the true and actual date for the fall and flight of Topiltzin was a year somewhere between 896 A. D. and 1011 A. D. Elsewhere in his writings *Ixtlilxochitl* gives the year 958 A. D.-959 A. D. for the end of the empire. In a summary entitled "Concerning the Tultecas," he says:

. . . many kings and lords rebelled against him [Topiltzin], especially three kings who were from the provinces *Quiahuiztlan* and *Anahuacac,* said and Cohuanacox—brave men and of great power. They came against him with armed hand to destroy him and for nearly twenty-six years they had very great and cruel battles in which many thousands of men died on both sides. God, who wished to punish them for their great wrong-doings, sent them great persecutions from heaven, and a general draught to their harvests and seeds and then great plagues—the greatest that there have been in this land—from which all were destroyed, that almost no man remained. *And their last destruction was in the year of ce Tecpatl, and in our [calendar system] year 958. . . .*

In a brief account entitled "Chichimeca History," *Ixtlil-xochitl* wrote:

When the signs appeared (and the priests and conjurers declared that they preceded the destruction of the Tultec monarchy), *Topiltzin* had his major domos called. He ordered that his treasures, which were the greatest that there were at that time, be delivered to them [the rival kings] so that they would withdraw themselves to the province of *Quiz-huixtlan*—being in fear of his enemy kings.

The draught was so great that it lasted 26 years.

In the flight of the remains of *Topiltzin's* defeated army, the first victims were the old king Iztacquauhtzin his father and with him lady Quetzalxochitl. . . .

Tochcueye, the nurse of Pochotl, saved him in the deserts of *Nono-alco*[3] where she was bringing him up.

To this end came the Tultec empire, which lasted 572 years: . . . and *this final destruction was in the year of ce Tecpatl, 959 A. D. . . .*

The late George Vaillant adopted *Ixtlilxochitl's* year, 959 A. D., as the date marking the end of Topiltzin's Tultec empire and the abandonment of the magnificent Teotihuacan.[4] This date receives some support from the *Annals of Cuauhtitlan*. The latter is one of the two chief documentary sources of information concerning Tultec history of central Mexico and the *Works*

---

[3] *Nonoales* is a district of Mexico City. Archæological excavations have been conducted there.
[4] George Vaillant, *Aztecs of Mexico* (1941), p. 53.

of Ixtlilxochitl is the other. Cuauhtitlan was a community on the west side of the great lake that once covered a considerable portion of the valley of Mexico. (*Ixtlilxochitl's* home was in Texcoco on the eastern, or opposite, side of the lake.) *The Annals of Cuauhtitlan,* like the *Writings of Ixtlilxochitl,* were derived from pre-Conquest native sources. The *Annals* date the end of Topiltzin's reign at 947 A. D., twelve years earlier than the *Ixtlilxochitl* date.

Topiltzin—His Religion and Accomplishments

As has already been pointed out, apparently the true and actual date of the collapse of the empire of the Tultecs, descendants of the ancient colonizers of Bountiful-land, was somewhere between 896 A. D. and 1011 A. D., and it is probable that the year 959 A. D. is the correct date. This latter date is strongly confirmed by Maya sources as the year of the defeat and flight of Topiltzin. It is noted that his flight was toward the Maya lands to the southeast—that is, he headed for ancient Bountiful-land, the home of his ancestors. To repeat *Ixtlilxochitl* on the point:

> Seeing the land totally destroyed, he went up to *Atlapallan* [Tlapallan or Huehuetlapallan], a province that reaches down to the South Sea [Pacific ocean]—a land very rich, prosperous and well settled. He said to his vassals . . . that *he was going toward the rising sun to some kingdoms and possessions of his ancestor, very rich and properous.* . . .

Where else could it have been that he was going but to ancient Bountiful-land below Tehuantepec? It is the only area that meets the description.

The Mayan accounts of Yucatan throw further light on the subject. They pick up the story of Topiltzin and continue from where *Ixtlilxochitl* left it. The time, place, and characters all remain the same: The time—about the year 959 and the years immediately following; the place—ancient Bountiful-lar.d to the east of Tehuantepec; the characters—the Tultec ruler from central Mexico with some of his followers.

The sixteenth century records of the Mayas of Yucatan reveal that a great Tultec king left Nonoual (*Nonoalco* of the valley of Mexico—see pages 384 ff.) during the score of years (katun—twenty years) from 948 to 968. The year 959 A. D., the date given by *Ixtlilxochitl* for the flight of Topiltzin, falls about midway in this Maya katun. The Maya accounts show that this great Mexican-Tultec king made his way from Nonoual to ancient Bountiful-land, home of his illustrious ancestors. In greater Bountiful-land (Tulapan-Zuyua), some Itzas—who, like himself, were descended from the early Nephite-Nahuas—were added to his company. He then proceeded with his retinue to the Itza stronghold in northern Yucatan—Chichen Itza. Appar- ently these Itzas who accompanied Topiltzin into northern Yuca- tan had lost the modified Hebrew and Egyptian tongues of their ancestors for history reports that they were speaking the "Maya" tongue at the time. As has been shown, the Maya language included some Hebrew elements. It was the main tongue of the victorious Lamanites in the southern homeland below Tehuantepec.

Topiltzin, the Tultec, stood for a decadent and degenerate "Judeo-Christian" culture. (The wickedness of his subjects at the time of his fall is mentioned by *Ixtlilxochitl.*) Topiltzin's religion was the religion of Quetzalcoatl in modified form. Doubt- less, he claimed to be a priest-follower of Quetzalcoatl and appar- ently he took upon himself the name "Quetzalcoatl," even as many unworthy persons in our present-day world take upon themselves the name "Christian." At any rate, on arriving in Yucatan he was referred to as "Quetzal-Serpent," or, in the Maya tongue, "Kukulcan." *Kukul* is the Maya term for *serpent. Kukulcan* is a translation of *Quetzalcoatl.*[5] Like his contemporary counterparts in European Christianity, and like many generations of ancient Israel, he practiced idolatry. In fact, he is credited with introducing idolatry into Yucatan. Apparently the "Chris- tianity" of the Itzas had not deviated as far from the original as had that of the Central Plateau Tultecs of the tenth cen- tury A. D.

The once-fallen and exiled Topiltzin-Kukulcan accomplished great things in northern Yucatan. He became the ruler of the great Itzan city, Chichen Itza. There he built a noteworthy temple-tower, palaces, and temples. The famous temple-tower at Chichen Itza, El Castillo as it is now called, is a monument to his industry. It was, of course, erected to Itzamna-Quetzalcoatl (Jehovah-Christ), but on one of the doorjambs leading into the temple on top of the pyramid is a profile representation of Topiltzin-Kukulcan himself. See the photograph of this low-relief carving, figure 51, p. 392.

---

[5] Alfred M. Tozzer, *Landa's Relacion de las Cosas de Yucatan* (1941 ed.), note 124. This is an excellent note with a rather full discussion of *Kukulcan.*

Fig. 51: Bearded Kukulcan (Topiltzin) of Chichen Itza, Yucatan

The bearded *Kukulcan*, tenth-century ruler of Chichen Itza, Yucatan, was a white man. Observe the profile line of his aquiline nose and the heavy growth of his beard. The feathers of the Quetzal bird protrude gracefully from his headdress—he claimed to be a priest of the Fair God who was symbolized by the Quetzal. *Kukulcan* was probably the Tultec king, Topiltzin, who left Teotihuacan and fled southeast. This likeness of him appears on a door jamb of the temple atop the temple-tower at Chichen Itza. *Photo by Ferguson.*

He built a mighty city, Mayapan, "Maya-capital." He also greatly modified the religon, art and architecture of Yucatan by introducing the Central Plateau styles and names and other-wise "Mexicanizing" northern Yucatan. Many are the references to the great Topiltzin (Kukulcan) in the historical works of six-teenth-century Yucatan. It will be enlightening to quote from several of them.

TOPILTZIN (KUKULCAN) AND ANCIENT SOURCES

Bishop Landa wrote in 1566 of Topiltzin (Kukulcan) as follows:

It is believed among the Indians that with the Itzas who occupied Chichen Itza, there reigned a great lord, named Kukulcan, and that the principal building, which is called Kukulcan, shows this to be true. They say that he arrived from the west; but they differ among themselves as to whether he arrived before or after the Itzas or with them. They say that he was favorably disposed, and had no wife or children, and that after his return he was regarded in Mexico as one of their gods and called Quetzalcoatl; and they also considered him a god in Yucatan on account of his being a just statesman; and this is seen in the order which he imposed on Yucatan, after the death of the lords, in order to quell the dissensions which their deaths had caused in the country.

This Kukulcan established another city after arranging with the native lords of the country that he and they should live there and that all their affairs and business should be brought there; and for this purpose they chose a very good situation, eight leagues farther in the interior than Merida is now, and fifteen or sixteen leagues from the sea. They surrounded it with a very broad stone wall, laid dry, of about an eighth of a league, leaving in it only two narrow gates. The wall was not very high and in the centre of this enclosure they built their temples, naming the largest, which is like that of Chichen Itza, the name of Kukulcan, and they built another building of a round form, with four doors, entirely different from all the others in that land; as well as a great number of others round about joining together. In this enclosure they built houses for the lords only, dividing all the land among them, giving towns to each one, according to the antiquity of his lineage and his personal value. And Kukulcan gave a name to this city—not his own as the Ah Itzas had done in Chichen Itza, which means the well of the Ah Itzas, but he called it Mayapan, which means "the standard of the Maya," because they called the language of the country Maya, and the Indians (say) "Ichpa," which means "within the enclosures." This Kukulcan lived with the lords in that city for several years; and leaving them in great peace and friendship, he returned by the same way to Mexico, and on the way he stopped at Champoton, and, in a memory of him and of his departure, he erected a fine building in the sea like that of Chichen Itza, a long stone's throw from the shore. And thus Kukulcan left a perpetual remembrance in Yucatan.[6]

⁶ Alfred M. Tozzer, op. cit., pp. 20-26.

In 1579-1581 Gaspar Antonio Chi wrote of Topiltzin (Kukulcan) as follows:

For a thousand years they did not worship idols, because the lords of Chichen Itza and their subjects wished it to be said that they were not idolaters. It is said that the first settlers of Chichen Itza [Itzas] were not idolaters until Kukulcan, a Mexican captain, entered these parts, who taught [them] idolatry.

The Itzas . . . founded Mayapan. This city of Mayapan . . . was very large, in the . . . province of Mani . . . And in it were to be seen many houses of stone, and a hill made by hand which was the temple of Kukul-can, the principal idol. . . .[7]

Francisco Hernandez made the following comment in 1545 A. D. about Topiltzin:

They also assert that in olden times, long ago, there came to the land [Yucatan] twenty men (he gave the names of fifteen of them), but because they were very poorly written, and furthermore as they do not have great importance for this report, I do not copy them. . . . The principal one was called Cocolcan, and they called this one the God of all kinds of fevers. . . . They all wore long gowns or mantles and sandals for their feet. They had long beards and wore nothing to cover their heads.[8]

From an ancient Yucatecan manuscript, the following is quoted:

Originally a god had been worshipped here who was the creator of all things, and who had his dwelling in heaven, but that a great prince named Kukulcan with a multitude of people, had come from a foreign country, that he and his people were idolaters, and from that time the inhabitants of this land also began to practice idolatry, to perform bloody sacrificial rites, to burn copal, and the like.[9]

The time of the arrival of Topiltzin-Kukulcan in northern Yucatan was fixed by the Book of Chilam Balam of Chumayel and by the Book of Chilam Balam of Mani. Further help comes from the Mayan Tizimin Manuscript. These complex native sources indicate the arrival of the great Captain was in a Katun 8 Ahau of the Maya Short Count. This, according to Sylvanus G. Morley, had the Long Count position: 10.6.0.0.0 8 Ahau 8 Yax, equivalent to our date 948 A. D.[10]

[7] Gaspar Antonio Chi, cited in M. Wells Jakeman, The Origin and History of the Mayas (1945), pp. 95-96.
[8] Cited in Tozzer, op. cit., note 124, p. 22. Observe that these tenth-century Tultecs were bearded and still wore the ancient garb of their ancestors from the Near East.
[9] Translated by Tozzer, op. cit., from the German edition of Edward Seler, Zeit. fur Ethnol., 30:377-410. (Coll. wks., 1:675) 1898, ibid., p. 23.
[10] Sylvanus G. Morley, The Ancient Maya (1946), pp. 86-87; Alfred M. Tozzer, op. cit., note 24.

Juan de Torquemada, writing in 1613 A. D., made some important observation concerning Topiltzin-Kukulcan. The discussion of this important and last Tultec ruler will be concluded with Torquemada's observations:

. . . Quetzalcoatl, according to true histories, was a great priest in the city of Tula . . . He determined to go to that place which was called Tlapallan. With this determination (which he now had because of the trickery and enchantment of the necromancer [Texcatlipoca]) he caused all the things to be burned which he had made of silver . . ., and soon afterwards set out on his journey, leaving his city, pursued by this necromancer and sorcerer who had overcome him, and arriving at a place which is called Quauhtitlan. . . . He continued on from this place, and whatever road he followed, many of the people whom he brought with him went along playing for him on flutes and other instruments. He arrived at another [place], which is a hill near the town of Tlalnepantla, two leagues from this city of Mexico. . . . In this manner, then, Quetzalcoatl went traveling along, continuing his journey on the road to the coast for the kingdom of Tlapallan, suffering some molestations from his enchanters his enemies, until he arrived at Cholula, where he was received . . . and afterwards worshipped as a god. . . . They affirm that he was with them [of Cholula] twenty whole years, after which he departed, continuing his journey to the kingdoms of Tlapallan, taking with him four young and virtuous nobles of the same city. And these he sent back from Coatzacoalco, a province distant one hundred and fifty leagues towards the sea from this city. And among other instructions which he gave them was that they should say to the inhabitants of the city of Cholula that they might hold for certain that, in the time to come, some white men with white beards, like himself, would come by the sea from the direction of the sunrise, and that they would be lords of these lands, and that those were his brothers. . . . The people of Yucatan venerate and reverence this god Quetzalcoatl, and they call him Kukulcan, and they said that he arrived there from the parts of the west. . . .[11]

There were no Tultec monarchs after Topiltzin. Since he took flight toward Cholula and Tehuantepec at the very time when Kukulcan made his way from the Central Mesa, it seems highly probably that Topiltzin was identical with Kukulcan. At any rate Kukulcan, if not identical with Topiltzin, was a Tultec prince from the Tultec kingdom.

COLLAPSE OF CENTRAL MESA TULTEC EMPIRE

The documentary sources mentioned above have dated the collapse of the Tultecs of the Central Mesa region about 950-960 A. D. They are supported by archæological findings in both the Central Mesa and northern Yucatan. Teotihuacan, To-

---

[11] Translation by M. Wells Jakeman, op. cit., pp. 74-75.

piltzin's great center, was abandoned in the tenth century, according to the archæological voices speaking from the dust of that great place. Vaillant comments:

> Ixtlilxochitl has related that religious conflict, revolt and crop failure contributed to the downfall of Teotihuacan. To some extent we can corroborate this statement from archæological interpretations. The architectural change has the appearance of having been made simultaneously, in contrast to the gradual development of the original city. Teotihuacan was built over hastily with the maximum use [by the victorious enemies] of original construction. The abrupt change in figurine styles suggests that a new god was honored by this new presentation.[12]

The great architectural changes wrought in the tenth century in Yucatan following the arrival of Topiltzin-Kukulcan and his Tultecs have already been discussed.

After the fall of Topiltzin, his famous Tula (Teotihuacan) was "a city of ghosts." The people who dominated the central plateau after the flight of Topiltzin did not occupy the state of Teotihuacan. Vaillant verifies this statement in the following comment:

> In Chichimec times the makers of the Mazapan culture occasionally crept onto the ruins to bury their dead, but they never disturbed the silence by building houses in the zone. A persistent tradition describes the great Aztec ruler Montezuma as visiting Teotihuacan to make sacrifices, but no evidence exists in the shape of ceremonial equipment left behind. The three or four Aztec potsherds found among the hundreds of thousands of Teotihuacan fragments certainly cannot be testimony to the pomp and ceremony of Aztec worship.[13]

TULTEC REMNANTS (959 A. D.-1520 A. D.)

With the flight of Topiltzin and the fall of his kingdom, a remnant of the Tultecs shifted across the lake to Azcapotzalco. The latter is about fifteen miles south of Cuauhtitlan. The *Annals of Cuauhtitlan* list the lineage of the rulers of the Tultecs of Azcapotzalco as follows:

Matlaczochitl	947 A. D.- 983 A. D.
Nauhyotzin I	983 A. D.- 997 A. D.
Matlaccoatzin	997 A. D.-1025 A. D.
Tlilcoatzin	1025 A. D.-1046 A. D.
Huemac	1047 A. D.-1122 A. D.

[12] George Vaillant, *op. cit.*, p. 64.
[13] *Ibid.*, p. 65.

In the twelfth century came the final, utter, and complete collapse and virtual extinction of the Tultecs. Tultec arts and crafts disappeared with the wind-up in Azcaptozalco. Only the name Tultec continued. Other peoples claimed it to lend them-selves prestige. The final destruction in the twelfth century came about as a result of civil war and religious strife as the earlier calamities of the fourth and tenth centuries had done. Those who claimed to hold the ancient priesthood of Quetzalcoatl were no more.[14]

About this time strange and ignorant nomads from the north were arriving in central Mexico.[15] Doubtless the ancestry of these newcomers was of the yellow race of eastern Asia—people who made their way into the New World by way of Bering Strait and Alaska; or they may have been Algonquins whose ancestors were a blend of Asiatic types. It is difficult or probably impossible to ascertain just when the first Mongoloids reached the New World. They were an illiterate people who left no records. Apparently they did not arrive in Alaska until near the time of Christ.[16] It took them hundreds of years to make their way from Alaska to Middle America. Not until they arrived in Mexico's central plateau area did they encounter high cultures. Certainly they left no trail of advanced culture behind—no mathematics, no astronomy, no architecture, no metallurgy, no polished red pottery, no fine textiles. They had none to leave or it would have been discovered by now.

It took the Mongoloids a long time to settle south of the Rio Grande. By the time they did arrive in Mexico they had mixed with the Algonquins, no doubt. And before their depar-ture from northeastern Asia a considerable amount of "mixing" had already occurred. To quote Harold Gladwin:

Where did these Mongoloids live before they came over here? Their physical makeup points quite clearly to eastern Asia, but eastern Asia covers a good deal of country and it contains many different types of people —short, stocky Japanese, tall Manchus, Chinese, short and tall, slim and stout—all sorts and conditions of Mongoloids. Of them all, the northern provinces of China will come nearest to filling the bill for the fifth migra-tion. It does not make the problem any easier, however, to realize each branch of Mongoloids that migrated to North America was entering regions which were being more and more thickly populated, and that as

<hr>

14 Ibid., pp. 67-70.
15 Vaillant, ibid., p .71, says "Dissolution set in as famine, religious disagreements and the incursions of strange peoples corroded the structure of Teotihuacan civilization."
16 Harold Gladwin, Men Out of Asia (1947), p. 185.

soon as they arrived they promptly began to mix with peoples already here, and in putting their stamp on the earlier types were themselves also changed. For the moment, the essential fact to remember is that the newcomers possessed broad Mongoloid skulls, and that no such heads had been known in any part of North, Central, or South America before the arrival of this fifth migration.[17]

Whatever the time when the Mongoloids first arrived in Middle America, it is apparent from a look at the faces of some of the people portrayed in Maya Old Empire sculpturing at such places as Copan, Honduras, and Quirigua, Guatemala, that a Mongoloid element was then present. See figure 33, page 253.[18] It also appears that nomads from the north were still finding their way into Mexico in the twelfth century. Apparently the Chichimecs and Aztecs, who succeeded the Tultecs, had strong strains of Mongoloid blood.[19]

CHICHIMEC PERIOD (1100 A. D.-1300 A. D.)

In the central plateau of Mexico, those who vanquished the Tultecs were originally called Culhuas. After the final collapse of the Tultecs, the Culhuas, also known as the *Chichimecs,* continued to dominate the lake region of the plateau. A number of cities, all within a radius of 300 miles of the present Mexico City, called Tenochtitlan, were occupied by them at various times. The Culhuas founded Culhuacan at a point between what is known today as Mexico City and Xochimilco.

The Culhuas were defeated by another city-state, Tepanec. That occurred in the fourteenth century. In the meantime, the Aztec center, Tenochtitlan, on Texcoco Lake, had become a city-state to be reckoned with. Texcoco, on the eastern side of the lake, home of *Ixtlilxochitl,* had become an important city-state by 1300 A. D. More cultured peoples from the Oaxaca area to the south had come up onto the plateau, giving the decadent Chichimecs a lift. The refined civilization of the extinct Tultec nation "disappeared before the infiltration of intruding tribes. The nomadic groups referred to in the chronicles have left no identifiable remains. Hunters reduced to the bare necessities which they can carry on their backs do not leave much trace of their presence."[20] The rate of degeneration had increased.

[17] *Ibid.,* p. 166.
[18] Jakeman, *op. cit.,* pp. 181-183.
[19] Since the Mongoloids were from the north, the northern people in the central plateau of Mexico would have encountered them before the Mayas to the south.
[20] Vaillant, *op. cit.,* pp. 76-77.

However, extensive trade was carried on with such remote regions as Guatemala and Yucatan. Mexican influence reached southward into the Maya-Zapotec-Lamanite centers.

The Aztecs came to power in Tenochtitlan and Culhuacan. They became powerful and important about 1300 A. D. They spoke what was referred to as the Nahuatl tongue—the language of the late Nahuas from the Cholula-Puebla area. The late Nahuas from Puebla are to be disinguished from the early Nahuas of the highlands of Guatemala—the first and original Nephite settlers who arrived in the New World by sea. The "Nahuas" of the fourteenth century, having come up to the Central Plateau from the Puebla area, probably had an earlier origin in the Maya-Lamanite country. Like some of the other inferior tribes of the fourteenth and fifteenth centuries who called themselves "Tultecs," they designated themselves by another of the names of the originally great Nephite nation that they had helped to destroy —"Nahuas."

The Aztecs, or late Nahuas, engaged in extensive formal religious rituals which included human sacrifice.[21] They introduced into the Central Plateau area distinctive gods and a formal type of war. Elements of Aztec religion reached as far northward as southeastern United States.[22]

Aztec Period (1300 A. D.-1520 A. D.)

During this period of 220 years, the history of the Central Plateau region of Mexico was a history of struggle and intrigue between city states. Tenochtitlan, the city state of the Aztecs, emerged as the great power. The other principal city-states were Culhuacan, Cuauhtitlan, Cuitlahuac and Texcoco. The Aztecs had no empire in the sense that we use the term in connection with European history. The Aztecs did not govern conquered cities and lands. They merely exacted tribute.

In 1428 A. D. Itzcoatl became king of Tenochtitlan, the fourth ruler of the city. He established a powerful religious hierarchy and built imposing temples to the Aztec gods. He conquered many tribes and cities in the Central Plateau. However, Texcoco, on the other side of the lake, was the city of Tenochtitlan's chief rival after it had for a long time been an ally.

---

[21] *The Book of Mormon*, p. 466 (Mormon 4:15-21). See Topic XCIV.
[22] For a more detailed summary of the Chichimec period see Vaillant, *op. cit.*, Ch. IV.

Itzcoatl died in 1440, after a reign of twelve years. He was succeeded by Montezuma I, a great soldier who made successful raids and conquests into Puebla, Vera Cruz, Morelos and Guerrero, getting assistance from Texcoco. Many important engineering projects were completed during his reign from 1440 to 1469 A. D., a period of twenty-nine years. He built a large dike and an aqueduct. Five years of famine occurred during his reign.

Montezuma I was succeeded by a son, Axayacatl, who reigned for ten years, 1469 to 1479 A. D. He added one more important city-state, Tlatelolco, to those paying tribute to Tenochtitlan. The great Aztec Calendar Stone, which many travelers have seen in the National Museum in Mexico City, was cut during his reign. It weighs approximately twenty tons and is an outstanding work of art.

Tizoc, a war chief, reigned from 1479 to 1486, a period of seven years. He accomplished little in the way of conquest and is believed to have been poisoned by one of his soldiers. Some engineering works were undertaken by him, including the reconstruction of the temple of the Aztec war god, Huitzilopochtli.

Succeeding Tizoc in 1486 was his brother, Ahuitzotl. The latter reigned from 1486 to 1503 A. D., dying of injuries received while working on an engineering project. Under his direction 20,000 captives from Oaxaca (former home of the Aztecs) were put to death in bloody sacrificial rites.

Montezuma II ruled from 1503 until 1520 A. D. It was he who witnessed the arrival of Cortez. The native accounts claim that he was killed by the Spaniards. The Spanish historians contend, however, that he was stoned to death by his own Aztec people for not resisting the Spaniards.

The defeat of this powerful king at the hands of Cortez is explained by a number of factors. First, Cortez was regarded by the people of Mexico as the "Fair God" who, in accordance with his promise, had returned; and this mistake on the part of the Mexicans enabled the Spanish soldiers to gain a foothold on the mainland. Further, it is explained, a number of the city-states subservient to Montezuma went over to the Spanish cause and aided Cortez with troops, supplies and other much-needed assistance. The Spanish military techniques were new and surprising to Montezuma and his commanders. In addition, the superior weapons and equipment, including guns, horses, steel swords and crossbows, gave the Spaniards a big advantage. It has also been suggested that it was harvest time when the principal fighting occurred and many of Montezuma's soldiers were occupied with farm work.

After the death of Montezuma, the heroic efforts of his successors, Cuitlahuac (who reigned only four months in 1520) and Cuauhtemoc (1520-1524) failed to repel the conquering Europeans.

Despite the cruel and inhumane practice of human sacrifice on the part of the Aztecs, there was much that was commendable and good in their society. Some of the better and higher religious sentiments, which came originally from the Judæo-Christianity of the Nephites, were transmitted through the Lamanite-Mayan people to the Aztecs and were found in a degenerated form when the Spaniards came to Mexico. Thus like a golden thread the divine and eternal truths persisted from age to age, although in blighted and dimmed forms.[23]

---

[23] For a more detailed summary of Aztec history from 1300 A. D. to 1520 A. D. see Vaillant, op. cit., Ch. V.

Chapter 33

MAYAS AFTER 385 A. D.

Mayan Old Empire

When the Tultec-Nephite people were driven from their ancient Bountiful-Zarahemla homeland in the fourth century, the area was left to the Lamanite-Maya people. According to *The Book of Mormon,* the Lamanites were left in control of the entire occupied area below the "narrow neck of land"— including greater Bountiful-Zarahemla (extending from the isthmus on the west to the East Sea on the east) and the highlands of Nephi on the south. The truthfulness of the foregoing is sustained by unimpeachable archæological sources. Through them evidence has been produced which shows that after 385 A. D. the area below the Isthmus of Tehuantepec—including ancient Tlapallan and the highlands of Guatemala on the south, was the land of the Mayas. See the maps, pp. 158 and 186. A few "Maya-speaking" Chols entered northern Yucatan at an early date and were already there when a colony of Itza-Nephites entered the area about 500 A. D. Chichen Itza in northern Yucatan was founded by those Itzas in 514 A. D.[1]

The Tzokal ceramic period of the Mayas extended from the departure of the Tultecs from Bountiful-land in 339 A. D. down to about 633 A. D. During that same period stone monuments and stone buildings (including some buildings with corbeled roof-vaulting) were erected on a rather grandiose scale. Such works were not produced during the Nephite-Tultec occupancy of the "Maya" region. The construction of great calendar stones (stela) and imposing buildings with corbeled vaulted roofs continued in the area until 987 A. D. when Maya culture came to a virtual stop except in northern Yucatan.[2]

---

[1] Sylvanus G. Morley, *The Ancient Maya* (1946), p. 79 and Chart V, opposite p. 80.
[2] *Ibid.,* Table III, opposite p. 40.

The practice of erecting dated stone columns at the end of five-, ten-, and twenty-year cycles was one of the most peculiar practices.that characterized the post-Book-of-Mormon Mayas. Some of their cities where the practice was followed are listed below and the time span covered by dated monuments found at each site is indicated in our time system:

Uaxactun (Guatemala) . . .	327 A. D.-889 A. D.[3]
Tikal (Guatemala)	485 A. D.-869 A. D.
Copan (Honduras) . . .	480 A. D.-800 A. D.
Xultun (Guatemala) . . .	509 A. D.-889 A. D.
Yaxchilan (Chiapas) . . .	509 A. D.-771 A. D.
Piedras Negras (Guatemala) .	509 A. D.-810 A. D.
Pushilha (Br. Honduras) . .	569 A. D.-810 A. D.
Tonina (Chiapas)	544 A. D.-790 A. D.
Chincultic (Chiapas) . . .	588 A. D.-844 A. D.

The foregoing list shows only the dates in which dated monuments were erected. The dates do not reflect, necessarily, the full period of occupancy of each city. In fact, they may have been occupied earlier than the discovered monuments indicate.

Beginning about 633 A. D., a new ceramic period began. It is called Tepeu. Dated monuments began to appear in Palenque, Chiapas, in 638 A. D. New cities where dated monuments have been found were established in the Maya area at this time, including the following:

El Tortuguero .	about	645 A. D.
Jaina	"	652 A. D.
El Amparo . .	"	665 A. D.
Etzna	"	669 A. D.
Tila	"	685 A. D.
Quirigua . .	"	692 A. D.
Tzendales . .	"	692 A. D.
Lacanha . . .	"	692 A. D.
Quexil . . .	"	692 A. D.

The great Itza people, the "Holy Men" of Itzamna, abandoned Chichen Itza in 692 A. D. after 178 years of continuous occupancy. The reason is not known. From that important religious center they moved down the west coast of Yucatan to Chakanputun in the Campeche area. There they remained until about the time of the great Kukulcan. In 948 A. D. Chakanputun was abandoned by the Itzan—Serpent-Men, and under *Holon Chan,* they returned to their former center, to

---

[3] Morley gives the Maya dates for each of these cities and includes a number of other cities in his list. *The Ancient Maya,* Fig. 2, preceding p. 65.

Chichen Itza in northern Yucatan. Chichen Itza was formally reoccupied by the descendants of the ancient Itzas, cultural leaders of the Yucatecan New Empire, in 987 A. D.

In the meantime the great centers in the Usumacinta River basin, in ancient Bountiful-land, and in the Peten of Guatemala were deserted. The great city-states in those zones which lay far to the south and southwest of Chichen Itza were deserted by about 900 A. D. and they never were rebuilt. The tropical jungle has enveloped them from that date until the present time.

There has been much speculation regarding the causes of the collapse of these wonderful city-states of the Mayas' "Old Empire." Failure of the agricultural system and war may have been the primary causes.[4]

The period in which the greatest number of time-cycle stones were set up and dated was that century from 731 A. D. to 830 A. D., sometimes referred to as the Golden Age of the Mayas. Many wonderful buildings of stone were erected; very excellent sculpturing was done (see figure 40, page 267); fine ceramics and textiles were made; Maya territorial expansion reached its maximum limits; and the Maya priest-rulers were actively engaged in astronomical, mathematical, religious and agricultural pursuits. Whether metallurgy, which had been important in the early Nephite-Mulekite-Tultec period, was of importance is uncertain. Little use appears to have been made of metals in the area (ore is non-existent in the Maya lowlands) during the period of Maya dominance. The chief industry of the masses was, of course, farming, the principal crop being maize. Government of the Maya city-states was by the priest-hood; therefore it was theocratic. Writing was done in the Maya hieroglyphs. And apparently the scripts and tongues used by the priest-historians of the early Nephite-Tultec people belonged to the past ages. Lands were held in common, as in Nephite times. Slavery existed. Tattooing and painting of the body were practiced, as in Book of Mormon times. Peoples of both light and dark skins comprised the population. Herbs were used in treating the sick, as was done by the early Nephite-Lamanite peoples. And a form of baptism was practiced. Baptism of the dead (as distinguished from baptism for the dead) was engaged in.[5] Temple towers were in use as places of worship, even as in the early period.

---

4 Morley, op. cit., pp. 67-72.
5 Ibid., p. 205.

Mayan New Empire (987 A. D.-1441 A. D.)

About the time Topiltzin-Kukulcan passed along the Gulf Coast of Tabasco and Campeche in southern Mexico, following his flight from the Central Plateau, a group of Itzas were beginning to head back to their ancient capital—Chichen Itza in northern Yucatan. Topiltzin-Kukulcan joined forces with some of those Itzas. He was related to them through his ancestry that went back to the common homeland, the land of Bountiful. He and some of the Itzas of Chakanputun[6] (see figure 20, page 163) made their way to Chichen Itza. There Topiltzin-Kukulcan, the Tultec prince, led a great renaissance movement. The up-

(c) N.G.S. COURTESY OF NATIONAL GEOGRAPHIC MAGAZINE

Fig. 52: Maya Women of Today

They still cling to the religious practices of their Lamanite-Lemuelite-Ishmaelite ancestors. The women shown here live in the original homeland of the earliest Nahuales in the highlands of Guatemala. (Courtesy of *National Geographic Magazine*.)

swing lasted for 200 years—until 1194 A. D. The reborn culture of the Mayas in northern Yucatan is referred to by historians as the "New Empire." The impetus for this regeneration was furnished by the Tultec element from central Mexico and by the Itzas returning from Chakanputun. Both elements stemmed from the early Nephites and Lamanites.

---

[6] Chakanputun was in the vicinity of the modern Champoton in Campeche, on the Gulf Coast. Morley, *op. cit.*, p. 84.

Topiltzin-Kukulcan founded the great city of Mayapan in northern Yucatan about the same time the city of Uxmal was established in that area. Uxmal was settled by a leader who had also come from the ancient Bountiful-plant-land region for he bore the title *Tul-tul-xiu*, that is *Tutulxiu*, which means "Bountiful-Bountiful-herbs." His full name was *Ah Ziutok Tutul Xiu*.[7]

A political-military league was organized about 1000 A. D., comprised of these three northern cities—Chichen Itza, Mayapan and Uxmal. It was known as the League of Mayapan. The beautiful *Castillo*, temple-tower of Kukulcan at Chichen Itza, the observatory at Chichen Itza, the great outer temple-tower

(c) N.G.S. COURTESY OF NATIONAL GEOGRAPHIC MAGAZINE

Fig. 53: MAYA MEN OF TODAY

Note profile of the one on the right. They are descendants of the sages who came by sea from the ancient East. Beautiful lake Atitlan is in the background. This lake lies in an early and important archæological zone in which artifacts dating back to the very early Miraflores-Usulutan period have been found. *Courtesy of National Geographic Magazine. Original Kodachromes by Luis Marden.*

and the splendid Palace of the Governors at Uxmal are all monuments to the Itza-Tultec leaders of the period.

---

[7] *Ibid.*, p. 88.

Civil war in 1194 A. D. brought an end to the happy league of Mayapan. The war occurred between Chichen Itza and Mayapan, starting from rivalry over a beautiful woman. The ruler of Mayapan imported mercenary soldiers from the former Tultec country in Mexico. Chichen Itza was the loser and its leaders and their descendants were kept captive in Mayapan until 1441 A. D. In the latter year the tyrants of Mayapan were killed and the city fell. The empire of the Itza-Tultec leaders had collapsed. The Itzas of Chichen Itza fled 300 miles south to Lake Peten in Guatemala, located on the eastern rim of ancient greater Bountiful-land.

The eighty years from 1441 until the coming of the Span- iards was a period of chaos and disunity among the Mayas of northern Yucatan.

Period of Independent States—1441 A. D.—Conquest

The period following 1441 A. D. has been referred to by students of Mayan history as the "Period of Independent States."[8] The era from 1441 to 1697 A. D. has also been spoken of as the "Period of Disintegration."[9] Many small and powerless petty states arose during that period.

About 1464 A. D. a great hurricane swept Yucatan, doing immeasurable damage. That catastrophe was followed sixteen years later by a plague or pestilence which swept the land and reduced the population. In 1496 A. D. another terrible war was fought; and between 1500 and 1520 smallpox killed many of the inhabitants of the land. Thus, by the time the Spaniards arrived the once mighty Mayas were destitute of power or strength. Their ancient Old Empire cities to the south and west of Yucatan were abandoned and jungle-buried, and their New Empire cities in northern Yucatan had lost their splendor, power, and glory.

The remnant of the ancient Itza-Christians which made its way from Chichen Itza to Lake Peten in Guatemala following the fall of Mayapan in 1441 A. D. was, however, still intact as an organized political-religious entity when visited by Spanish priests in 1695-1699. It is of interest to note that the Itzas

[8] M. Wells Jakeman, *The Maya States of Yucatan, 1441-1545*, Doctoral Dissertation, 1938, Univ. of California at Berkeley.
[9] Morley, *op. cit.*, p. 94.

resisted the Spanish military until about 1700.[10] At that late date the degenerate Itzan remnant of the "Christians" of ancient Middle America still had hieroglyphic books,[11] still held to some aspects of their ancient religion, and were still governed by priests. Fray Andres de Avendano y Loyola visited the Itzas in 1695-1696 A. D. His description of the physical characteristics of the Itzas, in which he stated that they were well-featured and, like mestizos, nearly all of a light complexion, of very perfect stature and of natural gifts, has been previously quoted.[12] The Itza nation numbered about 150,000 persons when finally subdued by the Europeans. Philip Ainsworth Means said of them: "The Itzas resisted successfully for a much longer time a power more their superior than was that of Cæsar to that of the Guals."[13]

The attempts of the Spaniards to Christianize the descendants of the ancient "Christians" of the New World is interesting. A modified form of the teachings of Jesus of Nazareth was being urged by the Spaniards upon a people who already possessed an altered brand of the same doctrines. Means made this interesting observation of available data:

> At the time when Cortez was at Tayasal [Itzan capital at Lake Peten] (1525) a tolerant attitude toward the white men was prevalent. Far from resenting the proposed change in religion, the Canek of that day seems rather to have welcomed the new (sic) faith, and one can readily believe that had Cortez been able to do all that he promised, an early Christianization of the Itzas would have taken place. Instead, however, as we shall see, their idolatrous ways were to continue for many decades, and their attitude was to suffer a great change which, we must concede, is largely to be accounted for by Spanish brutality and bad faith.[14]

Today in Middle America the descendants of the ancient Mayas, Itzas, Tultecs, Nephites, and Lamanites look upon the splendid ruins left by their ancestors and wonder concerning them. It is quite certain, however, that they realize that those ruins represent former ages in which their ancestors attained and passed through several epochs of high culture and that the archæological remains bear mute witness to the phenomenal history of those people. Very few of the inhabitants of Middle America

[10] Philip Ainsworth Means, History of the Spanish Conquest of Yucatan and of the Itzas, Peabody Museum of American Archæology and Ethnology, Harvard Univ. (1917), pp. 58, 184-185.
[11] Padre Avendano described the Itzan books as follows: ". . . books of a quarter of a yard high and about five fingers broad, made of the bark of trees, folded from one side to the other like screens; each leaf of the thickness of a Mexican real of eight. These are painted on both sides with a variety of figures and characters . . ." Means, ibid., p. 141.
[12] See p. 248.
[13] Means, op. cit., p. 58.
[14] Ibid., p. 59.

today, however, realize that God preserved for them a book which contains the history of their ancestors—a great people who worshipped God the Eternal Father through His Only Begotten Son, Jesus Christ. As has been pointed out, that divine and holy book came to the world through the Prophet Joseph Smith and the administration of angels. In the present volume (*Ancient America and The Book of Mormon*), the readers have observed the abundance of evidence presented from sixteenth-century documentary sources, as well as from archæologists, all of which sustain the teachings proclaimed in the Nephite and Jaredite records, and, therefore, all of these sources bear witness to the divine authenticity of *The Book of Mormon*.

Chapter 34

THE WORLD TODAY AND THE
BOOK OF MORMON

AN AMERICAN WITNESS AND JESUS CHRIST

The Book of Mormon lends itself to proof or disproof as does no other purported scripture—be it the Bible, Koran or *Popul Vuh*. Biblical archæologists have gone far in establishing the authenticity of much of Bible history. But even so the skeptic still questions whether Jesus came forth from the tomb as a living person.

On the New World side of the picture, if the authenticity of the historical portions of *The Book of Mormon* are proven to be true, it follows necessarily that the literal and physical resurrection of Christ occurred. His appearance and ministry in Bountiful-land is an integral part of the historical portion of *The Book of Mormon* and, we might add, of the *Works of Ixtlilxochitl* also.

Further, if the historical portions of the Nephite records are true, the resurrected Christ necessarily had everything to do with the coming forth and the translation of those records— for there can be no other explanation for the coming forth and the translation of *The Book of Mormon* in 1830 as a true account of the inhabitants of ancient America. Having preceded Kingsborough's edition of the *Works of Ixtlilxochitl* by eighteen years, Stephens' *Incidents of Travel in Central America, Chiapas, and Yucatan* by eleven years, and having been ahead of the most important archæological discoveries from Middle America by one hundred years, the claim of the book itself and of Joseph Smith that Jesus Christ was the moving power behind the entire project would seem to be entitled to much weight. The Man of Galilee must have been very much alive and very much interested in the progress of mankind in 1830; otherwise no such work as *The Book of Mormon* could have come to the world from western

New York by way of a very humble boy—the Prophet Joseph Smith. Nor could the boy-prophet have translated a dead Egyptian script without divine aid. In the light of present knowledge, only Jesus the Christ could have engineered that important project.

It is a fact that the evidence supporting the truthfulness and divine authenticity of *The Book of Mormon* is voluminous. Admittedly not all readers will be alike in evaluating the evidence for and against the book. The range of evaluations will probably run the following gamut:[1]

> Authenticity—absolutely certain
> Authenticity—practically certain
> Authenticity—reasonably certain
> Authenticity—extremely probable
> Authenticity—very probable
> Authenticity—probable
> Authenticity—rather probable
> Authenticity—doubtful
> Authenticity—rather improbable
> Authenticity—improbable
> Authenticity—very improbable
> Authenticity—extremely improbable

Regardless of which of the foregoing classifications the reader may check as being applicable to his present view of *The Book of Mormon,* the work is entitled to further investigation and careful reading or rereading. It deserves the attention of the world's best students of the civilizations of ancient America. No other book holds forth such claims and such a remarkable challenge as does the Nephite scripture and yet no other important work has been so completely ignored in archæological circles.

If the reading of *Ancient America and The Book of Mormon* has not convinced you that it is probable that *The Book of Mormon* is true (and even if you think it is false) then the writers can only urge you to watch future developments and discoveries in Middle American, Near Eastern, and Egyptian antiquities. Not all the evidence has come forth.[2]

---

[1] See Dr. M. Wells Jakeman's method of interpreting and evaluating sources of Maya history in his book, *The Origins and History of the Mayas* (1945), pp. 155-156.

[2] Scripts identical with those in use in the ancient Near East and in Egypt may yet be found. Bible archæologists have lately been turning up various scripts of the ancient Near East that had not been known to modern scholars. W. F. Albright, *From the Stone Age to Christianity* (1940), pp. 13-14.

OUR MODERN WORLD AND THE BOOK OF MORMON

On the one hand, progress in physics, chemistry, and related sciences has reached a point where mankind is quite capable of destroying the human family with atomic and hydrogen bombs. Also, retrogression in religion and morality, accompanied by the spread of pagan-communism, have become so marked that man is quite likely to eradicate himself. Today the world is divided into two monstrous armed camps. It makes one sad to reflect on the fact that the Communistic Camp is directed by a handful of provincial pagans whose burning mission in life is to establish a dictatorship over the entire world—and this they intend to do *by any means most likely to prevail*. They now have atomic weapons. All liberty-loving people must face those awful facts.

Standing in opposition to the forces of evil is the power of the United States of America. The power of this great nation is of two kinds—physical and spiritual. It is true that America will need all the strength it can muster—both physical and spiritual—to bring the world and mankind safely through the next fifty years. The fact is regrettable, however, that America's stockpile of atomic weapons apparently inventories better than her stockpile of spiritual powers. According to a nation-wide poll,[3] only twenty-six per cent of the people of the United States think of God in intimate relation to their own lives and behavior.

If *The Book of Mormon* will help to fortify spiritually the people of this nation, or if it will help to change the hearts of the Russian leaders, all honest-hearted Americans should possess it and endeavor to share it and any other spiritual resources that they have with the Communists.[4]

The world is at the Saturday night of history. It is really late. On February 5, 1950, the president of one of our greatest American universities said:

Survival of the human race is at stake. . . . What is the answer to the A-bomb? Or the H-bomb? No government and no people yet know, but they had better find out, and soon, for it is later than we think.[5]

Our age, or the "Fourth Age" described by *Ixtlilxochitl*, can come to an end with fire—atomic fire; and that can occur

---

[3] *Ladies' Home Journal*, Nov., 1948; *The Readers' Digest*, Jan., 1949, p. 33.
[4] It is realized that the latter suggestion may be futile. Mormon missionaries have lately been arrested and expelled from Czechoslovakia.
[5] Robert Gordon Sproul (president of the University of California), as reported in *The Oakland Tribune*, Feb. 5, 1950.

quickly even as predicted in the Bible and *The Book of Mormon*. The question would seem to be merely, who will survive to witness it? As John Foster Dulles has put it:

There is no doubt whatever in my mind but that moral force is the only force that can accomplish great things in the world. If you look back to the history of our own country, you will find that our finest institutions were primarily molded by the Christian belief of our founders. They believed that there was such a thing as moral law, and that there was a Creator who endowed men with inalienable rights. They believed, too, that this nation had a great mission in the world to carry those concepts of righteousness to other people—— . . . The problem is: Will humanity be saved? It can be saved if, in proportion to our numbers, we have the ten righteous men who would have saved Sodom.[6]

Lessons Taught by The Book of Mormon

The Book of Mormon is an American scripture that made a quiet and modest appearance in 1830 in the then-recently organized republic, the United States of America. When Jesus Christ selected a place for the debut of a New World scripture, it was quite natural that the newborn land of the free should have been the most likely choice. At any rate, Joseph Smith lived and died claiming to have made available a new witness for the divinity of Jehovah-Christ. A million of his followers now believe that from ancient America there has come to us through *The Book of Mormon* the very knowledge of the force that causes humanity to progress or to retrogress—the knowledge for which a distinguished present-day American archæologist hoped when he wrote the following to his colleagues concerning the study of the ancients of Guatemala:

If we do our work as we should, we may come to understand the meaning of that civilization's strange pulsations, we may learn what stimulated its successes and what brought about its failures. We may even glean some knowledge—and the Lord knows we need it—of the mysterious forces that in all ages and in all parts of the globe seem inevitably to have caused each hopefully flowing tide of human progress to halt and finally to ebb.[7]

The Book of Mormon gives a clear and precise picture of two great social experiments—the Jaredite story on the one hand and the Nephite-Lamanite-Mulekite story on the other. Through ancient eyewitness historians, people of our age

---

[6] John Foster Dulles, in *The Readers' Digest* (Aug., 1948), pp. 105-108. See W. F. Albright, *Archaeology and the Religion of Israel* (1941), pp. 33-35.
[7] A. W. Kidder (of the staff of The Carnegie Institution of Washington, D. C.), "Excavations at Kaminaljuyu, Guatemala," *American Antiquity* (Oct., 1945), p. 75.

see families led into a rich but isolated zone—far removed from an already corrupted Eastern world. There they watch these select communities grow from family units to nations. They perceive that their societies became complex, and then later divided into tribes and factions.

Throughout the entire course of *Book of Mormon* history it is clearly evident that the ancient Americans were assisted by Deity at every turn. Jehovah-Christ himself led them, ministered to them and taught them that the individual members of society must keep under restraint personal lusts and ambitions for power and self-indulgence. A study of those ancient Americans clearly shows that where individuals allow lusts for power, prestige, riches and weaknesses of the flesh to dominate, the results have had widespread destructive effects. As a general rule, the innocent, the good, and even the just were made to suffer along with the unjust and wicked. The perennial adage that "the rains fall upon both the good and the bad" is proven to be true. All the instructions which the Lord has given to his children through the House of Israel, including its New World branch, were designed to encourage men to resist personal immoral lusts and ambitions.

The Jaredite-Nephite experiments demonstrated a social law. When men followed the instructions of God by controlling and restraining themselves, as directed, the result was happiness, love, prosperity and progress. When men ignored the instructions, the result was sadness, hatred, retrogression and finally destruction. Emphasis should be placed on the thought that this rule is universal. It is an eternal law; therefore, it applies to our complicated modern world as well as it did to the societies of ancient America.

PRICE OF PEACE

The formula for peace and happiness, as given in *The Book of Mormon,* is plain and precious. It is simply this: "*Keep the commandments of the Lord.*"[8] It is most difficult to get people to do this—but *it is the price of peace.* The Nephite-Lamanite society succeeded at it for 288 years following the ministry of Christ in Bountiful-land; 288 years of continuous peace and prosperity is a world record. Their history demonstrates that the rule works when applied.

---

[8] See George Albert Smith (President of The Church of Jesus Christ of Latter-day Saints), "The Path of Peace," *The Improvement Era* (Oct., 1948), p. 617.

The Book of Mormon also demonstrates graphically, as was testified to by eyewitness leaders, that utter destruction and desolation of mighty people came following sensual uncontrolled release of lusts for power and self-gratification.

The same choices that were before the Jaredites and Nephites lie before our marvelous world of 1950. Our ascent can continue or our fall can be the greatest of all time. The human family needs only to keep the commandments of God to get the good result; but if mankind continues to live lustful, sensual, selfish lives, just as sure as the sun shines, misery and destruction await the world. *The Book of Mormon* is a remarkable semaphor. It must not be ignored.

WARNINGS TO THE WORLD IN "LATTER DAYS"

The true Gospel of Jesus Christ was restored to earth again a little over a hundred years ago through the instrumentality of the Prophet Joseph Smith. The Church that he organized under the direction of heavenly beings, known as the Church of Jesus Christ of Latter-day Saints, is endowed with the Holy Priesthood after the Order of the Only Begotten Son of God. All of the gospel ordinances and doctrine necessary for man's salvation and exaltation in the presence of God the Father and Jesus Christ have been restored to that Church. Thus the same Gospel that Jesus Christ taught in Palestine in the meridian of times and also that He taught the Jaredites and Nephites in ancient America has been restored to earth again.

Along with the restoration from the heavens of the true plan of salvation, an eternal decree has gone forth from the throne of Almighty God to the effect that if the inhabitants of the earth will accept the true Gospel as restored through the Prophet Joseph Smith they will enjoy peace, happiness, and great prosperity and the Lord Jesus Christ will come on earth to reign for one thousand years as Lord of lords and King of kings. But, on the other hand, if humanity rejects the restored Gospel of our Master, misery, suffering, calamities, and destruction await the inhabitants of the earth. Terrible and numerous are the calamities which shall be poured out on the human family prior to the second advent of Jesus Christ. God has spoken in definite terms through the Prophet Joseph Smith. Following are a few examples of the word of the Lord on this subject:

And the whole world lieth in sin, and groaneth under darkness and under the bondage of sin. . . . Verily, verily, I say unto you who now hear my words, which are my voice, blessed are ye inasmuch as you receive these things; the doctrines and ordinances of the Gospel of Jesus Christ; For I will forgive you of your sins with this commandment—that you remain steadfast in your minds in solemnity and the spirit of prayer, in bearing testimony to all the world of those things which are communicated unto you. Therefore, go ye into all the world; and unto whatsoever place ye cannot go ye shall send, that the testimony may go from you into all the world unto every creature. And as I said unto mine apostles, even so I say unto you, for you are mine apostles, even God's high priests; ye are they whom my Father hath given me; ye are my friends; Therefore, as I said unto mine apostles I say unto you again, that every soul who believeth on your words, and is baptized by water for the remission of sins, shall receive the Holy Ghost. . . . Verily, verily, I say unto you, they who believe not on your words, and are not baptized in water in my name, for the remission of their sins, that they may receive the Holy Ghost, shall be damned, and shall not come into my Father's kingdom where my Father and I am. And this revelation unto you, and commandment, is in force from this very hour upon all the world, and the gospel is unto all who have not received it. But, verily I say unto all those to whom the kingdom has been given—from you it must be preached unto them, that they shall repent of their former evil works; for they are to be upbraided, for their evil hearts of unbelief. . . .

Behold, I send you out to reprove the world of all their unrighteous deeds, and to teach them of a judgment which is to come. And whoso receiveth you, there I will be also, for I will go before your face. I will be on your right hand and on your left, and my Spirit shall be in your hearts, and mine angels round about you, to bear you up. Whoso receiveth you receiveth me; and the same will feed you, and clothe you, and give you money. And he who feeds you, or clothes you, or gives you money, shall in nowise lose his reward. And he that doeth not these things is not my disciple; by this you may know my disciples. . . . Nevertheless, search diligently and spare not; and wo unto that house, or that village or city that rejecteth you, or your words, or your testimony concerning me. Wo, I say again, unto that house, or that village or city that rejecteth you, or your words, or your testimony of me; For I, the Almighty, have laid my hands upon the nations, to scourge them for their wickedness. And plagues shall go forth, and they shall not be taken from the earth until I have completed my work, which shall be cut short in righteousness —Until all shall know me, who remain, even from the least unto the greatest, and shall be filled with the knowledge of the Lord. . . .

. . . warn the people . . . with the sound of my gospel, with a loud voice, of the desolation and utter abolishment which await them if they do reject these things. For if they do reject these things the hour of their judgment is nigh, and their house shall be left unto them desolate. . . . For, with you saith the Lord Almighty, I will rend their kingdoms; I will not only shake the earth, but the starry heavens shall tremble. For I, the Lord, have put forth my hand to exert the powers of heaven;

ye cannot see it now, yet a little while and ye shall see it, and know that I am, and that I will come and reign with my people. I am Alpha and Omega, the beginning and the end. Amen.[9]

Therefore, verily, thus saith the Lord, let Zion rejoice, for this is Zion—THE PURE IN HEART; therefore, let Zion rejoice, while all the wicked shall mourn. For behold, and lo, vengeance cometh speedily upon the ungodly as the whirlwind; and who shall escape it? The Lord's scourge shall pass over by night and by day, and the report thereof shall vex all people; yea, it shall not be stayed until the Lord come; For the indignation of the Lord is kindled against their abominations and all their wicked works. Nevertheless, Zion shall escape if she observe to do all things whatsoever I commanded her.[10]

And again more than one hundred years ago the voice of God warned the nations of the earth in the following firm decree:

Verily, thus saith the Lord concerning the wars that will shortly come to pass . . .

And thus, with the sword and by bloodshed the inhabitants of the earth shall mourn; and with famine, and plague, and earthquake, and the thunder of heaven, and the fierce and vivid lightning also, shall the inhabitants of the earth be made to feel the wrath, and indignation, and chastening hand of an Almighty God, until the consumption decreed hath made a full end of all nations; That the cry of the saints, and of the blood of the saints, shall cease to come up into the ears of the Lord of Sabaoth, from the earth, to be avenged of their enemies. Wherefore, stand ye in holy places, and be not moved, until the day of the Lord come; for behold, it cometh quickly, saith the Lord. Amen.[11]

Warnings to the inhabitants of ancient America came from God through the holy prophets to the effect that destruction awaited the Jaredite and Nephite nations if the people did not repent of their wickedness and turn unto the God of this land "who is Jesus Christ," and serve Him. History affirms, however, that the people continued in their wicked ways of living. In the case of the Jaredites, they paid no attention to the voice of God's Prophet—Ether; and in the case of the Nephites, they refused to heed the instruction of the Prophet Mormon. Therefore, complete destruction lay at their doors and two great nations were swept off the face of the earth.

Our twentieth-century world has had similar warnings and notice. The same choices are before us. It is hoped that humanity today will choose intelligently.

[9] *Doctrine and Covenants,* 84:49, 60-64, 74-76a, 87-90, 94-98a, 114b-115, 118-120.
[10] *Ibid.,* 97:21-25.
[11] *Ibid.,* 87:1a, 6-8.

If people will read *The Book of Mormon,* and read it with an open mind, it will serve as a guiding light to the human family. It is perhaps the most powerful witness in the world today, testifying that Jesus of Nazareth was resurrected and that He is the Messiah—the light, life, and hope of the world, and furthermore, of each person in the world. Each individual is indebted to Him personally for the earth on which we live and for life itself. Accordingly, everybody should worship God the Eternal Father and serve, honor, and obey His Only Begotten Son, Jesus the Christ, in harmony with the warnings which have come to us from the Prophets of ancient America as well as the admonitions of the latter-day servants of God. By doing so the world can be saved from destruction. *There is no other course!*

CHAPTER 35

CONCLUSIONS

INTRODUCTION

The story of the inhabitants of ancient America from the time of the erection of the Tower of Babel to the Spanish Conquest, according to the historical data obtained from several documentary sources, has now been told. The two principal documents—*The Book of Mormon* and the *Works of Ixtlilxochitl*—have furnished the writers the most extensive amount of historical information regarding the ancient inhabitants of this land of all sources used. Several sixteenth-century writings have also proven of much worth in the production of this book. However, by far the most complete and also most authentic of all documents used in compiling this volume was the Nephite record. Such is the case because it was written by holy prophets of God who were eyewitnesses of the events as they occurred in ancient times from the time of the migration of the Jaredites from Babel to 421 A. D. Also, the Nephite and Jaredite records were preserved under the direction of the Lord for approximately fourteen hundred years after the extermination of the Nephite nation for the purpose of giving to the world in the latter days a new witness that Jesus is the Christ and the Savior of the world. Thus, *The Book of Mormon* is a divine record of ancient America and an holy scripture.

ANCIENT SOURCES CONFIRM EACH OTHER

The Book of Mormon is in close parallel with the *Works of Ixtlilxochitl* on a multitude of things—both general and technical. There are so many close parallels that they cannot all be reviewed here. It is suggested that the reader may wish to go back and reread the introductory and summary statements at the beginnings and ends of the various chapters where they are found.

By way of summary and conclusion, throughout this book the fact has been mentioned several times that both accounts tell that there were three separate groups of cultured colonizers who migrated from the "Fertile Crescent" to Middle America in ancient times, bringing with them to the New World much of the cultural knowledge of the "cradle of civilization." Both tell many of the details of the history and culture of the settlers. Both furnish many specific dates for the happening of outstanding events. Likewise, each sets forth the names of important places, persons and peoples. There is remarkable agreement between *Ixtlilxochitl* and *The Book of Mormon* concerning most of those details.

Further, when third sources throw light on ancient Middle American history—whether those sources be documents such as the *Popol Vuh, Totonicapan, Sahagun* or *Torquemada,* or whether they be such archæological discoveries as the bearded "Uncle Sam" of La Venta, Tabasco, with his Semitic face and upturned shoes —they also all confirm our two primary accounts.

According to the evidence, it was Jesus Christ, or Jehovah of the Old Testament, who led the settlers to the New World, who watched over their activities here, and who personally appeared and ministered to the people of Bountiful-land shortly following His resurrection. In fact, the climax of the ancient history of Middle America was the appearance of the resurrected Messiah to the people in the land of Bountiful in 34 A. D. He was known in the sixteenth-century documents by the names of Quetzalcoatl, Gucumatz, and Itzamna. No more minute and exact parallels exist between *Ixtlilxochitl* and *The Book of Mormon* than those relating to this matter. Full support for the claims of both histories also comes from the third sources.

THE BOOK OF MORMON

What is the most significant and vital point in regards to this book—*Ancient America and The Book of Mormon?* The answer lies in the fact that the *Works of Ixtlilxochitl,* the *Popol Vuh, Totonicapan, Torquemada, Sahagun,* and other works quoted herein, as well as the archæologists cited, as has been pointed out, all corroborate the historical facts and doctrinal data contained in *The Book of Mormon.* Also, all of these sixteenth-century documents confirm the fact that the beliefs and practices of the ancient Americans came down through the ages in the histories and traditions of the Indians. Certainly many variations occurred as the years passed; but numerous resemblances to the original record also persisted. The logical conclusion to be drawn is that all the sources supply evidence which verifies *The Book of Mormon* to be an accurate and true history of the inhabitants of ancient America, as well as a divine and holy scripture, as that book and members of the Church of Jesus Christ of Latter-day Saints claim it to be. Furthermore, more than a hundred years ago the voice of God spoke from heaven on three different occasions and verified the foregoing to be true. He proclaimed:

Behold, thou [Joseph Smith] wast called and chosen to write *The Book of Mormon,* and to my ministry; . . .[1]

Which commandments ["the will and commandments of God," including the instruction to organize the Church of Jesus Christ] were given to Joseph Smith, Jun., who was called of God, and ordained an apostle of Jesus Christ, . . .

. . . God ministered unto him by an holy angel, whose countenance was as lightning, and whose garments were pure and white above all other whiteness; and gave unto him commandments which inspired him; and gave him power from on high, by the means which were before prepared, to translate *The Book of Mormon; which contains a record of a fallen people, and the fulness of the gospel of Jesus Christ to the Gentiles and to the Jews also.*[2]

And he [Joseph Smith] has translated the book, even that part which I have commanded him, *and as your Lord and your God liveth it is true.*[3]

It is the privilege of every person in the entire world who is honest in heart to know for himself or herself whether or not *The Book of Mormon* is a holy, divine, and true scripture, as it is claimed to be. When Moroni, the last writer on the Nephite records, was completing the job and preparing to hide the records for the purpose of having them brought forth in the latter days through the power of God, he made the following promise to you and me and to everybody throughout the world who would have faith enough to put it into effect:

And I seal up these records, after I have spoken a few words by way of exhortation unto you. . . . And when ye shall receive these things, I would exhort you that ye would ask God, the Eternal Father, in the name of Christ, if these things are not true; *and if ye shall ask with a sincere heart, with real intent, having faith in Christ, he will manifest the truth of it unto you, by the power of the Holy Ghost.*[4]

[1] Joseph Smith, *Doctrine and Covenants,* 24:1a.
[2] Ibid., 20:2a, 6b-9.
[3] Ibid., 17:6.
[4] *The Book of Mormon,* p. 520 (Moroni 10:2, 4).

Since the time of the publication or *The Book of Mormon* in 1830 A. D., thousands and thousands of people have put Moroni's admonition into effect and have received the result that he promised. They have found that Moroni stated a divine spiritual law which is irrevocable and which is just as real and exacting in its operations as are physical laws. Therefore, practically every member of the Church of Jesus Christ of Latter-day Saints today bears witness to the fact that he knows *The Book of Mormon* is a divine and sacred record of the historical events and religious teachings and practices of the inhabitants of ancient America, and that that record was revealed by the power of God to the people of the world in the latter days through the instrumentality of the Prophet Joseph Smith.

The Book of Mormon is the most authentic document in existence relative to the history of ancient America. All of the early Spanish and Indian documents used by the writers in composing this book *(Ancient America and The Book of Mormon)*, as well as the findings of the archæologists, have sustained the teachings of the Nephite record time and time again. In fact, they have been consistent in their continuous accord with that record on practically every point presented; therefore, they have all borne witness continuously to the divine authenticity of *The Book of Mormon*.

INDEX

A

Aaron, Lamanite king and general, 230, 352.

Aaron, Mosiah's son—teachings of, 235.

Abinadi, fulfillment of prophecies of, 229, 289.

Abraham, altar of, 267; father of Ishmael, 76; God of, 264; Guatemalans descendants of, 64.

Acamapichtzin, discoverer of Tulantzinco was, 374.

Acapichtzin, leader of Tultecas, 359.

Acapitzin, queen of Tulta, 375.

Aculhuas, of Chichimecas, 25.

Acxocuauh, son of Cuatlix, 386.

Adam, creation of, 234; fall of, 235; forbidden fruit partaken by, 213, 234; father of humanity, 89.

Adamic language, spoken by Jaredites, 29-30.

Aeronautical Chart Service Maps, utilized in Book of Mormon geography study, 146.

Agaba, Gulf of, 77.

Agates, Old Testament mention of, 302 ff.

Aguacatal, excavations at, 270.

Ahnitzotl, Aztec ruler & accomplishments of, 400.

Akish, wickednesc & destruction of, 41-42.

Alaska, Eskimos of, 239; Mongoloids came to America via of, 397.

Albright, William Foxwell, work on Isaiah scroll of, 100; clothing of ancient Israelites described by, 319.

Alma, priests ordained by, 155; quoted on Liahona, 71; religious leadership of, 148; teachings of regarding accountability for our words & thoughts, 324.

Alpha & Omega, God is, 417; Jesus Christ is, 192.

Algonquins, arrival of in Mexico, 397.

Alta Verapaz, archæological site at, 62.

Altar, Abraham building of, 267.

Altars, erection of by Israelites, 270; erection of by ancient Americans, 271.

Alvarado, city of, location and description of, 185.

Alvarado, Pedro de, location of Tlapallan given by, 166-167.

Amaleki, records given to King Benjamin by, 399; records kept by, 127.

Amalekites, Nephite dissenters, 275.

America, Columbus discovered, 241; Indians live in, 1, story of, 3; cultures from Near East, 8; journey of Lehi's group to, 242; ancient America compared with, 228-229.

America, ancient, architecture in, 264 ff.; Book of Mormon divine record of, 419; Book of Mormon true record of, 232; cotton brought to, 307-308; destruction in at time of crucifixion, 192-193; inhabitants' knowledge of Christ, 207-212; Jesus Christ visited, 195 ff., 202 ff., 216-217, 222, 420; law against black magic in, 291; people of admonished to repent, 417-418; people of had gospel, 422; peoples who lived in, 19; prophets in, 289; Quetzal-serpent symbolism in, 202; cross symbolism in, 202; races in, 239 ff.; settled by descendants of Jacob, 288; three migrations to, 55; wheeled toys of, 260; roads in, 261; white people in, 174.

America, Middle, 228; altars found in, 271; archæology of, 258; arts & crafts resemble those of Mediterranean world, 288; colonizers of, 67; gold refining process used in, 281; inscriptions on door jambs in, 271; metallurgical skills in, 283; Near East people came to, 249; plaster & cement used in, 269-270; temples in, 264-268; temple-towers in, 26, 267 ff.; Near East & Asiatic colonizers of, 283; Mongoloids migrate to, 397-398; Jaredites lived in, 121; Liahona had by people of, 72.

America, North, traditions of 2nd coming of Christ in, 215.

America, South, gold plates from, 280; traditions of 2nd coming of Christ in, 215; type of Indians found in, 239 ff.

Americans, ancient, directed by Deity, 414; social law demonstrated by, 414; dress of, 317; law of regarding war, 362; practices & doctrines of transmitted through ages, 421; skills of, 257 ff.; wars & peace of, 227; how peace achieved by, 228; wheels had by, 258-259.

43; description of complete destination of Jaredites in, 49 ff.; Jaredites battle grounds described in, 53; edition used, 15; fortifications described in, 273; geography of, 143-146; God's declaration of truthfulness of, 421; Moroni tells how to get a testimony of its truthfulness, 421; gospel contained in, 421; gold plates of, 277; greatest source for this book, 419; history covered in, 20; how quoted, 18; ignored by archæologists, 13; what does not contain, 13-14; information regarding Christ in, 207 ff.; Jaredites' history in, 121; uniting with Nephites, 122; knowledge concerning creation in, 21, 88; knowledge concerning flood in, 22, 91; most authentic document of history of ancient America, 422; documents used testify to divine authenticity of, 422; most complete story of Christ in, 272; Nephites' animals & fowls listed in, 308-310; summary statement regarding, 314; Nephites' armor described in, 273-275; quoted—Nephites came from Palestine discussed in, 276; Nephites had Liahona discussed in, 70-71; Nephites paid tribute to Lamanites told in, 87-88; contents confirmed, 88; Nephites' use of stones described in, 283 ff.; Nephites were of Israel, 84; new witness of Christ, 413; not influenced by Works of Ixtlilxochitl, 7; eyewitness record, 7; people described in, 19; popularity of, 11; far ahead of times, 11; details on early Americans in, 12; not fairly appraised, 12; possible location of Bountiful & Zarahemla indicated in, 167-169; pottery dated in period of, 171; preface of, 18-19; productivity of America described in, 38-40; proofs of divine authenticity of, 410-411; spiritual forces in, 412-413; lessons taught by, 413-414; quoted—bad arts practiced by Lamanites & Nephites, 289-290; quoted, Christ's departure, 218; quoted—description of Christ in, 210; cross symbol of, 211; Tree of Life, 212-213; quoted—description of peace, 229-230; date of, 231; destruction of Nephites predicted in, 216-217; quoted—Jesus teaching on speech in, 323; quoted—long period of peace, 223 ff.; quoted—Mulekites directed by God, 130-131; quoted, Nephite crops, 302-303; quoted—Noah's tower & garden, 329;

Nephi's garden & tower, 329; quoted—regarding Christ's visit to ancient America, 203-207; quoted—regarding color of Nephites & Lamanites, 240; quoted—ship building, 132; quoted—skills of Nephites, 257; quoted—sun standing still, 298-299; discussion of, 300-301; seven caves, "barges," 34; shows people of Bountiful-land were poets, philosophers, orators, 292; sorrow of colonists reported in, 69-70; spinning, weaving & dress of Nephites, 315-316; story of Lehi's journey in Arabia, in, 72ff.; story of Nephites in, 54 ff.; summary comparison with Ixtlilxochitl, 370-371; quoted—unity of Nephites & Mulekites, 127 ff.; sustained by Popol Vuh, 80, 93; temple-towers mentioned in, 26; term "precious stones" used in, 286-287; tests of truthfulness of, 195-196; third great calamity described in, 46-47; translation completed of, 105; three witnesses to, 104 ff.; eight witnesses to, 116 ff.; validity of witnesses to, 118-120; date of publication of, 120; Tree of Life, mentioned in, 213; uses of iron, copper, brass, claimed by, 276.

Boturini, Motolinia, statement—solar eclipse recorded by Tultecas at crucifixion of Christ, 198.

Bountiful, droughts in, 305; Fair God appeared in, 198; heart of Nephite-Tultec kingdom at, 366; change to Lamanite dominance at, 366; home of Nephites, 55; in Arabia, 58; land of, Nephite armies in, 177; meaning of, 151-153; Nephite armies gathered in, 178-179; Nephites arrived at, 74; Nephites lived in, 180; people of, 3, 57; precious stones carved by people of, 286 f.; point of embarkation, 81, 84; possible location of, 33, 124, 167-169, 175; ship built at, 80-81, 132 (Tullan), departure from, 87; white people of, 174; colonists from, 175.

Bountiful-land, abandonment of by Nephite-Tultecs, 369-370; arts & crafts of people of, 257 ff.; altars built by people of, 271; appearance of Christ in, 218, 220; Christ's ministry in, 221; colonists from, 285-286; dress of people similar to that of Bible lands in, 315 ff.; flight of Topiltzin to, 390; fortifications in, 273; Itzas came from, 248; knowledge concerning God of people of, 233 ff.; location of, 158 ff.; 165 ff.; 287, 390; ceramics found in, 287; manners &

had by, 310; origin of metallurgical skills of, 283; expert goldsmiths, 279-280; variety of physical types of, 239 ff.; white bearded God tradition of, 215; white ones of, 241.

Indian Ocean, Nephites crossed, 84.

Iron, Nephites' uses of, 258, 276; use by ancient Americans of, 276 ff.; Noah's palace ornamented with, 325.

Iron Age, date of, 276.

Irreantum, ocean named, 74.

Isabel, the harlot, 331.

Isaiah, quoted by Nephi, 100; problem of in Book of Mormon, 100; scroll of found in 1947, 100, 102; quoted—"mountain of the Lord's house," 267; quoted—regarding gardens & pools, 330; teachings of in Book of Mormon, 342.

Ishmael, family of joins Lehi, 64; sons of rebellion, 64, 69; death of, 73, 78; Arab-Israelite of, 75.

Ishmaelites, tribe of, 229, 230.

Israel, Nephites of, 55, 66-69; lost tribes theory of, 12-13; progenitors of Quiché, 63; scattering & gathering of, 66-67; Nephites branch of, 197; Messiah symbol of, 201; Jesus Christ God of, 204; ancient Americans were, 209; prophets of fought black magic, 290; of Caucasian race, 249; Nephites descendants of, 155, 221.

Israelites, plaster used by, 269; writings on gold tablets of, 279; led by Moses, 276; architecture of, 272 ff.; writing on brass & gold of, 277; mining activities of, 279; uses of gold of, 282; sandals of, 322; settlers of Bountiful-land descended from, 322; ornaments worn by, 326; mourning & fasting custom at death of, 326-327; cremation not practiced by, 328; meal schedule of, 328; gardens & towers of, 329-330; pools had by, 330; marriage age of, 335; law against marrying relatives of, 335-336.

Itzamna, bearded white God was, 68; Messiah of Yucatan, 91; God of Itzas, 214; (Christ), Tree of Life symbol of, 113; identical with Christ, 420.

Itzas, Tree of Life worshipped by, 213-214; Yucatan colonized by, 162, 165; home of, 174; described & identified as Caucasians, 252; white settlers of Yucatan, 248; Nephite settlers of Yucatan, 372-373, 402; high culture of, 405-406; Kukulcan ruler of, 393; descendants of Ne-

phites & settlers of Chichen Itza, 391; Spaniards resisted by at Lake Peten, 407-408, 156.

Itzalte, "tree of liquid amber," 214.

Itzamat, "God tree," 214.

Itzcoatl, king of Tenochitlan & accomplishments of, 399; death of, 400.

Ixanom, fruit Adam ate was, 213.

Ixtlilxochitl (Works of Ixtlilxochitl), first appearance in English of, 3; date of, 3-4, 6; source of, 6; publishing of, 3, 5-8; historical source of, 1; Works of—translated, 3, 5-9; location of home of, 390; no help from archæology, 8-9; writings of far ahead of time, 11; brief biographical sketch of, 15; far ahead of times, 11; details on early Americans in, 12; not fairly appraised, 12; date writings published, Spanish edition used of, 14; what does not contain, 13-14; how quoted, 18; people described by, 19-20; infers settlers were of Israel, 84; statement on Tultecas' knowledge of creation & flood, 21-22, 35, 89, 91; confusion of tongues in, 24 ff.; account of Ulmecas in, 121 ff.; account of Giants or Ancient Ones coming to America by, 33, 38; second great calamity described by, 41-44; third great calamity described by, 34, 48; description of destruction of Giants in, 46; destructions of Ancient Ones in, 49-54; colonizers of Bountiful-land discussed in, 60; coming of Ulmecas discussed, in, 123, 135; seat of kingdom given in, 167; quoted— Giants discovered by Ulmecas, 136 ff.; chosen land described in, 25; temple-towers mentioned in, 26; confirmed in location of Tulan, 174; pottery dated in period of, 171; destruction at time of Christ's crucifixion told in, 189-194; Christ's 2nd coming predicted in, 214-215; claims Bountiful settlers come from Near East, 256; colonizers from Near East, 250; quoted—regarding Quetzalcoatl's visit to ancient America, 203; quoted—description of Christ in, 210; quoted—long period of peace & its disruption, 223-224; quoted—Quetzalcoatl's prediction people pass through calamities, 216; quoted — Quetzalcoatl, departure, 218; skills of Tultecas, 257; iron used by Tultecas, claim of, 263-264; quoted—sacrificing of white children, 245; quoted—kings of Tlapallan were white & bearded, 240; Tultecas' armor described by, 273-274;

quoted—armor of Tultecas, 275; claimed Tultecas expert metal workers, 276 ff.; Tultecas' uses of stones described in, 283 ff.; bad & good arts parcticed by Tultecas, 289; ceramics dating in period of, 287-288; quoted—sun standing still, 298; discussion of, 300-301; quoted—weaving and dress of Tultecas, 315-316; Tultecas' crops listed by, 302; Tultecas' animals & fowls listed by, 308-310; summary statement regarding, 314; description of hair dress of ancient Americans by, 322; quoted—Tultecas spoke little, 323; quoted—Tultecas wore pearls, 324; quoted—burial customs of Tultec kings, 326; quoted—Tultecs' meal schedule, 328; quoted—divine book compiled by Hueman, 338; quoted—virtue, 330; quoted—Tultecas' gardens & pools, 329; statement regarding human sacrifice, 360; account of Tultecas & Nephites who survived Cumorah given by, 373 ff.; stay of Tultecas to Spanish conquest told by, 373 ff.; agreement with Book of Mormon, 153, 155, 194, 370-371; Book of Mormon confirmed by, 12, 287, 291, 157-158, 218-220; 29-30, 35, 232, 347 ff., 420; "Fourth Age" —fire—described by, 412-413; Tultec empire dating of, 388-389; second source for this book, 419, 175.

Ixtlilxochitl, ancestor of Ixtlilxochitl, Cortez accompanied by, 167.

Izcax, son of Texpolcatl, 381.

Izacatecatl, king of Tula, 376.

Iztachuexuca, Tultecas settled at, 374.

J

Jachin, pillar of, 264.

Jacinth, Old Testament meeting of, 287.

Jacob, birth of, 81; descendants of settled ancient America, 288; God of, 267; Guatemalans descendants of, 64; Hebrew name, 76; quoted—hardships of, 70; revelations received by, 97; teachings of regarding chastity, 330-331.

Jacobites, tribe of, 229, 231.

Jade, early pieces of & where found, 284-285; Montezuma's use of, 325.

Jakeman, M. Wells, extracts from Totonicapan published by, 56; meaning of Tutul-xiu given by, 151; new world cotton in Polynesian islands, 307.

James, King, Bible translation of, 277.

Japanese, all cattle in Philippines eaten by, 312.

Jared, Brother of, at Babel & migration to America, 24 ff.; language not changed, 25, 29-30; God's instructions to, 30; barges bulit by, 30-32; God praised by, 32; power in writing of, 297.

Jaredites, ancient homeland of, 370; archæology in land of, 175; home of, 176; artifacts of, 188; choice land of, 38-40; come to America from Babel, 33; complete destruction of, 49-54; definition of, 19-20; encountered by Mulekites, 34, 136-139; first settlers, 55; forces back of, 413; game hunted in Bountiful-land by, 182; history of on 24 gold plates, 97; translated by king Mosiah, 97; discovered by Lemhi's men, 97; homeland of, 172, 182; knowledge concerning creation of, 21; knowledge concerning flood of, 22-23; land of, 126; maize domesticated by, 303; map—landing place of, 37; migration of from Babel, 260, 419; migration to America of, 24 ff.; Nephites received ancient homeland of, 349, 356; no dated monuments found of, 187; ocean crossed by, 307-308; records of, 3; records of abridged by Moroni, 6, 340-341; records of preserved, 409; traveling to America of, 30 ff.; true gospel had by, 415; turkeys had by, 309; warning of prophets to 417.

Jasper, Old Testament mention of, 287.

Javelin, Nephites' use of, 258.

Jehovah, Christ known as to Hebrews, 420; commandment of, 67, 68.

Jehu, King of Israel, homage of to Shalmaneser & dress of, 319.

Jeremiah, quoted—regarding writing on silver & gold tablets, 279; signets worn on hand at time of, 326; teachings of prophets to on brass plates, 98.

Jericho, seige of, 34.

Jershon, colonizing of by Ammonites, 287.

Jerusalem, architecture of, 272; Ishmael came from, 64; people desire to return to, 64, 69; Jaredites came from, 121; Jews fled from, 79-80. Lamanites came from, 69; Lehi left, 235; Lehi lived at, 59; Mulekites came from, 123, 128; Nephi left, 208; Nephites came from, 55, 88, 241; people came from, 20; peoples' sorrow on leaving, 69; time measured from Nephites' leaving of, 27-

98; seeds brought from, 302, 305; small Nephite party left, 85.

Jerusalem, New, to be established, 220.

Jesus Christ, admonitions to people of, 191-192; law of Moses fulfilled by, 192; destruction at crucifixion of, 189 ff.; God of the land, 38; gospel of, 92, 416; people of Bountiful visited by, 157-158, 218; prediction of Nephite calamities of, 216; predictions regarding, 217; 2nd coming of, 214-215; Son of God's name, 62; visit to ancient America of, 203 ff., 67, 220-221, 216, 217, 420; introduces himself, 204; 12 selected by & authority given & instructions on baptism by, 205; doctrine of fasting by, 206; sick healed by, 206-207; was white, 241; baptized in name of, 223; Fair God of ancient America was, 194 ff.; Messiahship of, 194; to be rejected by Jews, 67; righteous works performed in name of, 224; other names of, 420; appearance to the Nephites of, 209; ask God in name of, 341; Book of Mormon new witness for, 413; birth & crucifixion of, 230; chastity teachings of, 332; children of, 225; Church of, apostasy from, 226; Church of established, 223; Church of in Old & New worlds compared, 228; colonization near time of, 175; departure of, 218; description of, 210; cross symbol of, 211; Tree of Life symbolism, of, 212-213; destruction at time of crucifixion of, 218; fasting established by, 119; sick healed by, 219; symbolism of, 219; promise to return, 219; Quetzalcoatl identical with, 199-200, 220; garden parable of, 330; God worshipped through, 409; Mayan temple erected to, 391; Mayan writings 3rd or 4th before 170; pottery about time of, 171; millennial reign of, 415; most complete story of, 222; must hear Gospel of, 229; Nephites were believers in, 243; Nephites who would not deny were killed, 372; peace following ministry of & its disruption, 223 ff.; description of appearance of, 219; teachings of, 219; plan redemption given by, 235; proof of resurrection of, 410; work of Joseph Smith directed by, 410-411; symbolism of, 199-203; quoted—on good shepherd, 198; on other sheep, 199; rejection of, 129; resemblances to teachings of, 373; resurrection of, 418; worship God through, 418;

scriptural knowledge of, 207 ff.; information in Book of Mormon of, 208 ff.; signs of birth of, 299; signs of death & resurrection of, 120, 220-221; statement other sheep by, 67; teaching of in Book of Mormon of, 342; teachings of regarding swearing, 323; regarding speaking little, 323; time of crucifixion of, 193-194; ways Quetzalcoatl resembled, 221; world created by, 296.

Jews, fled from Jerusalem, 79-80; marriage customs of, 333-335; persecutions of, 91; progenitors of ancient Americans, 68; would reject Jesus, 67.

Jonathan, gives his robe to David, 317.

Joneam, Nephite army led by, 363.

Joseph, birth of, 81; Hebrew name, 76.

Josephites, tribe of, 229, 231.

Joshua, City of, Nephite armies gathered at, 348, 351.

Joshua, Sun commanded to stand still by, 300.

Judah, Zedekiah, king of, 89-90.

K

Kaminaljuyu, archæological site at, 62.

King of kings, Christ to be, 415.

Kingdoms, to be rended, 416.

Kings, how appointed, 86.

Kingsborough, Lord, American Indians origin theory of, 13; biographical sketch of, 7; no help from archæology, 8; writings of, 5-8; publishing notes of, 410.

Kirtland Temple, Martin Harris custodian of, 112.

Ku, meaning of, 267.

Kukul, Mayan term for serpent, 391.

Kukulcan, characteristics of, 256; identified with Topiltzin, 395; idoltry introduced by, 67; Mayan term for Quetzalcoatl, 391; Topiltzin also known as, 391; picture of, 391-392; time of, 403; (See Topiltzin).

L

Laban, brass plates secured from, 98; sword of, 257; sword of to be shown to 3 witnesses, 105; witnesses seeing of, 107.

Lake Peten, Guatemala, settlement of by Itzas from Chichen Itza, 407.

Lachish, ceramics found dating at Lehi's time at, 288.

Lachoneus, colonists called back to Bountiful by, 179; Nephite army recruited by, 178; proclamation of, 262.

Lamah, Nephite army led by, 363.

Laman, 75; Lehi's son, 63; meaning of name, 76-77; murmuring of, 73; rebellion of, 64, 69; river named after, 64; wickedness & cursing of, 242-243.

Lamanites, armor of, 275; attitude of, 69; blending of with Nephites, 244; Mormon's prophesy regarding, 244; Bountiful-Zarahemla taken over by, 366; branch of Nephites, 55; cement used by, 263; ceramics of found in Guatemala, 288; contempt for Nephites of, 56; Cumorah battle survived by, 372; cursing with dark skin of, 240; didn't practice polygamy, 333; differences between Nephites &, 366; dominance of, 171, 370; got drunk, 140-141; horses used by, 262; battle of, 262; Jershon settled by, 287; knowledge of creation of, 92; land southward gained by, 177; land northward settled by, 178; Lemhi & people in bondage to, 181; land of, 184; Mayas were, 402; Nephites armed against, 257; Nephites banished & destroyed by, 347 ff.; Nephites being defeated by, 361; Nephites being overpowerd by, 360; Nephites destroyed by, 345, 350, 362-363; Nephites fortified against, 273; Nephites fought by, 299 ff.; Nephites paid tribute to, 303; Nephites would be destroyed by, 217; origin of, 241-242; cusing of, 243; peace with, 230; treaty with, 231; people of Ammon were, 177; practice of human sacrifice by, 350; riches of, 178; righteousness of, 223-225; wickedness of, 226; sorceries, witchcrafts & magic practiced by, 289-290; treaty—Bountiful-land received by, 354; tribe of, 229, 231; tribute received by, 87-88; war against Nephites of, 348 f., 358; Desolation captured by, 359; war began with Nephites, 351; war declared again on Nephites by, 357; who they were, 86.

Lamoni, king, chariot & horses of, 262, 311.

Land, choice, 25, 26, 30-33, 38-40, 51; narrow neck of, 181, 182, 187-188.

Land Northward, Book of Mormon requirements met, 187; called Mulek & Desolation, 178, 180; scarcity of timber in, 177; colonists went to, 177 ff.; missionary work in, 178.

Land of Many Waters, Cumorah located in, 350; referred by Ixtlilxochitl & Book of Mormon to, 370.

Land Southward, Lamanites gained control of, 177; called Lehi, 178; Nephite armies gathered in, 178.

Landa, Bishop Diego de, deluge knowledge of, 91; quoted — people of Yucatan descendants of Jews, 68; quoted—hair, dress of Tultecas, 322; quoted—Indians of Yucatan animals of, 310; quoted—Mayan law against relatives marrying, 336; quoted—Mayan marriage age, 335; quoted—Mayan mourning & fasting at deaths, 327; quoted—regarding Kukulcan in Yucatan, 393; quoted—regarding marriage, 333; statement regarding Mayas use of plaster of, 269; Mayas armor described by, 275.

Las Casas, Bartolome de, quoted—world to end by fire, 94; clothing of Americans described by, 318; statement—gospel resemblances given Indians by devil, 222.

Las Charcas, Guatemala, Lamanite ceramics found at, 288.

La Venta, archæological site—date of 173; Tabasco, "Olmec" ceramics found at, 287; "Uncle Sam," figurine discovered at, 133, 173.

Lawyers, Nephites had, 258.

Lehi, 209; altar built by, 77; arrival in America of, 241-242; brought brass plates to America, 98; Christ to visit descendants of, 217; coming of, from Near East, 288; colonizers brought to America by, 19-20; commanded to leave Jerusalem, 59; grains brought to New World by, 304-305; importance of Egyptian script to, 99; in Palestine, 290; inspired leadership of & following, 288; Jeremiah contemporary of, 279; land of, 124, 125, 179; land southward called, 178; leader in Nephi's account, 80; Liahona possessed by, 196; missionary work of in land northward, 178; name of discovered, 75; origin of his family named, 75-77; premonition of death of, 85; farewell address of, 85-86; death of, 86; prophesy of, 239-240; revelations received by, 68; river & valley named by, 63-64, 78; God spoke to, 64; settled land southward, 180; seven tribes of, 165; teachings concerning God of, 234.

Lemhi, king, bondage of, 181; scouts of find Jaredite remains, 181-182; Nephites brought to Zarahemla by, 140-141; men of discovered 24 gold plates, 97.

Lemuel, 75; Lehi's son, 63; river named after, 63; marriage of, 64; meaning of name, 76-77; murmuring of, 73;